James S. Coleman

'There are a very small number of people who end up defining a major part of the intellectual agenda for their times . . . An even tinier group of thinkers influence both intellectual and policy debate. James Coleman's work formed the bed-rock for scholarship and policy in education and sociology for a genera-tion' (*cited in the memorial service tribute to James Coleman by Senator Daniel Patrick Moynihan*).

This is the first book to debate critically James S. Coleman's work and contribu-tion to sociology and the social sciences more generally. It consists of eighteen major papers by twenty authors from six countries on a range of themes, including: childhood and adolescence; educational opportunity and achieve-ment; social scientific theory, method and policy research; social theory, rational choice and the unification of the social sciences. The volume is framed by an extended editorial introduction reflecting on the five year exchange of corre-spondence between James Coleman and the editor, together with two of Coleman's own works. There are four appendices, including a reproduction of all the speeches made at James Coleman's memorial service in May 1995, and Coleman's curriculum vitae, with a full bibliography of his published books and papers.

A reviewer in *Contemporary Sociology* wrote in 1994: 'the sociology profession still owes Coleman a comprehensive and ambitious, if ambivalent appraisal.' This book aims to fill that gap. It also gives a rounded and highly personal impression of James Coleman as a researcher, teacher, colleague, friend, squash player, cancer patient, and dedicated sociologist. Shortly before he died, Coleman described this book as 'an extraordinary set of papers . . . a major tribute to my work even though it shows warts and all.'

Jon Clark studied in Birmingham (UK), West Berlin and Bremen and researched in London and Paris prior to his appointment at the University of Southampton in 1978 where he is now Professor of Industrial Relations and Dean of Social Sciences.

Falmer Sociology Series

Principal Editor: Jon Clark

James S. Coleman
Edited by Jon Clark

Alain Touraine
Edited by Jon Clark and Marco Diani

Falmer Sociology Series: Consensus and Controversy

Editors: Jon Clark, Celia Modgil and Sohan Modgil

Robert K. Merton
Anthony Giddens
John H. Goldthorpe

Falmer Psychology Series: Consensus and Controversy

Editors: Sohan Modgil and Celia Modgil

Lawrence Kohlberg
Hans Eysenck
Noam Chomsky
Arthur Jensen
B.F. Skinner

James S. Coleman

Edited by

Jon Clark

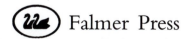 Falmer Press

(A member of the Taylor & Francis Group)
London • Washington, D.C.

UK   The Falmer Press, 1 Gunpowder Square, London, EC4A 3DE
USA   The Falmer Press, Taylor & Francis Inc., 1900 Frost Road, Suite 101, Bristol, PA 19007

© Jon Clark, 1996

The editor and publishers would like to thank the following for permission to reproduce their photographs on the cover of this book:
Front cover © Bruce Powell
Back cover © Shakeela Z. Hassan

First published in 1996

A catalogue record for this book is available from the British Library

Library of Congress Cataloging-in-Publication Data are available on request

ISBN 0 7507 0511 6 cased
ISBN 0 7507 0512 4 paper

Jacket design by Caroline Archer

Typeset in 10/12 pt Bembo by
Graphicraft Typesetters Ltd., Hong Kong.

Printed in Hong Kong by Graphicraft Typesetters Ltd.

Contents

Contents

Acknowledgments

First and foremost I would like to express my thanks to James S. Coleman, without whose commitment, support and courage this volume would not have been possible. From February 1995 Zdzislawa A. Coleman has added her indefatigable encouragement and support to the production of the book; the format of the editorial introduction and Appendix 2 owe much to her inspiration.

Thanks are due to James S. Coleman and Phi Delta Kappa Educational Foundation for permission to reprint his 'Reflections on Schools and Adolescents' (Chapter 2); Sarane Spence Boocock and Greenwood Publishing Group, Inc., for permission to reprint 'Games with Simulated Environments' (Chapter 10); the Department of Sociology, University of Chicago, and Transaction Publishers for permission to reprint James S. Coleman's 'A Vision for Sociology' (Chapter 21); Debra A. Milton for preparing Appendix 4 and facilitating, with great efficiency and tact, communication between myself and the Coleman family at a time of great difficulty; Roger Lawson (Head of the Department of Sociology and Social Policy, University of Southampton) for his encouragement, Glynis Evans for preparing a first draft of the consolidated bibliography, Elizabeth Leeks, Doreen Davies, Glynis Evans, Gwen Gordon, Jo-Anne Ireland and Eileen Upward (members of clerical staff in the Faculty of Social Sciences at the University of Southampton) for their general assistance; and Lyn Gorman for her high standards of copy-editing, proofreading and indexing.

Finally, I owe a particular debt of gratitude to Malcolm Clarkson, Managing Director, Falmer Press, for his unswerving confidence in the Falmer Sociology Series and his continued commitment to the highest standards of scholarship and professionalism in the editing and production of this volume.

Jon Clark

Acknowledgments

First and foremost I would like to express my thanks to James S. Coleman...

Jon Clark

1   Introduction

Jon Clark

James Coleman and the Evolution of the Volume

The first three volumes in the Falmer Sociology Series — on the work of Robert K.
Merton, Anthony Giddens and John H. Goldthorpe — were edited by myself, Sohan
Modgil and Celia Modgil. They were begun in 1986 and published in 1990. The idea
for this volume was conceived on 30 July 1990 at Nuffield College, Oxford. I had
arranged to visit Nuffield Official Fellow John H. Goldthorpe with Christine Cox,
the editor of the Falmer Sociology Series, to celebrate the publication of his own
Falmer volume. At this point nothing was further from my mind than the idea of
editing further volumes in the series on leading living sociologists. I was about to
begin fieldwork on a major new research project on 'managing an automated factory',
and had no intention of letting myself in for further editorial exhaustion of the kind
required when editing a series with large numbers of 'paired contributors' from
various academic cultures with very different definitions of that most elusive of
concepts, the deadline. Nevertheless, it was always good fun, and extremely revealing,
to ask colleagues whom among leading living sociologists they would choose if there
were to be further volumes in the series.

When Christine Cox and I arrived at Nuffield for a pre-prandial sherry, we were
met, not just by John Goldthorpe, but by his old friend and colleague (and one of
the contributors to Goldthorpe's Falmer volume), Walter Müller, who was coming
to the end of a year at the Center for Advanced Studies in the Behavioral Sciences
at Stanford University. We soon began talking about the links between US and
European sociology, and as soon as there was a short lull in the conversation, I asked
my standard question: whom would they regard as the best candidate/s for further
volumes in the Falmer series? Within one minute there was a clear consensus among
everyone present — Jim Coleman. To some extent this was influenced by the very
recent publication of his mammoth *Foundations of Social Theory*. But he also fitted the
bill of the series in many ways: his work was internationally recognized in the
discipline, was extensive in its thematic and methodological coverage, had excited
much controversy (the subtitle of the first three volumes was 'consensus and controversy'), and was highly relevant to the core of the discipline in the 1990s. The enthusiasm of John Goldthorpe and Walter Müller, together with that of Christine Cox,
persuaded me to reconsider my decision not to edit any more volumes in the series.

In just under two weeks I was due to attend the American Sociological Association (ASA) conference in Washington, DC, in part to host an eightieth birthday
celebration for Robert K. Merton on behalf of Falmer Press and to present him with
a leather-bound copy of his volume on behalf of the publishers. Jim Coleman had
contributed to the Merton volume, had already agreed to attend Merton's birthday

'bash', and so I thought I would try and arrange to meet him at the ASA and explore with him the possibility of a Falmer series volume. This was easier said than done. This was the conference at which he was finally elected to be president of the ASA (in 1992), and I was reliably informed by Robert Merton — who had prepared the ground for a meeting — that the only way to get some time with him was to ring his hotel room early in the morning and book a ten-minute slot in what was an horrendously full diary. This was duly done, but the slot then had to be cancelled and eventually we agreed to discuss the Falmer series volume informally at Merton's birthday celebration.

This was the only time I met Jim Coleman, although I had attended a packed session at the same ASA at which *Foundations* had been subject to detailed scrutiny by a panel of speakers (Harrison White, Randall Collins and Jeffrey Alexander), followed by a vigorous defence from the author and animated discussion from the floor. After this, and Randall Collins' description of Coleman as the 'Karl Marx of the twenty-first century', I was more convinced than ever that he would be an ideal subject for a Falmer volume. I decided to drop my 'rational' decision not to edit any more volumes in the series, borne along by the sheer intellectual excitement promised by an engagement with Jim Coleman's work together with the infectious enthusiasm and conviction of Goldthorpe, Müller, Merton and many others whom I had consulted. The previous day, I had also been able to speak with Aage B. Sørensen, who had assured me that the Coleman *festschrift* he was co-editing (Sørensen and Spilerman, 1993) would be unlikely to overlap with my projected volume.

At Merton's eightieth birthday celebration I only managed to speak with Jim Coleman — bottle of cold beer in hand — for around five minutes, but this was enough to gain agreement in principle to proceed with the volume and to correspond further about the details and timing. The one thing that remains very clearly in my mind from this meeting was Jim Coleman's answer to my request that he should write a concluding chapter to the volume within around three months of receiving the completed manuscript. He said that he had absolutely no difficulty in writing at present, and that as long as he had advanced warning he could easily turn it round in three months. I had no doubt that he meant it and that I would have no problems on this front.

The day after my return from Washington Malcolm Clarkson, Managing Editor of Falmer Press, confirmed his agreement to publish the volume, and a day later, on 17 August 1990, I wrote to Jim asking him to begin the process of identifying with me the ten or twelve themes in his work against which we would invite 'pro' and 'con' contributors. I also said that I was not sure how we would deal with *Foundations*, suggesting we could invite four or five stand-alone or overview contributions rather than a series of 'pro' and 'con' papers, as in the previous Falmer volumes. My aim was to go ahead fairly swiftly, seeking completed contributions by mid-1992 so that he would receive the manuscript around September 1992, just after the end of his year as ASA President. He responded on 31 August 1990 with an extended handwritten fax:

> First pardon the handwriting. I've got my secretary tied up with other things, and I wanted to get an initial response off to you before our long weekend.
>
> I'm certainly pleased to be invited to join the distinguished 'Falmer sociologists'. In some respects, however, I wish this had come a couple of years later, for a single reason: I regard the most lasting and most important

part of my work that which is represented by *Foundations of Social Theory*. I believe, however, that it will take a couple of years of discussion and debate before the implications of the book come to be out in the open, so to speak. What I mean can be compared to the reaction of people (including news analysts) to an event like the US invasion of Grenada, an event which initially created mixed reactions, and then resulted in a crystallization of opinion strongly backing the action and favoring the President's decision. The problem was that people didn't know how they felt until they knew how others felt. It took a lot of talking and listening, even by the broadcasters, until people came to have an idea just what the event *meant*, just how to interpret and react to it.

This is what one would call, I suppose, a social definition of reality, and it clearly depends on more than the content of the event. It depends also upon the social circles within which it reverberates. (As I write this, I am reminded of a picture on television news of frenzied crowds in Baghdad after the Iraqi invasion of Kuwait, while the definition of the event throughout the West was altogether different.)

This is the kind of phenomenon that will occur with that book. Someone writing a review or making comments on it now will do so without the benefit of the social definition of reality. It's not principally that they won't know which side to take. It is, rather, that their reaction will be a 'thin' one, without the kind of depth that a subsequent reaction will have after the book has been discussed at length, and after it has had a lot of people scratching through it, attempting to pick off the fleas, so to speak.

For this reason, I would not like to sign up Collins and White [who had discussed *Foundations* at the ASA session mentioned above, JC] to do something on the book now. Their critiques were o.k., but nothing profound. Over the next year, there will come to be critiques, both overall positive and overall negative, which will have a depth and richness that nothing written or done now will have. All that will emerge. But it needs time to percolate.

I have thought a little about the ten or twelve themes that you mentioned as a starting point, but I find that trying to do this is somewhat distressing. It is, in effect, attempting to sum up one's life in ten or twelve topics and leads one to say, 'Does it all come down to nothing more than this?'

As I try to do this it seems to end up consisting of separate themes for each of ten or twelve books. Partly this arises naturally, because around many of the books in particular, controversy circled, and it would be natural to have as a theme each of these (policy-related) topics. But at least on the others, it would seem peculiar to have the themes coincide with the books, rather than in some fashion crosscutting them. But on this I will think further — if you have any ideas or suggestions about how to go about this, please let me know.

The main reasons I wanted to write now were first to let you know that I got your fax, and second, to say that I think it's important to wait a while before signing anyone up on themes involving the big book.

Jim C.

P.S. Sørensen would be very good as one of the people for the volume.

After speedy consultation with Malcolm Clarkson and Christine Cox of Falmer Press, I wrote back on 7 September expressing complete agreement with his suggestion to postpone the volume pending the 'social construction of reality' around *Foundations of Social Theory*. In the light of his fax I also identified three possible organizing principles for the structure of the volume: the 'one-theme-per-book' approach, a thematic approach cross-cutting his books, or simply inviting individuals whom we agreed it would be good to include in the volume to select their own themes. At the back of my mind, too, was the wish to break away from the 'pro' and 'con' format, which had been invented by the two co-editors of the previous volumes, Celia and Sohan Modgil.

Jim wrote back on 11 September, again by handwritten fax:

> I'm pleased that you're willing to delay the volume until *FST* has had a chance to undergo, as you put it, the social construction of reality. As far as the rest is concerned, the work in sociology of education will, of course, play a reasonably large role (although my most important book before *FST* was *Introduction to Mathematical Sociology* in 1964, which has nothing to do with education). But on the education work, I will send you a draft of a piece I am writing for an education journal. This will give an idea of some themes within that theme.
>
> Jim

That piece 'for an education journal' was eventually published in 1991 as 'Reflections on Schools and Adolescents', and is reproduced with Jim Coleman's permission as Chapter 2 of this volume.

Around four months later, after I been able to delve more deeply into his writings, I wrote to Jim Coleman again on 7 January 1991 suggesting we should try and fix on themes for the volume which would encourage contributors to range more widely than simply discussing a single book. As examples I suggested themes such as 'the social experience of adolescence' or 'educational opportunity and school segregation' rather than book titles such as *The Adolescent Society* or *Equality of Educational Opportunity/High School Achievement*. I was also coming round to the view that *Foundations* would be best treated by a series of freestanding chapters, and not by the 'pro' and 'con' format. I concluded by asking Jim if he would make an initial attempt at some themes and contributors. He responded on 4 March 1991:

> I'm sorry about the delay in response to your letter of 7 January about the book on my work. I will try to respond with a few ideas about themes, and then a few names of people. I will first discuss themes independent of *Foundations*, then some things related to it, and finally some names.
>
> One theme would bring together *The Adolescent Society*, *Youth: Transition to Adulthood*, and *Becoming Adult in a Changing Society*, together with related papers. This has to do with the social organization of education, and of the period of adolescence and youth. It is broadly concerned with the question of how children grow into adults during the ages of about 14–20, and how the institutional structure in which they find themselves affects that. Some possible people for this would be Sarane Boocock, Aage Sørensen (both former students), Michael Rutter, Torsten Husén (Sweden).

A second broad area would be that represented by the Westview Press collection published in 1990, titled *Achievement and Equality in Education*. This covers not only *Equality of Educational Opportunity* and *Trends in School Segregation*, but also *High School Achievement* and *Public and Private High Schools: The Impact of Communities*, and a number of related papers. The last of these begins to move back in more sociological directions by examining the role of families, communities and religious institutions in education, and introducing the concept of social capital. This is possibly too broad an overall area and perhaps should be split. I have had lots of critics in this work, some more extreme than others, along with some who are not so critical. Some economists who have been in on this, from the less critical to the more critical, are Eric Hanushek, Myron Lieberman, Richard Murnane, Glen Cain and Harold Watts. Sociologists are Andrew McPherson, Peter Cuttance (both at Edinburgh), Aage Sørensen, Reynolds Farley, Barbara Heyns and Maureen Hallinan.

Related to this area is something about which I have not written much, but which enters into some of the above writings: the issue of parental choice vs assignment by school district in education. Lieberman from the above list, Charles Glenn, John Chubb and Terry Moe are people who know this work and have written in the area.

There have been several things in my career which have been relatively single-shot activities, though they have had a fairly extensive response. My early participation as a junior author in *Union Democracy* has had indirect effects on later work. That book has generated enormous response from sociologists over the years, but it is more attributable to Marty Lipset, the senior author. *Community Conflict*, a short monograph, and a couple of other related publications, is another minor direction. *Medical Innovation* and a couple of papers constitute still another.

There is one direction of work which is not greatly evident in my publications (there are only 6 or 7 papers in it). It concerns social simulation games, either as a teaching device, or as a form of social theory. This work, which I began about 1960 and continued until about 1973, was the path to the theoretical direction taken in all my theoretical publications since the late 1960s, and culminating in *Foundations*. There are several publications related to this, although not all of them discuss games. Most are in the general area of collective decisions. People who have done work in this area and who know my work are Erling Schild, Michael Inbar (both in Israel), Gudmund Hernes (Norway), Richard Duke (a political scientist), Benjamin Zablocki, Sarane Boocock.

One theme of a number of my publications has been the role of policy-related or applied research in the social sciences, and its relation both to social policy and social theory. This has been implicit, and sometimes explicit, in some of my work in education, and there have been some papers solely devoted to this. Some people who are relevant here are Peter Rossi, Walter Williams, Carol Weiss, Bob Boruch (a psychologist).

A major direction of my work from graduate school on has been the broad field of 'mathematical sociology'. My work in this area has been divided in two parts, the first mostly focused around stochastic processes, and the second mostly focused around models of purposive action, and market models. The former had little theoretical content, but consisted of mathematical models for a wide range of social processes. The latter is mathematics appropriate for the theoretical work in *Foundations*, and is to be found not only there (in Part IV), but in a 1973 book *Mathematics of Collective Action*, and in some papers in the Cambridge University Press collection. The former is in *Introduction to Mathematical Sociology* (probably my most highly-regarded book until *Foundations*) and *Models of Change and Response Uncertainty*, both in 1964, as well as the paper 'The Mathematics of Change', in 1968. People who would be possible authors in this 1955–1968 mathematical direction are Aage Sørensen, Seymour Spilerman, Gudmund Hernes (Norway), Michael Hannan, Nancy Tuma, Kazuo Yamaguchi, David Bartholomew (statistics, England). People who would be good for the 1973–1990 mathematical work are Hernes, Schild, Tony Tam, Piotr Swistak.

Now to come to *FST*. I believe one might think of the work in the book as falling into three or four areas. The one that is more easily separable is Part IV, Modern Society. This is least related to the conceptual foundation itself, and is more nearly a set of essays which draw out some of the principal implications of the perspective taken in the book. The theme of this section could well be seen as 'the rationalization of society', or 'the purposive construction of social institutions', or the theme which I've taken for the 1992 ASA meetings 'Sociology and the Reconstruction of Society'. It argues that there is a massive transformation of society away from primordial institutions towards 'rationalized' or 'single-purpose' or 'constructed' ones.

Part V is the next most separable section, not because the substance is unconnected with Parts I–III, but because it is a mathematical parallel to Parts I–III. Parts I and II are the more micro parts of the foundations, and Part III moves to the macro level, with chapters concerned with the construction of corporate actors and their destruction.

Throughout the book, but particularly in Parts I–III there is room for a critique from the perspective of political or moral philosophy. A philosopher concerned with 'rights' would probably be the best person to do that, for as Chapter 3 discusses, a particular view of the origin of rights underlies the whole work. Who is the right person here I don't know.

There ought to be an economist in the book because so much of *FST* is an extension of economic theory. I don't know who might be right. Perhaps someone from George Mason, in Buchanan's centre for public choice. Viktor Vanberg would be one possibility, though the mathematics of Part V would escape him. Gary Becker is not the right person, but he knows the book and would perhaps know the right person. Demsetz might be the right person.

Probably the treatment of *FST* ought not to be section by section, as I have intimated above, but as you have suggested: to have four or five people treat the work as a whole, with a subsequent interchange. If that is done, then I think it would be useful to have an economist, a political or moral philosopher, possibly a psychologist (perhaps a social psychologist) and one or more sociologists.

As far as sociologists who might be right for the *FST* part, I don't know. Of the reviews I've read, I've felt that Tilly, Stinchcombe, Smelser, White and Hechter have misunderstood the book, each in his own way. Only James Rule and Thomas Fararo have written reviews that I think show some insight into the book. Christopher Jencks might be a possibility. Richard Swedberg (Sweden) is a distinct possibility. Ron Burt is also a possibility.

I don't know how helpful these ruminations are, but I'll send them on.

Sincerely
Jim

Apart from its intrinsic interest, this letter makes it very clear that Coleman regarded his work on social simulation games, beginning in 1960, as one of the main factors which led him to rational choice theory and, ultimately, to *Foundations of Social Theory*. Rational choice theory was not something he had come to relatively late in life following his work on busing and his more systematic intellectual engagement with economics from around 1983 (this view is confirmed by Chicago economist Jim Heckman in a postscript to his chapter with Derek Neal in this volume).

Following our previous agreement not to proceed on the volume till after the 1992 ASA conference, I filed away Coleman's detailed letter of March 1991 and only came back to it in the summer of 1992. In the meantime, I had agreed to co-edit a further volume in the series with Marco Diani, then at the Paris Centre d'Analyse et d'Intervention Sociologiques (CADIS), on the work of the French sociologist Alain Touraine. On 20 July 1992 I wrote to Jim Coleman informing him of this and also that we had decided not to structure Touraine's volume in debate format but in a series of single chapters centred on five or six major themes. I asked him what he would think of structuring 'his' volume along the same lines, and, building on the thematic suggestions he had made in his letter of 4 March 1991, I proposed six main themes:

- social organization of education: adolescence and youth
- achievement and equality in education
- sociology of education and the concept of social capital
- applied research in the social sciences
- mathematical sociology: stochastic processes and models of purposive action
- *Foundations of Social Theory*.

He replied on 5 October 1992:

I'm sorry I've been so long in answering your letter of July 20. I am in agreement with much of what you suggest. The debate format can sometimes be artificial, and in such cases it doesn't work. The problem about the other (Touraine) format, which you've proposed for 'my' volume, is that it can get too much like a *festschrift*, in which each author takes a paper out of a drawer, adds an initial paragraph about the party in question, and ships it off. Altogether, it's difficult to get people not to do this, that is to write a new paper about anyone else's work, a problem which exists for both the debate format and the non-debate format. How you can overcome this is presumably a problem that you have successfully dealt with in the past, but it is one that would daunt me. It may be more easily handled, however, in the debate framework than in the non-debate framework.

I guess I would slightly prefer the debate framework, partly because I think it is appropriate for my work, since there has been a lot of conflict surrounding it, and partly because it may be easier to keep people on task in that framework. *However,* I think you should use whichever framework you find easiest to carry out, because either would be fine with me, and the task will be yours, not mine.

The themes you suggest seem fine to me. However, I think the third theme, 'the sociology of education and the concept of social capital', may not be enough of a separate theme to be included. I think it can be combined with the first theme. There are various papers and three books (*The Adolescent Society, Youth: Transition to Adulthood*, and *Public and Private Schools: The Impact of Communities*) which would be relevant to this combined theme. An alternative, in place of the current theme 3, would be 'Public and Private Schools', which would cover various papers plus two books *High School Achievement* and *Public and Private High Schools*, over the period 1980-present, or 'Choice in Education', covering the same papers and books.

Altogether, I defer to your judgment. Full speed ahead.

Sincerely
Jim

I faxed back on 12 October, suggesting a compromise format in which there would be five or six themes with between three and six contributions in each. Each contributor would also be asked to comment on all the other chapters in their thematic section. Pragmatically, this meant that I could retain some kind of debate format, but if one contributor dropped out, I would not be faced (as in previous volumes) with having to find another paired contributor. I also asked whether game theory/collective decisions should not be treated in a separate thematic section, and listed a whole series of names of potential contributors, asking for comments and additional suggestions. On 24 November I received a nine-page fax with fifty-three names and addresses (including a number of additional ones) for each theme, in 'rank order'.

In the following six months, I wrote to forty-four academics in seven countries (including some who weren't on the original list) in order to secure the eighteen chapters in the volume, some of whom ended up writing on different topics from those for which they were originally invited! By May 1993 a final list of contributors was agreed and formal invitations sent out with a deadline of summer 1994 for submission of manuscripts. By this time it had become clear to me that the idea of clearly delineated thematic sections with a roughly equal number of contributions in each was simply not going to work. It was at this point that I decided, on pragmatic grounds, to give up the idea of a comment or debate section on each theme, which had been a central element of the format of previous volumes in the series.

I wrote to Jim Coleman in May — and again in July — 1993 enclosing a proposed table of contents and asking for his curriculum vitae for onward transmission to contributors. However, it was not until 9 August 1993 that he responded, and told me for the first time of his prostate cancer: 'By the time I received your May letter I was in the midst of this health turmoil which I am still embroiled in. I have had time for nothing else, and the treatments have so sapped my energy and destroyed my concentration that my time has been useless anyway. I hope to get out of this mess; but I'm still in it now'. He had found time, though, to prepare both a full and a shortened vitae, which were sent to me, and thence to contributors, in September 1993.

The next contact was not until 1 May 1994, when I wrote that the volume was proceeding well and that I was intending to send the completed manuscript to him by the end of October 1994. This I did on 31 October 1994. At the same time I sent him an accompanying letter saying he could write anything between 10,000 and 30,000 words, and that ideally I would like his response by the end of January 1995. I knew from a number of colleagues in Chicago and elsewhere that Jim's health was not good, but also knew that he wanted to write his concluding chapter if at all possible, so all my letters were based on the assumption that he would complete.

My first letter from Jim since August 1993 was dated 19 January 1995:

> I suppose that you have felt secure in the belief that I am nearly done in my response to the volume you have created. If so, you are wholly wrong. In November, my illness got worse, and I have been unable to work since then. I have been able to read only about a third of the papers. I was in the hospital for 10 days, but am now out. I think there are two possibilities. One is the possibility that I will recover to the point of being able to prepare a chapter. That I should know within three weeks. The other is that I will never get back to the point where I could write a coherent chapter.
>
> I'm of course sorry about this, as you can imagine.
>
> Sincerely
> Jim

Just over one month later, on 20 February, Jim Coleman wrote again. He had, in the meantime, been able to complete his reading of the manuscript and had made a few first notes beginning to map out his conclusion:

> I am in a terrible pickle. I am still able to put sentences together, and perhaps even to make sense. I would like nothing better than to be able to write the concluding chapter to your volume, for I regard the volume as a major tribute to my work even though it shows warts and all.
>
> I will keep trying, but only if it makes sense for me to do so. If there is a time point (and there clearly must be beyond which the volume must go to press) then tell me I will stop trying.
>
> Unlike a *festschrift* this volume consists largely of papers describing some part of the honoree's work. Papers for a *festschrift* ordinarily consist of some piece of work of the author of the paper, which may bear a loose connection or no connection at all to the persons whom the *festschrift* is designed to honor. I think this is why *festschriften* are inherently uninteresting, and ordinarily sell poorly. Your book, however, is for me extremely interesting, and I think part of that interest goes beyond pure egoism. The papers reveal connected parts of a single man's work, seen through the eyes of those who are writing the papers. (Heyns is an exception, Husén, Alexander and Entwisle, Bartholomew, Abell, Inbar and Collins are partial exceptions.)
>
> What makes my 'conclusion' so difficult to write is not merely that I have a hard time writing, but that the work that authors are commenting on

is complex and diverse, attempting to contribute to empirical research, to social policy, and to social theory. One major problem is that there are a number of different ways to approach the whole thing, and it's difficult for me to devise which is going to be most useful. And I've changed my orientation midstream, which brings about complexity. Nevertheless, it is the single thing I work on, and I will continue to do so until you tell me the deadline is at hand.

Sincerely
Jim

This was the last major communication I received from Jim Coleman on the volume. In the last six weeks of his life, I communicated with him largely by e-mail via his secretary Debbie Milton. His last letter/fax to me, on 9 March, responding to my request of 5 March to include his full bibliography and his essay 'Reflections on Schools and Adolescents' in the volume, was short and positive on both counts. His final words to me were: 'full steam ahead'. Between 9 and 21 March, just four days before he died, he mapped out his conclusion and began writing the first section. Transcripts of what he wrote, together with a context-setting commentary by his wife, Zdzislawa A. Coleman, are printed in Appendix 2.

With the death of James S. Coleman the world of sociology has lost one of its finest, most prolific and most combative scholars. He was a committed theorist who was constantly wrestling with the 'inconvenient facts' thrown up by empirical investigation. He also believed fervently that sociologists should seek to apply their theories and relate their empirical data to questions of social and public policy. When I first met him in August 1990, he had just published his monumental *Foundations of Social Theory*. He regarded this book, as we have seen, as 'the most lasting and important part of my work' (letter to the editor, 31 August 1990), in some ways the summit of his life's work. Yet, being Jim Coleman, it was impossible for him to rest on his laurels. He always had unfinished work, including his conclusion to this volume, in which he intended to develop further his ideas on the way information at the level of individual actions could be used in the analysis of the way social systems and social institutions function.

His qualities, as a sociologist and as a person, are well captured in the following tribute from Robert K. Merton in a letter to the author of 13 April 1995: 'He was a fine, original, mind; a dedicated scholar and scientist who believed in (what is now often defined as the heresy of) trying to discover sociological truths; a courageous citizen who made his values and social judgments known (sometimes at considerable cost); and a gentle and constant friend'. We are all the poorer for Jim Coleman's untimely death. He had so much more to do.

The Contents of the Volume

This introductory chapter is followed by James Coleman's own 'Reflections on Schools and Adolescents' written in 1990 and first published in 1991 (nearly half the contributions to this volume are concerned with adolescence, youth and schools). In this short paper Coleman traces how a dinner conversation in the mid-1950s led to the production of a research proposal, which in turn resulted in his first major research project, an empirical study of adolescent subcultures in ten high schools in Illinois. The results were published in 1961 as *The Adolescent Society*. Coleman's 'Reflections' take us through the development of most of his major empirical research projects, finishing in 1990 with the question 'Now what?'. The answer was short and to the point: 'I am in the midst of tackling the difficult task . . . [of] incorporating the functioning of the informal social system among adolescents into an analysis of the effects of schooling on student outcomes'.

Coleman's 'Reflections' are followed by reflections of a different kind from the doyen of researchers on youth and adolescence, Torsten Husén, whose 1944 book on *Adolescence* and 1974 study of *The Learning Society* are already classics in their fields. Husén's chapter adopts a historical and cultural perspective on questions of youth and adolescence. It deals with two areas within educational sociology in which James Coleman's influence has been seminal: youth culture and the generation gap; and child and youth socialization in the context of the changing role and functions of the family. He locates Coleman's key contribution to the development of educational policy, including his work in the OECD strategy group in the early 1970s, as the analysis of the concept of equality of opportunity and its policy consequences for schooling.

Chapter 4 by Denise Kandel provides a systematic analysis of Coleman's research on youth and adolescence over thirty-two years, tracing the shifts in his views by reviewing in turn each of his major empirical studies. She identifies five main reasons why his work has been so important and influential. It generated important substantive findings and theoretical insights; developed innovative research designs; marked the beginning of large-scale social/sociological projects; illustrated the power of social science as a basis for policy-making; and heralded the age of the social scientist as media star. She sees the central thread in Coleman's work on youth and adolescence as a concern with the social factors that foster the formation of human capital.

In Chapter 5 Barbara Heyns examines the ideologies and strategies of educational privatization in Poland between 1989 and 1993 and compares them with those of private schools in the USA. In so doing, she examines propositions about the levels and sources of achievement in education that have been a major concern of much of Coleman's work in the area. She concludes that the value differences between Polish and American private schools, while not coincidental, are not causally related to achievement. The substance of values is much less important than their strength and consistency. On this analysis, social capital is not a consequence of a particular set of values, but of the social organization and networks — in families and communities, for example — that any set of values creates.

In Chapter 6 Karl Alexander and Doris Entwisle use data from the ongoing Beginning School Study (BSS) in Baltimore to revisit one of the major issues thrown up by the *Coleman Report* (Coleman *et al.*, 1966): the relative influence of schools and families on the educational achievement of children. They do this by examining the achievement disparities separating children of various socioeconomic levels, concentrating on schooling in the early primary grades (6- and 7-year-olds). While not underestimating the real and severe problems besetting urban education, the BSS data reveal not just that schooling is a powerful force in the lives of children of lower socioeconomic status, but that it is a positive force. The findings also emphasize the importance for children's development of the very earliest years of schooling.

Chapter 7, by economists James Heckman and Derek Neal, aims to uncover the diverse research styles of Coleman's research on education, in particular the tension between 'the two Colemans', the theorist and the empirical researcher. They argue that Coleman the rational choice theorist has consistently been concerned with the forces shaping personal and institutional choices, while Coleman the empirical social scientist has been less concerned about the consequences of some of those choices for the analysis of his data. They revisit the 'most controversial and least robust finding' of the 1966 *Coleman Report*, that integrated schools boosted the academic achievement of black students without affecting the achievement of white students. The US Civil Rights Commission introduced legislation into the US Congress based on this finding, which generated major controversies about 'peer effects', busing, and 'forced integration' of white and black students. Heckman and Neal conclude by suggesting that Coleman preferred to establish empirical regularities using simple methods without imposing a strong a priori structure onto his data through elaborate causal empirical models. Unfortunately, they argue, correlations of the kind identified by Coleman are often interpreted in popular discussion, despite multiple warnings, as implying strong causal links and used as 'scientific' justifications for particular social policies.

The chapter is followed by two short postscripts by James Heckman reflecting on numerous conversations he had with Jim Coleman in the final months of his life. (The postscripts were written following discussions with the editor in Chicago on Friday 19 May 1995.) The first reflects on the origins of Coleman's interest in rational choice theory, tracing it back to his research on adolescence and simulation games. The second provides a fascinating extension of the ideas in the conclusion of the Heckman/Neal paper on the nature of empirical social science, in particular on the relation between the kind of formal social science frameworks adopted by econometricians and Coleman's 'empiricist' refusal to adopt the false precision of scientific models in areas of social science where knowledge is still not settled.

In Chapter 8 Martin Bulmer examines in more detail James Coleman's sociological contribution to social policy research, exploring how and why he became involved as a national policy actor. He concludes that while other social scientists, such as Daniel Patrick Moynihan, have had a higher profile and achieved a similar national impact, what is distinctive about James Coleman is that he was 'throughout the researcher, insisting that the findings of social science research are the basis from which the policy debate must start'. Many of his findings were uncomfortable and inconvenient for Coleman himself. However, he never hesitated to point out their implications and often appeared to delight in the controversy to which his public interventions gave rise. Bulmer concludes that because of the strength of Coleman's challenges to the conventional wisdom over busing and public schools, his principled stance generated much fiercer public debate than if the results of his research had been presented more in conformity with the prevailing liberal consensus.

In Chapter 9 Sally Kilgore addresses the same theme, but concentrates on the political context of social policy research as exemplified by Coleman's work on educational opportunity and achievement. She is particularly concerned with the strict time constraints imposed by legislative agendas, and the propensity of legislators to adopt solutions before they evaluate systematically the needs to which the policy is supposed to be a response. She suggests that the key to bridging the gap between social research and public policy is to redefine the audience for such research towards the public at large and away from a predominant focus on policy-makers and legislators.

For Kilgore, it is the public at large's definition of the problem which will either breathe life into, or destroy, the programmatic preferences of legislators. If researchers address directly the multiplicity of interests embedded in most social problems, then controversy and/or surprising results will emerge naturally from their work and often lead to both academic and public policy redefinitions of the problem. She concludes: 'Coleman never simply informed legislators about a program or policy options; he always informed and stimulated public debate. More important, he made truthseekers of us all'.

In Chapter 10 Sarane Spence Boocock examines James Coleman's major excursion into applied sociology in what became known as the Academic Games Program (AGP) or the Hopkins Games Project. She examines the claims made for games with simulated environments, both as educational innovations in schools and as vehicles for sociological research. She also assesses the AGP and its intellectual legacy. She concludes that, in the current 'back to basics' educational environment, there is little enthusiasm for games and other enjoyable kinds of educational innovation. At the same time, developing workable simulation games is extremely time-consuming, and there is little hard evaluative research evidence which could demonstrate their educational value. Nevertheless, she argues that, should the intellectual climate become more receptive to educational experimentation and reform, the body of knowledge on simulation games pioneered by Coleman in the 1960s could reinstate them — using the wider accessibility and capabilities of new computer hardware and software — as a proactive vehicle for students to learn about their own social environment and even create their own social worlds.

Coleman's main application of simulation gaming to theory building was a study of collective decision-making involving the simulation of various elements of the legislative process. His objective was to show how rational self-interested actors could engage in collective decisions, without engaging in a war of all against all, by identifying the 'structural conditions under which collective decisions can be made without recourse to external power' (Coleman, 1975c: 406). In Chapter 11 Benjamin Zablocki addresses directly the problem of accounting for collective behaviour. He also addresses a central concern of Coleman's sociology, the social mechanisms which link micro to macro and macro to micro levels. He begins by explaining why understanding collective behaviour is an important sociological problem and reviews the status of our current knowledge about it. He then explains why he believes Coleman's approach (including the two chapters and multiple other references in *Foundations of Social Theory*) provides the most promising basis for achieving a solution to the problem. He concludes by outlining an agenda of theoretical extensions to Coleman's model of the 'acting self' and a set of guidelines for future empirical research. For Zablocki a successful solution to the understanding of collective behaviour could help confirm the efficacy of rational choice theory and methodological individualism as the foundations of a general theory of action in the social sciences.

Chapters 12–14 move to a different area of James Coleman's work, stochastic processes, measurement, and the use of mathematical models in applied sociological research. In Chapter 12 current President of the UK Royal Statistical Society David Bartholomew examines the use of stochastic modelling in mobility research, arguing that human populations exhibit the essential characteristics of a stochastic process in that their social structure develops over time in an uncertain manner. He suggests that James Coleman was one of the first to recognize this in his two books *Models of*

Change and Response Uncertainty (1964a) and *Introduction to Mathematical Sociology* (1964b). In particular Coleman anticipated later developments by using continuous time versions of the so-called 'Markov process'. Bartholomew's paper shows that if the essentials of the process of mobility are adequately captured by a Markov model, then the parameters of that model provide a complete description of the system. Since the point of constructing measures is to make comparisons, he argues that the more limited the choice of measure, the wider its use will be. The aim should be to settle on a small number of robust measures which, although possibly insensitive to the nuances of particular situations, will capture what is common to most.

In Chapter 13 Peter Abell brings together Coleman's pioneering work on the use of stochastic flow models with his more recent promotion of rational choice theory in an examination of recent British data on entry to, and exit from, self-employment. He begins with a critique of the econometric, psychological and sociological literatures on 'what drives' entrepreneurship. He then lays out the elements of a new approach to modelling entry into entrepreneurship through self-employment using elaborated versions of the 'Coleman diagram' in *Foundations of Social Theory*. Individual propensities to enter into, and exit from, self-employment are related to three macro variables (Gross Domestic Product, unemployment, and lagged entry and exit rate to and from self-employment), controlling for time, region and sector. Abell views entry and exit decisions as socially embedded in networks of social capital. His most consistent result is that past self-employment entry and exit rates have a net positive effect upon current rates, which operate by affecting the legitimacy of self-employment as espoused by the social contacts of any potential entrant.

In Chapter 14 Aage Sørensen examines questions of statistical methodology in Coleman's two major research projects on educational opportunities and school effects. He argues that the apparently conflicting conclusions of these two studies can be explained in part by the use of different statistical measures of the importance of schools, and in part by the presence or absence of theory to explain school effects. In his research on constructing mathematical models of social processes and social structure, Coleman established the basic principles for integrating theory and empirical evidence. However, according to Sørensen, Coleman did not follow his own principles in his educational research. Sørensen's paper is an attempt to do this. He presents a conceptualization of how school effects are produced, formalizes this in a simple model, estimates it, and discusses some of its main implications. He also shows conclusively that there is no such thing as a model or measure without a theory.

In Chapter 15 Michael Inbar examines the issue of rationality in individual judgments. For Inbar, the view that the human being is a purposeful actor runs through the whole of Coleman's work and lies at the heart of *Foundations of Social Theory*. He cites a key sentence from *Foundations* (1990a: 18): '[much] of what is ordinarily described as nonrational or irrational is merely so because the observers have not discovered the point of view of the actor from which the action is rational'. In the main body of his chapter Inbar illustrates the perspicacity of this view by showing how even the best documented psychological findings suggesting that people frequently make irrational choices and judgments are in fact not immune from rational explanation. For this purpose he provides an extensive analysis of one particular psychological task — the Linda vignette — and its interpretation by Tversky and Kahneman in terms of the so-called conjunction fallacy (1983).

Chapter 16 by Thomas Fararo provides a general introduction to Coleman's

Foundations of Social Theory. After a brief overview of its aims, methods and contents, he locates Coleman's work in the context of other 'foundation efforts' within sociology, especially those of George Homans, Talcott Parsons and Jeffrey Alexander. He shows how Coleman's views on explanation, theory and method in sociology led him to develop models within the umbrella of rational choice theory, and how he extended this theoretical model by adopting the general equilibrium theory from economics. He concludes by assessing the strengths and weaknesses of Coleman's general theory as formulated in *Foundations*.

In Chapter 17 Adrian Favell argues that *Foundations* marks a return to the terrain of general sociological theory to rival the 'grand foundational works' of Talcott Parsons and Robert K. Merton. He traces its formative influence to the fact that it reconnects sociology directly with the current debates and methodological concerns of analytical political science, policy studies and institutional economics. It thus restores to sociology a central place in the social sciences, creating, in Coleman's own words, a 'new social science' fit for the social scientists operating in the conditions of the late twentieth century. Indeed, Favell goes further and suggests that Coleman's *Foundations* can be read as a rival to the grand philosophical works — of Habermas, Rawls, Luhmann and Gadamer — which dominate much contemporary European social and political thought. Such works offer foundational systematic theories which ground normative concerns and applications in the long philosophical tradition of modernity.

Chapter 18 by Siegwart Lindenberg identifies a clear paradigm shift within contemporary sociology. The new paradigm is concerned with specifying the micro mechanisms which relate individual action to macro phenomena. The theoretical base generally used to achieve this task is rational choice theory. Lindenberg contrasts two different positions within the 'rational choice' camp: Coleman's view of the relation between social structure and social theory, and Lindenberg's own argument about the convergence of sociology and economics and its implications for social theory. In the main body of his chapter he applies these two approaches to a central substantive issue in sociology: the problem of order.

In Chapter 19 Richard Swedberg examines James Coleman's contribution to economic analysis. He begins by identifying the impact of the Columbia school of sociology, Coleman's discovery of rational choice (1957–61), and his debates with the ideas of leading economists such as Kenneth Arrow, Gordon Tullock, James Buchanan and Gary Becker. Coleman is one of the few leading sociologists who has engaged consistently with economic debates and also published in leading economic journals. Swedberg goes on to examine Coleman's analysis of the emergence of the modern corporation, comparing it with that of Max Weber. He also stresses the importance in Coleman's work of the analysis of the 'macro-micro-macro transition', in this case, the analysis of the corporation, then how it affects the individual, and then how individuals, by interacting, create an effect at the macro level. Finally, he discusses Coleman's analysis of the modern corporation and critique of contemporary organization theory in *Foundations of Social Theory*. He concludes by suggesting that the fusion of Columbia style sociology and rational choice analysis in Coleman's theory makes it into a powerful tool for analyzing economic phenomena.

In Chapter 20 Randall Collins asks whether rational action theory can unify social science, or less ambitiously, whether it can unify sociology or some significant 'slice of overlap' between social scientific disciplines. The first main part of his chapter examines the analytical possibilities of what might be accomplished along these lines. Collins identifies some degree of convergence between his own emphasis on the importance of emotions in micro motivational schemes and Coleman's attempt (in Chapters 10 and 11 of *Foundations*) to weave market and network considerations into a rational action theory of solidarity. The second main part of the chapter examines whether the multiple factions of the world of the sociology of science are capable of uniting under the single theoretical banner of rational choice theory. The sociology of science perspective reminds us that what we accomplish is done by a community of scholars. For Collins, Coleman's 'great synthetic work', *Foundations of Social Theory*, links social scientists backward across the generations and forward into the future as well. He concludes: 'that is why he has communicated, perhaps more than anyone, the sense of a broad unified movement, full of energy in its upward trajectory of growth'.

The volume concludes with a reprint of Coleman's 'A Vision for Sociology', written in 1994 in response to his receipt of the Phoenix Prize of the University of Chicago, and four appendices: 'Teaching James Coleman', a slightly revised version of Robert K. Merton's presentation at the Phoenix Prize conference in Chicago in April 1994; the transcripts of Coleman's own unfinished concluding chapter to this volume together with a context-setting commentary by Zdzislawa A. Coleman; the reproduction of the speeches made at his memorial service on Friday, 19 May 1995 in the Rockefeller Memorial Chapel, Chicago, by Marta Tienda (University of Chicago), Mark Siegler (University of Chicago Hospitals), Seymour Martin Lipset (George Mason University), Edward L. McDill (Johns Hopkins University), Sally B. Kilgore (Hudson Institute, Indianapolis), Edward O. Laumann (University of Chicago), Gudmund Hernes (Ministry of Education, Research, and Church Affairs, Oslo), Senator Daniel Patrick Moynihan, and Nobel prize winning economist and sociologist Gary S. Becker (University of Chicago); and Coleman's curriculum vitae (including a full bibliography of all his publications) prepared by Debra A. Milton. The endmatter consists of a consolidated bibliography for this volume prepared by Glynis Evans and the editor, a list of contributors and their affiliations, and indexes prepared by Lyn Gorman.

A recent review in *Contemporary Sociology* (September 1994: 761–2) concluded: 'the sociology profession still owes Coleman a comprehensive and ambitious, if ambivalent appraisal'. It is to be hoped that this volume goes some way to achieving this goal.

2   Reflections on Schools and Adolescents

James S. Coleman

My life as a sociologist concerned with education began one evening at the dinner table. I was near the end of my graduate studies at Columbia University and my wife and I had invited to dinner my fellow student and co-researcher, Martin Trow, and his wife. The talk turned to our high school days. As we described our experiences, it was clear that each of us had lived in a somewhat different kind of cocoon during that period of our lives. My wife had gone to high school in Shelbyville, Indiana, a school that when she was a junior had won the state basketball championship. Basketball was the focus of adolescent attention, rivalled only by the social escapades of the leading clique in school. Trow's wife had attended a private girl's school in Atlanta, a school designed to produce young ladies for the next generation of Atlanta social elite, but also a school in which scholastic pursuits were taken with serious interest. Trow had gone to Townsend Harris High School in New York City, a public high school (no longer in existence) that was highly selective on academic grounds. Graduates who returned to speak in assemblies or at commencement were Nobel prize winners or others who had distinguished themselves in intellectual pursuits; and the focus of current students was upon similar goals.

My own high school experience had been in Louisville, Kentucky, where there were two boys' public schools, Male (with a college preparatory curriculum) and Manual (with vocational and pre-engineering curricula). I attended Manual. Male and Manual were locked in a fierce football rivalry that culminated every Thanksgiving Day but flavored the whole school year. The boys who counted in the school were the first-string varsity football players. This environment had shaped my own investment of time and effort, intensely focussed on football, although arguably my comparative advantage lay elsewhere. (I had begun high school in a small town, Greenhills, in southwestern Ohio, where school life had, for a few of us, a more academic focus, in retrospect surprisingly so.)

The diversity among the different worlds that the four of us had inhabited during our high school years intrigued me — for each of us was shaped by the particular world each had inhabited, and me by the two sharply different worlds. That dinner conversation took place near the end of graduate school for me, as I was pondering upon the research direction I would take the next year. The conversation raised problems that interested me greatly: how did such different subcultures come into existence and persist, and what kind of impact did they have upon those young people who passed through them? As a research focus, it met three criteria important to me: First, it allowed study of variations among social subsystems, which the survey research that many of my fellow-sociologists were undertaking did not. Second, it had potential implications for policy, for something that would make a difference. Third, it held intrinsic interest for me, for it might help me understand better my own childhood experiences, which had taken place in four quite different social environments.

Stimulated by the dinner conversation, I wrote a research proposal which was subsequently funded by the newly created Cooperative Research program of the US Office of Education. The research, carried out in 1957–58, consisted of the study of adolescent subcultures in ten high schools in Illinois. During that year, I and my small research team visited these schools, interviewed students individually and in groups, talked to teachers and principals, and administered questionnaires at the beginning and end of the school year. The results were reported to the Office of Education in 1959 as 'Social Climates in High Schools,' and were published in 1961 as *The Adolescent Society*.

This research took a perspective on educational institutions that was distinctly sociological, and decidedly unlike that taken by researchers concerned explicitly with educational policy (such as, for example, the kind of research that had been carried out by Paul Mort of Columbia Teachers College, on characteristics of modernity in public schools). This research looked at high school life not in terms of the goals of educators, but in terms of the goals and interests of the adolescents occupying the school and constituting the largest part of its population. In this it contrasts not only with that of earlier researchers, but also with much of the educational research that has occupied me later in my career. The advantages of the perspective characteristic of *The Adolescent Society* are, I believe, great, for by getting inside the lives of those who pass through the schools, one can gain an understanding of why and for whom educational institutions fail, and what kinds of changes might lead them to draw the interest of the young people in them toward educational goals.

The last chapter of *The Adolescent Society* focussed on policy implications of the research results. One very clear result of the research was that the social structure of competition for sports activities in the high schools, organized interscholastically, led to social reinforcement of the activity on the part of other students: teams were cheered on, participation and effort was encouraged, and success was rewarded with popularity and the status of local hero. The social structure of competition in scholastic matters, by contrast, was not interscholastic but interpersonal, and a second clear result of the research was that this led to social suppression of the activity on the part of other students: good grades were not rewarded by hero status, but their recipients were chided for rate-busting. Academic achievement by itself did little to bring popularity.

A policy implication I drew from these results led to my next educational research, in 1961. If all the foregoing were true, then a reorganization of academic competition around teams, games, and interscholastic competition would create a structure that would lead to social encouragement of educational goals. I embarked on a program of development of academic games for high school and middle school students. These games, mostly social simulation games (but including one game for young children learning numbers) were intended to be part of a reconstructed curriculum, in which students would learn social studies through a structure which induced cooperation and social reinforcement. Our research group developed about six games, tested them in Baltimore schools, and disseminated them to teachers who came to share our enthusiasm for this reconstruction of the learning environment.

How successful was this strategy? The success was mixed. My vision of a re-shaped learning environment throughout American schools, with status systems where scholars brought glory to their school through success in academic games in inter-scholastic competition was, needless to say, not realized. Yet the kinds of effects we anticipated, in terms of social encouragement for learning, increased motivation, and intrinsic interest in the subject matter did occur. We saw a parallel program of activity developed by Layman and Robert Allen around games of logic (Wff'n Proof), algebraic operations, and other topics, have greater success, with interscholastic competition and a national 'Academic Olympics' that some schools continue to participate in. A broad-scale program of interscholastic competition (thus generating *intraschool* social support) has recently been initiated throughout the state of West Virginia. Initial results indicate that among other results, success in the academic games does, as predicted, increase popularity. A program at Johns Hopkins of 'Teams, Games, and Tournaments' was a spinoff from the Academic Games program, and the very successful cooperative learning curriculum that Robert Slavin has developed at Hopkins counts the Academic Games program among its forbears. The basic principles are clearly correct. (I saw my fifth-grade son last year energized to the study of mathematics by a teacher's introduction of mathematics games, which induced cooperation, discussion, and intense effort.) Yet academic competition in the schools remains largely interpersonal, and these principles find limited use in the schools. I remain puzzled about why this is so.

In the midst of the Academic Games program, in February 1965, I received a telephone call from Alexander Mood, a well-known statistician who was Assistant Commissioner of Education and Director of the National Center for Education Statistics. The 'phone call led, after extensive discussion and some hesitation on my part, to my accepting the task of directing a survey of equality of educational opportunity mandated in the Civil Rights Act of 1964. Ernest Campbell from Vanderbilt University and I directed this massive survey, which culminated the next year in *Equality of Educational Opportunity* (EEO). I saw this research as a detour in my research direction, but I undertook it for a combination of two reasons: It offered an opportunity to demonstrate the value of social research for policy issues; and it provided the potential for contributing to increased equality of educational opportunity for black children. As it turned out, both of these possibilities were realized: the research helped create the mold into which much succeeding policy research in education has been cast; and the results were widely used in school desegregation policy over a period of years following its publication.

The principal results of the research with policy relevance were two: First, that the usual measures of school quality regarded as resources for learning (per pupil expenditure, teacher education, size of school library, age of textbooks) showed little relation to achievement in school when students of comparable backgrounds were compared, while differences in students' family backgrounds showed a substantial relation to achievement. Thus to search for ways of equalizing educational opportunity through school 'quality' resources was not likely to prove successful. Second, another result related to equality of educational opportunity: A student's achievement was not only related to that student's own family background; it was related, less strongly, to the family backgrounds of other students in the school. This has obvious implications for strategies of equalizing opportunity through desegregation, implications which led to widespread use of the report in support of desegregation policy.

It is useful to contrast this work with that which led to *The Adolescent Society* (TAS). The EEO survey did not begin with the lives of children; it did not ask what was the school experience for black children and for white children in the varying school settings in which they found themselves. It began rather with administrative goals, and asked questions about how well these were met. How effective were schools for achievement? What were inequalities in the educational resources available to black and white children, and what were inequalities in the outcomes of schooling?

Were the policy-relevant questions better answered by taking this perspective, asking directly about achievement of administrative goals? Or would they have been better answered by starting with the lives of children, and asking what was the school experience for them? Could we have taken this other perspective? These questions remain difficult to answer, even twenty-five years later. The approach of TAS could not have been taken over wholesale, for that approach took the social system of the school, not outcomes for individuals, as its focus. But EEO, by largely ignoring the social system of the school, and taking the administrative perspective of the school as delivering services individually to students, may have missed the most important differences between the school environments in which black and white children found themselves.

One could imagine a combined perspective, in which the administrative goal, that is outcomes for children, remained the ultimate focus, but the social system of the school and its impact on children's investments of effort were not ignored. To take this combined perspective would involve a more indirect route: first, to use information from students (based on interviews, questionnaires, or observation) to reconstruct conceptually the functioning of the social system of the school, by determining the norms, the bases of popularity, the positive or negative status conferred by various activities, and the social location of each child in this system. Then this social system of the school is regarded both as dependent upon the policies and practices of the school staff and in turn as a factor that has consequences for outcomes for children. Most interesting and most important in the context of the policy issues surrounding EEO would be the way in which the social system of the school varied with the racial composition of the school (and with the interaction between racial composition of the school and school administrative policies and practices), and how this in turn affected the experience of the school for black and white children.

Had this been done — and its not having been done in EEO or in other research is in part a matter of lack of research vision, and in part a matter of the inherently greater difficulty of such research — our knowledge of how to overcome problems of racial segregation would be far more advanced than it is. The task of doing this, and doing it well, remains a challenge to sociological researchers, a challenge which, if met, would have important benefits for society.

This is not a trivial matter: With such knowledge, the policies of school desegregation as carried out from the late 1960s until today might have been far more beneficial for the lives of black and white children than they have been, might have led to more stably integrated schools, and might not have brought the backlash of the 1980s which has exacerbated race relations on some college campuses and in some large cities.

The reception of EEO by the research community and in the political arena involved me in controversy over a period of several years. However, another problem in the way we bring up our young began to occupy my attention. The time was the late 1960s and early 1970s, the emergence of the baby boom generation into youth and young adulthood, and the period of youth revolt. The events of that period focussed attention on the inadequacy of schools, as they came to envelop increasingly large fractions of young persons' lives, as a total environment for bringing young persons into adulthood. The problems are principally problems of the high school period, a segment of school which has never been satisfactorily organized since mass secondary education began in the 1920s and 1930s. The problems of how best to organize the processes of bringing the young into adulthood were not those which required new research, but nevertheless merited more serious attention than they had been given.

I was at the time a member of the President's Science Advisory Committee, and in that capacity organized a Panel on Youth which addressed these questions. We approached this task by reviewing the implications of existing knowledge for this transition period between childhood and adulthood. Our panel produced a report, *Youth: Transition to Adulthood*, published by the Federal government in 1972. As one of three or four similar reports on these questions appearing at about the same time, the report reinforced some of the restructuring of high schools designed to reduce the discontinuity between school and work, between dependency and economic independence.

Much later, in the mid-1980s, similar problems continued to beset a number of European countries (which had seen their youth unemployment rates rise and had continued to experience problems in their recently restructured secondary education). These problems led to a request from OECD to address, with Torsten Husén of Sweden, similar problems in a broader perspective. We prepared a report, published in 1985 by OECD, titled *Becoming Adult in a Changing Society*.

In 1974 another telephone call led to a new research direction related to the EEO-derived school desegregation policies. The call was from William Gorham at the Urban Institute in Washington, asking if I would contribute a chapter on urban education to a bicentennial book that he would be editing with Nathan Glazer. (The book, published in 1976, was titled *The Urban Predicament*.) One topic I wished to investigate in the chapter was trends in the racial integration of schools, given the massive desegregation policies of the late 1960s and 1970s. As it turned out, the Civil Rights Commission had been collecting, since 1967, yearly data on racial composition of schools across the United States, and had data available in machine-readable form for the years 1968–1973. With two research assistants at the Urban Institute (Sara Kelly and John Moore), I analyzed these data to examine these trends.

The results were published in 1975 by the Urban Institute as *Trends in School Segregation, 1968–73* (TSS). We found disturbing results: Although desegregation policies had led to central-city school districts that had less segregated schools, the large cities had experienced another change which tended to defeat desegregation policy. These schools experienced extensive losses of whites, primarily to predominantly white sub-urban districts. Most serious, analysis showed that loss of whites was most extensive where central-city desegregation had been most intensive. Thus the policies of school desegregation in central cities had acted to increase racial segregation between cities and suburbs. This, as one might imagine, was not welcome news, especially to those still working to extend those policies, and especially coming from a researcher who, since EEO, had been counted as an ally in the social movement to racially integrate America's schools. The familiar tendency to 'kill the messenger' led to another period of controversy, which made the earlier controversy over EEO pale by comparison.

Nineteen seventy-nine marked the beginning of my next major foray into re-search on schools. It was the time when the National Center for Education Statistics issued a request for a proposal on what would become High School and Beyond — a survey of tenth and twelfth graders in a sample of 1015 high schools throughout the United States. In the proposal we prepared at NORC, we planned not only data collection, but also ten initial analyses on topics relevant both to fundamental issues in education and to current policy questions. Five of these were approved, and in September 1980, after the data collection in spring 1980, we presented our analytical reports to the government. Included among these was a report on public and private high schools that I, with two research assistants, Sally Kilgore and Thomas Hoffer, had prepared. In spring 1981 the report was released by the Department of Education, and in 1982 it was published as *High School Achievement: Public, Catholic, and Private Schools Compared*.

As in EEO and TSS, this research challenged conventional wisdom, for it reported both that private sector schools did not increase the degree of racial segregation in education, and that achievement in private schools was higher than that in public schools for students who were comparable in background. That we found these results for Catholic schools, previously regarded as inferior, as well as independent schools, was particularly hard for some to accept. Again controversy erupted, controversy that only subsided when Thomas Hoffer and I showed (in *Public and Private High Schools*) with a second wave of tests on the same tenth graders as seniors that growth in achievement between grades 10 and 12 confirmed the results found for levels of achievement.

This last research, however, did more than confirm the results of the 1980 survey. We searched for an explanation of why the performance of children in religiously-grounded private schools was greater than that of comparable children in public or independent private schools. The answer involved going back to a more sociological conception of the school, back in the general direction I began in *The Adolescent Society*, and away from a conception of the school as an institution delivering services individually to a set of independent individuals. This time, however, the social milieu that was relevant for explaining the effectiveness of religiously-grounded schools was not the society of adolescents in the school; it was the community of adults outside the school. We found that when that community was strong, as it more often was in religiously-grounded schools, it provided a resource (which we then termed 'social capital') that was important for students' achievement and for their staying in school until graduation. This research again focussed attention on the point suggested in TAS, that educational outcomes are not merely independent consequences of institutional 'treatments' or 'delivery of services', but can be understood only as a complex consequence of the functioning of social systems of which the formal school activities are merely a part.

Now what? I am in the midst of tackling the difficult task referred to earlier: incorporating the functioning of the informal social system among adolescents into the analysis of the effects of schooling on student outcomes. I will report in my next *Reflections* in Phi Delta Kappan whether or not the attempt was successful.

Acknowledgment

This article first appeared in *Reflections*, edited by Derek L. Burleson, Bloomington, Indiana: Phi Delta Kappa Educational Foundation, 1991, pp. 62–70. It is reproduced with the permission of the author.

3   Youth and Adolescence:
A Historical and Cultural Perspective

Torsten Husén

My first contact with Coleman's work occurred at the University of Chicago, where I spent the fall of 1959 as a visiting professor at the Comparative Education Center. My sociology colleague Arnold Anderson gave me a report written for the US Office of Education by a young assistant professor by the name of James S. Coleman, who was at the time in the process of leaving Chicago for an associate professorship at Johns Hopkins. The report dealt with a study, supported by a grant from the US Office of Education, which Coleman had conducted in a number of high schools and later published in his book *The Adolescent Society* (1961). Since fifteen years earlier I had myself submitted a dissertation in psychology on adolescence at my home university of Lund in Sweden I read the report with particular interest. It proved to be a seminal work on youth culture, which provided a much better understanding of adolescence than the psychologists so far had been able to advance. I wrote an extremely positive review of the report for a Swedish journal.

However, personal contacts leading to a fruitful cooperation were not established until the late 1960s, when we both became members of the US National Academy of Education. In the meantime Coleman had published another important study, *Equality of Educational Opportunity*, in 1966. In the fall of 1971 Coleman, in his role as chairman of the President's Advisory Committee, invited me to attend a meeting of the Panel on Youth to be held in Washington, D.C. The immediate reason for the invitation was a discussion that we had had earlier that year in Stockholm while he was a visiting scholar at the Institute of International Education. He was injecting ideas into the analyses of data collected by the International Association for the Evaluation of Educational Achievement (IEA), which then had its headquarters in Stockholm. I showed him a critical essay, which had originally been given as a farewell lecture at the School of Education when I left to take over the Institute of International Education. The ideas in the essay were later spelled out in more detail in my book *The School in Question* (1979). He thought that these views, which were similar to his own, would be of interest to his panel.

I am embedding Coleman's work on youth and adolescence in these personal recollections, not least because he has been very influential on my own work in the field. When the OECD asked us to write a report on youth problems in the early 1980s, it was quite natural that we sat down to work together in Paris and Chicago respectively, as natural as it was later on to come together with other colleagues from both sides of the Atlantic to establish the International Academy of Education.

Another field of educational sociology where Coleman's work has been seminal concerns the role of the family as a 'social capital' together with problems of changing responsibilities for child rearing. When the *Academia Europea* asked me to set up a task force to identify major issues in European formal schooling and their ramifications, it was natural to draw upon Coleman's ideas in analyzing the changing relationships between home and school.

The present chapter will deal with the two areas in educational sociology in which James Coleman's influence has been seminal: youth culture and the 'generation gap', and child and youth socialization and child rearing against the background of the changing role and functions of the family in modern society.

Adolescence and Sociocultural Setting

To be acknowledged as a fully fledged adult varies considerably depending on socio-cultural setting. In 'primitive' societies, even with due consideration to the variation between them, the transition from childhood to adulthood occurs almost instantly at the time of physical sexual maturity, in some cultures after a short period — often a few days or weeks — of 'testing' or after certain initiation rites. The latter signify that the young person is ready to shoulder adult responsibilities in working life, to choose a sexual partner, to form a family, and to become familiar with the religious and mythical notions of the tribe and thereby adopt a *Weltanschauung*. The initiation ceremonies indicate that the individual passes from the position of being an economic liability to that of an asset. In some cultures the initiation ceremonies are centred on the boys, which signifies that they play a more dominant role in the economy, whereas in others the ceremonies are centred on the girls. In pre-industrial societies, then, there is no such thing as 'youthhood' as a period in its own right.

During the Middle Ages an apprenticeship system emerged as a means of learning a craft or a trade. The guilds of senior craftsmen prepared rather elaborate rules on how to take on apprentices and how and for what length of time they should be trained and examined. Rules were set for adopting journeymen (*Gesellen*), who had to find opportunities of further training by wandering from one place to another for an extended period before being regarded as qualified to open up their own shop.

In some countries the apprenticeship system almost disappeared when mass production enterprises with routine jobs were established. There was little opportunity to learn a complex craft or trade, and young people who began work in these enter-prises were taken on as handymen or errand boys. But the apprenticeship system as a means of socializing young people into working life has continued in countries such as Austria, Germany, Switzerland and Denmark, even in medium-sized or large enterprises. In such cases the learning of various industrial jobs has been achieved by a combination of working on the shop floor and attending 'vocational' schools. This dual system covers the age range 14–18 in Germany, where the young people work in the enterprises most of their time but attend classes in school some ten hours per week.

As noted above, in pre-industrial subsistence society of a tribal character the tran-sition from childhood to adulthood was a short process, sometimes a kind of 'instant co-option', sometimes after certain initiation ceremonies. It was during the Enlight-enment that adolescence began to be conceived as a separate development stage in its own right. It was Rousseau who, not so much with *Émile* as with *Le Contrat social*, founded the new way of thinking about adolescence. The 'common ego' (*moi commun*) that emerged from the social contract gave rise to a society that was lifted from the raw natural to a cultural stage. Young people were introduced into it by a 'second birth', or rather, youth became constituted as a result of the second birth. This conception of youth as a stage with its own intrinsic value was also fostered by German Romanticism. The very idea of the idealistic young person, who in Goethe's words was '*himmelshoch jauchzend und zum Tode betrübt*' (heaven high shouting from joy and depressed to death), and of youth as a stage of 'storm and stress' became generally accepted, not least in the literature of Romanticism. This was a precursor of the conception of adolescence developed in modern times by Erik Erikson (1968), who regarded the period of youth as one of identity crisis, a disequilibrium of the individual's conception of the self and an exploration of various roles.

Thus adolescence and youth as a distinctive period of development is a product of complex and differentiated industrial society, where a long period of schooling and preparation has to precede co-option into adult society, and where a wide range of options and the lack of consistency between the preparatory functions of various institutions — family, school, workplace — make the establishment of an adult identity both difficult and complex.

Changing Conceptions of Transition to Adulthood: Hall, Bühler, Mead and the Lynds

The monumental *Adolescence* by G. Stanley Hall, published in 1904 in two volumes and reporting studies based on questionnaire data, was the first major empirical study of this stage of development. Since at the time fewer than 10 per cent of young Americans entered high school and very few of them went on to college, the picture he obtained was rather selective. It reflected at best the views and reactions of adolescents of middle-class background.

As Stanley Hall confesses in his autobiography (Hall, 1922), Darwinian evolutionism was 'music to my ears'. He accepted as a biologically given, self-evident fact that adolescence was a long, troublesome transition period characterized by storm and stress. According to the Darwinian or Spencerian scheme, the stages of individual development (ontogenesis) were seen as a repetition of cultural development, which had its parallel in biological phylogenesis. Adolescence could thus be seen as a parallel to the 'heroic' stage of historical development, the stage of classical Greece (see Husén, 1944).

The next important study of adolescence was conducted by Charlotte Bühler in Vienna. Her seminal study, based mainly on diaries kept by young people from educated homes, *Das Seelenleben des Jugendlichen* (1921), was important in two respects. She made a distinction between puberty and adolescence, the first being the period of physiological maturity and the second the *Kulturpubertät* when the young person achieved the psychological and social maturity required for the culture to which he or she belonged. Her analyses of how young people reacted were based on diary data. Again, the subjects whose diaries were examined came from rather sophisticated and articulate intellectual circles in Vienna and could certainly not be construed to be representative of young people in general.

Subsequent anthropological studies of 'primitive' societies, for instance the one by Margaret Mead on Samoa (Mead, 1943), relativized the previous conception of adolescence. They showed that there was little 'storm and stress' in such societies. One began to realize that Hall's study of adolescence was in fact an ethnocentric portrait of young people of middle-class background in Western societies. Margaret Mead and other social anthropologists began to show how the dynamics and length of adolescence depended on the cultural setting. In so-called primitive, pre-industrial societies physiological puberty marked the transition to adult responsibilities. The change from childhood to adult status was symbolically emphasized by initiation rites. After a short period of learning and preparation, young people were ready to support themselves, establish a family of their own and exercise the religion of their elders. The surviving confirmation rites in rural Sweden reflected this. At the age of 14–15 the young people went through a period of religious instruction by the parish priest and were examined. The boys were thereafter supposed to wear long trousers (which emphasized their adult status) and expected to deal with age mates from the other sex. A dominant characteristic of the transition period in pre-industrial society was its brevity.

There was no need to go back to 'primitive' societies to find variations in the dynamics of adolescent development. When Stanley Hall in the 1890s studied adolescent 'crises' in America, he found that in many cases they tended to be resolved by religious conversions and deliberations. Studies conducted less than half a century later in America showed that the preoccupations were quite different. In their investigation of *Middletown in Transition* (1937), the Lynds, who took an anthropological approach, showed how the juxtaposition of old and modern values and the ensuing inconsistencies created problems about identities and roles among young people. These inconsistencies, defined as the 'generation gap', was one of the central themes of Coleman's first major work in the field, *The Adolescent Society* (1961).

Youth Culture and the 'Generation Gap': Coleman's *Adolescent Society* (1961) and Its Reception

From the beginning of the 1950s social psychologists and sociologists began to undertake systematic studies of adolescence. However, the Coleman study of 'youth culture' in ten middle-west high schools in the US, published in *The Adolescent Society*, had a particularly strong impact.

Adolescence, when it started to become a field of systematic study, was, as we have seen, conceived as a stage when the young person is trying to come to grips with him- or herself and thereby comes into conflict with adult authorities and institutions. The young tend to turn from their parents and to their peers. Empirical studies show how they gradually turn away from ideals embodied by persons in their close proximity to remote ideals, often literary figures far away from the tangible reality surrounding them (Husén, 1944).

It has been contended with some justification that this is a picture of adolescence in upper- or middle-class homes where young people attend school during their entire teens, as distinguished from those from working-class backgrounds who begin to work with adults and have to shoulder adult responsibilities much earlier. But in those societies where the great majority of young people attend school well into their late teens, the picture becomes more universal.

There exists a consensus among those who have studied adolescence that the lower limit of the period is defined by physiological criteria, puberty and a growth spurt in height and weight. There also seems to be a consensus about the social nature of criteria setting the upper limit, for instance taking on certain adult responsibilities, the ability to support oneself by work, and the readiness to vote and to marry. The problem, however, is that whatever criteria one chooses they tend to be rather spread out in time. Young people can be 'adults' in certain respects, for instance with regard to voting age, but dependent youngsters in other respects, for instance with regard to authority to conduct certain types of business.

There is further general agreement that adolescence and youth is a period when young people try to explore themselves and the future roles they want to play. Indeed, they often not only explore but also try out various options. It is a stage which Erik Erikson refers to as a 'psychological moratorium', a period in modern complex society which has become increasingly difficult because more options and alternatives (educational, vocational and marital) are open than in the more static, pre-industrial society. Young people need access to meaningful alternatives without premature commitments. This means by necessity that the age at which they assume adult roles more definitively has tended to be later. The scheme proposed by Charlotte Bühler (1921), in her seminal study of the psychology of the adolescent, proposes two stages of development. After the advent of puberty comes a period of psychological maturation, exploration and 'floundering'. Bühler distinguished between *Pubertät* and *Adoleszens*. Given that in many advanced industrial societies most young people are in institutions of formal education until their early 20s, it is clearly important to distinguish between adolescence and youth.

Coleman (1961a) talked about an 'adolescent society', others about a 'youth culture', 'age segregation' or 'generation gap' as typical of the status of young people in modern society. There has been as much controversy about the justifications for such expressions as there has been about the use of 'crisis' for the present situation in secondary schools. As always, controversy tends to stem not only from different perceptions but from different definitions as well. What criteria constitute a 'generation gap'? A gap between which generations?

We can distinguish here between more objective and more subjective criteria of distance, segregation or isolation. On the one hand, one can record the amount of contact young people have with adults as compared with their peers, as well as their participation in adult activities such as work tasks and leisure activities performed within the context of various voluntary associations. On the other hand, we have subjective criteria that in the first place relate to value orientation, expressed attitudes and preferences. Given these criteria, what evidence can be advanced for or against the existence of an 'age segregation'?

In presenting his theory of an adolescent society Coleman (1961a, 1974a) points out that only a small minority of young people chose the occupations of their parents, perhaps at most 10 per cent, whereas in pre-industrial society the main fields of work — such as agriculture, cattle-raising and artisan crafts — meant working 'at home'. The family was a unity of work and consumption, with the children working along with the parents from an early age. Since early industrialization most fathers work outside the home and many children have only a vague idea about what their fathers are doing during their absence. More recently, there has been a major increase in the number of working mothers. This means that children in a majority of homes not only are out of touch with the sphere of work which occupies their parents most of the day. In some countries they are increasingly being taken care of by institutions, such as day care centres. This has certain consequences in terms of shifting the responsibilities for upbringing from the family to impersonal agencies, 'corporate actors' to use Coleman's (1981a) expression, with all that that implies.

The most basic and undisputed evidence which supports the contention of age segregation is prolonged formal schooling. In 1945 some 80 per cent of 14-year-olds in Western Europe left school and joined the work force. The apprenticeship system was still a major way of introducing young people into the work force, and many gained their first experience of the world of work by being assigned simple tasks of an errand-running character at very modest salaries. Today some 80–90 per cent of the 14–18-year-olds are in full-time schooling. Mandatory school attendance in most countries lasts until 16, and the majority opts for upper secondary school for some additional years. Thus, whereas most teenagers of the 1940s and 1950s were to be found in workplaces with adult workers, their age mates of the 1990s are to be found at schools with adult contacts limited to teachers and with a quite different role from that of young people of their age some decades ago. Even though one's status was at the bottom of the hierarchy, work participation then was of a functional character. In principle, however, young people were involved in the work process along with adult workers and gradually had to take responsibility for their part of it. But the role of a school pupil means being a client, being taught and examined by somebody who plans the teaching-learning process for both partners, and without sharing functional responsibility for the work process.

Coleman's report on *Youth: Transition to Adulthood* (1974) has been criticized, for instance by Timpane *et al.* (1975), for using the contacts, or rather lack of contacts, with parental work as the sole criterion of 'isolation' or 'age segregation'. The critics refer to US statistics according to which since the early 1950s young people in the age range 16 through 24 have increased their participation in the labour market, both full- and part-time, in spite of increased participation in further education. The National Longitudinal Study of 1975 found that in the early 1970s 70–80 per cent of those in senior high school held summer jobs. A similar tendency can be observed in other countries.

Socialization and Changes in Responsibility for Child Rearing: Coleman's *Asymmetric Society* (1981)

Sociologists in central Europe, particularly in Germany, began to study youth problems soon after the Second World War. These studies were inspired to a large extent by the destruction of previous values and ideals by the German defeat in the war and subsequent revelations of atrocities. Much of the research in this field was referred to as 'socialization studies' and was influenced by the critical philosophy of the Frankfurt School of Social Research under the intellectual auspices of Horkheimer and Adorno, and later Habermas. The major concern was to map out how young people perceived their situation and what attitudes they were adopting in order to obtain a better basis for the work conducted by educators, youth leaders and others.

However, there was also a focus on socialization in terms of the learning of social roles, internalization of norms and beliefs and the learning of 'useful' social skills. For example, the German Shell Youth Foundation in 1953 decided to sponsor a study of the situation of German youth. Two reports were published in 1954 and 1955 entitled *Jugend zwischen 15 und 24* (*Youth between 15 and 24*). The same sponsor was behind a further major study which came out in 1965 under the title *Jugend, Bildung und Freizeit* (*Youth, Education and Leisure*). Some twenty questions given to the sample of young people in 1953 were kept in the interview questionnaire a decade later and were repeated on a third occasion in the 1970s.

In the 1970s the Shell Foundation provided further support for two major studies. The first was published in 1975, *Jugend zwischen 13 und 24* (*Youth between 13 and 24*) with the subtitle *Vergleich über 20 Jahre* (*Comparison over 20 Years*). The second study comprised representative samples of young people at 13, 17 and 23 from the Federal Republic of Germany, France and the United Kingdom and was thus cross-national in orientation. The title of the ensuing comparative publication was *Jugend in Europa: Ihre Eingliederung in die Welt der Erwachsenen* (1977) (*Youth in Europe: Its Integration into the Adult World*). The last two studies were explicitly oriented towards elucidating the socialization of young people. Thus in the preparatory stage, before designing the questionnaires and starting the data collection, five leading German sociologists were invited to spell out their views on the socialization process. It was decided to conduct what one of the participating sociologists called a 'panorama study' which could provide descriptive data pertaining to a broad range of problems, thus compensating for the 'lack of theoretical parameters', a euphemism for lack of consensus about the theoretical conception of socialization.

A comprehensive questionnaire was designed covering socialization at home, school, vocational training and out-of-school activities. The interviewees were some 1000 young people expected to be broadly representative national samples. The field-work was conducted by an opinion poll and market research institute, the *EMNID Institut für Meinungs- und Marktforschung.*

Consensus was achieved, however, about a classification of the questions to be included in the interview questionnaire. It was agreed that three domains of socialization should be investigated:

1   *primary socialization* occurring in the family, kindergarten and among playmates with the goal of achieving emotional stability, successful affective relations, cooperative abilities with peers and respect for non-parental authority;
2   *secondary socialization* brought about by the various stages of formal schooling, vocational education and leisure time activities with the goal of achieving cognitive competencies, readiness for continuous learning, political socialization and work discipline;
3   *tertiary socialization* conducted by various legal and religious organizations, voluntary associations, the mass media and by the political system with the goal of social integration, social recognition, readiness and capacity to assume new roles and to achieve responsibility and vocational competence.

In order to study the socialization process at these three stages, three age cohorts were selected: 12-year-olds, the age of transfer from primary to secondary school in the three countries, 17-year-olds, the age of transfer from secondary school to working life or tertiary education, and 22-year-olds, the age marking the end of apprenticeship or the attainment of the first university degree. A model was advanced according to which within the total context of socialization conditions were seen affecting the interaction between the socialisand and the socialisator.

In his book *When the Nettles Bloom* the Swedish author and Nobel laureate Harry Martinson presents experiences from his own childhood in a rural area. The mother had deserted the family and the children were taken care of by the local board in charge of the poor and desolate. They did what was common in earlier days, namely 'auction' the children to farming families in the area. The lowest bidder was charged with the task of taking care of a given child. Pending the transfer, the main character of the book spent some time in the home of the elderly of the parish, and after delivery to that home the lady in charge of it, wanting to comfort him, patted him on his head. As the author wrote: 'he felt that it was the communal pat'.

This episode illustrates a phenomenon that has become commonplace in all industrialized societies in recent decades: the shift of responsibility from the family to various social institutions and — in the final resort — to state and national agencies. An increasing number of children are growing up subjected to a different kind of 'communal pat'.

In his analysis of 'the asymmetric society' Coleman (1982a) showed that the institutions involved in child rearing today are not extensions of the traditional family, 'the last kernel of the old social structure to remain'. The family is in a way a 'legal anachronism' which is difficult to sustain in a society consisting of growing, powerful organizations where 'persons are transient and only the structure is permanent' (1982a: 122). There is a sharp discontinuity between the dominant social structure consisting of institutions on the one hand and the family on the other. The new structure is built upon activities and not on persons. Membership of a family is what sociologists used to refer to as 'ascribed', whereas membership in the organizations that Coleman refers to as modern 'corporate actors' is 'achieved', an outcome of initiative on the part of the individual or the 'corporate actor'.

Traditionally, the family is 'structured around authority over and responsibility for persons'. But the organization or corporate actor is structured around activities. Authority over a person, such as the one exercised by the family, means — or meant — responsibility for the welfare of that particular person. In earlier days the family had authority over a person as a whole. It also had responsibility for that person as a whole. In many advanced industrial societies new and specialized institutions have now moved in to take responsibility when the family is no longer exercising it. Children of pre-school age are taken care of in day care centres while their parents are at work. A system of welfare agencies guarantees that family members are taken care of during sickness, disabilities and old age. Schools assume responsibility for children from the age of 6–7 to their mid- and late teens. Each such institution with narrowly defined responsibilities is in charge of a particular segment of the person: as a child, as a patient, as unemployed or retired.

Earlier a large part of child rearing took place in conjunction with the productive activities performed jointly by the entire family. Now both the productive and child rearing activities have become specialized by function and are performed separated from each other. The consequences of this development for child rearing have already been hinted at. The role of the family and the parents has been substantially reduced. The school has taken over one limited part of the responsibility, but does not have the authority to exercise that responsibility efficiently in academic and disciplinary matters. There are other corporate actors who are exploiting the fact that young people represent a powerful group of consumers and try to sell their products via newspapers and television and create 'an admiration for high consumption' (1982a: 137).

The incompatibilities between the responsibility of the parents and the society represented by ever more powerful institutions, each with its responsibilities for one aspect or segment of the child, have brought about problems of crisis proportions, particularly among children who are growing up in what Martin Trow (1977) in his typology of youth refers to as disadvantaged and deprived milieus. The ecology of upbringing has become increasingly fragmented and impersonal, particularly for children growing up in large cities with large schools, particularly at the secondary level. For instance, studies conducted in the mid-1970s found that in five large cities in the United States 84 per cent of high school students were attending schools with an enrolment above 2000 students (Timpane *et al.*, 1975). Schools have increasingly become pedagogical factories.

Conclusion

James Coleman has contributed in a decisive way to our conceptual understanding of youth in modern society and of the role of the family in providing the cultural capital which plays such an important role in laying the ground for success or failure at school. Above all, he has developed the strategy of thinking that allows us to understand what has happened to upbringing in the transformation into modern urbanized society. Coleman was also one of the leading scholars in the field of educational research in 1970 invited by OECD to become a member of a so-called strategy group appointed to come up with ideas which would guide the OECD secretariat in its framing of educational policy. In this and other ways he has also contributed to strategic thinking in school policies, particularly by his analysis of the concept of equality of opportunity and its policy consequences.

4 Coleman's Contributions to Understanding Youth and Adolescence

Denise B. Kandel

Youth as a Theme in Coleman's Research

The study of youth is central to James Coleman's work. In turn, James Coleman's work on youth is central to our understanding of youth development in modern society. His work has been important for five independent reasons. It generated important substantive findings and theoretical insights. It developed innovative research designs. It marked the beginning of large-scale social projects. It played a pivotal role in policy and it illustrated the power of social sciences as a basis for policy. Finally, Coleman heralded the age of the social scientist as a media star. Each of these contributions made a major impact in the field, as reflected in other chapters in this volume, which discuss each of these aspects in greater detail. Coleman's work on youth was also central to my own career, as will become apparent in the personal postscript that I have included in this chapter.

Research careers generally follow one of two patterns, along the lines of Isaiah Berlin's (1953) elaboration of the hedgehog and fox distinction (Bierstedt, 1990).[1] One pattern, the hedgehog, is characterized by an almost single-minded focus on a limited number of themes to which the person returns time and time again. The second pattern, the fox, by contrast, involves divergent and changing commitments. 'The fox knows many things, but the hedgehog knows one big thing' (Berlin, 1953: 1). Paradoxically, Coleman's career fits both paradigms. He is the fox as hedgehog. Youth and adolescent development in schools has been the major focus of Coleman's research and policy writings and is represented by four major empirical studies and two policy reports. In addition to many journal articles, the studies are summarized in five books: *The Adolescent Society* (1961a), *Equality of Educational Opportunity* (Coleman, Campbell *et al.*, 1966), *High School Achievement: Public, Catholic, and Private Schools Compared* (Coleman, Hoffer and Kilgore, 1982), *Public and Private High Schools: The Impact of Communities* (Coleman and Hoffer, 1987) and *Parents, Their Children and Schools* (Schneider and Coleman, 1993). Both policy reports focused on the transition to adulthood. One, *Youth: Transition to Adulthood* (Coleman, 1973b), was written when Coleman was a member of the President's Science Advisory Committee. The second, *Becoming Adult in a Changing Society* (Coleman and Húsen, 1985), was written for the Organization for Economic Cooperation and Development (OECD).

Throughout, Coleman's concern has been on socialization influences, particularly the school, that determine a young person's development as a productive member of industrialized society. In such a society the school becomes the primary socialization agency, because other institutions, such as the family, have lost most of their influence

(Coleman, 1973b). Coleman has focused singlemindedly on a crucial aspect of youth development, namely academic and educational achievement. To use a concept that was not yet in use at the time Coleman started his research, he has been interested in social factors that foster the formation of human capital. In the thirty-two years spanned by this work, important shifts have occurred in Coleman's views about the important socialization influences in a young person's life. I trace this shift in this chapter by reviewing in turn each of the major relevant empirical studies. Because of Coleman's perspective, a discussion of his treatment of adolescence and youth becomes a discussion of his research on schools. This chapter perforce covers issues that are treated by others in this volume who discuss Coleman's school-related research.

Adolescent Status Systems and Subcultures

The Adolescent Society is Coleman's first work on the subject of adolescence. (A much shorter report from the study, *Social Climates in High Schools* (1961b), was published in the same year by the governmental funding agency.) He designed the study (and sought funding for it) while still in graduate school. But the study was not implemented until his first year on the faculty at the University of Chicago. Many of the themes that Coleman pursued subsequently were presaged in one way or another, theoretically as well as methodologically, by *The Adolescent Society*. This seminal book dealt with issues that have preoccupied Coleman throughout his career: the impact of schools on the development of youth, characteristics of schools that are favourable or detrimental to learning, equality of educational opportunity.[2] The study was motivated by a long-term concern with sources and consequences of status pluralism in social systems and the desire to investigate the problem with quantitative methods (1964c, 1990f, 1994b). The impact of high schools on adolescents appeared to provide an almost ideal system for such an investigation. The concern with the social climates of high schools may also have had its origin in Coleman's personal interest in understanding how he, having attended a technical high school, alone among his classmates had ended up as an academician.

An often quoted citation, which captured the imagination of the public and the scientific community, exemplifies the major message of the book: 'This setting-apart of our children in schools . . . has a singular impact on the child of high-school age. He is "cut off" from the rest of society, forced inward toward his own age group, made to carry out his whole social life with others his own age. With his fellows, he comes to constitute a small society, one that has most of its important interactions *within* itself, and maintains only a few threads of connection with the outside adult society' (Coleman, 1961a: 3). Adolescents form societies of their own with their peers and are immune from the influence of adults. 'It is their peers whose approval, admiration, and respect they attempt to win in their everyday activities, in school and out' (Coleman, 1961a: 11). The title *The Adolescent Society* reflected the book's message. Coleman's innovation was to describe on the basis of systematic survey data the social systems of different schools and their impact on adolescents. He identified the different values in these schools, how they were reflected in the characteristics of elites and the social networks among students, and how in turn the dominant values and the students' sociometric positions in these social systems affected the students' self-esteem and academic performance. The dominant values favoured leading crowds, athletics for boys and popularity and leadership in activities for girls. Those who were nominated by their peers as excelling in the high status areas had the highest self-esteem. Student scholars had very little prestige, were isolates, and generally had low self-esteem compared with their peers. The role of parents was not discussed, and by implication parents were assumed to play little role in their child's development. In the book itself and in subsequent writings in the decade following (1970a, 1973b), Coleman stressed the emergence of strong adolescent subcultures in modern society and the increased separation between parents and their adolescent children. As discussed in *Youth: Transition to Adulthood* (Coleman, 1973b), the emergence of these distinct subcultures was attributed to structural changes in the social organization of modern industrialized society: the age segregation of adolescents from younger children and from adults; their ecological segregation in schools where they spend most of their lives with peers of their own age; the lengthening of schooling; the reduced responsibilities for participation in the labour force. Insulation from parents and other adults was assumed to result in the elimination of parental ability to influence their adolescent children. There was, as subsequently proposed by Margaret Mead (1970), a generation gap. While *The Adolescent Society* had made some attempt to consider other aspects of a young person's development, such as self-esteem, besides those related to academic concerns, these efforts were abandoned subsequently.

Coleman made very little use of the survey data that he had collected from the parents themselves, except for documenting with a single table the differences in the value systems of parents and adolescents. No relational analysis was conducted that would consider simultaneously the values of parents and of peers or subgroups in the school in order to assess under what conditions peer and parental influences clashed or reinforced each other. The parental data, however, were used in a subsequent article with Edward McDill on the relative importance of parents and peers on adolescent educational aspirations (McDill and Coleman, 1965). In the freshman year of high school, parental self-reported educational aspirations for their child were twice as important an influence as high school social status on the child's own aspirations. Although parental influence declined over the four years of high school while the effect of social status increased, by the senior year parental influence was still stronger than peer influence, but only slightly so. This message is quite different from that conveyed by *The Adolescent Society*. Similarly, Coleman did not analyze the longitudinal data from the adolescent's peers, which were subsequently analyzed by Jere Cohen (1983). Yet such analyses are crucial in determining whether similarity in values and behaviours within a network reflects assortative affiliation or true influence. Curiously, several years later, when Coleman needed a sixteen-fold table for a chapter on mutual interpersonal influence that he was writing for a festschrift in honour of Paul Lazarsfeld (Coleman, 1979a), he used a cross-tabulation over time of patterns of marijuana use among adolescent friendship pairs from one of my studies (Kandel, 1978) rather than a similar table that he could have derived from longitudinal data collected as part of *The Adolescent Society*. Coleman was familiar with the table, having consulted with me regarding its analysis. Thus the table was more readily available than the comparable table he would have had to reconstruct from the data from *The Adolescent Society*. However, the use of another person's data may also reflect how strongly he perceived the book to be a study of social systems and not of individuals.

The Adolescent Society had a major impact on the conceptualization and understanding of adolescent development. This impact is reflected in many ways and, in

Figure 4.1.   Number of Citations for Adolescent Society by Year

Number of citations

Source: Social Science Citation Index (1961–93).

particular, in the citation patterns for the book. A plot of the number of citations since the book was published illustrates dramatically its continuing influence (Figure 4.1). Both in the number of citations and in the span of time over which they have occurred, the book is almost unique in sociology. An analysis of citations to socio-logical books carried out by the Institute for Scientific Information (Bott and Hargens, 1991) found that the average number of citations for books published in 1974 during the next eleven years (1974–85) was 41.4 (standard deviation = 63.9). In that same period, starting thirteen years after its publication, there were 546 citations to *The Adolescent Society*, close to eight standard deviations above the mean. The number of citations to *The Adolescent Society* remained at a peak level for ten years from 1970 to 1980, close to twenty years after the publication of the book, and declined slowly thereafter. In 1991 the number of citations was the same as it had been almost thirty years earlier in 1963. By 1993 *The Adolescent Society* had been cited a total of 1053 times. What is especially noteworthy about the citation pattern is its longevity. The citations to Coleman's next empirical monograph, *Equality of Educational Opportunity*, illustrate the remarkable longevity of the citation pattern of *The Adolescent Society* (Figure 4.2). At its peak the second book received many more citations than *The Adolescent Society*, but the number of citations declined sharply fifteen years after the publication of the report.

The notion of an adolescent society fuelled much subsequent work by others. Many attempts were made to refine the conceptualization of adolescent subcultures. Coleman had stressed leading crowds, athletics for boys, being popular and good looking for girls. Cohen (1979) reanalyzed data from one of the ten high schools

Figure 4.2.   Number of Citations for *Equality of Educational Opportunity* by Year

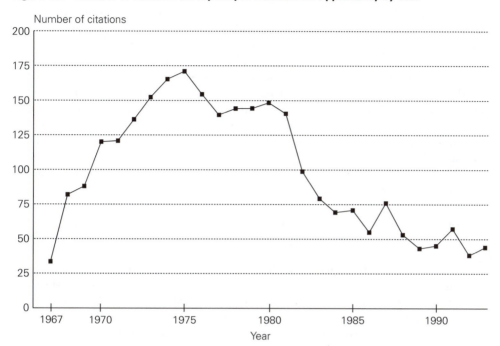

Source: Social Science Citation Index (1967–93).

sampled in *The Adolescent Society* and identified three subcultures: academic, fun, and delinquent subcultures. Attempts at refinement have culminated in Bradford Brown's recent (1992) work on multiple adolescent crowds, including nerds, jocks, brains, druggies. Coleman himself did not pursue empirically the nature of adolescent subcultures and their impact on young people.

Like all good stories in science, the story line in *The Adolescent Society* was somewhat simplified. Because no longitudinal analyses were conducted, the relationships that were observed between the social systems of schools and adolescent cliques with adolescent behaviours and values assumed a unilateral direction from the former to the latter and assigned the entire causal impact to the social context itself. Yet, in a clique, associations between like-minded persons reflect assortative pairing on the basis of prior similarity as well as increased similarity as the result of socialization due to continued association, as was documented by Cohen (1983) twenty years later in his analysis of *The Adolescent Society* data and by my own work (Kandel, 1978; see also postscript below). *The Adolescent Society* exaggerated the influence of the school and of peers on the development of a young person's values and activities. It did not take sufficiently into account the interpersonal influences occurring outside the school. This bias would be rectified, beginning with the very next work.

High Schools and Cognitive Outcomes in Adolescence

Following *The Adolescent Society*, and for the next thirty years, Coleman engaged in a relentless search to understand how schools affect the academic performance of young people, their verbal and mathematical skills, their ability to remain in school, their educational aspirations. The basic question was: what is it about schools that produces or fails to produce the desired outcomes? The desired outcome was the adolescent as 'Homo Scholasticus'. The focus on adolescent subcultures was abandoned in favour of a focus on structural characteristics of schools. The ultimate goal was to construct a just society that would provide equal opportunities for all its young people. The research was characterized by large national samples of students and schools, cross-sectional as well as longitudinal. The very large samples made possible the systematic study of structural factors in the school that could explain equality of educational opportunity, or rather reductions in inequalities (Coleman, 1969b). Paradoxically, the singleminded focus on schools would lead to recognition of the importance of the family in the formation of a young person as a successful and productive member of society.

Equality of Educational Opportunity (Coleman, Campbell *et al.*, 1966) followed the publication of *The Adolescent Society* by five years. Known as the (first) Coleman Report, *Equality of Educational Opportunity* was another landmark study.[3] Its design reflected Coleman's innovative and provocative premise that equality of opportunity should be measured by equality of outcome and not necessarily equality of input (Coleman, 1968c). The study assessed the students' achievements, as measured by standardized tests, as well as school resources, as measured by a series of indicators, such as per pupil expenditures, teachers' degrees or number of library books. It became possible to ask, 'How much do schools overcome the inequalities with which children come to school?' (Coleman, 1990b: 2). Chief among these inequalities was race. As the first mega educational study, the national sample included 639,650 students in grades 1 through 12, principals and teachers,[4] and 4393 elementary and secondary schools. The book reached conclusions that were startling and controversial. It emphasized that student learning was determined foremost by the student's family background and interests and by the characteristics and intellectual interests (especially racial composition) of the student's classmates. These factors were much more important than any other, including teachers or other school resources. Family factors were more important for high achieving (i.e., whites and orientals) than low achieving (i.e., minorities, blacks and Hispanics) students. Thus, while the achievement of minority children was improved by attending a school with high achieving white children, the achievement of white children was not affected downward by the mix in ethnic composition. The book generated much controversy, was attacked by academicians and politicians alike, and created a whole industry of critiques, counter-critiques and reanalyses. A distinguished group of statisticians and social scientists, led by Frederick Mosteller and Daniel Moynihan, formed the Harvard University Faculty Seminar on the Coleman Report and met for one year for the sole purpose of re-analyzing the data and verifying the original findings. Statistical reanalyses confirmed the original conclusions (Mosteller and Moynihan, 1969). This led to new hopes for maximizing the academic achievement of young people. What was required was social engineering at the school level rather than personalized attention at the individual level in order to increase the influence of schools relative to experiences out of school (Coleman, 1969a). The book became a central piece of empirical evidence supporting legal efforts at school integration and busing.

Because the findings suggested that inequalities of opportunity could only be mitigated by increasing the impact of the school relative to that of the family, the search for influential school-related factors continued. Coleman's subsequent works were designed to specify further the attributes of schools that determined a young person's intellectual achievement, controlling for background characteristics.[5] Following a pattern established by the prior publications, each new work generated novel insights and, perhaps as a consequence, much controversy.

High School Achievement: Public, Catholic, and Private Schools Compared (Coleman, Hoffer and Kilgore, 1982) provided a partial answer. An important characteristic of a successful school was that it was private, specifically a private Catholic school. The results again were based on a very large sample of students (N = 58,730) and schools (N = 1015), not quite as large as in *Educational Opportunity*, but still very large. Furthermore, the study was designed to be longitudinal, so that much of the criticism inherent in drawing causal connections between school characteristics and students outcomes, which could be due to self-selection, could be addressed. Controlling for initial family background, students in Catholic schools achieved at a higher level on verbal and mathematical tests than students in private public schools and also had higher educational aspirations.

These conclusions were strengthened (and enlarged) in a subsequent report that used longitudinal data collected two years later and reported in *Public and Private High Schools: The Impact of Communities* (Coleman and Hoffer, 1987). In addition to superior cognitive skills, students in Catholic schools were also less likely to drop out of school and to engage in destructive behaviours while in school. Coleman highlighted two features of Catholic schools which he believed were strongly tied to these differential levels of performance. One set of factors was inherent to the schools themselves and reflected major differences in their functioning: stronger academic demands and disciplinary standards in Catholic schools compared with public schools. In those public schools with academic demands and disciplinary practices that matched those of the private Catholic schools, the students' cognitive skills were equal to those of students in private schools. The reverse was also true. The second set of factors resided outside the schools in the kinds of family and communities to which the children belonged.

Social Capital and Family Influences on Academic Outcomes

Public and Private High Schools: The Impact of Communities (Coleman and Hoffer, 1987) marked a profound shift in Coleman's thinking about adolescent socialization. It marked a shift from concentrating almost exclusively on structural characteristics of schools to interactions within the family and between the family, the school and the larger community. Coleman proposed the concept of social capital, inherent in the *relations* between individuals both within the family and in the community, to describe these outside-school influences (Coleman and Hoffer, 1987; Coleman, 1988a, 1988b, 1990a). Social capital, which parallels the concepts of physical and human capital in economics, is assumed to be a crucial factor in the development of young people and the formation of human capital. Parents influence their children not only through transactions internal to the family but also through transactions in the community external to the child. Deficiencies in social capital, whether internal or external to the family, are detrimental to the development of youth. Internal deficiencies can be structural, e.g., single parent, or functional, e.g., decreased parental involvement with the child or family activities. Deficiencies in social capital outside the family are reflected in lack of intergenerational closure, the extent to which adults in the community interact with one another, and especially with the parents of their children's friends and with the children's friends themselves. 'The social capital for a young person's development resides in the functional community, the actual social relationships that exist among parents, in the closure exhibited by this structure of relations, and in the parent's relations with the institutions of the community. Part of that social capital is the set of norms that develop in communities with a high degree of closure' (Coleman, 1988b: 387).

Thus closed networks give rise to functional communities, favour the development and enforcement of social norms, which foster the child's conformity to school norms and academic interests and restrain the child's involvement in deviant activities. Because of a lack of interactions between parents and children and between parents and other adults, open networks, by contrast, lead to lack of communication, lack of enforcement of norms and an erosion of these norms and of family control. Diminution of social capital creates diminished possibilities for the formation of human capital and greater possibilities for the development of antisocial behaviour in the children. In this way social interactions within and across generations underlie the genesis and maintenance of positive and conforming or deviant behaviour in the children.

As *The Adolescent Society* had done almost thirty years earlier, the concept of social capital seized the attention of the social science community and proved useful not only to account for the achievement of academic goals but for other aspects of a young person's functioning, including delinquency and extreme political attitudes (Hagan, Merkens and Boehnke, 1994; Sampson and Laub, 1993; Steinberg *et al.*, 1993). While *The Adolescent Society* had stressed the importance for adolescents of adolescent subcultures and of the school, social capital stressed instead the out-of-school influence of the family as it interacted both with the school and the larger community. This represented a complete intellectual shift on Coleman's part.

The concept of social capital became a major focus of Coleman's next school-related empirical activity, a collaboration on a multiwave longitudinal study of a national sample of high school sophomores in the United States (NELS'88). Again, large samples of students, parents and teachers were sampled over time: 14,599 eighth graders were sampled from 1057 schools. A recently published monograph from that study, *Parents, Their Children and Schools* (Schneider and Coleman, 1993), reflects the increasing emphasis placed by Coleman on the role of the family in the development of a young person's cognitive skills. Consisting of several chapters written by different collaborators, the report focuses on the nature and consequences of parental involvement in activities related to their child's schooling: the types of involvement in home, school and community; the impact of parental involvement, family composition and maternal employment on cognitive outcomes; the characteristics of schools that foster or impede parental involvement in school; and the factors that determine parental choice of schools. Structural deficiencies in families, represented by non–intactness, can be overcome by functional strengths, as reflected in parental involvement with the child. In the concluding chapter Coleman discusses how expanding parental choice of school might increase equality of educational opportunity for disadvantaged students.

While the role of the family on adolescents' academic achievement is now explicitly acknowledged and the processes underlying its influence partially explained, how family influence relates to or is integrated with the influences of peers and of adolescent subcultures remains to be understood. One such effort at integration would consider the role and influence of parents in their children's peer affiliations. There are at least two such types of influences. One, most often emphasized and best documented, arises from factors and processes *internal to the family* itself, namely parental behaviours and quality of parenting. Lack of parental monitoring, lack of closeness between parent and child and poor disciplinary practices foster affiliation with deviant peers (Brook *et al.*, 1990; Brown *et al.*, 1993; Dishion *et al.*, 1991; Dishion *et al.*, 1992; Elliott, Huizinga and Ageton, 1985; Kandel and Andrews, 1987; Patterson *et al.*, 1992). A second class of indirect parental influences arises out of processes *external to the family*. This is where the concept of social capital becomes especially important. These indirect effects might operate through the extent of parental social capital in their communities. Parents' decisions to settle in certain neighbourhoods and to establish ties with other parents and institutions in the community contribute to indirect peer selection effects. To the best of my knowledge, there are no data available to enable us even to make a guess as to what the extent of these influences could be. Were these indirect parental influences on peer selection taken into account, the relative influence of parent versus peers would be further increased (Kandel, 1995).

Toward an Integration

More than in any other component of his work, Coleman's research on youth and adolescence combines the two major influences to which he was exposed as a graduate student at Columbia. From Lazarsfeld he learned the importance of systematic large-scale empirical social surveys and sophisticated quantitative statistical analyses. From Merton he learned the power of sociological concepts, the importance of the social system, of roles and statuses for understanding the functioning of these systems and their impact on their members. If one reflects on Coleman's work, Merton's influence seems to have been even more pervasive than that of Lazarsfeld. This may explain both the strengths and perhaps some of the limitations of the work for understanding adolescent development. As he announced at the very beginning of his career, Coleman has been primarily interested in the functioning of social systems. As regards the young people in these systems, *The Adolescent Society* constitutes Coleman's most dynamic treatment of adolescent development. Subsequently his empirical research has centred exclusively on levels of youth's cognitive skills and educational aspirations. His basic concern has been with the social factors that determine the formation of social capital. It is important to recognize, however, that even when Coleman acknowledges the importance of the family in fostering the child's cognitive development, his concern throughout is how to maximize the school's influence on the child. In the end the school is a most powerful magnet for the hedgehog.

Yet understanding the development of young people as productive members of society requires understanding more than simply their interests in academic pursuits. The picture of youth as reflected in Coleman's empirical work is somewhat restricted and ignores other aspects of a young person's psychosocial development, which are important not only in their own right but also because they impinge on the development and performance of academic pursuits. One needs to know not only about the development of a young person's ability to perform as a productive member of society but also about the development of the person's ability to perform the other major roles of adulthood, including the establishment of close interpersonal relationships. Coleman recognizes the importance of these other aspects of young people in his policy writings (Coleman, 1973b). However, from reading Coleman's empirical work, we know nothing about the adolescent's social relationships with parents, peers and others in the community, we know nothing about their sexual behaviour, delinquency, health, or psychological strengths and deficits. From Coleman one comes to understand a great deal about the nature of the social forces that impinge on the young person; but one understands very little of the young person's experiences in these settings.

Coleman himself emphasizes an aspect of his work which he feels deserves further elaboration, namely: how do individuals themselves come to determine the norms and values of the social systems to which they belong? This becomes the fundamental issue in sociological analysis: how does one move from the micro to the macro level of analysis? There is no better way to make the point than to quote from two of Coleman's recent essays. Because it is not readily available, I quote at length from a short statement on 'Sociology of Education in the Year 2000' written in 1992 for the newsletter of the section on the Sociology of Education of the American Sociological Association:

> I believe that many sociologists of education have been more attentive to government and general societal orientations to problems in education than they have to sociological orientations. I know that has been true of my own work, at least that after the earliest (*The Adolescent Society*) and before the most recent (*Public and Private Schools: The Impact of Communities*). What has been ignored in much of sociologists' work on schools is the fact that the classroom is a social system, the school is a social system encompassing the classroom, the family is a social system intersecting the school and classroom, and the community is a social system encompassing school and family. Within all this is a set of age-specific subsystems, distinguished by grade in school, and by youth vs. adult. A full recognition of this social location within which education takes place would lead to the recognition that much of the explanation of educational outcomes (grades in school, dropout, attendance, misbehavior, and plans for further education), depend greatly on the functioning of those systems, and the role of the child within them. What we think of as 'educational outcomes' are residues of processes that result from the incentives which relate individuals to social systems. These systems, the child's position within them, bring about these outcomes as well as certain attitudes, such as attitude to school, to education in general, and to specific subjects. (1992: 4)

In his 1994 essay 'My Vision for Sociology' (reprinted as Chapter 21 below), Coleman writes further:

> My vision for sociology . . . shares . . . both a focus on the social system and quantitative methods. But it includes some additional points . . . it . . . is willing to take not only system behavior, but also individual actions as proper phenomena for sociological study, but it sees them as closely intertwined, individual actions generating system behavior, and system properties in turn affecting individual actions.
>
>   Thus it requires going beyond both the kind of analysis . . . which concentrated on the social system, and used individual actions primarily as indicators

of system functioning, and the kind of analysis . . . in which properties of the individual (and sometimes the 'context') are used to account for individual actions . . . in order to pursue that vision, I need to assume a theory of action rather than to focus, like Durkheim, on social and moral density as the prime mover . . . I see as the most formidable task of sociology that of developing theory for moving from the micro level of action to the macro level of norms, social values, status distribution, and social conflict. (1994b; 9, 10, 13)

This new theoretical development, and ultimately its incorporation in empirical investigations, would bring about a true organic merger of the Mertonian and Lazarsfeldian perspectives. Lazarsfeld not only developed the quantitative survey and sophisticated methodologies, but in his empirical work he searched for motives underlying individual behaviour. When this vision is fulfilled, we will indeed approach a deeper understanding of adolescent development in modern society.

A Personal Postscript

James Coleman's work influenced my own work, as will become apparent in this personal postscript. Following a postgraduate fellowship in psychiatry and social sciences at the Harvard Medical School, I obtained a position to direct a project for Gerald Lesser, a psychologist on the faculty at the Harvard School of Education. Jerry had obtained a grant to carry out a comparative study to replicate *The Adolescent Society* in Denmark. Having been an admirer of the book, I was delighted to have an opportunity to work on the study. While a postdoctoral fellow, I had become interested in issues related to family functioning. The work with Jerry Lesser spurred my interest in the relative influence of parents and peers on adolescent development. I had felt, as noted earlier in the chapter, that Coleman had not made sufficient use of the parent and peer data that he had collected. I was determined to explore this aspect of our data in greater detail than had been done in *The Adolescent Society*. Jerry Lesser and I enlisted Jim Coleman and Ed McDill as consultants and carried out the study which was published as *Youth in Two Worlds* (Kandel and Lesser, 1972). The purposefully ambiguous title referred both to the two cultures of America and Denmark and to the two worlds of peers and parents to which young people belong. As noted earlier in this essay, Coleman's thesis was that adolescents were insulated from adults. Insulation from parents and other adults was assumed to result in the elimination of parents' ability to influence their adolescent children. An alternative theme held that parents and peers were not necessarily in antagonism to each other, that parents and their adolescent children could maintain close relationships with each other, that there was continuity of behaviour and values across the generations, and that a proper evaluation of relations across the generations must be area-specific. Having found, contrary to Coleman's thesis, that parental and peer influences were domain-specific, and that parents were more influential than peers with respect to future life plans, while peers were more important for current adolescent concerns and lifestyle issues, I became very interested in initiating a new study in which the influence of peers would predominate. This was the late 1960s, the beginning of the so-called drug epidemic. The use of drugs would be an ideal behaviour to compare with future life plans for understanding socialization influences on adolescents. I designed a longitudinal study, sampled a representative sample of New York State secondary school students, and obtained data from fathers as well as mothers, although only a single parent per household, as well as nominations of the adolescent's three best school-friends. Adolescents had been asked for these nominations both in the fall and spring of an academic year. Some of the friendship pairs were the same at both times, others were unstable. Because I had sampled entire schools at a six-month interval, for these unstable friendships I had serendipitously obtained samples of triads composed of the two friends at each period plus the friend-to-be at Time 1 (in the fall) and the former friends at Time 2 (in the spring). This analytical sample, which has yet to be replicated by others, enabled me to disentangle the relative influence of selection and socialization underlying similarity observed at one point in time in adolescent friendships (Kandel, 1978). I examined four adolescent behaviours: marijuana use, delinquency, political orientation and educational aspirations. Coleman was a methodological consultant for the analyses. The results suggested that selection and socialization were equal in importance. Thus estimates of peer influence based on cross-sectional data overestimate friends' influence by a factor of two, at least, a conclusion confirmed by Cohen from secondary analyses conducted on unpublished data from *The Adolescent Society* study (1983). There are also other sources of bias, which further reduce the size of what may be the 'true' effects (Kandel, 1995). The sixteen-fold table based on the cross-tabulation over time of the two friends' marijuana use was analyzed by several social scientists, including Duncan (1985), Davis (1978), Lazarsfeld (1978) and by Coleman himself (1979a), in a chapter written for a festschrift for Lazarsfeld.

This cohort of New York State high school students has now been followed for nineteen years and has been a major focus of my work over the last two decades. I expanded the concern with interpersonal influences in adolescence to other phases of the lifecycle, to include partners and friends in adulthood. I found by examining a longitudinal subsample of individuals from adolescence to adulthood, for whom I had data on their best school-friend in adolescence and their spouse or partner in early adulthood, that there were persistent variations in individuals' predispositions to associate with others similar to themselves. Those who affiliated with congruent peers in adolescence were more likely to marry or choose as partners in adulthood individuals who were like themselves. When Kazuo Yamaguchi, a student of Coleman, joined me in 1982, he became interested in applying the notion of selection and socialization to the participation in the social roles of adulthood (such as entry and exit of family roles: Yamaguchi and Kandel, 1985a, 1985b) and to the interpersonal influence of spouses on each other over time (Yamaguchi and Kandel, 1993). After spending several years at the University of California in Los Angeles, Kazuo Yamaguchi returned to Chicago as a tenured member of the faculty in the Department of Sociology. Although he left New York more than ten years ago, we are still collaborating. Thus the issues of selection and socialization have played themselves out in my own life, as they have in my own work, and forged an intellectual and personal link with James Coleman and his work.

Acknowledgment

Work on this chapter was partially supported by a Research Scientist Award KO5 DA00081 from the National Institute on Drug Abuse to Denise Kandel. I wish to acknowledge the assistance of Jay Cross, a Lazarsfeld Fellow in the Department of Sociology at Columbia University, who carried out the citation analyses to Coleman's works.

Notes

1 Jon Clark reminded me that Bierstedt, who traced the distinction to the Greek philosopher Archilochus, used it also to describe Robert K. Merton's career in the previous volume on Robert K. Merton in this series. Bierstedt concluded that Merton was a fox.
2 Although Coleman himself (1990b: Preface) traces the beginning of his research into equality and achievement in education to a subsequent work, *Equality of Educational Opportunity* (Coleman, Campbell *et al.*, 1966), the implicit framework that generated *The Adolescent Society* was the attempt to understand the education of young people in a rapidly changing modern industrial society 'committed to equality of opportunity' in contrast to a stable farming society (Coleman, 1961a: 2). See also the more detailed treatment of this point in Coleman (1968c).
3 I only discuss here briefly the implications of the work with respect to Coleman's contribution to the understanding of adolescent development. I do not discuss the enormous impact of the work on policy, its landmark status as research specifically commissioned by Congress to inform governmental policy and one of the first such studies following those conducted done on the military during the Second World War (Coleman, 1990b: 1).
4 To my surprise, I could not find in the main report (Coleman, Campbell *et al.*, 1966) a reference to the specific number of students who were surveyed.
5 I do not discuss the work on white flight which followed from the desegregation policies derived from *Equality of Educational Opportunity* (1966).

5   This Little School Went to Market: Private Schooling in Post-Communist Poland[1]

Barbara Heyns

One of the most fascinating developments in post-communist education is the emergence of private schools and reform movements at every level of schooling. Ideologies in support of private education resonate with the liberal, market-oriented philosophies prevailing in the region; the policies of private schools promote and legitimate anti-state rhetoric and echo the themes of renewal and transformation heard in other policy realms. Virtually every institution favours democratization and decentralization; the monopoly of the state over the provision of goods and services must be broken. Rigid educational hierarchies must be replaced with schools and teachers who are more responsive to the needs of individual parents and children. The curriculum needs to be completely overhauled; all traces of ideological indoctrination must be expunged. The organization and financing of schools should be lodged in democratically organized community groups; schools should be controlled by the families who can best monitor the education their children receive. Schools must be liberated not only from communist doctrine but from the state as a whole; a free market for schooling should replace state control. These themes lead directly to the assumption that the only workable strategy for eradicating state control of education is to establish new, independent private schools under the control of parents' groups.

This chapter reviews the ideologies and the strategies of educational privatization in Poland. Poland provides an intriguing contrast with the processes of privatization in other countries. On the one hand, private schools are a grass roots movement, rather than an effort at government retrenchment. Although the emphasis is on diversity and choice, the values embodied in Polish private schools do not necessarily represent those of the marketplace. The next two sections are devoted to a description of the schools and their particular ideologies. The conclusion views the findings on Polish private schools in comparative perspective, examining propositions about the sources of achievement in education that have dominated the intellectual work of James Coleman for much of his career.

Private Education as School Reform

Społeczne Towarzystwo Oświatowe, which literally means the Civic or Social Education Association, or STO, is the best example of the school reform movement in Poland. It has had phenomenal success in challenging the monopoly of state schools and in creating new educational alternatives. In the first year, 1989, thirty-five non-state or semi-state schools of various sizes opened their doors; in September 1993, 130 or more 'social' schools were in operation, organized by some thirty-six different local educational associations and 160 educational foundations. STO currently claims over 10,000 members, as well as many sympathizers and several international affiliations. The primary schools tend to be quite small and represent only a tiny fraction of the student population; the new secondary schools, however, now constitute 10 per cent of all post-primary schooling. With few exceptions, these new schools resemble the traditional elite lyceum, offering university preparation and a modified, even trendy, version of the standard lyceum curriculum.

The term 'social' as applied to private education in Poland is curious, but illuminating. The term is used in contrast to 'state', and it includes virtually all independent or non-state education, whether religious or non-denominational. Social is sometimes translated as 'civic' — or even 'public' — education; the critical distinction, however, is the opposition to 'state' education. As in England, public has little to do with funding. The term 'public school' in Britain captured the contrast between the two forms of education favoured by elite families — private, home tutoring and public boarding school. The financial basis was private, but irrelevant. Only a handful of the new private schools are wholly supported by private funds, but all proclaim the essential right to establish autonomous educational institutions, subject to democratically elected self-governments. Politically, these schools must meet the standards of educational quality that apply to state schools, and they must provide the core, or minimum, required curriculum. By law, the new private schools can be organized and run by 'non-state self-governments, legal or natural persons', but virtually all the new schools are still fiscally dependent on the state.[2] In practice, social schools have been organized by foundations, by private companies, by the church or one of the various convents, and by private individuals.

The style and the rhetoric of STO clearly owe much to the political opposition in Poland. Virtually all the founders of the organization had belonged to Solidarity, and many were very active. The beginnings of the educational movement might even be traced to the Commission of Experts of Solidarity who developed special classes for the public schools aimed at moving away from a centrally determined program. The success of the movement is surely attributable in part to the collapse of the communist state, although the organization itself antedated the change of government. As an organization, STO was the result of the decision made in 1987 to try to register an association of parents explicitly claiming the right to control the education of their children and the right to establish private schools. In theory, these rights were guaranteed by Polish law, under a statute passed in 1961; but official permission was needed to exercise such rights, and such permission had never before been granted. In December 1987 neither the Ministry of National Education nor the twenty-three signers of the petition asking for official sanction believed that an organization like STO would be allowed to exist.

When the petition for registration was denied, the fledgling organization appealed the decision through the courts. After a brief legal battle, STO and two affiliated groups in Wrocław and the Małopolska region won their suit; in December 1988 they were formally registered with the intent of establishing private schools. STO was registered as an official organization, but opening such schools still had to be formally approved. The stage was set for private alternative schools under the auspices of democratic, non-state control and authority.

The first petition requesting official permission to open a private school was submitted to the Ministry of National Education in June 1988. The minister responded quickly and as predicted, rejected the petition, arguing that it would be against the Polish Constitution to collect fees for education. The Krakow parent, Anna Jeziorna, who had submitted the petition, then appealed this decision to the High Administrative Court. This case understandably attracted considerable attention; it was the first time in which a group of concerned parents had challenged the right of the ministry to determine where and how their children would be educated. The timing was, of course, fortuitous. Plans for the roundtable talks were underway, and Solidarity was about to be reinstated as a key actor in the negotiations between state and civil society. The political changes were not lost on the legal system. On 23 February 1989, at almost the same moment that the roundtable talks were beginning, the High Court handed down its decision: the state administration was wrong to deny parents the right to organize schools. Parents did have the legal right to open private schools in the People's Republic of Poland. The right to found private schools, as it turned out, would outlive the 'People's Republic of Poland'.

The 'social' or civic schools take democratization as both their fundamental purpose and their principal grievance with state schools. The chief impetus behind STO, and a central motif in the schools that have been formed, is democratic education. Although STO does not endorse any particular educational philosophy except democratic pluralism, the STO schools share basic assumptions.[3] First among these is the importance of enhancing the education of children by expanding the private sector, and breaking the state monopoly on education. The state system is described as overly centralized, hierarchic and inhumane. In the words of Katarzyna Skórzyńska, 'Education in Poland in the post-war period was subordinated to ideology and politics. Educational management consisted of the Minister of Education subordinated to the Central Committee, school superintendent to voivode who was a kind of provincial Communist governor, with the teacher at the very end of the ladder of official dependence. No wonder then that schooling favoured passive and conformist behavior'. Pedagogically, the ethos of the 'social' schools most resembles that of progressive education in the West. Teachers should respect and attend to individual differences and the needs of particular children. Parents should be actively involved in the education of their children at every stage. Schools should be open institutions, fostering community participation and parental involvement. The only sure way to rid schools of socialist dogma, to change the subservient attitudes and behaviour associated with the past, is to establish new and different institutions, institutions that are tolerant of individual differences and freedom. The curriculum should be modernized and facilities updated, but the essential educational reforms consist of the qualities that create an open school. Open does not, however, mean disorderly or indifferent to academic achievement. For STO members, open schools are not the same as 'free schools', and reformed does not mean that standards should be lowered or the curriculum should be intellectually diluted. The parents who have so ardently supported these new schools do not want their children to be at a competitive disadvantage with the graduates of state schools.

Ironically, thus far it seems easier to privatize state education than state industry; and it has been easier to found new schools than to alter the organization and structure of those already in existence. Education under communism was both highly centralized and quite hierarchic. It is not yet clear what organizational framework will define the governance of education in the future. It is possible that the new private schools will become models for democratic education generally; it is possible that they will not survive the present economic crisis. The current government clearly favours both local control and local funding. New public educational boards, School Councils, are in place. These boards are democratically elected, from three slates that are equally divided between parents, teachers and students. The councils also often include a few eminent leaders from the community, either religious or lay. These boards are mandated to provide local oversight, they can propose educational policies, and they now control that part of the school budget that is locally collected. At present, however, only the new 'social' schools receive a significant portion of their funds from non-state sources. In the state schools the local boards are not particularly responsive to parent or community groups yet; at the same time, parent and community groups often have no idea of how to use them to improve the quality of education or to influence programs.

The civic schools incorporate forms of education that were unavailable under state socialism. The schools tend to attract parents with elite aspirations, if not backgrounds, and both the formal and the informal curricula are conscious of status. English has replaced Russian as the dominant language; computer training is offered, although most schools do not yet have any computers. Even in sports there are changes. Several new schools offer tennis and swimming.[4] The socialist schools had stressed team sports and low-cost recreation, such as soccer or gymnastics. Soccer, like most team sports, requires minimal individual coaching and much less expensive equipment for each student. Gymnastics can be taught in a vacant room furnished with a few mats; when the weather is inclement, these courses provided good indoor exercise, but at relatively low cost. The supplemental athletic activities in civic schools provide access to training that, under socialism, was reserved for private classes paid for by parents.

There are no blueprints available for shaping post-communist society or post-communist educational policy. The social schools have elicited an uncommon amount of energy and activity from parents. The STO '*Koła*' or 'circles' undoubtedly pursue democratic decision-making in their schools and communities. The thrust of their efforts, however, seems to be oriented toward discrediting state control in all aspects of educational planning and financing. At the moment they have succeeded in realizing a balance between state funding and local control, but this may not be a stable formula in the long run. Privatization in Polish education represents at present an idealistic, democratic alternative to traditional state schools; the founders see STO schools as models for democratic education and egalitarian participation. The question remains, however, how and whether such schools will support educational equality and the public interest in the future.

Financing Private Schools

The new private schools have been quite innovative in soliciting different types and sources of funding, but it is fair to say that virtually all of them are seriously beleaguered by inflation and limited revenues. The attitude toward state funding for private schools among the STO activists is surprising, at least to an American observer. One hears again and again the argument that the state is constitutionally responsible for funding private schools. Education should be provided free to all children, and be-cause the STO schools are shouldering the burdens of administration, they deserve special subsidies. Moreover, because the new government has shown some reluctance in this respect, it is regarded as derelict in its duties. Second, activists maintain that without state funding, STO schools are in grave danger of becoming 'merely schools for the rich'. Both attitudes are extremely common, and both are typically expressed in an indignant, even outraged tone. These are two of the three reasons most often heard in the parliament in support of increased funding for private schools. A third is sometimes mentioned, but less vehemently; private schooling is part of the Polish educational tradition and should be 'restored' to its rightful place. The state has re-fused to provide tax credits to parents or exemptions for non-religious private schools. The government does provide subsidies for accredited private schools, however, of 'up to 50 per cent' of the amount it costs to educate a child in an equivalent state school. The difference is paid by parents, or sometimes by private donors. Estimates from the STO office in Warsaw suggest that state subsidies and reimbursements cover less than 20 per cent of the actual costs of running the schools.

The costs of private education have risen much faster than inflation or revenues. Initially, school start-up costs were low, and volunteers provided much of the time and effort needed to renovate classrooms or assist in instruction. Many schools began in someone's home; they then renovated space, rented parish buildings, or in some cases offered classes in the regular state schools. The first schools could rely on in-kind contributions from parents and other community groups, for desks and other school furniture, books and even microcomputers; contributions do not pay rent or teacher's salaries, however. For many schools, the choice has become to raise fees and tuition or to bankrupt and close.

Teachers in the STO schools make slightly higher salaries and tend to have smaller classes than in the state system; however, much more time and energy is required of them if the school is to make good on promises made to parents. Parents, moreover, have a difficult time not interfering with the operation of the schools they 'own'. The examples are legion. Teaching in the STO schools involves intensive, prolonged contacts with both parents and pupils, which takes a lot of extra time. Many of the teachers are paid an hourly fee, rather than a salary; their positions are not covered by the Teacher's Charter, and their pension and benefits are uncertain. As the transition period wears on, more and more people feel an extreme financial pinch and become more aware of alternative possibilities. The commitment to making private schools work may yet fall victim to what one might describe as the mania of rational choice. Initially, there were many teachers willing to make sacrifices for the pleasure of teaching and belonging to a STO *koła*; now the turnover rate is higher than in the state schools. STO schools still attract many qualified young teachers; but they expect them to spend many more hours with students than their counterparts in the public sector. Moreover, many teachers find it necessary to moonlight exten-sively. The skills that STO schools aspire to offer are in short supply — languages or knowledge of computers, for example — and they can be sold in the urban market-place for much more per hour than in any school, state or civic.

A second problem is the excessive demands of parents and students in the STO schools. Teachers are required to make a large commitment of time and energy, and they must negotiate the fine but perilous line between responding to parents who believe they 'own' the schools they pay for, and are the employers of the teachers they hire, and reaching out to include parents who prefer to delegate all educational responsibility to the school. It is hard to fault teachers who earn less than $300 a month in their state job from accepting private, informal fees; at the same time, a school that aspires to provide individual attention to all pupils, to have several meetings a month with parents, and to organize a large number of extracurricular events and outings cannot compete with the state schools in terms of pedagogic autonomy or limited hours.

A recent issue of *Edukacja i Dialog* talks about the limitations of dialogue, and the lack of understanding many parents have about educational programs. The authors, predictably, conclude that parent education is needed, and that there should be a clear demarcation between didactic and administrative responsibilities. The former are assumed to be those that concern teachers' professional responsibilities.

At one time the schools could rely on legal, accounting and even managing by volunteers; this was often enough to get accreditation and recognition from the *Curatoreum*. As business has grown, however, such volunteers have tended to evaporate. Moreover, there are problems in defining intellectual property, such as new curricula, which are in great demand. Are such materials owned by STO, or by those who develop them? Should all STO schools have free access, or pay? The schools are caught between the need to provide the 'core curriculum', common to all state schools, and the need to offer something more, something exceptional, to parents who are being asked to pay ever-increasing costs. STO schools contribute 1 per cent of their base budget to the central organization, but these funds must be used to develop new courses and curricula, to provide outreach to international organizations and foundations, and to arrange exchanges, motivational seminars and conferences for teachers and parents.

The schools are also subject to an increasing array of requirements. Non-profit organizations are not yet tax-exempt in post-communist countries, although legislation is pending. Private organizations are required to pay taxes, even if they are nominally exempt, because the regulations are not yet in effect. Since taxation is the norm for all private institutions, even those that are or should be exempt, the institutions or rather the legal bodies that 'own' them must declare all revenues, expenses and deductions — and risk breaking the law by not paying taxes. State schools are not, of course, under any such strictures. The position of private education in Poland, as in most other countries, depends on events in the state sector. To this we now turn.

State Education in Transition: Decentralization, Funding, Values

The founders of private schools were among the first to advocate decentralizing socialist education, but they were surely not the last. The state has begun a policy of decentralizing schools. Beginning in 1991, the responsibility for managing education was turned over to local provinces and communities. Pre-schools were the first, followed quickly by elementary schools and even some secondary or vocational schools. By the beginning of the 1991–92 school year, 5.3 per cent of the state schools had been transferred to local government, or 935 schools, out of 17,653 in the entire country. By 1993–94 localities had assumed control of over 3000 schools; 14.8 per cent of all elementary education was controlled and funded by local government (OECD, 1994).

Funding for these schools is, however, still largely the responsibility of the central government. Formulas were established to calculate subsidies; these were initially based on previous levels of funding and on the expected increase; however, over the period in question it became necessary to adjust these figures several times, to take account of varying state revenues and as various new 'economizing' measures were put in place. Subsidies to the localities that had taken over schools early in the process were exempt from new budgetary reductions. Moreover, local governments could decide to take over some or all of the schools in their territory independently. The full extent of the fiscal anomalies resulting is not yet known. However, it is generally believed that this process of piecemeal decentralization benefitted urban centres and the most affluent regions differentially, since they tended to be quick to seize control and because they seem to have a better grasp of financing. Given the incentive structure, many localities were eager to assume responsibility for especially viable schools, such as those that had received capital improvements in recent budget cycles. The Ministry of National Education is reviewing the various subsidy schemes, and no doubt some corrections will be made. The general conclusion, however, that decentralization has introduced substantial new inequities in state funding, seems unavoidable.

The financing of education in post-communist countries is a topic that could take us very far afield. In Poland the best estimates suggest that total state support for education has declined since 1990, in real terms and as a percentage of Gross Domestic Product. Teachers' salaries have fallen, and less money is spent on either facilities or the physical plant. Moreover, enrolments have risen dramatically in the same time period, in large part because many vocational schools and apprentice programs that were operated by state enterprises have been closed or transferred to the Ministry of National Education. State schools, as well as those in the private sector, now scramble for extra money and special donations. Moreover, a fair number of schools are deeply in debt. Local governments have contributed some additional funding, but the most substantial portion of the shortfall appears to fall on individual families. Estimates suggest that the average Polish family now spends 17 per cent of their total earnings on education-related expenses (Gmytrasiewicz, 1993). Although precise comparisons cannot be made, the data suggest that rising costs and declining equity may be an even larger problem for the state sector than for the private schools.

The state schools have also reformed the concept of values in education in another way that is likely to have long-term effects. In 1990 religious education was added to the minimum number of courses that all schools must offer, and funding was provided for at least one religious instructor, typically a priest, in every school. Although these courses are not compulsory for students, in practice the vast majority attend.

Religion in schools was not an issue that STO supported, despite their emphasis on values and choice. STO private schools were, after all, quite secular, and most intended to stay that way. As an organization, however, STO was beholden to the church for facilities and general support. The position taken by many STO activists was ecumenical; but for others the issue became intensely divisive. The question most often asked was whether schools and parents could choose the type of religious instruction offered, and the answer was generally no. The church was responsible for the assignments, and not the schools. Under socialism, religion had been enormously important for Poles, and most parents enrolled their children in special religious classes at their own expense. In previous times the church expected parents to decide such

·matters, and in all urban areas the choices were diverse. One could, for example, find priests who did not regard divorce or abortion as mortal sin, and who taught broad humanistic political values. Quite suddenly, it seemed, many parents realized they could be denied the choice of the value alternatives offered to their children.

The question of values in the curriculum has created enduring rifts among STO schools and STO parents. Moreover, the private schools may have lost a valued ally and support against the state. STO schools aim to be pluralistic, and to have a basic philosophy that is secular, rather than anti-religious. Several private schools that had close ties to the church broke with STO in order to offer more extensive religious training and to take advantage of religious support.

Successful private school movements, like so many ideologies, seem to contain the seeds of their own destruction. Without state funding, they must compete by offering diverse educational alternatives, parental choice and values that include a coherent critique of the established order. Diversity and choice are values, of course, but they do not necessarily lead to cohesive, integrated programs with a consistent point of view. Even those movements that manage to survive internal conflict risk having their unique point of view absorbed by the mainstream. A trenchant critique of the state system loses considerable power when the public schools reform by embracing the very values the private schools identified as unavailable.

School Reform after Five Years

Education is a beleaguered institution in post-communist Poland. The new private schools, like the public schools, face spiralling costs and shrinking budgets. In March 1994 Wojciech Starzynski, the president of STO, characterized the STO schools as exhibiting 'more professionalism, but less enthusiasm' (see Wieckowski, 1994). He hastened to point out, however, that the majority of STO schools were still enthusiastic after five years, despite that fact that in most cases they were still staffed by their founders.

Despite the enthusiasm, STO has gradually relinquished its position as the organizational hub of private education: STO claims only 130 private schools in Poland, and does not expect to provide resources or guidance for many new ones. This decision was based on the fact that the organization could not provide services to all those who wished to affiliate, nor could it monitor their progress effectively. The very diversity of the private school sector means that no single organization, however knowledgeable or charismatic, can fully represent independent schools. The efforts of STO are concentrated on helping schools deal with the supervision and monitoring of the *Curatoreum*, which varies tremendously by region, and with settling conflicts and 'trouble shooting' within existing STO schools. Although STO remains the group most identified with private education in Poland, the organization sees no need to grow. The STO journal continues to publish innovative educational ideas, and to offer a forum for educators of diverse points of view in both the private and state sectors. The materials and curricula developed in and by STO schools are widely disseminated; perhaps half of the 500 or more independent schools in Poland have sought a connection or affiliation with STO. From any standpoint, STO has accomplished a great deal to broaden education, to bridge diverse views, and to help in the reconstruction of civil society in Poland.

Privatizing Higher Education

A second example of how market ideologies influence education is illustrated by Polish business schools. The rationale for higher educational reform has been clearly laid out in a number of publications. The version presented here has two pertinent advantages: it is a particularly lucid exposition; and it has been translated and is available outside Poland (see Beksiak, Chmielecka and Grzelonska, 1992). The policies and recommendations, as well as the rationale for markets, that follow depend heavily on this document.

In virtually all the materials regarding educational reform, including *Academic Economic Education in Change* (Beksiak, Chmielecka and Grzelonska, 1992), the case for markets in education is made by contrasting the system under the former regime with that considered ideal. Although the ideal has yet to be fully realized, pursuing market reforms is argued to be the best way of bringing it about. For example, the educational reformers — in this case Janusz Beksiak, Ewa Chmielecka and Urszula Grzelonska — distinguish three types of schools, defined theoretically as ideal types, but bearing a strong resemblance to existing schools in contemporary Poland. First, they identify schools that are strictly commercial endeavours, in which skills such as shorthand or computer programming are marketed and purchased, generally for a specific vocational purpose. The authors assume that such proprietary schools are largely irrelevant to their primary concern, which is the reform of state education; hence they conclude that these programs can be organized in whatever fashion seems expedient, either as independent establishments or as an annex to more traditional schools. The authors suggest that such schools may complement, or even provide some competition for, regular programs.

Second, there are schools that operate according to autocratic principles. Although defined theoretically, the logic of autocratic schools is clearly based on the socialist educational system, which 'for many years predominated' in Poland. These schools are primarily 'outcome oriented', in that their educational goals are formulated exclusively as desirable outputs or products, such as the 'so-called model graduates, e.g., the well trained and ideologically fit director of a socialist enterprise, or the technocratically oriented and dynamic manager'. In autocratic schools the entrant becomes a subordinate, and is reduced to being the 'object of a particular treatment'. The achievements of the school are evaluated strictly in terms of the number of students trained or the number of certificates granted. If a student changes faculties or quits before completing the degree, this is viewed as 'raw material' that was 'wasted'. The emphasis, the authors assert, is on the product and not on 'the intellectual development of a human being'. The curricula in autocratic schools consist of rewards and penalties attached to various well defined career paths, including appropriate courses and sequences, degree requirements, number of examinations and teaching hour quotas; these, in turn, are generally standardized and quite uniform.

Autocratic schools are inevitably hierarchical and overly centralized. Arbitrary and whimsical decisions can be, and are, made at any level, although they can be appealed and reversed by higher authorities. For example, while teachers give marks and passing grades, deans can annul the decisions of the former; the Faculty Board may be authorized to grant degrees, or it may lose such power; central committees approve — or withdraw approval — of degrees granted; still another central body confers professorships. The authors concede that various elements of hierarchic organization may be needed in elementary and secondary education, but not in the higher schools. Moreover, autocratic controls constitute 'the main obstacle to progress in education' of any form. Hence the authors define 'our major negative task is to remove — or at least undermine — the whole aggregate of the above mentioned rules'. The primary purpose of reform is to transform higher education by dismantling bureaucratic controls.

The third alternative, which is considered ideal, is a school formed on the basis of a 'contract for joint action'. Such a contract is based on the voluntary cooperation of teachers and students, 'with the division between them consisting mainly in differences in knowledge, professional competence and authority, but not in power'. This relationship, it is stressed, is not one of subordination. 'It is', the authors maintain, 'a system of mutual commitments and benefits'. A faculty member is the master, a student the disciple; but the relationship is completely voluntary on both sides. The possibility must exist for both master and disciple to 'freely choose the conditions of their cooperation'.

Thus education consists of the sum of the contracts made between faculty and students. The context, or school, that results can be easily — and the authors acknowledge, correctly — recognized with 'reference to the medieval university of feudal traditions'. The authors refer to these sites of learning as 'corporations' formed to realize particular goals; however, they are not just companies established to pursue economic interests; they have little, if anything, in common with the economic establishments that are called corporations in the 'contemporary jargon adopted from America'. The universities envisioned are communities, or a group of people 'with common goals pursuing common interests'. Among the interests that might be pursued, two are salient. The 'twin goals' of cultivating learning and preparation to perform a specific role in society, although not identical, 'should not be separated altogether'. In size these 'educational corporations' could consist of a single master and disciples, comparable to the Japanese *sensei* relationship, or it could take the form of the *katedra*, or academic chair in Poland. This form of corporation is, in the authors' assessment, the 'most promising' for carrying out desirable changes in Polish education.

The authors also describe the several principles that govern the formal organization of such programs, determining who should be admitted and how their studies should be organized. In theory at least, admission should be open to 'everyone who is properly prepared, willing to study, and who can pay for the education'. The authors acknowledge two exceptions. The first concerns especially talented students without the secondary certificate; such students should be allowed to enrol early. While the authors believe that such cases will be more common in mathematics than in economics, the corporation should avoid becoming too rigid with respect to age or exact preparation requirements.

The second exception concerns the troubling question of who should pay. The answer given is 'those who benefit', whether from their own resources or from the public purse. The state 'may decide to support some or all students, but the state cannot regulate admissions, or determine access'. The schools, however, should not be burdened by 'the necessity or the obligation' to educate everyone who applies. Nor should schools concern themselves with financing their operations. Funding should, therefore, be arranged independently of the schools. Scholarships or vouchers for study should be given to students directly, rather than through the schools. Higher education should not be, in the words of the authors, a 'kind of social welfare agency'.

The authors defer the complicated philosophical questions about funding to the last chapter of their report. However, they firmly support the idea that the purpose of education is knowledge acquisition, rather than credentials. Students forced to discontinue or delay their schooling, who drop out of the program for whatever reason, should not be considered failures. Access should be easy; there should be no sanctions or penalties for interrupting or resuming studies at will, except perhaps supplementary or renewed exams. Moreover, the higher schools should not be held accountable for the success of individual students. Since pursuing knowledge is an individual choice, higher schools should not, and cannot, accept any obligation to teach particular skills or subject matter. Vocational preparation need not, and should not, concern universities. In terms of career preparation, higher schools can only provide students with basic knowledge or the chance to attain it. Even the most distinguished diploma does not ensure that graduates will be admitted to practise, or to enter a 'given professional circle'. Schools can provide only the opportunity to become a candidate for a professional position. The authors are quite explicit on this point.

> It is just impossible to fill somebody with knowledge without his or her active cooperation. The process of learning is not external to a person; it proceeds inside, although cooperation of other people can be helpful or even necessary. We think that such commitment — often declared by various courses and schools — is neither honest nor reliable, even with regard to young children or simple skills.

The thrust of the reforms recommended follows from these observations. The assumption is that culture and learning, although public goods, can be efficiently rationed and transmitted via an open market, without any supervision or interference by the authorities. The schools should be allowed to charge for their services, and they should conduct their financial affairs responsibly, 'according to market principles'. The schools should be allowed to decide for themselves whether to invest in their own improvement or to reduce their fees. So long as the schools and professors maintain high professional standards, they should be allowed to profit from the market for their services. Although education is not, the authors admit, identical to a profit oriented business, schools should be allowed to claim full compensation. It is reasonable for prestigious institutions to charge more for their services, because they are in greater demand. State control, however, is anathema, whether for purposes of accountability or quality control.

It is not possible, the authors assert, to attach a price to all aspects of education, or to charge what the market can bear; hence, as a valued public utility, state funding for education may be an unavoidable necessity. Higher education is a resource for society, and some minimal standard of material resources is a prerequisite deserving of support by society as a whole. Universities should be considered as valued public utilities, like libraries or hospitals. 'Services', the authors note, 'may be available, but only utilized services are of value. A master without disciples is no longer a master; science embodied in unread books is no longer anyone's knowledge'. The authors do not really consider the question of how much support is needed, or what should happen if 'society' preferred some other expenditure over education. The value of education is assumed to be inestimable; the only restriction is the scarcity of time by the professional faculty, not inadequate demand.

The authors do note that 'the traditional school of the authoritarian type attempts to counteract this by imposing the obligation to utilize services, making lectures compulsory and ordering books to be summarized'. While such policies have the 'possible merit' of teaching disciplined work habits, they also produce the reverse effect, 'making contact with books and participation in academic disputes repugnant'. The ideal higher school is one composed of faculty and students pursuing individualized courses of study voluntarily. Such a school should be neither 'profit oriented, nor gratuitous'.

Financial issues are frequently mentioned in this report, but only in the concluding pages do the authors present their position. The authors proclaim themselves in favour of 'possibly wide privatization of the existing higher schools and in favour of supporting the institution of private higher education'. Four possible objections are mentioned. Private universities might become commercialized, and 'hunt for profit instead of serving society's good and the development of education'. Second, it is not possible to price all the services provided by universities. Third, state control may be useful or even necessary for some matters, like accreditation. Finally, the state or other non-educational institution can protect the poor, ensuring them access at all levels. Each of these objections is dealt with succinctly, as being either counterfactual or manageable within existing state institutions. The authors conclude that privatizing higher education is the best way to guarantee institutional autonomy and academic freedom, and that state support, without strings of course, should make it feasible.

In Poland installing a free market for education apparently means both institutional independence and full funding. No contradiction is perceived between economic dependence and political autonomy; the arguments are made for both positions by the same authors and in the very same breath. There are now thirty-three private universities or post-secondary schools in the country, compared to ten in 1991–92 and eighteen in 1992–93. The accreditation of schools is not equivalent to certifying the credentials offered, however, and many of the new private schools have admitted students before receiving authorization to give them a particular credential. Enrolments have soared, despite the crisis in funding. Although the Polish constitution still prohibits charging student fees in state schools, tuition can be charged for night courses, 'irregular' students or extracurricular offerings, and these classes are a growth industry. The attitudes expressed in the report *Academic Economic Education in Change* may well be, at least in part, a function of the robust market for economics and business courses that the authors perceive in Poland at the moment.

Polish private schools at all grade levels embody a new conception of the place of economic and political values in education. But do these values and these schools have much in common with private schooling in other countries? To this question we now turn.

Private Schools and Achievement

In Poland market ideologies influence the structuring, or restructuring, of education. Private schools can illustrate, if not test, propositions about the source of achievement that are fundamental to the normative and intellectual theories central to Jim Coleman's work.

In both Poland and the US the private schools enrol and seemingly produce pupils with higher levels of achievement than the public sector. The conventional explanation for this in both countries is that private schools are selective and recruit the highest achieving pupils from advantaged families, with strong interests in the children's schooling. Yet in both countries there is substantial evidence that the most successful schools are not necessarily those with the highest fees or the most select student bodies. Despite the conventional wisdom, Catholic schools in the United States tend to be more racially integrated than those in the public sector. In Poland STO schools are quite heterogeneous compared to the highly stratified public sector, and they seem to be particularly effective in dealing with students who have problems adjusting to state schools. In both countries successful private schools enhance achievement more for 'high-risk' students, rather than the most able, 'adding value' to their products, whatever the initial levels of achievement. The outcomes of private education in both countries would seem to be higher levels of achievement and greater equality. Conclusive evidence on these points is not yet available for Poland, and even though it has been demonstrated decisively by Coleman and his associates, it is still controversial in the United States.

Market mechanisms do not seem to be the source of the private school advantage. In both Poland and the United States independent schools depend on private fees; in neither country, however, can one understand their role by reference to their economic niche. In both countries the private schools work because they construct community, and not because they maximize either profit or achievement. In Poland, and I will argue in Coleman's work as well, markets are assumed to be an instrumental device for realizing particular goals, and not the goals themselves; markets are a means rather than the end. Jim Coleman is usually regarded as an advocate of unregulated markets in education, and his concepts of effective school organization are widely discussed, even in Poland. But the rationale offered for supporting private schools is educational rather than economic; his seminal contributions to rational choice theory link the organization of schooling and parental choice and control first to the issues of achievement, and only secondarily to efficiency or enhanced productivity.

In contemporary Poland free market policies are central to the rhetoric of school reform, but private schools gained adherents for political reasons, because they represented an assault on state authority, rather than a special market or an exclusive enclave. In education, markets can be instrumental for achieving or restoring other valued goals, such as community, democratic institutions or civil society. Even in business and economics, where the logic of markets constitutes both the subject matter and the organizational rationale, unregulated markets for schooling are premised on an unlimited demand for schooling. The educational marketplace would seem to work on social rather than economic principles; competition and efficiency are less important than the values they embody for students and for the society.

Although private schools enhance achievement in both countries, the process seems to be related to cohesive, community ties among parents and the commitment and devotion of teachers. In both countries one might conclude that commitment to community, or dedication on the part of a teacher, are 'irrational' behaviour, reflecting acts of altruism and self-sacrifice rather than self-interest. In both countries state schools provide higher rewards and less demanding working conditions for teachers; monetary incentives for investing extra time and effort are few and far between. Private schooling in both Poland and the United States would not seem to be rational choice for either parents or teachers. Despite the market ideologies expressed, the mechanisms promoting achievement in private schools are difficult to understand within the assumptions of economic theory. A more parsimonious explanation for the origins of private schools is a critical mass of families and teachers sharing educational values that are not given voice or allowed expression in the public sector. Values dictate establishing markets in both contexts, but markets alone have little to do with the quality and equality of educational outcomes. For both Coleman and Polish educational reformers in Poland, private schooling provides an alternative model of education; markets are an essential, if radical, remedy for the dismal existing state of affairs.

Do educational reform efforts in Poland have much in common with the history and controversies surrounding private education in the United States? What conclusions might one draw for the issues of educational policy that have figured so prominently in the intellectual work of James Coleman?

Schools, as James Coleman has so often remarked, are socially constructed, purposive organizations. In both Poland and the United States schools are institutions that embody values and ideals; as such, they are constructed, reformed and reconstructed to suit the societies in which they are found. The origins of private schools in both countries can be traced to a set of alternative values that were not represented or given voice in the public sphere. The private schools in both countries have active, dedicated supporters and much higher levels of satisfaction among both students and parents than public schools. Despite the fact that the great majority of the private schools face serious financial difficulties, private education in both countries is still widely believed to offer an alternative model for what public sector schooling ought to be. Finally, in both Poland and the United States private schools have a much more profound influence on pedagogic theory and practice than one would predict, knowing only their enrolment share or their resources.

The values actually espoused by the private schools, however, are quite different. Polish private schools aim, first and foremost, to liberalize education for students, rather than to increase discipline, homework or rigour. They are intentionally much more unstructured, less hierarchic and authoritarian, and a great deal more democratic than Polish public education. Their educational goals include reducing control over both students and teachers, removing rigid course requirements and surveillance, and broadening student horizons. Polish private schools aim to personalize attention and individualize instruction, to reduce competition and stress in favour of cooperation and encouragement, to enliven classroom instruction and liberate children's interests and innate love of learning. The state system, as well as being a monopoly denying parents choice, is portrayed as harsh, punitive and unduly concerned with selection at all levels. Virtually all the examples cited previously, suggesting that STO resembles an alternative schools movement more than a campaign for private schools, could be reiterated in support of this point. Although university reformers mention high standards in a perfunctory way, the thrust of reform is to increase electives and student choice. Private schools in Poland are, in short, a reaction to the narrow instrumental goals pursued by the communist regime.

In contrast, American debates on pedagogy and private schools adopt precisely the opposite polarities in terms of both diagnosis and cure. The public system is criticized for being lax, undemanding and apathetic to the point of neglect; while private schools are extolled for maintaining high standards, strong values and rigorous discipline. As Jim Coleman and his associates have convincingly shown, on most counts the private sector, and particularly the Catholic schools, do much better by their students than do the public schools. Moreover, their most telling successes are not with 'their own', whether this is defined by class, race or religious upbringing.

Catholic schools in the United States may be one of the few remaining 'functional communities', capable of integrating children into a set of shared values, common expectations regarding achievement and intergenerational closure. The effectiveness of Catholic schools is argued to be a consequence of the psychic support and affiliative bonds such communities can offer students. In transient, contemporary America, with many disrupted or dysfunctional families, a strong school community can be a critical asset to a child or to a broken or impaired family, with more human capital available than social capital. Despite the emphasis on a community with shared values, Coleman's work is usually invoked in support of a particular kind of community, one that embodies strict, traditional values, rigorous discipline, hierarchical control and order. Too often these are the aspects of Catholic education that are assumed to produce academic achievement, and not community.

The private schools in Poland embody very different values, values that on the surface do not seem to have much in common with American Catholic schools or with achievement. The STO schools emphasize individual choice, personal freedom and the secular, humanistic traditions of the Enlightenment. Authority relations between staff and students are casual, at least relative to those in the state sector. Students are encouraged to be critical, to study diverse and perhaps irrelevant topics, and to question all received ideas and dogma. Creativity is valued more than rote learning; active participation is more rewarded than obedience or docility. Moreover, these values are claimed to be those responsible for enhanced student achievement.

In both countries the private schools represent alternative values and a coherent critique of the existing system. In both countries private schools embody strong values in opposition to those of the mainstream. However, the failures addressed and the remedies advocated in Poland are the mirror image of those pointed to in the United States. In the realm of practice, if the reforms advocated by private schools were to be adopted by public education, they would move the system as a whole in diametrically opposed directions. In Poland the state system would have to become more child-centred and would have to allow students greater freedom. In the United States the public system would have to become more rigorous, more value-conscious and more demanding.

The substance or content of values, I would argue, is much less important than their strength and consistency. The value differences between Polish and American private schools, while not coincidental, are not causally related to achievement. Private schools in both societies compete with the dominant educational system. They must articulate and reflect a distinctive set of values, sufficiently at odds with those attributed to the public sector to be recognizably different. Moreover, the values endorsed should have a logical connection to the goal of achievement, and should foster participation and community. Social capital, in such a model, is not a consequence of a particular set of values, but of the social organization and networks any set of values creates. Even in Poland, a society that retains strong families, traditional values and intergenerational closure, communities defined by a shared commitment to particular educational values seem to embody resources that enhance achievement.

Notes

1   Information regarding the independent schools movement is based on interviews with members of the Ministry of National Education and STO activists in Warsaw. The

philosophy of the movement, and the views of prominent spokesmen, are reprinted in various issues of the STO journal, *Edukacja i Dialog*, published since 1989.

2   In January 1990 the Minister of National Education agreed that the state should subsidize social schools to the amount of half the current costs per child in state schools in the region. Schools sponsored by foundations or business concerns do not qualify for state subsidy, although denominational schools do. The tuition paid by parents is quite modest by Western standards, amounting to between $10 and $12 per month. However, even fees of this order represent 10 per cent of the average monthly salary.

3   The STO journal is eclectic pedagogically, but quite consistent politically. The ideas of Montessori, Steiner, Korczak and Freinet are frequently mentioned.

4   The first Civic High School in Warsaw supplements the state curriculum with the teaching of 'swimming, skiing, skating, horseback riding, and the rudiments of self-defence' (*Edukacja i Dialog*, 26/27, March/April 1991, p. 31).

6 Early Schooling and Educational Inequality: Socioeconomic Disparities in Children's Learning

Karl L. Alexander and Doris R. Entwisle

Well into the present century Americans believed schooling was the chief remedy for inequalities in social and economic opportunity. Over the last three decades, however, leaders and laypersons alike have become increasingly disturbed by the persistent pattern of low school achievement and underachievement among children in families of low income and in some minority communities. Dropout rates have gone down in recent years in the nation as a whole and test scores of minority youngsters relative to whites have improved somewhat (see Bracey, 1991), but these advances are over-shadowed by the problems that remain. In fact, a sense of crisis continues, especially in central city school systems with largely minority and poverty level enrolments where dropout rates of the order of 50 per cent are common (Hammack, 1986).

Schools cannot be expected to make up for all inequalities in other spheres of life, but focusing narrowly on school reform, as is often done, runs at least two risks: confusing 'schooling' with 'learning'; and thinking of schooling in terms of students, rather than in terms of the setting which frames their learning. Confusing schooling with learning results in out-of-school problems like the consequences of low family income being mistakenly cast as school problems because they are manifest in lower test scores, dropout and the like. Second, overlooking the profoundly social nature of schooling has tended to perpetuate practices that do not serve either the students' or society's interests. Students work for social approval and somehow that motive has to be harnessed.

To his credit, Coleman understood these two risks much earlier than most. Virtually alone in the 1950s, he focused on the social dimensions of schooling. *The Adolescent Society* (1961) portrayed American high schools as places where peer sub-cultures and reward systems were almost orthogonal to the value and reward systems that educators used to motivate students. He pointed out that students worked hard to gain prestige in the eyes of their classmates, and in some high schools doing so meant actively avoiding high grades. Though the adolescent society described by Coleman has a decidedly early 1960s, small-town USA flavour, his insight is as relevant today as it was then: a serious price is paid when students' value systems pull against the school's (e.g., Ogbu, 1988, 1992). Small wonder that after this pioneering work, and soon after the passage of the Civil Rights Act of 1964, Coleman was chosen to lead a national study of equality of opportunity in US schools. Space does not permit a summary of even the major findings of the EEO Report (Coleman, Campbell *et al.*, 1966), but good sources are readily available (e.g., *Harvard Educational Review*, 1968; Hodgson, 1973; Levine and Bane, 1975; Mosteller and Moynihan,

1972). Most immediately relevant here is one of the report's major insights: the importance of out-of-school factors for children's cognitive development. It concluded that family and other non-school influences explain a major part of 'school' effects and that differences among schools matter less for student achievement than differences among students within those schools. Although these conclusions were controversial and sharply questioned, they have stood the test of time (see sources in Mosteller and Moynihan, 1972) and are now generally accepted.

As with any landmark study, some of the report's insights have been distorted or misunderstood, however. The report was misread by many as implying that 'schools don't make the difference, families make the difference' (see Hodgson, 1973). Eventually, however, the research community has come to realize that families being important does not mean that schools are unimportant, or that they have no effects at all.

This chapter revisits one of these issues by examining the achievement disparities separating children of various socioeconomic levels. That children whose socioeconomic status (SES) level is low are 'at risk' for academic failure is well established (Natriello *et al.*, 1990). The question addressed here is how schools fit into this picture: do they function so as to offset the out-of-school circumstances that put such children at academic risk; do they magnify children's difficulties by reinforcing outside patterns of advantage/disadvantage; or are they essentially irrelevant, in line with the 'schools don't matter' point of view?

The perspective used in this chapter to examine the nature of schooling is unusual in two respects. First, we focus on *schooling in the early primary grades*. The EEO Report (Coleman, Campbell *et al.*, 1966: 293–306) dealt mainly with children in higher grades, six and up, and more recent research (e.g., Coleman, Hoffer and Kilgore, 1982; Coleman and Hoffer, 1987; Schneider and Coleman, 1993) also has had little to say about children in the primary grades. However, as we have argued elsewhere (Entwisle and Alexander, 1989, 1993), early schooling may be precisely the time when schools exercise their greatest influence. For one thing, the rate of children's learning of verbal and quantitative skills is perhaps ten times as large in first grade as it is in high school (Jencks, 1985). Also families probably weigh in most heavily in the first few grades, when children are making the transition to formal schooling. Six- and 7-year-olds depend on their families to get them to school, and, even more important, families in one way or another select the schools children will attend. For these and other reasons, socioeconomic influences on educational outcomes may be stronger in the early primary grades, when children are just acclimatizing to the school routine, than later on, when achievement patterns are already well established (e.g., Alwin and Thornton, 1984).

Second, we try to divide *in-school* from *out-of-school learning*. Typically sociologists of education assess the joint influence of home and school on learning by examining how resources linked to each setting map onto measures of achievement. Most often these measures of achievement are end-of-year cognitive test scores or gains in test scores over one- or two-year intervals. Studies of this genre, including the EEO Report, conclude that differences in measurable characteristics of schools make only a small contribution to differences in how much students learn when out-of-school factors are controlled. A different approach is to try to isolate the school's unique contribution. We accomplish this division by comparing how much students learn over the summer months, when schools are not in session, with how much they learn during the school year.

In the United States children attend school about 180 days a year, for perhaps six hours a day. Tests to measure children's achievement are usually given once a year. Still, the large majority of children's time during the year is spent outside school, so unless one assumes that no learning occurs when children are outside school, there is obviously a major confounding of school effects with effects of the other contexts children experience. Since it is hard, indeed usually impossible, to compare children who attend school with others who do not attend at all, there is no straightforward way to calculate the effect of schooling per se.[1] Yet, whenever unschooled children can be found, it turns out that they have mastered many of the skills they need in daily life, including complex concepts of the kind ordinarily thought to be inculcated in school. For example, Brazilian 10-year-olds who sell candy on city streets, and *who have no schooling whatsoever*, price their wares in ratio form (Saxe, 1989). They also change their prices regularly to take account of inflation. Other unschooled Brazilian children, who live in rural areas, weave straw in ways that demonstrate a deep under-standing of the topology involved in the path of a two-dimensional strand set in a three-dimensional space. The kinds of knowledge possessed by these children who have not attended school dramatize the difficulties that confront researchers who study schooling: much of children's learning can, and probably does, occur outside the classroom.

Considering the many settings in which learning occurs has led us, like Heyns (1978), to question the findings from typical models of schooling. First and most important, small differences across schools cannot be taken as evidence of negligible effects of schools altogether. Children are continuously learning, in school and out of school, and since students spend much more time outside school than inside, family or other background factors have more of an opportunity than do school factors to influence achievement. Also, as already suggested, it is possible to separate home and school influences by contrasting pupils' achievement when schools are in session with their achievement when schools are closed. By this means we can isolate the unique contribution of the school.

Illustrative Data from the BSS

Using data from our ongoing, Baltimore-based, Beginning School Study (BSS, see below), we will examine patterns of cognitive growth over the elementary and middle school years according to children's socioeconomic standing. Since achievement dis-parities at the point when formal schooling begins reflect largely the out-of-school circumstances that children have experienced during their pre-school years, we begin by noting the differences in children's test scores according to their families' socio-economic levels at the time they began first grade. Not surprisingly, the BSS data show that family socioeconomic status can explain much of the social patterning of cognitive differences when children begin school (Entwisle and Alexander, 1990). We next plot achievement trends annually over the first eight years of the BSS cohort's schooling, and find that the achievement gap separating upper SES level from lower SES level children, which was present when children began first grade, increases substantially over time. This pattern of increasing disparities usually is taken to mean that schools do little to offset differences in children's out-of-school learning resources, and hence that schools have, at best, small effects. *When achievement trends are plotted season by season however, the children of high and low SES gain at much the same pace during the school year.* Over the summer months, however, like Heyns (1978, 1987) and Murnane (1975), we find that poor and minority youngsters do not learn nearly as much as do their more privileged counterparts (Entwisle and Alexander, 1992, 1994). For the BSS children, furthermore, the first two summers dividing the early primary grades stand out as especially critical. From this perspective, then, schools and families are complementary — and possibly competing — influences on educational attainment. Only when schools are not in session do poorer children fall behind.

A few words are needed about the Beginning School Study (BSS), which has been monitoring the academic progress and personal development of a cohort of about 800 youngsters who began first grade in Baltimore City public schools in September 1982. Selection of schools and pupils for participation involved a two-stage process. First, twenty elementary schools throughout the city were selected at random from within strata defined by racial composition (segregated white; segregated African-American; integrated) and community SES level (white collar; blue collar); then pupils were sampled randomly from 1981–82 kindergarten rosters and fall 1982 first-grade rosters. All regular first-grade classrooms in the twenty schools were included in the sampling. Only 3 per cent of parents of children so selected declined to have their children participate in the project.

The resulting sample of beginning first graders was 55 per cent African-American, 45 per cent white; 47 per cent of children were in single parent households; 67 per cent of the children's families qualified for reduced price meals at school, indicating low income; and 38 per cent of the study children's mothers did not finish high school. A large majority of those who remained in Baltimore's public schools through the end of middle school (about 60 per cent of the entire group) were African-American (71 per cent), and these youngsters were more disadvantaged still: 52 per cent in single parent households as first graders; 76 per cent receiving meal subsidies; 42 per cent high school dropout mothers. All these characteristics are well documented academic 'risk factors' (Natriello *et al.*, 1990). Overall, the families of BSS children, especially those who did not leave Baltimore City, reflect high levels of socioeconomic disadvantage even though schools in upper income and predominantly white communities in Baltimore were oversampled to enable comparisons across SES and racial/ethnic lines.

Table 6.1 shows how family socioeconomic status level maps onto selected school achievement indicators in first grade: test scores, marks, retention and special education. The SES composite is an average of five indicators, scaled as Z scores: each parent's educational level (originally coded as years of school completed); each parent's occupational status (coded in the Featherman-Stevens SEI metric, 1982); and the child's eligibility for the federal school lunch program. (Eligibility, determined by family income relative to family size, indicates low but not necessarily poverty-level family income.[2])

The 'high,' 'middle,' 'low' distinctions used in Table 6.1 lead to half of the sample being classified as 'low' SES, about a fourth as 'middle' SES and another fourth as 'high' SES.[3] The mother's education averages for the three groups are 10.4, 12.0 and 14.6 (pooled SD = 2.6); father's education, 10.4, 12.1 and 15.1 (pooled SD = 2.7); mother's occupation, 26.5, 40.5 and 60.1 (pooled SD = 19.7); father's occupation, 22.6, 31.1 and 60.4 (pooled SD = 22.4), and the percentages of children in the groups receiving free or reduced price meals are 95.1, 53.7 and 13.0 respectively

Table 6.1. Comparison of Beginning School Study Students' First Grade School Performance, by Socioeconomic Status Level: California Achievement Test Scores in Reading Comprehension and Mathematics Concepts/Reasoning, Plus Marks in Reading and Math

	SES level		
	Low	Mid	High
Fall 1982 reading comprehension (CAT-R):			
Avg	272.6	279.6	300.3
[SD]	[36.0]	[38.1]	[47.0]
(N)	(342)	(169)	(164)
Fall 1982 math concepts/reasoning (CAT-M):			
Avg	282.1	296.8	312.3
[SD]	[27.2]	[27.4]	[35.8]
(N)	(357)	(172)	(164)
First quarter reading mark:[a]			
Avg	1.7	1.9	2.3
[SD]	[.61]	[.62]	[.79]
(N)	(350)	(173)	(173)
First quarter math mark:			
Avg	2.0	2.3	2.7
[SD]	[.79]	[.77]	[.84]
(N)	(356)	(174)	(172)
Percentage of students retained in first grade:	22.2	12.9	7.4
[SD]	[41.6]	[33.6]	[26.2]
(N)	(396)	(201)	(190)
Percentage of students receiving special education in first or second grade:	16.7	11.0	9.0
[SD]	[37.3]	[31.3]	[28.6]
(N)	(396)	(201)	(190)

a   1 = Unsatisfactory; 2 = Satisfactory; 3 = Good; 4 = Excellent.

(pooled SD = 47.4). Fifty-four per cent of the low SES youngsters were in single parent households at the start of first grade, versus 40 per cent of middle SES youngsters and 28 per cent of high SES youngsters. Two parent households include stepparents, biological parents and families with other adults in residence along with two parents.

The first comparisons in Table 6.1 involve reading comprehension and math concepts standardized test scores from the California Achievement Test (CAT) battery, Form C, Level 11, administered in the fall of first grade. The test averages closely parallel SES resource differences, in that they strongly favour high SES youngsters. The California Achievement Test reading comprehension (CAT-R) and California Achievement Test math concepts/reasoning (CAT-M) differences between children in the high and low SES groups are 27.7 and 30.2 points respectively, corresponding to about .68 and .95 standard deviations.

These huge disparities in entry-level academic skills are mirrored in the marks teachers gave children on their first quarter report cards in first grade (Excellent = 4, Good = 3, Satisfactory = 2 and Unsatisfactory = 1). Low SES children's first reading marks averaged below satisfactory (1.7); their math marks were just satisfactory (2.0). Middle SES youngsters did somewhat better in both areas. Upper SES youngsters' initial marks were highest: 2.3 in reading, 2.7 in math. The high SES-low SES marking difference of 0.6 units in reading corresponds to over 0.8 standard deviations; the 0.7 unit difference in math represents about the same relative gap. Lower SES youngsters also were three times as likely to be held back at year's end (first grade retention rate of 22 per cent versus 7 per cent among those from high SES households) and were almost twice as likely to be referred for special education services (17 per cent versus 9 per cent),[4] so children's profiles are consistent across a range of early academic indicators. Test scores, marks, retention and special education needs all point in the same direction: family resources, and presumably related differences in out-of-school learning opportunities over the pre-school years, are strongly correlated with children's academic standing when their formal schooling begins.

The data presented in Table 6.1 give a sense of the importance of the range in children's school readiness, and this range is probably a 'minimal' estimate in that the upper SES extremes are not well represented in the BSS archive. But what happens after first grade? If out-of-school opportunities to learn were the only consideration, we would expect the gap separating children in high SES households from those in low SES households to continue to widen because the same family resources that favoured upper SES children at the start of their schooling will continue to confer an advantage all along the way (e.g., Hess and Holloway, 1984; Slaughter and Epps, 1987). The next sections check this hypothesis by plotting achievement trends over time by SES level.

Achievement Trends from First Grade through Middle School

A key strategy for understanding academic development is to monitor the *same* children's progress over time. The problems with cross-sectional studies like the EEO, which sample children at different grade levels at a single point in time, when used to address causal hypotheses are well known. Several large-scale panel studies of children's schooling (e.g., NLS-72, HSB, NELS-88) have been conducted since the EEO survey but the earliest of these starts at eighth grade. The period of early schooling thus has received little attention in research on children's learning from a sociological perspective, yet educational trajectories are highly stable from first grade onward (Alexander *et al.*, 1994; Husén, 1969; Kraus, 1973), and, as mentioned, the pace of cognitive development in first grade may be ten times as great as it is in high school. This implies that growth in the early school years produces relatively much greater variance between students than does growth later on. For these reasons and others, the crucible early years of children's schooling are critical for understanding long-term patterns of development, and perhaps especially for understanding patterned inequalities across socioeconomic cleavages (Entwisle and Alexander, 1988, 1993).

Table 6.2 presents CAT averages and SES comparisons year by year for the BSS students over their elementary and middle school years.[5] Entries in the first column repeat the achievement test data from Table 6.1 for the fall of first grade. The rest of the entries in Table 6.2 are test averages which rate children's standing near the

Table 6.2. California Achievement Test Averages and Differences in California Achievement Test Averages by Socioeconomic Status Level, from the Fall of First Grade through the Spring of Year 8

	Fall Year 1	Spring Year 1	Spring Year 2	Spring Year 3	Spring Year 4	Spring Year 5	Spring Year 6	Spring Year 7	Spring Year 8
Reading comprehension (CAT-R)									
Full sample avg	281.1	340.2	390.2	417.7	455.3	481.9	504.1	517.9	552.9
(N)	(675)	(732)	(644)	(556)	(539)	(566)	(496)	(446)	(405)
Low SES avg	272.6	327.9	378.0	400.2	434.3	462.3	485.4	494.1	527.4
(N)	(342)	(369)	(334)	(310)	(299)	(321)	(290)	(261)	(234)
High SES avg	300.3	359.6	416.8	456.4	504.6	530.0	553.1	582.2	618.1
(N)	(164)	(178)	(152)	(119)	(110)	(102)	(92)	(76)	(71)
High-low SES difference	27.7	31.7	38.8	56.2	70.3	67.7	67.6	88.1	90.7
Difference as percentage SD	0.68	0.70	0.82	0.98	1.00	0.92	0.92	1.13	1.14
Math concepts/reasoning (CAT-M)									
Full sample avg	292.1	341.0	384.2	413.6	446.7	476.0	498.5	515.8	542.7
(N)	(693)	(722)	(639)	(556)	(538)	(560)	(490)	(437)	(399)
Low SES avg	282.1	330.6	373.2	399.0	429.2	458.5	481.7	493.5	516.3
(N)	(357)	(365)	(330)	(310)	(299)	(315)	(284)	(255)	(226)
High SES avg	312.3	355.8	406.0	446.6	484.9	511.3	533.0	574.4	598.8
(N)	(164)	(174)	(151)	(119)	(109)	(102)	(92)	(76)	(73)
High-low SES difference	30.2	25.2	32.8	47.6	55.7	52.8	51.3	80.9	82.5
Difference as percentage SD	0.95	0.69	0.87	0.98	1.01	0.86	0.80	1.15	1.16

end of each school year. For children promoted each year, these eight years extend from the start of first grade through the end of eighth grade. Eighth grade is the *base-line year* for the NELS-88 project. The trends depicted in Table 6.2 thus are not seen in the large, national studies of schooling. The key importance of securing data for the early years is highlighted by the fact that when the BSS youngsters reached Year 8, the large cleavages in test scores across SES levels already had existed for a long time.

The pooled data reported in the first row for reading and math show that average test scores increased year by year, as would be expected, but there is a sharply decelerating trend in the number of points children gained each year, especially over elementary school. The nine month fall-to-spring first grade gains (59 points on the CAT-R; 50 points on the CAT-M) are the largest in the table. Next largest are the twelve month gains from the spring of Year 1 to the spring of Year 2. After Year 2, annual gains become smaller until the end of middle school.

Because the average gain on tests decreases year by year, the variance in *gains* inevitably shrinks. (The variance in scores, of course, increases steadily over the years.) This developmental phenomenon, namely the relatively larger variance in gains early in children's school careers, is easy to see but seldom looked for. Still, if the aim is to understand the nature of schooling, attending to life periods when variance in outcomes is relatively large affords the best chance of achieving that understanding. Put another way, the early years of schooling are a more strategic time to investigate the forces leading to growth in achievement than are the later years. A second implication of the decelerating growth rate is that differences among children established in the early years will tend to persist, if only because they are relatively larger. Growth during the first year, for example, equals or exceeds most *two-year* gains over Years 4 through 7.

Comparisons by SES level over the eight years have similar implications. Table 6.2 gives the differences in scores comparing high and low SES groups in the spring of each year. The second order differences by SES become *larger* over the first four years. For example, the difference in Year 2 minus the difference in Year 1 is just four points on the CAT-R (31.7–27.7). The second-order difference increases to seven points over the Year 3–Year 2 interval, then further increases to seventeen and fourteen points over the next two periods. Over Years 4 to 8, however, second order differences are small, almost constant, suggesting that a parallel linear pattern of growth emerges around ages 10 to 11. The point here is not to describe these trajectories — that is a topic for another paper — but to stress that once children are launched on a given trajectory, strong forces continue to channel them, so that the gap between trajectories widens over the elementary years when children are making their most substantial gains. The cycling down of the rate of growth over the elementary years, however, suggests that much of the difference in school achievement associated with SES in the upper grade levels *must* be attributed to what has transpired in earlier periods.

The clear trend in test score averages shows that lower SES youngsters fall farther and farther back as time passes, whether we look at simple scale score differences in test averages or at differences relative to the variance in test scores. For example, in the fall of first grade, lower SES youngsters on average are 0.68 standard deviations below upper SES youngsters on the CAT-R. After first grade and through the rest of elementary school, their relative shortfall holds steady in the vicinity of 0.8–1.0

standard deviations. This holding pattern continues into Year 6, when most of the cohort has made the transition into middle school.[6] After that, in Years 7 and 8 the test scores of low SES children trail by well over a full standard deviation in both reading and math, their largest shortfall over the entire period. Considerable other evidence suggests that student performance tends to fall off in the middle grades (see Eccles and Midgley, 1990; Stipek, 1984; *Harvard Education Letter*, 1992), and the test scores in Table 6.2 suggest that such problems may be especially severe for lower SES youngsters, whose academic foothold has been tenuous all along the way.

Over time, then, the cleavage across SES levels in the competencies tapped by the two CAT subtests widens substantially. It might be concluded from this trend that schools over these years have not served lower SES youngsters especially well. But we cannot tell from these data what the *unique* contribution of schools is. Schools are not the only developmental context that these students have experienced over the eight years in question. Table 6.1 shows that some children have a substantial edge at the start of their schooling, and they are the ones in higher SES families. It is reasonable to assume that these favourable circumstances continue to confer benefits. The trends by SES seen in Table 6.2 reflect *all* the influences in children's realm of experience, not just influences present in schools. To determine the schools' unique contribution requires a different approach.

Achievement Trends Season by Season

Comparing school year gains and summer gains isolates the school's unique contribution. When testing is done every fall and spring (the testing schedule used when BSS children were in elementary school),[7] the impact of schooling should be reflected in improvement during the fall-spring interval. During the time school is in session, both in-school and out-of-school influences are combined in unknown proportions. The spring-fall testing interval reflects gains over the summer break, however, when children are not in school.[8] By comparing gains children make in winter with gains they make in summer we can approximate a natural experiment: the influence of schools is withheld for part of the year (summer), but all other sources of influence on children's cognitive development are operating.[9] Since schools are not implicated in summer gains but are implicated in winter gains, differences between summer and winter in the amount of learning can suggest how much schools specifically contribute to cognitive growth.

Table 6.3 reports seasonal gains over the first five years of children's schooling.[10] Winter gains exceed summer gains by a wide margin each year. The difference in gains is even clearer when gains are expressed in units per month rather than in units per season (roughly eight months in the winter, four months in the summer). The average monthly gain on the CAT-R for low SES children in the first winter is just over 7.0 points (i.e., 56.7/8 = 7.1) compared to an average *loss* over the first summer (four months) of 0.9 points per month (−3.7/4). The corresponding monthly figures are 7.6 (60.8/8) and 3.8 (15.0/4) for high SES children, both positive.

The winter gain over first grade for the high and low SES groups is almost the same: the difference is only 4.1 points, corresponding to just 0.09 standard deviations (the SD for winter gains the first year is 46.07). When school is in session, then, there is very little difference in the amounts children learn, irrespective of their SES standing.

Table 6.3. School Year and Summer California Achievement Test Gains over the Elementary School Years by Socioeconomic Status Level

	Socioeconomic status level				Socioeconomic status level		
Reading comprehension (CAT-R)	Low	Mid	High	Math concepts/reasoning (CAT-M)	Low	Mid	High
Winter gains				*Winter gains*			
Year 1	56.7 (327)	68.6 (165)	60.8 (161)	Year 1	50.0 (340)	52.9 (166)	45.0 (158)
Year 2	48.0 (323)	45.4 (151)	40.1 (151)	Year 2	42.9 (322)	43.5 (154)	42.2 (150)
Year 3	31.2 (294)	35.6 (120)	33.7 (118)	Year 3	36.0 (296)	35.9 (120)	35.6 (118)
Year 4	33.1 (291)	41.0 (128)	31.7 (109)	Year 4	33.2 (291)	33.6 (128)	35.7 (108)
Year 5	24.3 (315)	29.1 (142)	24.6 (102)	Year 5	24.7 (307)	30.7 (141)	27.8 (102)
Total winter gains	193.3	219.7	190.9	Total winter gains	186.8	196.6	186.3
Summer gains				*Summer gains*			
Year 1	-3.7 (318)	-2.1 (159)	15.0 (154)	Year 1	-4.8 (321)	-6.8 (160)	8.8 (151)
Year 2	-3.5 (295)	1.8 (126)	8.5 (123)	Year 2	-5.2 (294)	-0.6 (127)	3.3 (123)
Year 3	1.6 (299)	2.5 (123)	14.9 (114)	Year 3	-1.9 (299)	5.1 (123)	1.3 (114)
Year 4	4.5 (285)	1.6 (126)	10.4 (91)	Year 4	4.9 (283)	4.8 (125)	5.6 (90)
Year 5	2.0 (274)	-4.1 (113)	-2.2 (88)	Year 5	-0.9 (277)	1.6 (110)	5.9 (87)
Total summer gains	0.8	-0.3	46.5	Total summer gains	-7.9	4.0	24.9

The summer pattern is quite different, however, as the total score difference of almost nineteen points amounts to almost 0.5 SDs, and the low group actually loses ground. Even though the summer period is only half as long, the advantage created for the high SES children is striking, and the pattern is very much the same for math (CAT-M).

The last entries in each panel show how the SES advantage cumulates over the five elementary years (see 'Total gain' entries in the last row for each panel). Across all five summers, the high SES group gained forty-six points in reading comprehension and about twenty-five points in math, while the middle and low SES groups essentially stood still in reading and either gained a little or lost a little in math.

In winter periods, by contrast, total gains over the five elementary years are less than five points apart for the high and low SES groups in both reading and math. *The difference between the high and low SES groups that develops over the five-year period can thus be attributed almost entirely to differential gains made when school is not in session.* When school is in session, all children are learning at much the same rate.

Several other studies in various parts of the country (David, 1974; David and Pelavin, 1978; Hammond and Frechtling, 1979; Hayes and Grether, 1969; Murnane, 1975; Pelavin and David, 1977) likewise find that lower SES and/or minority youngsters gain much less than their more advantaged peers during the summer. In a national longitudinal study of over 100,000 elementary students, Heyns (1986), for example, found a consistent relative loss over the summer among the least advantaged children. African-American elementary school children in New Haven (Murnane, 1975) and middle school children of both races in Atlanta show similar seasonal patterns (Heyns, 1978). All these studies show the same kind of severe deficit in summers that we observe, but the BSS data, to our knowledge, are unique in that they estimate *winter* learning over a substantial time interval. Furthermore, contextual analyses reported elsewhere (Entwisle and Alexander, 1992, 1994) that cover the first two years of BSS children's schooling conclude that SES background much more than school contexts or family configuration is responsible for producing differences in children's summer achievement. It is important to be able to rule out these factors, since children of lower SES are also more likely to attend segregated schools and to come from one parent families than are higher SES children.

Before proceeding a word is in order about measurement issues. Note particularly that since gains (by definition) control for initial test scores, we can sidestep issues related to initial group differences in 'mental ability'. Also the CAT-R and the CAT-M subtests show little indication of ceiling constraints for the BSS sample in the early grades. The CAT tests used in this analysis can be compared to published norms intended to apply to all public school districts with eleven or more students and to all Catholic schools. The composite means for the BSS sample are below the fiftieth percentile at the beginning of grades 1, 2 and 3, and at about the fiftieth percentile at the ends of grades 1 and 2, suggesting that students' scores are not depressed because of insufficient range at the top of the test.

Another notable feature of the BSS data involves lack of fan-spread in seasonal gains. Children's gains in the school year show an *inverse* relationship to test score levels at the beginning of the observation period, because low SES children have the lowest scores at the beginning of the year, but during winter periods gain as much as do their classmates who start with higher scores. Some accounts of achievement differentials across ethnic boundaries cite 'fan-spread' as a major reason for increasing cleavages in attainment levels with age (Coleman, Campbell *et al.*, 1966). Here we do not see fan-spread because during the winters children whose test scores were the highest to begin with tended to gain less than others did. Nor is there evidence of regression effects. Gains that are maximal for one end of the test score range in winter and maximal for the other end of the range in summer do not lead to a pattern consistent with a regression interpretation. As far as we can determine, the seasonal patterns seen in the BSS cannot be attributed either to peculiarities in the psychometric properties of the tests or to idiosyncrasies of the BSS research design.

Discussion

Seasonal comparisons can help distinguish the unique influence of schooling on young-sters' academic development. Children learn year round, yet most studies, with a few exceptions (e.g., Heyns, 1978; Murnane, 1975), neglect the summer decrement in children's learning rates. To our knowledge, only in the BSS is it clear that winter learning rates are virtually equivalent across SES groups. As the *Coleman Report* (Coleman, Campbell *et al.*, 1966) emphasized, families do indeed make a difference, as shown in the large variance across SES levels in children's test scores at the start of first grade (Table 6.1) and in their cognitive gains over the summer (Table 6.3). But patterns of winter learning provide compelling evidence that schools also make more of a difference than the *Coleman Report* and subsequent large-scale studies credited them with. Schools cannot compensate for differences in out-of-school resources in summer when they are not in session, but during the primary grades it appears they come close to levelling the playing field when they are in session, at least for the kinds of verbal and quantitative skills captured in the CAT-R and CAT-M subtests.

Differences in learning rates linked to SES may be most important in the first few grades, before the age when most sociological studies of educational attainment begin. In the primary grades children are learning foundational skills — sounding letters, basic math operations, counting blocks, how to tell time, make change and the like. Many such learning activities are part of everyday life and occur in school and out, summer and winter. Correspondingly, much of the curriculum in the early grades can be, and often is, mastered outside school. This confounding has made it hard to know what school and home each contribute uniquely to early cognitive growth, and there-fore how to evaluate effects of economic deprivation and other forms of social dis-advantage on schooling. Seasonal variation in learning may be particularly important for understanding achievement differences that are linked to stratifying conditions in the larger society — racial/ethnic differences, differences across socioeconomic levels and the like, because children from disadvantaged circumstances are more likely to spend the summer in environments where resources to support learning are scarce.

The impressive season by season differences seen in the BSS are obscured when comparisons across groups are made using only year-end test scores or when test score gains are computed spring to spring as is typical in most studies. When BSS data are pooled across seasons, we see the usual positive correlations between SES level and learning or achievement found in all the earlier large-scale studies, including the *Coleman Report*. There are no real guidelines about how to select the time intervals over which to measure any kind of change, but the units of time over which change is assessed are exceedingly important. Disadvantaged children in the BSS keep pace when they are in school, or come very close to keeping pace, so school plays a strong positive role for such youngsters, effectively offsetting tremendous out-of-school differences in learning opportunities available to children in the extra-school hours. It seems that economically disadvantaged youngsters stop learning or slow down when they are out of school in summer, when the only resources to support their development are those available in their home and community environments. Children reared in upper SES settings advance year round, almost as much in summer as in winter. They appear to be not nearly as dependent on schools for the experiences that help move them forward.

Sketching out the positive and productive role that schools play for low SES students gives a far different picture of urban education than that typically portrayed. The BSS, of course, reflects children's experience in just one city school system, but the summer patterns that come through so vividly in Table 6.3 appear to be quite general — they also appear to characterize children's achievement in several other large city school systems, although fewer summers and fewer grade levels are available for inspection in other data sets. What the BSS adds to fill out this picture is the complementary winter pattern suggesting that less advantaged children do as well or better than the advantaged when school is open. Urban school systems specifically have been faulted for failing to serve the interests of disadvantaged and minority youth, but the comparisons in Table 6.3 suggest they are doing a better job than is generally appreciated.

Another insight offered by BSS data is that the largest seasonal disparities were registered in the first two years of children's schooling. Unlike the junior high transition, the transition from 'home child' to 'school child' has excited little curiosity among sociologists of education. As we note elsewhere (Entwisle and Alexander, 1993), however, life-stage and developmental considerations heighten young children's sensitivity to early school influences, while pressures associated with social role transitions (from 'home' child to 'school' child) challenge them. This coupling of key physiological changes with a life-stage transition, which is also true for the junior-high transition, makes a hurdle especially difficult. When rates of growth are computed annually, as is usually done, complex interactions between in-school and out-of-school learning, home background and other factors camouflage the nature of the transition.

Lower SES children seem especially vulnerable during this transition, and that vulnerability is plain to see in BSS children. With gender and race controlled, children who were on meal subsidy, signifying low family income, were 41 per cent more likely to be held back than were children not on subsidy (Dauber *et al.*, 1993). Even allowing for their lower beginning test scores, those on subsidy still were 21 per cent more likely to be held back. Once held back, children are effectively 'off-time' and in a lower school track from that point forward (Alexander and Entwisle, 1994).

It is almost thirty years since Coleman and his colleagues undertook the survey now known as the *Coleman Report*, and in a very real sense this pioneering survey set the agenda for research on educational attainment over the next two decades. In the last decade there has been a shift from input-output models to a life course perspective, in part prompted by some other work of Coleman (1984c) on the transition from school to work. Research on the school to work transition mounts steadily (see Pallas, 1993), but to our knowledge the BSS is still the only study of the first grade transition that covers children across a wide span of socioeconomic backgrounds.

We have been exploring a number of topics related to the first grade transition: the circumstances that support exceptionally good first-grade outcomes (Pallas *et al.*, 1987); teachers' sentiments, patterns of pupil-teacher interaction and marking practices (Alexander, Entwisle and Thompson, 1987; Entwisle and Alexander, 1988); advantages associated with full-day kindergarten (Entwisle *et al.*, 1987); children's behavioural style, like interest/participation and attention span/restlessness (Alexander *et al.*, 1993); social supports and other resource differences in home and school (Alexander and Entwisle, 1988; Entwisle and Alexander, 1988; Entwisle *et al.*, 1989; Thompson *et al.*, 1989; Entwisle and Alexander, 1990; Thompson *et al.*, 1992); the role of school racial composition (Entwisle and Alexander, 1992; 1994); and effects of retention (Alexander *et al.*, 1994; Cadigan *et al.*, 1988; Dauber *et al.*, 1993) and of other forms of educational tracking (Entwisle and Alexander, 1993; Pallas *et al.*, 1994; Alexander and Entwisle, 1994).

The BSS research points to an important outcome: schools can make a difference for poor children, because children's schooling offsets the dearth of learning resources in low SES youngsters' home environments, at least in the early years. But exactly what are the home learning resources that the school replaces in winter? While we cannot go very far in unpacking this variable, we do know from other BSS analyses that family structure and school racial composition are not major considerations, at least for BSS youngsters (Entwisle and Alexander, 1992, 1994). One obvious consideration involves differences in specific learning materials, educational toys, books, etc. These no doubt play a role, but here we wish to comment on several other kinds of SES-linked resources that might not be so obvious. The first has to do with the emotional climate in homes where finances are short. The second has to do with the world view of parents of different social levels. The third hinges on how parents react to information about their children's progress in school.

Some authors report that children who live in poverty experience double jeopardy, first because they are exposed more frequently to medical illnesses, family stress and other negative life conditions; second, because they experience more serious consequences from these risks than do children of higher SES, particularly if their poverty is long-term (Parker *et al.*, 1988). It is difficult to reconcile the BSS data with this perspective, however. We have data showing that in BSS families the number of negative life events for low SES children exceeds the number of such events for high SES children, but when school is in session the two groups gain at about the same rate. This parity in school outcomes for children from different backgrounds suggests that in addition to seeing the school as a forum for learning, where teachers mobilize resources and so prompt pupils to achieve, we may also conceive of the school as a social environment that neutralizes or buffers home stresses. Elder's (1974) research with children reared during the Great Depression found that adolescents (the Oakland cohort) who were old enough to work and who therefore spent significant amounts of time away from home did well — in fact, the long-term outcomes for the deprived males surpassed those for the non-deprived. But younger boys in the Berkeley cohort, born just as the depression started, did suffer the consequences of a negative emotional climate in the home created by their out-of-work fathers (Elder *et al.*, 1984). By similar means, attending school may help low SES youngsters in part because it provides a setting where family stresses are temporarily screened out.

A second possibility emphasizes the different roles that parents of various SES backgrounds set for themselves with respect to their children's education. Middle-class parents conceive of themselves as active partners in the education of their children, while working-class parents prefer leaving the role of educator to the school (Lareau, 1987). If so, the strong seasonal patterns in test scores for BSS children could reflect parental involvement for better-off children, which, when school is in session, tends to be redundant with school effects but which, when school is not in session in summers, adds importantly to student achievement. High SES parents take over the role of teacher in summer and because of close contact with school in winter they know the level and kind of experiences their children are ready for. From this stand-point the summer decrement in children's progress is not so much a consequence of a dearth of material resources in low SES homes as of a lack of a special kind of 'human capital'.

A third possibility relates to still another kind of human capital. In every BSS analysis so far, we have found that parents' expectations are powerful predictors of children's performance, irrespective of SES level. Other researchers corroborate our findings, even reporting parents' expectations to be more potent than the child's IQ in predicting school performance (Parsons *et al.*, 1982). Low SES parents are just as likely to hold high expectations for their children as high SES parents are, but parents' expectations for high SES children are much more in tune with the child's perform-ance level than are those of low SES parents (Alexander *et al.*, 1994). High SES parents, for example, recall their children's marks on prior report cards more accur-ately than do low SES parents. In other words, high SES parents are good at pro-cessing information furnished them by the school that will help them monitor their child's schooling. Perhaps because high SES parents are more informed about what to expect, their expectations are stronger predictors of the child's actual performance, or, put another way, high SES parents' expectations are a more useful resource for the child. Children probably have a good sense of their parent's monitoring ability because in some earlier research (Entwisle and Hayduk, 1982), also with first graders in Baltimore, lower SES children were influenced by their parents' expectations *only* in the first semester of first grade. Later on parents' expectations had much less in-fluence on these children, perhaps because they found their parents' expectations were not particularly useful as sources of information. Higher SES children, on the other hand, continued to respond to their parents' expectations as far as they were followed (through third grade).

We do not wish to suggest that any of the explanations proposed are necessarily correct or that the list is exhaustive. The data in this chapter can suggest only that the home resources found in high SES families have some role in promoting young-sters' achievement in the summer. These resources could encompass books, games, trips to museums and zoos, special lessons and organized summer activities, but em-phasizing material resources may be deceptive. The human resources that usually ac-company material resources may hold the key. Whatever the case, we need to define the circumstances that make it possible for children to make a smooth transition into first grade and then to continue to move forward even when schools are closed.

Conclusions

Our purpose in directing attention to schooling's positive contributions to disadvan-taged children's learning is not to paper over the very real, very severe problems that beset urban education but rather to call attention to the positive role that schools seem to be playing. In the years since the EEO Report was mistakenly read by many as implying that 'schools don't make a difference', we have come to understand better what it is about schools, schooling and home–community–school relationships that do make a difference. In a very real sense the *Coleman Report* mobilized the sociological profession to study education. The Beginning School Study in Baltimore is heir to that tradition. The seasonal learning perspective on the schooling of primary grade children offered by BSS data reveals, not just that schooling is a powerful force in lower SES children's lives, but that it is a positive force. It emphasizes the importance of the very earliest years of schooling, and the importance of SES for children's development.

Acknowledgments

Data collection for this research was supported by the W.T. Grant Foundation, Grant No. 83079682 and National Institute of Child Health and Development Grant No. 1 RO1 16302. The analysis was supported by National Science Foundation Grant No. SES 8510535 and National Institute of Child Health and Development Grants No. 1 RO1 21044, 5 RO1 23738 and 5 RO1 23943. We thank the children, parents and teachers who gave us such splendid cooperation in all phases of this research.

Notes

1 For an overview of the research that has attempted such comparisons, see Ceci, 1991. Such 'natural experiments' usually only occur when wars or natural disasters disrupt the normal routine or when societies are undergoing rapid social change.
2 Just under half the sample (46.9 per cent) had data on all five indicators, 18.1 per cent were covered by four indicators, 19.5 per cent by three indicators, 9.7 per cent by two indicators and 5.4 per cent, or forty-three youngsters, by one indicator (for thirty of these, the one was mother's education; for ten others it was the meal subsidy measure). Only three of the 790 children were missing data on all five indicators.
3 SES scale scores 0.5 SDs or more above the sample wide mean comprise the 'high' group. The lower bound for the 'middle' group is the lowest scale value that yields educational averages above 12 (i.e., high school graduate) for both parents.
4 These figures apply to the first two years of children's schooling. Since we initially sampled regular classrooms only, special education placements are underrepresented in the first year data. The percentages reported combine assignment to separate special education classes and pull-out programs from regular classes.
5 These testing data come from BCPS records, so children only are covered so long as they remain in the city school system. Over the eight years covered in Table 6.2, case coverage falls off substantially over time, by about 40 per cent. However, patterns displayed in Tables 6.2 and 6.3 are unchanged when averages are computed just for the youngsters who remain in city schools over the entire period.
6 The school transition issue is complicated, as children in the lowest SES group are much more likely than those in the middle and upper groups to be held back in elementary school. Because of this, barely half (52 per cent) are in sixth grade in Year 6, compared to 70 per cent of those in the middle SES group and 82 per cent of those in the upper SES group (for a general overview of these children's complicated 'pathways' through the elementary and middle school years, see Alexander *et al.*, 1994, Ch. 2).

7   After elementary school (project Years 7 and 8) testing was done in spring only.

8   In the primary grades, formal summer programs are uncommon.

9   Although exactly how they affect development might vary throughout the year.

10 The interval covered here is shorter than in Table 6.2 because the BCPS discontinued fall testing after project Year 6.

7 Coleman's Contributions to Education: Theory, Research Styles and Empirical Research

James J. Heckman and Derek Neal

This essay describes an intellectual odyssey. The story begins more than thirty years ago when James Coleman began work on a study of high schools that formed the basis for *The Adolescent Society* (Coleman, 1961a) and followed this with the equally path-breaking *Coleman Report* (Coleman, Campbell *et al.*, 1966). This research would be the beginning of a lifetime of productive and influential research on education. This chapter is an intellectual history of these major works and their aftermath. We place Coleman's contributions in context. We consider how well his early work on education has stood the test of time and examine the impact of his research on public policy. Few social scientists have been as effective as Coleman in shaping public policy discussions about education. He has repeatedly mounted successful challenges to the conventional wisdom.

Coleman has used schools as a laboratory for a study of society at large. His work on education has been motivated by theoretical questions at the core of sociology. From the beginning he has been concerned with the social organization of schooling — the organization of activities within schools and classrooms and of the relationship between schools and society. His longstanding interest is founded on the premise that patterns of reward within a social system shape the motivations and behaviour of members of that system. The effective design of social systems, including those that educate and socialize the young, requires that the structure of incentives promotes desirable ends for members of the social system and maintenance of the system over time. Early on Coleman stressed the importance of incentives in schools — a theme only recently accepted by the avant-garde of the educational research community (see Hanushek, 1994).

Throughout his career Coleman has stressed the value of rewards in motivating outcomes. He has always viewed social actors as goal-directed and purposive, and assumed that they would direct their energy in the ways they saw fit. Consequently, he has always argued that designers of social systems have to take into account the choices of agents structuring incentives in ways that would effectively motivate persons. Although Coleman the choice theorist is best known for his magisterial *Foundations of Social Theory*, analysis of the response of persons to incentives has been a main theme of much of his research in education since his early work on schooling. However, in his recent work on rational choice theory Coleman is much more formal and explicit in treating incentives than he has been in his earlier work. Unlike many theorists, Coleman has actively been engaged in the analysis of public policy questions. Such questions are often ill-posed. In each area where he has worked Coleman has helped to clarify the discussion by defining and delineating the relevant issues, shaping the agenda for his own work and that of other scholars.

Motivated by an interest in the relationship between schools and society, Coleman has carried out extensive empirical research. His major studies in education have been based on large data sets. In his empirical research he operates like a true inductive scientist. He not only brings his own vision to a project but also learns from the data, and revises his vision in the light of the evidence. Each major empirical project has produced a series of papers and monographs that generalize and refine the main empirical regularities unearthed in the original large-scale studies. Each project has been an intellectual odyssey of its own, as data and core ideas are turned over and re-examined from a fresh perspective. The element of surprise both for himself and his readers is always present in his work.

Like many great scholars, Coleman has multiple intellectual personalities that develop at their own rate and express themselves in different ways. In seeking to digest his immense body of work on education, we have been struck by the diversity of his research styles. Coleman the empiricist is clearly not the same person as Coleman the theorist. Both are excellent but in different ways. The evidence affects his theory, and his theory affects his interpretation of the evidence. Coleman the empiricist is no demographer-drudge who churns numbers without insight. Coleman the theorist is definitely also not in the post-modernist mode — his theory is grounded in empirical reality. These features make his work fascinating and yet hard to synthesize. We chronicle the contributions of both Colemans in this essay, and point out a contradiction between them. Coleman the rational choice theorist has consistently been concerned with the forces shaping personal and institutional choices. Coleman the empirical social scientist has been less concerned about the consequences of some of those choices for the analysis of his data. Any neglect caused by the second Coleman has been more than compensated by the first Coleman. Coleman has been a successful and effective empirical scholar because each empirical study has been accompanied by a convincing and insightful interpretation of the evidence.

The Adolescent Society

Coleman's first major work in the area of education was *The Adolescent Society*, published in 1961. This work was empirical in nature, but Coleman made many important generalizations about the functioning of incentives within schools. He began this work because of his interest in the structure and functioning of social systems. He thought that high schools could be a research site for the study of sources of status in social systems (Coleman, 1964c). This research focused on ten high schools in northern Illinois, including the celebrated New Trier system. The schools were chosen to provide variation in size, in type of community location and in the informal status system operating among students. Although he documented differences among the ten high schools he studied, his most important finding was the existence of a common adolescent culture in all schools with values different from those espoused by parents and teachers. Adolescents attached importance to acceptance by peers, and such acceptance was determined more by participation in athletics and extracurricular school activities and by personality, clothes and attractiveness to the opposite sex than by scholastic achievement.

The twentieth century expansion of participation in secondary schooling created a new phenomenon: adolescence as a distinct stage of life during which youth were segregated in formal institutions set apart from society. Informal social systems emerged within schools which fostered values which were to a considerable degree in conflict with the values of the formal institution. Restricted from activities outside school that would integrate them with the larger society and require them to take greater respons- ibility, adolescents looked to each other rather than to the adult community for their social rewards, and the influence of parents and the general community relative to peers in school declined. The values of the adolescent society, however, were shaped in part by the larger society through the mass media, whose dominant themes and heroes influenced adolescent attitudes, and through the structuring of school activities — for example, the use of high school sports as community entertainment and for contests between communities — and through restrictions on adolescent activities outside school.

To redirect adolescent choices, Coleman argued for change in both the structure of school activities and the relationship between the school and society. He observed that in contrast to scholastic activity, which involved interpersonal competition for grades that was not highly visible, athletic activity involved highly visible inter- scholastic (and intramural) competition where the athlete was part of a collective effort, doing something for the school and the community. To make academic activity a more important source of status among adolescents, and thereby use informal group rewards to reinforce the aims of education, he argued that interscholastic (and intra- mural) competition in scholastic matters be substituted for interpersonal competition for grades. These policies are widely advocated today. For example, the greater per- formance of students in Hungary has been attributed to intermural competitions that are a routine part of that country's scholastic culture. So has the greater performance of students in Iowa schools where interscholastic competition is an important aspect of the state scholastic environment. Coleman also argued that the relationship be- tween the school and society should be changed to integrate adolescents with the adult community and give them opportunities for responsibility. Recent proposals to motivate performance in school by linking work and education in apprenticeship programs are based on insights like this.

These conclusions derived from his first work on *The Adolescent Society* influ- enced Coleman's subsequent work. In the early 1970s he chaired the Panel on Youth of the President's Science Advisory Committee, which advocated that youth become more integrated into society at an earlier age and assume greater responsibility through participation in the workplace (Coleman, 1974a). *The Adolescent Society* provided important evidence in support of the idea that individuals respond to incentives. He found that there was more emphasis on scholastic achievement in schools where the students came from higher socioeconomic backgrounds. His evidence on the impor- tance of families in motivating children anticipated a major finding of the *Coleman Report* (Coleman, Campbell *et al.*, 1966).

The structure of incentives in schools has changed little since Coleman's work on *The Adolescent Society*. Most schools do not motivate most students to learn. The mass media continue to exert a strong effect on adolescent attitudes. Positive parental influences appear to have declined further as a result of adverse changes in family structure. His insights continue to be relevant to contemporary American education. (See the essay by Denise Kandel in this volume for further discussion of this work, and our discussion of incentives below.)

James J. Heckman and Derek Neal

The *Coleman Report* and Its Aftermath

Coleman's work on *The Adolescent Society* was followed by his work in the 1966 *Coleman Report*, which is a watershed in social science research. In one report Coleman and his colleagues changed the terms of the debate regarding inequality in schooling and defined new ways to think about inequality. They challenged a major premise of Lyndon Johnson's Great Society in its heyday — that increased spending on education could easily remedy social deficits. The research also demonstrated the value of large-scale data sets and empirical social science for evaluating social programs. The report had an enormous impact on contemporary policy discussions and inspired volumes of spirited attacks and rejoinders. Leading figures in the economics and sociology of education such as Sam Bowles, Christopher Jencks, Eric Hanushek, Hank Levin and Richard Murnane teethed on the *Coleman Report*. An entire research community devoted to the evaluation of educational reforms emerged in the wake of the study. One central empirical finding of the report — that blacks who attended integrated schools appeared to benefit in terms of their test scores, while whites who attended those schools did not appear to lose anything on their test scores — helped to trigger wide-scale busing programs to exploit 'peer effects'. Ever the vigilant observer of society, Coleman noticed that busing and forced integration led to white flight from central cities and resegregation of schools. Within one decade of the publication of his report, Coleman was an active and effective spokesman against forced integration programs that had been spawned by his report.

Unlike *The Adolescent Society*, the *Coleman Report* was not a traditional academic research study. The report was mandated by an act of Congress. The agenda shaping the study was narrowly defined. Time pressure to complete the study was enormous. It was to his credit that Coleman satisfied the mandate of the Congress and moved beyond it to refocus all future discussions of equality of opportunity in schooling away from the traditional emphasis on measuring inputs to an emphasis on measuring outputs. Neither the pressure of time nor the narrowness in the vision of the government bureaucrats monitoring the study encouraged systematic tests of competing social theories. The findings that emerged from a simple analysis of the data were so striking that a refined and closely qualified summary of the evidence would only have diminished the impact of the major findings from the study. Yet it is remarkable that all of the major findings — save one — held up under intense scrutiny by an army of social scientists.

The Main Findings of the 1966 Coleman Report

The Coleman group conducted the first broad inventory of the inputs and outputs of public education ever undertaken in the United States. A wide array of 3100 schools representing over 600,000 school children was interviewed in 1965. Measures of a variety of test scores, the qualifications of teachers, the backgrounds and attitudes of administrators, the backgrounds of students and their attitudes, the composition of student bodies and measures of the inputs used in schools were analyzed. The work was conducted in a brief period. Only ten months elapsed from the time questionnaires were administered to the publication of the final report. No study of this type had ever been undertaken in the US or elsewhere.

The factual description of American education circa 1965 was never challenged — except for one major point discussed below (see Jencks' (1972) thoughtful reanalysis). The report documented that most American school children were enrolled in racially segregated schools. There were pronounced regional disparities in access to educational resources, but outside the south there was no evidence that white children were favoured over black children. The disparity in the south was surprisingly small. However, minorities scored substantially lower than whites on achievement tests even in the first grade, and the gap between blacks and whites widened with grade level.

More controversial were the results relating schooling inputs and outputs. The single most important and enduring contribution of the study was to change the focus of discussions of inequality in education away from inequality in inputs, which had previously occupied centre stage and had been the focus of most school desegregation cases, to inequality in outputs, where output was measured by test scores. (Verbal scores received the most scrutiny, but other tests were also administered.) This change in emphasis signalled a revolution in thinking about education because for the first time school outcomes were being evaluated. The report implicitly questioned the efficiency of public schools in converting inputs to outputs. Goals 2000 and all of the recent initiatives regarding performance in schools are direct consequences of Coleman's change in emphasis from inputs to outputs. So are the widely publicized evaluation systems that monitor the test scores of public schools.

The second most important and enduring contribution of the Coleman study was to demonstrate the essential contribution of pre-school factors and out-of-school factors such as family and community to variation in the performance of children in schools. By emphasizing the role of families, and general social environments, in shaping learning, Coleman instructed 'Great Society' planners that much of what influenced academic achievement was beyond their control because schools operate in contexts that strongly influence academic success. Of equal importance was the finding that measured schooling inputs such as expenditures per pupil, school size, volumes per student in the school library, guidance counsellors, presence of tracking, accelerated curricula and teacher characteristics, such as their performance on an achievement test, their education and experience, and the proportion of white teachers, explain very little of the variance in student test scores, controlling or not controlling for family background. This was true for all racial groups, but differed somewhat among racial groups. There was a stronger effect of inputs on outputs for blacks than for other groups (Jencks, 1972).

However, Coleman's empirical claim about the importance of peers in schools for the educational performance of children did not hold up in subsequent reanalyses of the Coleman data (Smith, 1972; Hanushek, 1968, 1972). As noted by Smith (1972), a simple coding error produced much greater evidence of peer effects than was found in analyses of the corrected data. Unfortunately, this evidence on peer effects had considerable impact on policy and served as an important catalyst for busing and forced integration programs. Since home environments are less easily influenced by policy, Coleman's evidence was cited as evidence that forced integration was the most expeditious policy for raising black achievement.

The report never claimed that teachers — or school inputs — do not affect test scores, just that their contribution to variance within racial groups was small compared to the contribution of home environments. However, Coleman (1967b) strongly suggested that school inputs did not contribute much to the formation of cognitive achievement. Subsequent analyses challenged the order of importance (in explaining variance of test scores) of the non-home environmental variables but never challenged the dominance of environmental variables in accounting for variation in test scores.

Two central objections to the report raised by economists Eric Hanushek and John Kain (1972) concerned (a) the meaning of 'importance' to be assigned to the variables used in the regression studies and (b) the causal interpretation to be placed on Coleman's evidence. Hanushek's 1972 book presents a comprehensive statement of what a more completely specified causal model for analyzing Coleman's data would look like. Hanushek's analysis is the basis for the 'value-added' approach to the evaluation of schools currently in widespread use (see also Levin, 1970, and Bowles and Levin, 1968, for a discussion of this issue).

One of the most controversial features of Coleman's approach to analyzing the data was his method of accounting for the 'importance' of background, schooling and peer effects. He took it for granted that the contribution of a regression variable to the overall variance in an outcome variable is a proper measure of the importance of the variable. Economists (e.g., Bowles and Levin, 1968; Cain and Watts, 1970; Hanushek and Kain, 1972) were quick to note that with inter-correlated regression variables, no unique contribution of any single variable to the overall fit of a regression equation is an appropriate measure of importance. Step-wise procedures for accounting for importance depend on the order in which the variables are entered into a regression equation. Further, procedures which account for importance based on the 'unique' (regression adjusted) contributions of variables to total variance produce decompositions that do not fully account for all of the explained variance.

Coleman's response to the factual aspects of this criticism (1972b) has withstood the test of time. Using a variety of decompositions and methods for allocating joint variance, the central finding that parental environmental variables drive the explained variance in test scores remains unchallenged. Some of the subsidiary findings of the report were successfully challenged in the more refined analyses, and his defence of variance explained as a measure of importance was not widely accepted.

A more serious challenge to the *Coleman Report* was the one posed by Hanushek (1968, 1972), Cain and Watts (1970) and other economists. The *Coleman Report* and related studies have a distinctly empirical flavour. Long lists of regressors are used to establish empirical regularities with little effort made to justify a causal interpretation for them. Accordingly, it is difficult to use Coleman's evidence in any interpretive manner or to use it to suggest particular policy interventions, as Coleman himself acknowledged (Coleman, 1968c). His inductive approach to the analysis of his data often ignored the possibility that his regressors were determined in part by the outcomes. Decisions by parents to pick high quality (i.e., high achievement) schools and high quality student peers for their children were ignored and treated as inconsequential to his analysis, despite the fact that the relatively strong peer effects estimated in the *Coleman Report* could be a consequence of such choices. Decisions by school districts to devote more resources to problem areas could also produce understated estimates of the effects of measured inputs on pupil performance. Empirically strong family background effects of the sort found in the report may arise in part because bright parents have higher incomes, higher levels of education and more family resources, and may provide richer home learning environments for their children. They may also arise from genetic mechanisms through which the intelligence of the parents is passed on to the child. Since no serious attempt was made to separate spurious correlation from genuine causation, the report could not be used as the basis for any serious evaluation of specific policy proposals.

Hanushek's (1968, 1972) program for causal inference was based on linking outputs of schools to well defined inputs. Coleman related academic performance to contemporaneous values of inputs. However, it is important to recognize the cumulative nature of learning and to link current outputs to all previous inputs. A compromise adopted by Hanushek, and now widely accepted as the 'value-added' approach to educational evaluation, measures the contribution of contemporaneous inputs to changes in outputs. Coleman could not implement this approach in the 1966 report because he lacked longitudinal data or repeated cross-section information on the same schools.

In arguing for the valued-added approach, Hanushek noted that students move across school districts and that contemporaneous school quality measures are likely to misstate previous levels of inputs experienced by students. Thus conventional arguments based on measurement error in regression models suggest that, if parents with better environments tend to send their children to better schools, the impact of measured home environments on measured outputs is overstated in conventional regression analyses because home environment appears in its own right and also stands in for the more poorly measured schooling quality in estimating the output of schools. This argument helps to explain one of Coleman's central findings: that measured inputs have weak effects on outputs.

There is an important distinction between an empirical relationship estimated between output Y and inputs X and a causal relationship connecting Y to X:

$$Y = F(X). \tag{1}$$

This distinction arises when some or all of the X are measured with error, or when some of the X are not measured at all, or when the relationship mapping X to Y is misspecified due to an incorrect choice of a functional form for F. An entire literature in econometrics discusses alternative methods for estimating (1) under different maintained assumptions. Unless (1) is clearly specified and can be plausibly estimated using the available data, it is difficult to interpret or use estimated empirical relationships of the sort reported in the *Coleman Report*.

Estimates of the educational production function F are only the first step for determining how inputs raise outputs. Rational choice theorists motivated by utilitarian criteria or conventional economists using cost-benefit analysis would not only ask how X affects Y, but also how that effect is valued (i.e., how does Y translate into income, occupation, education, welfare participation, or perhaps even 'happiness' or utility) and what the costs are of changing X. An ordering of inputs in terms of their contribution to net benefit may be very different from the ranking of variables by their contribution to variance that is used in the *Coleman Report*. A variance ranking procedure (a) ignores costs altogether, (b) does not claim to estimate F, or the causal responsiveness of Y to X, and (c) instead establishes an empirical relationship between Y and X that has no clearcut causal interpretation. Unfortunately, the full cost-benefit program proposed in the aftermath of the *Coleman Report* remains to be implemented for the evaluation of schools. Cost functions for schools are rarely estimated because the requisite data are rarely collected in disaggregated form or made available to scholars. Coleman was wise not to claim to produce a full cost-benefit analysis of school inputs because the data were not available to perform such an analysis.

Research after the Coleman Report

Three different lines of research originated as responses to the *Coleman Report*. One line, begun by Hanushek (1972) and continued by Murnane (1975) and others, directly responded to the popular interpretation that the *Coleman Report* had shown that teachers do not matter. As previously noted, the report never made that claim, but it was picked up as a main finding in popular discussions of the report and is still widely held in scholarly circles.

A second line of research initiated by Welch (1966, 1967) and carried on by Johnson and Stafford (1973) and Wachtel (1976), Betts (1995a), Card and Krueger (1992a, 1992b) and others looks at earnings — rather than test scores — as an outcome measure of schooling expenditure. A third line of research built on what turned out to be the most fragile finding of the report: that peer effects were more important than school effects. Subsequent reanalyses by Smith (1972) and others successfully challenged this finding. Nonetheless, it motivated and was used to justify school desegregation and busing plans. Coleman's later evidence on the consequences of forced integration led him to oppose it — taking a major intellectual force out of the busing movement. Coleman documented the importance of accounting for parental choice. Parents voted with their feet in response to changes in the schooling opportunities offered to their children. This sometimes led to greater segregation in schools as whites fled inner cities to avoid busing problems.

Do Teachers Matter? The literature immediately spawned by the *Coleman Report* focused on the crude interpretation given to it in the popular press: that teachers and other schooling inputs do not matter much. Both Hanushek (1972) and Murnane (1975) found that individual teachers matter in the following sense: certain teachers seem to produce — or be associated with — higher quality students. They do not distinguish between these two possibilities. It is possible that, within a particular school, good students are systematically assigned to certain teachers so that sorting may explain this evidence.

At the classroom and school level, individual teachers appear to matter in affecting outcomes. Yet there is so much heterogeneity across the environments in classrooms and schools that estimates of the effect of measures of teacher inputs on outcomes show no effect. As the level of aggregation of the measure of schooling inputs is increased, however, strong quality effects on outcomes tend to emerge in estimated empirical relationships, as we document below.

Early on, a theme still current in debates over the impact of schooling quality was sounded. Aggregative measures of schooling quality bear little relationship to measured outcomes. Yet teacher inputs matter. The performance of schools is not necessarily improved by changing the aggregates — what matters is improving the incentives to motivate individual teachers and the organization of schools (see, e.g., Levin, 1970; Hanushek, 1991; or Hanushek, 1994, for a modern statement of this view; see also Coleman, 1994c). The focus in the recent debate on improving education has shifted from a focus on inputs to incentives. Inputs matter, but only if they are efficiently utilized. Increasing the resource aggregates available to schools does not necessarily increase schooling outputs (see Hanushek, 1994).

The Impact of Schooling Quality on Earnings.   Coleman and his immediate critics judged schools by their performance in boosting test scores. However, there is little interest in test scores per se. Interest focuses on what higher test scores predict in terms of completing schooling, attaining success in the labour market or in other aspects of social life. In fact, much recent research indicates that the verbal test scores extensively analyzed by Coleman are weak predictors of earnings compared to maths scores, which seem to do a better job in predicting wages (Murnane, Willett and Levy, 1995). To conduct more interesting cost-benefit studies, it is advantageous to utilize more clearly defined benefit measures.

An entire companion literature emerged in economics that addressed one of Coleman's central questions but changed the metric of outcomes from ordinal test scores to cardinal earnings. This literature came in two waves: an early wave stimulated by the *Coleman Report*, and a more recent wave stimulated by the influential work of Card and Krueger (1992a, 1992b). Comprehensive surveys of this literature are presented by Card and Krueger (1994) and Betts (1995b). Unfortunately, the surveys do not agree about what the literature has found.

The level of aggregation in the measure of schooling inputs differs greatly across various studies. Coleman *et al.* (1966) estimated relationships at the level of individuals and schools — relating school characteristics to individual test scores. Altonji and Dunn (1990) and Betts (1995a) also pursue this approach. All this work is more aggregative in nature than some of the early studies by Murnane (1975) and Hanushek (1972), which examined the performance of individual teachers and classrooms.

In contrast, Card and Krueger (1992a, 1992b) pursue an even more aggregative approach used by many economists in showing that *state* average school characteristics are related to individual earnings. Their rationale for using such aggregative measures of schooling inputs is partly based on expedience and partly motivated by conceptual concerns. With US census data, it is only possible to locate the state of birth of persons. State average measures of schooling quality are assigned to persons; so are average measures of family background. One conceptual defence for their approach is that estimates of quality — outcome relationships based on state aggregates — are less vulnerable to the consequences of self-selection decisions by parents and schools that we previously discussed and are more robust to measurement error. States vary greatly in their educational spending levels for reasons assumed to be unrelated to the unobservable components of the subsequent realized earnings of school children.[1]

The Card and Krueger evidence indicates that estimating relationships between school quality and earnings at this level of aggregation produces strong empirical relationships. However, Heckman, Layne-Farrar and Todd (1995; 1996) re-examined this evidence and found that when the assumptions of linearity in the schooling-earnings relationship and the absence of selective migration, on which the study is based, are tested, they are rejected. The evidence of strong quality effects weakens when these assumptions are relaxed. Nonetheless, Card and Krueger (1994) summarize a variety of different studies and claim that different data sets and different statistical models produce the same average effect of aggregate quality on earnings. Betts (1995b) is not willing to make this claim. He demonstrates that recent estimates by himself (1995a) and others using measures of quality at the schools actually attended by students find little relationship between measures of schooling quality and earnings. Altonji and Dunn (1990) report similar evidence.

Although many issues remain to be sorted out, the following summary is a fair description of the consensus view.

1 Using quality measures constructed at the level of the individual teacher and the classroom, individual teachers appear to matter. All of this evidence is for test scores. This level of aggregation is finer than that used by Coleman *et al.*, who relate school-level measures of inputs to individual test scores.

2 Using quality measures constructed at the level of individual schools, there is at best weak evidence relating schooling inputs to test scores or earnings. This evidence is consistent with a central finding of the *Coleman Report*. Estimated effects of *school-wide* aggregate measures on student outcomes are weak.

3 Using quality measures constructed at the *state* level, there is more evidence of an effect of school quality on earnings. (There are no comparable studies for test scores.) Yet this evidence is problematic because of the level of aggregation and the assumptions on which the research is based (see Heckman, Layne-Farrar and Todd, 1995; 1996).

4 Evidence of quality effects on outcomes is stronger for older cohorts when dispersion of inputs among geographic units is greater and the mean level of quality is lower. Reduced dispersion in quality and diminishing returns to schooling make it less likely to find any statistically significant effect of school quality on outcomes in more recent data. Reduced dispersion in a regressor variable makes it harder to estimate a precisely determined effect of the regressor on outcome measures. Diminishing returns to schooling quality makes estimated input–output relationships weaker.

Recall that Coleman had found that schooling inputs were roughly evenly distributed across racial groups within regions. An exception was for southern blacks, for whom he found the strongest effects of schooling inputs in accounting for the variance of test score outcomes (see Smith, 1972). Like all southerners, this group also had lower levels of schooling inputs than persons in other regions, so diminishing returns were less likely to be operative for this group.

The evidence in the *Coleman Report* is thus not necessarily at odds with the evidence for earlier cohorts assembled by Card and Krueger (1992a) and Hanushek and Harbison (1992). When there is greater dispersion in measured schooling inputs, there is stronger statistical evidence of quality on outcomes.

Peer Effects, Busing and Forced Integration. The most controversial and least robust finding of the *Coleman Report* was its claim that integrated schools boosted the academic achievement of black students without affecting the achievement of white students. The US Civil Rights Commission introduced legislation into the US Congress based on this finding. Evidence from the *Coleman Report* was introduced into numerous lower court cases during the period of federal circuit court judicial activism on school desegregation in the late 1960s.

Marshall Smith (1972), Eric Hanushek (1968, 1972) and others questioned the empirical robustness of this finding. Subsequent research on schools that had recently desegregated (St John, 1975; Crain and Mahard, 1979) found no support for peer effects. The absence of estimated peer effects is not necessarily surprising. We have already noted that simple sorting mechanisms could easily produce estimated peer effects as statistical artifacts rather than as causal outcomes. Students from good homes are more likely to attend the same schools and display higher performance on achievement tests.

Although Coleman did not note that parental choice could have generated what he called 'peer effects' in his original report, he saw how parents responded to the policies that his report spawned. Coleman's evidence in support of peer effects was used to justify forced integration of schools, but Coleman (in Coleman, Kelly and Moore, 1975; Coleman, 1979b, 1979c), more effectively than anyone else, demonstrated that forced busing produced white flight from inner city schools subjected to busing. People responded to what they perceived to be adverse changes. If the perceived quality of urban schools declined, whites could migrate to white suburban schools producing resegregation of the urban schools and generating increased residential segregation in inner cities. Coleman's research demonstrated that people can evade unwelcome regulations, and that effective regulation must account for their powers of evasion. Stringent regulations mandating desegregation could heighten segregation of schools and communities.

Subsequent long-term follow-up analysis by Welch and Light (1987) confirmed Coleman's qualitative evidence on white flight. Whites fled jurisdictions imposing stringent racial desegregation plans, and flight was especially high during the periods when plans were being instituted. In the school systems subject to forced integration there were proportionately fewer majority students, and the reduction in majority participation was attributable, in part, to the introduction of forced integration. In this sense forced integration of schools led to their segregation.[2]

Inequality, Education and Moral Philosophy

Using the academic freedom available to him after completing the *Coleman Report*, Coleman (1968c, 1972b, 1974b) clarified the various concepts of inequality of educational opportunity and both drew on and clarified the concepts of inequality being debated in the late 1960s and early 1970s.

In his 1968 *Harvard Educational Review* article Coleman (1968c) emphasized the contrast between an input-based measure of inequality of educational opportunity and an output-based measure. This distinction was at the heart of the 1954 US Supreme Court decision in *Brown vs. Topeka Board of Education* that struck down the 'separate but equal' doctrine of *Plessey vs. Ferguson*. The 1966 *Coleman Report*, which found equality within regions in schooling inputs but inequality in outputs, gave solid support to the empirical importance of the distinction made in *Brown*. Its central finding that families and communities were major contributors to inequality in schooling outcomes demonstrated that factors other than schools were major contributors to producing achievement in schools. This evidence suggests that equality of opportunity may be hard to define or achieve. Full equality would entail full equalization of all family and cultural factors, possibly including genetic contributions.

Coleman made a notable contribution to social science by examining and modifying the concepts of inequality and social justice advanced by Rawls (1971) and Nozick (1974). He tested the relevance of their abstract theories to the debate over inequality in opportunity in education and found them to be wanting (Coleman, 1976b). He challenged sociologists to participate in conceptual discussions regarding the formation of norms regarding inequality and their enforcement. He questioned whether society would ever voluntarily embrace conclusions emerging from application of Rawls' 'veil of ignorance' as a principle for solving social problems.

He is most explicit on these issues in Coleman (1974b, 1976b). He contrasts the policy implications emerging from application of the principles advocated by Rawls (1971) and Nozick (1974) to produce equality of educational opportunity. Given the importance of the family in producing educational outcomes found in the *Coleman Report*, equality of opportunity in Rawls' sense would require state orphanages to equalize initial conditions. (However, even orphanages could not equalize genetic disparities.) In a Rawlsian world, initial endowments and family birth rights would become the property of the state and equality would be the norm as long as the move to equality did not reduce aggregate productivity so much that the welfare of persons in the lower tail of the income distribution would be adversely affected.

Equality of opportunity in Nozick's sense would require that initial endowments of family and ability would be respected and that any move toward equality would be agreed to by all parties. In one extreme version of Nozick's society, there would be no public schools. Parents would provide for their own children unless altruism towards others played an important role.

Coleman suggested a third scenario through which public schools might emerge without embracing extreme Rawlsian egalitarianism. Society would compensate persons to associate with others if such associations were deemed to be 'socially productive'. Social productivity may arise due to altruism or simply as a consequence of the public good aspects of basic education. Coleman rejects Rawls' extreme egalitarianism and seeks a voluntary organization of schooling that recognizes initial inequality in endowments and the rights of individuals and families to control those endowments. However, Coleman provides no mechanism for implementing this scheme which would seem to be vulnerable to free-rider problems.

In a similar vein Coleman dismissed Rawls' veil of ignorance as a valid starting point for solving social problems. He formulates an alternative 'partial veil of ignorance' theory that recognizes the need to reconcile conflicts among actors in society who can partially anticipate and affect their outcomes in any particular resolution of the problem of social choice. The key distinction is that in his scheme, unlike Rawls', agents anticipate outcomes that are at least partly dependent on their initial position. Under these circumstances viable social contracts that would be universally accepted would have to respect individual incentives and initial endowments and account for how individuals respond to their private information. Only under special conditions of extreme homogeneity or high mobility rates over time in social status would a Rawlsian veil of ignorance emerge as a universally accepted point of departure for social decision-making.

Coleman presents a theory of the evolution of norms about inequality which predicts what type of societies choose to define equality in Rawlsian and in Nozickian ways. Characteristic of his style, Coleman developed a positive theory of adoption and acceptance of social norms regarding inequality. Decentralized societies stressing individualism tend to adopt Nozickian norms of equality of opportunity. Centralized societies of homogeneous individuals devoted to common objectives tend to adopt Rawlsian norms.

In his discussion of equality of educational opportunity Coleman (1968c, 1976b) raised another issue to which he would return in his study of public and private schools. He characterized early American public schools as redistributive 'common schools' that provided equal opportunity to all children with resource levels determined by local communities. (Racially segregated schools were an obvious exception.) These opportunities were available to all persons irrespective of family wealth and individual ability. He contrasted the diversity of student backgrounds in common schools with the more homogeneous student bodies in the schools that emerged as a consequence of post-Second World War suburbanization. Offsetting this trend, he noted the centralization of school finance which led toward greater equalization in schooling expenditures across schools. In his later work on public and private schools he claimed that Catholic schools were the new common schools that served to equalize inequality in family backgrounds.

Public and Private Schools

Within a year of the release of the *Coleman Report*, Coleman (1967b) began to speculate in public about the broader questions raised by his findings. He explicitly discussed the problems of monopoly in the provision of public education. He presented specific proposals for introducing competition into schools by subcontracting to private vendors who would be compensated on the basis of their performance. He also extolled the virtues of parental choice among schools. However, it was not until 1981 that Coleman and two colleagues, Sally Kilgore and Thomas Hoffer, presented the first hard evidence on the performance of private schools compared to that of public schools in *Public and Private Schools*. They collected a large new data set to address this question — used data from the High School and Beyond survey — and evaluated the relative performance of public and private schools. This survey provided background information and several achievement test scores for approximately 50,000 high school sophomores and seniors. Just as in the original *Coleman Report*, Coleman and his coauthors went creatively beyond the narrow mandate issued by the government agency funding the project. Coleman and his coauthors (CHK) argued that Catholic and other private schools produce better cognitive outcomes than public schools. Further, they argued that the selection of superior students into the private sector cannot fully explain sectoral differences in student performance. They concluded that private schools are more effective institutions of learning.

A 1982 follow-up survey provided achievement data for seniors who had been tested as sophomores in the original study. In 1987 Coleman and Hoffer (CH) published *Public and Private High Schools: The Impact of Communities*, which presents not only an analysis of the data from the follow-up survey but also a theory of school performance. The book offers additional evidence that private schools — especially Catholic schools — enhance cognitive outcomes compared to the performance of public schools. The results also show that Catholic schools substantially reduce high school dropout rates among students of similar backgrounds and ability levels. Although Coleman and his coauthors investigated non-Catholic private schools, the samples available to him on such schools were too small to be the basis for any precise inference for such institutions, and so we do not discuss the evidence on those institutions here.

In both studies the authors claim that Catholic schools are better than public schools in approximating the ideal of a 'common school' — the neighbourhood school of small town America that taught a common curriculum to all children, irrespective of their background. They argue that students from disadvantaged backgrounds benefit most from Catholic schooling because the family background of students has comparatively less effect on outcomes in Catholic schools than it has in public schools. This finding appears to justify private schools as remedies to a basic problem raised in the *Coleman Report*: that the family plays the dominant role in producing the outcomes in students of public schools. Common schools serve to minimize the role of family background in producing student achievement. Catholic schools and associated communities appear to offset disadvantages due to bad families. Communities are sources of 'social capital' producing and reinforcing values. Coleman later generalized the notion of social capital in *Foundations of Social Theory*.

Recent research on public and private schools follows up Coleman's pioneering studies by defining more precisely what is meant by a 'school effect' and by investigating more thoroughly the empirical consequences of parental choices. We first summarize Coleman's claims about Catholic schools and academic achievement. We then consider the objections raised by his critics. There are two central findings: first, sophomores in Catholic schools score about as well as public school *seniors* in both reading and vocabulary and are slightly better in math. Thus Catholic school sophomores are approximately two grade equivalents ahead of public school students. Second, measured family background characteristics account for roughly 60 per cent of these differences in achievement. When adjustments for background are made, Catholic school sophomores are almost one grade equivalent ahead of observationally similar students in public schools.

Coleman also claimed that Catholic schools more closely approximate a 'common school' than do public schools. Achievement differentials between Catholic and public school students are greatest for disadvantaged students. The largest differentials are for minority students and students from low SES backgrounds. In addition, dropout rates are lower for private schools than public school students, and minorities and disadvantaged students benefit most from this advantage of Catholic schooling. The results regarding dropout rates have held up in several studies that employ different data sets and methodologies (see Evans and Schwab, 1994; Neal, 1994; Sander and Krautmann, 1994).

Goldberger and Cain (1982) and Noell (1982) criticized the Coleman group for not considering the consequences of parental choices on their statistical results. The Coleman group did not allow for the possibility that children in Catholic schools systematically differ from children in public schools due to factors not available to analysts from the surveys conducted. Goldberger and Cain (1982) also cast doubt on Coleman's conclusion that Catholic schools achieve a 'common school' ideal. They note, 'the selectivity argument suggests that students with unfavorable measured backgrounds who nevertheless enter the private sector are precisely those whose unmeasured academic proclivities were unusually favorable'. Coleman ignored the consequences of choice for the interpretation of his estimates. Missing from his analysis is any discussion of the choices facing the parents of majority and minority students, and the consequences of these choices for the statistical evidence.

In their analysis of the 1982 follow-up survey Coleman and Hoffer (CH) made a stronger case for the proposition that Catholic schooling enhances academic achievement.

Their follow-up data provide observations on the same students in both their sophomore and senior years. CH performed analyses of senior achievement using sophomore achievement and family background characteristics to control for student ability. Both Williams (1985) and Alexander and Pallas (1983) performed similar analyses, and all three groups of scholars report similar conclusions. Catholic schooling is associated with statistically significant gains in verbal skills, mathematics and writing, but not in science or civics. The estimates imply that four years of a Catholic high school education produces the achievement associated with six years of public secondary schooling.

CH also demonstrate that sophomore-senior achievement gains associated with Catholic schooling are greatest for minorities and students from low SES backgrounds, vindicating the conclusions of the earlier Coleman group study. Catholic secondary schooling is associated with real achievement gains, and these gains are greatest for minority students and students from disadvantaged backgrounds.

CH also explicitly address selection bias in their analyses of the follow-up data. They split their sample into percentiles according to predicted probabilities of attending a Catholic school, and then perform their analyses within these subsamples (see Heckman and Robb, 1985, for a statement of the assumptions required to justify this approach). They report evidence that there is no selection bias in their data using one definition of that term.

Selection Bias and Causal Inference

The discussion of selection bias in both of Coleman's monographs and the corresponding critiques of his work raises some important questions. All the criticism and discussion of selection bias dealt with the simple hypothesis that students who attend Catholic schools are more able or motivated than students who attend public schools. However, this is only one form of selection bias. Holding student ability constant, there might remain differences across students in how well they are suited to particular types of school environments. Students who choose Catholic schools may be indicating by their choice that they are well suited to an environment created by Catholic schools. Therefore, any estimate of the benefits of Catholic schooling derived from data on students who chose Catholic schools will likely overstate the benefit available to a randomly selected public school student or a randomly selected person in the population.

There are two ways to define a 'Catholic school effect'. The first involves the benefit associated with Catholic schooling for a randomly selected student. The second involves the benefit for a randomly selected person who actually chooses Catholic schooling. Only under the special condition that everyone has the same response to Catholic schooling would the two definitions be the same.[3]

Most of the literature on public and private schools implicitly assumes that estimates of the first type of effect are sought. However, this type of effect is hard to estimate. It is difficult, if not impossible, to determine how students from families hostile to organized religion would fare in Catholic schools, or how well Jewish or Muslim children would perform in such an environment. Available data tell us little about this issue because Jews, Muslims and atheists are seldom found in Catholic schools. We cannot confidently estimate an expected 'Catholic school effect' for a randomly chosen person when the data provide so little information about the match between Catholic schooling and students from many segments of the population that are never found in Catholic schools. A more prudent strategy is to focus on estimating the benefit derived from Catholic schooling by those who actually attend Catholic schools. Besides, this is the appropriate question to ask in evaluating the impact of Catholic schooling choices on the achievement scores of those who choose Catholic schools.

Coleman implicitly assumes that his estimate of 'Catholic school effects' provides information about the benefits available to a randomly chosen student. In his analytical framework he implicitly assumes that the effect of enrolment in Catholic school is the same for everyone, so there is no distinction between the effect for those who attend and the effect for a randomly chosen person.

Accounting for Choices in a Broader Setting

Neal (1994) demonstrates that the effect of Catholic schooling on high school graduation rates is greatest for urban minorities. He shows that Catholic schooling dramatically raises graduation rates for urban blacks and hispanics. Among urban whites and suburban residents of all races, the effect of attending Catholic schools is much smaller. Urban minorities benefit most from Catholic schooling because they often face the worst public schooling alternatives.

This evidence suggests that it is not enough to ask, 'What are the benefits of Catholic as opposed to public schooling?' Even if one is willing to assume that most Catholic schools are of similar quality, this question begs another question, 'Which public schools constitute the alternative to private schools for different racial and ethnic groups?' This is a difficult question to answer because families often make residential and schooling decisions jointly. A proper answer requires estimating a model of joint schooling-residential location decisions — a task that remains to be accomplished.

Within a choice-theoretic framework, empirical analyses of public and private schools do not provide enough information to evaluate analytically the two options even for the subset of persons who attend Catholic schools. Taking as given that Catholic schools produce higher achievement for those who attend them, we are still left with the following questions. What do these gains imply about prospects for future success in post-secondary schooling or the labour market? At what *cost* are these gains achieved? How much subsidy is entailed in the production of Catholic schooling? If Catholic schools are more cost-effective, what features of the institutional and technological structure produce these gains? Until the ingredients of costs, preferences and endowments are identified, it is not possible to use Coleman's results on Catholic and public schools as a guide to formulating policy.

Incentives in Schools

In a recent paper (1994c) Coleman goes back to the topics considered in *The Adolescent Society*: the problems of motivating students and schooling organizations to perform. He develops explicit models of individual and organizational incentives, building on the formal framework of individual choice presented in *Foundations of Social Theory*.

He demonstrates the value of imposing external standards on school organizations. Separating the task of defining acceptable performance from the task of motivating persons to meet the standards enables teachers to gain the sympathy and support of their students while maintaining a high level of performance. He also considers models of peer influence and student motivation, providing an analytical structure for the peer effects that received so much attention in *The Adolescent Society*.

These models formalize his earlier work. Schools are modelled as a collection of interconnected individual students, teachers and small organizational units making choices in competition with each other for scarce resources. Students compete for the respect and attention of teachers. Teachers attempt to motivate students to learn under different institutional and environmental conditions. This vision of schools is a more fine-grained analysis of the mechanisms operating within schools than the implicit input-output model of schools that shaped the analysis of the *Coleman Report*. Incentives and organizational structure are now on centre stage as the main factors affecting the transformation of inputs into outputs.

The Two Colemans: How to Do Successful Empirical Work in Social Science

We have chronicled Coleman's contributions to the study of education. His research has made many enduring empirical and theoretical contributions. He pioneered the use of large-scale micro data sets for evaluating social programs and shaped the research agenda for an entire generation of social scientists. It would make for a neat story if we could document a linear evolution in Coleman's thinking about education; but no simple story seems possible. Coleman has thought deeply about personal and social choices, and how they are affected by constraints and environments, since the beginning of his work on education. The foundations of the *Foundations* can be seen in his earliest work and in the work on games described by Boocock in this volume. At the same time Coleman's large-scale empirical exercises have largely been conducted ignoring some of the statistical consequences of personal, parental and institutional choices in generating his data.

There is no inconsistency here. The *Coleman Report* was commissioned by the government to describe inequality in educational opportunity. Strict guidelines were imposed and rigid deadlines were enforced as is typical of much government contracting activity. It is amazing that a report that redefined the very premise of the commissioned study was accepted by government bureaucrats who as a group are not notable for their intellectual curiosity or their flexibility. It would be asking too much to expect that causal models could have been developed or would have been accepted under the circumstances.

The same excuse cannot be made for Coleman's other empirical studies. The plain fact is that Coleman uses simple empirical methods to tell simple causal stories and does not develop elaborate causal empirical models. It is interesting in this regard that Coleman (1970e) once confronted this issue in print. In an exchange with Cain and Watts (1970) who — among other things — faulted him for failing to develop a clear causal empirical model in the *Coleman Report*, Coleman rejected the empirical

paradigm of the elaborately specified 'structural' econometric model of causal inference because it was ill-suited for exploring rich new data sets. Rejecting the almost
certainly false precision of a misspecified 'structural' model, Coleman indicated a
strong preference for establishing central empirical regularities using simple methods
without imposing strong a priori structure onto his data. This is a time-honoured
position in empirical social science that is almost always accompanied by a time-
honoured slogan that 'correlation does not imply causation'. The trick is that in
popular discussions, and in many circles in social science, correlation is often interpreted causally despite all warnings about doing so.

A good piece of empirical social science is always accompanied by a good interpretive story. Coleman's empirical work is always accompanied by insightful, often
brilliant interpretive stories. It is this feature of his research that makes Coleman's
empirical work of such lasting value.

Acknowledgment

Heckman's research was supported by NSF-SBR-91145, NSF-FES-9224079, a grant
from the Mellon Foundation, and a grant from the American Bar Foundation. Neal's
research was supported by an Olin Faculty Fellowship from the Center for the Study
of the Economy and the State, University of Chicago. We thank Eric Hanushek,
Christopher Jencks, Lynne Pettler and especially Margaret Mooney Marini for
comments.

Notes

1 In the language of econometrics, state quality averages are 'instrumental variables' for the
   micro quality.
2 However, in another sense forced integration was successful. Most school systems became
   more racially balanced at a new lower level of white participation. The remaining whites
   were more equally distributed among schools within systems.
3 See Heckman and Robb (1985), Heckman (1992) and Heckman and Smith (1995) for
   more on the definition of treatment effects and the distinctions made in the text.

Postscript 1: Themes in Coleman's Research
James J. Heckman

The first version of this chapter had a better plot line than the version you have just
read. Based roughly on the Road to Damascus story in the New Testament in which
Saul — later St Paul — sees the light and is converted to Christianity, I imagined that
the busing episode had turned James Coleman toward rational choice theory and the
flirtation with economics that characterized the last ten years of his life. The idea was
this: once Coleman realized that the response to forced integration motivated by his
erroneous evidence on peer effects was white flight from the central cities, he began
to realize that people made choices in response to incentives.

This version of the story did not play very well, especially with Coleman. In
the final months of his life we had numerous conversations about how he became

interested in rational choice models, and how his ideas on education evolved over time. He was eager to make three points which are not developed at any length in the preceding essay.

The first point was that his work on games described by Sarane Boocock in this volume had a major influence on his thinking about rational choice theory. In order to teach people how democracy worked, through building a game called Democracy, it was necessary for him to build a model of how democracy worked and to consider how people made choices under different democratic rules. Developing his teaching games thus forced him to model the subjects of his games and hence stimulated him to produce models of social phenomena. He expressed strong feelings about the importance of this work not only in shaping his own thinking, but also in teaching students basic ideas about how society operates. Like most scholars, he felt that some of his best work was also his most neglected work.

The second point was first impressed on me by Peggy Marini who kindly read the 'Road to Damascus' version and properly took me to task for failing to discuss *The Adolescent Society*. Reading that work, I recognized that Coleman's analytical framework in that study was clearly grounded in principles of rational choice theory. Students respond to the incentives facing them. Isolating adolescents from the realities of the adult world created the ersatz high school culture with values and norms of its own that were remarkably similar across high schools with students from very different socioeconomic environments. His stress on the influence of the environment on the actions of school children was classical sociology. His analysis of the choices of children in response to their environment is modern rational choice theory.

One of Coleman's last papers, 'What Goes on in School: A Student's Perspective' (Coleman, 1994c), comes back full circle to *The Adolescent Society*. In that paper there is a formal mathematical model of peer influences in high schools that he discussed in his early book. In both studies the same general rational choice framework is present. Students make purposive choices and incentives affect student performance. The later work is more formal, but the content of the paper and the book is similar. Any notion that Coleman was converted to rational choice theory by the busing episode or his later close contact with economists at Chicago can be dismissed by carefully reading his first book on education and then reading its formalization thirty years later.

A third point that Coleman was eager to emphasize was that no simple account of his evolution as a social scientist can be told. Like many distinguished scholars, he pursued a number of different styles and lines of research, often at the same time. Many pots were always on the stove, and they were not all cooking the same stew.

This is especially true for Coleman because he was fundamentally empirically oriented. He was easily distracted from pursuing any preset agenda by his confrontations with unexplained social phenomena. Unlike many rational choice theorists, Coleman was motivated by a profound interest in what goes on in society. He did not attempt to impose an a priori vision onto the world he saw, nor did he have messianic ambitions for a particular methodological approach. Rather, he sought to learn about the world using whatever tools he could find. The fundamental empirical motivation for his research gave his work spontaneity and unpredictability that is difficult to chart in any linear fashion. What is clear is that the seeds of many of his most important ideas were sown early in life and came to harvest at different times over his career.

Postscript 2: Coleman's Approach to Empirical Social Science
James Heckman

As an empirical economist wedded to the notion that precisely defined economic models inform empirical research, one of the most difficult features of Coleman's work for me to understand was his fairly casual use of empirical evidence and his failure to use formal social science frameworks explicitly to guide the interpretation of his data. In the course of preparing my paper for this volume I had many exchanges with him about his views on empirical research. I summarize that exchange in this postscript.

One explanation for his failure to develop explicit empirical models for rational choice could have been that he came to rational choice theory late in life, before he had time to execute an empirical research project with his new tools. The discussion in Postscript 1 rules out that possibility. Moreover, a careful reading of his defence of the *Coleman Report* refutes any such argument, for he confronted this issue explicitly in his exchange with Cain and Watts (1970).

Econometricians espouse an ideal that few true empiricists embrace. It is a vision of induction informed by well defined deductive models founded on articulated axioms. Many would call it a scientific ideal, but others would call it scientism — a form of cargo-cult science worship. The standard theory of consumer demand is a paradigm for many econometricians. A clearly stated set of hypotheses flow from basic assumptions about the choice structure facing agents who are maximizing their welfare subject to constraints. This theory and its parallel development for firms is the motivating force for many theoretical and empirical studies in economics.

Separation between the act of constructing a model and the act of verifying it is held up as a paragon in many fields of economics. The whole literature on the 'identification problem' in economics or the problem of 'observational equivalence' is premised on making this separation. Models are either 'identified' or not, depending on whether they can be distinguished in terms of their predictions on *the available data*. Two fundamental assumptions underlie this approach: first, that the set of available models is known prior to looking at the data; and, second, that the set of consequential facts is fixed in advance of conducting an empirical test. Such is the domain of the econometric paradigm of the identification problem.

This a priori deductive-inductive approach to formulating principles for acquiring empirical knowledge does not describe much empirical research activity, nor should it. It rules out an evolutionary interaction between theory and data that is central to the act of creation of empirical knowledge. The set of available models used to analyze the data is never fixed in advance of looking at it. The data may suggest new models and the models may in turn suggest new data — or more careful examination of old data — in the light of new theoretical advances (what some call 'letting the data do the talking'). While there are well known problems in using the data that suggest a theory to test it, there are more important problems that arise from refusing to learn from the data in revising models. The standard model that guides much econometric research also assumes that objective statistical 'tests' can be conducted to falsify a model. Any serious scholar of the philosophical foundations of statistics (see, e.g., Hacking, 1995) will recognize the difficulties in using classical (or Bayesian) testing theory to falsify hypotheses.

The econometrician's stylized view about using data assumes that (a) all knowledge about a model is acquired in advance of looking at the data; (b) the act of looking at data does not generate new hypotheses and models; and (c) acceptance or rejection of a model should be based on 'objective' statistical tests.

In most areas of social science there are few precisely formulated models that are known in advance of looking at the data. Usually a lot of vague notions coexist. Many precisely formulated models may exist as well, but usually these are based on ad hoc axioms, without much intuitive or empirical support. In the case of the *Coleman Report* there were no well articulated models at hand, nor were specific functional forms of estimating equations suggested by any theory. The data were the first of their kind to be collected on such a wide scale. Adopting a false precision for the sake of 'looking scientific' and following a particular empirical program would not have been good science or social science. It would have been acting foolishly in a precise way.

Coleman — like most true empiricists — chose not to adopt false precision to satisfy the methodological desiderata suggested by the econometric literature on the identification problem. He also exploited the possibility of looking at the data and being surprised by it, and he reformulated models in the light of discoveries from the data. Who could have forecast that family and community variables would have been so important in explaining schooling outcomes in the data used to produce the *Coleman Report*? The data suggest possibilities not thought of in advance of looking at them. The standard econometric framework rules out such surprise. The Bayesian framework is no better in this regard, having fundamental problems with outcomes deemed a priori to be impossible, i.e., complete surprises.

Coleman was too good a social scientist to let 't' values or 'p' values solely or even primarily determine the interpretation of a body of evidence. He knew that a coherent social science explanation was worth 10,000 data points and fifty points of statistical significance. He was not taken in by the myth of 'objective' statistical testing. He was well aware that only fresh data, generated under new circumstances, could confirm or deny any model constructed from a given set of data.

The econometric paradigm of the identification problem and the separation of theory from evidence does not apply to most areas of social science where knowledge is not settled. It may describe a mature science built on numerous previous empirical studies conducted under other research paradigms where empirical regularities about a phenomenon have accumulated. In this regard the domain of applicability of the paradigm of the identification problem may be viewed as a limit state for a mature field. Econometric theorists too easily forget that a priori theories specified in advance of looking at the data are often just condensations of accumulated empirical knowledge, acquired using crude empirical methods.

Coleman worked in areas too uncharted and too uncodified to follow rigid econometric conventions developed for mature fields. There is no inconsistency for a rational choice theorist not to do formal 'structural' econometrics, especially in research areas where central empirical regularities remain to be determined.

None of this says that Coleman — or any other scholar — would not have benefitted by taking more care in defining terms and using data. This point is especially relevant in his analysis of Catholic schools. Part of his style was a consequence of his desire to focus on main points, leaving details to the side to avoid diversions. Part of his style was also a consequence of his desire to reach a wide audience, and for that reason to appeal to basic intuitive principles rather than to elaborate formal criteria. Part of his style of weaving evidence with interpretation reflected a conscious rejection of the Popperian empirical model that models should be formulated independently of the data. The style he adopted is an expression of his acute sensibility that good empirical social science is primarily good social science and is not necessarily good statistics.

Coleman's critics were legion. Some faulted him for not being a more careful statistician or econometrician. Others faulted him for going outside his data — what some might call creative leaps, like his concept of 'social capital' — that emerged from a few fragments of evidence in his 1987 book with Hoffer. What is remarkable is that despite these criticisms, the main lessons from most of his empirical studies survive to this day. By focusing on core issues and finding new insights in the data, his work has lasted whereas most of the nitpicking 'careful' criticisms of his work are now properly forgotten.

Shortly before he died, I told him that one of his most vociferous critics had called him 'lucky with his evidence' because so much of his empirical work had held up under close scrutiny. Coleman laughed and told me that it wasn't luck at all. He said that every empirical finding he reported was tested in many different ways using simple methods. Only when a finding survived such a battery of tests would he report it. I told him that this was exactly what Nobel economist Simon Kuznets told his student, Nobel laureate Robert Fogel, to do in his PhD thesis, and that Fogel asked his students to do the same. Coleman laughed again and said he was glad to be in such good company.

8   The Sociological Contribution to Social Policy Research

Martin Bulmer

The modern sociologist is generally uncomfortable as an adviser to policy-makers. Sociology and social policy as academic fields are relatively uneasy bedfellows. In Britain the two subjects are institutionalized in most universities in separate departments, of sociology on the one hand and social policy and administration on the other. Much of the British empirical policy oriented social research carried out in independent institutes, government and market research firms is untouched by the influence of sociological ideas, and many academic sociologists are indifferent to such research, preferring to pursue their own more theoretical and disciplinary concerns. In the United States the links are somewhat closer in some cases. Leading sociologists, of whom James Coleman was a prime example, have undertaken major studies with national policy relevance, and the discipline of sociology is characterized by greater intellectual rigour and methodological sophistication. Even in the United States, however, the pursuit of policy research is a minority activity among sociologists. It is, therefore, of some interest to understand how and why such an energetic and encyclopedic sociologist as James S. Coleman became involved as a national policy actor.

James Coleman wrote that in 1951, at the age of 25, he gave up working as a chemist to enter graduate school at Columbia University and embark upon a sociological career. In doing so, he shed almost all his prior associations and entered a new life as a sociology graduate student. He left behind his previous world, and relatives apart, never interacted further with those among whom he had lived up to that age (Coleman, 1985). Did a further transformation occur fourteen years later in February 1965, when a telephone call came to him at Johns Hopkins University from Alexander Mood, assistant commissioner for statistics at the US Office of Education? This call was the first step to the invitation which led Coleman and Ernest Campbell of Vanderbilt University to embark upon the study which became famous as *Equality of Educational Opportunity*. 'It was the beginning, for me, of research into equality and achievement in education. It was also the beginning, or nearly so, of a new relation of social science to government policy, and the beginning, or nearly so, of a new orientation to research on the quality of education provided by schools' (Coleman, 1990c: x). It came near the beginning of a period of extensive change in the relation of social science to social policy, of which Coleman was a leading practitioner. This chapter examines certain aspects of this relationship.

Coleman's Early Work

Coleman's publications prior to embarking on *Equality of Educational Opportunity* do not suggest a strong concern with policy. His main Columbia teachers, Robert

Merton and Paul Lazarsfeld, imparted a strong interest in theory and methodology (Coleman, 1990d). His main substantive research at Columbia, participation in the printers' study, *Union Democracy* (Lipset, Trow and Coleman, 1956), was a classic test of middle-range theory, and his developing methodological and substantive interests were in areas like mathematical sociology, statistical modelling (stochastic processes) and relational analysis using survey data. Although Paul Lazarsfeld was involved in much applied research, this was much more oriented to the mass media and less toward social policy. Moreover, Lazarsfeld's interests became more academic in his later years. The empirical and theoretical studies of Coleman's post-Columbia period — *The Adolescent Society*, the study of medical innovation, and *Community Conflict* — were addressed to sociological problems with little direct policy relevance. Potentially some of the methodological problems with which Coleman continued to wrestle, particularly the problems of using social survey research to study social organization, had considerable policy relevance, but he was pursuing them more in the spirit of trying to use methods which were inherently individualistic, even atomistic, to study larger collectivities (Coleman, 1970d). As he observed, it was

> an interesting footnote in the sociology of knowledge that none of the social and intellectual forces impinging on the discipline was conducive to the development of these analytic tools. My own efforts in this direction were diverted in 1965 by the demands of government for policy research, which resulted in *Equality of Educational Opportunity*. (Coleman, 1986b: 1315, n 8)

Policy Research in Education: Three Major Studies

James Coleman's substantive contribution to the study of education and educational policy is embodied in three notable sets of studies over two decades, his studies of equality of educational opportunity in 1965–66 (hereafter Coleman I: Coleman, Campbell *et al.*, 1966), of school segregation, busing and white flight in 1973–76 (hereafter Coleman II: Coleman, Kelly and Moore, 1975) and of public and private schools in 1979–81 (hereafter Coleman III: Coleman, Hoffer and Kilgore, 1982). Our purpose here is to understand the development of his ideas about the relationship between sociological research and social policy over the course of three studies. The first, Coleman I, involved responding to Section 402 of the Civil Rights Act of 1964 to conduct a survey 'concerning the lack of availability of equal opportunities for individuals by reason of race, colour, religion or national origin in public education institutions at all levels in the United States' (Ravitch, 1993: 129). A large research team collected data from over 4000 public schools in the autumn of 1965 and the report followed in July 1966.

The second, Coleman II, a decade later, 'Trends in School Segregation, 1968–1973', presented to the American Educational Research Association (AERA) in April 1975, concerned busing to reduce racial segregation in schools, and suggested that legal intervention was contributing to white flight from major cities and to resegregation of urban districts. The most controversial conclusion was that

> The extremely strong reactions of individual whites in moving their children out of large districts engaged in massive and rapid desegregation suggest that

in the long run the policies that have been pursued will defeat the purpose of increasing overall contact among races in schools. . . . Thus a major policy implication of this analysis is that in an area such as school desegregation, which has important consequences for individuals and in which individuals retain control of some actions that can in the end defeat the policy, the courts are probably the worst instruments of social policy. (Quoted in Ravitch, 1993: 135)

This report set off a tremendous furore, the significance of which will be discussed later in the chapter. It centred on what was seen as Coleman's apostasy in casting doubt on the effectiveness of busing, and criticizing a major plank of the liberal agenda in contemporary race relations.

The third study, Coleman III, *Public and Private Schools*, published in 1981, based on the longitudinal study *High School and Beyond*, covered nearly 60,000 high school students in 1016 schools, as well as their principals and teachers. Its controversial conclusions pointed to the superiority of private over public schools in a number of respects and suggested that private schools, including Catholic parochial schools in urban areas, provided a more effective education than public schools on average. This set of findings became the subject of heated public controversy.

The Development of Sociological Research for Policy in the United States

The Chicago School

The historical significance of Coleman's work can be related to his own view of the development of policy research in sociology. For he himself is located within a period of change in which social policy research has assumed increasing salience. The controversies in which he has been involved in relation to all three pieces of educational research have highlighted the importance which such studies and interventions can have.

The first group of studies which Coleman identifies as having an impact upon American public policy were the sociological community studies of the first third of the twentieth century. These are inescapably identified with the urban sociology of Robert Park and Ernest Burgess at the University of Chicago, and include such classics as *The Polish Peasant in Europe and America*, *The Negro in Chicago*, *The Gold Coast and the Slum*, *The Gang*, *The Ghetto*, *Organized Crime in Chicago*, *Negro Politicians*, underpinned by theorizing about the ecological structure of the city and internal differentiation into natural areas with distinctive characteristics. There were other studies of this period, including one or two local community studies carried out at Columbia University even earlier, the work of the Institute of Social and Religious Research in New York in the 1920s and most notably Robert and Helen Lynd's study of Muncie, Indiana, *Middletown*, published in 1929.

These studies were produced in a society which was largely locally focused upon its own problems, extending at the furthest extent to the state or the region. Thus the Chicago School studies were investigations, in the main, of social structure and process in the city of Chicago and its environs, including Cook County but scarcely extending into the rural areas of the state of Illinois. Social relations were still principally those of a local society, politics were locally-based, the 'nation', except in time of war, still had relatively little meaning for the individual citizen. The model of research utilization underlying such research was weakly developed. Such studies, as in the case of local social surveys, were seen either as a means of societal self-understanding, or as contributing to basic social science. At its strongest sociology was seen in Robert Park's terms as contributing to the illumination of 'public opinion', indirectly feeding back into the self-control of society, but not conceiving research as having a primarily utilitarian purpose. Many of the philanthropic sponsors of this early social research held such views.

The Rise of Columbia Sociology

Beginning in the 1930s, this began to change. A national economy began to replace the local economy for many products. Nationally manufactured washing machines replaced locally constructed washboards, refrigerators replaced iceboxes. Radio, national magazines, the movies and in due course television created national communication media (Coleman, 1993b). To monitor and understand the nature of these national markets, audience research and market research developed. These general trends in society coincided with the development of techniques of social survey research which made possible the investigation of national markets. After the debacle of the *Literary Digest* poll in 1936, the superiority of probability sampling methods showed that social surveys using small samples could provide snapshot pictures of the views of market members at relatively modest expense (Converse, 1987: 111–27). The first corporate actors using this research were large corporations in the advertising and media industries, some of whom commissioned research from Paul Lazarsfeld. Much of his work in the two decades after his arrival in the United States was geared to this market, particularly the academic studies of media effects and influence.

With these economic and communication changes, the individual's points of reference extended from the locality to the national level. The historian Barry Karl has traced in the same period the slow development of the reality of the American state, and the reluctance of Congress to take action which might be interpreted as the extension of state power beyond the boundaries of the minimalist role which was considered appropriate in peace-time (Karl, 1987). The slow shift toward a national polity and society, which gathered pace during the Second World War and accelerated thereafter, had consequences of considerable import for sociology.

> Survey research, mirroring the social change it measured, held centre stage in sociology throughout the 1940s and 1950s and into the 1960s. Symptomatically, research in stratification, which in the 1920s and 1930s and 1940s had focused on single towns or cities (Middletown, Elmtown, Yankee City), in the 1960s reflected a shift to the national economy. In the United States a marker for this shift is Blau and Duncan's *The American Occupational Structure* (1967). This work was based on a nationally representative sample, characterising stratification not in a given locality but in the country as a whole. (Coleman, 1993b: 6)

In terms of the history of sociology, the Columbia department in which Coleman was trained, and its associated Bureau of Applied Social Research, was at the centre of this shift in the development of sociology in relation to policy (Coleman, 1980a).

The Third Phase: Social Policy Research

In the third phase, however, Coleman himself has been a major actor. Current social policy research for government, of the type that Coleman himself has undertaken, is an outgrowth of the earlier audience and market research. Although originally academic centres such as Denver and Chicago (NORC), Michigan (ISR), Columbia and Princeton were the primary loci for such applied survey research, increasingly such work has tended to shift either to the market research sector or to non-profit or for-profit independent research institutes. Coleman I took only sixteen months from commissioning to publication. The massive fieldwork for Coleman I was done in a very short space of time, which an academic centre would have found difficult to accomplish. Coleman II was undertaken in cooperation with authors from the Urban Institute.

From the 1960s onwards there was also a shift in responsibility from the local and private to the national and public level. The altered structure of the economy and communication increasingly generated change on the national government and an assumption that the national government would assume responsibilities which hitherto it had avoided. Thus, for example, in the field of race relations the South remained the last bastion within the United States of the local, community oriented society, with norms and sanctions governing interracial relations derived from the dominant local white society proving resistant to change. This race relations order was reinforced at the state and regional level. One type of social change occurred through the legal system, particularly in the wake of the *Brown* decision of 1954, where the NAACP used the Supreme Court as an instrument of exogenous change (Tushnet, 1994). More direct political intervention took place as a consequence of the Civil Rights movement, when protests in southern states met oppressive responses from the local police and National Guard, prompting in some cases federal intervention to prevent further violence. In the longer term congressional legislation such as the Civil Rights Act of 1964 and the Voting Rights Act of 1965 modified the pattern of race relations and ended certain types of behaviour — such as black disenfranchisement — which the local communities had wished to maintain.

The creation of a national society and the extension of the responsibilities of government, which occurred with particular intensity during the 'Great Society' period of Lyndon Johnson's presidency and during which Coleman I was commissioned, led to the development of a new type of social research: social policy research. All three of Coleman's educational research projects were of this type, and they represent a new type of social research in several respects.

> . . . research with a much more direct linkage to policy began to emerge. Contracts, initiated through Requests for Proposals (RFPs) and much more specific in their timing and product requirements, began to replace grants. Large grants, requiring a responsible and multi-skilled organisation, replaced

small projects that tolerated the irresponsibility and narrower skills of a single investigator. Research began to be commissioned not merely by 'research funding' agencies (like NIMH and NIE) but also by operating (i.e., policy-making) agencies like the Departments of Housing and Urban Development, Transportation and Labor. Agencies like NIE, without direct responsibility for projects, began to initiate demonstration programs and other 'mini-policies' (sometimes on the principle that successful programs would be continued by local authorities, sometimes on the principle that successful programs could be incorporated into legislation at the national level). (Coleman, 1980a: 343–4)

Such work had several new features. First, a considerable range of methodologies and research designs had been employed, wider than used hitherto, extending the frontiers of the social sciences. Although survey methods remained the basic method of collecting data, the designs became much more varied; social experiments, evaluation research and secondary analysis became characteristic modes of inquiry. Second, the institutional locations were different from previously, when most research was carried out by academics. As research became more salient in government, speed of response became of considerable importance. Many academic researchers found difficulty in meeting the short timescales, and profit and non-profit organizations such as Rand, the Urban Institute, Abt Associates, Mathematica, Westat and SRI (Stanford Research Institute) grew up or expanded to meet the demand, particularly from the federal government. A variety of organizations at state and local levels are now engaged in program evaluation (Nathan, 1988). In Britain a similar tendency is observable on a smaller scale, with research bodies like the Policy Studies Institute and Social and Community Planning Research undertaking major policy research for government (Bulmer, 1993). Government, of course, is not the only client, which includes voluntary organizations, trades unions, commercial organizations and others; but government is the most significant commissioner. Third, as Coleman has repeatedly observed, the new social policy research has brought corporate actors into the picture, who seek information enabling them better to pursue their interests. This has major political and normative dimensions which are considered further below. It also changes the role of sociology.

The shift toward individualism was accompanied by a growing structural asymmetry in Western society, with large corporate actors (corporations, governments) on one side and individuals (not communities, not neighbourhoods, not families) on the other, linked together by mass media rather than direct communication. In this social structure, a new kind of social research has arisen, as part of the articulations between corporate actors and persons, first in the form of market research and then in the form of social policy research. With this move, social research has come for the first time directly into the functioning of society — no longer standing outside it but instead modifying the articulation between corporate actors and persons — primarily as the agent of corporate actors. As such, it becomes not only part of sociology but also properly an object of social theory, as part of the large task of social theory to characterize this articulation between actors of different types and very different size and power. (Coleman 1986b: 1320)

The Relationship between Sociology and Policy

The emergence in the 1960s of social policy research, to use James Coleman's term, implied a different relationship between sociology and society. In the Chicago and Columbia traditions the impact and use of research were implicit, informing public opinion in Park's view, playing the role of social critic adumbrated in Robert Lynd's *Knowledge for What?*, aiding the commercial interests and developing the mass media interests in the case of Lazarsfeld's applied work, but usually at a considerable distance from government and the state. The most extensive inter-war study for government was commissioned by President Hoover but paid for by the Rockefeller Foundation. *Recent Social Trends* (1933), the report of a presidential committee in which sociologist William Ogburn played a major part, confined itself to a severely factual account of the state of American society, without any attempt at causal analysis or indeed inter-pretation of any kind (Bulmer, 1983).

War created different circumstances. Just as the First World War had given a powerful impetus to applied psychology in the form of psychological testing used in recruitment to the armed forces (Sokal, 1987), so the Second World War provided opportunities for sociologists to develop applied work. The major study of army life and personnel, published after the war as *The American Soldier*, directed by Samuel Stouffer (Stouffer, 1949), was an early example of the potential for applying socio-logical research methods in the study of public issues. In the history of survey research it is part of a lineage which leads to the education studies of James Coleman in the 1960s, 1970s and 1980s. Was it social policy research? In Coleman's terms it was not, because it was not seeking to provide systematic information for social policy. It was intended to be useful to the Army in the conduct of the war, but it was a small unit which conducted the research, fighting its corner with the support of General Osborne and under fairly regular threat of being closed down (Converse, 1987: 161ff).

It is the history of economics and its application, rather than the history of sociology, which provides a key to understanding the rise of social policy research. Politically it flourished to a greater extent in the more receptive American climate than in Europe, partly perhaps because of the greater influence of economists (par-ticularly in the 1960s in the Office of Economic Opportunity [OEO]). Macroeconomic theorizing about the economy, from the time of Keynes's *General Theory*, worked with an implicit model of how the different parts of the economy interacted, and how they could be adjusted and controlled. The model when applied to the real world came to approximate control theory in physical systems. The government makes economic decisions, the consequences of the policy are systematically observed and fed back to the decision centre, which modifies policies on the basis of the feedback. Of course, in trying to influence the course of the economy there are many variables (models of the economy which economic theorists create contain hundreds of vari-ables), and there is a high degree of imprecision compared to the physical control system. Intervention is highly imperfect and may not lead to the anticipated results. But economists since the Second World War have operated with such a model of the macro economy, and developed measures, such as price indicators and measures of inflation, which they use to monitor changes in the economic system.

This is only indirectly related to James Coleman's conception of social policy research, but there is a connection. For out of the confidence that the economists could construct a working model of the economy came the optimistic view that other aspects of society were susceptible to modelling and empirical investigation. This found most obvious expression in the 1960s in the movement, influenced by the economists in OEO, toward large-scale social experimentation, producing studies like the New Jersey–Pennsylvania and Seattle–Denver income maintenance experiments. The rationale for the approach was elegantly sketched by psychologist Donald T. Campbell in his paper, 'The Experimenting Society'.

The Experimenting Society?

Campbell posed the question whether the open society can be an experimenting society. He pointed out that social policy researchers tended to encounter continual frustration within a political system that seemed designed to prevent social reality testing. In frustration, social policy researchers then resorted to proposals which amount to designing a new political system. Campbell criticized the prevailing mode of policy advice from social scientists, in which a variety of experts (for example, sociologists of poverty or psychologists of child development) provided advice to government which incorporated analysis of their problem plus recommendations about appropriate courses of action to follow, thus engaging in a considerable degree of overadvocacy. More modesty would be appropriate, following the physical sciences, in the spirit of trying policies to see whether they worked or not. What was needed, Campbell argued, was an '"experimenting society" that would vigorously try out possible solutions to recurrent problems and would make hard-headed, multidimensional evaluations of outcomes, and when the evaluation of one reform showed it to have been ineffective or harmful, would move on to try other alternatives' (Campbell, 1987: 291). There are affinities between this position and that argued by Moynihan (1969), who suggested that social scientists operating in the policy arena needed to shift their attention from the causes of social problems to evaluating the effects of intervention, since causation was so multifactorial that it was very difficult to identify clear causal paths.

Locations for Policy Research: The Academic World and the World of Action

Coleman acknowledged that working at the macrosociological level alone was not adequate. Much more microsociological work was needed to make social structural analyses of the generation and disposition of social policy research, showing how the results and utilization of social policy research are affected by the social structure within which it is generated, executed and generated. One of these structural features is the context in which the research is carried out. There were systematic differences among the world of academic disciplines, the world of sociological knowledge in which research takes place and social theories are developed, and the world of action, in which policies are made and consequential events occur. The norms and values of the disciplinary world favour disinterested inquiry, the search for truth and full communication of inquiry. Such work is not time-bound, or answerable to outsiders. By contrast, in the world of action there are interested parties, whose view of the research may not coincide, and there is a time-bound process, whereby actions which occur later are dependent on those which have happened earlier. Thus, for example, policy-making processes depend upon actions, such as legislation or executive orders, which are preceded by a series of investigations, discussions, consultations with affected interests, etc. which follow a sequence and which in turn lead to policy action, and in turn the action is monitored and its effects upon the system are observed and reported. This constraint of time is combined with the characteristics of the world of action which are the opposite in some respects of those of academic research: secrecy, privacy, pursuit of interests and diversity of values. Because the world of action contains interested parties, the policy researcher is ordinarily an agent of one of those parties.

Coleman's colleague at Johns Hopkins, Peter Rossi, drawing on his experiences as director of NORC at the University of Chicago, pointed out in the early 1960s some of the incompatibilities between the academic and practitioner research orientation. In a memorable passage he described the lack of fit between the academic orientation to prescribed teaching duties, research according to what was expected by local norms, and the ability to choose what else to do and when, with the requirements of the large social survey organization, tight timescales to work to, and a complex interdependent division of labour. These requirements all dictated the development of research institutes separate from the conventional departmental structures of universities (Rossi, 1964).

There are countervailing pressures. In the USA the demands of those who pay for policy research have tended over time to favour the creation of independent research organizations. A similar tendency is observable in the UK. On the other hand, the danger exists that he who pays the piper will call the tune. The university's role is

> to provide the autonomous base for social policy research. Nearly all the examples I know in which policy research has arrived at results that throw doubt on federal policies and has insisted that the results be publicly available, are cases in which the analyst was *not* in a contract research organisation wholly dependent on government funds, but a university faculty's member. (Coleman, 1982b: 99)

Academic Freedom?

Coleman's position here does not seem entirely consistent. For the reasons which Rossi set out, university teaching departments are not suited to fostering large-scale research enterprises. It may be possible to institutionalize research centres outside departments, and in the case of the large survey centres this has been done with considerable success. But in substantive research areas, maintaining an institute poses greater difficulties. Moreover, the way in which Coleman I was conducted appears to contradict the generalization Coleman offers. It is true that the principal investigators (Coleman and Campbell) were based in universities, but the study was carried out at, and with the participation of staff of, the National Center for Educational Statistics in the US Office of Education. The Educational Testing Service of Princeton, New Jersey, a national for-profit educational research organization, carried out the major survey of public schools. The Census Bureau of the federal government administered the non-enrolment study as part of the October 1965 Current Population

Survey. Case studies of education for minorities were carried out in ten cities through a contract with Raymond Mack, a sociologist at Northwestern University, who in turn enlisted ten sociologists to carry out these city studies (Coleman, Campbell *et al.*, 1966: 1). Coleman II was carried out in part in collaboration with staff of the Urban Institute, a policy research institute outside academia. Coleman III was commissioned by the National Center for Education Statistics, which had commissioned Coleman I. The analysis of the data was carried out by Coleman and his associates, Sally Kilgore and Thomas Hoffer, on the campus of the University of Chicago, using the facilities of NORC.

Thus none of the three studies was carried out wholly within a university, and although a university was the location for the data analysis for Coleman III, much of the work for Coleman I and II was done outside universities in government or independent research institutes. What is the relationship between institutional setting and the character and quality of the social policy research carried out? Coleman's argument about only universities providing an autonomous base is substantiated by his own involvement: he remained an academic throughout, acting as a consultant to government bodies and independent institutes, and he would never have abandoned this institutional location. Arguably, however, Coleman I and possibly Coleman II would not have been carried out rapidly, fitting into the public policy agenda in the way that they were, if the entire study had been done within a university. The time-scales of universities are not adapted to such policy work, unless semi-autonomous institutions are created which can undertake such work at relatively short notice. In the case of Coleman I, for example, a period of only a few months intervened between the first phone call from the Education Department and fielding the main survey. Most social science academics find it impossible to operate in that way because of year-long teaching and other research commitments, which cannot easily be substituted in the short term.

The implication of the argument that only academics can provide the critical distance to challenge the assumptions of policy orthodoxy is possibly true, but is countered by the tendency of these very academic experts to disagree among themselves. The furious debates which accompanied all three Coleman reports, with most of the flak coming from his professional colleagues, not from independent researchers or government officials, suggest that the picture of a detached, critical body of scholars in academia motivated by a disinterested desire to know the truth is an idealized one, and that academics both hold value standpoints and have interests at stake, particularly on issues of high public saliency such as inequality in education and life chances and their intersection with race and religion. We shall return to this below.

The Problem of Values

At this point it is useful to link Coleman's analysis of the emergence of social policy analysis as a mode of policy research with his developing social theory, and particularly his view of power and of the relationship between corporate actors and individual persons in modern society (Coleman, 1974c; Coleman, 1990a). Research on educational inequality is pre-eminently about individual persons, in the sense of the outcomes of educational careers for the individual passing through the educational system. At the same time these individuals are located within a system. Coleman has discussed the problems which arise in a political democracy in achieving adequate information about the policy issues which are being decided by the various interested parties in a political system.

> In a political democracy, feedback from policy is necessary . . . but that feedback must provide information relevant not only to the goals and interests of the central political authority, but also to the goals and interests of all interested parties. Yet policy research, as it is now initiated and conducted in political democracies, is not so structured as to achieve this. (Coleman, 1975a: 305)

The paradox with James Coleman's three major pieces of educational research is that, although it might be anticipated that the major question of impact lay outside academia, in the public realm, much of the controversy generated, particularly about Coleman II and III, was generated by Coleman's academic peers, who contested both the findings and the value implications of the research which he had conducted.

An unresolved issue in James Coleman's interventions as a social policy researcher has been the value implications of his research. Coleman has criticized social policy researchers, in terms similar to those of Donald Campbell, for insinuating value prescriptions into supposedly objective analyses of particular social issues. 'The social scientist's recommendations about policy contain a combination of factual information based on research results, *together with* a value premise, which is often implicit. A major part of the problem lies in the difficulty of untangling the facts from the value premise, and making the latter explicit' (Coleman, 1978: 702n29). This has been true of his own research as well as that of others, but he has taken an unusually robust stance in relation to the implications of his findings, which has landed him in enduring controversy.

Coleman I was published at the height of American sensitivities to racial divisions in the society, and highlighted racial segregation in American education, the greater advantages enjoyed by white schools, the gap in academic achievement between white and black pupils, and the importance of family background as a determinant of school achievement. Different interests drew different conclusions from the report, but there was a tendency for its findings to be used to advocate social change. Some concluded that changing schools was less important than intervention in family and community. Others claimed that racial integration would improve black educational performance. Still others suggested that black community control would improve the performance of black children. Most significantly, it was argued that its findings supported court-ordered efforts to reduce educational segregation by race and achieve racial balancing in schools, an ironical situation in the light of the subsequent controversies over Coleman II.

When Coleman I was published, James Coleman was already a leading American sociologist. The report established his reputation as a national figure. Its data were the subject of reanalysis by professional colleagues, and a major seminar at Harvard was devoted to its evaluation (Mosteller and Moynihan, 1972). Qualifications which Coleman made to the central findings of the report were ignored and

> he continued to be celebrated by journalists as the social scientist who had definitively established the educational gains that would flow from racially

balanced schools. Among his peers he was a towering figure, a man who had reached the pinnacle of his profession. To the public he was the nation's foremost sociologist, probably the only one whose name was regularly mentioned in editorials and news stories. (Ravitch, 1993: 134)

Coleman's research on busing in the early and mid-1970s met a different reception. Coleman I was in general warmly supported by those who took a liberal or reformist stance towards American race relations, as providing evidence for intervention in the direction of greater racial equality. The subsequent work on busing (Coleman II), the major report on which was released at the AERA conference in April 1975, met with a very different reception, and resulted in a national campaign to impugn both the research and Coleman's professional credibility. Coleman II's conclusion that court-ordered school desegregation contributed to white flight from inner city to suburb, and fostered the resegregation of urban schools, provoked bitter attacks from civil rights activists, the media and professional colleagues. Although ultimately his findings were borne out, in the aftermath of Coleman II he suffered a period of intense isolation and professional obloquy, including an unsuccessful attempt to censure him by the President of the American Sociological Association (this is recalled in relative tranquillity in Coleman, 1989b). Few sociologists ever had to endure the high profile public controversy which swirled around him in America at this period.

No friend of political correctness, and not easily categorized on the political spectrum, Coleman III on public and private schools (Coleman, Hoffer and Kilgore, 1982) engendered further national controversy. Among its findings were that, compared to public (i.e., publicly financed) schools, private schools produced better cognitive outcomes. Even after controlling for social background, private schools provided a safer and more disciplined environment for pupils and enrolled a smaller proportion of blacks. There was also less racial segregation within them, and pupils in private schools had higher self-esteem. Supporters of public schools were enraged by his conclusion that Catholic schools (the main type of private school in racially mixed inner city areas) 'more nearly approximate the "common school" ideal of American education than do public schools in that achievement levels of students from different parental educational backgrounds, of black and white students and of Hispanic and non-Hispanic and white students are more nearly alike in Catholic schools than in public schools' (quoted in Ravitch, 1993: 138). Once again Coleman had challenged enshrined beliefs and had not hesitated to say that the evidence cast doubt on the superiority of an institution which for many liberal Americans was an article of faith, the superiority of public education. Coleman III was in effect an argument for the pursuit of certain school policies, an interesting modification of Coleman I which had downplayed the importance of the school as an influence on educational outcomes.

The saga of the three major Coleman studies is instructive from several points of view, including the history of educational research, the political context in which American educational policy is conducted, the influence of social science upon policy-making, and the value-laden nature of public debate about the significance of findings produced by sociologists. It is the last which is our focus here. One conclusion which Coleman drew in his 1989 retrospective view was that he had only been able to withstand the onslaught of criticisms of Coleman II and Coleman III because in addition to holding a tenured university post he had enjoyed 'tenure' (i.e., a sufficiently strong reputation) in the discipline. It also led him to reflect about the place of values in social policy research, and the need to develop systems which would ensure that presentation of the findings of the research was not simply reduced to arguments about values and political positions. Reflecting the inflammatory responses to Coleman II and Coleman III, he asked in 1989:

> What is threatening to the discipline about such research that it provokes these reactions? If we could answer that question, we could perhaps create a structure to combat these norms and the sanctions they generate. If we could develop such a structure, it would be a service not only to our field (the sociology of education) but to sociology as a whole; and not only to sociology as a whole, but to the whole scientific enterprise. (Coleman, 1989b: 5)

Citing Max Weber's editorial on taking over the *Archiv für Sozialwissenschaft und Sozialpolitik*, he wrote after Coleman II, distinguishing between scientific analysis and social action:

> To apply the results of . . . analysis in the making of a decision, however, is not a task which science can undertake; it is rather the task of the acting, willing person: he weighs and chooses from among the values involved according to his own conscience and his personal view of the world. Science can make him realize that all action and naturally, according to the circumstances, inaction imply in their consequences the espousal of certain values — and . . . the rejection of certain others. (Weber, quoted in Coleman, 1978: 689–90)

The resulting distinction between the scientific investigator and the 'acting, willing person' is underlain by a further feature of the social sciences, that the selection of problems for investigation is influenced by practical questions in the world, which are very likely to be value-laden. The social scientist thus occupies two quite different positions, very often in the same person, one as a scientific investigator, where values are excluded, the other as the selector of the problem to be investigated and making arguments or recommendations about the policies to be pursued, where values enter in. The former pertains in terms of Coleman's analysis of social policy research, cited earlier, to the world of the discipline, the second to the world of action.

Maintaining the Sociologist's Credibility

Perhaps reflecting his own experiences, Coleman comments that the social science expert who contributes knowledge to an issue gains credibility in the eyes of others which gives his value statements unwarranted power. A prime example was the way in which natural scientists involved in the design of the atomic bomb became involved in the aftermath of 1945 in giving advice about the use of atomic weapons, creating the *Bulletin of the Atomic Scientists* as a vehicle for doing so. Although analytically Weber's distinction in quite clearcut, empirically the separation of the two roles is extremely difficult.

It may be necessary to devise institutional means for bolstering the first of the roles, that of the technical expert. A *sine qua non* is the existence of strong methodological standards which will ensure that the data on which analysis is based are of the requisite quality. In the Coleman controversies this has been generally the case; argument has raged over the interpretation of the data, not the quality of the data. However, this is a very important baseline requirement for social policy research. Second, reanalysis of the data should be routinely undertaken, something which has been much more common in the United States than in Western Europe, partly due to the greater sophistication of American quantitative social science. It is no longer true that British sociology lacks the plurality of openly competing institutions in which the results of educational research can be rigorously scrutinized and reanalyzed (Hope, 1978: 260), but the quantity of secondary analysis in American educational research and the rapidity with which it is carried out remain significant. This occurred with Coleman I and was part of the process of professional reception of the report.

Coleman has argued, however, that one needs to go further. There is a need to recognize the existence of different interests in relation to policy issues, and to ensure that the results of research are presented in ways which can be used by these different interests in the policy process. Research is often initiated under the sponsorship of one of the interests involved (often, but by no means exclusively, government) but needs to be presented in a way that is not simply in terms of the interests of that party. The discipline needs an institutional structure which ensures that the information provided by social research will be equitable to the various interests involved, in both the questions asked and the implications drawn (Coleman, 1976a: 257). Coleman argues, however, that the adversary procedure characteristic of the legal system is not the answer as to how to proceed. Experience of a number of scholars in the case of the busing research was that the parties to lawsuits each sought their own professional experts, and that in the longer run the technical questions were only resolved by further analysis in the comparative calm of academia rather than in the courtroom.

Coleman has also pointed out that despite the initiation of much social policy research by governments and those in positions of political authority, the results of such research often seem to provide more solace and ammunition for their critics than for those who sponsored the research. Carol Weiss has pointed to the use of social science research as providing political ammunition (Weiss, 1986: 36–7), and in part this is what is happening. But it is also that research which evaluates the effectiveness and outcomes of government policy will tend to draw attention to the lacunae, failings and lack of realization of intended outcomes of such policies, messages which show up the gap which commonly exists between aspiration and reality. Thus the furore over public and private schools arose in part because the research findings challenged the conventional wisdom in liberal circles about public schools, their value and effectiveness. Social policy research may have the effect of weakening the authority claimed by those in charge of a system — in the case of education, the legislators, administrators, school superintendents and teachers who run the system. The verdict is open. David Cohen suggested many years ago that the net effect of American research in the sociology of education had been to render matters more complicated and even opaque from the point of view of the non-specialist, as ever more complex findings, often qualified and increasingly complex methodologically, appeared (Cohen and Garet, 1975; Cohen and Weiss, 1977). More research did not mean more enlightenment, in and of itself. These issues are pursued further in the next chapter by Sally Kilgore.

Contesting Research Results

One concrete proposal which Coleman has put forward is for more explicit recognition of competition in the planning and presentation of social policy research. Although he does not talk of a market in social policy research, his proposal amounts to introducing elements of competition into the process of presenting research results. One suggestion is of the value of forums in which the scientific merits of the findings could be released before research results entered into public debate through the mass media, provided that it is established impartially and with rules to prevent it being 'packed' by particular interests. Having participated in seven such events in connection with Coleman II and Coleman III, his view was that those which were preceded by data reanalysis and were kept closed and small were the most useful (Coleman, 1984a: 136n2).

A more radical step would be to institutionalize the review of research findings in a more formal way. Economists have mechanisms of this kind, for example, when it was established in 1920, the National Bureau of Economic Research in New York had two boards. The purpose of one board was to use representatives of a wide range of interests including employers and trade unions to review publications of the institute and attempt to eliminate possible bias. In 1975 Coleman advocated that a forum be created within the National Institute of Education,

> a research initiation council on desegregation, with explicit representation from all the legitimate interests that might be affected: civil rights groups, black parents and white parents with children in public schools that would be extensively affected by desegregation, representatives of large city school administrations, from the teachers' unions, and from city administrations. Unlike legislatures in which policy decisions are made, which have geographic constituencies, or regulatory agencies which are intended to have no constituencies, such representation would be explicit interest representation. While such a body could hardly be expected to make equitable policy decisions . . . it could, I believe, generate the variety of research questions that would provide information relevant to all the affected interests. (Coleman, 1975a: 310–11)

A year later he advocated more explicit recognition within the sociological profession of the need for a quantitative macrosociology which could be used in policy analysis, for the need to train new cadres of researchers skilled in the necessary quantitative methods, the possibility of careers as a sociologist in such research, and the development of new institutions mid-way between detached scientific inquiry and adversary procedure (Coleman, 1976a: 261).

Conclusion

James Coleman's contribution to the emergence of a professional sociological contribution to social policy research has been immense in the last thirty years, since that phone call from Washington in February 1965. However, such research has been only a part of his contribution to sociology and stands alongside his contributions to the development of theory, of methodology and in substantive analysis. It is nevertheless distinctive. Few of his contemporaries, with exceptions such as William Julius Wilson in the fields of race and urban policy, have done research with such national impact. Other social scientists with as high or higher public profiles, such as politician Daniel Patrick Moynihan, have achieved that by means other than sheer research. James Coleman has been throughout the researcher, insisting that the findings of social science research are the basis from which policy debate must start. Many of these findings were uncomfortable, and although sticking closely to the findings, he has not hesitated to point out their implications if they were.

At times James Coleman has seemed to delight in the controversy to which his public interventions gave rise. Unlike some of his contemporaries, however, he has pursued an individualistic line consistent with his general social theory. He has pursued a lone furrow, not engaging in political partisanship or the espousal of normative standpoints, but believing that more effective social research would lead to more efficient social policies.

> Coleman rarely made his personal commitment on social matters clear to his students. During the 1960s when civil rights protests were at their peak, several students from the [Johns Hopkins] department participated in Freedom Rides in the South. There was of course much discussion among students, from which Coleman generally remained aloof. But one day a picture appeared in the *Baltimore Sun* showing Coleman and his young son being arrested at a civil rights protest. (Sørensen and Spilerman, 1993: 7)

A distinguishing characteristic of his approach as a sociologist has been one of scholarly detachment in relation to the political and value dimensions of major public issues, believing that the scientific analysis of the issues involved was sufficiently problematical without moving into the realm of policy recommendations. Because of the strength of his challenges to the conventional wisdom over busing and public schools, the outcome of this principled stance has, nevertheless, been to generate much fiercer public value conflict than would have been the case had the results of the research been presented more in line with the liberal consensus.

9   The Political Context of Social Policy Research

Sally B. Kilgore

Few, if any, sociologists in this century have had more impact on public debates in the United States than James S. Coleman. Beginning in the 1960s with the federal report on equality of opportunity, proceeding in the 1970s with a study of school busing, and then in the 1980s with two studies on public and private schools, Coleman has persistently sparked debates about educational policy. Seldom, if ever, did his work on education confirm commonly held assumptions in the research community. Instead, it challenged many assumptions and thereby stimulated waves of additional research seeking to refute the conclusions he reached. Thus the effects of his work have been twofold. First, his work drew social science research into the arena of public debates — in news magazines, television and, of course, in legislative and judicial decisions. Second, his work legitimated whole new arenas of research as scholars sought to refute, or simply explore, his claims.

Throughout the history of his work in education scholars have challenged not only Coleman's conclusions but also the forum in which he chose to report them. Some critics contended that scholarly work should be released first to scholars, then the public. Others argued that the work was offered prematurely: Coleman should have waited for additional data that would allow for more thorough investigation. Yet others consider direct communication between a scholar and the public inappropriate. Although not well developed, this secondary debate about the forum in with research is released led Coleman to try to formulate a set of principles about policy research. This chapter reviews and expands upon Coleman's work, identifies some dilemmas for policy research, and suggests that while controversy in policy research is an essential requisite for truth-finding, limiting it to legislative debates may constrain the usefulness of policy research as well as its legitimacy. Some alternatives are suggested, some likely to be more palatable to social scientists than others.

Social policy research refers to research that is oriented by questions in social policy, or that is designed to inform choices in societal action. It is distinguished from theoretical research by the nature of the questions posed, the former driven by debates and issues in the political arena, the latter by issues generated by social theory.

The formation of sound social policy — which, at a minimum, is defined as a policy which generates its intended effects — is more readily achieved when empirical evidence of the anticipated consequences of the policy is available. A simple policy objective, such as ensuring that all people have food, can be achieved with greater or less effectiveness depending on the instruments chosen to achieve it. Putting food on the corner of every residential street, for instance, could put food in reasonable proximity to every person. Costs aside, though, the practice might not achieve its intended effects in that one person might seize the food assigned to a given area and charge exorbitant prices to others for access to it. For sound policy formation to occur, the probable consequences of all policy options should be known before one option is selected over another. In the arena of policy formation that can never occur. Always some inferences are required. But the central question remains: how much empirical evidence versus wild conjecture is available to inform the decision? Policy research can increase the amount of empirical research available to inform such decisions.

Given that a number of interests — often competing — should be taken into account in formulating social policy for a democratic polity, a parallel corollary should be met: the empirical evidence should inform all interests that will be affected by a policy before a sound one can be formulated. It is this corollary that has persistently concerned Coleman (1968a, 1972a, 1976c, 1989b). Policy research should, he argues, enable all actors within the political arena to have a better understanding of which policy choices are most likely to achieve their respective objectives.

As Coleman (1980a) notes, American social scientists initiated social policy research as part of a more general trend of pursuing research that informed specific decisions, such as determining market niches for a product or separation policies in the military. In each instance, though, the audience for this research consisted of a limited number of decision-makers within an organization. Some of the best work of twentieth century social science emerged under these conditions. Elihu Katz and Paul Lazarsfeld's (1955) work on personal influence and Stouffer's (1949) work on the American soldier are two important cases. Although their research eventually had a broad impact on social science, their initial work, as well as that of others, informed some, but not all, of the interests of persons affected by a policy or practice.

This earlier research usually addressed one part of the issue: will a policy have the intended effect? When the requirement is simply to evaluate the likelihood that a given policy will have the effects intended, then the practice of conducting research that answers the questions of a limited number of decision-makers is satisfactory. In fact, such circumstances do exist. For instance, where a legislative action establishes a mandate, such as increased parental participation in education, it may be appropriate to commission research that focuses on ways to implement the intent of the legislation.

However, the most significant role for policy research is related to legislative action itself: the formation of policy where competing interests must be adjudicated. Legislative debate is, in fact, about the probable effects of a proposed policy on the various interests represented in a democratic polity. As Coleman notes (1980a), this role for policy research is parallel to those provided by lobbyists in the United States. A lobbyist's role is to inform 'legislators and administrators of the anticipated consequences of [pending] legislation' (Coleman, 1980a: 305). Taken collectively, lobbyists represent a multitude of interests, but not all interests, in a democracy. Coleman argues that this institutional structure is inadequate in two respects: first, it does not represent all interests of the polity; and, second, 'lobbyists cannot be depended upon to show accurately the consequences of a projected policy' (Coleman, 1980a: 305). Policy research can address both of these inadequacies.

To determine the circumstances in which multiple interests become informed by policy research, three questions will be considered: who should ask the questions; who should conduct the research; and who should be the audience? In each case, an attempt is made to determine how various options affect the degree to which all parties improve their understanding of the consequences of various policy options in terms of their interests.

Who Should Ask the Questions?

Coleman argues that anyone assigned the task of asking questions has an interest in the issue, an interest that leads that person to have greater curiosity about some aspects of an issue than others. Bureaucrats, for instance, are likely to have a different set of interests about an education issue than do parents. On the issue of school choice, government officials may want information on the effects of choice on the racial composition of schools, while parents may be more interested in the types of students who benefit from a certain type of school. Taxpayers may be concerned about the relative costs of different choice systems. Bias, such as it is, arises not in the process of research, but rather in framing the questions to pursue. A set of research questions can, and often does, address a limited set of interests. (I would argue that bias most often occurs in the omission of questions, not in distorting data or in constructing leading questions.) To the extent, then, that questions are restricted to a limited set of interests, only a limited set of actors can learn, and therefore benefit, from the answers.

By the mid- to late 1970s Coleman began writing about a model 'pluralistic policy research' (Coleman, 1976a), where a broad range of interests shape the formulation of research questions. The inclusion of a broad range of interests requires that definitions, cause and consequence be evaluated from a number of theoretical perspectives and interests. Coleman, however, was aware of this challenge much earlier, at least as early as the work on equality of educational opportunities in 1965. The legislative directive for the research required a 'survey, and report, concerning the lack of availability of equal educational opportunities by reason of race, color, religion, or national origin.' In 1972 Coleman reports: 'the first research task was an investigation of what [the words] meant to those who imposed the directive (Congressmen) and to those who could have an interest in the research results' (1972a: 7). In the end the staff generated five different understandings of inequality of opportunities that were evident in the interviews with congressmen and interest group representatives:

1 different types and levels of inputs (or resources);
2 racial composition (since the US Supreme Court had ruled that segregated schools were inherently unequal);
3 intangible characteristics of school and community, such as teacher morale and expectations;
4 consequences of the schools for students with equivalent backgrounds, where one would expect equality of results;
5 inequality of consequences for those with unequal backgrounds.

Although Coleman's work (Coleman, Campbell *et al.*, 1966) focused on the fourth definition, it attempted to provide information on all five definitions of inequality of opportunity. Similarly, in the study of public and private high schools Coleman and his colleagues attempted to provide information that would address criticisms and assertions of both those who opposed any aid to students attending private schools and those who supported such aid.

Coleman's decision to secure data on all five definitions of equality of educational opportunity received some legitimate criticism: it unduly burdened the study's sampling design. Requiring school and student level data, 'the study attempted to do too much', argued Hanushek and Kain (1972). Coleman aptly notes that to have limited the study to one definition unduly legitimates and 'reinforces' one point of view over another. In fact, Coleman argues, the major impact of the study was to shift attention from the traditional definition — equality of input — to concern for output and 'the effectiveness of inputs for bringing about changes in output' (Coleman, 1972a).

To what extent has Coleman's concern for multiple interests influenced the direction of educational policy research in the United States? In one respect the effect has been substantial. By the late 1980s federal education officials in the United States routinely made use of this principle in determining the specific items to be included in large data collection activities in education. For instance, the national longitudinal studies sponsored by the National Center for Education Statistics are the product of extensive meetings with a broad range of interest groups and researchers. Equally important, the analytic capacity of the data in the most recent longitudinal initiative on education (NELS, 1988) was increased through an expansion of the number of private schools selected for the study. Private funding allowed the survey to be augmented to include a sample of private Christian schools, and funding from another public agency expanded the scope of the teacher survey to allow for the collection of college transcripts.

More recently, the 1993 reauthorizing legislation for the Office of Education Research and Improvement (OERI) established a research advisory council composed of five practitioners, five researchers and five policy-makers. While this representation provides an additional forum for various interests — particularly practitioners, it is far from exhaustive. No positions are reserved for the clients of education: parents and employers, for instance, are notably absent. Moreover, using official representatives from interest groups generates its own dilemmas. The leaders of such interest groups — teachers' associations, administrators' organizations — have interests that are not always parallel with the interests of their members. Indeed, as leaders of organizations, they may have a number of interests they share among themselves, but not with their respective constituencies.

These moves to engage the broader public in the formulation of research questions, while addressing the problems identified by Coleman, remain quite limited in their impact. While a pluralist model appears to be fairly institutionalized in routine data collection activities, it does not appear to be common practice among those who analyze data — an issue which leads to the second question.

Who Should Conduct Research?

Both Coleman and his critics would agree that, at least insofar as publicly funded research is concerned, researchers with analytical expertise are preferred to those lacking such skills. But beyond that condition, does the variation in authorship affect the degree to which multiple interests are addressed? Embedded in the question of who should conduct the research are two issues: the environment or setting in which the research is conducted; and the controls introduced by those who support the research financially.

   In the United States the environment in which research is conducted can be of at least four types: a university, a governmental agency, a think tank, and an interest group organization. The setting can affect the apparent impartiality of the research, the pressures exerted, and the capacity to be responsive to time deadlines often required in policy analysis. The funding sources affect, most importantly, ownership of the data — where contractual relations usually, but not always, imply some control over publications and possibly ownership of them. On the other hand, grant relations with a funding source generally assign ownership and publication rights to the researcher.

Impartiality.   Apparent impartiality refers to the preconceptions that the public (and policy-makers) hold about the degree to which interests within the setting will affect the direction of the research. Only one setting appears to be disadvantaged consistently by perceived impartiality: interest group organizations. For instance, in the US the National Education Association collects a considerable amount of information about teacher salaries, but this author's experience suggests it is utilized with great reluctance by other organizations and federal agencies. Most audiences assume that whatever is 'authored' by an interest group is designed to serve the clients of that organization. Given that interest groups, by virtue of their charter, serve a limited set of interests, such organizations appear to be less desirable settings of policy research than others.
   Think tanks in the US vary substantially in their reputation for impartiality. Recent efforts to classify think tanks along a conservative to liberal spectrum by the media would suggest that, to some degree, their perceived impartiality is fairly vulnerable. Most US governmental statistical agencies have acquired a reputation for impartiality, in part because they avoid policy research. In the past decade Washington policy-makers have generally accorded the most respect to policy research performed in governmental agencies that are relatively independent of executive branch policy-makers: the Government Accounting Office and the Congressional Budget Office. University-based research is generally treated as an impartial source primarily because of the apparent disinterest of researchers that reside there. However, it is unlikely that that view would be consistent across all spectrums of political orientations in the US.

Timelines.   Coleman notes (1972a) that the world of action requires information at a particular time. After that specified time (i.e., when a legislative decision is made) information is largely irrelevant. Thus some evidence at an appropriate time (prior to a legislative action) is better than full information (i.e., evidence) at a time after legislative action. Who should do the research is dictated, in part, by those actors who can respond within the timeframe dictated by the 'world of action'.
   Academics in a traditional university are not in an environment that responds easily to a time-sensitive product (Coleman, 1972a). Academic structures do not foster such responsiveness. All other environments appear to have a greater capacity to respond to deadlines. In general, government and interest group environments probably have the best understanding of the nuances associated with timing in the legislative arena.
   Is time, in fact, a critical variable? Yes and no. Legislatively, of course, all deliberations have some time parameters; but some are more tightly constrained than others. Legislation in the US Congress that reauthorizes existing programs has very predictable and firm timelines. Reauthorizing legislation must precede the expiration

of existing legislation — although, even here, it is possible to extend the period of deliberation. Other legislation, authorizing new programs, is quite variable. Presidential initiatives, such as health care, can have very short time horizons. In education, where the turnover in executive officers is quite high (several months to two years is quite typical), research can only serendipitously inform policy proposals. Each officer seeks to make a quick 'mark' on the executive agenda and move elsewhere (Hill, 1980).

On the other hand, legislation initiated by a few minority members of Congress can languish for years, never reaching the floor for debate. Within this range, policy research that informs reauthorization is clearly the most feasible. Policy research that informs the formulation of new initiatives is less feasible for a number of reasons — and time is only one of several variables that affect it. Finally, research that informs the regulatory component of policy formation can have a very short time horizon, since most regulations must be developed within a year of the authorizing legislation. Thus policy research in the US can address, most consistently, reauthorizating legislation. As discussed in the closing section of this chapter, the use of policy research in these circumstances is highly circumscribed.

Controls. The issue most pertinent to Coleman's principles of sound policy research is that of the control or pressure exerted either by actors within the organizational setting for the research or by the agency or organization providing funding for the research. Coleman (1972a), for instance, argues that university environments have less pressure than governmental ones to serve a limited set of interests. Paul Hill (1980) refines our understanding of the governmental environment, noting that two types of clients exist in government: the executive branch and the legislative branch. It must be noted, however, that legislative clients are generally (with some major exceptions) served within the executive branch environment. Federal researchers in the executive branch gain a measure of freedom when they serve under the direction of the legislative branch. Serving two authorities, one gains a measure of freedom from each (Simmel, 1950).

Coleman's experience in the 1960s with a congressionally mandated study on equality of opportunity is somewhat different from Paul Hill's work in the 1970s on a congressionally mandated study of compensatory education. In Coleman's case the executive branch sought to shape the presentation of the results to conform with their program. In Hill's case the executive branch simply wanted access to the 'truth' prior to Congress receiving the material — a struggle precipitated by the desire to get credit for solutions, not by a desire to control the presentation to the public. In the mid-1980s, when this author had oversight of a congressionally mandated study on compensatory education, the legislative client restricted the scope inquiry — the legislative staff did not want to risk acquiring data that would give ammunition to the critics of the program. The executive branch had numerous interests in the results and sought to influence the outcome, but they lost interest as it became apparent that those interests were not addressed by the study. The study in the 1980s differed from earlier ones in one respect: it was completed with a Democratically controlled Congress and a Republican controlled executive branch. In the other cases the Democratic party controlled both Congress and the executive branch. In the 1970s Hill's work was commissioned to inform a conflict among legislators about the efficacy of targeting money by poverty levels versus achievement levels. In the other two instances actors had a number of preconceptions for which they sought confirming evidence.

Although motives varied, in all instances researchers in the government setting operated under substantial pressures. In two cases (1960s and 1980s) those pressures were directed toward the substantive content — and implicitly affected the degree to which multiple interests could be informed. All three experiences suggest that pressures to conform to either the administrative or the executive branch interests can realistically be resisted only if researchers lack any long-term interest in remaining in the government. If that condition is absent, then researchers will inevitably move toward compliance with some interest groups and fail to serve multiple, and presumably competing, interests.

In 1972 Coleman noted that university-based researchers were in an environment that had less pressure than government environments to serve a limited set of interests. This may, in fact, be a case where Coleman has changed his mind. Adapting a phrase from previous sociological eras, Coleman (1989b) argues that the need of academics to display 'conspicuous benevolence' to disadvantaged groups has created a powerful taboo in pursuing research questions that might not serve the interests of those who are less fortunate in society. The question is this: how can academics presume to know the interests of these groups a priori? It is a curious conceit to invade the life of academics.

It was such a conceit that led scholars to discourage their colleagues from publishing findings suggesting that busing might have negative effects on the children it was intended to serve. What entitles the researcher to conclude that he or she knows more than the data? In the case of busing, reporting of the apparent negative effects on minority children might have led to restructuring the program to greater advantage of those children, or the ensuing controversy might have generated further studies that identified beneficial effects. University settings, then, appear to have acquired pressures to serve a particular set of interests, even if the understanding of those interests is 'ill-formed'.

Given that neither university nor governmental settings appear to very hospitable environments in which to pursue research that addresses a multitude of interests, what alternatives exist? At least two alternatives have been considered. First, one could support the pursuit of policy research by numerous groups representing multiple interests. Coleman, for instance, has demonstrated in action, if not by words, that other researchers, and even interest groups, should have access to data that can allow them to frame the argument and analysis in ways that address alternative interpretations.

In the study of equality of opportunity Coleman made the data available to anyone who wished to do further analysis. While precedent-setting, it was not his last effort to increase access to data. In a 1988 proposal submitted to the National Center for Education Statistics to collect the High School and Beyond longitudinal data, Coleman proposed to establish a permanent research team that could conduct the empirical analysis required by any question a member of the public might generate — assuming, of course, that the question was addressed in this broadly-based longitudinal study. Thus a local school board member might want to know about disciplinary problems, nationally or regionally. The member could call the research team, ask for the data broken down by, say, gender. Under these conditions all actors in a polity have 'equal access' to data that could inform their work and practice. Although the proposal was accepted and funded, the provision for data analysis services to the public was quickly abandoned by the contracting agency.

Even if Coleman's efforts had been successful, it is not clear that the consequences would be altogether positive. Recalling the credibility of interest group research, how would the public respond? The secondary consequences would be most problematic. Relying on interest group research to provide information on competing interests implies that any position in policy debate can generate preferred empirical results to support a claim — a practice of an effective lawyer. Such a position is dangerous to the extent that it fosters the public perception that 'anything can be said with statistics'. For, unlike a court of law, no rules of disclosure exist. Instead, much truth can be obscured as those who pursue research encounter results that fail to confirm their predispositions and subsequently withhold those findings. As Coleman (1978) notes, commissioned studies seldom, if ever, confirm the initial assumptions that drive the research.

Alternatively, competing arguments about a public issue could be explored concurrently (Coleman, 1972a). For instance, researchers, with different arguments as to the cause of a given phenomenon or as to the consequence of a given policy option, could be engaged simultaneously to analyze the same data. To date, federal officials in education have persistently rejected, or sometimes never considered, this strategy. At least in the 1980s this author found that federal officials viewed such strategies simplistically and regarded simultaneous efforts on a topic as a duplication of effort. Paul Hill (1980) notes a similar position in the 1970s. Given that controversy can be very costly to an agency, it would be necessary to find another venue in which to foster such work.

Unlike the issue of formulating the research questions, the question of who should conduct the research has no easy answers. This analysis emphasizes, instead, the limitations of numerous settings. As is argued in the concluding section, the answer resides within the norms of academe. But first, the issues of audience must be reviewed: who should hear the debate?

Who Should Be the Audience?

A persistent claim by some researchers is that the public should not be exposed to research findings until they have been reviewed by other scholars. The specific intent here is to argue that peer-reviewed publications should constitute the forum in which public policy research is reported. The issue is not who should listen, but rather how to ensure a quality product. This is a legitimate concern and one with far-reaching implications.

Public agencies, when serving as a contractor for research, often perform the quality control functions of the profession. They may commission outside reviewers or review the research internally. The problem with this procedure is that the issues of quality control inevitably become entangled with political interests. Whether or not the work of a researcher is regarded as sound, then, is affected by the degree to which it supports the policy preferences of those in office. Peer-reviewed journals sometimes generate highly negative reviews motivated by the discipline-based norm of 'conspicuous benevolence'. Thus, with both referees, one faces the dilemma that analytical weaknesses can be exaggerated to control the release of the analysis. There are no easy answers or solutions.

The notion that the public needs some protection from unwarranted claims is a good one. The question is whether filters through peer review journals or public agencies are the most effective ones or whether they introduce problems greater than the one they solve.

To address the issue of audience properly, and provide some solutions to quality control, I must digress to define the legislative audience that is the presumed target of policy research. Theoretically, legislators and other public policy-makers represent the scope of interests found in their constituency. Coleman's early (1972a) formulation of the role for policy research reflected that assumption. However, reality is shaped somewhat differently and affects how public policy is utilized. A few examples of the actions of policy-makers will illustrate the dilemmas.

Beginning in the 1970s, the US federal government sponsored annual studies of learning known as the National Assessment of Education Progress (NAEP). Fearful of invidious comparisons, legislators required that the sampling be done in ways that prevented state by state comparisons. Then in 1983 Secretary of Education Bell released the first wall chart — a state by state listing of indicators on the status of education. Among the indicators chosen was the Scholastic Aptitude Test (SAT) which is taken by *some* of the students interested in attending college in the United States. It was not too many months before various media ranked states by their average SAT scores. State officials were understandably upset. It took six years before state officials agreed that the federally sponsored NAEP studies should be conducted in ways that allow for state by state comparisons. As a federal official at the time, I marvelled at the power of a pitiful indicator. It was only the introduction of an indicator that did not serve the interests of states that changed their opinion of how NAEP should be administered.

In the 1980s allowing students to choose a school they would attend (rather than being assigned on the basis of residential location) emerged as a major debate, nationally and locally in the United States. Various legislative proposals emerged in the US Congress: tax credits for those attending private schools and special support for schools that accepted students from across a school district (magnet schools). Despite the great interest and debate regarding choice, Congress persistently refused to fund studies that might evaluate the efficacy of choices in schooling. While this inertia was in most respects a trivial event, it was a highly informative one — because, at best, legislators implicitly said that they would prefer no information to risking the appearance of information that did not reflect their preferences. At worst, legislators (largely Democratic) believed that those with interests different from their own (the Republican administration) would generate research that did not favour or inform their interests.

How does history square with either of these interpretations? As Coleman (1978) notes, research commissioned by governmental agencies or legislative bodies seldom serves their interests or confirms their preconceptions. If the facts informed legislators debating research on choice, they should not perceive risks to their interests. Either a problem in understanding the nature of social science research exists, or legislators, at least, just do not want to know.

Other data suggest that legislators do not want to know. Policy research, to be useful to legislators, has to fit within the framework of political discourse. As it currently stands, this constraint puts severe limits on policy research and may, in fact, undermine its legitimacy. James Q. Wilson (1994) argues that politicians adopt solutions before they determine the needs they are trying to address: 'It is a characteristic of political discourse, I think, everywhere that we embrace solutions first and then look for problems they might solve, in much the same spirit as a person holding a hammer looks for anything resembling a nail' (Wilson, 1994: 13). Thus political campaigns at their best consist of promoting a particular program, such as Head Start for pre-schoolers, rather than committing themselves to finding solutions to the problem, say, of children's readiness for school. Wilson argues that this happens because politicians define problems 'so as to make them amenable to solutions they favor for ideological or moral reasons'.

This problem is far more pervasive and destructive than one might initially suppose. The compensatory education research of the 1980s (referenced earlier) had not included any evaluation of student achievement. When I assumed an oversight role, I was informed that congressional staff had explicitly requested that such questions not be pursued in this congressionally mandated study, and the researchers had complied with the request. My surprise was only an indication of my naiveté. The legislators were not interested in data that would force them to debate the merits of the program, but, rather, in data that would identify incremental changes that might improve the delivery of services. Commitments are made to programs first, then to ways to make the program function satisfactorily. Within such a framework, evidence from policy research at best becomes ammunition for defending or denouncing the viability of a specific program in the legislative arena. The statement of the problem, if it exists, resides in the heads of the constituents who support a candidate on the basis of these programmatic commitments.

Using research evidence as ammunition may appear innocuous. It falls within the legitimate discourse of legal debates, where evidence is selected to support a particular claim and the truth is supposed to emerge as competing claims are evaluated by an impartial jury. However, this is not the forum in which such research ammunition is shot. In the political arena the claims go largely unanalyzed. Politicians, as a class, are woefully incapable of challenging statistical data. They seldom challenge distortions of percentage increases, much less the latent variables utilized by a researcher. Political forums provide limited forums for policy research. The risk to social science research, in general, is also great. For it is a forum, as it now stands, that maximizes the likelihood that participants acquire the disdainful conviction that 'you can say anything with statistics'.

When one combines the practices of legislators discussed above with certain forms of advocacy practised by social scientists, then the legitimacy of social policy research may be at risk. Drawing on Weber's (1949) classical work, Coleman (1972a) enumerated several governing principles for policy researchers. Among them was this principle: 'Those stages of policy research that lie in the world of action, formulation of the research problem, posing conditions for communication of the research results back into the world of action and making policy recommendations based on the research results, should be governed by the investigator's personal values and appropriately include advocacy' (1972a: 14). Advocacy by policy researchers is not problematic. What is interesting, problematic in fact, is the way in which social scientists construct their advocacy. Some social scientists appear to be comfortable in constructing their advocacy independently of their research evidence.

Take, for instance, the debate on the value of private schools. One expert witness before Congress sought to refute Coleman, Hoffer and Kilgore's findings by arguing that there was no difference in achievement between the public and private sectors and no difference in student effort in the two sectors. Yet, despite this apparent lack of advantage for students in private sector schools, the expert witness invoked his general expertise as a psychologist to *support* federal funding of private schools. (This must have been especially confusing to legislators since another expert witness, providing evidence on the benefits of private schools to low income students, concluded that the evidence provided lacked policy implications for federal funding of private schools.)

The problem with this incident is that the advocacy, supported by Coleman and the traditions of social science, arises independently of the research results. What can legislators think when the convictions of social scientists work independently of their evidence? Certainly, Coleman did not anticipate such liberties. Advocacy by social scientists conducting policy research should never ignore the evidence garnered by the research. A social scientist cannot be so named without allowing evidence to inform his or her own judgment.

Two factors have contributed to certain problems of legitimacy for policy research in the United States. First is the problem of political discourse and how evidence is used. Legislators restrict its usage to advocacy debates regarding a particular program. Second is the problem that some social scientists allow their advocacy to function independently of their evidence. Should we be surprised when a chief legislative specialist, in defending his disinterest in educational research, asserts: 'you can say anything you want with research'?

Are there solutions to this morass? How can it inform our understanding of the proper audience and quality control? For over a decade Coleman (1978) and others proposed the introduction of an independent review panel, such as that used by the National Institute of Health (NIH). These panels seek to identify best practice for medical practitioners. NIH convenes a panel of researchers who are *not* specialists in the field under question — say, liver transplants — and asks them to serve as jurors. Specialists in liver transplants present their competing evidence on best practice. After hearing the evidence, jurors are asked to prepare a statement on best practice, given the evidence on liver transplants. These statements then become part of the 'official statements' from NIH. Applying such practices to social science could limit the use of statistical data in legislative debates to that defined and endorsed as credible (Coleman, 1976c). While that procedure may resolve issues of legitimacy and conform to the constraints of political discourse, it is a less than satisfactory solution in some respects because the information needs are confined to the preconceived solutions of legislators. If we move outside the box of political discourse, other alternatives may seem equally reasonable.

Changing the Parameters of Policy Research

Given the strict time constraints imposed by legislative agendas and the propensity of legislators to adopt solutions before they evaluate the needs, it is reasonable to ask whether alternative conceptualizations of the proper audience for policy research can mitigate the disadvantages associated with the time constraints of the legislative process and legislators' restricted interest to evidence which supports specific programs — proposed or existing.

Part of the answer lies in Coleman's own account of his work on the equality of educational opportunity. As noted earlier, Coleman sees the major impact of his study as shifting the public debate from an exclusive concern for equality of input to a concern for the 'effectiveness of inputs for bringing about changes in output'. In essence, Coleman was redefining the nature of the problem. It is in this context, of defining the problem and the probable causal linkages, that the full potential of policy research can be utilized.

However, to target that stage of policy formation requires several changes, many of them a derivative of one fundamental shift in the framework for policy research: the audience for public policy research cannot be limited to policy-makers or legislators. Instead, the audience must be the public at large. For it is their definition of the problem that breathes either life into or destruction upon the programmatic preferences of legislators. If, however, one takes the public as the appropriate audience, the constraint of time becomes even more peculiar. Acquiring a public audience requires the use of media. In that medium, research either has to create news (as in the case of Herrnstein and Murray's (1994) work on intelligence) or follow the news (as in the case of Chubb and Moe's (1990) work on public and private schools).

Creating news is easiest, although always somewhat unpredictable, when the results contravene common sense, stimulate controversy, or uncover some surprising relationships. In essence, the old media adage applies: man must bite dog. Following the news, as a means to address the larger public, does have precedence, but the average researcher would be hard pressed to follow it. A major think tank in the United States, known for its bland reports, has — at least during certain parts of its history — held many of its reports for release at a time when they could 'follow the news'. Thus the report might be released when the findings directly contradicted the recent claims of a public official. Time, here, for the think tank, was rendered irrelevant. It was just a matter of waiting for the appropriate moment. However, for most researchers in the US, who require external support for the pursuit of their work or an active publications list, the luxury of such a strategy is seldom within reach.

Many researchers might recoil at either strategy of reaching a public audience. Something crass and unprofessional seems to be buried in either strategy. However, that is not entirely the case. If, in fact, researchers take seriously the dictum that their work address the multiplicity of interests embedded in a problem, then controversy or surprising results will naturally emerge from their work. It is the failure of modern academics, not the vagaries of modern forums for public debate, that must be reassessed. For nothing, it seems, could be a more noble act for those who call themselves scholars than an act which requires a citizenry to reflect upon their commonly held assumptions, or an act which encourages that same citizenry to become active truth-seekers. Advancement of knowledge should not be restricted to the halls of academe.

Scholars, at least in the US, subscribe to archaic norms that were appropriate in pre-democratic societies where advancing knowledge required only that a limited few understand new discoveries in science and philosophy. For now, more than ever, the gap between the knowledge found within academic disciplines and that of the general public can be too great for either a democratic society or its academic institutions to function effectively. Environmental and educational policy, for instance, are issues that a citizen can, and should, have a means to realize his or her preferences. Yet the scientific base underlying the policy options is largely inaccessible to the general public. Such a critical gap puts all institutions at risk.

The problem is that the incentives of academy in the United States directly undermine the pursuit of such public discourse. Researchers in the academy risk censor, informal though it may be, if they pursue questions or publish results that violate the norm of 'conspicuous benevolence'. Considering these risks, Coleman's career in public discourse and controversy was remarkable. Coleman never simply informed legislators about a program or policy options; he always informed and stimulated public debate. More important, he made truthseekers of us all. Like the irritating grain of sand that generates the pearl, the product of Coleman's research was greater than his effort and unique in its formation. It was unlike sand in that Coleman stood as sui generis in his efforts to address those interests and thereby stimulate public debate about commonly held assumptions. While sociologists in particular do not favour one-man theories of social change, we face not just the simple evaluation of that unique contribution, but also the difficulty of asking how academic disciplines can predictably generate practitioners who will see, understand and address the multiplicity of interests associated with any given social policy.

It requires that academics take seriously the dictum of Albert Einstein, shown on his statute in Washington, D.C.: 'The right to search for truth implies also a duty. One must not conceal any part of what one has recognized to be true'. Social scientists cannot in this context hold to the conceit that they know what question is best pursued, or which findings are best suppressed, to protect or advance the interests of disadvantaged groups. It is a conceit that reinforces the paternalism they so often condemn. Instead, they must be willing to challenge conventional wisdom of their colleagues, allow controversy to come to their table, and accept their errors or more adequate interpretations of their data. In so doing, they may achieve the noble calling of their profession. It is only in changing the norms of the academy that we can remove our dependence on unique individuals, such as Coleman, to challenge our understanding of a problem.

10 Games with Simulated Environments: Educational Innovation and Applied Sociological Research

Sarane Spence Boocock

In his introduction to a pair of issues of *American Behavioral Scientist* devoted to the topic 'Simulation Games and Learning Behaviour', Coleman asked this question: 'Why should self-respecting sociologists, who could be working in research directions that would gain far more recognition from colleagues, instead toy with games in a field — educational sociology — that has long languished in the cellar of the discipline?' (1966c: 3). Answering that question was a major preoccupation throughout the 1960s and early 1970s, and led to the diverse set of research and development activities that came to be known as the Academic Games Program, or sometimes the Hopkins Games Project, and that constituted Coleman's major excursion into applied sociology.

When the project began, there existed a small literature on the role of games in the socialization process, including Herbert Spencer's (1873) exposition of the surplus energy theory of games; John Huizinga's (1955) classic analysis of the 'play element' in human culture and civilization; George Simmel's study of the contribution of games to 'sociability' (1950); and, of course, George Herbert Mead's essay on 'Play, the Game, and the Generalized Other', with its famous analysis of baseball as a means of developing the social self (1934: 152–64). The claims made for the socialization functions of games are diverse. 'Various social theorists have proposed that play and games are the means by which individuals develop creativity, achievement motivation, independence, personality stability, a sense of self, an understanding of the function of rules, knowledge of culturally defined roles, feelings of efficacy, and empathy' (Livingston *et al.*, 1973: 10).[1] Coleman, however, provided the first rationale for treating games and gaming — in particular, the construction and observation of games with simulated social environments — as a mainstream sociological research methodology.[2]

To his own question — why games should be of interest to sociologists — he offered two answers. First, because they change the social organization of schools and schooling, academic games could 'transform the techniques by which children learn in schools and thus transform children that schools presently leave untouched or mildly "educated"'. Second, because a simulation game is a 'kind of caricature of social life', gaming constitutes a research tool for sociologists analogous to, and as powerful as, the use of experiments by psychologists and physical scientists (Coleman, 1966c: 3–4).

This chapter examines the claims made for games with simulated environments as educational innovations and as vehicles for sociological research, reviews the major activities comprising the Academic Games Program, and assesses the intellectual legacy of the program.

Rationale 1: Simulation Games as Learning Devices

Coleman introduced the notion of academic games in the concluding chapter of *The Adolescent Society* (Coleman, 1961a), and expanded upon this preliminary statement in a series of subsequent papers and reports. The basic argument was that classroom activities organized like athletic contests could remove major impediments to academic motivation and achievement by correcting certain defects in the structure of secondary education; in particular, 'a focus upon future needs which are not made real to students, a rigid system of assignments and grading which does not reward high levels of achievement or effort, and emphasis upon the "judging" aspect of the teacher's role' (Boocock and Coleman, 1966: 235).

Perhaps the principal defect in formal schooling, as Coleman saw it, is the disparity, in time and space, between the school and the outside world: 'The child is being taught for a future whose needs have not yet impressed themselves upon him; hence he sees little need to focus his energies upon learning' (*ibid*.: 217). Coleman compared the ease with which most young children learn the language (sometimes languages) of their own society, and some adults learn a foreign language when they find themselves in situations where their native language is not understood or spoken, with the dismal results of most school foreign language training, where students may study a second language for many years without acquiring any real fluency. The problem is that most school assignments do not utilize the principle that people learn what they need to know in order to survive in their immediate environment. The solution to the problem is, as Dewey put it, to 'reproduce the conditions of real life' in the classroom (1916: 292).

The kind of simulation games envisioned by Coleman would serve this function, by surrounding the student with a simulated environment that is

> artificial for the present, but realistic for the future. His academic task is not to carry out assignments, but to 'survive' in this complex environment. In playing a management game, a child is forced to turn to economic texts, not to get a grade, but for economic survival in this complex environment. In a consumer game [s/he] must learn both economics and mathematics, as well as the necessity to defer gratification. More generally, a boy or girl will be able to play at those roles that he must play in earnest once he becomes an adult, and enters the complex modern society of adults. (Boocock and Coleman, 1966: 218)

A second effect has to do with the structure of rewards and punishments. In most high schools, 'grades are almost completely relative, ranking students relative to others in the class. Thus extra achievement by one student not only raises his position but lowers the position of others' (Coleman, 1965: 77). Given this zero–sum reward structure, a student's rational response is to discourage outstanding performance by anyone in the group. Moreover, the locus of rewards is external to the learning itself. Grades do not teach students anything (except perhaps how the school system operates). They are essentially a means of motivating students to learn things, and, as we have seen, they can have the opposite effect on many students. Thus the student's attention and efforts are focused not upon the learning activity itself, but upon the grades or other rewards she will receive after the learning activity is over. Games, on the other hand, are inherently appealing to most children — playing a game is in some sense its own reward. Thus they may be capable of inducing the kind of concentration and effort observed often on the athletic field but seldom in the classroom.

Unlike many educational critiques of the 1960s, Coleman's did not view competition per se as harmful. Rather he contrasted the pure individualistic reward system of the classroom, which pits student against student, with the combination of individual and collective rewards offered by interscholastic and intramural athletic contests, where spectacular individual performance is encouraged as long as it contributes to the success of the team as a whole. The skilled football or basketball player not only gets the prestige accorded an athletic star, but his skill can also bring rewards of victory to his teammates and, vicariously, to the whole student body (in some communities even adults can share in the satisfaction of having a winning team at 'their' high school). Even if academic games were played solely on the classroom level, students would have the experience of learning as a group enterprise. However, Coleman saw the greatest potential of games for affecting student motivation and performance: they were organized as intramural and interscholastic events, so that they could benefit from the larger audience, and some of the attendant publicity, that athletic contests command (Coleman, 1961a: 322; 1965: 86).[3]

The dual role of the teacher as both teacher and judge is a third structural defect of the school. Not only does the teacher have a monopoly on power in the classroom, but a teacher's judgment of a student can greatly affect that student's future. Such a relationship is more likely to produce hostility and alienation than initiative and creativity among students (Boocock and Coleman, 1966: 217–18; see also Coleman, 1961a: 324).

This kind of role relationship is not, however, inevitable. Again Coleman turns to the athletic program, where a coach can instruct without at the same time acting as disciplinarian, judge and jury. The athletic contest in 'self-judging, the outcome decides the winner, and a player knows that he has won or lost by his own actions'. Games are also self-disciplining; players know that they must obey the rules, not just to please a teacher or coach, but simply for the game to continue (Boocock and Coleman, 1966: 219).

How Games Teach

While Coleman believed that games with simulated environments were superior to traditional teaching methods in certain respects, he also pointed out that the process by which learning occurred — and by implication what was learned — was quite different in the two situations. Most school learning tasks involve the following sequence of steps:

1 reception of information through a symbolic medium, e.g., a lecture or book;
2 assimilating the information via a general principle;
3 particularizing, or inferring how the general principle applies in a particular instance, or what general principle applies to a particular instance;
4 acting, or using the information and general principles learned in previous steps (Coleman, 1973a: 2–3).

Coleman compares the above process, which he terms the 'information processing' mode of learning, with the learning process characteristic of simulation games, which he terms 'experiential' learning:

1   acting in a particular instance;
2   understanding the particular case, i.e., the effects or consequences of the action performed in Step 1;
3   generalizing, or attempting to understand, the general principle that applied to, or explains, Steps 1 and 2;
4   acting in a new situation or set of circumstances. (Coleman, 1973a: 3–5)

The final step in both processes involves action, but in experiential learning it comes at the beginning as well, and the actor draws upon that experience, even if in somewhat different circumstances. Information is generated through the sequence of steps themselves rather than through a symbolic medium. 'Understanding of the general principle does not imply, in this sequence, an ability to express the principle in a symbolic medium, i.e., the ability to "put it into words"'. It implies only the ability to see a connection between the actions and effects over a range of circumstances' (Coleman, 1973a: 4). Indeed, a typical observation of someone who has learned something through experience, real or vicarious, is that 'he can't verbalize it, but he can do it' (1973a: 7).

Coleman points out that each of the two learning processes has advantages and disadvantages. Information processing can be very efficient, reducing the time and effort needed to learn something new, while experiential learning 'may require actions over a range of circumstances to gain experience beyond the particular instance and suggest the general principle' (1973a: 4). However, only the information processing mode of learning depends heavily upon artificial or external motivation; since action comes only at the end of the learning process, 'there is no incentive for learning until the connection between the information and the action becomes clear — thus motivation must be extrinsically supplied, as, for example, by grades in school' (1973a: 5–7). Things learned through experience appear to be less easily forgotten than things learned through a symbolic medium, since 'the associations which embed it in memory are associations with concrete actions and events to which affect was attached, and are not merely associations with abstract symbols' (1973a: 9). The weakest link in the experiential learning process appears to lie in Step 3, in generalizing from the particular experience to a general principle applicable in other circumstances. Experience alone may not be sufficient to make students aware of what they have learned.

Unfortunately, this comparison of alternative learning processes was buried in one of the many reports issued by the Johns Hopkins Center for Social Organization of Schools during the 1970s, and it was not published elsewhere. Perhaps more important, most evaluation research, at Johns Hopkins and elsewhere, did not really test the areas of learning in which simulation games would be expected to excel. As we shall see, failure to do so has undoubtedly contributed to the rather inconclusive results of most research on the effects of games, adding to the difficulty of making a compelling case for their inclusion in the school curriculum.

Rationale 2: Simulation Games as Research Devices

Although most of the activities of the Hopkins Games Program focused on the design and testing of simulation games for educational purposes (probably because most of the financial support for the program came from agencies and organizations interested in the educational functions of games), Coleman was equally interested in their potential as mechanisms for the construction of social theory.[4] An important feature of games with simulated environments is that they model important aspects of social life while remaining distinct from it. On the one hand, 'certain social processes are explicitly mirrored in the structure and functioning of the game' to the extent that 'it induces, in a restricted and well-defined context, the same kinds of motivations and behaviour that occur in the broader contexts of life when we play for keeps' (Coleman, 1968b: 29). On the other hand, because they 'pluck out of social life generally (including economic, political, and business life) a circumscribed arena, and attempt to reconstruct the principal rules by which behaviour in this arena is governed and the principal rewards that it holds for the participants', games abstract and simplify the phenomena they simulate (Coleman, 1966c: 4; see also Coleman, 1968b: 30).[5]

Perhaps the most important parts of a game from the sociological perspective are the rules. Indeed, the rules of a game may be viewed as the designer's model or assumptions about the social phenomenon being studied.[6] The rules of a game specify those 'properties of individuals that are relevant to performance of the player's role', and play of a game generates data about the interactions among persons in social roles and between individuals and the systems of which they are members — i.e., about social organization (Coleman, 1975b: 389–90). Coleman identified five types of rules that, he argued, are characteristic both of games and of social organization generally: first, procedural rules, which specify how the game is put into play, the general order in which play proceeds, and how conflicts or impasses are to be resolved; second, behaviour constraints, parallel to real-life obligations, which specify what actions are prescribed, permitted and proscribed; third, rules specifying the players' goals and the means of attaining them; fourth, environmental response rules, which specify the probable responses of persons, groups and organizations not represented by players in the game; and fifth, police rules, which specify the consequences to players of breaking a game rule (Coleman, 1968b: 32–5).

While Coleman believed that the construction and observation of simulation games constituted a research methodology for sociology comparable to the physical scientist's or the psychologist's use of experiments, he noted:

> This methodology contrasts sharply to those that sociologists presently use as avenues toward social theory. In contrast to survey research and observations in natural settings, it depends on the creation of special environments, governed by rules that are designed precisely for the study of the particular form of organization. In contrast to experiments, with their experimental probe or stimulus and the consequent response, the principal element in game methodology is the construction of rules which can elicit a given form of social organization. The involvement of persons in a game is also different from the use of persons (or 'subjects') in psychological experiment. In a game, the goals of each player and the incentive to play must be generated by the rules of the game itself. The players are not passive subjects, but active participants or players. As in any social subsystem, the players in a game find their rewards in the game itself, while an experiment ordinarily merely uses the services of its subjects for a period of time. (1975b: 387)

Just as educational games teach by direct experience rather than by use of language or other symbolic media, so construction of simulated environments leads the sociologist toward formal theory by a different path:

rather than abstracting concepts and relations from the system of action observed in reality, the construction of a game abstracts instead a *behaviour process*, describing through the rules the conditions that will generate that *process*. An important virtue of this path is that one learns, by malfunctions of the process. As a consequence, extensive corrections to the theory can be made in making the game function, even before the conceptualization that follows play of the functioning game.[7] (Coleman, 1968b: 50–1)

Thus simulation games appear to be most useful in the intermediate stages of theory development — between 'verbal speculation and a formal abstract theory'. Ultimately, Coleman believed, it would be possible to develop a formal 'theory of rules', which would enable the researcher to 'create systematic variations in games, rather than merely ad hoc ones' (Coleman, 1975b: 393–4). Finally, Coleman shared with a number of game designers the view that simulated environments provided a medium for exploring innovative or hypothetical societal forms (Coleman, 1968b: 47).[8]

Development and Testing of Games with Simulated Environments

The first year of the Academic Games Program (1962–63) was devoted to the design and testing of a computer-based game simulating a national presidential campaign.[9] Students in two Baltimore high schools were divided at random into campaign teams of six or seven individuals, whose purpose was to see their candidate voted into office. At each stage of the campaign, team members had to decide what position their candidate would take on several issues, and how to spend the campaign fund allotted to the team. Each day's decisions were rushed back to the university, where they were fed into a computer programmed with the results of polls taken in Baltimore during a previous election. The next day students were given feedback in the form of computer output on the state of their candidate at that point in the campaign. The game ended on the fourth day when the computer calculated votes and winners were announced.

The first year's experience indicated that the game clearly created interest and involvement among the high school students who participated, but that the difficulties of using the computer (originally believed to be an important element in the game's appeal) far outweighed its advantages. Without more rapid feedback, students' exploration of the simulated environment and their learning from the game were severely limited. Thus the group turned to developing games with greatly simplified social and economic environments that did not require any elaborate equipment. During the next decade a variety of such games were designed, seven of which were eventually published.[10]

New games were tried out in meetings that eventually evolved into a weekly seminar of the project staff and other games enthusiasts. Games that survived the critical review of the seminar were then tested in schools and other educational organizations. A long-term relationship was developed with several Baltimore high schools, in one of which a paid panel of some twenty students met regularly to try out games in various states of development and to assist in their revision. As might be expected, the schools that were most likely to adopt simulation games were schools with a special mission that led them to experiment with a number of non-traditional teaching materials and methods, for example, the North Carolina Advancement School and Nova High School (in Fort Lauderdale, Florida). A particularly fruitful collaborative relationship was established with the national 4-H Clubs, which made simulation games an integral part of their programs and provided access to large numbers of young people at national and local conferences.

From the more constricted perspective of the 1990s it is difficult to conjure up the heady combination of enthusiasm and idealism, the commitment to social reform and the spirit of improvisation that fuelled a project like the Academic Games Program. For most of the project staff, the decision to disseminate games and gaming technology nationwide resulted in a first encounter with applied sociology — and with the world of lawyers, accountants and expense account lunches, designers, marketing experts and the mass media (during 1966–67, the Hopkins Games Program was the subject of two television specials, and articles in *Newsweek, Time, Saturday Review, The New Republic* and *Readers' Digest*). There was also a feeling of being part of a larger process of reform in schools and society in general. The Hopkins Games Program paralleled the development of other educational innovations, including programmed learning, team teaching, the open classroom and free schools. Many social scientists believed that American society was on the threshold of a major societal transformation, and that they would play an important role. Interviewed by *Newsweek* in 1966, Orville Brim, then president of the Russell Sage Foundation, predicted that social science knowledge would change the world 'as drastically as did nuclear weapons', and that in thirty years' time Americans would have the knowhow to produce the kind of individuals and societies that they chose (15 August 1966: 82). The same article included a discussion of the Hopkins Games Program. Naive as such predictions sound in the current era of diminished expectations, Brim's views were widely shared at the time, and they reflect the intellectual and moral background against which the Hopkins Games Program operated.

Evaluation of the Effects of Games with Simulated Environments

Although, as we have seen, Coleman was not the first to make claims for the value of games and simulations as educational and research devices, until the 1960s there was little testing of these claims. While most of the efforts of the first few years of the Hopkins Games Program went into developing new simulation games, even at that early stage efforts were made to field test each new game in a wide variety of settings and to gather data on its effectiveness, with at least some of the evaluations conduced by persons other than the game's designer.[11] After the establishment of the Center for Social Organization of Schools (CSOS) in 1967, this aspect of the program was greatly expanded via studies of the socialization effects of game playing (including the unsupervised sports and games children play in their free time, as well as instructional games, both simulation and non-simulation), the effectiveness of games as a method of teaching, and the feasibility of games as environments for social and behavioural research and theory building.[12] Following is a brief overview of major findings.

Student Motivation and Interest

Most, though not all, students who participated in games expressed enthusiasm about their experience. They described it as more interesting than what they usually did in class, and they especially liked the opportunities for interaction with their classmates. Some of the games appeared to have positive responses, and there was little evidence that the interest aroused by a particular game resulted in increased interest in other classroom activities or other courses. Teachers were generally enthusiastic about the games, but this finding is tempered by the fact that a high proportion of the games were tested in classes whose teachers had volunteered to participate in the project.

Cognitive Learning

Neither the Academic Games Program nor any comparable program has ever demonstrated consistent and/or significant advantages of simulation games over other teaching methods in the acquisition of factual knowledge, general principles or learning skills; most of the studies showed no difference or a statistically insignificant difference in favour of games. Perhaps the most positive conclusion that can be drawn from research on the effects of games on cognitive learning is that 'although there is little evidence that students learn more when taught by games than by conventional methods, there is no evidence that they learn *less*. . . . Hence games seem to be at least as effective as other modes of teaching, and further studies may show yet more significant results' (Greenblat, 1975b: 282).[13]

As noted already, a major weakness in this research is that it seldom takes account of the fundamental differences between gaming and other teaching methods (further evidenced by the near-zero-magnitude correlation of performance in games and in conventional classroom work). In a generally critical review of three books on educational gaming (including Boocock and Schild, 1968), Shirts points out that games cannot really be expected to compete successfully with 'traditional didactic methods' in the teaching of the sort of factual information that is measured by 'objective' tests, because 'books and lectures present carefully processed ideas and facts to the student in grade-A, enriched, homogenized form. The students, in turn, have been trained by many years of conditioning to accept this rich diet and to return it to the lecturer on demand' (1970: 82).

A generally overlooked finding of the CSOS research is that experience in a simulated environment tended to improve students' performance on tasks 'similar' to those practices in the game. This finding was not really followed up — for example, by research specifying the nature of this similarity and attempting to measure it more precisely. Thus an important opportunity to demonstrate the value of simulation games as learning devices may have been lost.

Attitudes

Another frequently expressed claim was that experience in a well designed simulated environment could have positive effects on players' attitudes, in particular, increasing empathy and understanding for the real-life persons whose roles they took in the game. The empirical evidence regarding this claim is mixed. For example, students playing Ghetto, a game simulating conditions in a low-income urban neighbourhood, were significantly more favourable toward the poor after playing the game, though there was no change in the players' factual knowledge, and a small decline in interest in the subject matter occurred. Similarly, election and legislative games generally produced some changes in political attitudes, in the direction of believing that congressmen should vote according to their constituents' preferences rather than their own convictions, agreeing that sending letters to congressmen is a waste of time, and accepting the practice of 'log-rolling' as a necessary element in the legislative process. They did not, however, increase students' interest in politics and the legislative process; in fact, the game experience tended to make players feel less positive toward politicians and less likely to want such an occupation for themselves. The prediction that experience in a simulated situation would produce feelings of efficacy or control with regard to the situation simulated, which would in turn lead to enhanced academic performance, was not clearly supported. Some studies reported increases on measures of efficacy, but others showed a reverse effect, and there was no evidence of linkage between feelings of control and learning factual information (Livingston *et al.*, 1973; see also Greenblat, 1975b).

Whatever they felt about and learned from a particular game, most players found the simulated environment realistic. A frequent postgame comment from players was that they had felt they really were in the role or situation simulated. Indeed, the verisimilitude of many of the simulated environments and the tendency of players to trust the experience raises concerns that do not apply to other, less convincing modes of instruction. As one analyst put it: 'the danger arises that games — most of which mirror political and economic institutions as they are — may encourage quiescent and conformist attitudes. One may question whether this spurs critical thinking, since success is premised on accepting the "simulated reality" as it is rather than on examining what is wrong with it' (Carlson, 1967: 83). Another critique warned that games simulating war, race relations and other controversial social issues may not teach what their designers intended:

> Most students report that the experience of planning, announcing, threatening, and conducting wars is great fun. . . . Such an experience could be viewed as a valuable learning technique; it could also be viewed as a means of habituating students to the idea of war. Unfortunately, the reward of conducting a simulated war is much greater than the pain suffered from the simulated consequences. [Similarly, there is] a real danger that games about the black community, which are generally written by persons from the suburbs and are based on a series of unfounded cliches about what it is like to be black, not only encourage stereotyping but create an attitude of condescension toward blacks. More importantly they can give students a false feeling that they actually know what it is like to be discriminated against or what it is like to be black. (Shirts, 1970: 82)

Both Carlson and Shirts argued that postgame discussions and other activities (in the case of a game like Ghetto, Shirts recommended extensive input from the black community) were needed to uncover and counteract the simplistic and stereotypic thinking that might be encouraged by the game experience. The game kits marketed by the Hopkins Games Program did include suggested readings, films and discussion questions, but it is not known whether and how these materials were actually used, and the CSOS research reports do not indicate any clear effects of postgame activities on learning or attitudes (Livingston *et al.*, 1973: 27).

Player Characteristics

It seems reasonable to assume that learning outcomes of simulation games would be affected by player characteristics, such as race, sex, prior attitudes and experiences, and academic ability. Differences in the play patterns of girls and boys are well documented (Lever, 1978; Paley, 1984; Elkin and Handel, 1989), and CSOS studies on children's unsupervised 'natural' games revealed gender and racial differences, both in choice of games and in relationships between types and frequency of game play and academic attitudes and achievement (Stoll, Inbar and Fennessey, 1968a, 1968b). However, the effects of these and other background characteristics on the outcomes of the games developed in the Academic Games Program have never been systematically examined.

It was also hypothesized that games with simulated environments would have special value for students who did not perform well in the conventional classroom setting, and would thereby narrow the gap between high- and low-achieving students. It has generally been concluded that the research evidence does not support this hypothesis, that like most other methods of instruction, simulation games are more effective with students of high academic ability than with students of lower ability. Closer inspection of the findings reveals, however, that the advantage of the former over the latter appeared to lie in their greater facility in articulating what they had learned from the game and in drawing analogies to the real world, not in their actual game performance. This finding exemplifies one of the major dilemmas in evaluating the effectiveness of simulation games as learning devices, which is that many players feel they have learned from the experience but cannot say just what it is they have learned (Greenblat, 1975b: 277).[14] This discrepancy is especially noticeable in the game behaviour of students who perform poorly on conventional classroom assignments and standard tests of achievement.

> One sees them making very shrewd moves — and making them repeatedly so as to show that they are not simply random or lucky moves. Such students are, however, seldom able to explain in words what they did. . . . Of course, the highest order of understanding means not only being able to act effectively but also being able to say what you are doing. What we wish to make clear here, though, is that these are two distinguishable kinds of performance, and for young people with academic backgrounds of deprivation and failure, the former alone may represent a real intellectual victory. (Boocock and Schild, 1968: 257)

Games as Research Environments

Although use of simulation games as research and theory-building devices was designated as one of the major concerns of the Hopkins Games Program, the output in this area was relatively sparse. Coleman's major application of simulation gaming to theory building was in a study of collective decision-making based upon construction and play of the set of simulations of various aspects of the legislative process comprising the Democracy game. His objective was to 'show the way in which rational self-interested actors can engage in collective decisions without engaging in a war of all

against all . . . [by identifying] structural conditions under which such collective decisions can be made without recourse to external power' (Coleman, 1975c: 406). His
theory was revised and extended through repeated plays of the game which revealed
additional phenomena that were not part of the original design of the game, for
example, exchange of votes or other favours between competing players (Coleman,
1968b: 50).

A few other CSOS projects utilized games as research environments. For example, one tested hypotheses derived from Erving Goffman's analysis of the effects of
role and structural constraints in the situations he termed 'game encounters', using
data generated by play of Generation Gap, a simulation of family interaction (Stoll,
1968); another utilized play of Ghetto as an environment for measuring and testing
hypotheses about the spread of emotional arousal in a group (Kidder, 1971). Although
the results in each case appeared to validate simulation games as environments for
theory testing and development, this remained the most underdeveloped area of the
program.[15]

Discussion

By the late 1960s many writers — including those who had reservations about certain
aspects of simulation gaming — believed that they would achieve (indeed, had already
achieved) an established status as modes of instruction and research. Concerning the
former, one review of the field concluded: 'The burgeoning market for games reflects
further movement away from two long-time staples of the classroom: unrealistic and
idealized textbook views of American life, and the old teacher-pupil relationship in
which the former hands down pronouncements to be regurgitated by the latter'
(Carlson, 1967: 83). Concerning the latter, the author of a major monograph on
simulation and gaming proclaimed that although before the mid-1960s a social
scientist speaking about this technology 'had to explain what he meant', simulation
gaming was now 'in', and 'likely to become a standard research technique' (Raser,
1969: viii, ix).

If games with simulated environments were ever truly 'in' — a debatable point
— that is clearly no longer the case. Granted, the number of published simulations
and games continues to grow, and professional associations and journals continue to
churn out papers and reports. Still it would be hard to argue that simulation gaming
is in the mainstream, educationally or sociologically. It has certainly not replaced textbooks or teachers; most schools do not use simulation games at all. Nor has gaming
become part of the standard sociological research repertoire, along with surveys or
controlled experiments. Few sociologists routinely use simulated environments to
study socialization and social organization, and Coleman himself does not seem to
have followed his earlier advice about how to construct social theory. There is, for
example, no mention of games or simulation in *Foundations of Social Theory* (1990),
his most comprehensive theoretical opus.

Why have games with simulated environments failed to fulfil their early promise?
First, with regard to educational applications, the intellectual atmosphere has shifted.
What brought an end to enthusiasm for educational innovations like simulation games
was not so much a lack of conclusive evidence about their effectiveness, but a change
of social climate. In American schools, periods in which experimentation flourishes

alternate with 'back to basics' periods in which maintaining discipline and academic standards are central. The straitened economic circumstances of the 1990s, as well as an abiding suspicion of any mode of instruction that involves fun, also explain the lack of interest in simulation games among most educators today.

Second, developing a workable simulation game, for educational or research purposes, is very hard work. This may seem obvious, but Raser, who believes that 'periodically in his career, every scholar should try to build a comprehensive simulation of the phenomenon in which he is interested', also reminds us why most scholars do not:

> It is too humiliating. He who wishes to build a simulation must formulate his assumptions explicitly, state the parameter values, and specify the relationships among variables in mathematical or other equally precise form. Unfortunately, most social science theories crumble before such a test, a painful consequence for the social scientist who has put his trust in impressive sounding but vague generalizations or in overwhelming piles of data connected by nothing more tangible than his own interest in them. (1969: 72)

Third, most evaluation research is still of poor quality, and some of Coleman's arguments have yet to receive an adequate test. As Greenblat has repeatedly pointed out, most claims about games are still based upon anecdotal rather than empirical evidence, and most evaluation research is seriously inadequate with regard to sampling, operationalizing and measuring concepts, and even defining the appropriate goal of a particular simulation experience (Greenblat, 1975b: 279; 1989: 272). The piles of data presented in the CSOS reports document, among other things, how difficult it is to say anything conclusive about any game, let alone about variations from one game to another, or about games in general.[16] Finally, while the need to develop tests that measure more accurately the kinds of learning that occur in games is widely acknowledged, few games designers have the inclination or the resources to produce new evaluation instruments as well.

Fourth, some important but implicit elements of Coleman's model have never been adequately explored. For example, almost all game designers agree that they learn a great deal about social process through their efforts to simulate it, regardless of what the players learn or do not learn from the game. One implication of this observation is that for students as well as for sociologists, the maximum benefits of simulation games will be obtained through taking an active role in creating them. Using games in this way is very much in line with Seymour Papert's work with children and computers. Dissatisfied with most so-called 'computer-assisted instruction', in which the computer teaches — or programs — the child, Papert envisioned turning the process around so that '*the child programs the computer* and in doing so, both acquires a sense of mastery over a piece of the most modern and powerful technology and establishes an intimate contact with some of the deepest ideas from science, from mathematics, and from the art of intellectual model building' (Papert, 1980: 5). The computer program LOGO was created partly so that elementary school children could write their own programs and thereby control their own learning environment. Just as Papert wanted to enable the child 'to speak the language of computers as naturally as she could speak her native language' (Turkle, 1984: 97), so taking Coleman's model of how games teach to its logical extreme would have students learn the language of simulation gaming in order to create their own social worlds, as well as experience social environments designed by others.

In the 1990s the field of simulation gaming might be described as in a stage of partial but not full eclipse. Still, the repertoire of simulation games and the body of knowledge regarding their construction and their effects continue to accumulate, and the more grandiose early claims are gradually being replaced by more realistic expectations. Sooner or later the current intellectual climate will yield to one more receptive to experimentation and reform. When that happens, the time may be ripe for a re-examination of Coleman's pioneering venture, and some new answers to the question he posed in the 1960s.

Acknowledgment

This chapter first appeared under the title 'Games with Simulated Environments: Educational Innovation and Research Technology', in A. Sørensen and S. Spilerman (eds), *Social Theory and Social Practice*, Westport, CT, Greenwood, 1993, pp. 143–61. It is reprinted with permission of Greenwood Publishing Group, Inc., Westport, CT.

Notes

1   For a fuller review of the theoretical literature on games and hypotheses concerning their role in socialization, see Inbar and Stoll (1968) and Boocock (1968).

2   The terms 'game', 'simulation' and 'simulation game' have been variously defined. For a systematic discussion of definitions and distinctions, see Greenblat (1975b) and Raser (1969), Ch. 1.

3   The emphasis upon competition and winning is that aspect of Coleman's rationale that received the most severe criticism, on the grounds that it 'may mislead the player as to the real objectives of learning. That is, the short-term pressures generated for popular success may lead the player to conclude that the ultimate virtue is simply a workable and, at the same time rather manipulative strategy. So while gaming may produce an academic hero, doubts remain whether the values underpinning his emergence will be any less superficial than those that have glorified the athlete' (Carlson, 1967: 83).

4   The fullest expositions of his ideas on this subject are in Coleman (1968b, 1975a, 1975b).

5   Another way Coleman expressed this similarity but separation between games and real life is via the concept of 'time out'. He argued that just as games make provision for breaks in the sequence of play, during which the rules do not apply, games themselves constitute a kind of time out from real life: 'Play and games "don't count" in the normal sequence of life activities, just as activity during time out in a game "doesn't count" in the game' (Coleman, 1975a: 384). To put it another way: 'the general category of activities that are described as games, these times out from life, can, because of their peculiar resemblance to life itself, be important elements in the construction of social theory' (1975a: 385).

6   Coleman notes that the games developed in the Academic Games Program have a special kinship to exchange theory, as exemplified in the work of Thibaut and Kelley, Homans, and Blau. This theoretical stance is individualistic, purposive and goal oriented. Each party to an exchange expects to gain something from it, although the 'currency' of an exchange is likely to be intangible, such as deference, acceptance, autonomy, aid and especially control over actions, rather than physical goods. Similarly, the Hopkins games take as their starting points the self-interested individual. In most, the goal is to maximize individual

satisfaction, and gains and losses — whether of votes, jobs, personal safety, or the right to choose one's own friends and dating partners — are calibrated into a 'satisfaction' scale by which success in the game is measured (Coleman, 1968b: 44–6).

7 Coleman credits von Neumann and Morgenstern (1953: 32) as the source of this view about the relation of games to social theory. A similar argument is made by Raser (1969: 30–7).

8 See also Greenblat (1975a), who suggests that games may be 'good vehicles for social planning or "future testing"', by virtue of allowing players to 'try out alternative forms of social organization, resource allocation, communication, etc., within a simulated context to "test" the efficacy of their ideas, the costs and rewards of various options, and the difficulties of going from the present structure to the desired future one' (1975a: 380).

9 The Academic Games Program was supported for the first six years (1962–68) by a pair of grants from the Carnegie Foundation. In 1966 it became one of the five programs of the Johns Hopkins Center for Social Organization of Schools, a research and development centre supported by the US National Institute of Education. At about the same time Coleman and three partners founded Academic Games Associates, a non-profit corporation for the licensing, production and marketing of Hopkins games, and royalties from the sale of games provided additional support for the program.

10 The seven games, originally published by Western Publishing Company, later sold to Bobbs-Merrill, were Democracy, a game simulating the legislative process, in which players negotiate to have bills passed or defeated in accordance with their own beliefs and their constituents' interests; Life Career, which simulates certain features of the labour market, the education market and the marriage market, in which players plot the life of an imaginary individual with specific personal qualities; Consumer, which simulates the problems and economics of instalment buying, and players take roles of credit and loan managers as well as consumers; Disaster, a kind of civil defence exercise, in which players in the roles of public officials and citizens of a simulated community hit by a hurricane, tornado, earthquake or other disaster must balance the demands of saving themselves and their families with general social responsibilities for helping the community respond to the emergency; Generation Gap, which simulates the interaction between a parent and an adolescent son or daughter with respect to certain issues on which they may have opposing attitudes; Ghetto, which simulates the pressures experienced by the urban poor, and the choices open to them as they seek to improve their life situation; and Economic System, in which players in the roles of workers, farmers and manufacturers attempt to maximize their welfare as they move through the stages of producing, marketing and consuming food and manufactured goods.

11 Results of this first phase of the Hopkins Games Program and of similar projects at other institutions are discussed in the two issues of *American Behavioral Scientist* devoted to papers on 'Simulation Games and Learning Behavior' (Coleman, Boocock and Schild, 1966a, 1966b), and the subsequent volume edited by Boocock and Schild (1968).

12 A full listing of thirty-seven CSOS reports relating to the Academic Games Program, produced between 1967 and 1972, and summaries of major findings can be found in Livingston (1972) and Livingston *et al.* (1973). Most of the reports are also available through the ERIC system.

13 Similar conclusions were reached in the reviews of research findings by Rosenfeld (1975) and Cherryholmes (1966).

14 The finding is also consistent with Coleman's distinction between experiential vs. information processing modes of learning, discussed on pages 135–6.

15 For discussion and examples of theory-building efforts at other research institutions, see Raser (1969), Chs 4 and 5.

16 On this point, see also Rosenfeld (1975).

11 Methodological Individualism and Collective Behaviour

Benjamin Zablocki

It's amazing to me that the problem of accounting for collective behaviour has still not been solved. The phenomenon of elementary collective behaviour (riots, panics, expressive crowds, hostile mobs, fads, religious frenzies, etc.) has been kicking around the fringes of sociological theory for a long time. It has always seemed to be one of the potentially easier problems to solve even by the exacting and convoluted standards of the social sciences where every solution seems always to be up for rhetorical grabs. It looked like sociology was on the brink of fully explaining the phenomenon thirty years ago when Roger Brown (1965) threw a startling but brilliant light upon the subject by approaching it for the first time from an internally consistent perspective of rational action theory and methodological individualism. Brown's approach, though necessarily sketchy, provided a theoretical framework within which a concerted program of research could be launched with the aim of solving the problem of collective behaviour. But then, as so often happens in our discipline, the problem was half solved and we lost interest in it and went on to other things.

A review of James Coleman's curriculum vitae shows that Coleman has been interested in the problem of collective behaviour from the very beginning of his career as a sociologist. Some of his very earliest publications (Coleman, 1957; Coleman and McPhee, 1958; Coleman, 1961c) represent early attempts to understand aspects of crowd behaviour and the closely related phenomenon of the diffusion of innovations. Although collective behaviour phenomena have never been at the forefront of Coleman's research agenda, it is fair to say that the problem has been on his back burner consistently throughout the years. The problem of collective behaviour lacks direct policy significance, except perhaps in 'very interesting times' and is thus important primarily for its potential contribution to basic theory rather than to applied social research. As Coleman has taken quite seriously his own admonition that sociological research be policy relevant, other more urgent issues have always seemed to direct his attention away from making a concerted attack on the problem of collective behaviour. For example, Coleman gives only scant attention to collective behaviour in his *The Mathematics of Collective Action* (1973), being concerned in that work with the mechanisms (such as voting) happening in more self-consciously deliberative collectivities.

It is not until recent years, along with a growing attention to theoretical fundamentals and theoretical synthesis, that Coleman has again trained his sights on a solution to the collective behaviour problem. He has indicated the importance he places on collective behaviour by the fact that he gives it two full chapters in his *Foundations* book (Coleman, 1990a: Chs 9, 33) as well as discussing it in passing throughout the rest of the book. For Coleman, collective behaviour is not important in and of itself but rather for its strategic significance in the development of a rational choice-based theory of social interaction. It seems clear to me that Coleman has provided a necessary and sufficient framework for the solution of the problem. In doing so, he has reaffirmed the fruitfulness of methodological individualism as an approach for studying collective behaviour. However, the insights offered by Coleman, unless complemented by a concerted program of research, cannot possibly provide a full solution. I will argue that Coleman's theoretical framework needs elaboration in at least two specific areas if it is to lead us all the way to a full understanding of collective behaviour. Coleman's approach needs a more workaday set of connections to empirical sociology as it is currently practised, and it also needs a slightly more elaborate model of the acting self than Coleman has thus far provided.

For a working definition of collective behaviour I will use Coleman's taxonomic classification of the phenomenon as a subtype of purposive behaviour. Coleman defines collective behaviour as a subtype of the more general class of purposive action in which transfer of rights or resources occurs. He argues that this general class of purposive action extends along three principal dimensions according to (1) whether or not there is an ongoing system of relations proximate in time and space; (2) whether or not there occur unilateral transfers of rights and resources; and (3) whether or not there exists a system of rights to control action. In terms of these dimensions he then defines collective behaviour as that subtype in which the answers to the first two questions are 'yes' and the answer to the third question is 'no' (Coleman, 1990a: 34ff).

Such a definition of collective behaviour has the advantage of deriving from a more general theory rather than from an evolving set of empirical generalizations. Incidentally, it illustrates the power of such theoretically-based definitions by helping us to understand some of the hitherto more puzzling examples of collective behaviour (e.g., saturnalia, potlatches) that arise precisely when there is a sudden, often institutionalized shift along the third dimension from a well developed system of rights to control actions to one in which that system of rights is abrogated, reversed or loses legitimacy.

Coleman goes on to note that collective behaviour phenomena observed at the system level have certain empirical indicators in common: 'They involve a number of people carrying out the same or similar actions at the same time. The behavior exhibited is transient or continually changing, not in an equilibrium state. There is some kind of dependency among the actions; individuals are not acting independently' (Coleman, 1990a: 198). He leaves open, as I shall here, the question of whether the class of phenomena defined typologically is in all cases identical to that defined in terms of the above empirical indicators.

Although the above indicators are no doubt valid to locate collective behaviour as a class of events, I question how useful they are to empirical sociologists attempting to locate, enumerate and catalogue such events in the field. Thus, anticipating an argument that I will make below, I want to offer a complementary set of defining characteristics for collective behaviour in terms of the kinds of data that are more typically available to empirical researchers. In these terms, an instance of collective behaviour may be said to have begun whenever a sudden change occurs in the distribution within a collectivity of the values placed by individuals on a specific resource or set of resources. This change consists of a simultaneous raising of the mean level of value given to this resource and a lowering of the standard deviation in the value given to this resource. In other words, all instances of collective behaviour, I conjecture, are characterized by a sudden and simultaneous inflation and increased homogeneity with regard to the value placed on some resource. The instance of collective behaviour would be said to be ended when these parameters return to something approximating their previous levels. The intensity of the experience can be measured in terms of the amount of change that occurred in these parameters. These indicators probably do not result in any significant variations from those suggested by Coleman in terms of criteria of inclusion or exclusion of specific events. However, I offer them here out of a conviction that theory, to be of use in solving empirical problems, has to go out and meet current practices in empirical research more than half way.

In this chapter I have attempted to do four things. First, I have sketched out a description of what I think a full solution to the collective behaviour problem would look like and why we have reasons to find such a solution as well as reasons to be optimistic about finding it. Second, I briefly review the status of our current knowledge (and ignorance) about collective behaviour. Third, I describe Coleman's approach to the problem and argue that it is the most promising approach for achieving this solution. Fourth, I delineate an agenda of both theoretical extensions to Coleman's model of the acting self and a set of guidelines for empirical research that are likely to lead to the desired solution.

What a Solution Might Look Like

What would a solution to the problem look like? It must involve the discovery of mechanisms and measurable parameters. It is important to recognize at the outset that we are looking for two distinct levels of explanation. First, we are looking for a general explanation of collective behaviour phenomena as a subclass of collective phenomena in which purposive action occurs. We wish to be able clearly and unambiguously to account for the occurrences of such phenomena. We wish to be able always to distinguish this type of phenomenon from other related types.

However, we also want our solution to provide us with insights that can be used for the explanation of surprising aspects of collective behaviour, the prediction of its incidence and natural course, and the control of its outcome. In other words, a solution to this problem would have to be empirically accurate as well as analytically precise. Moreover, such empirical accuracy should give us the power to explain, to predict and to control such phenomena.

Specifically, what are some of the things we would want a complete solution to allow us to explain? A very partial list would include the following: Why does collective behaviour happen at all? Why does it often produce zeal? Why does it sometimes engender regret? Why is it sometimes addictive? Why does it stop? Who are more likely to participate, i.e., who are the differentially vulnerable? Is there a critical mass? What are the characteristics of amplifiers?

A complete solution to the problem would give us power at the explanatory level, the predictive level and the control level. Most important from the perspective of its contribution to a theory of collective action would be the explanatory level: to be able to understand, at a level sufficient for accurate modelling and simulation, just what happens in a collective behaviour experience. This would include, at a minimum, the specification of two mechanisms, the micro to macro mechanism that initiates collective behaviour and the macro to micro mechanism that sustains it. Although both of these puzzles need further input from empirical research, the first is undoubtedly the easier of the two. Coleman (1990a: 912ff) has given us a good model of what such a specification might look like for the case of escape panics. The second specification of how collective behaviour is sustained (at least briefly) once initiated is more difficult and has so far proven refractory to this kind of precise modelling. Beyond the specification of these two mechanisms, a complete explanation of collective behaviour would also have to indicate who is susceptible for recruitment and under what conditions and what, if any, are the after-effects.

Although explanation at the mechanism level is important, predictivity is proof of the pudding. So many of the earlier explanations of collective behaviour have been revealed as rhetorical facades concealing a device devoid of empirically realistic mechanisms, that we need proof that the approach through rational choice theory and methodological individualism is not merely another one of these solutions that sounds good but really doesn't fit the complexities of the phenomenon. We should not, however, expect a level of prediction like that of classical mechanics or the theory of pure gases. Collective behaviour has more in common with a meteorological type phenomenon. Exact prediction may well not be possible because tiny individual level variation (random or near random) could be decisive at the systemic level. However, a great increase in assignment of probabilities or likelihoods is feasible.

Finally, we would like to have insight at the control level. This is a level of understanding sufficient not only to predict when a collective behaviour event is likely to happen but also to create such an event at will and to prevent and/or abort such events when they are deemed undesirable. An understanding of mechanisms at a level to allow at least the attempt at control can be a valuable tool in any effort to fine tune our understanding of a phenomenon. Of course, as much can be learned from instances of attempted control that fail to work as from those that succeed. Given a complete solution to the collective behaviour problem, our ability to explain, predict or control might still fall short in any particular situation, but these shortcomings should be traceable to specific areas of ignorance about the facts and/or inaccuracies of estimating specific parameters.

Is it realistic to expect to be able to solve this sociological problem (or any sociological problem) at this level of completeness? I would argue that we have reasons to be optimistic about being able to find such a complete solution coming from both literature and charismatic ethnomethodology. The fact that there seems to exist a high level of lay expertise in the prediction and control of collective behaviour suggests that we can do as well.

Literature abounds in dramatic examples of the control of collective behaviour. Although literary examples don't prove anything, they suggest, by their plausibility, that shared wisdom finds these examples reasonable. One example drawn from Tolstoy's *War and Peace* (1957: 854ff) is instructive here. As the Russians retreat before Napoleon's invasion in August 1812, the peasants on the estate of Prince Bolkonsky rebel immediately following the death of the old prince, an event which has created a vacuum of legitimate authority. This sets the stage for the dramatic rescue of the helpless Princess Maria by the young Nicholas Rostov. What is significant for us is how easily Nicholas is able, virtually single-handedly, to abort the peasant rebellion. He knows exactly what he is doing and he is successful; and nobody is surprised, least of all the peasants. Many other examples can be found, both in literature (e.g., Lee, 1960) and in real life (e.g., Shellow and Roemer, 1969) of a single, determined individual or agency successfully controlling the behaviour of an entire crowd.

Even literary situations where attempts to control crowd behaviour are not successful suggest a high level of potential predictivity of crowd behaviour. The results are bizarre but not surprising to us. For example, when Henry Fonda fails to face down the angry lynch mob in *The Oxbow Incident* (Trotti, 1943), probably the most intelligently nuanced and sociologically sophisticated instance of collective behaviour in the movie genre, nobody is surprised either. What is striking about this movie is how many of the subtle characteristics of the Coleman model of collective behaviour it conveys: the simultaneous production of free riders and zealots; the presence and mutual interdependence within the mob of leaders, followers, amplifiers and independents; the sluggishness of the mob as it lags in its reaction to feedback; the continuous mutual surveillance of the crowd members in attempting to determine whether to continue to cooperate or to defect. Even the sham 'majority vote' to determine whether to lynch or not to lynch, which is in many ways the dramatic climax of the film, indicates, through its very hypocrisy, the confidence which all of the participants (and the audience) had in their ability to determine precisely how this supposedly out-of-control social collectivity was going to act.

However, surprisingly little progress has been made toward a predictive model. As we have seen, folk wisdom suggests that this is a particularly amenable subject for predictive theory. Sociology ought at least to be able to predict what clever lay observers of the passing social scene can predict. So, when the old sheriff in innumerable cowboy movies says to his deputies, 'Boys, there's going to be trouble tonight. Just mark my words', this is a challenge to us as sociologists to do as well.

In fact, sociology does not do nearly as well. A good part of this deficiency can be blamed on the fact that sociology does not do well with slow or fast phenomena. There are obviously certain interesting empirically observed regularities associated with the rise and fall of civilizations, but these occur on too glacial a timescale for sociology to be good at incorporating them into our theories. The same is true at the other end of the timescale. Phenomena that happen too rapidly — riots, panics, fads, etc. (collective behaviour) — leave us blinking our eyes and scratching our heads. It's all over before the questionnaires can even be duplicated, let alone administered. However, another place where the fault can be laid is at the mismatch between theory and empirical research. During the 1950s and 1960s, when ethnographic descriptive research on collective behaviour and attempts to survey participants in the aftermath of collective behaviour were at their height, there was no guiding theory to which research results could be agglomerated. Now that there is such a theory, research has not kept pace; nor have theorists done as much as they could to build bridges to the world of the empirical researcher.

What Do We Know and Not Know about Collective Behaviour?

Brief Review of the Literature

Do we know more now than we knew when Roger Brown (1965) wrote? Not a whole lot. Interestingly, this identical complaint was made by Anselm Strauss (1947) when he surveyed the previous several decades of research on collective behaviour almost half a century ago. A great advance occurred when Brown's formulations exposed the superficiality of theories based upon irrational surrender to emotional contagion. Upon this rather simple foundation, Coleman has built a much solider structure with robust links to economic theories of markets and political theories of coalitions, voting and authority relations. But this structure, as of yet, is broader than it is tall, having successfully predicted so far only a few major empirical facts about collective behaviour.

What we do know more about now is a range of approaches that do not work. The successes of collective behaviour research have largely been in dispelling myths. The myth of the outside agitator, the myth of hysterical, paranoid or other emotional contagion, the myth of uniformity of participation — all have been exposed by careful research (McPhail and Wohlstein, 1983; Oliver, 1993).

The classic solutions of Freud (1971) and Le Bon (1952) are theoretical dead-ends. They do not satisfy the minimum criterion of disprovability. Their hypotheses are not testable by methods available to the social scientist. However, the mechanisms that they posit in terms of amplification of affect and transfer of affect are worth keeping in mind. It is still an open question as to whether affect needs to be incorporated into the model in order to achieve predictivity.

Smelser's (1962) value-added approach to collective behaviour is an improvement in this respect in that it offers empirically testable hypotheses. In fact, Quarantelli and Hundley (1969) were able to provide what was perhaps the first thorough testing of a comprehensive theory of collective behaviour using the results of a careful analysis of an actual collective behaviour situation, partially disconfirming Smelser's hypotheses. However, regardless of whether the Smelser hypotheses turn out to be confirmed, they constitute a dead-end from the point of view of our search for a solution to the problem in that they do not attempt to explain the phenomenon at the level of mechanisms. In this sense the Smelser theory may be seen as merely descriptive, although the description is highly structured and comes out of a well developed theoretical rationale. But without any hope of discovering mechanisms, the potential results of such theories are severely limited. The same can be said for the simple rational actor solutions (e.g., Berk, 1974) that have assumed that the explanations could be found at the network level.

The symbolic interactionist perspective, best typified by Blumer (1953) and later elaborated by many others, most notably Goffman (1974), does attempt to specify mechanisms but lacks rigorous criteria of testability. Although we do not need to look in this direction for leadership in model building, it would be good if there were more mutual influence between the symbolic interactionists and the rational choice theorists. Rather than being competing perspectives, they are more accurately to be viewed as looking at different parts of the elephant. Since we ultimately want some degree of insight into the whole elephant, the formulations of this school, and most particularly Erving Goffman (1974), are not to be dismissed.

Finally, the resource mobilization perspective (Zald and McCarthy, 1979) and Lofland's (1985) interesting synthesis of interactionist and resource mobilization deserve mention here. If there is any real rival to the rational choice perspective in the field of collective behaviour today, it must be located here. This somewhat eclectic perspective is deficient in the deductive rigour of its theoretical structure but so far has been much richer in its ability to offer convincing middle range explanations of a wide range of collective behaviour phenomena.

Known Empirical Properties

In the 1950s and 1960s much of the theoretical work on collective behaviour was devoted to cataloguing recognizable empirical types and certain stages (or phases) of collective behaviour. This work was fruitful, and a broad level of consensus exists today on both of these descriptive issues. These are briefly summarized as follows.

The major types of collective behaviour are generally identified around some combination of the goal or organizing principle of the collectivity and the dominant display of emotion made by the collectivity. In these terms, the major types of collective behaviour are usually thought to be the panic, the hostile crowd and the craze (Lofland, 1985), each of which gives rise to two or more subtypes. The panic is further broken down by Coleman (1990a) into the bank panic (single stage) and the escape panic (sequential). Recently, attention has also been focused on an entity known as the moral panic (Goode and Nachman, 1994). However, this, despite its name, is better categorized as a kind of fad or craze. The hostile crowd is broken down into the following types: riot, protest demonstration, mob. Finally, the craze is broken down into the celebratory demonstration, the fad and the fashion. A solution to the collective behaviour problem should yield a set of similar mechanisms yielding results of explanation, prediction and control for all these diverse phenomena.

The phases of a collective behaviour experience will obviously be different for different types of collective behaviour. Nevertheless, certain general sequential phases can be identified for which the specific types offer more or less close approximations. These are the following: milling, collective focus, queuing, collective locomotion and collective vocalization (McPhail and Wohlstein, 1983). The milling stage is particularly important for our theoretical understanding of mechanisms. This is so because it is likely that it is in this stage that the individual makes his first and sometimes his only decision as to whether or not to participate.

In addition to descriptive knowledge about types and stages, there has also been an accumulation of certain interesting and non-obvious properties of collective behaviour. One of them is its limnality (Turner, 1969), the sudden and temporary collapse of all institutionalized systems of inequality. Another is its capacity for creating zeal, defined by Coleman (1988c: 53) as 'an excess of incentive to contribute to the common cause'. I group these apparently unrelated phenomena together here because both are examples of new resources created by the collective behaviour process, and both therefore have an effect upon exit costs. An unwillingness to give up the limnal state and an unwillingness to give up the new-found zealousness in oneself and others help to explain the often considerable momentum attained in some instances of collective behaviour.

Finally, we know something about the after-effects of collective behaviour, mainly that these are weak to non-existent (McPhail and Wohlstein, 1983) even in cases such as mass religious conversions where longer-term effects might be expected. The lack of enduring structural consequences of collective behaviour cuts two ways. On the one hand, it explains the tendency to relegate these phenomena to the fringes of a policy oriented sociology. On the other, it offers the social theorist an opportunity to account for a sociological phenomenon which is both relatively simple and relatively self-contained.

Some Things We Don't Know about Collective Behaviour

There is much more, of course, that we still do not understand about collective behaviour. I do not have the space here to attempt a systematic accounting of this ignorance. Instead I shall mention briefly four specific holes in our knowledge that, in my opinion, offer high likelihoods of short-term strategic payoff.

First on the list is the triggering mechanism. Particularly at the predictive level we know next to nothing about this. There is reason to suspect that we may never approach a deterministic theory of the triggering mechanisms for collective behaviour. Many researchers (e.g., Granovetter, 1978; Lichbach, 1994) have suggested the existence of a rather broad grey area in which small unpredictable random shocks to the system may determine whether or not an instance of collective behaviour erupts. However, note also Oliver's (1993) critique of such deductions made from Granovetter's threshold theory. My own hunch is that we should not be so quick to give up on the possibility of being able to predict outbreaks of collective behaviour. Even an ultimate failure to do this may teach us more about the phenomenon than if we did not try.

Second, we know very little about the feedback loop involved in sustaining collective behaviour when it occurs. In other words, we know more about the micro to macro inference than the macro to micro inference. One aspect of macro to micro feedback that cries out for attention is the question of the operation of ephemeral and sui generis authority structures in collective behaviour. In the past our tendency has either been to ignore the existence of authority in collective behaviour or to use it to explain away the phenomenon. However, the work of Michael Hechter (1987) has suggested that we look for (possibly ephemeral) systems of authority and social control underlying any development of group solidarity. To the extent that we observe solidarity in collective behaviour, we have reason to suspect that someone or something is manipulating exit costs. It is probable that this observation and subsequent misinterpretation of transient but powerful authority structures quickly arising and disappearing within collective behaviour situations have caused portions of the mass media to overemphasize consistently the role of 'outside agitators' in trying to explain the eruption of panics or demonstrations in hitherto quiet communities.

Third, we are relatively ignorant about the role that relational network ties play in collective behaviour. This is an area rich in conjecture but poor in research findings. Although the potential payoff is great here, the technical problems of mapping relational networks in such rapidly shifting collective situations are staggering. Granovetter (1978) has shown the enormous payoff to be gained from considering even the most rudimentary aspects of network structure. We have reason to suspect that structural holes (Burt, 1992; White, 1992) tend to disappear during collective behaviour and that this is one of the major sources of the resulting shift from aggregate to collective action. But we don't know how this occurs, whether it always occurs to the same degree, and whether it is a necessary characteristic of collective behaviour.

Finally, we know that regret and addiction are two possible outcomes of the collective behaviour experience for individuals. But we know nothing about the personal or the collective behaviour characteristics that make specific individuals susceptible to one or the other of these consequences. This area of ignorance is particularly accessible to remedy because it does not require the fast footwork that direct observation of collective behaviour often does. What are needed here are retrospective interviews with participants in collective behaviour experiences investigating, as soon after the fact as possible, feelings about participation and possible plans for future participation.

The Value of Coleman's Approach to the Problem

'Theoretical conjecture is usually a matter of choosing the least worst among a set of competing possibilities' (Abell, 1992: 189). This is a point that Coleman takes so for granted that I think he sometimes fails to stress it enough to silence some of his critics. A good part of the heuristic value of attempting to model collective behaviour as a set of interactions among optimizing individuals is that it allows for a possibility of identifying a residue that is not explainable in this way.

Collective behaviour involves a clear case of both micro to macro and macro to micro effects operating. All explanations of the phenomenon have rested on the assumption that individuals somehow get caught up in a collectivity, this collectivity sustains itself for a period of time, and then spews the individuals back out, usually little the worse for wear. McPhail (1991) has shown that there are rarely enduring effects of participation in collective behaviour events. Even in revival meetings which are designed more than other collective behaviour experiences to change the sub-sequent course of life, little difference is found between the subsequent lives of those who rush up to be saved and those who do not.

Although Coleman gives less attention to it in his models, the macro to micro effect is also quite important to the understanding of collective behaviour. Not only Coleman but all recent analysts have used feedback imagery to account for the fact that, at some point, the group seems to take on a life of its own. Collective behaviour involves a clear case of micro to macro and macro to micro mechanisms. Although it is possible to quarrel with some of the particulars of Coleman's arguments, it is not possible to deny the need to understand the mechanisms happening (very quickly) at both of these levels. Of these, the micro to macro mechanism is better understood, although the macro to micro mechanism is the more difficult and mysterious.

Collective behaviour is a particularly good problem for the Coleman paradigm to cut its empirical teeth on. To the extent that it can succeed where other paradigms have failed, to explain, predict and control collective behaviour events, it will have clearly demonstrated its usefulness as a tool for understanding more complex and stable social phenomena. Coleman lists the following eleven readily testable hypotheses about collective behaviour (Coleman, 1990a: 239f):

1 In a physical escape panic the greater the focus of attention on one or a few persons (that is, the greater the heterogeneity with respect to focus of attention), the less likely a panic will occur.
2 In a bank panic (single stage of action) there should be no such effect.
3 In a hostile crowd the greater the focus of attention on one or a few persons, then the more likely it is that the crowd will take some hostile or expressive action, and the more organized that action will be.
4 In a hostile crowd the greater the heterogeneity among individuals with respect to their normative constraints (holding constant the average degree of normative constraint and the commonality of interests), the more likely it is that the crowd will break out into hostile or expressive collective action.
5 Training persons to exit in an orderly fashion and to direct attention to a designated leader will be valuable for preventing escape panics (sequence of actions) but not bank panics (single stage of action).
6 In an escape panic the more prominent individual's position in the crowd

(the greater the attention directed to him), the more likely he will be to exhibit orderly exit behaviour.

7 The larger a crowd is in absolute numbers, the more likely it is to break out into hostile or expressive collective action.

8 The larger a crowd is in absolute numbers, the greater is the likelihood that a panic will occur in a physical escape situation.

9 Such a relation will not hold for bank panics.

10 Physical escape panics (sequence of actions) should show greater variability in outcome when circumstances are similar than is true for bank panics (single action).

11 Contagious beliefs should arise at times of extensive social change, when rights of control have been withdrawn from institutions that have power.

What is to be noted about all of these propositions is that they are all deductions from a theory that makes surprisingly few assumptions about the individual actor and none at all about the pre-existing social structure. This is a win–win situation assuming that enough research is carried out to test these propositions. Each hypothesis that is confirmed increases our confidence in the underlying theory. Each hypothesis that is disconfirmed points us to an area of the theory that needs elaboration or modification. Either way, our knowledge of the subject benefits. We thus find ourselves in a situation which is commonplace in the more established sciences but only rarely found as yet in sociology in which good research cannot help but drive knowledge forward.

Methodological Individualism

The genius of Coleman's achievement in bringing us to such an enviable situation is to be found not so much in the intricate complexity of his formulations but in their simplicity. Steering a middle course between the black hole of psychological reductionism on the one hand and what Michael Hechter (1987) calls normativism and structuralism on the other, Coleman puts all of his theoretical money on the individual actor who is conceptualized as little more than a black box for revealed preference. The concept of methodological individualism, which is the heart of this radically simplifying strategy, is based upon the obvious but powerful premise that it is only individuals who ultimately take action. In Abell's pungent words: 'Things happen in the social world because individuals do and do not do things, and they are the only things that do or do not do things. All statements that attribute "doing" to other things can, in principle if not in practice, be translated without loss into statements about individuals doing things' (1992: 191).

Methodological individualism is defined in terms of: (1) all social phenomena related to individual level mechanisms and (2) the individual defined in a minimally reductionist way. It is important to note that methodological individualism is not psychological reductionism, nor does it imply reductionism in any way. Quite the contrary, methodological individualism can fairly be called psychologically minimalist in that it starts with an absurdly rudimentary model of the acting self and then borrows from psychology only the barest minimum required for fitting this model to observed social reality.

Methodological individualism does not imply rationality at the actor level but is generally associated with that assumption. In terms of a mechanical model, for illustrative purposes, the black box of methodological individualism now becomes a black box with an attached gauge with an ordinal scale from which preferences can be read off and the optimal preference selected as a behavioural choice. Implicit in this theory's interest in rational action rather than merely rational preference is, of course, the requirement that a motor be connected to the box so that preferences may be acted upon. Implicit in Coleman's premise that control over one's own actions may be transferred to others is the requirement that there be a coupler/decoupler allowing this motor to be disconnected from one's own black box and connected to the box of others. However, control over the coupler/decoupler remains inalienable in Coleman's theoretical framework. All of Coleman's propositions about purposive action both individual and collective stem from assumed properties of this simple four-component model of the acting self.

Methodological individualism has been criticized for leaving out the importance of norms and thus of socialization; but this misses the point. Methodological individualism does not deny the importance of norms in shaping behaviour. Rather it places its bets on the possibility of deriving those norms from micro to macro and macro to micro processes. Indeed, Coleman (1973c, 1990a) has been successful in showing how norms can arise from the interactions of discrete individuals each acting rationally in his or her own interest. However, neither Coleman nor any other rational action theorist has been notoriously successful, thus far, in being able to derive the specific norms that we observe even in fairly simple large collectivities from assumptions about individual interactions. This has prompted Coleman, among others, to conjecture that the basic four component model of the acting self discussed above may need to be extended.

Coleman has briefly explored, in the final chapter of *Foundations* (1990a), the idea of extending the simple model of the acting self by opening the black box of preference formation and modelling within it an internal constitution with properties similar to those that Coleman has located at the corporate actor level. Coleman's ideas for extending the basic model of the self by reasoning by analogy from the level of corporate actors does not seem to be the best way to accomplish this. Instead, let me suggest that we follow Coleman's earlier lead of psychological minimalism and add to the model of the acting self only those elements necessary to allow it to function in the solution of a sociological problem. For example, if the primitive Coleman self is inadequate to deal with the macro to micro mechanism in collective behaviour, an interesting question would be: what are the minimum extensions that have to be made to the primitive Coleman self to enable us to involve it in empirically testable models of macro to micro feedback in collective behaviour?

Our knowledge of positive feedback systems in general should suggest that no individual (as a system component) can continually adjust without buffers to changes in the intensity of feedback from the system. This suggests an extension of the self in which we posit a thermostatic device to regulate (lag) response to the system. McPhail's (1991) concept of a reference signal emitted by the collectivity as a result of the actions of a critical mass of individuals, to which these individuals then respond, is relevant here. Transitory norms (precisely the kind we find in collective behaviour phenomena) then can be located in the thermostat. Or, to paraphrase T.S. Eliot, between the feedback and the reaction falls the norm. The twin concepts of calibration and feedback

(Bateson and Bateson, 1987) might be powerful in accounting for the very rapid shifts that seem to occur in collective behaviour between individual level strategic assessment and collective participation. It is extremely doubtful if such a model could be of use in accounting for more enduring norms, let alone whole patterns of culture. But this simple extension of the Coleman acting self may be all that is needed to model fully the more primitive phenomenon of collective behaviour. It might help to account for one puzzling but frequently observed property of collective behaviour, sluggishness of response.

The Outline of a Research Agenda

If rational choice theory is to become something more than another 'grand theory' of sociology, it has to learn to meet empirical sociology more than half way. This is easier said than done. To take an example from another field within sociology, despite Goffman's (1974) efforts to delineate a method of frame analysis as a link to empirical research, his sociological paradigm has evolved in a way that is theory rich but research poor. If the same thing is not to happen to rational action theory, it will have to do a better job of building bridges to the community of empirical research.

The current structure of sociology as a science in some ways works against the ability of theory to guide research. If journals were organized around theoretical paradigms rather than methodological predilections, there would be more incentive for reports of research to take theoretical stands. As it is, the rational approach for a report writer seeking acceptance from a major journal is currently to hedge theoretical bets and appeal to all major competing paradigms.

Careful investigation of instances of collective behaviour as they arise is labour intensive and requires quick reaction time. It has tended, therefore, not to be a popular area of investigation. Each practitioner, moreover, has tended to fashion his or her own tools. The kind of careful painstaking research done by Lofland (1985) or Quarantelli and Hundley (1969) or Heirich (1971) is not done nearly as often today as would be needed to make significant headway into the problem. Let me sketch briefly here five areas in which better bridges can be built between rational action theory and empirical research in their common goal of solving the problem of collective behaviour. These are: first, the development of hypotheses regarding role differentiation; second, the development of hypotheses regarding temporal and spatial variations in the occurrence and form of collective behaviour; third, the development of hypotheses regarding double crowds; fourth, the sensitizing of the theorists to the beliefs about collective behaviour of lay experts in the society; and, fifth, the development of technical tools that will make the study of collective behaviour less intractable. I will touch briefly on each of these areas.

Empirical research is good at finding out things, but often the things that it finds out are not relevant to the hypotheses deduced from theory. This seems very much to be the case with respect to collective behaviour. The eleven hypotheses that Coleman deduced, quoted above, are interesting and important, but they do not for the most part involve the kind of data that survey researchers or ethnographers are used to collecting. It would be quite reasonable to respond that survey researchers and ethnographers should learn to collect different kinds of data. This is true, but it ignores the fact that there is a pre-existing culture of empirical research with powerful enduring norms of its own, and these norms do not always rank service to theory as the highest priority. Coleman has recognized the need of sociological theory to be constantly involved in building bridges of mutual understanding and reciprocity with the world of social policy if theory is to be both supported and relevant. If theory is to avoid the fate of becoming grand theory, there is a parallel need with regard to the world of empirical research. Of course, I hope it goes without saying that such accommodation should be mutual and that researchers need to do more to frame their investigations in ways that will be useful to theory builders.

One thing that researchers are good at is identifying role differentiation. To the extent that a theory of collective behaviour generates hypotheses that call for comparing and contrasting one type of person with another, they have generated problems that researchers can sink their teeth into. One such problem would involve survey research in the task of identifying the observable characteristics of leaders, followers, amplifiers and independents in collectivities engaging in collective behaviour. How do these differ from one another? Is it personal characteristics or structural position that determine role? Another aspect of role differentiation that could be a fruitful meeting ground between the interests of theory and the interests of researchers is the development of reliable and valid techniques for observing zealous and free riding behaviour in rapidly moving crowd situations. Aspects of role differentiation that do not themselves arise from theory could also be useful to study. For example, little has been done within the field of collective behaviour to distinguish differences between the ways men participate from the ways women participate.

Second, systematic variations in the form, duration, incidence and virulence of collective behaviour in historical time and geographical space are greatly in need of investigation. Thanks to a rich body of work by historians (Rudé, 1964) and by historical sociologists (Tilly, 1978), we know a lot more about historical variations than we do about contemporary differences across cultures. However, careful recent work in Eastern Europe (Oberschall, 1994) and in China (Zhou, 1993), to cite just two of many examples, helps to build up our catalogue of events by culture. Unfortunately, differences in data presentation and analysis still impede the comparison of events across cultures, even among studies based upon rational action theory. Historical and cross-cultural standardization in reporting methods would help a great deal to make this rapidly accumulating mass of material more useful.

A third area involves Canetti's (1966) concept of the double crowd, defined as two temporally and spatially proximate crowds of roughly equal size and power that feed off each other. Although at first sight this seems a more complex phenomenon than the single crowd, the observation of competing crowds of about equal power (e.g., fights at sports events) could simplify our understanding and estimation of some of the key parameters in collective behaviour. This would be particularly true of the poorly understood process of feedback. Whenever possible, the rare case of male versus female crowds would be particularly useful to observe. In any case, sensitizing researchers in the sociology of sports to the perspective of collective behaviour could be of use.

Researchers are also good at asking people their opinions in great depth. Society is full of collective behaviour experts and we can learn from their opinions. We can learn much from the strategies developed ethnomethodologically by collective behaviour experts in the society. Among these are experts in the marketing of fads and fashions, religious experts in recruitment and control mechanisms (Zablocki, 1980a,

1993), law enforcement experts in crowd control, officers of fiduciary institutions charged with maintaining trust at high levels, and charismatic leaders in all situations (Frank, 1973; Zablocki, 1980b).

Finally, work is needed on the development of ethnographic tools for improving systematic observation of collective behaviour. Very few graduate departments of sociology offer opportunities to learn techniques of observation from helicopters, for example, although this is frequently the best and sometimes the only way to observe a rapidly developing instance of collective behaviour. Perhaps more practically speaking, part of the training of students in sociology should include techniques for making crude estimates of the size of collectivities. In general, a whole range of skills involving rapid response to quickly developing social situations falls completely outside the scope of research methods as they are currently taught to sociological researchers.

Conclusions

I have argued that collective behaviour is a solvable problem within sociology, that the Coleman paradigm offers a plausible strategy for solving it, and that the solution to this problem is well worth the effort that would be needed in terms of its potential payoff. The solution to the problem warrants high priority and a concerted effort not only, or even primarily, because of the value of understanding collective behaviour but mainly because of the value that such a success could have for confirming the efficacy of rational choice theory and methodological individualism as the foundations of a general theory of action in the social sciences.

I have noted that two obstacles to the solution have to do with the need for further bridge building to empirical research as it is currently practised and the need for extensions to the model of the acting self sufficient for the explanation of feedback loops. With regard to the former, rational choice theory, if it is to escape the fate of becoming a new 'grand theory' of sociology, is probably going to have to do more to meet the ethnographers, the ethnomethodologists and the survey researchers on their own terms. Rational choice theory can offer two things in this regard: first, an agenda of new techniques and instruments for standardizing the collecting of data that are capable of confirming or disconfirming the hypotheses generated by the theory; and, second, a greater effort to generate hypotheses in terms of parameters that can be estimated by research, given the limitations of its current methodology.

With regard to extensions to the model of the self, I have pointed to the possibility of incorporating mechanisms of feedback delay into Coleman's elementary model of the acting self. Another possibility, of course, is to extend the model along the lines that Coleman himself suggests in the final chapter of *Foundations of Social Theory* (1990), opening up the black box of motivation at the core of the self via the mechanism of internal constitutions. Of these two, the mechanism of feedback delay is the more parsimonious, whereas the mechanism of internal constitutions is the more powerful. My hunch is that something like internal constitutions may well be needed for understanding more complex institutional social action but that feedback delay may be adequate to allow for the modelling of the more transient events that we call collective behaviour.

12   Mobility Measurement Revisited

David J. Bartholomew

Sociology and Stochastic Processes

The term 'stochastic process' entered the statistical vocabulary in the 1950s, although the study of such processes goes back to the origins of probability theory. Feller's *Probability Theory and Its Applications, Vol. 1* appeared in 1950 and was both a definitive landmark and a stimulus to much of what followed. The applications of the title were of a rather academic kind, but epidemiology and biology generally soon provided a rich field for applied work. Human populations also exhibit the essential characteristics of a stochastic process in that their social structure develops over time in an uncertain manner. In retrospect, at least, it is obvious that there was a great opportunity to apply the newly developed theory to sociology.

James Coleman was one of the first to recognize this and his two books, *Models of Change and Response Uncertainty* (1964a) and *Introduction to Mathematical Sociology* (1964b), include much of his early thinking. Changes of state over time characterize many social processes; attitudes and preferences provide one example, and occupational and social mobility another. Both received Coleman's attention and in both cases he anticipated much later developments by using continuous time versions of the Markov process. It is pertinent to remark in passing that Coleman recognized that failures in fitting models can often be just as illuminating as successes.

Most of these early developments were directed away from another longstanding and fundamental concern of quantitative sociology, namely measurement. Without measurement of some kind, mathematical analysis is hardly possible, and so, as one would have expected, this matter is prominent in the first two chapters of the *Introduction to Mathematical Sociology*. The emphasis there is on the nature of the measurement process itself, although it is significant that the measurement of social prestige, which is used as an example, is shown to need theoretical underpinning. Models, however, were seen primarily as tools for understanding how social variables were related to one another and to give insight into the dynamics of systems.

Once stochastic modelling had taken root in social science it soon became evident that it could throw light on some of the more recalcitrant problems of social measurement. As early as 1955 Prais (1955) had used results from the theory of discrete Markov chains to construct measures of social mobility. His point of departure on the empirical side was Glass and Hall's social mobility table for England and Wales published in Glass (1954). That began a model-based approach to measurement culminating in Brummelle and Gerchak (1982), and it is this line which we trace in the present chapter. There is a second and major branch of research deriving from the same root exemplified by Goldthorpe (1987) and Erikson and Goldthorpe (1992). This adopts a more empirical approach to the study of patterns of social mobility.

These two branches have remained almost entirely separate and a rapprochement is perhaps now due.

The measurement of social and occupational mobility provides a good case study for showing how the obscurities which so often cloud discussion of such matters can be clarified by recognizing that something like mobility is a property of a stochastic process. It is a topic which has attracted interest over a long period, and a position has now been reached where lessons can be learnt which have relevance beyond this particular application. In the present context it also establishes a link with another of James Coleman's interests in equality. Mobility is the process by which social structures are changed, and although he has not, so far as I am aware, explored this connection himself, it illustrates the rich interconnections of his interests.

Social mobility is concerned with the movement of individuals or families between social classes. Since class is usually defined in terms of occupation, it may equally be described as occupational mobility. However, these two terms are often used to make another important distinction. This is between inter- and intragenerational mobility. Individuals may change their job, and hence their occupational class, several times during a working lifetime, and this may happen at any time. This is intragenerational mobility and the timescale of interest is usually relatively short. Intergenerational mobility takes a longer view and incorporates a natural unit of time — the generation. In both cases measures of mobility are needed to make comparisons either between societies at the same time or for the same society across time. A measure of mobility therefore needs to represent some quantifiable characteristic of a society which persists, though in varying degrees, in space and time.

But what is mobility? The complex flux of movement across class boundaries seems to defy summarization in a single number. Yet if we were to admit a vector-valued measure, the possibility of simple comparison would be lost and the whole point of the exercise nullified. It is here that a model comes to our aid. If we can establish that the essentials of the process are adequately captured by a Markov model, say, then the parameters of that model provide a complete description of the system. By identifying what role each of the parameters plays we can hope to see which parameter, or combination of them, best embodies the concept of mobility.

Mobility Tables

Most empirical mobility tables, whether inter- or intragenerational, relate to transitions over a fixed interval of time. In the case of intergenerational mobility this will be the generation, but otherwise it will be some arbitrary period, often determined by extraneous circumstances. We adopt the notation set out in Table 12.1. The rows refer to the beginning of the interval and the cell frequencies in any row show how the members of that class are distributed across the classes at the end of the time interval. The row totals are the numbers in the classes at the beginning and the column totals are the numbers at the end.

Although much can be learnt about the pattern of mobility by inspecting the frequencies, the task is simplified by expressing the frequencies in terms of proportions. Dividing the row and column totals by n gives us what we shall call the *class structure*, and a comparison of the row and column structure will reveal whether the system is in a steady state. The cell frequencies may be treated in two ways. If we

Table 12.1. Transition Frequencies

I\II	1	2	3		k	Totals
1	n_{11}	n_{12}	n_{13}	....	n_{1k}	$n_{1.}$
2	n_{21}	n_{22}	n_{23}	....	n_{2k}	$n_{2.}$
3	n_{31}	n_{32}	n_{33}	....	n_{3k}	$n_{3.}$
.	.	.	.		.	.
.	.	.	.		.	.
.	.	.	.		.	.
.	.	.	.		.	.
k	n_{k1}	n_{k2}	n_{k3}	....	n_{kk}	$n_{k.}$
Totals	$n_{.1}$	$n_{.2}$	$n_{.3}$	....	$n_{.k}$	n

divide the elements in a row by the row total, the resulting vector shows what proportions of the members of a class move to other classes. These are transition proportions and they play a major part in mobility studies. The second way of viewing the cell frequencies is as proportions of their column totals. The proportions in any column will tell us in what proportions the members in a class at the end of the interval have been drawn from the other classes. This second way of looking at a mobility table is less familiar but is, we shall argue, an equally important way of describing the mobility process.

The duality represented by these two ways of looking at the table relates to the distinction sometimes made between pure (or exchange) and structural mobility. If the mobility process is unconstrained, individuals in any class will be free to move anywhere, and hence the class numbers at the end of the interval will be whatever the mobility process happens to generate. In contrast these moves may be constrained by other factors determining the class structure at the end of the interval. If the table relates to occupational mobility, the actual numbers in the classes will be, partly at least, determined by the labour needs of the economy. If, for example, automation reduces the relative number of unskilled jobs available, then some individuals will be forced out of the unskilled categories. This is described as structural mobility because it is generated by the changing structure. Roughly speaking, therefore, we can distinguish two forces driving mobility. There is the individual element whereby someone by effort, qualification, good or ill fortune moves from one class to another, and then there is the environmental pressure resulting from the occupational needs of the society. In the one case mobility changes the structure, and in the other the changing structure generates the mobility. We shall argue that these two kinds of mobility need to be modelled in different ways and this has consequences for how we measure mobility.

There are questions to do with how the data are obtained which bear upon inferences which may be drawn from a mobility table. These are not major questions for our purposes but they should be noted. When studying intergenerational mobility through the male line, we could draw a sample of men and inquire about the class of their father. In this case we would be first constructing the column totals and then for each column determining the distribution in the columns. This method would, if the sampling were random, give a proper estimate of the sons' class distribution but not of the fathers' because fathers with several sons would be more likely to be selected than those with fewer. If we were to sample fathers (which would not be straightforward) and inquire about their sons, we would obtain a valid estimate of the fathers' class distribution but not of the sons'. A third possibility would be to sample families. This would give valid estimates of both distributions if the family were a stable and readily identifiable unit. If a population is not growing or declining, each father will have, on average, one son, and it can then be shown that the problems just outlined are not serious.

Similar difficulties arise in occupational mobility. In a prospective study we can take a sample of individuals at the beginning of the period and observe their new occupational group at the end of the period. Or we can take a sample at the end and look back at their occupation at the beginning. The problem here is that members join and leave the population and so not all will be present at both ends of the interval. In this case we can account for all movements by augmenting the mobility table with a $(k+1)$th column to record losses from the system and a $(k+1)$th row to record entrants.

Having drawn attention to these matters, we shall leave them on one side as their effects will not, in general, be serious enough to invalidate the treatment which follows. It would be possible to generalize the models to accommodate these complications but this would tend to obscure the central points which we wish to make.

From an empirical point of view the problem of measuring mobility is to find some mapping from the set of mobility tables onto some convenient interval of the real line. Much work has been done on these lines, the various indices proposed by Yasuda (1964) being good examples. The alternative course, to be followed here, is first to construct a model of the process and then to base a measure on the parameters of that model.

Two Markov Models of Mobility

The summarization of the mobility table by transition proportions immediately suggests a Markov chain model. If a proportion n_{ij}/n_j move from i to j, it is natural to suppose that each member of i was subject to a transition probability p_{ij} of making that transition. Any family line or occupational history is then generated by the set of probabilities $\{p_{ij}\}$. If we suppose that the same set of transition probabilities applies to all members of the population, we can describe the aggregate behaviour by reference to the Markov chain with transition matrix $P = \{p_{ij}\}$.

This simple model is the basis of almost all theoretical work on mobility, and the problem of measuring mobility has been posed as that of choosing a suitable function of the elements of P. The measure is then *estimated* from estimates of the transition probabilities. This model goes back at least to Prais (1955); here we shall merely summarize some of its salient features before introducing our second model. First, however, we introduce a modification of the traditional Markov chain notation used above. Henceforth, instead of p_{ij} we shall write $p(i \mid j)$. This makes clear that j is the conditioning event and will subsequently enable us to distinguish between two kinds of transition probability corresponding to the two ways of forming proportions in the mobility table.

A transition matrix P has rows summing to 1. We denote the class structure at the beginning of the period by $p(0)$ and at the end by $p(T)$ where T is the length of the interval. These vectors may be thought of as the expected proportions in the classes and they are related by

$$p(T) = p(0)P \tag{1}$$

where class vectors are written as rows. A stationary structure, p, is one satisfying

$$p = pP \tag{2}$$

Two special cases of P play a key role in setting up a scale of mobility. The first is when $P = I$, the identity matrix, since this allows no movement at all. The second is when P has identical rows; any such matrix will be denoted by P^*. In such a system the probability of moving to class j is the same whatever the initial class. Since an individual's destination is uninfluenced by class origin, this is sometimes described as characterizing a perfectly mobile society. If the common row of such a matrix is denoted by p, then p is also the stationary structure as is easily verified. The stationary structure is also the limiting structure in the sense that, provided that P is regular, it is the structure to which the system converges after many time periods if P remains constant. A matrix is regular if any state can be reached from any other state in a finite number of steps. For most mobility tables any state can be reached from any other in a single step, so the condition is certainly satisfied. To construct a measure of mobility for the interval $(0, T)$ we are not interested in the long-run behaviour. For this model the problem of measuring mobility is that of constructing a suitable summary measure of the elements of P; we take up this question in the following section.

The second Markov model starts from the structural perspective and assumes that the class distribution is fixed by factors outside the system. It models the flow of vacancies rather than people. Suppose at the *end* of our observation period there are $v_i(T)$ jobs to be filled in class i ($i = 1, 2, \ldots k$). These may be thought of as vacancies to be filled from those in the system at time 0. The decision to fill a vacancy in class j by moving a person in class i is equivalent to the vacancy moving from j to i. To every move of a person in one direction there is an equal and opposite movement of a vacancy in the reverse direction. The changing state of the system can, therefore, equally be described in terms of vacancies.

A Markov model for vacancies supposes that vacancy moves are generated by transition probabilities and hence that the flow of vacancies is an aggregated Markov chain. We denote by $q(i \mid j)$ the conditional probability that a vacancy in j moves to i and the matrix of such probabilities we denote by Q. Everything we did for the 'forward' process can be done for the 'backward' process, and so we use q to denote a stationary row vector and Q^* a matrix with identical rows.

From this perspective we regard the mobility table as having been generated as follows. The vacancy numbers at T were fixed externally and, since these vacancies were subsequently filled, the column totals $n_{.j} = v_j(T)$, ($j = 1, 2, \ldots, k$). The vacancies in j are then distributed among the k classes according to the transition probabilities $\{q(i \mid j)\}$ ($i = 1, 2, \ldots, k$). The total number arriving in j from all sources will thus be the number of vacancies in j at time zero, and this must be the same as the numbers n_j who were already there. The cell frequencies are equal to the vacancy flows and so we may write

$$n_{ij} = v_{ji} \quad \{i, j = 1, 2, \ldots, k\}$$

where the reversal of the order of the subscripts for v reflects the fact that vacancies move in the opposite direction.

For a single mobility table there is no way of telling which model is appropriate if all we have is the numbers. We could, therefore, equally well base a measure of mobility on Q. The two special cases of Q, $Q = I$ and $Q = Q^*$ have similar meaning to their counterparts in the forward process. $Q = I$ implies there is no movement and $Q = Q^*$ means that selection among the classes for transfer is the same for all destination classes. In other words one's original class is irrelevant. If we had data over a succession of periods, we could test which of the two models provided the best representation of the data. In the absence of this we must consider how to choose between the models or to effect a compromise between them. As a preparation for this we examine the relationship between the two processes more closely.

Suppose first that the 'true' model is the forward Markov chain with transition matrix P. If we were mistakenly to treat this as if it were a vacancy model, we can easily work out the connection between the two sets of transition probabilities. Thus by Bayes' theorem

$$q(i \mid j) = \frac{p_0(i) \, p(j \mid i)}{q_T(j)} \, (i, j = 1, 2, \ldots k) \tag{3}$$

where the subscripts on p and q refer to the two ends of the time period. If the process is a forward chain, then $q_T(j) = p_T(j)$, the probability that an individual is in j at T. From (3) we infer that the backward process will be Markovian but, in general, it will be time-dependent. It will be time-independent only if $P_0 = P_T$, that is, if the structure is stationary. In that case we have

$$q(i \mid j) = \frac{p(i)}{p(j)} p(j \mid i) \tag{4}$$

In matrix notation we may write this as

$$Q = (\text{diag } p)^{-1} P' (\text{diag } p) \tag{5}$$

where diag p is a diagonal matrix with the elements of p along its diagonal.

The matrices P and Q are not, in general, identical, but it is easy to show that they have the same stationary distribution. Thus if p is the stationary structure of P,

$$pQ = p(\text{diag } p)^{-1} P' (\text{diag } p) = 1 P' (\text{diag } p)$$
$$= 1(\text{diag } p) = p \tag{6}$$

so that p is also a stationary structure of Q. For a stationary system where the class structure is not changing, the two models are totally confounded and each therefore has an equal claim to be made the basis of a measure.

In practice it appears that P and Q are often very close. This was so in twenty cases examined by Sommers and Conlisk (1979). In such cases the chain is said to be reversible and this has rather implausible implications. Rewriting (4) as

$$p(j)\,q(i \mid j) = p(i)p(j \mid i) \tag{7}$$

and substituting $p(i \mid j) = q(i \mid j)$, the left-hand side is the probability that a randomly chosen person moves from j to i and the right-hand side the probability of a move from i to j. Multiplying both sides by n, we have the requirement that the expected number of moves from i to j is the same as that from j to i. It has seemed puzzling that such a strict coupling of moves should be implied by what we usually find in practice. It is as though every move from teacher to policeman, say, must be balanced by a move in the opposite direction. It seems more natural when the same requirement is viewed in the vacancy perspective. From that point of view the number of places in each occupational category is fixed, and then it is clear that any move requires a space to move into. It is still somewhat surprising that the balance has to be struck in every pair of categories rather than just overall, but this is, nevertheless, implied by the fixed transition matrix.

Measures of Mobility

We have identified two matrices which may be relevant in describing the mobility process. The forward matrix P for describing the movement of people and the backward matrix Q for the flows of vacancies. We have noted that the two types of model cannot be distinguished if the system is in a stationary state because both have the same steady state distribution. In practice there may well be elements of the two processes in operation, and, as already noted, Sommers and Conlisk (1979) have pointed out that the two matrices are often very close numerically. This suggests that it might be reasonable to take the average of the two and base our measure of mobility on that. There is a further theoretical reason for doing this because for a stationary system the matrix

$$R = \tfrac{1}{2}(P + Q) = \tfrac{1}{2}\{P + (\text{diag } p)^{-1}P'(\text{diag } p)\} \tag{8}$$

has some attractive properties. It has the same stationary distribution as P and Q but, unlike them, its eigenvalues are always real. We shall shortly see that the eigenvalues of the transition matrix play a key role in constructing measures of mobility and this fact gives R some advantages. To keep the discussion as simple as possible, we shall conduct it in terms of P because this has some expository advantages, but Q or R could be used instead.

It is clear from the analysis so far that the transition matrix P generates all movement and thus characterizes the mobility process. It follows that any scalar measure of mobility should be some function of the elements of P. The problem of measurement lies in identifying which such function best captures what we understand by the term 'mobility'.

One line of approach starts with the fact that we have already fixed two points on the scale. There will be no mobility at all if $P = I$ and therefore the unit matrix must map onto one endpoint of the scale. The second fixed point occurs when P has identical rows, meaning that son's class is independent of father's class. All matrices of this form, denoted by P^*, should therefore map into the same point on our scale of measurement, but, unlike $P = I$, it is less clear that this is an extreme point. The reason for this can be seen by looking at the following three matrices.

$$\begin{pmatrix} 1 & 0 \\ 0 & 1 \end{pmatrix} \quad \begin{pmatrix} .75 & .25 \\ .75 & .25 \end{pmatrix} \quad \begin{pmatrix} 0 & 1 \\ 1 & 0 \end{pmatrix}$$

$$\text{(i)} \qquad\qquad \text{(ii)} \qquad\quad \text{(iii)}$$

The matrix (iii) would involve more movement than (ii), and hence it could be argued its mobility measure should be greater than that of (ii). However, if we think in terms of the degree of dependence between father's and son's class, then (ii) represents an extreme. The matrix (iii), like (i), exhibits a total dependence between father's and son's classes, the difference lying in the direction of the dependence. In (i) the correlation is positive and in (iii) it is negative. We must, therefore, decide whether the sign of the correlation is relevant. If not, (i) and (iii) would map onto the same point but otherwise they would be at opposite ends of the scale. This simple example shows that there are two distinct aspects to the notion of mobility. One has to do with the degree of social inheritance and the other with the amount of movement between classes. The two are closely intertwined but cannot both be adequately represented by the same measure.

Measuring the Amount of Movement

The obvious way to do this is to compare P with I, the matrix representing the extreme of no mobility. In a rough sense the 'farther' P is from I, the more movement there will be. Perhaps the simplest scalar measure of the distance is the sum of the absolute differences between the pairs of elements of the two matrices. Thus we may define a measure

$$\Delta_1 = \sum_{i=1}^{k} \sum_{j=1}^{k} | p_{ij} - \delta_{ij} |$$

where $\delta_{ij} = 1$ if $i = j$ and is zero otherwise. A simple calculation yields

$$\Delta_1 = 2\sum_{i=1}^{k} (1 - p_{ij}) = 2(k - traceP) \tag{9}$$

This ranges from $\Delta_1 = 0$ when there is no mobility to $\Delta_1 = 2k$ when all members change their class. In the intermediate case when $P = P^*$, trace $P^* = 1$ and $\Delta_1 = 2k - 2$. Unless $k = 2$, the case of no correlation does not occur at the mid-point of the scale. We could easily make Δ_1 lie in the interval $(0, 1)$ by dividing by $2k$.

This measure has the merit of simplicity and direct intuitive appeal and has often been used in practice. Since the trace is the sum of the eigenvalues, it is linked with the wider class of measures treated below. There is, however, some arbitrariness in the way that the distance between P and I is measured. One effect of this is that the measure takes no account of the destinations of the moves. A move from the bottom to the top of the social scale would count for no more than a move to an adjacent class. If we chose to use a squared measure of distance, instead of the absolute value, we would obtain

$$\Delta_2 = \sum_{i=1}^{k} (1 - p_{ii})^2 + \sum\sum_{i \neq j} p_{ij}^2$$

$$= k - 2 \ trace \ P + \sum_{i=1}^{k} \sum_{j=1}^{k} p_{ij}^2 \tag{10}$$

This too involves the trace, but the last term introduces a distinction according to how equally those moving out of a class are distributed among the other classes. A society in which most of those leaving a class go to the same class would have a higher Δ_2 than one in which they were distributed among several classes. This seems counterintuitive and Δ_2 has no other obvious advantage over Δ_1.

A serious objection to both Δ_1 and Δ_2 is that they do not necessarily reflect the gross amount of movement over any generation or time interval. If, for example, the off-diagonal elements in the first row of the matrix are relatively large, they will contribute substantially to Δ_1, but the number of movements out of that class will also depend on the numbers already in that class. If the class is virtually empty, there will be very little movement out of it no matter how large the transition probabilities. Only if, initially, there are equal numbers in each class will Δ_1 be proportional to the expected number of moves. The difficulty in remedying this defect is that the numbers in the classes change. If we want a purely transitory measure of mobility, this might not matter, but if our initial intuition that mobility should depend on P alone were correct, then there are problems. The solution is to use the stationary class structure associated with P. We can then compute the expected flows that would occur if the system were in a stationary state. For example, the expected proportion in the population who will change state over any interval is

$$1 - M_1 = \sum_{i=1}^{k} p_i p_{ii}$$

$$= \ trace[(diag \ p) P] \tag{11}$$

The elements of the matrix whose trace is used here are the joint probabilities of having a father in i and the son in j; that is, they are the expected values of the n_{ij}'s of the mobility table.

As defined by (11) M_1 is actually a measure of immobility so we have taken its complement. There is a technical difficulty about the extreme of immobility. For if $P = I$, any distribution is stationary but, regardless of what we choose, $M_1 = 1$. At the other extreme, when all members of every class move, the measure is zero. At the intermediate point when $P = P^*$, $M_1 = \Sigma p_i^2$ and thus the case of perfect mobility does not correspond to a single point on the scale. This is of no consequence if it is the amount of movement we are interested in because different members of the class P^* will clearly involve different amounts of movement. But if we wish our scale to have a single point corresponding to total lack of social inheritance, M_1 will not do.

Since most systems of social or occupational classification involve, at least, a partial ordering of the classes, we may wish our measure to reflect the distance moved. A move between distant classes ought to carry more weight than one between adjacent classes. Both Δ_1 and M_1 can be modified by the introduction of weights. Thus if we were to attach a weight d_{ij} to the transition from i to j reflecting the distance apart of i and j, we would arrive at

$$\Delta_3 = \sum_{i=1}^{k} \sum_{j=1}^{k} d_{ij} \mid p_{ij} - \delta_{ij} \mid$$

and

$$M_2 = \sum_{i=1}^{k} \sum_{j=1}^{k} d_{ij}\, p_i\, p_{ij}.$$

Later we shall meet a method by which suitable values of d_{ij} might be determined, but if the aim is to have a readily interpretable measure, there is much to be said for choosing $d_{ij} = \mid i - j \mid$ which is the number of class boundaries crossed in moving from i to j. In the case of M_2 we then have the expected number of class boundaries crossed in a stationary population with transition matrix P. This meets our need for a simple, easily interpretable measure which depends only on the transition matrix.

Measuring Social Inheritance

Social inheritance is essentially about the degree of correlation between fathers' and sons' classes in successive generations. The natural 'zero-point' for such a scale occurs when the two are independent; in other words, when $P = P^*$. The measures of movement considered so far lack the most basic requirement for such a measure that all matrices with identical rows should map onto the same point on the scale. The form of the empirical social mobility table immediately suggests using one of the many measures of correlation, or association, which are available for contingency tables. To gain more insight into the theoretical implications of doing this, we shall work with the expected cell frequencies given by the matrix (diag p)P. Again we have supposed the system to be in a stationary state, but many of the possible measures turn out not to depend on p. To illustrate the point, we consider the two–class system in which the matrix of expected transition numbers will be

$$\begin{pmatrix} p_1\, p_{11} & p_1\, p_{12} \\ p_2\, p_{21} & p_2\, p_{22} \end{pmatrix}$$

It is well known that reasonable measures of association should be functions of the odds ratio

$$(p_1 p_{11} \times p_2 p_{22})/(p_2 p_{12} \times p_1 p_{21}) = p_{11} p_{22}/p_{12} p_{21}$$

which is independent of the starting structure.

Measures of association in contingency tables may be classified according to whether or not the classes are ordered. When they are ordered, grouped versions of

Spearman's and Kendall's rank correlations are available, but these do not appear to have been used in social mobility studies. In any event the possibility of ordering can be covered by a more general approach. We approach this in two stages, starting from the fact that any transition matrix can be expressed in the following form

$$P = 1'p + \sum_{h=2}^{k} \theta_h v_h' u_h \tag{12}$$

where 1 is a vector of 1's, p is the stationary vector of P, $\theta_2, \theta_3, \ldots, \theta_k$ are eigenvalues of P (excluding $\theta_1 = 1$) and $\{v_h\}$ and $\{u_h\}$ are the left and right eigenvectors associated with the eigenvalues. The matrix $(\text{diag } p)P$ can thus be expressed in a similar form with the leading term becoming $p'p$ and with the remaining terms similarly modified. Since $p'p$ is the set of expected transition proportions in the absence of social inheritance, it is clear from (12) that the eigenvalues $\{\theta_h\}$ play a key role in the assessment of how much P differs from $p'p$.

This fact has led to a number of proposals to use various summary measures of the set of eigenvalues. We have already noted that the sum of the eigenvalues leads to Δ_1, which was the only one of the measures proposed in the last section where independence corresponded to a fixed point on the measurement scale. Another widely canvassed proposal is the second largest eigenvalue in absolute value. The smaller this value, the closer is P to $p'p$ and max $|\theta|$ conveniently ranges over the interval (0, 1). The use of the modulus conceals the sign of the correlation. If we refer back to the 2×2 tables discussed above, (i) and (iii) have max $|\theta_1| = 1$. In the case of (i) the two eigenvalues are both unity, and in the case of (iii) they are 1 and -1. If we retained the sign, it would indicate the direction of the correlation, but then we would be in difficulties if the value were complex. In practice this is extremely unlikely to occur, but one advantage of using the average matrix R is that its roots are always real.

The absolute value of the second largest eigenvalue arises out of the more general approach to the analysis of association in a contingency table known as correspondence analysis. This may be motivated in a variety of ways. One is directly linked to (12). We noted that premultiplying both sides by diag p gave us an expansion of the expected frequency of transition matrix in terms of its value under the hypothesis of independence and a series of further terms the size of whose coefficients determines the deviation from independence. The successive terms of this expansion provide an analysis of the dependence structure of the data. An alternative approach was used by Sommers and Conlisk (1979), although without any recognition of its links with correspondence analysis. Here we introduce scores $x_1, x_2, \ldots, x_k$, one for each class representing the status value of the class. If we had some independent basis for choosing the x's, we could use the product moment correlation as our measure. This will usually be lacking, so an alternative is to determine what scores will maximize the correlation coefficient. Since the correlation does not depend on the origin or scale of the x's, we may fix them arbitrarily to have the values 0 and 1 respectively. The correlation coefficient is then

$$\rho = \sum_{i=1}^{k} \sum_{j=1}^{k} p_i \, p_{ij} x_i x_j \tag{13}$$

171

David J. Bartholomew

Sommers and Conlisk (1979) showed that the maximum value of ρ, subject to the constraints of origin and scale, is given by the absolute value of the second largest eigenvalue of the matrix R. Exactly the same solution is obtained if we use the matrices Q and R instead of P. If one had views a priori about the ordering of the classes, (13) could be maximized subject to order restrictions on the x's, but this avenue is yet to be explored. The minimum possible value of ρ without order restrictions would clearly be zero, so the question of whether it is desirable to allow negative values does not arise.

The fact that the two ideas behind mobility — amount of movement and degree of social inheritance — are not separable is apparent on noticing that (13) is also a member of the class M_2. For if we write

$$x_i x_j = \tfrac{1}{2}\{(x_i - x_j)^2 - x_i^2 - x_j^2\}$$

and remember that the marginal variances are unity, then the essential correspondence follows by setting

$$d_{ij} = \tfrac{1}{2}(x_i - x_j)^2.$$

The best measure to choose will evidently depend on the use to which it is to be put. The fact that there are several competing indices merely reflects the many faceted nature of the concept of mobility. For general purposes, the measure based on M_2 with $d_{ij} = |i - j|$ provides a simple intelligible measure of the movement taking place, and the second largest eigenvalue of P is, perhaps, the best available measure of social inheritance.

Some Questions of Validity

Our approach to constructing measures has been firmly rooted in the idea of a stochastic model generating the mobility process. But having identified the transition matrix as the relevant basis, we have proceeded informally. A more formal approach was adopted by Shorrocks (1978) when he attempted to embody the essential requirements of a measure in a set of axioms. One might hope that such a set would eliminate all but a very small number of possibilities. This proved to be impossible in the strict sense, because no known measure satisfied all his axioms. However, we can use such a set of axioms as a guide to the validity of a proposed measure. If it fails to satisfy any axiom, we can conclude that our measure does not conform to the idea expressed by that axiom.

Many of the measures we have mentioned fail this test, including the two that we have particularly recommended. It is important, therefore, to decide whether the fault lies with the measure or the axiom. The monotonicity axiom says that if we increase any off-diagonal element in P at the expense of its diagonal element, then the measure should increase. Increasing the potential for movement surely increases mobility. The trace measure Δ_1 of (9) does meet this requirement, but those measures which explicitly involve p do not. The reason for this is that changing P also changes p and so an increase in an individual p_{ij} may be more than offset by a decrease in p_i. Here the fault lies in the axiom. The role of p was to provide a 'typical' distribution.

172

Any other distribution with claims to be typical could have been used instead and that would not have been affected by the change in *P*. We are asking about the number who would be expected to move if the initial distribution were *p*. To ask the same question when *P* is changed requires us to use the *same* initial distribution if we are to compare like with like. Increasing the potential for movement will then increase the value of indices such as M_2 or max $|\theta|$.

A second axiom is referred to as having to do with period invariance. In intergenerational mobility this does not arise because the generation provides a natural unit of time. With occupational mobility, on the other hand, the time period is arbitrary. Other things being equal, the longer the interval, the more movement there will be. To make valid comparisons, we therefore need to estimate the mobility tables for a common time period. In principle this is straightforward. If the real process is continuous in time, as it must be if we can arbitrarily choose the time interval, then we may treat it as a continuous time Markov process. If this is the case and the transition matrix for an interval of length *T* is *P*, then that for $aT (a > 0)$ will be P^a. Powers, fractional or otherwise, of a matrix can be computed directly from the expansion of (12) by replacing θ_h by θ_h^a. In this manner we can reduce all transition matrices to be compared to a common time interval.

The axiom of period invariance says that the mobility measure of a matrix should not depend on how this unit of time is chosen. This holds for max $|\theta_i|$ but not for the other measures we have discussed. However, if the prime purpose of the analysis is to order populations according to their degree of mobility (in whatever sense), this may not matter. For many purposes, therefore, the axiom of period invariance is too strong.

A final point is more loosely related to the idea of validity. Brummelle and Gerchak (1982) have proposed a very general family of measures which includes all that we have discussed and many more besides. Within this family one can choose measures to emphasize many different facets of mobility. This propensity to increase the number of potential measures may be seen in other fields such as measuring inequality of incomes or wealth, but it is misguided. The main point of constructing measures is to make comparisons. If each situation requires its own individual measure, no comparisons will be possible. The more limited the choice of measure, the wider will be its potential use. The aim should be to settle on one or two robust measures which, although they may be insensitive to the nuances of particular situations, will capture what is common to most.

The two branches of mobility research which we identified at the outset have, to a large extent, been complementary. It would be entirely in the spirit of James Coleman's approach to the study of social phenomena if the insights of the one were brought to bear more directly on the other.

13 Self-Employment and Entrepreneurship: A Study of Entry and Exit

Peter Abell

Amongst the innumerable contributions which Jim Coleman has made to sociology are his early and pioneering works on the use of stochastic flow models (Coleman, 1964a, 1964b) and, more recently, his promotion of rational choice or action theory (Coleman, 1990a). In this essay in honour of Coleman — surely the outstanding sociologist of his generation — I shall bring together certain aspects of the two, by analyzing the entry to and exit from self-employment. In so doing, I shall make use of Coleman's well known diagram (Figure 13.1) which provides him with an organizing framework for his monumental work on rational choice theory — RCT (Coleman, 1990a).

He invites us to understand the causal interplay between four types of analysis using a rational choice perspective at the individual or micro level. Entry into self-employment (particularly when, in the process, it provides employment for others) I shall construe as an individual level entrepreneurial action which, when aggregated, determines an entry *rate* and in turn (along with the exit rate) shapes the national self-employment rate. The individual propensity is, however, shaped, first, by GDP, second, by the unemployment rate and, third, by the self-employment rate at an earlier period. These macro level variables have their effect, however, through three identifiable individual level social networks (which may overlap) providing respectively 'legitimacy', 'opportunities' and 'resources'. I follow Coleman (1990a) in another respect by regarding these networks as forms of *social capital*.

In choosing to study entrepreneurial entry I examine actions which some have concluded defy the attentions of RCT; and certainly, as we shall see, the theoretical and empirical literature offers little support for the belief that entry can be systematically understood, let alone brought within the ambit of RCT. My argument will be that by viewing the entry and exit decisions as socially embedded in networks of social capital we maybe can secure a firmer understanding of these potentially complex processes. This chapter is, however, only suggestive of the analytical power of such an approach; if the conclusions drawn are correct, then it opens up a line of inquiry rather than settles any issues.

Despite the manifest importance of the supply of entrepreneurial skills for any economy, little of a reliable nature seems to be known about the factors — personal and environmental — which encourage people to take on entrepreneurial roles, however we care to define them. One can find many scholarly attempts to define entrepreneurship in something like its full complexity (what it is that entrepreneurs do, or what it is that they supply — see Casson, 1982, for a review; in this respect there is an economics, a psychological and a sociological literature). I shall not start, however,

Figure 13.1. The Coleman Diagram

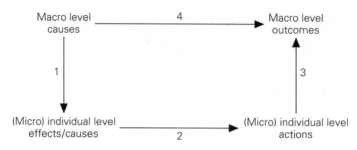

by seeking something which has proved elusive for a multitude of scholars. Rather, I shall operationally define an entrepreneur as someone who (either individually or with others) sets up (and owns) a new enterprise, especially when it provides employment for others. I shall then seek to model the decision process which eventuates in such behaviour within the general framework of the Coleman diagram (Figure 13.1). The analysis will also involve the exit decision, although this will be given less attention here.

Explaining Entrepreneurship

It is a sobering thought that despite a number of major econometric and other studies concerning the determinants of entrepreneurial entry, we are little wiser as to the nature of the processes involved (see Blanchflower and Meyer, 1990, for a succinct summary of the econometric studies). For instance, the average variance explained (when reported) in these studies does not amount to more than a few percent, even where several exogenous variables are involved. Correspondingly, an (Austrian inspired!) argument we must keep in sight avers that entrepreneurial entry is largely an unpredictable phenomenon.

Entrepreneurial entry is but one among several modes of entry and in many industries the least prevalent (in terms of both gross entry numbers and market shares). The other modes of entry include: first, entry by an existing firm which opens up a new plant; second, entry by a firm which purchases a plant/firm already in an industry; third, entry by an existing firm which changes the use of a plant; and, fourth, entry by an entrepreneur who buys or inherits an existing plant/firm.

My simple definition of entrepreneurial entry has a number of obvious limitations. First, it is clear that in a modern dynamic economy many 'managerial' roles possess an entrepreneurial component (intrapreneurship). This is particularly so where managers are charged by their parent enterprise with the responsibility for opening up new plants and markets, or with aggressively improving market shares. Second, the currently fashionable practice of extending equity options to managers and others can also be considered as a way of spreading entrepreneurial risk/uncertainty to hitherto unaffected employees. Third, statistics show that significant numbers of individuals inherit going concerns which they then continue to run. Entrepreneurial entry, as I propose to use the term, misses these aspects of the wider conception. On the other hand, it could be argued that our definition is too broad. Curran (1986), for example, urges that: 'The great majority of those who start, buy or inherit a small business should not be seen as entrepreneurs in any strict sense. If the term "entrepreneur" is to have any meaning . . . it might be properly reserved for those who create a new successful enterprise based on a novel product or service and/or organizational means for producing a good or providing a service and/or the novel marketing and distribution of goods and services. Most small business owners are simply cloning an existing well proven form of enterprise'.

Curran's approach is not, I believe, the most useful for several reasons. First, it would be analytically unwise to identify entrepreneurship with the creation of 'successful' enterprises. Most new enterprises are not successful, if by success we mean to imply a life expectancy beyond five years and/or a significant market penetration. Indeed, much of the research into entrepreneurship is vitiated precisely because it rests upon samples with an inbuilt selection bias in favour of success (Crouchley *et al.*, 1994; Mosakowski and Carroll, 1985). Sociological and psychological researchers are particularly guilty of this; they have usually seen fit to examine only the characteristics and circumstances of those who either become entrepreneurs (self-employed) or even successfully self-employed, failing to pay comparative attention to those who do not, those who fail and those who sell up.

The second reason for resisting Curran's definition follows from his insistence that most new small businesses are merely 'clones' of market incumbents and should accordingly not be seen as entrepreneurial in any significant sense. There may, notwithstanding, be circumstances where product markets are not exhausted by incumbents and cloning is an effective entry strategy (e.g., with expanding markets or as a consequence of temporary disequilibria — Baumol, 1993).

It is convenient to consider briefly a related set of issues raised by alternative conceptions of entrepreneurship which are advocated by various economists. Schumpeter (1939) conceived an entrepreneur as someone who provokes change by inducing disequilibria. The entrepreneur creates new opportunities by finding 'new combinations in production'. The role of entrepreneur is distinct from that of capitalist, labourer or inventor, although the entrepreneur may coincidentally assume any one of these roles also (Stinchcombe, 1990). Specifically, the entrepreneur, though an innovator, is not an inventor. Furthermore, in locating new ways of combining the factors of production, there is, *ex ante*, an inherent uncertainty (or risk) in the commitment of resources. Again, though the entrepreneur may choose to embrace all or many of the uncertainties involved, this is incidental to her role. The entrepreneur is not essentially a bearer of uncertainty or risk. This usually falls to those who see fit to provide the non-entrepreneurial factor inputs.

Kirzner (1973) and Schultz (1980), while agreeing with Schumpeter that the bearing of uncertainty is only adventitiously related to entrepreneurship, in contrast to him regard entrepreneurs as those who adjust to (exogenously) generated opportunities (disequilibria). For Kirzner entrepreneurs are 'alert' to the uncertain opportunities which exogenously created disequilibria offer. From a psychologist's standpoint, it is not clear to what extent 'alertness' is a motivational or a cognitive concept. One might reasonably ask whether, perhaps among other things, it is the motivation to search which distinguishes the entrepreneur from others or whether the entrepreneur is, for exogenous reasons, more favourably placed to recognize the going opportunities. I shall return to these issues.

By contrast to the authors just mentioned, others, notably Kanbur (1982), Kihlstrom and Laffont (1979) and Grossman (1984), have promoted positive attitudes to risk (uncertainty) as the discriminating factor accounting for entrepreneurial propensities. Thus the key factor in accounting for the adoption of entrepreneurial roles is neither a 'motive to innovate' nor an 'alertness to opportunities' (both of which are assumed to be widely distributed dispositions) but a willingness to absorb risks or uncertainties (risks in Kanbur). Let us now look more closely at these suggestions from a RCT point of view. I shall, in part, follow a development of Coleman's diagram (Figure 13.1) set out in Coleman and Fararo's edited collection, *Rational Choice Theory: Advocacy and Critique*, by myself (Abell, 1992).

Entrepreneurial Motivation

The potential entrepreneur must in some sense be motivated to establish an enterprise; this much is obvious. Given her resources (including her own human capital) and her perception of various opportunities (including, of course, non–entrepreneurial opportunities), we may assume that entry is her optimal choice. As far as I know, nobody has seriously proposed that we should depart from the optimality assumption of rational choice theory in trying to model entrepreneurial entry, unless, as with some psychoanalytically oriented writers (e.g., de Vries, 1977), we regard those beholden to their unconscious motives, which eventuate in entrepreneurial behaviour, as behaving suboptimally. Rather, the debate concerns whether we need to invoke distinct motivations or utility functions for entrepreneurs; that is, either distinct arguments or distinct weightings — or both.

Economists, insofar as they have addressed the issue, appear divided. On the one hand, there are those who would allow exposure to opportunities to do all the explanatory work; no special motives need to be adduced and an individual becomes an entrepreneur if she believes that her own use of (exogenously) available resources can yield a higher risk discounted expected income flow when compared with the possibility of hiring them to others. Entrepreneurs on this reading are motivationally just like the rest of us. For good measure also, exposure to opportunities is not a variable which is responsive to motives in any special way. Entrepreneurs are not assiduous beyond the average in their search behaviour. What drives entrepreneurial entry, according to this view of things, is an individual's exposure to opportunities. Furthermore, if this exposure is essentially random with respect to identifiable personal characteristics, then we are dealing at the individual level with an unpredictable process (*pace* our earlier observation concerning the low predictive performance of the existing studies). Here the rate of entrepreneurial entry largely depends upon the exogenous rate of production of opportunities which picks up individuals at random. There is no need of a theory of entrepreneurship beyond this. This view can, however, be somewhat softened by allowing that either cognitive skills or information asymmetries might affect the perception of opportunities.

Other economists, by contrast, seem happy to ascribe discriminating motives (or at least beyond average weightings of conventional motives) to those who seek entrepreneurial entry. Schumpeter speaks of 'building dynasties', 'the will to conquer' and 'the exercise of ingenuity' and Knight (1921) of 'overweening self-confidence': Casson (1982) reviews, in passing, many such motives which have to be spoken of in one place or another. It is not entirely clear, however, what we should do with these suggestions. Many of them seem more appropriate to the shaping of post–entry performance, for example, the adoption of aggressive market penetration and growth policies. But, when considering how they might shape the entry decision, it is not clear whether we should do more than assume they imply very low leisure preferences, high risk/ uncertainty bearing attitudes or above average search effort. It might be that a number of these routinely ascribed dispositions can fruitfully be construed as being spuriously related in terms of a distinct and discriminating underlying entrepreneurial motive. If such could be found, it might play an important role in the bottom left-hand corner of the Coleman diagram.

It is the psychologists who have pursued the idea of special entrepreneurial motives in this sense, and we might sensibly look in their direction for help. A protracted search has taken place to find the entrepreneurial character or personality (Burch, 1986; Brockhaus, 1982; Chell, 1985), and in some cases to root out its social and/or psychodynamic causes. Chell (1985) in a useful review distinguishes between what she terms the 'psychodynamic approach', the 'developmental model' and the 'trait model'. Although the details are different, all of these authors emphasize the traits which motivate and enable (a skill variable) people to take judgmental decisions. It is not easy to see though how these profiles discriminate between entrepreneurs, however defined, and others taking on judgmental roles.

Perhaps the most influential view derives from McClelland (1961) who postulated that entrepreneurs are disproportionately endowed with a 'need to achieve'. However, even though he was able to find support for his ideas, often utilizing highly ingenious indirect measures, and in a variety of cultural settings, others have found it difficult to be so enthusiastic (Leff, 1979). Again, although a need for achievement will be differentially distributed in a population, it is unlikely that it will pick out entrepreneurs from others occupying roles which also require above average drive.

Other special motives/traits have variously been ascribed to entrepreneurs; Hornaday and Bunker (1970) listed twenty-one. However, a smaller number seem to be mentioned most frequently:

— internal locus of control (Evans and Leighton, 1989);
— a need for power or domination over others;
— a need for independence of the domination of others (Blanchflower and Oswald, 1990);

Chell (1985) notes that despite repeated attempts empirically to establish the salience of one or more of these motives/traits, the results are disappointing, producing a mass of weak and contradictory evidence. Furthermore, many studies suffer from selection bias, failing to compare entrepreneurs with those who do not take on an entrepreneurial role or those who fail as entrepreneurs. Unfortunately, we have to draw the conclusion that despite the wide-ranging nature of their research, the 'psychologists' have failed to provide a convincing picture of distinctive entrepreneurial motives/traits.

It may be that the motives which lead people to become entrepreneurs are so widely distributed that their presence or absence is only a marginal discriminator. Indeed, there is some considerable indirect evidence that this might be so. Blanchflower and Oswald (1990), when analyzing the British Social Attitudes Survey (BSA), find that, of those employees who were asked if they have ever considered becoming self-employed, about 30 per cent answered affirmatively. Although survey answers of this sort might be of questionable reliability, it is difficult to discount them entirely. There may (in Britain) be large numbers of these with the requisite motives to become entrepreneurs, given the right circumstances, but who are not so engaged. Such reasoning would push us in the direction of searching for variations in the rate of matching between 'circumstances' and those with latent predispositions. Any matching mechanism would then find an upper-bound in terms of the proportion of the population with the appropriate predispositions (motives).

As far as I know, there is no sound evidence to suggest that entrepreneurs are more keen than others to take risks (or judgmentally to embrace uncertainties), although there is a theoretical literature proposing this to be the case and some weakly suggestive empirical studies. Kihlstrom and Laffont (1979) see low risk aversion as the key differentiating feature of the entrepreneur. They assume, in the spirit of full information, that entrepreneurial opportunities are visible to all and each with an estimable risk. Further, entrepreneurs have standard arguments in their utility functions. Low risk aversion is promoted to do all the explanatory work. Brockhaus (1982) could, nevertheless, find no evidence suggesting that risk orientation separates entrepreneurs from managers. Blanchflower and Oswald (1990) also find some contrary evidence (although given their data, it is a weak test) in that the self-employed are no more likely to gamble than others. They are, however, sufficiently confident of the negative finding not to include 'risk bearing' in their subsequent modelling, where they urge that 'attitude to risk is not a central characteristic which determines who becomes an entrepreneur' (1990). In their analysis of the BSA survey they did, nonetheless, find that respondents cited risk as a deterrent to self-employment: some 20 per cent of the respondents mentioned risk (capital constraint headed the list). A number of authors (see Brenner, 1987) opine that those who lose status (utility) are more likely to take risks. This fits well with Kahneman and Tversky's (1979) finding that the marginal disutility of loss is greater than the utility from an equivalent gain.

There seems to be no good reason to exclude the possibility of low risk/ uncertainty aversion as a potential explanatory variable for entrepreneurial entry. It is, nevertheless, important to recognize that entrepreneurial entry may vary in its level of inherent risk/uncertainty for two distinct reasons: first, some opportunities are more risky/uncertain than others; and, second, the entrant may be able to shift the risk/uncertainty onto others. There is some psychological evidence that the latter is a skill (persuasiveness) that entrepreneurs disproportionately possess (Casson, 1982).

The literature unfortunately offers little solace to those who might like to find robust explanations of the individual propensity to enter entrepreneurial roles in terms of distinct types of motivation (utility argument). No doubt such exist and, moreover, will play some role in selecting entrepreneurs from the population at large; low risk aversion may also feature in this respect. It does not, however, appear sensible to search in this direction for strong effects; the outcome of many years of research seems to rebut any ambitions of this sort. Furthermore, from an RCT perspective, if distinct utility arguments over and above the standard ones of risk discounted income, were to be invoked, they would need themselves to be explained (endogenized). In terms of the Coleman diagram (Figure 13.1) the arguments would then occupy the bottom left-hand corner of the diagram and invite a type 1 explanation (RC theorists usually assume that standard discounted income utility arguments are not in need of explanation, as they are both stable and universal). But if this is so, we must look to differential exposure to knowledge of opportunities to explain differences in individual behaviour.

There is, however, an endogenized motivational concept which will prove useful in the analysis presented below. I believe there is a strong demonstration or imitation effect steering entrepreneurial entry. Other things being equal, those exposed to entrepreneurial opportunities (below) who also have contact with others either entering into or already in entrepreneurial roles are more likely to avail themselves of the opportunity. Initially I called this 'motivational confidence', but following the population ecologists, I shall now call it *legitimation* (Hannan, 1992) and propose that legitimation increases monotonically with the probability of contact with others in (entering) entrepreneurial roles. This probability is then, in turn, a function of the 'local' lagged self-employment (entry/exit?) rate. I shall not, however, make explicit use of a simple density dependent growth model, although the agency of a counteracting competition effect, as the time series for self-employment (with and without employees) gives no impression of equilibrating at a carrying capacity equilibrium. Population ecology models probably work reasonably well for specific sectors or markets where the technology is relatively fixed. The aggregate self-employment market with frequent technological shocks is another matter. I shall return to the modelling strategy later in the chapter and now turn to the mechanisms which match individuals to opportunities which, if I am correct, need to be legitimated by a contagion process. Another way of viewing the contagion, again following Coleman's (1990a) lead, is by interpreting the legitimation which contact with others in entrepreneurial roles brings as a form of *social capital*.

Exposure to Opportunities, Social Capital and Social Networks

We may assume that entrepreneurs are those who are, for whatever reason, exposed to or matched with entrepreneurial opportunities. Some of Coleman's recent work has drawn our attention to matching mechanisms. Granovetter (1973, 1982, 1985) has shown quite convincingly that in their search for employment, individuals characteristically make use of what he termed weak ties. A weak tie is a relationship to another person/group/organization which is one of superficial acquaintance and which carries little overall affect. They are to be contrasted with strong ties, where the relationship is close and usually affect-positive, engendering trust and the possibility of immediately unreciprocated exchanges. With weak ties, if *a* is linked to both *b* and *c*, then it is unlikely that *b* and *c* are themselves linked. Furthermore, weak ties can go through intermediaries, so if *a* is linked to *b* who in turn is linked to *c*, then *a* and *c* might be seen as weakly tied. Strong ties by contrast exhibit more closure; if *a* is related to both *b* and *c*, then it is likely that *b* and *c* will be similarly linked. Strong ties form relatively complete structures, whereas weak ties, though creating connected structures, are not as complete.

Following suggestive analyses by Aldrich, Rosen and Woodward (1986) and Greve and Foss (1990), we propose to see individuals as located in various networks of relationships which can encourage them to enter self-employment. We have accumulated considerable case study evidence, using the method of comparative narratives (Abell, 1987), that entrants are rarely the sole originators of ideas about entrepreneurial opportunities but are rather embedded in networks of contacts within which the opportunity is widely recognized. In this sense the entry decision is almost invariably not one that is well modelled by assuming a heroic Schumpeterian isolated individual. Rather, the entry is highly social. In the approach adopted here entrepreneurs are those who have distinct social networks. Entrepreneurial entrants are not motivationally distinct but 'structurally' distinct, and entrepreneurship is more a question of social contact than anything else. It could be argued that entrepreneurs are those who are motivated to generate the appropriate structures, but this would, once again, require the postulation of a special motive and we have seen there is little support for such a procedure. We take 'structure' as generated by factors beyond the actor's control. Such a procedure is entirely consistent with a rational choice perspective which usually assumes that resources are exogenously given to the actor, and structural links are here deemed a resource — social capital.

It is necessary to see how this way of looking at things bears a relationship to more conventional sociological approaches to entrepreneurship. Sociologists have sought to explain the probability of somebody becoming an entrepreneur in terms of their 'social positions' or origins. For instance, it is well established that those coming from a 'petit bourgeois' background are, some other things held equal, slightly more likely to become entrepreneurs themselves (Goldthorpe, 1987; Curran, 1986). More ambitiously, attempts have been made to explain entrepreneurial entry by examining the work history (a sequence of positions) of individuals (Mosakowski and Carroll, 1985). In addition, searches have been made for a relationship to religious affiliation, to ethnic status, and to social marginality or downward mobility. Unfortunately, like the psychologist's attempts to find some special discriminating motivation, this work has proved disappointing. Relationships are at best very weak, although research designs have also often been inadequate (poor or no controls, selection bias and small samples of dubious representativeness). The approach we are promoting here would dispense with these broad and explicit typifications of 'social position', replacing them with the idea of locations in complex networks. This is not entirely to discard the conventional sociological approach since, for instance, 'social class of origin' might be taken to imply something about the networks in which an individual will find herself. Similarly, social marginality might imply something about the ratio of weak to strong ties.

There is some evidence that contacts of one sort or another are important in both entry and subsequent growth. Birley (1987), for instance, in an examination of 'the top 100 owner-managers' in Britain found that 70 per cent were 'influenced' by family, friends (strong ties) and their previous employer. Pickles and O'Farrell (1987), using Irish data, find that self-employment is significantly related to being married. Others have, nevertheless, failed to find such relationships.

Our proposal is to conceive of three broad types of network as follows:

1 *Legitimation networks.* As suggested in the previous section of the chapter, ties of a focal individual with others in self-employment (entrepreneurship) which confer 'legitimacy' upon the entry decision. These may be weak.
2 *Opportunity networks.* Relations or ties to (experience of) individuals in sectors in an evolving economy which offer varying levels of opportunity for entry.
3 *Resource networks.* Relations or ties to others with (a) material resources (b) appropriate human capital. The ties may be variously weak or strong.

This enables us to make a first simple elaboration of the Coleman diagram (Figure 13.1) as depicted in Figure 13.2. Their individual actions are construed as 'caused' by

Figure 13.2. An Elaborated Version of the Coleman Diagram

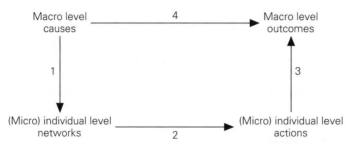

the location of the individual in networks of one sort or another (cf. Abell, 1992). Although this viewpoint is not entirely without difficulties, it provides a useful way of connecting the individual to her own local social structure which may then, in turn, be caused by certain macro variables (type 1 explanation in Figure 13.2). In any event this is the standpoint which will be explored here, and we now turn in the direction of opportunity networks, since we have already covered legitimation networks in the previous sections.

Quite a lot is known about the market and industry conditions which appear to facilitate exposure to opportunities and thus encourage entry, including entrepreneurial entry. Two salient aggregate features of entry stand out: its relatively high incidence; and its hazardous nature. Many attempt the journey but few survive for more than a few years. As Geroski and Schwalbach (1990) graphically put it, 'the average entrant is ... basically a tourist and not an immigrant, enjoying a life that is often nasty, brutish and above all short'. Entry appears to be relatively easy; it is sustained market penetration which proves more difficult. Net entry is rather low, sometimes negative, and this pattern appears to be repeated in most low and average growth economies. Industry patterns are also shown by Cable and Schwalbach (1990) to be similar in a number of countries. Most entrants are also small when compared to industry averages, and, of course, we are here concerned with individual entry (albeit often with employees). Our own studies suggest that those entering self-employment (particularly with employees) tend to stay in the sectors with which they have previous experience (employment).

The literature also suggests a number of industry-specific variables which may shape the pattern of opportunities and therefore the entry rate:

1 *The average profitability of the industry.* There are numerous theoretical and empirical studies pointing to a positive association between rates of entry and sector profitability (see, for instance, Geroski and Schwalbach, 1990). It may be, though, that potential entrants look at extreme or selective cases rather than at averages. There is also the problem that recent profit levels may reflect short-term disequilibria and not be a good guide to longer-term expected levels. Sophisticated entrants might estimate/guess accordingly. Potential entrants might also concentrate upon the performance of recent small entrants (profitability and market penetration). Be this as it may, we might expect (other things equal) that those with some relationship (perhaps through previous employment) with individuals in high profit sectors will disproportionately encounter self-employment opportunities.

2 *Growth (rate?) of the market; size of the market; elasticity of demand productivity.* As far as I can tell, market share dynamics are not well understood, but my knowledge of the literature is patchy. It may be asking too much to assume that entrants have very much in their heads! Clearly, if a market is growing, then penetration need not be at the expense of others, and incumbents might be less ferocious. The possibility of product differentiation may be important in creating niches in markets. Entrepreneurial entry of this sort brings us close to the inventor entrepreneur. Since most mature markets (old industries) which have reached an equilibrium size are dominated by longstanding incumbents (market share), in these circumstances entry will, if sustained, have to be at the expense of others (i.e., induce exit by replacement). Replacement will be easier in large markets with a large number of small concerns (low concentration).

3 *The number/proportion of small firms in the industry; more generally the degree of concentration.* A robust finding is that entry rates are higher in industries where the average size (employees) is small. This partly springs from lower set-up costs but may reflect also a lowered likelihood of collusion among incumbents against potential entrants. In general concentration will reduce the collusion costs to incumbents. Small firms are also more responsive to the state of the labour market which can clearly ease the path of entrants.

4 *The number of small firms in the local labour market.* Entry seems to be enhanced by the number of local small firms (even controlling for sector: Johnson, 1986). Gould and Keeble (1984) emphasize 'incubator plants' where employees obtain wide general experience and become attracted to running their own show. Sociologists and others speak of local entrepreneurial cultures (Burrows, 1990; Mason, 1990).

5 *Minimal optimal size.* Opportunities will decrease in feasibility as the minimal optimal size increases.

6 *The capital requirements for entry.* Blanchflower and Oswald (1990), Evans and Leighton (1989), and Evans and Jovanovic (1989) provide convincing evidence concerning the probability of entrepreneurial entry and access to capital — see below.

7 *Sunk costs.* Recent literature following Baumol, Panzer and Willig (1982) and Sutton (1992) has pointed to sunk costs as a barrier to entry; capital specificity and durability interact and increase sunk costs (see Geroski and Schwalbach, 1990); advertising intensity may be significant here.

8 *R and D intensity; internal/external technical change.* Entrepreneurial access is diminished if the flow of inventions is internal to established corporations: Audretsch and Acs (1990).

Our current research attempts to measure the intensity of either direct contact of individuals with sectors with varying levels of opportunity derivative of the above factors or with others so placed. We shall not make use of the measure here but the ideas are incorporated into the overall model depicted in Figure 13.3 which will guide the empirical study presented below.

We now turn to resource networks. Networks can be mobilized to procure resources, notably capital but also human capital. There seems to be copious evidence that entrants draw upon the skill of those with whom they have strong ties, particularly the immediate family (Casson, 1982) and ethnic communities in the case of minorities (Curran, 1986). A number of econometric studies have also demonstrated the importance of access to capital in the entry decision (Evans and Leighton, 1989; Evans and Jovanovic, 1989). Blanchflower and Oswald (1990) model the intrinsically uncertain credit market and inherited or gift capital and conclude that access to capital bears a non-linear relationship (concave) to the likelihood of being (and becoming) self-employed. Since the capital market is inherently uncertain, creditors seek collateral. Thus it is the capital market which ultimately constrains entrepreneurial entry. This is an interesting contribution as most of the literature on entry appears to concentrate upon barriers on the product side (Geroski and Schwalbach, 1990).

The literature reporting attempts to find relationships between either 'levels of education' or 'skills acquired on the job' and entrepreneurial entry gives no clear leads. Schultz argues that entrepreneurs (particularly successful ones) are likely to be of above-average education (Schultz, 1980). Storey (1982) finds no relationship between education and success; likewise, Gilmore (1972) and Birley and Norburn (1987). Curran (1986) and McGuire (1976) claim that self-employment offers a path to social mobility for those without formal education. The balance of the evidence is for an impact of 'education' on success but not on entry. Rees and Shah (1986) find no significant relationship with entry. Pickles and O'Farrell (1987) find evidence for an impact of 'incomplete secondary education' in an Irish sample. Borjas (1986), in samples from the US, finds that education increases self-employment. Blanchflower and Oswald (1990) seem to find no relationship.

One would expect the relationships, if they exist, to be affected by the sophistication of the undertaking. Casson (1992) gives a lengthy list of the skills which the entrepreneur needs (self-knowledge, imagination, practical knowledge, organizational ability, search skills, foresight, computational skills, communication skills), and some of these should be responsive to formal education! However, it is probable that education opens up so many non-entrepreneurial avenues that the motivation to exploit the relative attraction of risky entrepreneurial opportunities is somewhat stilled.

Cross (1981) emphasizes the importance of learning by trial and error on the job. Thus entrants — particularly successful ones — are likely to have an appropriate work history. Bannock (1981) suggests that most successful entrants have an entrepreneurial failure behind them. Others claim that second-time triers are no more successful. There seems to be fairly sound evidence that those with managerial skills are more likely to attempt entry, and the more senior (and perhaps general) the managerial experience, the greater the likelihood of success. Johnson (1986) shows that (in the UK) the probability of self-employment falls off as one moves from managers to the skilled to the unskilled. It may be that prior managerial experience not only facilitates entry, through the provision of the requisite skills, but also builds up facilitating networks which enable the neophyte entrepreneur to draw upon the skills of others. There is some evidence that entrepreneurs are able to acquire human capital in this way (Casson, 1982). Also it appears that joint entrepreneurial ventures are more likely to succeed than lone ventures. If entry into entrepreneurial roles is a matter of the human capital that can be accessed through networks, then it is perhaps not surprising that models which bring the qualifications of the individual entrant into the equation are not very successful.

Summing Up So Far

Unfortunately, despite a rather extensive literature in each of the three main social sciences, one can have little confidence that bringing them together in their present form is going to achieve a great deal. They do not appear to provide a series of partial but substantial truths that can be combined. The econometric models, though most reliable in the sense that controls are brought in when testing for significant relationships, reveal our ignorance of what drives entrepreneurship. There is no model which explains more than an insignificant percentage of the variation. This is partly attributable to the fact that research has had to rely upon data gathered for other reasons. But I suspect it is also attributable to a failure to take account of the social complexity in the entry decision. The sociological and psychological literature one might have thought would address the latter point, but once again our conclusions are not encouraging. For every study which promotes a determining variable (usually without adequate controls and/or sampling) there is usually another which finds contrary 'evidence'. There are perhaps two views one can take towards this rather negative picture: first, we may conclude that we are dealing with an inherently noisy process; second, that the process has not been adequately conceptualized.

In the course of the critical review we have begun to lay out the elements of a rather different approach to modelling entry into entrepreneurship through self-employment. In the first instance we propose not to invoke any special motives, but to rest content with simple (implicit) RCT assumptions. Second, we propose exploring the idea of micro causality (type 2, Figure 13.2) through the impact of three types of network upon entrants. Figure 13.3 gives a further development of the Coleman diagram incorporating the ideas developed so far and also some which are contained in the forthcoming sections of the chapter concerning the macro-micro linkage. The network variables are portrayed as interacting rather than as additive; whether this will prove to be a sensible construction only further research will tell.

In this chapter the network variables are treated as unmeasured and intervening (in our future research they will be measured directly). They may be interpreted in each case as the probability that a social contact (weak or strong) either legitimizes self-employment (the legitimacy network) or reveals opportunities for self-employment (the opportunity network) or provides resources, including human capital (the resource network). The measurement of these variables poses a number of problems which will not be taken up here as they are treated as unmeasured.

The incorporation of 'network' causes in type 2 explanations is, in effect, to admit the possibility of both exogenous and endogenous autocorrelation, i.e., individuals are not independent of each other in entering (and exiting) self-employment. This being the case, to exclude such causes in any estimation equation would introduce specification bias. This might account for the very uneven results in the econometric studies where individual level variables are brought into the regression model without controls for their autocorrelation. The present study proxies the legitimating and opportunity network effects by the macro level causal variables (Figure 13.3).

Self-Employment

In this section we report upon an empirical study of the flows (entry and exit rates) of individuals into and out of various states of self-employment. Although the definition

Figure 13.3. A Further Developed Coleman Diagram

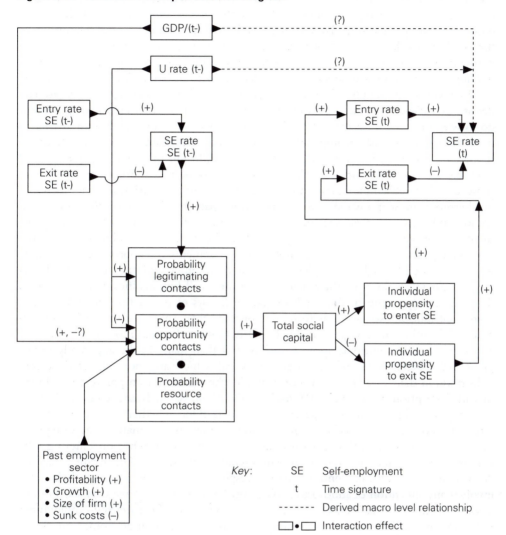

of self-employment is not entirely uncontroversial (see Hakim, 1989), we are led by definitions pertaining to available data sets — primarily the Labour Force Survey (LFS) (Campbell and Daly, 1992; Daly, 1991).

Our main concern is to disentangle the impact of prior changes in GDP and movements in the unemployment rate and self-employment upon the rate of self-employment in Great Britain (Figure 13.3). The current literature, pertaining to both Britain and other OECD countries, leaves us in considerable disarray on this matter. We shall approach our objective by separating the impact upon the rate of self-employment into those components operating through the entry and exit rates which, in turn, account for changes in the self-employment rate itself.

It is not unreasonable to suppose that entry into self-employment may bear some relationship to the supply of entrepreneurship and, whatever other merits there may be in studying self-employment, attempting to understand its significance from this standpoint seems worthwhile. The relationship is, however, by no means straight-forward. Certainly being self-employed is neither a necessary nor a sufficient condition for entrepreneurship. By any reasonable definition much entrepreneurship in the modern world is carried out by employees within the confines of established corporations or other organizations. When this is the case, is it sometimes dubbed 'intrapreneurship'. Such observations have led many to question the relevance of self-employment to the supply of entrepreneurship and, what is more, to predict ultimate demise of self-employment. Without doubt many of those entering self-employment do so with only the most modest of claims to possess any credentials as entrepreneurs, if by the latter we wish to imply they supply some significant innovative activity. It should, nevertheless, be borne in mind that the diffusion of established practices to new markets is of substantial significance, and it may be that appreciable numbers of those entering self-employment make an entrepreneurial contribution in this sense. Furthermore, most innovations are by no means path-breaking but rather modest in nature, and it may be that particularly those entering self-employment from employment (as opposed to unemployment) are often the carriers of modest innovations.

New products, processes, organizational arrangements and approaches to marketing are frequently highly complementary to each other and the incremental improvements in products or their delivery may be small but significant. If we care to designate entrepreneurs as those who organize factors of production (including their own contribution) so as to increase net output, then many of the self-employed would fall within the compass of this broad definition. Indeed, movement into self-employment may contribute more to net output than many of the apparently entrepreneurial machinations in the corporate world which are more directed at rent redistribution than value creation. For example, the market for corporate control may fit this description rather well (Baumol, 1993; Abell, Samuels and Cranna, 1994).

It proves difficult from large surveys to determine whether or not movement into self-employment embodies significant innovations. An alternative way of tapping the idea of entrepreneurship is to distinguish between those who, on entering self-employment, do and do not create employment for others. The former may be deemed to be 'significant' entrepreneurs irrespective of whether or not their entry involves any invention or innovation. Not least because the available data sets push us in this direction, we have chosen to concentrate on those who enter self-employment with employees. This could involve errors of both commission and omission. Some of those entering self-employment with employees may well be mere redistributors of rents currently available in the economy (Tullock, 1989). On the other hand, some highly inventive individuals may enter self-employment and never directly create employment for others. There is some evidence to suggest that the number of such one-person shows is increasing with the quickening incidence of corporate downsizing and contracting out. Be this as it may, by emphasizing the employment generating aspect of the movement into self-employment we are close to the commonsense picture of the entrepreneur as someone who establishes his own enterprise, which grows steadily by taking on new employees.

Studying Self-Employment

Although the entry to and exit from self-employment is a process continuously distributed in time, available data sources almost invariably impose a discrete time structure upon the available data, usually describing figures for yearly or quarterly intervals. It is correspondingly convenient to conceive of movements in discrete time. The LFS enables us to locate the labour market status of samples of individuals at the time of the survey and one year previously. The samples are drawn over a period of years, and the surveys generate a time series of one-wave cross-sections. They have been administered at varying intervals in Britain since 1973 and are also administered in a number of other European countries.

We have chosen to study flows (entries and exits) between the following states of the labour market:

— self-employed with employees (i.e., with at least one employee);
— self-employed without employees;
— employed;
— unemployed;
— outside (i.e., student, retired, houseworker or other).

Unfortunately, the LFS does not permit us to distinguish between differing levels of employment provided by the self-employed.

In addition the self-employed (with and without employees) are disaggregated by sector as follows:

— agriculture SE(A);
— energy and water SE(P);
— manufacture SE(M);
— construction SE(C);
— services SE(S).

In a previous paper analyzing the aggregate time series of the (log) of the ratio of self-employment to employment and unemployment respectively (Crouchley, Abell and Smeaton, 1994), we showed that the 'determinants' of the series, for females and males, are rather different, and we thus continue, where appropriate, to desegregate by gender.

The LFS data at our disposal enable us to study samples at the national level but also to disaggregate to regional figures. Assuming independence of the regions, the latter enable us to increase the number of observations, and thus the reliability of estimated coefficients. An earlier study of the SCELI (Social Change and Economic Life Initiative) data (Smeaton, 1992) suggests that most of those entering self-employment are not geographically mobile, which lends limited credence to such a procedure. Again, where appropriate, we use regional data, but any conclusions drawn will not depend exclusively upon the regional analysis.

Much of the analysis which follows is based upon a series of turnover tables distributed across time, each recording the labour market state of individuals in that year (rows) with a 'year ago' (columns). Appendix 13.1 gives the national level tables for Britain for 1991. Similar tables are available, though not included here, for earlier years generating over half a million observations.

These and similar regional tables enable us to make estimates for each table of:

— the absolute flows between any pair of labour market states;
— the expected flows given an assumption of independent marginal distributions (i.e., the distributions one year ago and in the current year);

Figure 13.4. Unemployment and Self-Employment in Britain, 1951–91

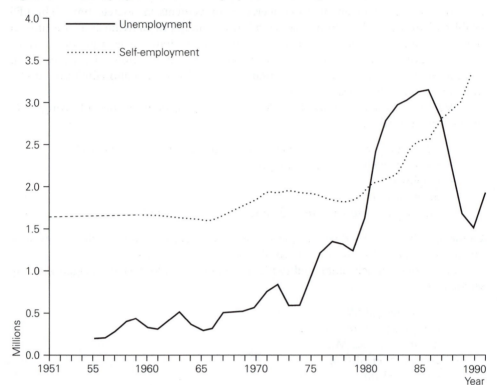

— the proportionate flows per cell based upon the table total entries, or the row, or the column (marginal) totals.

It is a straightforward matter to estimate entry and exit rates. The tables may be viewed as providing estimates for a discrete approximation to a continuous-time stochastic process. Such processes were first introduced systematically to sociologists by Coleman (1964a, 1964b).

Self-Employment: Recent British Experience

The trends in both the proportions and absolute number of self-employed and the unemployed in the British workforce are shown in Figures 13.4 and 13.5 (OECD figures). The numbers and proportions of self-employed decline from about 1971 to 1979 followed by a rather dramatic increase. This pattern seems equally true both for the total figures (agricultural and non-agricultural combined) and for the non-agricultural figures when taken in isolation. 1979–90 is not the only period of increase; between 1966 and 1971 there was also a sharp increase in numbers. It is worthy of note that the dramatic increase in self-employment during the 1980s still left the rate figure under the average for the OECD (= 9.8 and for EC12 = 13.2) countries. These patterns are, by and large, replicated at the regional level (not reported here but contained in Abell *et al.*, 1995).

Figure 13.5. Unemployment, Non-Agricultural and Total Self-Employment in Britain, 1959–91

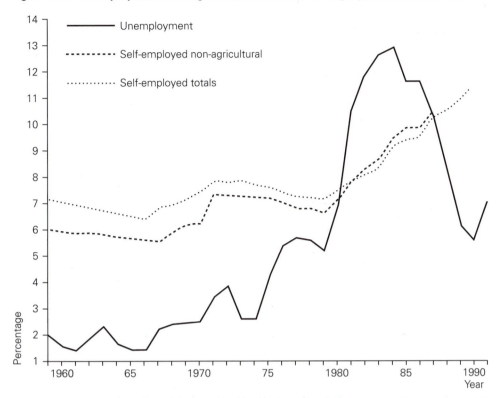

Figures 13.6 and 13.7 show the trends in the proportions of males and females in the workforce in self-employment (from 1977 only) in one case with, and the other without, employees. The '1979 upturn' and 1991 downturn are evident in each case. It is significant, however, that the upturn is sharper for both the male and female self-employed without employees than it is for those with employees. Apart from the upsurge from about 1979 onwards one of the puzzling features in both the national and regional figures is the growth in self-employment (rate) during the depression of the early 1980s and the expansion later in the decade, followed by a decline in the recession of the early 1990s. Numbers (not reported) are now (1995) climbing again.

Figures 13.8 and 13.9 show the time trend in proportions of the workforce in the various categories of self-employment, with and without employees respectively. We now turn to examine the impact of the three macro variables appearing at the top left-hand corner of the modified Coleman diagram depicted in Figure 13.3.

The Level of Economic Activity

It has long been held that there is in all the advanced economies a decline in self-employment rates, in both the agricultural and non-agricultural sectors, with economic development (per capita GNP or GDP). Theoretical reasons for this are not difficult to find. Lucas (1978) offers evidence for a model of development where the average size of firms increases with national wealth, if the elasticity of substitution

Figure 13.6.   Self-Employed Males as a Percentage of Workforce, 1977–91

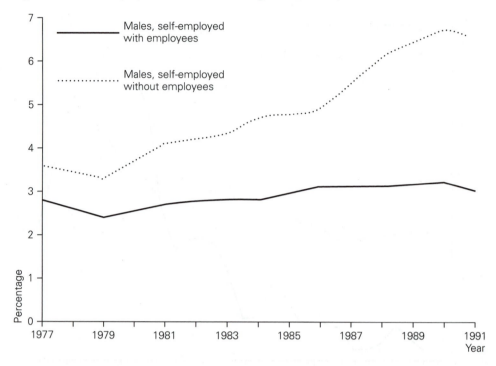

Figure 13.7.   Self-Employed Females as Percentage of Workforce, 1977–91

Figure 13.8.   Proportion of Workforce in Self-Employment with Employees, 1974–92

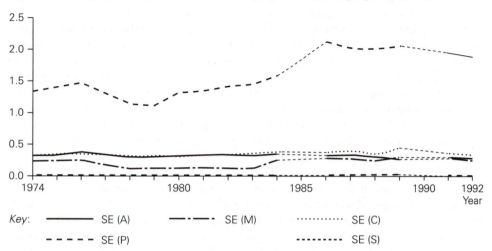

Figure 13.9.   Proportion of Workforce in Self-Employment without Employees, 1974–92

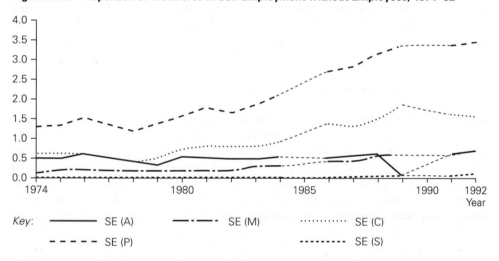

between capital and labour is less than one. More generally, economic development may be deemed to confer advantages upon larger firms through improvements in the infrastructure which decrease the relative costs of distributing goods and services. Be this as it may, recent tendencies for large corporations to downsize and subcontract may both confer scale advantages and increase the opportunities for small-scale enterprises and self-employment.

Acs *et al.* (1992) found, for a 1986 cross-section, that a 10 per cent increase in GNP per capita is associated with a 4.2 per cent decrease in self-employment rate (OLS, 22 observations, standard error of 1.3 per cent); thus supporting the long-held view. Longitudinal analysis of the data from the same sample of countries (1975–90) pointed in the same direction, although not as strongly; a 1.5 per cent decrease being associated with a 10 per cent increase in GNP per capita. These authors are of the view that the long-term tendency in self-employment rates is downwards.

Analysis of the British data (1966–91) does not, however, easily lead to the same conclusion. There is no significant relationship between the two variables for this period. As Figure 13.4 might suggest, for the period 1966–79 the relationship is (just) negative, but the later period shows a reversal of sign. Crouchley, Abell and Smeaton (1994), using a three-state model (employed, self-employed and unemployed), find no relationship, for males, between the time series of GNP per capita and the logs of the ratio, of self-employment to employment or alternatively unemployment, in each case controlling for a number of other variables (notably, a (significant) dummy for Conservative/Labour government and the unemployment rate). There is, however, a significant negative relationship (with one-year lag) for women upon the log of the ratio of self-employment to employment.

Changes in the proportion of self-employed in the national economy reflect the relative magnitudes of the entry and exit rates, and it seems sensible to ask what the impact of economic development is upon each of these variables and how they, in turn, constitute the overall proportion. This is precisely what is implied by the model in Figure 13.3. There, GDP is deemed to have an effect upon individuals' opportunity networks which is of indeterminate sign. The network, in turn, impacts upon individual level propensities to enter and exit self-employment, which accordingly aggregate to the macro entry and exit rates. So, at the aggregate (macro) level, the direction of the impact of GDP (ceteris paribus) depends upon the sign of the macro-micro linkage upon the 'opportunity network'.

Cyclical Effects: Unemployment

It is intuitively possible to conceive of both a positive and a negative impact of any short-term variations in the unemployment rate upon the rate of self-employment (Figure 13.3; Storey, 1991). On the one hand, increasing unemployment reduces the average opportunity cost of being in self-employment (increasing the number of contacts promoting the relative attraction or legitimacy of self-employment) and may, therefore, encourage entry to and discourage exit from self-employment respectively, to and from both employment and unemployment. The net effect will be to increase the rate of self-employment. In Figure 13.3 the unemployment rate is thus allowed to impact positively upon the legitimacy network. As unemployment increases (national or regional — see below), an individual's social contacts who are prepared to 'promote' self-employment increase. On the other hand, unemployment is likely to be associated with a (possibly lagged) reduction in opportunities which may depress entry and boost exits; the net effect will be to reduce the self-employment rate (see Figure 13.3). Unfortunately, we have at our disposal no independent measures of the 'legitimacy' and 'opportunities' variables and, therefore, cannot discriminate the paths; all we can do is look for the net balance of the positive and negative effects.

The empirically-based literature concerning the impact of unemployment rates upon the rate of self-employment is inconclusive. Negative (Blanchflower and Oswald, 1990; Evans and Leighton, 1989), positive (Acs *et al.*, 1992; Hakim, 1989) and zero (OECD, 1986) effects have all been reported, working variously with cross-section and longitudinal designs. Furthermore, some studies are at the individual level, while others are at an aggregate level. Yet others contain cross-level effects describing the impact of rates of unemployment upon the individual's propensity to self-employment

(Blanchflower and Oswald, 1990). Some studies are difficult to interpret as they adopt the ratio of self-employment to employment as the endogenous variable (Bogenhold and Staber, 1990), making it impossible to disentangle the impact of changes in unemployment upon the numerator and denominator. Studies of company birth rates seem also to lead in opposing directions. Hamilton (1989) suggests that self-employment rates are concave onto unemployment rates. Meager (1992) invites us to inspect entries to and exits from self-employment independently of each other. Crouchley, Abell and Smeaton (1994) hint at hysteresis.

Acs, Audretsch and Evans (1992), using both cross-sections and time series cross-sections of national level rates (fourteen OECD countries), find a consistent positive impact of unemployment rates upon self-employment rates, both in bivariate and multivariate models (the latter including a number of controls in the equation and taking the log of the self-employment rate). A first differences model (over five years to allow for significantly large movements), controlling for country-specific effects, however, reverses the sign and significance of the unemployment rate.

Steinmetz and Wright (1989), working with a US time series, suggest that an earlier significant impact (negative) of unemployment rates upon self-employment rates is no longer evident. Crouchley, Abell and Smeaton (1994), using UK time series, disaggregated by gender, of the (log) of ratios of self-employment to employment and self-employment to unemployment, find evidence consistent with the insensitivity of self-employment with the cyclical movement of unemployment.

An informal inspection of the self-employment rate and the business cycle in Britain from 1965 to 1992 suggests that self-employment rates tend to increase with expansion and decrease with recession, with the sole exception of the 1979–93 recession. Perhaps the incoming Conservative administration of 1979 changed things. It is important to appreciate what is and what is not at dispute in these matters. As inspection of any of the turnover tables like the one depicted in Appendix 13.1 will quickly confirm, a clear majority of those entering self-employment do so from employment. There can be no doubt that the individual probability of being in or entering self-employment is positively related to prior employment. This should not be at issue. The question is whether, and if so how, these individual level propensities are, or are not, influenced by the ambient unemployment rate operating through social contacts (Figure 13.3).

Entry to and Exit from Self-Employment

We start by inspecting the entry to and exit from self-employment respectively by the status of origin and destination of those making the moves. Figures 13.10 and 13.11 in turn portray the self-employment entry and exits from and to employment and unemployment respectively and in both cases from 1975 to 1991. Figures 13.12–15 present the same data but disaggregated by gender. The notable features seem to be:

— the domination of entry over exit from/to employment, particularly post-1979, for both men and women;
— the relatively flat exits to employment post-1979, irrespective of gender;
— the upturn in entry from employment around 1977;
— the peak entry around 1979 and 1989 from employment, with a trough in between;

Figure 13.10. Self-Employment Entry from and Exit to Employment

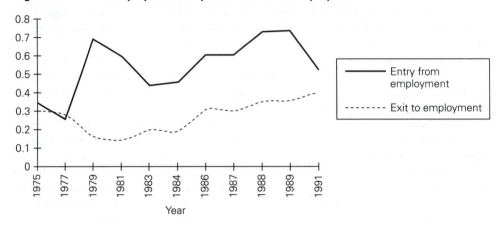

Figure 13.11. Self-Employment Entry from and Exit to Unemployment

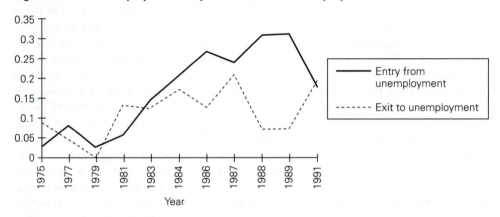

Figure 13.12. Male, Self-Employment Entry from and Exit to Employment

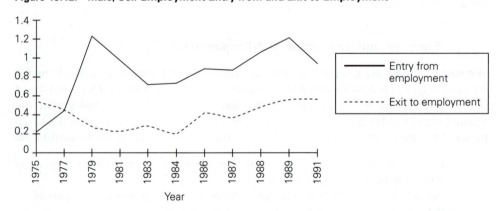

Figure 13.13.   Male, Self-Employment Entry from and Exit to Unemployment

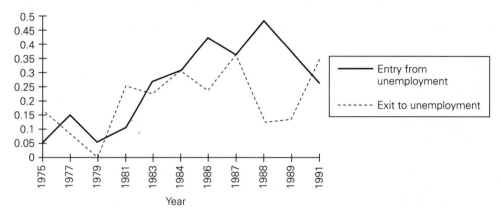

Figure 13.14.   Female, Self-Employment Entry from and Exit to Employment

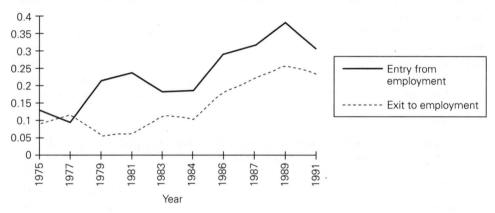

Figure 13.15.   Female, Self-Employment Entry from and Exit to Unemployment

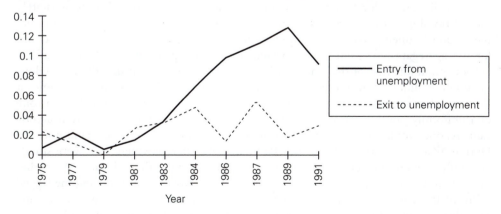

Table 13.1. Mean and Variance for Entry to and Exit from Self-Employment, 1975–91

	Entry rate	Exit rate
Total N = 106	0.0154 (0.049)	0.089 (0.012)
Agriculture	0.042 (0.020)	0.031 (0.011)
Private — Water, etc.	0.019 (0.008)	0.009 (0.006)
Manufacture	0.090 (0.018)	0.057 (0.011)
Construction	0.157 (0.020)	0.105 (0.018)
Services	0.445 (0.073)	0.25 (0.027)

Note: Those with and without employees are combined.

— the post-1979 jump in entry and exit from and to unemployment;
— the much greater variation in exits to unemployment than to employment;
— the drop, across the board, in entry in the recession of the early 1990s.

Figures not reported here show similar patterns when entry and exits are disaggregated by the labour market sector of the self-employed. Regional variations are also similar and will be reported elsewhere.

Table 13.1 gives the summary statistics for both the entry and exit rates for self-employment. The figures demonstrate that the mean entry rate (1975–91) is higher than the mean exit rate for all the categories of self-employment. The resultant changes in the self-employment rate (Figure 13.4) for the period studied are thus more driven by entry than exit. This may, however, not be true for an earlier period.

The Impact of Unemployment, GDP and Lagged Entry and Exit Rates upon Entry and Exit Rates

Our attention now shifts to the nature of the relationship (if any) between both the entry and exit rates to and from self-employment and movements in the unemployment rate, and *prior* entry and exit rates to and from self-employment and GDP (Tables 13.2 and 13.3).

Initially, an exploratory bivariate analysis was conducted investigating separately the relationship between the entry and exit rates to and from self-employment and the (national) unemployment rate and GDP. These analyses were first carried out for the aggregate rates, and then repeated distinguishing the status of origin of the entries and destination of the exits (see Table 13.2). They suggest that the unemployment rate is almost uniformly positive in impact, although also uniformly insignificant (the exception is entry from unemployment). The picture in relation to GDP is one of a uniformly positive impact on both entry and exit rates, though usually insignificant. As one would expect, very little can be divined from these results (and note the Durbin-Watson statistic). When both GDP and the unemployment rate were simultaneously brought into both the equations for the entry and the exit rates, the earlier bivariate results were largely confirmed (Table 13.3). However, introducing the lagged value of the entry (exit) rates begins to alter the picture. The unemployment rate, though not significant, now has a negative impact upon the entry rate and positive impact upon the exit rate; GDP remains positive, and is now significant, for both the entry and exit rates. These results would, if generalizable, deliver a net negative

Table 13.2.   Some Bivariate Models for Entry to and Exit from Self-Employment

	Exit rate	Entry rate
Constant	0.592(1.869)	1.016(2.031)
Unemp.	0.063(0.0868)	0.096(0.833)
D-W	1.127	2.229
Constant	−1.778(2.416)	−1.001(0.620)
GDP	0.007(3.588)*	0.006(1.496)
D-W	2.853	2.951

	Exit to unemployment	Exit to employment	Entry from unemployment	Entry from employment
Constant	−0.033(0.5)	0.308(3.208)	−0.042(0.66)	0.499(3.805)
Unemp.	0.022(1.63)	−0.016(0.71)	0.040(2.658)	0.0003(0.010)
D-W	2.047	0.827	1.107	0.887
Constant	−0.206(0.9)	−0.317(1.11)	−0.596(3.16)	−0.655(3.805)
Unemp.	0.001(1.22)	0.001(1.975)	0.002(3.81)*	0.003(4.85)*
D-W	2.514	1.04	0.981	2.046

Note: D-W is the Durbin-Watson statistic.

Table 13.3.   Multivariate Results: Entry to and Exit from Self-Employment

	Entry rate	Exit rate
Const	−0.951 (0.559)	−1.772 (2.226)
Unemployment rate	0.048 (0.398)	0.005 (0.090)
GDP	0.005 (1.207)	0.006 (3.157)*
DW	2.813	2.842
Const	1.507 (0.0807)	−3.412 (2.742)
Unemployment rate	−0.112 (0.835)	0.036 (0.610)
GDP	0.011 (2.011)*	0.011 (3.093)*
Entry rate (t–1)	−0.735 (1.955)	—
Exit rate (t–1)	—	−0.505 (1.306)
DW	1.51	2.77

Note: ( ) = t values.

impact of the unemployment rate upon the rate of self-employment, i.e., the proportion of self-employed in the working population (Blanchflower and Oswald, 1990). They must, however, be handled with extreme caution; the simple models are specified at the aggregate level and take no account of serial correlations, time trends or period-specific effects.

To begin to address these issues, a number of logit analyses were conducted (score 1 for entry or exit, zero otherwise), in effect dropping the unit of analysis to the individual level and allowing the unemployment rate to enter as a contextual (cross–level) variable impacting upon the individual's propensity to enter into or exit from self-employment (Figure 13.3). This analysis was carried out in two stages. First, the impact of the national unemployment rate, past self-employment entry and exit rates and GDP upon the individual propensity to enter and exit self-employment was studied. Second, the data were redisaggregated by region and the individual propensities were related to the regional unemployment and past self-employment entry and exit rates. In each case the data were aggregated over the period 1975–91 and the analyses were carried out for:

1   those in self-employment *with* employees;
2   those in self-employment *without* employees.

The analyses were also conducted separately for men and for women. Finally, rather than incorporating a dummy variable in the appropriate equations for either the source or destination of the entries and the exits respectively, the analyses were carried out for specific channels in the turnover tables (see Appendix 13.1). Thus for entries and exits the channels respectively from and to both employment and unemployment were analyzed in separate equations. All the logit equations contain a term for the time trend (1975–91) and also for year-specific dummies, allowing for year-specific effects. In addition, the regional equations contain regional dummies, allowing for regional-specific effects. The equations for flows from and to employment also contained sector-specific dummies to control the sector-specific effects in Figure 13.3. Estimated equations are not reported here, there being so many of them, but some of the main results are qualitatively summarized in Tables 13.4–13.5.

We may use the national level results in an attempt to draw conclusions about the impact of GDP upon entry to and exit from self-employment. However, no systematic conclusions can easily be drawn, perhaps accounting for the differing results about the impact of GDP upon the *rate* of self-employment in the existing literature (see also Figure 13.3).

Looking first at Table 13.4, we note that the only significant results for the impact of GDP (with no gender segregation) are upon the entry from both employment and unemployment into self-employment without employees and the exit from self-employment without employees to unemployment. When we disaggregate by gender, though, the entry rate to self-employment with employees from employment is significant and negative on GDP for both men and women, and the entry from employment into self-employment without employees, for women, is significantly positive.

What lessons can we draw from this rather complex and inconclusive picture? First, it is unlikely that any very secure statements (predictions) can be made about the likely movement of self-employment rates with advancing GDP. The rates, other things being equal, as constituted by entries and exits will be sensitive to the participation rates by women and the self-employed with and without employees which exhibit different patterns. It should, nevertheless, be borne in mind that the analysis of entry and exit rates is based upon a time series which only goes back to 1975. As Figure 13.5 suggests, the period prior to that would have in all likelihood produced different results.

Table 13.4 does exhibit a fairly consistent pattern in describing the impact of the lagged entry and exit rates to and from self-employment upon the individual propensities to enter and exit. Tracing the postulated signs of the relationships down the appropriate paths in Figure 13.3, we see that the rate of entry at t- should have a *positive* impact on current individual propensity to enter and *negative* impact upon the individual propensity to exit. Conversely, the rate of exit at t- should have the opposite effects. Table 13.4 conveys this pattern, although the relationships are not always significant. For males, however, there are significant relationships, particularly for those providing employment (all the signs are again in accordance with the

Table 13.4. National Level: Individual Propensities (logit) to Enter and Exit from Self-Employment

		All		Men		Women	
	Independent variable	1 Self-employed with employees	2 Self-employed without employees	1 Self-employed with employees	2 Self-employed without employees	1 Self-employed with employees	2 Self-employed without employees
Entry to							
Entry from							
Employment	U rate	-ns	[-S]	[-S]	-ns	[-S]	+ns
	GDP	-ns	[-S]	[-S]	-ns	[-S]	[+S]
	Entry rate t-	+ns	+ns	[+S]	-ns	-ns	-ns
	Exit rate t-	-ns	-ns	[-S]	-ns	+ns	-ns
Unemployment	U rate	-ns	+ns	-ns	-ns	-ns	-ns
	GDP	-ns	[+S]	-ns	+ns	-ns	+ns
	Entry rate t-	+ns	+ns	[+S]	+ns	+ns	+ns
	Exit rate t-	-ns	-ns	[-S]	-ns	-ns	+ns
Exit from							
Entry to							
Employment	U rate	+ns	[-S]	-ns	-ns	+ns	+ns
	GDP	+ns	[-S]	+ns	-ns	+ns	+ns
	Entry rate t-	-ns	-ns	[-S]	-ns	-ns	-ns
	Exit rate t-	+ns	+ns	[+S]	+ns	-ns	+ns
Unemployment	U rate	+ns	-ns	+ns	+ns	+ns	[+S]
	GDP	-ns	-ns	+ns	-ns	-ns	-ns
	Entry rate t-	-ns	-ns	[-S]	-ns	-ns	-ns
	Exit rate t-	+ns	+ns	[+S]	+ns	+ns	+ns

Table 13.5. Regional Level: Individual Propensities (logit) to Enter and Exit from Self-Employment

Men only			
Entry to Entry from	Independent variable	1 Self-employed with employees	2 Self-employed without employees
Employment	U rate	+ns	[+S]
Unemployment	U rate	[+S]	−ns
Exit from Entry to			
Employment	U rate	[+S]	[+S]
Unemployment	U rate	[+S]	[+S]

Women only			
Entry to Entry from		1 Self-employed with employees	2 Self-employed without employees
Employment	U rate	−ns	−ns
Unemployment	U rate	−ns	−ns
Exit from Entry to			
Employment	U rate	+ns	−ns
Unemployment	U rate	+ns	+ns

Key to Tables 13.4–13.5

−	=	negative impact of independent variable
+	=	positive impact of independent variable
s	=	significant (5 per cent)
ns	=	not significant
U rate	=	unemployment rate (national or regional)
Entry rate t-	=	the entry rate into self-employment a year ago
Exit rate t-	=	the exit rate from self-employment a year ago

Control variables:
— trend
— year-specific dummies
— industry-specific dummies for flows involving employment
— regional dummies Table 13.5

predictions of Figure 13.3). For women, the mechanism through legitimation does not appear to work.

From the regional analysis (Table 13.5) of the impact of unemployment upon entry to and exit from self-employment, the exit propensity from each of the two categories of self-employment is significantly and positively related to the (regional) unemployment rate for men only. For women the results are still by and large positive but not significant. These positive results are consistent with the simple national (no time trend or dummies) model in Table 13.3. We feel fairly confident in asserting that the individual propensity to exit from self-employment is positively related to the ambient unemployment rate, although women, who are an increasing proportion of the self-employed, are less subject to the generalization. The propensity to enter tells a less certain story. For women the impact of unemployment is universally negative but insignificant. For males the impact is usually positive but not always significant. It is clear, therefore, that the impact of unemployment upon the overall rate of self-employment will be crucially affected by the distribution of the genders in the flows. The effects of the lagged values of the regional self-employment entry and exit rates are not reported in Table 13.5, although the results were by and large consistent with the national level analyses.

Putting together the most general picture, we can ascertain the impact of unemployment upon the individual propensities to enter and exit self-employment. For males both the propensities to enter and exit are positively related to the unemployment rate. Women, on the other hand, exhibit a negative impact upon the entry propensity and a mixed but predominantly positive impact on the exit propensity (both insignificant). These results are identical for the self-employed both with and without employees. Finally, the impact of the unemployment *rate* upon the self-employment *rate* will be negative for women. For men, however, an increasing unemployment rate will increase exit (to both employment and unemployment) but also tend to increase entry. The net effect will depend upon the stronger of the two constituent effects. In fact the former is stronger so, once again, we predict a negative impact of the unemployment rate upon the self-employment rate.

Conclusion

Although this empirical analysis only scratches the surface of a patently complex dynamic process, it is suggestive of the ideas which are collected in Figure 13.3. These draw heavily upon Coleman. Our future work, which will attempt to measure the 'intervening' network variables directly, should substantiate the view that entrepreneurial entry is a social process in which the embeddedness of an individual in complex networks of social capital offers the key to understanding.

Coleman in his early work taught us to think in terms of flows of individuals between various possible states and in his later work to understand how macro level variables might impact upon these flows which, in turn, aggregate to produce new values of the macro level variable (Figures 13.1, 13.2 and 13.3). If the sociological enterprise is essentially concerned with the elucidation and estimation of the relevant importance of the macro-micro and micro-macro 'explanations' in accounting for macro-macro explanations, we need to control for the individual (micro) level causes of action which have no macro causes and ask how important type 1 (macro-micro) explanations are in determining the causes of individual action, and ultimately of actions themselves. This is, in effect, what has been attempted in this chapter. Individual propensities to enter into and exit from self-employment have been related to three macro level variables (GDP, unemployment and lagged entry and exit rate to and from self-employment), controlling for time (trend and year-specific dummies), region and sector. The most consistent result is that past self-employment entry and exit rates have a net positive effect upon current rates. It is argued (Figure 13.3) that they operate by affecting the legitimacy of self-employment as espoused by the social contacts of any potential entrant.

Appendix 13.1. Turnover Tables, 1991

	SE(A)	SE(P)	SE(M)	SE(C)	SE(S)	S(A)	S(P)	S(M)	S(C)	S(S)	EMP	UNEMP	STUD	RET	HSE	OTHERS	ROW TOTAL
SE(A)	249 0.3	0 0.0	0 0.0	0 0.0	1 0.0	26 0.0	0 0.0	0 0.0	0 0.0	0 0.0	3 0.0	0 0.0	0 0.0	0 0.0	1 0.0	1 0.0	281 0.3
SE(P)	0 0.0	26 0.0	0 0.0	0 0.0	0 0.0	0 0.0	1 0.0	0 0.0	0 0.0	0 0.0	4 0.0	0 0.0	2 0.0	0 0.0	0 0.0	0 0.0	33 0.0
SE(M)	0 0.0	0 0.0	238 0.2	0 0.0	0 0.0	0 0.0	0 0.0	25 0.0	0 0.0	0 0.0	7 0.0	2 0.0	0 0.0	0 0.0	0 0.0	4 0.0	276 0.3
SE(C)	0 0.0	0 0.0	0 0.0	307 0.3	1 0.0	0 0.0	0 0.0	0 0.0	41 0.0	2 0.0	11 0.0	0 0.0	0 0.0	0 0.0	1 0.0	1 0.0	364 0.4
SE(S)	0 0.0	0 0.0	0 0.0	0 0.0	1648 1.7	0 0.0	1 0.0	0 0.0	3 0.0	103 0.1	92 0.1	16 0.0	1 0.0	2 0.0	12 0.0	10 0.0	1888 1.9
S(A)	10 0.0	0 0.0	0 0.0	0 0.0	1 0.0	574 0.6	0 0.0	0 0.0	0 0.0	2 0.0	22 0.0	10 0.0	3 0.0	0 0.0	1 0.0	7 0.0	630 0.6
S(P)	1 0.0	0 0.0	0 0.0	0 0.0	0 0.0	0 0.0	56 0.0	0 0.0	2 0.0	2 0.0	5 0.0	2 0.0	0 0.0	0 0.0	5 0.0	3 0.0	76 0.1
S(M)	0 0.0	0 0.0	24 0.0	0 0.0	1 0.0	0 0.0	0 0.0	458 0.5	6 0.0	5 0.0	60 0.1	18 0.0	4 0.0	0 0.0	11 0.0	9 0.0	596 0.6
S(C)	0 0.0	0 0.0	0 0.0	40 0.0	2 0.0	2 0.0	0 0.0	9 0.0	1393 1.4	5 0.0	97 0.1	32 0.0	6 0.0	0 0.0	3 0.0	13 0.0	1602 1.6
S(S)	1 0.0	0 0.0	1 0.0	0 0.0	100 0.1	2 0.0	1 0.0	5 0.0	19 0.0	2625 2.7	317 0.3	92 0.1	32 0.0	10 0.0	98 0.1	36 0.0	3341 3.4
EMP	4	0	3	8	58	15	6	33	99	168	55,074	1073	1690	111	1087	513	59,942

	SE(A)	SE(P)	SE(M)	SE(C)	SE(S)	S(A)	S(P)	S(M)	S(C)	S(S)	EMP	UNEMP	STUD	RET	HSE	OTHERS	TOTALS
UNEMP (count)	2	3	8	5	7	4	15	89	52	0	1480	918	110	2	49	195	2939
UNEMP (%)	0.0	0.0	0.0	0.1	0.0	0.0	0.0	0.1	0.2	0.0	1.5	0.9	0.1	0.0	0.1	0.2	3.0
STUD (count)	0	0	1	0	3	0	0	5	0	9	308	151	3061	0	120	105	3761
STUD (%)	0.0	0.0	0.0	0.0	0.0	0.0	0.0	0.0	0.0	0.0	0.3	0.2	3.1	0.0	0.1	0.1	3.9
RET (count)	1	0	0	0	3	6	0	18	0	26	667	17	0	5203	144	7	6095
RET (%)	0.0	0.0	0.0	0.0	0.0	0.0	0.0	0.0	0.0	0.0	0.7	0.0	0.0	5.3	0.1	0.0	6.2
HSE (count)	0	0	0	0	0	2	1	26	0	33	632	144	0	0	7642	152	8855
HSE (%)	0.0	0.0	0.0	0.0	0.0	0.0	0.0	0.0	0.0	0.0	0.6	0.1	0.0	0.0	7.8	0.2	9.1
OTHERS (count)	0	2	1	10	4	7	0	33	0	0	1276	259	49	0	7	4035	6981
OTHERS (%)	0.0	0.0	0.0	0.0	0.0	0.0	0.0	0.0	0.0	0.0	1.3	0.3	0.1	0.0	0.0	4.1	7.1
TOTALS (count)	268	26	271	370	1847	631	71	560	1666	3050	59,454	2779	4980	6071	10,364	5252	
TOTALS (%)	0.3	0.0	0.3	0.4	1.9	0.6	0.1	0.6	1.7	3.1	60.9	2.8	5.1	6.2	10.6	5.4	
GRAND TOTAL																	97,660
GRAND TOTAL (%)																	100.0

Key:
SE(A) Self-employed, *with employees*, in Agriculture
SE(P) Self-employed, *with employees*, in Water, etc.
SE(M) Self-employed, *with employees*, in Manufacture
SE(C) Self-employed, *with employees*, in Construction
SE(S) Self-employed, *with employees*, in Services

S(A) Self-employed, *without employees*, in Agriculture
S(P) Self-employed, *without employees*, in Water, etc.
S(M) Self-employed, *without employees*, in Manufacture
S(C) Self-employed, *without employees*, in Construction
S(S) Self-employed, *without employees*, in Services

14 Educational Opportunities and School Effects

Aage B. Sørensen

James S. Coleman started a heated debate and inspired volumes of educational re-search with the main conclusion of the first *Coleman Report*. The conclusion was that school characteristics explain very little of the variance in academic achievement scores: students' family backgrounds explain most of the variance (Coleman, Campbell *et al.*, 1966). This is usually taken to mean that schools have little or no influence on educational achievement relative to the influence of family background. The con-clusion is upsetting to educators and to educational researchers who make their living from finding ways to make schools important, and therefore the interpretation usually given to the findings of the report continues to be challenged, including by Coleman himself.

According to other research by Coleman, both before and after the first *Coleman Report*, the conclusion of no school effects is wrong: it *does* matter to which school a parent sends a child. Coleman (1961a) showed that *the social systems associated with schools matter a great deal* for the values and aspirations of a student, and Coleman clearly believed that the different values and adolescent societies created in high schools matter for learning. Following the first *Coleman Report*, the claim of important school effects is voiced even more forcefully. In Coleman's most important educa-tional research after the first report, that on private and public schools (Coleman, Hoffer and Kilgore, 1982; Coleman and Hoffer, 1987), the conclusion is that the choice of school matters. Not only is it shown that schools matter for variables that are likely to influence academic achievement, such as values, as in Coleman (1961a),[1] but the recent research concludes that the choice of school matters directly for academic achievement, at least when the choice is between a public and a Catholic private school (Coleman, Hoffer and Kilgore, 1982). The results of Coleman, Hoffer and Kilgore (1982) also inspired much criticism, but now the tables are turned. It is no longer Coleman, but his critics, who argue that school characteristics, in particular whether they are private (Catholic) or public, do not matter. (See, for example, the articles in the 1982 special issue of *Sociology of Education*, Vol. 55, No. 2/3.)

There are several ways to reconcile Coleman's apparently conflicting conclusions about school effects. One can point to the choice of variables used to characterize schools in Coleman's various studies, to the choice of statistical measures employed, or to the different theoretical frameworks used to interpret the evidence.

The choice of variables is clearly relevant. The first *Coleman Report* showed that those characteristics of schools one can purchase with money did not account for much variation in student achievement. Yet the characteristics of schools used to ex-plain the difference between private and public schools — nuns, parental involvement and discipline — are not among the characteristics that one can easily purchase with money. So perhaps there is no difference to reconcile, and Coleman's educational studies before and after the first *Coleman Report* show that there are indeed school effects, only these effects are not associated with the variables used to measure school characteristics in Coleman, Campbell *et al.* (1966).[2]

It is not completely satisfactory to explain the varying conclusions about school effects by the choice of variables characterizing schools. Jencks *et al.* (1972) conclude that schools have little impact on measures of academic achievement, no matter which school characteristic is focused upon. This conclusion is based partly on a reanalysis of the data used in the first *Coleman Report*. There is other research, using other data, that claims to show very small between-school variation, after the variation in family background is considered (e.g., Hauser *et al.*, 1976). Their analyses focus on all the between-school variance, regardless of source, net of student characteristics. In studies focusing on partitioning of explained variance, there seems to be consensus that only a quite small proportion of the variation in academic achievement lies between schools. This, of course, does not preclude that a few schools may be unusually outstanding or that there are characteristics of schools reliably related to student learning. In any event, the choice of variables describing school characteristics seems unimportant for the amount of variance explained.

There are important differences in the statistical methodology of the two studies that may be relevant for the conclusions. Coleman, Campbell *et al.* (1966) and Coleman, Hoffer and Kilgore (1982) use different statistical measures of the importance of schools. The former research focuses on explained variance, the latter on the existence of the effect of school sector (private versus public). The reason for the shift in methodology was that by 1982 the variance-accounted-for measure of effect was abandoned by most researchers as a metric for the establishment of an effect. Attributing the variance explained to a group of variables is an ambiguous exercise when a substantial amount of the total variance explained is shared among the independent variables — a key issue in the debate over the 1966 *Coleman Report*.[3] Further, the amount of variance explained came to be regarded as a suspect measure of effect because of its dependence on the variances of the variables involved (statistical significance also depends on the variances involved, but this does not seem to have bothered anyone in the private/public school debate).

The difference in statistical measure suggests that there is not necessarily any real difference between the two sets of results. It is, of course, possible to have a statistically significant difference between two groups of schools net of student characteristics and still find that school characteristics only account for a modest amount of variance in student outcomes. The choice of variables measuring school characteristics and the differences in the statistical methodology used do not unambiguously explain the conflicting conclusions about the existence of school effects. There remains one important difference between the studies on school effects: the use of theory. Coleman, Hoffer and Kilgore (1982) present a persuasive argument for the existence of a school effect. It is an argument about how schools create different learning environments — through homework, discipline and effective social capital — and therefore produce differences in learning. No such reasons are presented why the school characteristics measured in Coleman *et al.* (1966) would or would not have an effect.[4] Thus a main difference between the two studies is the presence or absence of a theory about school effects.

The existence of school effects in Coleman's educational research appears to be a matter of theory and not of empirical evidence. Both the main studies find some effect of school characteristics on learning. It is the presence or absence of an argument for why schools should make a difference that determines the conclusion about the existence of school effects. Those who disagree with Coleman's argument about the advantages of Catholic schools see the evidence as suggesting only a marginal difference between the two types of schools — a difference that probably would disappear altogether if more controls for the self-selection into private schools had been used. Those who agree with the argument find the evidence sufficient to support the idea that there are important differences between schools. In the debate over the 1966 research the roles were reversed. Coleman then did not find the amount of variance explained by schools sufficient to warrant constructing an argument about why schools made a difference. It is not at all clear that the evidence for school effects is any stronger in Coleman, Hoffer and Kilgore (1982) than in Coleman, Campbell *et al.* (1966), but Coleman saw things in 1982 that he had overlooked in 1966 so the theoretical argument is there.[5]

This resolution of Coleman's conflicting conclusions about school effects suggests that the relationship between theory and evidence is one where theory decides what we take as evidence and therefore our conclusions about what exists. This tendency to see differences only when they are supported by an argument seems quite common in sociological and educational research, but it is perhaps especially common when such research is used for policy purposes. This is not a satisfactory state of affairs. Naturally we would like evidence to be strongly linked to theory so that the evidence decides when we will believe a theory rather than the theory deciding when we will believe the evidence.

Coleman himself presents the principles for how theory and evidence should be integrated in his work on constructing mathematical models of social processes and social structure (Coleman, 1964b, 1968d). The basic idea is that theory is formulated in models with parameters to be estimated so that the estimates speak to the validity of the theory.

Coleman did not follow his own principles in his educational research. Instead, he went from some theory to no theory about school effects from 1962 to 1966, and then went back to some theory in 1982. The integration of theory and evidence was never completed. There is no explicit statement about how schools may influence learning in any of the studies, only suggestions about how private schools may be more effective than public schools. Therefore, one cannot translate ideas about how school effects come about into parameters of models of the educational process that could provide precise measures of the effectiveness of schools.

This chapter is an attempt to apply Coleman's own principles about the link between theory and evidence to the study of school effects. It presents a conceptualization of how school effects are produced, formalizes this conceptualization in a simple model, estimates the model, and discusses some implications of the model.

School Effects and Change in Achievement

School effects presumably are effects on learning or on outcomes that depend on learning, such as educational attainment. Such effects would show up in measures of change in variables measuring the level of learning achieved, or academic achievement, at a certain point in time. Indeed, the most persuasive demonstration of private/public school effects, presented in Coleman and Hoffer (1987), uses growth in academic achievement as the dependent variable, where growth is measured as the gain between sophomore and senior year in high school.

To statistically oriented researchers, and this is the large majority, the difference between level and change matters little. The issue for them is the statistical significance of the between-school differences. However, there is an important conceptual difference between focusing on *gains* in academic achievement and focusing on the *level* of achievement. This difference is fundamental for our understanding of what school effects are about.

In his treatise on the mathematical study of change Coleman (1968d) considers the basic structure of the most simple change processes. Consider a time dependent variable $y(t)$. If change can take place in any interval of time, the appropriate formulation of the change process is in continuous time, so that the rate of change $dy(t)/dt$ is the quantity of interest. Applied to learning in schools, this quantity is the amount of learning taking place in a small interval of time. In the simplest model for a change process, the amount of change in a period is assumed constant, or $dy_i(t)/dt = a$ for all individuals i — everyone learns the same amount in a period of time. This is seldom realistic. An obvious modification lets the magnitude of this change vary among individuals, or whatever the unit of analysis, or $dy_i(t)/dt = s_i$; where s_i is a variable characterizing individual i. This means that the amount of learning, $dy(t)/dt$, depends on an individual characteristic, say ability. In this simple formulation, the amount of change does not vary over time, although it varies among individuals. However, it is apparent that many growth processes have the property that the amount of change depends on the level achieved of the change variable. This will result in change depending on time, through $y(t)$, so that the change process will be $dy_i(t)/dt = s_i + by_i(t)$. Coleman (1968d) argues that the quantity b often is negative, so that the rate of change is constrained by $y(t)$. In the application to learning this would mean that the amount of additional learning to take place in a small interval of time is constrained by the amount already learned.

The simple linear model for change, $dy_i(t)/dt = s_i + by_i(t)$, is the main topic of Coleman's treatise. The above reasoning suggests that this model is a reasonable candidate for a model of learning. The next section shows that this model can indeed be given an interpretation as a model for learning, an interpretation that is very useful for the conceptualization of school effects.

A Model for Learning

Sørensen and Hallinan (1977) propose a theory for growth in academic achievement. The theory conceives of learning as the product of students' abilities and efforts and their opportunities for learning. The basic idea is that students can only learn what they have the opportunity to learn. This means that a student ordinarily will not learn what is not covered in class. Students may learn different fractions of the material covered. How much students learn of what they had the opportunity to learn is governed by their abilities and efforts, or their resources for learning. How much is taught is governed by curricula and by teacher effort and ability. The resulting opportunities for learning vary by school, teacher, classroom and ability group within the classroom.

Let $y(t)$ denote the level of achievement displayed by a student in some domain, for example trigonometry, at time t. This quantity presumably is measurable with some academic achievement test. Time, t, is measured from the start of a period in which the teaching of the material covered in the test began, when $t = 0$. The amount of material covered in period t can be denoted $v(t)$, where $v(0) = 0$ at the start of the period. For each lesson, $v(t)$ increases by new material being taught until $v(t)$ reaches a value v^* at the end of a curriculum unit (say a school year). In other words, v^* is the total amount a teacher will cover in a curriculum unit of subject matter, and $v(t)$ is the amount covered by time t before the end of that period. The quantities v^* and $v(t)$ will vary by teachers, schools and instructional groups, but students in an instructional group (a classroom, or an ability group within a classroom) will all be exposed to the same $v(t)$ and v^*.

Students learn some fraction of the amount taught in period t. The size of this fraction depends on their resources for learning. Let s denote a variable providing a comprehensive measure of a student's ability and effort. This quantity will vary over time. Ability is partly a function of 'innate ability', partly a function of past learning and of developmental influences to which students are exposed. Also effort will change over time because of changes in incentives. These over-time changes will be ignored and s assumed to be a constant.

In a small period of time, dt, a small amount of new material, $dv(t)$, will be taught and a small amount of learning will take place, $dy(t)$. By definition, s determines how much of $dv(t)$ will be learned, so that

$$dy(t) = sdv(t) \tag{1}$$

This very simple formulation of the relationship between the amount students learn, their resources and their opportunities for learning has a very reasonable property: if there are no opportunities for learning, there will be no learning. The solution to equation (1) gives a simple linear relationship between $y(t)$ and $v(t)$ with a slope reflecting the level of a student's resources. The time trajectory would depend on how $v(t)$ depends on time; that is, how the presentation of material is organized in time.

Direct measures of the opportunities for learning are rarely available.[6] By assuming a particular dependency of $v(t)$ on time, it is possible to derive a formulation of the relationship between $y(t)$, time, and measures of ability and effort. The desired formulation is obtained assuming the amount of new material $dv(t)$ presented in a small period will decline over time. Teaching consists of the presentation of instructional material, mixing new material with the repetition of old material in a lesson. At the beginning of a curriculum unit most of the material is new; toward the end of the unit most is repetition of material already presented. In other words, the process of change in $v(t)$ is one where less and less new material is presented as the curriculum unit is completed, or $dv(t)$ declines with $v(t)$.

If the proportional decline in $v(t)$ is the same in all periods of time, then the process of change can be conceived of as governed by the equation

$$\frac{dz(t)}{dt} = -b'z(t) \tag{2}$$

where $z(t) = dv(t)$ and b' is a parameter that governs the rate of decrease in the amount of new material. This quantity presumably is related to the amount that is to be covered in the curriculum unit. Integration of this expression will provide a solution

$$z(t) = ke^{-b't} \tag{3}$$

where k is the amount of material presented in the first period. Without loss of generality one may set $k = 1$ and the integrated constant $k' = 0$. Inserting $z(t)$ will give the implied time trajectory of $v(t)$ since $z(t)$ is defined to equal $dv(t)$. This trajectory becomes

$$v(t) = \frac{1}{b'}[1 - e^{-b't}] \tag{4}$$

Time is here defined so that $t = 0$ at the start of the curriculum unit when $z(t) = 1$. At the end of the unit everything is repetition, or $z(t) = 0$. When this happens, $v(t)$ will become v^*. It follows that $b' = 1/v^*$ so that b' measures the total amount of new material presented.

Solving the differential equation (1), gives the simple relationship $y(t) = sv(t)$, assuming $y(0) = 0$, that is, nothing is learned when nothing is taught. Inserting the expression for $v(t)$ into this solution and letting $b = -b'$ gives

$$y(t) = \frac{s}{b}(e^{bt} - 1) \tag{5}$$

This expression may be estimated using measures of $y(t)$ at two points in time and a measure of the intellectual resources of individual students, s, or a formulation of the dependency of s on measured variables, as shown below. With such a specification and with over-time measures of $y(t)$, one can obtain estimates of b that would reflect variation in opportunities of learning among schools, classrooms and teachers. It would also be possible to see how characteristics of schools and teachers might relate to a student's ability and effort.

Note that if (5) is differentiated with respect to t, the result is

$$\frac{dy}{dt} = s + by(t) \tag{6}$$

which is the simple linear model for change treated in Coleman (1968d) discussed above.

Equation (5) is the desired model of learning. It separates the influence of student characteristics on learning from the opportunities for learning provided by instructional settings. It is clear from this formulation that schools may affect learning and measured academic achievement in two main ways.

First, schools create opportunities for learning. Schools are largely responsible for students' opportunities for learning. Some things are taught by families, by peers and by experience, but schools are largely responsible for the teaching of the knowledge and skills that are measured in academic achievement tests. If some schools try to teach more than other schools, students may learn more in these schools, and the schools that try harder will provide an advantage for students attending these schools. Other things being equal, the parameter b should be smaller in absolute value in schools providing more opportunities for learning than in schools providing fewer opportunities.

Second, schools may cause change in ability and effort, measured by s in equation (1). Such changes are ignored in equation (5), where s is assumed constant. However, changes in s presumably do take place over longer time intervals and schools may affect both components of s. Schools affect effort by creating social capital and discipline, as celebrated in Coleman, Hoffer and Kilgore (1982), and by creating the values and social systems analyzed in Coleman (1961a). Schools affect the ability to learn by developing learning skills and aptitudes. As noted above, the ability to learn is partly a question of genes and partly a question of acquired skills. The latter is especially important in subject areas such as mathematics where the ability to learn some material depends on the mastery of other material. Since schools decide whether skills needed to acquire other skills and knowledge are being taught, over time they will affect intellectual development. Of course, intellectual development will in turn depend on the opportunities for learning. Thus, through the opportunities for learning they provide, schools will both directly affect learning, by determining how much is taught, and indirectly affect learning, by developing the ability to learn.

The model proposes that opportunities for learning and a student's intellectual resources combine in a multiplicative manner to produce learning. There is simple reasoning behind this: the model assumes that nobody can learn material they were not presented. The assumption of a multiplicative relationship is nevertheless an important departure from the models assumed in past sociological and educational research on the effects of schooling where school characteristics and individual characteristics are assumed to add in some manner, suggesting that schools somehow will produce the same amount of learning in bright and less bright students. This additive specification is, of course, the rationale for the partitioning of the variance and for the search for significant main effects of schools that have dominated the research on school effects.

These ideas have important implications for the study of school effects, both for the measurement of these effects and for our understanding of the processes they reveal. These implications are discussed below. However, first it is necessary to establish empirically the validity of these ideas and to show how they establish school effects on learning. In the present context it is natural to focus on private/public school differences. This analysis is presented next.

An Empirical Analysis of Private–Public School Differences

The proposed model for learning cannot be estimated directly since the dependent variable is an infinitesimal quantity. The differential equation can be approximated by a difference equation, and this is often done in social research. Another approach is to solve the differential equation to obtain relationships among quantities that can be measured. Because of the linearity, the solution will be similar for any time interval, not only the interval from the beginning of a curriculum unit, as implied by equation (5). The solution is straightforward. With Δt denoting a time interval, $t_2 - t_1$, the solution is

$$y(t_2) = e^{b\Delta t}y(t_1) + \frac{s}{b}(e^{b\Delta t} - 1) \tag{7}$$

where $y(t_2)$ is academic achievement at time t_2 and $y(t_1)$ the academic achievement at time t_1. The $y(t)$ variables would be, for example, the senior and sophomore test scores for the 1980 sophomore cohort from the High School and Beyond Study, used in Coleman and Hoffer (1987) and in the analysis presented below. This solution assumes that the s variable remains constant over the interval Δt. Thus there should be no marked and systematic change in the students' intellectual resources over the period of observation. It is difficult to say whether this assumption is satisfied over the two years between the measurement of achievement in the High School and Beyond Study. If the assumption is not satisfied, there are ways to deal with the change, as shown in Coleman (1968d). However, over-time observation is needed for the relevant independent variables, effort and ability to learn, and these observations are not available in the High School and Beyond data.

To estimate the model, measures are needed of the two main components, ability and effort, or of their antecedents. Measures of the students' family background are of particular interest because the question of school effects is usually conceived of as a question of the importance of schools relative to the students' family background — probably as a result of the manner in which variance was partitioned in Coleman, Campbell et al. (1966). Genes and culture make these family background measures — parents' education, the family's social status, etc. — relevant for the development of both components of the student's intellectual resources.

Assume now that s is a linear function of a set of variables directly measuring ability and effort, or of variables measuring antecedents of student intellectual resources, such as family background. Or, $s = a_0 + a_1x_1 + a_2x_2 .. + a_nx_n$. This will give this formulation of the solution (7)

$$y(t_2) = e^{b\Delta t}y(t_1) + \frac{a_0}{b}(e^{b\Delta t} - 1) + \frac{a_1}{b}(e^{b\Delta t} - 1)x_1 + \ldots \frac{a_n}{b}(e^{b\Delta t} - 1)x_n \tag{8}$$

where again it is assumed that the x variables are constant over time. This expression can be written as

$$y(t_2) = a_0{}^* + b^*y(t_1) + a_1{}^*x_1 + a_2{}^*x_2 + \ldots a_n{}^*x_n \tag{9}$$

where $a_i{}^* = a_i/b \,(\exp(b\Delta t) - 1)$ in terms of the fundamental parameters of the process.

Equation (9) is a lagged model of the type commonly estimated with panel data. The learning model thus suggests the type of regression analyses of gains in achievement done by Coleman and Hoffer (1987), using sophomore and senior test scores as measures of $y(t_1)$ and $y(t_2)$ respectively. However, Coleman and Hoffer do not estimate the specification suggested here, and their results do not inform about the validity of the proposed model for learning. Most importantly, Coleman and Hoffer (1987) effectively treat school sector (Catholic vs. public) as an x_i variable; their focus is on gains adjusted for differences in family background. Therefore, their analysis will reveal at best only school effects on the intellectual resources of students and not differences in opportunities for learning. Further, an effect of school sector, measured

Table 14.1. Ordinary Least Squares Estimates of b* by School Sector

	Public		Catholic		Elite private		Other private	
Test	b*	s.e	b*	s.e	b*	s.e	b*	s.e
Vocabulary	.757	(.006)	.719	(.014)	.422	(.062)	.691	(.037)
Reading	.714	(.006)	.736	(.017)	.619	(.063)	.672	(.043)
Mathematics 1	.829	(.006)	.817	(.016)	.651	(.055)	.798	(.038)
Mathematics 2	.572	(.007)	.604	(.020)	.446	(.060)	.640	(.047)
N	16,031		2048		258		313	

Note: Estimates of b* are obtained from a regression of senior test scores on sophomore score, race and a comprehensive measure of family background (BYSES).

as an x_i variable, might only mean that there are differences between the two sectors in the abilities and efforts of students, created by self-selection into the two sectors. Such pre-existing differences were the main concern in the controversy about the public versus private school difference.

The learning model proposed here allows for the estimation of school sector differences in opportunities for learning even when there is self-selection. Over a relatively short time span, these differences in opportunities are likely to be the main source of learning differences among the various types of schools. Indeed, the substantive argument in Coleman and Hoffer (1987) is about the better opportunities for learning to be found in Catholic schools. Differences in opportunities for learning between private and public schools would show up as a difference in the b parameter for the two school sectors. Estimates of this parameter are not provided by Coleman and Hoffer.

It is clearly of interest to estimate the school sector differences in opportunities for learning. These estimates may inform about the validity of the model and they may provide an evaluation of Coleman's argument about the superiority of private schools that is less vulnerable to selection bias. Using the High School and Beyond data, Table 14.1 presents estimates of b* in four different school sectors and for four academic achievement tests.

It appears that estimates of b depend on which test of academic achievement is used and on the school sectors compared in a way that does not provide much support for Coleman's argument about the superiority of private schools. Recall that $b = \log b^*$ and that b* is non-negative and usually less than 1. If the model is correct, a larger b* should mean more opportunities for learning (b is closer to zero and there is more growth in academic achievement). The results suggest that elite private and other private schools provide fewer opportunities for learning in all areas but advanced mathematics (the Math 2 test). Catholic schools provide more opportunities for learning than public schools in reading and advanced mathematics and fewer opportunities in vocabulary and elementary mathematics. This pattern might mean that the theory and proposed model are wrong, or that Coleman's theory about the superiority of the various school types is wrong, or that some methodological problem prevents a simple test. It is not possible to disentangle these three explanations using the results presented in Table 14.1.

To see if some methodological problem is present, it is useful to start with a replication of the Coleman and Hoffer (1987) analysis. Table 14.2 presents estimates

Table 14.2. OLS Regression of Senior Test Scores on Sophomore Test Scores, Family Background, Race and School Sector

Test score	Vocabulary		Reading		Mathematics 1		Mathematics 2	
Independent variables	b^*	s.e	b^*	s.e	b^*	s.e	b^*	s.e
Sophomore scores	.752	(.005)	.716	(.006)	.828	(.005)	.576	(.006)
BYSES	.714	(.037)	.606	(.038)	1.068	(.054)	.578	(.026)
White	.934	(.058)	.821	(.056)	.727	(.834)	.481	(.040)
Catholic	.840	(.077)	.606	(.081)	1.065	(.113)	.248	(.054)
Elite private	.230	(.210)	−.113	(.218)	.152	(.304)	1.003	(.147)
Other private	.618	(.187)	.747	(.195)	.465	(.272)	.360	(.134)
Constant	2.764		2.680		2.872		1.194	
R^2	.656		.554		.680		.409	
N	18,650		18,507		18,324		17,998	

of school sector effects on achievement gains, controlling for measures of family background and race. This is the type of analysis done by Coleman and Hoffer (1987: 76–9), although they present the results in a quite different way than here; they show the predicted gains in scores for students with similar backgrounds.[7] The difference in mode of presentation should be unimportant for the results.

Table 14.2 suggests that students in Catholic schools gain more than public school students on all four tests. Elite private schools appear to be no better than public schools, except with respect to performance on the advanced mathematics test. Other private schools are better than public schools with respect to scores on vocabulary and reading, but not with respect to mathematics learning. These results remain puzzling, yet they do suggest the superiority of Catholic schools argued by Coleman and Hoffer (1987). However, one should think that elite private schools would be even better, and clearly they are not, according to Table 14.2. One likely reason is strong ceiling effects in the test scores. This problem with the data is discussed in some detail by Coleman and Hoffer (1987) and by Coleman, Hoffer and Kilgore (1982). These ceiling effects presumably are strongest in elite private schools (omitted from Coleman and Hoffer's analysis apparently for this reason) and in the tests other than the advanced mathematics test.

The results of estimating b^* in Table 14.1 were also particularly strange for elite private schools, suggesting that dealing with the ceiling problem might improve the fit between the arguments about the superiority of private schools and the estimates of b. However, before an attempt is made to correct for the ceiling effect, it is useful to try to remove more of the ambiguities from these comparisons by establishing validity of the interpretation of b and the model of learning. The estimates of b^* in different school sectors only allow one to draw conclusions about the differences in opportunities if one believes the interpretation of b. Academic tracks in high school presumably try to teach students more academic material than non-academic tracks. Therefore, we should find that b^*, estimated for students in an academic track, should be closer to 1 (so that b is closer to 0) than b^* estimated for students in other tracks. Table 14.3 presents the results of estimating b^* by track.

The results from OLS regressions presented in the first panel suggest that academic tracks provide more opportunities for learning in advanced mathematics and

Table 14.3. Estimates of *b** from OLS and Tobit Regressions by Academic Track

	OLS estimation				Tobit estimation			
Track	Academic		Other		Academic		Other	
Test	*b**	s.e	*b**	s.e	*b**	s.e	*b**	s.e
Vocabulary	.722	(.008)	.736	(.007)	.755	(.008)	.744	(.007)
Reading	.709	(.009)	.680	(.008)	.724	(.009)	.683	(.008)
Mathematics 1	.798	(.008)	.798	(.007)	.823	(.008)	.802	(.007)
Mathematics 2	.612	(.010)	.499	(.008)	.641	(.010)	.506	(.008)
N	7126		11,524					

Note: Estimates of *b** are obtained from ordinary least squares and maximum-likelihood estimation of censored regressions of senior test scores on sophomore scores, race and a comprehensive measure of family background (BYSES).

Table 14.4. Tobit Estimates of *b** by School Sector

	Public		Catholic		Elite Private		Other Private	
Test	*b**	s.e	*b**	s.e	*b**	s.e	*b**	s.e
Vocabulary	.772	(.006)	.744	(.014)	.654	(.084)	.739	(.040)
Reading	.721	(.006)	.751	(.017)	.655	(.067)	.679	(.044)
Mathematics 1	.841	(.006)	.829	(.016)	.758	(.064)	.823	(.039)
Mathematics 2	.587	(.007)	.617	(.020)	.519	(.060)	.672	(.049)
N	16,031		2048		258		313	

Note: Estimates of *b** are obtained from maximum-likelihood estimation of censored regressions of senior test scores on sophomore scores, race and a comprehensive measure of family background (BYSES).

reading, but not in vocabulary. Advanced mathematics was the test where the earlier results suggested that the ceiling effects were less important. The first panel of Table 14.3 does not do anything about the ceiling problem and it clearly seems important to do something about it. There are several approaches. A straightforward solution is to estimate using maximum likelihood, a Tobit-like model where the observations of students scoring the maximum value are treated as censored observations (see Amemiya, 1985). The results of this estimation are presented in the second panel of Table 14.3. All the estimates now show the expected difference between academic track students and others. The differences are largest for reading and advanced mathematics, suggesting that the Tobit estimation reduced some, but not all, the bias caused by the ceiling effect. With the correction for ceiling effects, the interpretation of *b** seems validated. Therefore, we might now expect less ambiguous results from estimating the model in the various school sectors, using Tobit regressions.

The results still do not suggest a clearcut pattern of differences between public and private schools. According to Table 14.4, there should be more opportunities for learning reading and advanced mathematics in Catholic schools and fewer opportunities for learning vocabulary and elementary mathematics in Catholic schools. Elite private schools should provide fewer opportunities than other sectors, and other private schools are like Catholic schools except in reading achievement. It seems that the impact of the ceiling effects has not been removed completely.

Table 14.5. Tobit Estimates of b* by School Sector: Students Scoring Below the Median as Sophomores

Test	Public		Catholic	
	b*	s.e	b*	s.e
Vocabulary	.709	(.014)	.786	(.046)
Reading	.576	(.016)	.649	(.052)
Mathematics 1	.718	(.013)	.794	(.047)
Mathematics 2	.321	(.017)	.380	(.059)
N	8412		795	

Note: Estimates of b* are obtained from ordinary least squares and maximum-likelihood estimation of censored regressions of senior test scores on sophomore scores, race and a comprehensive measure of family background (BYSES).

There is a simple method for reducing the remaining ceiling effect. One can estimate the models on samples that are unlikely to reach the ceiling. These would be students who score low at time 1. I chose students scoring below the median at time 1. It is difficult to imagine a systematic source of sample selection bias for this sample that would invalidate the comparison between school sectors. This sample may produce estimates of gains in achievement that are too high because of regression to the mean. However, the size of the gain is not the issue here, only the comparison between sectors. At most, regression toward the mean would affect this comparison by biasing the results in favour of public schools.[8] The approach does have one strong disadvantage. It is simply not possible to obtain an adequate-sized sample of students below the median in elite private and other private schools. Therefore, only the public versus Catholic school comparison is performed. The results are in Table 14.5. Now all the differences are in the direction of suggesting more opportunities for learning in Catholic schools. This is Coleman and Hoffer's (1987) conclusion, so one may wonder what has been gained by this elaborate exercise.

The evidence for the conclusion here is less ambiguous than the evidence presented by Coleman. I have estimated school effects on a quantity — opportunities for learning — that schools can do something about and where effects are likely to be detected. Further, I have estimated the school effect so that it is not confounded by sample selection or by misspecification of the model for how change in academic achievement is produced. That the model is correct is only evident to those who believe in its validity. The analysis also presented evidence for the validity of the model using a comparison of opportunities for learning provided to students in an academic track with those for students in other tracks.

Methodological Implications

The proposed model has many methodological and theoretical implications for the study of school effects. First I will discuss the implications for the measurement of school effects and for the design of studies directed at measuring school effects, or, for that matter, any other organizational level effect on learning, be it at the level of the classroom, the ability group, the track, the school or the school district.

For the measurement of school effects the most obvious implication is that no simple measure of the difference in achievement among schools or of the gain in achievement over time will identify school effects on learning. With cross-sectional data, school effects must be established comparing schools. However, the variation in academic achievement across schools is a result of both differences in opportunities for learning among schools and differences among schools in student ability and effort. I will show below that cross-sectional data cannot identify the relative importance of the two sources of learning, even when measures of student ability are available. Longitudinal data can identify the two contributions to learning from estimates of the parameters of the proposed model; but the simple gain measure will not allow the identification of the two contributions. It is instructive to show why a simple measure of gain, such as that used by Coleman and Hoffer (1987), will not identify the sources of differences among schools in effectiveness.

The overall gain in achievement attributed to the advantage of private over public schools is measured by Coleman and Hoffer (1987) as the gain $\Delta y'$ that would obtain if students in Catholic and public schools had the same family background. In the framework of the proposed model, Coleman and Hoffer estimate a measure of the advantage of Catholic schools relative to public schools that can be seen as a coefficient to a dummy variable for Catholic schools, say x_p, in a regression of either the achievement gain, or the senior scores, on sophomore scores and family background measures. The size of $\Delta y'$ directly reflects the magnitude of a_p^*, similar to the estimates presented in Table 14.1 above. According to equation (9), this quantity can be expressed as $a_p^* = a_p/b \; (exp(b\Delta t) - 1)$. Here the coefficient a_p measures the difference between Catholic and public schools in students' initial intellectual resources and in the growth of these resources over the period Δt. The larger this difference, the larger a_p. In models controlling for the intellectual resources at time 1 (sophomore year) a_p measures change in intellectual resources. If these controls are not adequate, a_p also measures self-selection into the two school types.

The gain in achievement attributed to school sector depends not only on a_p but also on b and Δt. The quantity b measures opportunities for learning. However, $\Delta y'$ is estimated for the combined private and public school sample, so these opportunities are the opportunities for all students, that is, an average of the opportunities in the two school types. The adjusted gain estimated by Coleman and Hoffer (1987), therefore, says nothing about the difference in opportunities between the two sectors. In fact, if the public sector provides fewer opportunities for learning (as argued by Coleman) than the private sector, the average b will be larger in absolute magnitude than the b estimated for private schools alone. It follows that the larger the public sector is relative to the private sector, the smaller the estimated a_p^* will be and the smaller the adjusted gain $\Delta y'$ used by Coleman and Hoffer to show the superiority of private schools.[9]

Estimates based on cross-sectional analysis are even more difficult to interpret. As suggested by Coleman (1968), the model for change can provide cross-sectional analysis with an interpretation, in the following manner. Estimates of a_i^* depend on the length of the time interval Δt. As Δt increases a_i^* approaches the values $d_i = -a_i/b$, so that equation (9) becomes

$$y(m) = d_0 + d_1x_1 + d_2x_2 + \ldots d_nx_n \tag{10}$$

This is the cross-sectional formulation estimated in numerous studies regressing academic achievement on a set of individual variables. The formulation obtains from the model for learning when $y(t)$ reaches a value $y(m)$ that Coleman (1968d) calls the equilibrium value. This value is clearly the maximum academic achievement scores obtained by a student in subject matter.

It is not clear what is meant by (10) in the present context. The assumption of $y(m)$ having been reached amounts to assuming everything has been taught about the topic and that students learned as much as they could from this material. This is unlikely to happen often, and the use of the cross-sectional formulation (10) seems suspect on purely conceptual grounds. If the formulation is used, the estimates should depend importantly on the omitted variables, time and initial achievement (since equation (9) presumably is the correct formulation for an ongoing learning process).

Both the cross-sectional and the lagged models estimate as coefficients to independent variables quantities that depend on both a_i and b. All observed effects of independent variables on learning or academic achievement will depend on the opportunities for learning through b. The richer these opportunities, the larger the observed effects. When cross-sectional or lagged models are estimated for a set of schools, coefficients to independent variables will vary across schools in such a manner that they will be largest in the set of schools that provide the most opportunities for learning.

Ever since the publication of Coleman, Campbell *et al.* (1966), the school effects question is usually formulated as one of comparing the effect of school characteristics with the effect of students' family background. The dependence of effect estimates on b in cross-sectional and lagged regression equations has important implications for the outcome of this comparison: the estimate of the effect of family background will depend on the opportunities for learning. Thus the amount of variance explained by family background variables will be largest in the set of schools providing the most opportunities for learning. In schools providing very few opportunities for learning, student characteristics relevant for learning, including family background, have little to act on, and family background will explain little of the variance. The variance partitioning assumes an additive relationship between schools and families in generating academic achievement. If the true relationship is a multiplicative one, as assumed in the proposed model for learning, the partitioning of variance does not in any way separate school influences from other influences on learning.

The measurement of school effects by the amount of variance explained by schools relative to the amount of variance explained by family background only makes sense if the only way schools would affect learning is through influencing the abilities and effort of students. However, it is impossible to conceive of schools affecting the development of students' abilities through other means than by providing opportunities for learning. Thus partitioning of variance between blocks of independent variables may be the poorest conceivable way to measure school effects on learning.

The modelling issues discussed here are not the only methodological implications of the proposed model for learning. The simple idea that no one can learn what they have not been taught suggests that measures of learning or academic achievement should provide measures of what has been taught in schools, if these measures are meant to provide information that allows the assessment of the effectiveness of schools. This seems an elementary requirement. Nevertheless, it is not satisfied in the research discussed here, and in similar research involving large-scale surveys of students and schools. These studies use measures of academic achievement that seem to have very little to do directly with what is taught in schools. Quite general verbal and mathematical ability tests are used that seem to measure students' aptitudes and abilities rather than the specific skills and knowledge that students actually learn because there is no uniformity in the curricula in American schools. One cannot compare students from different schools in terms of how much they have learned; one can only compare their aptitudes for learning. These aptitude measures miss most of the variability between instructional settings. This alone could account for the finding of small school effects in large-scale surveys of schools. The achievement test scores analyzed in the previous sections provided clear examples of the problem. I simply could not find tests that would allow a meaningful comparison of opportunities for learning between elite private and other schools.

As a result of the lack of comparability in what schools do, the achievement measures are most likely to detect school effects on the development of students' intellectual resources, especially their abilities to learn. These are the school effects that are least likely to be dramatic. Schools and teachers seem mostly concerned with providing effective teaching not with changing students' mental capacities. Students and teachers test their performance by tests measuring the students' retention of what has been taught, not by measuring change in intellectual capacities. In sum, there is an important discrepancy between what schools are trying to do and what much educational research measures.

That schools seem to be primarily concerned with teaching and not with changing ability distributions has important implications. Effective schools will create more inequality in learning outcomes than will less effective schools. The next section discusses the implications of the proposed model for our understanding of the processes that create inequality and equality in schools.

Inequality of Educational Outcomes and Inequality of Educational Opportunities

Hauser (1978) argues, going against the model for learning, that it is unreasonable to assume that school effects are produced primarily by opportunities for learning. He suggests that there may be considerably more learning going on in a boot camp where relative achievement levels are in flux than in a perfunctorily led high school class where relative learning differences persist. Evidently Hauser conceives of learning as change in student ability and effort only. Further, Hauser will only allow school effects to be effects that change students' relative positions in terms of their intellectual resources. This is an unreasonably restrictive definition of school effects: schools only matter if they make the bright dull and the dull brighter. It is, however, the effect detected by the variance partitioning in cross-sectional models.[10]

Hauser (1978) conceives of schooling as a process whereby schools somehow add to, or subtract from, the intellectual resources of students. This is an attractive scenario, for it implies that schools would be able to produce gifted students and equal educational outcomes for all. At least all students attending the same schools would come out pretty much alike, and all students in America would become equal if schools are equally equipped with the things that mould young minds. This in turn would mean that schools could create equality, as well as equality of educational opportunity, if those who are in charge of schools think this is an important goal.

This conception of the educational process and of the role of schools is an important one in American culture. The comprehensive system of secondary education, or the 'common school' (Cremin, 1951), is a unique American institution designed to achieve a basic equality of educational outcomes. The institution has been imitated in a number of European countries, as a replacement for, or alternative to, the very selective and highly differentiated European school systems, designed originally to achieve the opposite of the American schools: the maximum feasible inequality in educational outcomes.[11]

The American goal is not an easy one to achieve, at least not if it is taken literally. Presumably, schools can only add to the intellectual resources of children by teaching and thus by creating opportunities for learning. If equal intellectual resources are desired, these opportunities should be allocated so that the least able receive the most opportunities and the most able receive the fewest. This is not what usually goes on in schools. One main reason may be that such an allocation of opportunities is in direct contradiction to another popularly accepted educational goal: the goal of providing each student with the opportunity to achieve to the maximum of his or her potential.

Providing students with more opportunities for learning produces more inequality in academic achievement. This is easily seen from the conception of learning and teaching proposed here. Opportunities for learning determine the parameter of equation (5) in such a manner that the variance of $y(t)$ in the long run will become $\sigma^2_{y(max)} = (-1/b)^2\sigma^2_s$. Here $y(max)$ is the eventual academic achievement, and σ^2_s is the variance in student intellectual resources. Clearly, as more opportunities are provided, more variance or inequality in academic achievement will be created, for given inputs. From equation (5), it can also easily be seen that the variance in achievement will increase over time until it reaches the value $\sigma^2_{y(max)}$. There is empirical support for this prediction about the increase in inequality in test scores in the form of a phenomenon called 'fan-spread'. For example, Willms and Jacobsen (1990) report that while students tend to maintain their initial position in the distribution of mathematics achievement from Grades 3 to 7, there is an increase in the variance in the scores completely consistent with the predictions suggested here.

In fact, the goal of providing each student with the opportunities to achieve to the maximum of his or her potential has stronger implications. Such a goal implies that those with the greater intellectual resources should have the more favourable opportunities for learning. For this reason, we get ability grouping and similar arrangement in the lower grades and often elaborate curriculum differentiation in the higher grades. Good schools with the most opportunities given to the most able are also schools that maximize the differences among students in academic achievement.

The goal of making students achieve the maximum of their potential therefore implies the maximization of inequality of educational outcomes. It is not easy to reconcile this with the goal of making schools equalizers. This may be well understood by educators and educational policy-makers, although it is often hidden in a rhetoric of schools as equalizers. If policy-makers understand the relationship between school performance and inequality, then by the term 'equal' they presumably mean not equality of outcomes, but equality of opportunities. Presumably it is possible to maximize inequality and minimize inequality of opportunity at the same time. However, it is not easy. The problem is that good schools, in terms of providing opportunities for learning, also tend to have higher inequality of opportunity than do less good schools. This follows directly from the relationship between the observed effect of an independent variable and opportunities for learning discussed above. The more opportunities for learning are presented to students, the higher the observed effect of an independent variable x_i will be, including a variable measuring an ascriptive attribute of a student such as his or her race, ethnicity or family background. In other words, good schools are likely to increase observed inequality of opportunities by magnifying differences among students. The simplest way to create equality of opportunity is to teach very little.

While these fundamental relationships between opportunities and equality may be well understood by parents and educators, apparently they are not so well understood by the sociologists and others doing research on schools who continue to estimate school effects by relying on boot camp models of how teaching and learning take place, where schools are assumed to be able to change the relative abilities of children (cf. Hauser, 1978). This evidently must produce estimates of school effects suggesting schools are quite unimportant.

Conclusion

The model for learning described here suggests that learning is created when students use their intellectual resources to take advantage of opportunities for learning presented by schools. This is a simple and very plausible idea. The idea means that the relationship between opportunities and intellectual resources is multiplicative: if there are no opportunities for learning, no learning will take place. The model implementing this idea has a number of methodological and theoretical implications for research on school effects on learning and academic achievement. In particular, I have shown that neither the amount of variance explained by school characteristics, nor the variation among schools in gain scores, can identify school or individual contributions to learning. The simple additive regression models used in all research on school effects thus cannot identify school effects, if these effects are produced by teaching.

The model for learning represents an attempt to implement the ideas proposed by Coleman (1964b, 1968d) about how to link theory and empirical evidence in models of social processes. Coleman himself never used these ideas in his research on schools. Instead he relied on the standard additive models sociologists almost universally use in their empirical research. There are presumably two reasons for the use of these models.

First, the additive models have become the standard framework for relative magnitudes of the contribution of various variables or groups of variables for some outcome. Multiplicative models cannot say what is most, or not so, important relative to something else, since both components in a multiplicative relationship are essential for something to result — learning cannot occur without both opportunities *and* ability. Relative importance was an important issue in Coleman, Campbell *et al.* (1966), where the main concern was the relative contribution of school characteristics versus student family background. The additive model required for the partitioning of variables suggests that schools, in principle, should be able to create learning with students who have no ability, but I shall not pursue the matter here of what is really meant by relative contribution, as ascertained in an additive model.

Second, the additive model is the choice of statisticians in the absence of compelling theoretical reasons for some other functional form. Statisticians are not empirical scientists so they have a good excuse for preferring simple additive models over models with a theoretical justification. Sociologists and educational researchers are presumably involved in scientific research and have theories about how the processes they investigate are constructed. However, sociologists rarely provide a theoretical rationale for the choice of models and almost never dare to provide a theoretical rationale for a functional form in an investigation that matters, for example, for policy. In these situations sociologists will inevitably defer to the statistical rationale that simpler and additive models are better than other models. Sociologists seem never to have enough confidence in their own theories to base a choice of model on a theoretical argument. This is especially unlikely when, as in the analysis of school effects, the choice of functional form makes a real difference in how empirical evidence is obtained and analyzed.

Especially in large-scale research projects, and in research that has policy implications, sociologists will insist on statistical analyses that are 'robust' and statistically 'sound'. Additive models are considered robust and they are regarded by the large majority of quantitative sociologists as more sound than more unusual forms, because almost all quantitative sociologists have more confidence in statisticians than in social theory. Hauser's criticisms of the model described here demonstrate this (Hauser, 1978). Clearly, Coleman had little choice in the matter. A model that implemented his own ideas about the integration of theory and empirical evidence in mathematical models would never have been accepted by the discipline.

It is widely believed that since we do not have very good theories about anything, sociologists should stick to empirical analysis that uses models supposedly requiring no theory. However, there is no such thing as a model or measure without a theory. Any model or measure assumes something about the process being focused upon or the concept the measure taps. I gave an example of this above when I showed that simple gain scores misinform about the difference private and public schools make for learning. Additive models are just as strong a theory as multiplicative models, except perhaps to statisticians. Social research may profit a great deal from accepting the fact that there are no free lunches in empirical research with respect to theory, and, though social theory may be inadequate, there are no such things as measures and models that do not assume some theory about a process.

Acknowledgments

For valuable comments and suggestions I am indebted to James S. Coleman, Peter van der Meer, Ulrich Pötter, Annemette Sørensen and the participants in a seminar held in the Forschungsbereich Schule und Unterricht at the Max-Planck-Institut für Bildungsforschung.

Notes

1 While in Coleman (1961a) the determinants focused upon were adolescent values, the determinants studied in the private/public schools research are discipline, homework and curricula.
2 Coleman, Campbell *et al.* (1966) showed that peers mattered, consistent with Coleman (1962), but peers were not seen as a school characteristic (neither were teachers).
3 See the contributions to Mosteller and Moynihan (1972).

4   This does not mean that Coleman, Campbell *et al.* (1966) made no theoretical contribution. They created the very concept of academic achievement being determined by individual family background, the family background of peers and the schools. This partitioning among family, peers and school is now basic in educational and sociological research, and Coleman, Campbell *et al.* (1966) may be said to have created the basic vocabulary for research on these matters. To introduce a concept that becomes the basic vocabulary for a discipline is, of course, a major achievement. The concept was also of major importance for educational policy (Moynihan, 1993). However, this partitioning is not a theory of what goes on in schools.

5   Hanushek and Kain (1972) argue that Coleman tried to do too much in Coleman, Campbell *et al.* (1966) by doing (1) a major survey of the distribution of inputs to the educational process in the form of school and student characteristics, (2) a survey of the distribution of educational outputs, and (3) research on the process that links educational inputs and outputs. Hanushek and Kain also argue that Coleman, Campbell *et al.*'s model for the educational process is theoretically unsatisfactory.

6   An instructive exception is provided by Barr and Dreeben (1983). They obtain measures of the amount of material taught in reading and mathematics, and they obtain very interesting results about the variation in opportunities for learning among schools, classrooms and ability groups.

7   Coleman and Hoffer (1987) base their tables on estimates of models where the dependent variable is the gain in test score between sophomore and senior years. Here the estimates are for models where the senior scores form the dependent variable. This makes no difference for the estimates of the coefficients to the x_i variables including the dummy variables representing school sector as $y_2 - y_1 = a_0 + by_i + a_i x_i$ can be written as: $y_2 = a_0 + (1 + b)y_1 + a_i x_i$ with no change in a_i.

8   If the public school students below the median tend to score lower than Catholic school students below the median (for all students), this approach will tend to bias the results in favour of the public schools.

9   Of course, should public schools provide more opportunities for learning, Coleman and Hoffer (1987) will be overestimating the private school advantage.

10 A number of implications for policy of the debate between Hauser and myself about the nature of school effects are developed by Hoaglin *et al.* (1982).

11 Kerckhoff (1993) presents an exemplary illustration of the contrast in an empirical analysis of schooling processes in the UK, emphasizing the long-term consequences of processes creating inequality.

15 The Violation of Normative Rules and the Issue of Rationality in Individual Judgments

Michael Inbar

The Problem

Introduction

The view that the human being is a purposeful actor runs through Coleman's work (see his *Individual Interests and Collective Action*, 1986). In his *Foundations of Social Theory* (Coleman, 1990a) this notion takes centre stage. To justify his choice of theoretical outlook, Coleman considers possible objections to it at some length. One of them stems from a large body of research in psychology which suggests that people frequently make choices and judgments that appear to be irrational. Thus they often seem to make inconsistent decisions or to break fundamental rules of normative choice in some other way (cf. Coleman, 1990a, in particular pp. 14–15, 505–6). Obviously, the image of man that such characteristics suggest does not sit well with an approach to social theory which assumes a rational actor as its analytical building block. Coleman recognizes this, and after discussing the general nature of the problem, notes, without elaborating, that while the deviations from rationality demonstrated in the psychological literature are serious, they do not substantially affect the social theory that he presents (1990a: 505).

From his previous discussions of the issue, one may infer that Coleman has two reasons in mind for making this statement. One is related to the fact that, while recognizing that people may make mistakes and unreliable judgments for a number of reasons, and that some of their acts are best conceived as expressive or impulsive rather than purposeful, Coleman does not view this as constituting a theoretical problem. Instead, he regards these difficulties as reflecting the practical limits of the usefulness of this, as of any, analytical construct, an issue which must be empirically determined. The second reason is related to Coleman's position regarding the philosophical aspect of the issue of human rationality. While he recognizes the relevance of the evidence from psychological and other research, he is unwilling to draw too drastic conclusions from this evidence. His rationale is the belief that: '[M]uch of what is ordinarily described as nonrational or irrational is merely so because the observers have not discovered the point of view of the actor, from which the action *is* rational' (1990a: 18; emphasis in original).

I am in complete agreement with this view. In the following pages I propose to illustrate its perspicacity by showing how even the best documented psychological findings of the kind just alluded to are not immune to it. I shall focus for this purpose on one particular psychological task — the Linda vignette.

Let me preface my undertaking with a semantic clarification. In most discussions of the notion of purposeful action, there is one aspect of the meaning of this idea which remains implicit — including Coleman's own explication of this notion (1990a: 13) — and which needs to be elucidated. As I interpret it, the idea of purposeful action does not merely refer to the mechanical pursuit of a goal, but implies its rational pursuit, at least in some general sense. For an act to qualify as purposeful, the actor must regard it as relevant to the goal s/he seeks to achieve with it, and s/he must abide by the constraints s/he has subscribed to (exceptional circumstances excluded). To the best of my understanding, this interpretation conforms to Coleman's usage of this notion in the commonsense acceptation of the term that he defines (1990a: 13); a fortiori, it agrees with the economic acceptation in which he generally uses the construct (1990a: 13–14). In this chapter I use the terms 'purposeful actor', 'rational actor', and their cognates interchangeably in this general sense.

The Linda Vignette

The judgmental task on which we shall focus involves the following vignette and question:

> Linda is 31, single, outspoken, and very bright. She majored in philosophy in college. As a student, she was deeply concerned with discrimination and other social issues and participated in anti-nuclear demonstrations.
>
> Please rank the following statements by their probability, using 1 for the most probable, and 3 for the least probable.
>> Linda is active in the feminist movement. [F]
>> Linda is a bank teller. [T]
>> Linda is a bank teller and is active in the feminist movement. [T & F]

The critical research question is how people rank the two last statements, [T] and [T & F]. As it turns out, between 35 and 95 per cent of all subjects generally choose the statement [T & F] as more probable than [T]. The typical figure among college students with little or no statistical training is 80 per cent ± 10 per cent. This figure is about the same for the population at large. Among statistically literate subjects (e.g., graduate students in the social sciences with several statistical courses to their credit), it is sometimes, although not always, lower (see, for instance, Tversky and Kahneman, 1982: 91–3; Wolford *et al.*, 1990: 52). In one study carried out at the University of Stanford and at the University of California at Berkeley, it was found to be 36 per cent (Tversky and Kahneman, 1983: 300).

This pattern of choice (i.e., of [T & F] over [T]) is known as the *conjunction fallacy*, or in its formal isomorph, the *disjunction fallacy*. It is also referred to as the *conjunction effect* by authors who wish to signal a neutral stance regarding the normativeness of the response.

Many tasks have been shown to produce the conjunction effect, but the Linda vignette has achieved the status of a paradigmatic example of the phenomenon. A cursory look at the literature indicates that it is the problem which is most commonly used to illustrate this effect (e.g., Morier and Borgida, 1984; Carlson and Yates, 1989;

Wolford *et al.*, 1990; Gavanski and Roskos-Ewoldsen, 1991; Dulany and Hilton, 1991; Bar-Hillel and Neter, 1993). Generally, the typical pattern of response is construed as evidence that puts in doubt the theoretical value of conceiving human beings as rational decision-makers.

The rationale underlying this view is that the typical response violates the extension rule of probability theory. The usefulness of the theory of probability built on the principle that P (A) $\geq$ P (A & B), leaves little doubt that, other things being equal, the validity of individual judgments can be assessed by their conformity to this elementary yet fundamental rule.[1] On the basis of virtually undisputed assumptions, the relation P (T & F) > P (T) constitutes a normative impossibility; no matter how we look at it, the probability of two events conjointly occurring cannot possibly be greater than that of the least likely of them.

The demonstrative power of the Linda vignette findings for questioning the conception of human beings as rational actors stems from the compelling nature of the model that underlies the normatively correct answer,[2] as well as from a couple of additional reasons. One is the strong intuitive appeal of the typical answer subjects give; even when the correct answer is suspected, and often after it is realized, the mistaken one continues to have a sort of magnetic appeal, something which has suggested that there is a parallel between cognitive and perceptual illusions (Tversky and Kahneman, 1983: 313). Another is that many replications have demonstrated the robustness of the findings, as well as their generality, established by the use of a variety of judgmental tasks. Lastly, its demonstrative power stems from the strong case that Tversky and Kahneman have made in support of the fallacy interpretation in the ground-breaking papers in which they originally reported their findings (Tversky and Kahneman, 1982; 1983).

The logic of their argument remains to this date the best source for understanding the issues which must be addressed when scrutinizing the fallacy interpretation of the conjunction effect. I turn below to a review of this argument. Henceforth, and with only a few exceptions explicitly indicated whenever they occur, I always refer in my discussions to their main article on the conjunction effect (Tversky and Kahneman, 1983).

The Case for the Fallacy Interpretation

Tversky and Kahneman's interpretation of the conjunction effect rests on the notion that people often replace the complex task of estimating the probability of features or events by the simpler one of assessing their similarity to some salient pattern — a strategy they label the *representativeness heuristic* (Tversky and Kahneman, 1983: 294–6). In the case of the Linda vignette, this heuristic leads us to assess the *similarity* between the image we have of Linda and the stereotype we hold of a feminist bank teller, and to substitute this judgment for that of the *probability* that she is both a bank teller and active in the feminist movement. The problem, of course, is that the latter judgment is bounded by the probability we attribute to Linda being a bank teller, while the similarity judgment is not. When judgments of similarity and probability yield incompatible answers, the representativeness heuristic produces erroneous decisions.

On the strength of this rationale, Kahneman and Tversky undertake to show that it is the use of the representativeness heuristic, rather than some other explanation, which accounts for the conjunction effect. In the part of their research which concerns us, they report a series of studies involving the Linda vignette that they describe as increasingly desperate attempts to induce subjects to obey the conjunction rule. The object of these studies is to make the applicability of this rule increasingly transparent. The experiments include a number of manipulations (not necessarily presented in their chronological order):

A Making the relationship of inclusion increasingly obvious by using an intrapersonal design (rather than an interpersonal one), and by reducing the problem to two alternatives. In the authors' first studies, the two critical alternatives [T] and [T & F] were embedded in a set of eight occupations and activities that subjects were asked to rank. In later studies the task was simplified. In one experiment one of the relevant alternatives plus one common filler statement were the only ones given to the subjects; some respondents assessed the likelihood of [T] (or [T]*, see below) and of the common filler, and others that of [T & F] and of the common filler. In an even more transparent manipulation (a within-subject design), respondents were merely asked to rank the two juxtaposed alternatives [T] and [T & F]. (This format, together with its three-statement variant illustrated above, is now the one to which the Linda vignette standardly refers.)

B Tversky and Kahneman also examined the possibility that the conjunction fallacy might stem from the contextual interpretation of [T] as 'Linda is a bank teller and *not* a feminist'. Thus in one study they instructed respondents to *rate* the alternatives along a nine-point scale (rather than to *rank* them). In a related study subjects were given the task of assessing the probability of [T]* and [T & F], where [T]* was formulated as 'Linda is a bank teller whether or not she is active in the feminist movement'.

C Finally, to eliminate the possible problem of not having the correct response available, subjects were given a recognition task. In one experiment they were asked to choose between the two following answers:
   1 Linda is more likely to be a bank teller than she is to be a feminist bank teller, because every feminist bank teller is a bank teller, but some women bank tellers are not feminists, and Linda could be one of them.
   2 Linda is more likely to be a feminist bank teller than she is likely to be a bank teller, because she resembles an active feminist more than she resembles a bank teller.

Overall, these manipulations did little to help subjects avoid the conjunction fallacy. A full 82 per cent of those who rated (rather than ranked) the alternatives, and 57 per cent of those who assessed [T]*, gave a fallacious response. Among the subjects who were given the recognition task, 65 per cent chose the fallacious resemblance argument. Finally, replacing a between-subject design with a within-subject one had no discernible bearing on the magnitude of the effect. In short, a majority of respondents committed the conjunction fallacy in all treatments, including when the alternatives involved the glaringly transparent formulation [T]* in a within-subject design.

Tversky and Kahneman also studied the effect of framing the problem as a betting task. Although this treatment, like some of the foregoing ones, had some effect, 56 per cent of the subjects still gave a fallacious response.

In sum, under all conditions investigated, the responses of a majority of subjects were compatible with the conjunction fallacy interpretation. Only one factor proved influential, in relative terms at least. In one experiment involving statistically literate respondents, most subjects (64 per cent) gave the normatively correct answer.

Tversky and Kahneman conclude this series of analyses with a discussion of their implications for the issue of people as rational actors. On the non-controversial premise that we often rely on rules of thumb to deal with complex decisional tasks, they argue that their findings show that people fall prey to the conjunction fallacy because they use the representativeness heuristic. They note that, while there is nothing wrong in principle in relying on rules of thumb, a normative problem does arise whenever heuristics are not overridden when they should be. They observe also that post-experimental debriefings suggest that the judgmental failure of the great majority of subjects cannot be attributed to their lack of understanding of the extension rule, or of its applicability to the Linda vignette. Rather, the evidence indicates that subjects' failure stems from the fact that they do not relate to this rule as a *compelling* one in the process of decision-making. It is only in the course of the debriefing session that subjects (or most of them) do recognize it as such — usually as soon as this is pointed out to them and with some signs of embarrassment.

Given that the subjects investigated are what most of us would consider intelligent people, the authors conclude that the evidence does not support the assumption of a rational model of human beings in theory building. The basic reason is that people exhibit a strong tendency to ignore the *necessity* of applying normative rules of even an elementary nature in everyday decision-making. This opens the door to mismatches between theory and behaviour resulting from mismanagement of the basic 'tension between compelling logical rules and seductive non-extensional intuitions' (Tversky and Kahneman, 1983: 313–14).

Other Interpretations of the Conjunction Effect

Tversky and Kahneman's findings, and the strong case they made for interpreting them as evidence of a reasoning fallacy (a case that, I should stress, I have very incompletely summarized and hence to which I have only partially done justice), have triggered a wealth of replications. The bulk of this work shows how robust their findings are, and how hard it is to dismiss their interpretation for an alternative one, try as one may. A few studies suggest, however, that neither the conjunction effect nor the representativeness heuristic may be as impossible to reinterpret as was thought at first.

Certain studies show that the representativeness heuristic does not necessarily explain the typical way people actually reason when they deal with the Linda problem. For instance, Carlson and Yates (1989) claim that people use a variety of strategies in solving conjunction or disjunction problems, only one of which is the representativeness heuristic. They argue that one strategy people often use is a signed averaging model, in terms of which the likelihood we attribute to a conjunction or a disjunction is a step function of the probability we attribute to the marginals of the conjuncts or disjuncts. The data they present support their view. Gavanski and Roskos-Ewoldsen (1991) go one step further, proposing that some form of averaging of the conjuncts is the *predominant* strategy that people use in making their judgments. Using an ingenious design, in which, for some problems, the representativeness heuristic is not a plausible theoretical explanation for subjects' reasoning, they present data which support their contention.

Other studies question the very existence, or scope, of the contended fallacy, arguing that it may be a byproduct of certain features, or of the language, of the instructions given to the subjects. For instance, Dulany and Hilton (1991) argue that, in keeping with the principle that anomalous questions invite reinterpretation, one can think of a number of legitimate ways in which subjects can interpret many conjunction problems, the Linda vignette being a perfect case in point. This vignette is anomalous by design, in that it calls for a conclusion which is at variance with what, by conversational implicature, her background suggests. But, the authors argue, only answers which depart from coherence from the particular viewpoint or interpretation chosen by a subject (provided it is legitimate) can be properly called fallacious. In this light they present data supporting the view that the incidence of the conjunction fallacy, properly speaking, is a minority phenomenon, which in their experiments never exceeds 38 per cent and is sometimes as low as 0 per cent.[3] Obviously, these figures cast a very different light on what the answers to the Linda vignette are normally construed to tell us about the typical subject's rationality.

A study by Wolford *et al.* (1990) is another attempt to show that the typical response to the Linda vignette should not be interpreted as a reasoning fallacy. This study endeavours to demonstrate that, in giving the answer they do, most subjects use a strategy that is not only legitimate but even normative. Wolford and his colleagues propose a theoretical distinction between the task of predicting known and unknown outcomes. On the basis of this distinction, they argue that subjects should be expected typically to interpret the question they are given to be about the probability that a feminist bank teller is Linda (P [L/F&T]), rather than about the probability that Linda is a feminist bank teller (P [F&T/L]), as the experimenters normally assume. By the authors' own account, however, their experiments are only moderately successful in supporting this view (see also Bar-Hillel, 1991).

The work of Gigerenzer and his associates is another example, perhaps the most radical one in its implications, of the attempts to show that subjects' typical response to the Linda vignette should not be interpreted as a reasoning fallacy. The gist of the argument is in this case that probability theory is only meaningful if it is given a frequentist interpretation. In a frequentist interpretation, however, the notion of probability is hollow in the case of single events, and hence there is no normative way to assess subjects' answer to problems of the kind investigated by Kahneman and Tversky. For such an assessment to be valid, a different formulation is required. Gigerenzer (1991) presents studies which suggest that the required formulation (from a frequentist perspective) significantly reduces the percentage of fallacious answers given by subjects, including in the case of the Linda vignette (Gigerenzer, 1991: 90–2).

To put in perspective the ongoing debate that these studies were meant to illustrate, I should point out that their lines of research and findings are, for the most part, neither new nor non-controversial. For instance, both Wolford *et al.*'s explanation and the Gricean core hypothesis on which Dulany and Hilton's study rests were anticipated and considered at some length by Tversky and Kahneman (1983: 302–3, 311–12). Moreover, in a study which matches in ingenuity that of Gavanski and Roskos-Ewoldsen's (1991), Bar-Hillel and Neter (1993) have shown that the formers' conclusion must be qualified: combination rules cannot always account for the conjunction fallacy, and the representativeness heuristic must sometimes bear the burden of doing this alone.

Taking everything into account, I believe that two generalizations accurately describe the present state of affairs. The first is that, on the whole, the conjunction/disjunction effect is regarded as a judgmental fallacy. The second is that while the representativeness heuristic is not viewed as one of the necessary causes of this fallacy, it is regarded as one of its demonstrable causes. This can be clearly seen, for instance, in Plous' (1993) award-winning *The Psychology of Judgment and Decision Making*, which also provides an excellent illustration of the paradigmatic status achieved by the Linda vignette. In the opening pages of this volume, the reader is asked to answer a preliminary thirty-nine-item questionnaire to establish a benchmark for assessing the mistakes s/he will learn to avert. The Linda vignette is the first problem in this questionnaire.

The Present Research

The purpose of the experiments discussed in this chapter is to examine whether the typical response to the Linda vignette should be construed, indeed, as teaching us something about 'the senses and limitations of [our] rationality, [which is] the deeper concern that animates this and a number of related literatures', as Dulany and Hilton (1991: 87) aptly put it. The answer I wish to propose to this question is 'no'.

The Linda vignette is, I believe, a particularly good example for making a basic point which has already been made many times but obviously to little avail. Perhaps making it more explicitly than it tends to be made, and illustrating it with a concrete and detailed example, as I propose to do, will help to make it more convincingly. The point is this: in principle, no rule, including a formal one, is ever compelling — in the sense that its application is perceived in human reason as being *necessary* — outside the strict confines of a purely mathematical or logical discourse. Neither the application of a rule, including a normative one, nor the conclusion which follows from it, is ever automatically rationally self-evident without a rigorous adherence to an artificial and formal vocabulary, and outside the boundaries of a purely theoretical argument. That is, in practice, no rule is ever compelling except in a problem space massively simplified by a host of assumptions and presumptions.

Pragmatic reasoning in a natural language — the kind of reasoning in which subjects given the Linda task must engage — excludes this possibility in principle. There are two related reasons for this. The first is the well known fact that a natural language is inherently an ambiguous medium of communication and problem-solving, both because the concepts of such a language are ill-defined, and because its use introduces a plethora of presumptions in the definition of a problem. The second is that, in contrast to a theoretical problem, a practical one is never actually given. For a human problem-solver, a problem is always in the first place a *situated* task whose definition must necessarily be constructed — or at least completed. In the kind of experimental situation at hand, subjects must complete the definition of the problem by selecting one of the many possible interpretations of the instructions and of the description given. Moreover, they must choose the spirit in which to engage in the task, as well as the personal aims they wish to achieve by performing it.

The difficulty in assessing the rationality of subjects is that their choice of definition of the problem which results from these processes can only be defined after the fact. More importantly, it can only be determined in proportion to the subjects' insight into what they did and their willingness and ability to convey this information, which are notoriously limited, in particular the latter (cf. Nisbett and Bellows, 1977; Nisbett and Wilson, 1977; and for a qualification of this view, see Ericsson and Simon, 1980). In short, people have a great number of degrees of freedom for defining their task, and the choices they make in defining it are difficult to determine, both before and after the fact. In such a situation, a priori considerations — and among them formal or normative ones — provide but a tenuous basis for calling a judgment irrational when it does not match the expectations one has developed on their grounds. The nature of human information-processing being what it is, all likely alternative explanations would have to be *simultaneously* controlled in order to leave irrationality as the sole reasonable explanation of a subject's response. But the number of alternative interpretations which may be seriously entertained is in principle so great that, in all but exceptional situations, this is an impractical proposition. A serious leap of faith is thus inherently required for concluding with some certainly that an answer is irrational — unless the person who gives it grants the fact in credible fashion. The prevalent interpretation of the findings generated by the Linda vignette provides a good example of the hazards involved in taking such a leap, even in a case when the evidence for doing so appears convincing.

The investigation which illustrates this, and to which I now turn, involves a total of 473 subjects (some of whom answered two questions) who participated in what are conceptually five studies. All respondents were undergraduates, freshmen through seniors, studying in two faculties at the Hebrew University of Jerusalem. They answered the question(s) given to them at the beginning of one of their regular class meetings. Students who might have been exposed to a version of a particular experiment in the framework of another course were asked to identify themselves and excused. All others had the freedom not to answer the anonymous form handed out, or not to return it. Approximately a dozen students availed themselves of this opportunity. In addition, three returned unclearly marked forms. The 473 subjects included in this research are those who returned properly filled questionnaires.

I should emphasize that many of the findings discussed below result from experiments or treatments in which only a small number of subjects were involved (typically between twenty and thirty, but on a couple of occasions fewer). The results must therefore be accepted with some caution; until they are replicated on larger samples, and by other investigators, I cannot claim for them more than suggestive value.

The first two studies are conceptually a sensitivity analysis of the scope and robustness of the typical response to the Linda vignette under three conditions: first, in the present population of subjects; second, in experiments conducted by the present author; third, with treatments which investigate a couple of traditional alternatives to the representativeness heuristic explanation.

Study 1

In what is conceptually perhaps their most transparent manipulation, Tversky and Kahneman provided their subjects with two pre-formulated answers (see above, p. 230). Study 1 replicates this investigation with a slight modification. Its rationale is the following.

As I have indicated above, from a pragmatic perspective the normatively justified answer is merely a legitimate one, not necessarily the only or most rational one. In particular, inferences may have reasonable justifications which include rationales that are not well defined by reference to the normative outlook. For instance, some subjects who used some rule or heuristic other than the representativeness heuristic may have chosen the normative answer as the better of two unsatisfactory and non-descriptive alternatives of what they felt their reasoning process had been. Conversely, some subjects who chose the representativeness heuristic answer may have done so more as an expression of their rejection of the normative alternative (for some reason to be determined, possibly one which co-varies with the use of the representativeness heuristic), than because of the fallacious reasoning that such a choice is customarily interpreted to reflect.

The first study was designed to explore this general possibility. The logic of the experiment is straightforward: it involves diversifying the alternative with which the criterial answer is associated. Thus subjects were presented with the standard Linda vignette described above and given the following instructions (in this and the other variants of this study, the order of the questions was not counterbalanced, owing to the small number of respondents).[4]

Consider the probability of the two following statements about Linda.
1   Linda is a bank teller.
2   Linda is a bank teller and is active in the feminist movement.
Please indicate which one of the following four arguments you find the most convincing by marking it with a 1.

(.06)   *Linda is more likely to be a bank teller* than she is likely to be a feminist bank teller, because every feminist bank teller is a bank teller, but some women bank tellers are not feminists, and Linda could be one of them.

(.03)   *Linda is more likely to be a bank teller* than she is likely to be a feminist bank teller, because the probability that a person is both a bank teller and active in the feminist movement is lower than that of being either.

(.38)   *Linda is more likely to be a feminist bank teller* than she is likely to be a bank teller, because she resembles an active feminist more than she resembles a bank teller.

(.53)   *Linda is more likely to be a feminist bank teller* than she is to be a bank teller, because if we assume that she is a bank teller, with her background she is more likely than not to be also active in the feminist movement.

The first and third alternatives are the original formulations offered by Tversky and Kahneman (1983: 299) as operationalizations of the normative and representativeness heuristic answers respectively. Alternative 2 is a filler, another normatively framed answer designed to counterbalance the addition of the critical answer in this experiment, alternative 4. This answer operationalizes in colloquial language one of the possible ways of looking at the percentages of a cross-tabulated set of data, namely P (F/T).

The question of interest is how many subjects will choose the answer which operationalizes the use of the representativeness heuristic (alternative 3) rather than the identical conclusion, but differently justified, provided by alternative 4. The percentages at the left of each alternative give the answer to this question obtained in a group of thirty-two students.

The first observation of interest is that these data unambiguously replicate one aspect of Tversky and Kahneman's basic finding. Dichotomizing the answers into two groups, viz., answers 1 and 2 versus 3 and 4, shows that 91 per cent of the subjects fail to prefer the presumed mandatory answers 1 and 2; this percentage is quite similar to the typical findings reported in the literature. But an additional finding also emerges. The majority of subjects who chose alternatives 3 or 4 selected the latter rather than the former. That is, holding the conclusion constant, when respondents are given a choice between a difficultly tenable rationale and a more defensible one (if one simply assumes that they reinterpret the probabilities they are asked to assess), the majority prefers the latter. The possibility arises, therefore, that the percentage of subjects who commit the conjunction fallacy strictly speaking may amount to a large minority (38 per cent), rather than to a large majority (80 per cent ± 10 per cent), as the literature suggests.

Two variants of this study give plausibility to this interpretation. In the first, alternative 4 was formulated as follows (the other three remaining unchanged).

> *Linda is more likely to be a feminist bank teller* than she is to be a bank teller, because given her background she is in any event more likely than not to be active in the feminist movement — including if she is a bank teller.

Of the twenty-five subjects who participated in this variant of the experiment, 10 per cent chose alternative 1 and 6 per cent alternative 2 (one subject checked both, noting that s/he felt that they were identical), while 28 per cent and 56 per cent chose alternatives 3 and 4 respectively. That is, the two major conclusions suggested by the first experiment are also supported by these data: a majority (84 per cent) of the respondents did not prefer the presumed mandatory answers 1 and 2 to the others; likewise, when offered an alternative to answer 3 involving the same conclusion but with a more tenable rationale, only a minority of the sample (28 per cent) chose the original formulation.

In the second of these two variants, alternative 4 was formulated as a colloquial expression of P (L/T & F). As in the variant just discussed, the other three answers remained unchanged. The phrasing was as follows.

> *Linda is more likely to be a feminist bank teller* than she is to be a bank teller, because given her background she is more likely than most bank tellers to be also active in the feminist movement.

Two groups of subjects responded to this version of the experiment. In the first group (n = 22), 23 per cent chose the first answer, and 5 per cent the second. Alternative 3 was chosen by 27 per cent, and alternative 4 by 45 per cent. That is, once more a majority (72 per cent) did not prefer alternatives 1 and 2 to the other two answers. And once more only a minority (27 per cent) chose the original formulation offered by Tversky and Kahneman. The data of the second group (n = 30) replicate these results: 7 per cent and 3 per cent respectively chose alternatives 1 and 2, while 40 per cent selected alternative 3 and 50 per cent selected alternative 4.

Taken together, these results underscore the following conclusion: a minority of subjects only (in absolute as well as relative terms) appears to endorse the representativeness heuristic explanation when a more tenable one is offered for the same conclusion. This stands out clearly in the percentages obtained by combining the four experiments we have examined into a conceptual sample of 109 subjects. Doing this yields the following results: 34 per cent of this composite sample chose the representativeness explanation when offered one of the alternatives to it we have discussed, while 51 per cent chose the answer paired to it, and 15 per cent chose answers 1 or 2.

These findings are consistent with the following observation, which is the main conclusion I wish to draw from this study. What the majority of subjects, or in any case a majority of those choosing answers 3 or 4, finds persuasive need not be the representativeness heuristic rationale per se, but may be the proposition that, under the circumstances (which include relevant features of the communicative situation), Linda is most likely to be both a bank teller and a feminist. That is, the finding originally reported by Tversky and Kahneman should not be hastily interpreted to mean that the majority of their subjects recognized or subscribed to the reasoning that these authors attached to the chosen alternative. This reading leaves open, of course, the question of the general rationale (as opposed to the process of individual interpretation), if any, which accounts for the subjects' massive choice of answer 3 in the original study, and of answers 3 and 4 in the present one, or, alternatively, for the respondents' overwhelming rejection of alternative 1 in the original study, and of alternatives 1 and 2 in the present one. I shall return to this question in the context of another study.

A last finding pertaining to the one under discussion needs to be mentioned. It illustrates the sensitivity of the results just reported to the wording used — a phenomenon often observed, first by Tversky and Kahneman (1983: 309) themselves, and then by others (see Fiedler, 1988; Dulany and Hilton, 1991; Schwarz *et al.*, 1991). The finding is related to a variation in phrasing associated with the first experiment discussed. In this experiment the reader will recall that alternative 4 was designed to express, in colloquial terms, P (F/T). This was also the intention in an experiment run parallel to it, in which alternative 4 was formulated as follows.

> *Linda is more likely to be a feminist bank teller* than she is to be a bank teller, because assuming she is a bank teller, it is more likely that she is also active in the feminist movement, than that she is just a bank teller.

In retrospect, the major semantic difference between this wording and the one reported earlier (and all the others discussed for that matter) appears to be that, in this instance, there is no reminder of Linda's background as a justification of the conclusion offered. Be this as it may, in a group of twenty-four respondents this phrasing produced the following results: 20 per cent chose alternative 1 and 8 per cent alternative 2, while in the critical set 46 per cent chose alternative 3 and 25 per cent chose alternative 4. That is, in this instance the trend we have observed until now is reversed in the critical set.

This result could be accidental, of course. But whether it is or not, the finding is of interest for two reasons. The first is that it completes the report of all the experiments that I have run under the rubric of the present study. (Note that the finding does not affect the main conclusion indicated earlier. Adding the data just reported to the conceptual sample indicated above makes this obvious: of the consolidated sample of 133 respondents which results, 36 per cent chose the representativeness heuristic explanation, while 47 per cent chose the alternative paired with it, and 17 per cent chose answers 1 or 2; it will be recalled that the previous percentages were 34, 51 and 15 respectively).

The second reason is that the finding serves as a useful reminder that subjects' interpretations are sometimes extremely sensitive to seemingly inconsequential cues. A study designed to explore this general question is our next topic.

Study 2

When Kahneman and Tversky started their program of research on human judgmental biases, Grice's ideas were not widely known. In the early 1980s this was no longer the case. In a retrospective comment on their work written at that time, Kahneman and Tversky take note of this development by observing that 'the conversational aspect of judgmental studies deserves more careful consideration than it has received in past research, our own included. . . . [Indeed, it] is often difficult to ask questions without giving (useful or misleading) cues regarding the correct answer and without conveying information about the expected response' (Kahneman and Tversky, 1982: 504).

This lucid remark is particularly relevant in the present case, for while the background information offered in the Linda vignette is irrelevant to the answer which counts as correct, conversational conventions suggest otherwise. As Dulany and Hilton (1991: 87) observe, in such a situation we can expect to find operative the principle that 'anomalous questions invite reinterpretations'. The experiment we consider next illustrates this phenomenon. Its purpose is to provide a sense of the global effect of the implicit assertions intimated by the way Linda's background is standardly formulated.

The following description was used:

> In the bar of a hotel in which the National Feminist Movement holds a convention, you run into an acquaintance who works as a bank teller. She introduces you to her friend, Linda, who is 31 year old, single, and turns out to be an outspoken and very bright person. You learn during the conversation that Linda majored in philosophy in college, and that as a student she was deeply concerned with discrimination and other social issues and participated in anti-nuclear demonstrations. As the chat goes on, you wonder: Is Linda by any chance active in the feminist movement? a bank teller? perhaps both?
>
> Please rank the following 3 occurrences by their probability, using *1 for the most probable*, and *3 for the least probable* (if you find it *impossible* to order two alternatives, give them both the same rank).

The reduced assertiveness of the relevance of Linda's background to the judgmental task, by comparison with the standard formulation, is obvious and requires no elaboration. Note that equal rankings are allowed in this experiment; this holds true in all the experiments reported in this section, including the control groups. The advantage of this procedure is that it provides the information required for excluding the answers P (T & F) = P (T) from the count of conjunction fallacies, and for classifying them as normatively valid answers. The rationale for doing so is discussed in Morier and Borgida (1984: 245).

The experiment yielded the following results: 47 per cent of the subjects (n = 34) answered P (T & F) > P (T), while in the control group (which was given the standard vignette) 80 per cent (n = 25) did so. A replication of this experiment yielded essentially the same results; the corresponding figures were 52 per cent (n = 29) and 89 per cent (n = 28).

Other studies have documented effects of similar and even greater magnitude. For instance, in a direct probe of people's interpretations, Dulany and Hilton (1991: 94–6) asked subjects to explain how they understood the statement 'Linda is a bank teller' that they had just assessed. One of the pre-formulated answers subjects could check was 'Linda is a bank teller — whether or not she is active in the feminist movement'. As the authors point out, this interpretation is a prerequisite for commit- ting the conjunction fallacy. However, only 52 per cent of the respondents presented with the standard form of the Linda vignette chose it, and only half of them (26 per cent) actually gave a fallacious response. The other respondents who judged P (T & F) > P (T) selected an interpretation (e.g., 'Linda is a bank teller — and she is *not* active in the feminist movement') which absolved them of the accusation of irration- ality. Dulany and Hilton (1991: 96, 103) found that taking into consideration legiti- mate interpretations, the incidence of conjunction fallacies across all their experiments ranged from a low of 0 per cent to a high of 38 per cent. Here it is of interest to note that there are other studies which suggest that these figures may be a good estimate of the order of magnitude of the conjunction effect when semantic factors are taken into consideration. Thus Fiedler (1988) found that only between 26 per cent and 29 per cent of his subjects fell prey to the conjunction fallacy when he substituted the term 'frequency' for that of 'probability' in the instructions.

Studies like the foregoing deal with the effect of what may be called experimental commission — i.e., using a particular phrasing rather than another in communicating Linda's background and the task instructions. The issue of experimental omission is theoretically no less important. The problem in this case is not what the experimenter is doing, but rather how subjects are filling in missing information and resolving am- biguities. The difficulty in this case is this. The fact that subjects frequently make use of seemingly irrelevant aspects of a communication is often implied to be evidence that they are erratic, and thus irrational decision-makers. This is arguably a problem- atic view, in that it disregards the important consideration that people's constant search for cues is in principle eminently rational. It also overlooks the fact that, in practice, the specific cues they choose are often of indeterminate rationality, rather than clearly irrational. The rest of this section is devoted to an elaboration of these remarks and a concrete illustration of their implications.

That we are less than perfectly reliable information-processors is beyond ques- tion. However, this does not detract from the fact that we should be expected to be extremely *sensitive* processors, *especially* assuming that we are rational. This follows directly from the implications of the following three characteristics: the complexity of our information-processing and mental activities; the slowness of our conscious de- cisions; and the real-time constraints that the environment sets on effective responses. Together, these characteristics create the need to make countless assumptions in even the simplest judgments we make, a need which is met by the logic of our information- processing architecture: in the absence of indications to the contrary, we make the necessary assumptions by default, most of the time automatically, at below awareness level.

Obviously, it would be irrational for a system operating in this manner not to be constantly on the alert — whether deliberately or automatically — for cues suggesting the necessity to override the assumptions it continuously makes as part of the logic of its mode of operation. Two more considerations are relevant in this connection. The first is that many of the decisions about the assumptions we make are not uniquely determined by the nature of the task we perform, or by relevant rules or conventions, and in this sense they are discretionary. The second is that in almost any problem no amount of explicit instructions (whether in real life or in the laboratory) can possibly deal with more than a small fraction of the assumptions which need to be made.[5]

Together, these observations suggest that it is not only the privilege, but the obligation of a problem-solver to make the discretionary decisions by default that the task requires him or her to make — *or which have been made discretionary by the experimenter's failure to give explicit instructions to the contrary*. Moreover, the subject is rationally entitled to make them as s/he pleases, guided by two things: the existence (or absence) of the cues s/he chooses to regard as significant (with many degrees of freedom, because in the last analysis few cue rationales can be compellingly rejected), and the logic of the definition of the problem — determined, in part, by the discretionary decisions s/he made.

Two sets of experiments discussed below illustrate some of the practical consequences that these observations have. These experiments deal with the consequences of the silence of the Linda vignette and its instructions with respect to two of the many decisions that subjects must make (whether consciously or not). One of them relates to the temporal aspect, the other to the contingency or independence of the events which are to be assessed. The first deals with the question of whether Linda is assumed to have been a bank teller, a feminist, or both for a long time (say for years, rather than for days). The second is whether the judgment which is called for is that of the probability that these developments — should they have occurred — occurred contingently or independently. Of course, from a normative perspective, the reply to these questions — and to many others — is irrelevant to the correct answer. But, as we shall see in a later study, this is so under an implicit assumption which cannot be taken for granted.

Leaving these considerations aside for the moment, let us consider the experiments of interest, the first of which involved an honours class of undergraduates, who were presented with the following description (in English):

> Linda is 31, single, outspoken, and very bright. She majored in philosophy in college. As a student, she was deeply concerned with discrimination and other social issues and participated in anti-nuclear demonstrations. [Recently//Some time ago] her company moved, and she lost her job. A close friend has tried to talk her into coming to work for the bank where she is a teller. A relative has suggested that this was her opportunity to do what she had always wanted to do, become active in the feminist movement. This was [ten days ago//two years ago].
>
> 1 Please rank the following 3 occurrences by their probability today, using *1 for the most probable*, and *3 for the least probable* (if you find it *impossible* to order two alternatives, give them both the same rank).

The three alternatives which followed were the standard ones (see above, p. 228). Thirty-five subjects assessed the ten–days–ago version, and thirty-four assessed the two-years–ago one.

Before considering the results, a preliminary remark is in order. I must emphasize that I do not assume that the subjects normally make the decisions which are investigated in the present experiment in conscious fashion. What I do assume is that these decisions are, by definition, part of our system's repertory[6] — as are countless others which, like these, are instantaneously recognizable as familiar or can be made or reviewed consciously. As an information-processing system, we necessarily make them one way or the other, and the present research merely investigates the consequences of people making, consciously or not, one of the assumptions that I have selected for investigation, among many possible others.

With this in mind, the findings of this experiment were the following: of the subjects given the two-years-ago vignette, 71 per cent judged P (T & F) as greater than P (T), versus 54 per cent in the case of those in the ten-days-ago treatment. Two replications of this experiment (with Hebrew material) confirmed these trends. In one case (n = 26), the respective figures were 83 per cent (n = 12) and 64 per cent (n = 14). In the other (n = 39), they were 63 per cent (n = 19) and 60 per cent (n = 20).[7] The similarity of the results produced by the two-years-ago treatment to those typically obtained in experiments using the standard vignette invites the speculation that most subjects presume they have to assess the probability of lasting states having come into existence at some relatively distant point in the past, and not necessarily contingently.[8]

However, the really interesting result is another finding generated by a related experiment. Before considering it, a word of clarification is in order. All the investigations discussed thus far are within-subject designs. In these studies the critical alternatives for determining the conjunction effect ([T], and [T & F]) are juxtaposed. From the standpoint of the subjects, this procedure is transparent, i.e., facilitative, because when a set and its subset are juxtaposed, the mistake involved in making a normatively incorrect judgment is, in principle, glaring. In a between-subject design, in contrast, subjects judge only one of the critical statements. Tversky and Kahneman (1983: 311) observe that within-subject studies may not be as representative of the gravity of conjunction effects outside the laboratory, because in real life many important judgments have the logic of the between-subject design. Their sense of the situation is that, because of considerations of feasibility or practicality, in everyday life '[t]he physician, judge, political analyst, or entrepreneur typically focuses on a critical target event and is rarely prompted to discover potential violations of the extension rule'.

On this backdrop, the finding alluded to above results from the following experiment. After completing the task of ranking the statements (T) and (T & F), some subjects were asked to answer the following question:

2 Please give a scale value to your judgement of the likelihood that Linda is [a bank teller/a bank teller and active in the feminist movement]. Under the circumstances, this is:

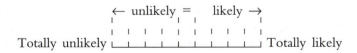

Half the subjects in the ten-days-ago treatment of the experiment administered in English were given the bank teller scale, and half of them the bank teller and active in the feminist movement scale (quantified as nine-point scales). This procedure created a between-subject experiment juxtaposed to the within-subject design reported above. This experiment produced the following results: P (T) received a mean rating of 5.70, versus 4.71, for P (T & F) (*t* = 1.52).[9] That is, contrary to expectation, Linda was *not* judged to be more likely to be a bank teller and a feminist activist than to be a bank teller.

This result is surprising for several reasons. As the prefatory remarks to this experiment have indicated, theoretical considerations (supported by all the currently available evidence, incidentally) suggest that, if anything, a between-subject design should sharpen the observableness of the conjunction effect. In the present case, in contrast, we find not only that P (T & F) is not judged to be strictly greater than P (T), but there are even indications of the *converse* trend occurring — even though the majority of the same subjects (54 per cent, see above) made judgments producing the conjunction effect. In other words, not only does the between-subject design fail to (re)produce the expected effect, but it appears to act as a relatively *facilitative* design.

A replication and elaboration of this experiment with the two groups of subjects given the Hebrew material confirms this finding. In these two groups, all subjects were administered the foregoing nine-point scales. In the first group (n = 26), the subjects in the ten-days-ago treatment gave a mean rating of 6.14 to P (T) versus 4.43 to P (T & F) (*t* = 1.54); in contrast, in the two-years-ago treatment, the corresponding figures were 3.83 for P (T), and 5.83 for P (T & F) (*t* = 1.82). The same pattern of findings recurred in the second group (n = 39): the subjects in the ten-days-ago treatment gave a mean rating of 5.00 to P (T) versus 4.28 to P (T & F) (*t* = .63); in the two-years-ago treatment, the corresponding ratings were 3.75 for P (T), and 5.25 for P (T & F) (*t* = 1.32). In other words, the finding obtained in the first between-subject experiment repeated itself in both groups. Moreover, the data obtained in these additional groups from the subjects in the two-years-ago treatment strongly suggest that we are confronted with a full-blown interaction effect.

Barring an unsuspected problem with the data reported, the foregoing findings have an important implication which stems from two possible explanations for them. Either a within-subject design does not operationalize transparency (in comparison to a between-subject one), or one of the assumptions on which the transparency argument is based is mistaken. In either case, contrary to the presumption found in the literature, the fact that a majority of subjects commit the conjunction fallacy in a within-subject design apparently does not guarantee that in a parallel between-subject study this effect will be documentable.

These remarks, and the questions they raise, complete the discussion of the two preliminary studies mentioned at the outset of this part of the chapter. While these studies replicate the central finding with which we are concerned, I believe that they also support the following conclusion. Upon close examination of the conjunction fallacy phenomenon, there is evidence to suggest that this effect may not be as unassailable, nor as unambiguously interpretable, as may have seemed at first sight.

The next two studies are conceptual linking pins in the overall argument. The first is an attempt to estimate the minimal conjunction effect that the Linda vignette may be expected to induce in the population investigated. The second illustrates how subjects resist adopting the extensional perspective that one would expect them to adopt, and conversely, how readily they engage in the desired mode of reasoning when, on a certain assumption, they can be expected to *elect* to do so.

Table 15.1. A Notional Set of Data

		Linda(s)		Caroline(s)		. . .	Total
T	F	8	[A]	1	[C]	. . .	9
	−F	2	[B]	19	[D]	. . .	21
	[subtotal]	[10]		[20]		[. . .]	[30]
−T	F	60	[E]	10	[G]	. . .	70
	−F	30	[F]	70	[H]	. . .	100
	[subtotal]	[90]		[80]		[. . .]	[170]
Total		100		100		. . .	200

Notes: T = bank teller; −T = not bank teller; F = feminist; −F = not feminist.

Study 3

Consider Table 15.1, which presents a notional set of data describing women with particular backgrounds (Linda, Caroline, etc.), classified by two attributes: being or not being a bank teller (T, −T), and being or not being or a feminist (F, −F). One way to look at this table is to focus on its columns. If we focus on Linda's column (using its total as a basis), Table 15.1 expresses the arbitrary estimate that, given her background, Linda has (or a sample of 100 women responding to Linda's description have) a 10 per cent chance of being a T, a 68 per cent chance of being a F, and an 8 per cent chance of being both T & F. Obviously, as long as we keep our focus on the Linda column and on its total, by the nature of this table P (T & F) can never exceed P (T), because the value of cell [A] cannot possibly exceed that of cells [A] + [B] combined (the two respective numerators in the same quotient of these probabilities). The two likelihoods can be at most equal in the limiting case where [A] = [A] + [B], i.e., where cell [B] is empty (a situation which holds true for the subjects who believe that, given her background, the probability that Linda is a bank teller and *not* a feminist can be taken to be zero, rather than 2 per cent, as in Table 15.1).

But there are other ways to look meaningfully at Table 15.1. One is to interpret the probability that Linda is a bank teller and a feminist as P (F/T), that is, as the probability that Linda is a feminist given, or assuming, that she is a bank teller. While we still focus on Linda's column, the basis of reference involved in this interpretation is the first subtotal (10), and the likelihood of Linda being a feminist and a bank teller is 8/10 — a far greater value than that of her being a bank teller, which remains 10 per cent.

Another possibility is to look at the table horizontally, in particular to focus on the first row and on the total of this row. Doing so amounts to interpreting the probability that Linda is a bank teller and a feminist as P (L/T & F), that is, as the probability that a bank teller who is active in the feminist movement should be Linda, rather than someone else (say, Caroline). This probability is 8/9 in the case at hand, again a much higher probability than that of Linda being a bank teller, no matter how we choose to compute this likelihood (given the marginals used in Table 15.1).

The point of these observations is that there is no a priori correct way to look at Table 15.1. The context, task and cultural conventions suggest in any particular situation — and within situations, in subsituations — what may be the appropriate way (horizontally or vertically) and basis (the total or some subtotal). However, because of the degrees of freedom that subjects have in defining and redefining a task, and because of the ambiguity of language, there may be in any particular combination of task and circumstances an irreducible amount of errors by some reasonable standard that people make in selecting a particular focus — errors which have conceptually nothing to do with the notion of rationality or irrationality.

Assuming for the sake of argument that this is the case, the question arises as to what is a good estimate of the frequency of these errors in the case of the Linda vignette. Stated differently, and by analogy with the notion of explainable variance or with the function of a control group, what is the minimum percentage of errors we can expect to find under the best of circumstances in the task at hand? In particular, what is this percentage when possibilities of misunderstanding are reduced to a theoretical minimum because subjects are in effect *told* how to look at Table 15.1? In the literature the implicit assumption is that this percentage is zero.

To check whether this is the case, an experiment is needed involving as unambiguous a formulation as possible for conveying that the judgmental task calls for interpreting the probability that Linda is a bank teller and active in the feminist movement as P (T & F), i.e., as [A]/100 in terms of Table 15.1.[10] To this end, I presented subjects with the standard Linda vignette and asked them to rank the probability (or state the equiprobability) of the following two statements:

Linda is a bank teller.
Linda is a bank teller only if she is active in the feminist movement.

In terms of a representation of the problem which is isomorphic with Table 15.1 (which I assume the subjects can set up and inspect at their discretion in their minds), this formulation probably comes close to specifying as exactly as is colloquially possible the probability in which we are interested. Admittedly, it is awkward and open to criticism for obvious reasons. I can only state that, without the benefit of the conventional symbolic notation, I found it surprisingly difficult to come up with a relatively succinct and colloquially precise way (in the context) to specify the probability of interest. Perhaps this difficulty is an indication that the desired focus is in some way, or in some contexts, a rather unusual one — a possibility that others have already alluded to (cf. Gavanski and Roskos-Ewoldsen, 1991: 192), and which may explain the absence of a satisfactory ready-made linguistic form to refer to it.

Be this as it may, this study involved a total of sixty subjects, thirty-five of whom were given the experimental treatment, the other twenty-five serving as controls. Both groups performed the task under the same conditions, the difference being that the critical statement was formulated in the standard way for the control group (i.e., 'Linda is a bank teller and active in the feminist movement'). The results were as follows: 80 per cent of the subjects in the control group compared with 26 per cent of those in the experimental group ranked P (T & F) > P (T).[11]

It is evident that the results are in the expected direction: a comparison between the percentages of conjunction effects in the experimental and in the control groups clearly shows that the intended message was adequately communicated. However, it is also surprising to find that the manipulation was not fully effective. The residual figure of 26 per cent is far from suggesting 0 per cent as a theoretical anchor of errors. Moreover, this figure obtains in a situation where, in light of the experimental treatment, most of us would probably be reluctant to accept the subjects' continued use of the representativeness heuristic, and in general their irrationality, as a satisfactory explanation for the errors.[12] Rather, the nature of the formulation used in the manipulation, as well as the similarity of the figure obtained with the results reported by other researchers using different methods (cf. Fiedler, 1988) suggests that, in the population studied, some 25–30 per cent of the subjects may well typically rank P (T & F) ahead of P (T) for any of a number of reasons independent of the notion of rationality, including inattention, random checking, playfulness, misunderstanding, attempts to outguess the experimenter, dyslexia and so on.

It may be felt that 26 per cent is a high figure for a residual category. To put this concern in perspective, recall Asch's study on conformity to group pressure. Although we often forget this, he found (experiment 1) that the control group made no less than 7.4 per cent of errors (compared with 33.2 per cent in the experimental group). As he points out, this happened in a situation where the judgments called for were simple and where '[t]he deviations . . . from the correct values [were] considerable, ranging from ¼″ to 1¾″' (Asch, 1957: 454, 457). Keeping this in mind, the finding I have documented may not be so surprising. In any event, I assume that the percentage reported is an estimate of the miscellaneous errors that we can expect to find in the performance of the Linda task in the population of college undergraduates with which we are concerned. Operationally, I take a value of up to about 30 per cent of conjunction effects as the threshold below which there is little theoretical interest in trying to explain the phenomenon, when discussing the subjects' rationality.

Study 4

Assume that a group of subjects are asked about the probability that 'Linda is a bank teller and a feminist' in the case not of one person, but of several. What should one expect the percentage of conjunction effects to be in this situation? One plausible hypothesis is that, as the number of Lindas increases, so will the number of subjects who interpret the critical probability to be assessed to be P (T & F), and in parallel so will the number of people who find that P (T) < P (T & F) decrease.

The experiment described below was designed to investigate this conjecture. It is part of the second study indicated above on p. 242, whose purpose was to probe factors affecting people's willingness, or resistance, to adopt an extensional perspective. In this experiment one group of subjects, which served as controls (n = 30), was given the standard vignette, while another group (n = 29) was presented with the following formulation:

> Linda and Eve are 30-year-old identical twins. They are single, outspoken, and very bright. Both majored in philosophy in college, but at different schools. As students, they were deeply concerned with discrimination and other social issues and participated in anti-nuclear demonstrations.
>
> Please rank the following 3 statements by their probability, using *1 for the most probable*, and *3 for the least probable* (if you find it *impossible* to order two alternatives, give them both the same rank).

Linda and Eve are active in the feminist movement.
Linda and Eve are bank tellers.
Linda and Eve are bank tellers and active in the feminist movement.

An additional group (n = 30) was presented with the same vignette, except that it described a triplet.[13]

The results of this experiment were as follows: 80 per cent of the subjects in the control group judged that P (T & F) > P (T), while in the twin and triplet conditions the figures were 79 per cent and 83 per cent respectively. That is, the manipulation failed to induce the extensional thinking anticipated to any discernible extent. Moreover, on the face of it the results are compatible with the representativeness heuristic explanation and even buttress it.

Looking at the result from a different perspective, however, and keeping in mind some of the findings discussed earlier, which suggest that the representativeness heuristic may not be as general or as unproblematic an explanation as appears at first sight, the very nature of this finding seems anomalous. Barring a statistical quirk as an explanation, why should the conjunction effect, which weakens significantly under some of the manipulations we have considered above, reappear in full strength under the present one? Could there be some other explanation for the result than a capricious or idiosyncratic use of the representativeness heuristic by the subjects? In particular, could the results be reflecting the operation of a basic process — perhaps correlated with the representativeness heuristic, but different from it in nature, especially with regard to its implications for the issue of rationality? Is it possible, for instance, that because we tend to overlook this process, and yet normally activate it (or deactivate it, for that matter), the consequences it controls give the appearance of being erratic? And if so, is it possible that this oversight is partly perpetuated by the fact that we have become so accustomed to explaining all phenomena which fit the representativeness heuristic in terms of this explanation, that we rely on it even when it ceases to be functional to do so — somewhat like subjects do in the Luchins task?[14]

The answer I wish to propose to this line of thought is that there is indeed a very basic process at work, similar in its effect to the use of the representativeness heuristic, but whose theoretical rationale is very different. By its nature, the difference puts the conjunction effect in a very different light with regard to the inferences that we can draw about the rationality of subjects in tasks of the Linda type. To specify the character of this process, it is useful to return to Table 15.1. As we have seen, there is no a priori correct way to look at the table. Moreover, we have also noted that the way we process information rests fundamentally on the use of defaults. These observations suggest that there is an important dissimilarity between what researchers normally assume the task to be in the Linda problem and what the subjects take it to be.

We customarily assume that subjects approach the inspection of Table 15.1 in the frame of mind of people who seek to decide how to look at it. Our previous discussion suggests, in contrast, that they should be expected to approach it with a way of looking at it by default. A reasonable default is arguably one which is grounded in the subjects' experience and/or in shared practice or cultural conventions. But whether by this criterion or a related one, the more rational the default is by its standard, the more likely subjects are to assume that it is through its prism that they are expected to relate to the task. Moreover, the better the default, the more we should expect subjects to overlook a discrepancy between it and what some aspect of the task or communication suggests, correcting it as an error or slip, unless the situation or communicator makes it unequivocally clear that the default is, indeed, to be overridden. In short, an effective cue or instruction should be commensurate with the experienced or otherwise known validity of the default to be overridden.

Thus what seems to be a clear cue from a particular standpoint, or in the perspective of a particular subculture, may be in many situations too weak an indication, or an improperly formulated one, for inducing people to override a normally appropriate default. People are aware of this and act accordingly in everyday life; in particular, it is an everyday experience that they can predict a probable default and use this knowledge to pre-empt its application and effectively communicate by what to replace it.

There is, however, another aspect of the situation which is less recognized. Communication of a sufficiently unambiguous cue for overriding a default requires an understanding of what this default is in the situation, as well as its general validity, for this factor determines the default's robustness and likely resilience to disturbances. As it turns out, this is not as simple a requirement as it may seem.

Consider the following task: to fill in missing information regarding the National Education Budget, you ask two aides, A and B, for estimates of the unknown figure. Aide A responds 20 to 40 billions; Aide B responds 18 to 20 billions. Later you find out that the correct answer is 22.5 billions. Which of the two estimates is better? In one study carried out by Yaniv and Foster, 80 per cent of the subjects said that 18 to 20 billions was a better estimate, despite the fact that the alternative range, but not the selected one, includes the correct value (cf. Bar-Hillel and Neter, 1993: 1123). This pattern of findings is general and robust (Yaniv and Foster, 1993) and reflects a basic dilemma: in making judgments about uncertain values in a probabilistic environment, people must trade off between two competing goals: accuracy and informativeness. The finding illustrates the principle that most people 'are willing to accept some error in order to obtain more informative judgments of uncertain quantities' (Yaniv and Foster, 1993: 29).

The issue of whether this choice (which appears to be regulated by the grain size of the error, see Yaniv and Foster, 1993) is rational or not as a default strategy is beyond the scope of this chapter. As an indication of the complexity of the issue, consider one simple problem and ponder what strategy is more rational for an intelligent information-processor constrained by limited time and resources, but endowed with peripheral vision, to adopt: searching for a lost needle on the floor of a large building, guided by the certain knowledge that it is there, or searching for it within a ten-inch area with the knowledge that it is possible, perhaps even certain, that it lies just outside the limits of the marked area?

How these considerations bear on the issue at hand is easy to illustrate. Consider the following vignette:

> Jonathan is a violent young mugger, well known to the local police, who often hits his victims, even when they don't resist. A policeman on his daily beat has just seen him coming out running from a street, a couple of hundred yards ahead. As the policeman reaches the corner of this street, he notices at some distance an elderly lady cringing on the ground. She gestures for help. As he runs towards her, he contacts the police station with his walkie-talkie to make a preliminary report.

Please indicate which of the following 3 reports is most likely to be true, using *1* for indicating *the most likely*, and *3 the least likely* to be true (if you find it *impossible* to order two alternatives, give them both the same rank).

The elderly lady has been the victim of an accident or assault.
$[A_1$ or $A_2] = A_0$
The elderly lady has been the victim of an assault and mugged.
$[A_2$ & $M] = a$
The elderly lady has been the victim of an assault. $[A_2]$

The third statement is obviously a subset of the first, as the second [a] is of the third $[A_2]$. From an extensional perspective, therefore, the probability of statement [a] cannot exceed that of either of the other two. Nevertheless, 47 per cent of the subjects (n = 19) presented with this vignette ranked the probability of statement [a] higher than they did that of one or both of the other two statements.

Another group of subjects — for whom the foregoing group served as a control — was presented with the same vignette, except that a second paragraph was inserted after the first one, and the instructions were modified, as follows:

While the policeman begins making his report, the warning of his captain echoes in his ears: 'I am interested in the truth, not in guesswork; I do not want reports which afterwards turn out to be mistaken'.

Please indicate which of the 3 following statements the policeman is most likely to make, assuming that he wants to increase the probability that his report will be true in any event; use *1* for indicating the report that he is *most likely* to make, and *3* for indicating the one that he is the *least likely* to make (if you find it *impossible* to order two alternatives, give them both the same rank).

In this treatment 18 per cent of the subjects only (n = 17) ranked the probability of statement [a] above that of one or both of the other two. That is, the percentage of responses compatible with the conjunction fallacy interpretation fell below what I have suggested may be threshold of errors it is useful to try to explain in the class of judgmental tasks and in the population under consideration.

Two replications of this experiment lend support to this finding. In the first, 65 per cent of the subjects produced the conjunction effect in the control group (n = 17), while only 17 per cent did so in the experimental group (n = 18). In the second, the figures were 61 per cent (n = 18) and 0 per cent (n = 17) respectively.

Owing to a planning mishap, I have no data to support an additional hypothesis related to this experiment. Let me nonetheless state it. I speculate that, if statements 1 and 3 had been modified by the addition of '. . . whether or not she had been mugged' (cf. Tversky and Kahneman's manipulation noted earlier, see above, p. 230), this would not have been as effective an inducement for subjects to rank third the probability of statement [a] as was the treatment just discussed. If subjects actually confront the dilemma between informativeness and truth discussed by Yaniv and Foster, the most effective way — perhaps even the only effective one — to induce subjects to override the strategy by default these authors have documented is to address squarely the weight that subjects should give to each of these conflicting goals. Indeed, if the game people play is normally that of informativeness, rather than one which is isomorphic with a gamble, then it may be useless to remind them that the more precise a guess is, the more likely it is to be mistaken. Such a warning is apt not to register or to be perceived as an irrelevant truism. It is important to realize, moreover, that in a game of informativeness involving the differential payoffs for precision and safe truths suggested by the work of Yaniv and Foster, the issue of what a rational strategy is, by the standard of people's subjective expected utility, may have no prescriptive answer.

Let us take stock of what the discussion has achieved to this point, and bring out a couple of propositions with which, I believe, it is compatible. Recapitulating from the beginning, we have seen that when subjects select the representativeness explanation in a dichotomous situation (the issue examined in the first study), this does not necessarily mean that they endorse that explanation. Rather, what many subjects may be doing is rejecting the alternative offered to them as even less reminiscent of what they do. They may do so for two basic reasons, which are not necessarily mutually exclusive. First, they may interpret the question as relating to the comparative assessment of P (T & −F) and P (T & F),[15] or of a conditional probability such as one of those we have considered (e.g., P (F/T).[16] Second, they may give priority to the goal of informativeness, as the research of Yaniv and Foster suggests, and reinterpret the question accordingly.

A second proposition is that the logic of Tversky and Kahneman's argument may not be as compelling in the case of the Linda vignette as one might have thought. In contrast to these authors' assumption, some opaque situations (i.e., a between-subject design) may *not* induce a conjunction effect, while the parallel, more transparent one, does, as was shown by the last experiment in study 2. The strength of their argument, which rests in part on the distinction between opaque and transparent situations, is consequently weakened.

A third proposition is that recognizing that subjects use defaults even more generally than they do heuristics provides a different perspective on their rationality in judgmental tasks directly comparable to the Linda vignette. In this altered perspective, their judgments are still at variance with prescriptive models, but their sensitivity to cues and the resulting unreliability they often exhibit cannot be readily taken as evidence of a shortcoming of reasoning; nor can many of their judgments, for that matter. Based as these are on the processing of noisy cues about the possible need to override generally valid procedures, the case for irrationality hinges on this account on the clarity and validity of the cues offered, rather than on the correctness of subjects' decisions by the standard of the experimenter's knowledge or intention. If people normally place a high value on informativeness, then they are entitled to expect from a communicator (including an experimenter) who wishes to engage them in a different game that s/he will clearly and forcefully convey this — as explicitly and emphatically as the contrast between the general validity of the default and the atypicality of the request justifies.

The reader will have recognized in these remarks the rationale underlying the Jonathan vignette. Obviously, while this rationale is consistent with our discussion, it does not follow from it; more precisely, it does not follow from the experiments we have considered. The last study to which we now turn attempts to remedy this problem to some extent. To anticipate, let me indicate that this study does not establish the argument either. But I believe that it provides an important piece of supportive evidence for it. Specifically, it shows that, in the case of the Linda vignette, subjects' typical avoidance of what is generally regarded as the prescriptive answer is not merely

Table 15.2. Hypothetical Distributions of Visits and Presents

		A Present Yes	No				B Present Yes	No				C Present Yes	No	
Visit	Yes	9	1	10		Yes	8	2	10		Yes	7	3	10
	No	0	2990	2990		No	0	2990	2990		No	0	2990	2990
		9	2991	3000			8	2992	3000			7	2993	3000

		X Present Yes	No				Y Present Yes	No				Z Present Yes	No	
Visit	Yes	1	9	10		Yes	2	8	10		Yes	3	7	10
	No	0	2990	2990		No	0	2990	2990		No	0	2990	2990
		1	2999	3000			2	2998	3000			3	2997	3000

the reflection of idiosyncratic judgments, nor does it depend on the use of the representativeness heuristic as an explanation. Rather, in responding as they do, many subjects may be conforming to a common practice whose irrationality is not as easy to determine in the class of problems illustrated by the Linda vignette as Tversky and Kahneman's framing of their findings suggests.

Study 5

Imagine the following situation: in the almost ten years following his divorce a man has paid exactly ten visits to his daughter. Sometimes, but not always, he has brought her a present on these occasions. Table 15.2 describes a sample of possibilities consistent with this hypothetical situation.

Suppose that the actual situation is described in Table 15.2Z. That is, the father paid ten visits to his daughter, and on three of these occasions he brought her a present. Under these circumstances, what is the event most likely to have occurred: (1) the father came to pay a visit to his daughter, or (2) the father came to pay a visit to his daughter and brought her a present? Assume now that the situation is that described in Table 15.2A, that is, the father brought his daughter a present nine out of the ten times he paid her a visit. Now what is the answer to this same question?

If you are like the group of informants with whom I pre-tested this sketch of a vignette, your answer is that, while the question is trivial in the first instance, in the second it depends on what it is taken to mean. In particular, should it be interpreted as a question about P (V) and P (V & P),[17] or about P (V & -P) and P (V & P) — or, once this possibility is taken into consideration, as a (loosely formulated) question about P (P/V) and P (-P/V)? The source of the ambiguity arises in this case from the fact that whereas the answer is the same in the case of Table 15.2Z regardless of the interpretation one chooses, this is not so in the situation depicted by Table 15.2A. With the numerators of our illustration, the probability of a visit (n = 10), or of a visit without a present (n = 7), is always higher in the first instance than that of a visit with a present (n = 3), while in the second case this no longer holds true.

The point is this. Interpreting the probability of a visit and of a present as a question about the conjoint probability of the two events makes the distinction between Tables 15.2A, 15.2B and 15.2C, on the one hand, and 15.2X, 15.2Y and 15.2Z, on the other, irrelevant. However, if we interpret the question as involving either the probability of a visit without a present or the conditional probability of a present as one element of the comparison, then the distinction between the two sets of situations becomes crucial. Obviously, barring a clear indication to the contrary, it makes a great deal of sense to presume, when one plays the game of informativeness, that a question is about an issue which makes the distinction relevant and, in case of ambiguity, to interpret the probability based on this assumption.

On this account, leaving subjects to their own devices for resolving such an ambiguity is a way to document the default that they use for doing so, and this may well be what the Linda vignette teaches us. On this hypothesis, the Present and Visit vignette outlined above provides the means of an instructive test. If we are willing to assume that normally competent persons understand, *in the course of task performance*, that in a game of chance — or in a situation which is transparently isomorphic to it — betting on an outcome which has ten chances to occur rather than one which has only nine chances to occur is a dominating strategy, then the test of interest is the following. Letting subjects resolve the ambiguity noted above as they choose, one can expect to clarify how they resolve a conflict between heeding cues which suggest that a question is about a gamble and abiding by the code of the game of informativeness.

Given the evidence generated by the Linda vignette, the logic of this test can be framed in terms of an analogy. Sherlock Holmes observed that, once you have eliminated the impossible, whatever remains, however improbable, must be the case. In a similar vein, if we believe that subjects are fundamentally rational, and that the Linda task neither overtaxes their mental capabilities nor is compellingly compared to a visual illusion, then the possibility arises, however improbable, that they will assert in response to the Visit and Present vignette that betting on an event which has nine chances to occur is better than betting on one which has ten chances to occur. Obviously, if this should be the case, the subjects' reinterpretation of the task that this would imply would cast a very different light on the conjunction effect in the particular class of tasks on which we focus, and would provide an explanation for it which (the context permitting, cf. Table 15.2) would not impugn the subjects' rationality.

To investigate this far-fetched possibility, subjects (n = 25) were presented with the following vignette:

Eve is 31, energetic and very friendly. She is married with two children. Talking about her youth, she recalls that as far back as she can remember, she saw her father a grand total of 10 times. And each time it was at most for an afternoon. But he would always bring her a present. In fact, only once did he fail to bring her one. This was when she was sixteen. After that visit he vanished, and she never saw him again.

In light of Eve's recollection, please rank by their probability the following statements: (indicate the statement with the highest probability with a 1; if you find it *impossible* to order the two statements, give them both the same rank).

    Eve's father will pay her a visit.

    Eve's father will pay her a visit and bring her a present.

As the reader will have guessed from the prefatory remarks, this experiment produced a most surprising result: 76 per cent of the subjects ranked the probability of the second statement above that of the first.[18]

To ensure that the critical information which was communicated actually registered, and to reduce the likelihood of unplanned interpretations, an additional experiment (n = 19) was run in which the second paragraph was modified to read as follows:

> In light of Eve's recollection, please rank by their probability the following occurrences, keeping in mind the two main features of the situation: Eve's father paid her 10 visits and brought her 9 presents during her youth (indicate with a 1 the occurrence which, in retrospect, has the highest probability; if you find it *impossible* to order the two statements, give them both the same rank).

A surprising 53 per cent of the subjects still produced the conjunction effect in this treatment.

In a last attempt to disambiguate still more the intended message, this vignette was further modified by underscoring the connective 'and' in the second statement. The statement was typeset to read:

> Eve's father will pay her a visit *and* bring her a present.

The results in this treatment were identical to the previous one: 53 per cent of the subjects (n = 17) gave answers which produced the conjunction effect. Pooling the results of the three treatments to obtain an average measure, the figure we obtain for the study as a whole is 62 per cent of conjunction effects (n = 61).

On the assumption that these results are not artifactual, I believe that the study warrants the following observations. First, what seemed implausible in the extreme turns out to be the case. Second, and more importantly, many subjects apparently do not interpret extensionally a statement in a natural language which expresses unambiguously the idea of P (X & Y), at least on some occasions. The nature of the study which demonstrates this phenomenon strongly suggests that these subjects fail to do so not because of faulty reasoning, but because they do not take some statements at face value; rather, they reinterpret them (and/or the proposed task) in terms of the basic goal they pursue or problem frame in which they operate.

If these conclusions are correct, the two dominant explanations found to date in the mainstream literature on the conjunction fallacy are probably misconceived for at least the class of vignettes that the Eve vignette illustrates. With college students as respondents, we can hardly attribute subjects' answers to the Eve vignette to the use of suboptimal procedures of reasoning or to their being irrational in the normal sense of the term; under the circumstances, such an explanation would raise more questions than it would help answer. It seems more tenable to interpret the data produced by the Eve vignette as evidence that the conjunction effect stems in certain classes of tasks from features of communicative conventions and natural languages, as well as of social situations, of which we are obviously not yet fully cognizant.

Discussion

The time has come to take an overall look at the discussion. I propose to do this by summarizing the principal aims I have attempted to achieve in this chapter. As a preamble, however, let me first clarify what I have *not* attempted to do.

I have not attempted to show that the representative heuristic is an invalid explanation of people's judgments. In fact, I believe that this explanation is a useful one for many judgments in some tasks, and for some judgments in many tasks — at least paramorphically (cf. Hoffman, 1960). I have no doubt, either, that people can be irrational, and not only on occasion. I am quite convinced also that cognitive blindness and illusions are very real phenomena. But these are not the issues I have attempted to address in this paper. My concern, instead, has been with three questions. Two are related to the issue of people's rationality at two levels of analysis, while the third is concerned with Coleman's (1990a: 18) cornerstone assumption in his *Foundations of Social Theory* mentioned at the outset of this chapter.

The first aim is a specific one. In the concluding part of the section in which Tversky and Kahneman (1983: 300) report their findings on the Linda vignette, they intimate that the failure of people to give the normatively expected answer is comparable to the failure of children in the preconservation stage to give the correct answer in the famous Piagetan experiment. They point out that the children's problem, as that of the typical subject in the Linda task, is not that they are blind to the argument of the conservation of volume in one case, or to the validity of the laws of probability in the other; as some of their remarks suggest, they are not. The problem is that they fail to recognize the *decisive* nature of the appropriate rule under the circumstances.

This conceptualization is problematic because, while some experiments that Tversky and Kahneman have run may be comparable to the conservation of volume study, in my view the Linda one is not. Rather, I believe that it is conceptually akin to the Eve experiment.

If the reader concurs in this judgment, then an implication follows. The issue of whether or not an answer is mistaken does not hinge on the applicability in some situation of a context-free rule — for no such rule exists in normal human transactions, the prior issue being always whether a rule is acceptable (i.e., is viewed as both valid and relevant/appropriate)[19] — but rather on the rule which applies *in the particular game* subjects are engaged in. Obviously, Tversky and Kahneman's (1983: 300, 304) observation that most subjects recognize, during debriefing, that they have made a mistake and *should* have known better (their emphasis) does not demonstrate the appropriateness of their analogy with the Piagetan situation, contrary to what these authors make of this admission. Such a reaction is arguably the common way people often express themselves when they realize that they have made an error of interpretation, and may even be a more typical response in this situation than when they realize that they have made an error of reasoning.[20] Thus it is a ubiquitous remark people make whenever they draw a conclusion or make a response that turns out to be inappropriate, because they made it on the assumption, say, that the conversation was carried out in one mode (e.g., a humorous one) when it was actually carried out in another (say, a serious mode). In such a situation, thinking and saying that we should have known better than to make the particular assumption we did does not imply that we, or others, consider the mistaken response *fallacious*. We may blame ourselves, or be blamed by others, for being inattentive, negligent, insufficiently knowledgeable, or for failing adequately to think out the issue or communication, but these are different matters. The same applies to subjects' answers in the case of the Linda or Eve vignettes. They may not have realized that the experimenter engaged them in a game of statistics rather than in the conventional one of informativeness, but the defective sagacity they showed in doing so does not justify viewing their responses as *irrational*.

The fundamental point is this. Because of the private and social games we always play in interpersonal exchanges, we normally lack a criterion directly comparable to a physical one (e.g., volume) for determining the rationality of people's judgments. This is, in effect, the proposition that Jonathan Cohen defended several years ago (Cohen, 1981) in a debate which, incidentally, he lost. But he lost it for two basic reasons unrelated to the claim itself. The first is that he partially built his case on the unconvincing proposition that Baconian probability theory is a useful complement or alternative to the conventional (Pascalian) theory for analyzing the kind of judgments we are interested in. Even more problematic was the second reason: he used people's untutored intuitions as a criterion of judgmental rationality — a fatal flaw in his argument. This brings me to my second point, which is the crux of the matter.

In the final section of their major paper on the conjunction fallacy, Tversky and Kahneman (1983: 313–14) state that their program of research demonstrates that people disobey a fundamental principle of normatively inspired theories of decision-making. They observe, then, that these theories are consequently descriptively inadequate, while psychological analyses which ignore the appeal of normative rules are incomplete.

It is non-controversial that Tversky and Kahneman have magisterially demonstrated the first of these two propositions, and most people would probably also agree that their second point is well taken. But then comes their final conclusion. In it, they define the question which results from their two observations. This conclusion is that there is a theoretical need to deal with what, by implication, they suggest their research has demonstrated, namely, 'the tension between *compelling* logical rules and *seductive* nonextensional intuitions' (Tversky and Kahneman, 1983: 314; emphasis added).

The conceptualization rhetorically conveyed in this concluding statement is the second and main issue with which I have been concerned in this chapter. This characterization is problematic in the extreme because, in case of a clash between a rational conclusion and our intuition, I do not believe that we can or should propose as a general principle (or, if you prefer, as a rule by default) that reasoned conclusions should be viewed as the voice of truth and intuitive conclusions as a lure. This view does not follow unarguably from their research, nor from a priori considerations, at least not when tutored intuition is involved, the main intuition with which I am concerned here.

Let me elaborate this remark with two brief observations. The first, a preliminary one, is that we often forget that the issue of who shall arbitrate our intuition (cf. Kahneman, 1981) has no ready answer. If one insists upon a response nonetheless, then at least as good a case can be made in support of intuition as the final arbiter of the intertwined workings of reason and intuition as can be made in support of reason. No amount of logical reasoning can produce a sound conclusion if the premises involved in it are mistaken, while incoherent reasoning, not to mention a good data bank, *may* produce the correct solution in *any* situation. Which kind of procedure one prefers under such conditions as an ultimate arbiter depends on the weight we give, in general or in some particular situation, to the danger of reasoning illogically versus the danger of proceeding from mistaken premises, or both. Goodman's principle (see note 19) may well be the best characterization of what intelligent people

— and in the first place philosophers and mathematicians — do under these circumstances, as well as of what one *ought* to do in general. On this account, i.e., with Goodman's principle viewed also as a normative precept, intuition and reason taken separately are potentially dangerous voices. Only when they speak in accord can we be sure that we have achieved the best conclusion of which we are capable as human reasoners.

The second is this. Intuition, like taste, may be conceived as a continuum — which may be very short or very long — ranging from untutorable, or almost untutorable, to highly tutorable, and, within these limits, as another continuum ranging from completely untutored to highly tutored or educated. Irrespective of the exact point at which we dichotomize this second continuum, research suggests that tutored intuition differs from untutored intuition in significant fashion (see, for instance, Glaser and Chi, 1988).[21] Under such conditions it is obviously of great importance to distinguish adequately between the premises and conclusions for which intuition is likely to be a useful check of reasoned conclusions or judgments, and those for which this is not the case.

I have assumed two kinds of intuitions in the discussion, and I have conjectured that each is potentially a warning against a different kind of erroneous conclusion. The first is the subjects' intuition. In this case I have not hypothesized that their intuition may tell us something of interest about normative reasoning per se. Rather, I have assumed that it may tell us something of interest about the possibility that, under perhaps some widely shared assumptions and in interaction with the complex operation of defaults, a different answer is conversationally (and more generally, functionally) possible or appropriate in the case of the Linda and Eve vignettes than the one which is deemed to be mandatory in typical research on the conjunction phenomenon.[22]

The second intuition with which I have been concerned is that of a number of students of judgment and decision-making. In this case I have been concerned with the lingering feeling of some researchers that it is a mistake to interpret subjects' failure to give the normatively expected answer as resulting from a *reasoning* fallacy, at least in a number of instances. This intuition is, so to speak, a second-order one.[23]

Several findings generated by the research reported in this chapter give some substance to both kinds of intuitions. They do so because, along with some of their shortcomings, these findings have the advantage of resulting from a study which scrutinized one of the experiments in which Tversky and Kahneman have made the most efforts to eliminate alternatives to the explanation they propose and, by implication, to its interpretation.

If I have made my case, the investigation I have reported shows that the untutored intuition of many, and the tutored intuition of some, may not have been deceiving them, but rather insistently telling them something all of us had overlooked. On this assumption, some of the findings reported here are one more illustration of the principle that tutored intuition can be a match for the best reasoned case, and evidence that this holds true even in the interpretation of judgments which fail to conform to expectations derived from the normative approach to decision-making. This should not come as too much of a surprise. Like all rules and schemes of reasoning, the normative framework of analysis is but a model, depending for its intrinsic validity, for its valid application, and above all (in the case at hand) for its valid *mandatory* application, on a multitude of assumptions, most of which are implicit presumptions. Overruling the warning of even a single tutored intuition that one of these presumptions may have been violated can only be validly done on the strength of the application of what Grice (1989: 189–94) calls 'reassurance conditions', an open-ended list of procedures of verification which, by their nature, are non-mechanizable (e.g., 'go over the argument again', 'look out for a possible omission [or] mistake'). By the character of these procedures, intuition can evidently call for as many iterations of their applications as it feels justified, without warranting viewing this, or an interim judgment, as irrational, even if the provisional judgment should heed intuition rather than reason.[24]

Finally, my third aim was to show that there are good reasons for subscribing to one of the theoretical propositions on which Coleman premises his *Foundations of Social Theory*. The reader will recall that Coleman uses this proposition to justify his choice of theoretical orientation in the face of some of the findings reported in the literature of which the conjunction fallacy is a part. The proposition is reproduced here: '[M]uch of what is ordinarily described as nonrational or irrational is merely so because the observers have not discovered the point of view of the actor, from which the action *is* rational' (Coleman, 1990a: 18; emphasis in original).

Some of the results reported in this chapter show that this assumption is not just a matter of faith, but has tangible validity. Together with the discussion, these findings illustrate concretely that there are serious and basic reasons for casting doubt on the possibility to infer with reasonable certainty from current research on human judgment and decision-making that human beings are not rational actors. The result of the studies is thus a testimony to the perspicacity of Coleman's view, as well as to the wisdom of the practical guiding principle it implies. If the reader concurs in this judgment, I have achieved my aim.

Concluding Remarks

There is no question that many people's judgments and decisions are inadequately modelled by the normative approach. It is also beyond question that the evidence presented in Tversky and Kahneman's (1983) main paper on the conjunction fallacy, as well as in some current corroborative research (e.g., Bar-Hillel and Neter, 1993), shows that in some cases the representativeness heuristic is a convincing theoretical explanation. Tversky and Kahneman's work in general, and their work on the conjunction fallacy in particular, also shows that this heuristic is in any event an effective paramorphic model (cf. Hoffman, 1960) for predicting human judgments in a great variety of probability tasks, whatever stand one adopts about the theoretical explanatory value of this heuristic. If only for these reasons, Tversky and Kahneman's classic report on the conjunction phenomenon on which I have focused is a remarkable achievement.

However, contrary to what some passages in this remarkable study intimate, and perhaps even more grievously to what it is often used by others to argue, Tversky and Kahneman have not non-controversially established that the answer typical subjects give to some conjunction problems show that they are irrational. The fundamental difficulty is that such a claim is probably undemonstrable (although not unarguable), not only in practice, but also in theory. In all fairness, one should hasten to add that Tversky and Kahneman's grounds for the foregoing view involve much more than the Linda vignette. But then, in all fairness, so does the case I have argued. Let me conclude by indicating one reason this is so.

March (1978: 598, 601) has observed that human beings have 'unstable, inconsistent, incompletely evoked, and imprecise goals . . . [and] find meaning and merit in [their] actions after they are taken and the consequences are observed and interpreted'. If one subscribes to this characterization, and if one grants that rationality depends critically for its assessment on the goal(s) a person pursues, then this portrayal is by itself enough to cast doubt on the feasibility of determining the rationality of an actor with any degree of certainty, in all but very unusual circumstances. Indeed, this characterization raises the question of *when* the rationality of a decision will be determined. In theory, this is possibly an even more problematic question than the traditional one of who shall determine its rationality.[25]

Of course, whether people should be viewed in the last analysis as inherently rational, or better, *fallibly* rational (for reasons that it is of course vital to document and become aware of), rather than in some other way, depends on one's definition of rationality. Let me sign off by making explicit the general conception of rationality I have assumed in the discussion.

Following Johnson-Laird (1988: 354–7; 1983: 451–77), I have assumed that rationality is a property of our highest conscious faculty of control, and is inherently linked to the parallel architecture of our information-processing system. On this account, the main function of rationality is to act as the ultimate agency for resolving conflicts that arise during task performance in the hierarchy of parallel processors which constitute our mental faculties. Unresolved conflicts between two or more parallel processors are referred to the conflict-resolution agency as a last resort (and experienced as one kind of 'intuition') when the attempts of the system to resolve them as part of its normal, non-conscious mode of operation have all failed. Our rational faculty then gives them attention, possibly serial and conscious consideration, and disposes of them in a manner consonant with the set of goals which is active in the system. A ubiquitous challenge of rationality so conceived is to interpret the problems which are inherently opaquely indicated by the calls for conflict resolution (cf. Johnson-Laird, 1983: 464–5). Another is to determine if these calls can be disregarded with little consequence or rather deserve serious attention as warnings that something may be wrong in a global outlook or on closer inspection (i.e., at one of the levels of information-processing at which much of the relevant knowledge we have is brought to bear on the task we perform by the logic of parallel information-processing (cf. Newell, 1990: 129–34, 90), or where a particular detailed computation takes place).

In such a system it is obviously perilous to follow the rule which views as a lure (or as the voice of truth, for that matter) requests for a review or creative solution for dealing with a mismatch between our knowledge base (or a particular computation) and the input or output expected by a standard procedure. Elsewhere (Inbar, in preparation) I call the attempt to justify the validity of such a principle an instance of Heisenberg's fallacy. As the name is intended to suggest, it is the error of going beyond the grain size at which it is appropriate to analyze a phenomenon for some purpose without denaturing it.[26]

When all is said and done, the fundamental point is this. People's rational faculties are unquestionably sluggish and fallible, and theoretical models which posit that they are rational actors, or that they maximize utility, are therefore bound to fit their behaviour only approximately. Tversky and Kahneman (1983) have compellingly shown the extent to which this must hold true, and perhaps never intended to do or claim much more. But the literature, in part inspired by their work, is full of examples where this is certainly not the case. By re-examining a paradigmatic experiment, I hope to have shown how problematic such an attempt is, in principle as well as in practice. To the extent that I have been successful in my undertaking, I have shown that Coleman's basic assumption in his *Foundations of Social Theory* (1990a: 18) is not only legitimate, but expresses a profound insight whose importance transcends the limits of this major work.

Notes

1   For a dissenting view about the usefulness of the standard theory of probability for assessing human judgments, see Cohen (1981: 317–30, 359–67; 1979: 387–93).
2   Through the paper I use this notion in the Bayesian interpretation that normativeness has in the current human judgment and decision-making literature. It should be noted, however, that there are those who dispute the validity of this interpretation (for instance, Gigerenzer, 1991).
3   They also present findings which suggest that while subjects predominantly use the vocabulary of the representativeness heuristic, the fact that they explain their judgment in these terms is unrelated (in fact, is negatively related) to making a fallacious judgment. In their study subjects who framed their judgments in this manner never used simultaneously an extensional interpretation of the problem.
4   All the research instruments in the investigation discussed in this chapter were administered in Hebrew. The formulations in the text are translations of this material, with one exception: it involves two experiments, discussed later, in which English materials were used with honour students. These experiments are identified at the proper place in the discussion.
5   See, in this connection, the perceptive discussion offered by Kahneman and Tversky themselves (1982: 501–2).
6   For an elaboration of the view that intuition and recognition are indicators of the problem-solving and decision-making processes we have in our repertory and normally carry out at below awareness level, see Simon (1986); for a shorter discussion see, for instance, Simon and Kaplan (1989: 41) or Searle (1970: 41–2).
7   The Hebrew versions used involved two slightly different phrasings:

> . . . [Recently/Some time ago] the company in which she worked moved its head office to Haifa, and she lost her position. A friend tried to talk her into coming to work for the bank where she is a teller. A relative suggested that this is an opportunity for her to do what she has always wanted to do — become active in the feminist movement. This was [ten days ago/two years ago].

And,

> . . . [Recently/Some time ago] the company in which she worked moved its head office to Haifa, and she lost her position. A friend tried to talk her into coming to work for the bank where she is a teller. A relative suggested that this is her opportunity to begin doing what she has always wanted to do — be active in the feminist movement. These conversations took place [ten days ago/two years ago].

8   This conclusion assumes, without this being necessary for my main argument incidentally, that an answer which implies that should Linda have become a bank teller and active in

the feminist movement, it was certainly within a very short period of time, is a view which is more likely to be associated with the assumption of a possible link, perhaps of a compensatory nature, between the two events, than is a view in which there is no necessary temporal association between the two events.

9   This and the other *t*'s I report below are of differences of means, a specification I omit for brevity's sake.

10 Note that Tversky and Kahneman's experiment in which T was formulated as 'Linda is a bank teller whether or not she is active in the feminist movement' (see above, p. 230), while related to our present concern, deals with a different question. This formulation insures that the set of events labelled T will be understood to include the subset of events labelled T and F. The experiment then rests on the assumption that T & F which is asserted in the next statement will necessarily be understood to refer to the subset of T just specified. For some reason, however, subjects obviously fail to make this connection. The question is what happens when the set inclusion is directly asserted in the target sentence itself in a manner which makes it unambiguous that the judgment called for is P (T & F) rather than some other one, say, P (F/T).

11 The experimental group (n = 35) was also administered the scales described in Study 2 to generate a between-subject design superimposed on the present one. The results of this between-subject experiment present no surprise: the mean rating of P (T) was 3.56, versus 2.64 for P (T & F) (*t* = 1.70). In other words, there is no indication of a conjunction effect in this experiment.

12 Under the circumstances, we seem to be left with no choice but to call them just that: errors.

13 The vignette read in this case as follows:

> Linda, Eve and Lydia are 31-year-old triplet sisters. They are single, outspoken, and very bright. All three majored in philosophy in college, but at different schools. As students, they were deeply concerned with discrimination and other social issues and participated in anti-nuclear demonstrations.
> Please rank the following 3 statements by their probability, using *1 for the most probable*, and *3 for the least probable* (if you find it *impossible* to order two alternatives, give them both the same rank).
> Linda, Eve and Lydia are active in the feminist movement.
> Linda, Eve and Lydia are bank tellers.
> Linda, Eve and Lydia are bank tellers and active in the feminist movement.

14 The Luchins task involves using one or more empty jars holding *A*, *B*, and *C* quarts of water to obtain *D* quarts. All problems are soluble with the same general solution (*B* − *A* − 2*C* = *D*) but, as the task proceeds, some problems are also soluble by an even simpler arithmetic procedure. The results of this experiment illustrate that solutions which have proved successful under certain circumstances tend to interfere with seeing a better one, later, in what looks like identical conditions (see Berelson and Steiner, 1964: 204–5).

15 This remains a possibility, despite Tversky and Kahneman's finding discussed earlier (see above p. 230 and note 10), as that finding results from an experiment which may be an unsatisfactory test of the explanation under consideration. It will be recalled that this test involved adding '... whether or not she is active in the feminist movement' to the T statement. As some researchers have noted (e.g., Dulany and Hilton, 1991: 97), in context this makes the sentence sound awkward or anomalous. Insofar as oddities tend to either attract attention or be disregarded as noise, it is quite conceivable that this formulation is generally viewed as a noisy addendum, and not even taken into consideration by many subjects for overriding the normal aim of informativeness.

16 Tversky and Kahneman (1983: 303) recognize that this possibility cannot be ruled out in the case of the Linda vignette.

17 The probability of a visit, and of a visit and a present, respectively.

18 Eighteen subjects ranked this statement above the first, while one gave equal rank to the two probabilities. In the present study the latter response was included in the count of conjunction effects, as subjects did not have to estimate the probabilities of V and P and their values rule out the possibility that $P(V) = P(V \& P)$.

19 Nelson Goodman aptly expressed this fundamental principle as it applies to reasoning in his famous saying that 'rules and particular inferences alike are justified by being brought into agreement with each other. *A rule is amended if it yields an inference we are unwilling to accept; an inference is rejected if it violates a rule we are unwilling to amend.* The process of justification is the delicate one of making mutual adjustments between rules and accepted inferences, and in the agreement achieved lies the only justification needed for either' (Goodman, 1983: 64; emphasis in original).

20 A good case can be made that saying that 'I should have known better' does not normally signal recognition of a logical error, but rather of an inaccurate presumption. Indeed, while it seems natural to say that one *should* have known the answer that an interlocutor expected, it sounds awkward to say that one *should* have known (or should have known a procedure to establish) that from the premises, say, that 'All Frenchmen are wine drinkers' and that 'Some wine drinkers are gourmets', it does not follow that 'Some Frenchmen are gourmets' — to borrow an example from Johnson-Laird (1993: 125).

21 Although the literature suggests that the intuition of experts is normally superior to that of naive people, on occasion the intuition of the latter is found to be more valid. This sometimes happens, for instance, when experts become set in their ways and too sure of themselves, and do not sufficiently check their intuitive responses; or in situations in which expertise is a misnomer, because the knowledge in the field of expertise does not impart any objective advantage to its practitioners.

22 While I have couched my argument in terms of the goal of informativeness, in many situations there is at least one other major rationale which is conceivable as an explanation of some conjunction effects. This rationale is that of *identification*. Although space does not permit me to elaborate this explanation here, let me briefly indicate its logic. Many definitions of situations (or tasks) may set up the goal of identification (of some object or event) as the guiding principle or 'game' to be played. Operating rationally under such a governing goal implies interpreting the probability of an event as one in which the proper way to look at an array of data isomorphic in its substantive organization with Table 15.1 is horizontally. Many conjunction fallacies reduce to conjunction effects if we assume that this is the way by default (by its nature, it will be recalled, resistant to possibly very noisy and inconsistent cues) in which subjects relate to some problems.

23 The rebellious intuition of some of these investigators stems in part from scepticism about the very value of the normative model itself. Indeed, some students of human judgment and decision-making feel not only that the current normative approach is often misapplied, but also that its normativeness is open to question (see, for instance, March, 1978: 593; Lopez, 1981: 385), if for nothing else, because the wrong statistical approach is used as a criterion (Gigerenzer, 1991).

24 Many iterations could be impractical, and in this sense requests for more 'reassurance' may be unreasonable in practical contexts, but this is irrelevant in a scientific context (cf. Coleman, 1972: 3–4). This remark implies, of course, that there may be very few questions, perhaps none, which can be securely settled in practice by human reason — except after there has been an adequate opportunity for self and critical others to review the conclusion or judgment of interest. But there is nothing new in this realization (cf. Hamblin 1970: 250). Whatever our conception of rationality, it obviously cannot involve disregarding this characteristic of the human condition.

25 The theoretical question alluded to here is whether, in the last analysis, it is legitimate to characterize a decision as irrational before it has been subjected to the full process of

rational review. By 'full', I mean that the decision-maker must have had a chance carefully (and repeatedly, if need be) to consider the decision of interest over some period of time and in conditions which are adequate for evoking, adequately realizing and pondering all the alternatives whose rejection s/he is called upon by self or others to justify. Evidently, most decisions are, by these standards, only interim decisions and embryonically rational. A sad aspect of the human condition is that we often become committed to them by the march of events or the logic of social situations. While such judgments and decisions can fail to be veridical or correct by the standard of some criterion, it is doubtful that there is much to gain by viewing them as irrational. We should not forget that this notion is operationalized by the failure of a process rather than by its non-application, and this process normally requires a long time to unfold. It does so because we need time to become fully aware of all the relevant factors which need to be taken into account in a problem, and we need time to conceptualize and ponder them sufficiently so as to bring them to bear adequately on a properly considered decision. The upshot is that calling a person irrational is legitimate (on this account) only if, and as long as, s/he refuses (without good reason; see, in particular, Raz, 1978) to consider changing a judgment s/he has made when s/he realizes, or is made to realize, that it is erroneous by a standard s/he accepts. Avoiding the error before the review of the decision is completed is on this view a question of perspicuity, wisdom or knowledge, rather than of rationality. Note that the conception of rationality that these remarks imply is the simple idea that a rational actor should not knowingly choose an inferior alternative.

26 Zeno's paradoxes about Achilles and the Tortoise and about the Arrow are probably the earliest recorded and best known examples of this fallacy.

16 Foundational Problems in Theoretical Sociology

Thomas J. Fararo

In this chapter the aim is to discuss Coleman's *Foundations of Social Theory* (1990). After a brief overview of its aims, methods and contents, I proceed to locate this work in the context of other foundation efforts within sociology. For the sake of keeping the discussion suitable to a chapter-length treatment, I place special emphasis on several selected formulations, especially Homans and Parsons among the postclassic theorists and Jeffrey Alexander among the more recent writers on the foundations of social theory. I then try to show how Coleman's considered views on explanation in sociology and on theoretical methods lead him to a particular mode of analysis in which he formulates theoretical models within the rational choice 'umbrella' theory. Then, in treating how Coleman constructs and extends these theoretical models, I focus especially on the idea of adopting the general equilibrium model from economics. I conclude the essay with an assessment of the strengths and weaknesses of the general theory formulated in this major work.

Overview

Foundations of Social Theory builds upon and deepens virtually all of Coleman's extensive earlier sociological research, including studies of community conflict, union politics, high school social structures, social diffusion, equality of educational opportunity, corporate actors, and, not least, pioneering works in the mathematics of social processes and social action. Although this is a unique book, a landmark in the history of social theory with depth and precision of analysis, like many other massive works, it has problems. There are problems of organization in terms of how its many model building efforts relate to each other; there are conceptual problems in terms of the interpretation of the framework; and there are theoretical problems in terms of the scope of its explanatory efforts. In the following brief summary, I will be making some appreciative remarks, but I reserve my critical reactions to a later point in the paper.

The key metatheoretical premise that Coleman articulates is that sociology's subject matter is the behaviour of social systems and that such behaviour is 'macro' relative to states and behaviours of individuals. There is a general form for linkage of these two levels, and much of this book shows how it works when we start with the assumption of purposive action. This is a form of methodological individualism: human beings are purposive actors whose interdependent actions generate, regenerate or change social systemic outcomes. More generally, since such outcomes include corporate actors, these too are treated as purposive actors. In detailed formulations the purposive action is treated as rational in a well specified sense.

Apart from a short orientation chapter treating the metatheory, the book consists of five large parts, treating elementary actions and dyadic social relations; structures of action such as authority systems; corporate action; modern society; and the mathematics of social action. The first four parts are almost entirely free of mathematics so that the main theory is accessible to all readers, although such readers will miss important ideas presented only in the mathematical chapters.

The simplicity of its starting point is one attractive feature of the theory. There are two kinds of entities: actors and resources. Connecting these are two types of relations: control and interests. When control and interest configurations are considered together, they imply two macro properties: the values of resources and the power of actors in the system of action. Coleman includes in-depth conceptual discussions of these notions and such important allied ideas as rights to control action as a type of resource.

In one aspect, that closest to the part of the theory that Coleman has been able to develop formally, what Coleman is doing is constructing a social theory which generalizes general competitive market equilibrium theory in economics. For instance, prices and wealth are special cases of values and power respectively. Data are provided illustrating the application of the generalized theory to classroom situations in which populations of student-teacher pairs constitute the generalized market with such resources as grades and time spent on homework.

This generalized theory is itself just a starting point for at least two types of extensions to cover social phenomena outside the scope of the generalized market equilibrium theory. First, Coleman's conception of a perfect social system uses the same basic elements, but with indivisible events instead of divisible resources. This allows a treatment of collective decisions and of the transition from internal power struggles in an organization to its revealed preferences as a unitary corporate actor engaged in interactions with other external actors. Second, dynamic theoretical models are introduced that treat complex patterns of interdependent behaviour as well as transient or unstable states, allowing detailed analyses of such topics as revolutions, collective behaviour and norm emergence.

There are also chapters on the history and current state of applied social research in relation to the role of theory in the 'new social science', one which aims to generate and transmit a scientific understanding of modern social structures to all the relevant actors, not just to privileged corporate actors that sponsor such research. A metatheoretical idea appears here also: that sociology is a reflexive discipline — it is an activity which is part of its subject matter. This means that there is a constraint on the form that theory can take: namely, it must make the behaviour of the theorist intelligible. Classic sociological theories, Coleman thinks, were deficient in this respect. Such theories emerged with the fundamental transformation of modern society that Coleman delineates in great detail: from primordial to purposive, now featuring large corporate actors whose interests are not necessarily the same as those of natural persons acting as their agents. But, according to a clearly stated normative premise, the interests of natural persons have ultimate priority. Using such normative premises and his analytical theory, what Coleman does, in effect, is to construct a critical theory of modern society. A detailed analysis of the situation of children under the old and new types of social structures illustrates the critical capabilities of this sort of theory.

So Coleman combines general-theoretical, world-historical and critical modes of thought within one framework.

Given this brief appreciative summary, let us turn to a deeper analysis of the ideas, placing them in the context of other foundational ideas in the tradition of sociological theory.

Foundation Ideas in Sociology

We can think of sociological thought in terms of three phases: classic, postclassic and recent. After a very brief statement concerning classic foundation ideas, I will turn to a more extended treatment of the later two phases.

Classic Foundation Ideas: Weber and Pareto

In the classic tradition Weber ([1922] 1978: Pt 1) formulated a 'conceptual exposition' of sociology as a science whose causal explanations are grounded in a concept of action and on a methodology of ideal types of actions. Rational-purposive action was treated as one particularly important type, but his analysis implied that charismatic domination related to affective action and traditional domination to habitual action, other ideal types of action. Also he regarded rational-purposive action as involving deliberation with conscious selection of means and/or ends, to be contrasted with the rational pursuit of an ideal, regardless of the consequences, a type of action he called value-rational.

Thus, for Weber, the theory of action employed in economics — given by the postulation of rational-purposive action in regard to means to given ends — was a very significant action model but only one such model among others. However, Weber did not resolve the problem of working out formal methods for constructing action-theoretical models from which social outcomes could be logically derived.

Weber was an economic historian who turned to sociology. By contrast, Pareto was an economic theorist who turned to sociology. He too regarded rational action as only one among a roster of possibilities and was even more sceptical of it as a basis for general social theory than was Weber. His own developments (Pareto, 1935) in analyzing non-rational action, however, did not exercise the same influence on subsequent generations of theorists as much as Weber's conceptual exposition and his allied substantive writings.

Postclassic Foundation Ideas: Parsons and Homans

When Parsons (1937) formulated his foundation of social theory he began with a close analysis of these ideas of Weber and Pareto, as well as those of the economic theorist Marshall and, of course, those of Durkheim. One of his criticisms of Weber's action foundations is its ideal type methodology. An action may well exemplify *elements* of any combination of the ideal types. For instance, an action might have an affectual element as well as a purposive-rational element. Thus Parsons regarded 'rational action' as analogous to 'heavy body', to be contrasted with theories employing rationality and mass, respectively for social science and for mechanics, as variables or analytical elements. A purely rational system of action is a logical possibility, but, he argues, the history of social thought shows that such a system would be unstable: no social order could really exist if all actions were purely rational. This phase of his treatment of action reflected the strong influence of Durkheim's ideas on this subject. This principle of the instability of purely rational action systems implies that the general equilibrium of an economy, as formulated in economic theory using a purely rational action model, can only be realized in the world by embeddedness in a wider system of action featuring Weberian value-rational and non-rational aspects.

A peculiar aspect of Parsons' movement beyond economic theory is that he tends to retain the phraseology of 'maximization' and 'optimization', although at no point in his theoretical canon can we find a genuine deduction from such premises. This is a point of very significant contrast with the foundation work of Coleman, who employs maximization arguments at the core of the quantitative version of his theory.

The long and arduous development of Parsons' ideas upon these foundations can be characterized as synthesizing in spirit, drawing into the theoretical framework ideas and findings from such diverse sources as behavioural learning theory, Freud's psychology, modern economics, cultural anthropology, Wiener's cybernetics and even, in his later years, modern linguistics — and this is only a limited listing. Out of this remarkable effort came a conception of what I will call 'a tree of theory' in the sciences treating human behaviour. This was never spelled out as such but appears to be as follows. The root of the tree is called the theory of action. The next level consists of four branches, corresponding to the AGIL scheme worked out by Parsons in the 1950s: culture theory (L), social theory (I), personality theory (G) and behaviour theory (A). Recursively, any such theory can be treated as a node with four subtheories. Focusing on the I node and social theory, we obtain four special social theories corresponding to IX, for X = A, G, I and L: economic theory (IA), political theory (IG), social integration (or 'solidarity') theory (II) and fiduciary theory (IL). With his passion for abstract symmetries, Parsons construes 'sociological theory' as the II theory, the theory that takes the solidarity of a social system as a theoretical problem. Another term for the II dimension of a social system is 'communal' (Fararo, 1989a: Ch. 3), and Parsons himself used the term 'societal community' for the II subsystem of a society. The problem of 'social theory', on the other hand, relates culture, personality and behaviour to social interaction. In particular, taking culture and personality states as exogenous, the problem of social theory is to take social relational expectation states as endogenous and account for order in their interrelations. Abstractly (see Fararo, 1989a: Ch. 3), the problem is to set out theoretical models that allow us to prove theorems about the cultural and psychological conditions necessary and/or sufficient for a stable social equilibrium: that is, to show how the very existence of non-transient states of social interaction is possible. An example of this idea is Parsons' conjectured theorem that no social state is stable unless there is an internalization in personalities of conceptions of the desirable formulated in the relevant cultural tradition. Thus a necessary condition for social order is that cultural and psychological parameters satisfy certain conditions.

Another postclassic theorist devoted his professional life to comprehensive theory, to general theoretical synthesis: George Homans. In his first synthesis Homans (1950) drew upon classical empirical studies (e.g., Whyte's pioneering 1943 study of a gang) and classical ideas (e.g., Pareto's on method and on action), embedding them in a common language and a systems framework. This work had a massive influence on social psychological experimentation — along with other influences in the 1950s — and led Homans (1961, 1974) to a second synthesis aiming to explain the earlier propositions and the new findings. For instance, earlier Homans had formulated a mutual dependence relation between liking and interaction; in the new synthesis, this relation is accounted for, but also qualified. The shift from the first synthesis to the later synthesis was accompanied by a considerable muting of the system idea that informed the early work. In place of thinking of a dynamical system, on the model of a set of differential equations, Homans thinks in terms of sentences arranged in a deductive system. But the deductions are weak because the ideas are not formulated in mathematical terms. Here is a second contrast with Coleman's foundation work which, while not written in axiomatic style, includes explicit mathematical formulations, some of which involve dynamical systems.

Returning to Homans, we can construct an implied 'tree of theory' image found in Homans' writings (especially Homans, 1967, with its methodological and presuppositional focus). But it is best to call this a 'tree of explanations', because, for Homans, there is only one theory: a system of explanations, with a common core of general principles applied to various distinct circumstances. These principles deal with the behaviour of organisms. In action-theoretic terms they deal with the unit act in a situation as their basic subject matter, accounting for choices in terms of the effects of past experiences. The same principles apply whether the situation is social or not, but when other organisms are the salient entities in the situation of action, then we have 'social behaviour'.

Homans' fundamental idea is that we explain social behaviour with the same principles as we explain non-social behaviour. It is a more complex explanation, however. Thus the first level built on the behavioural psychological foundation contains two branches: explanations of non-social behaviour and the more complex explanations of social behaviour.

Given a focus on the explanation of social behaviour, then a focus on 'the social individual' is one branch of theory, applying behavioural principles to the development of an organism in a social environment. Depending upon the biological givens, this produces one or another pattern of development: for humans, language and self emerge in the normal social situation. As is implied in Mead's (1934) foundational studies, language and self are normal emergents for *human* organisms but not for other organisms. This implies a biological parameter, or set of parameters, taken as exogenous, as *given* for social analysis. Although the emergence of the self involves interaction, the focus is on the over-time recursive generation of language skills and self-other interaction skills of the focal organism. Analytically, we are explaining the emergent behaviour of the social individual.

When multiple individuals are considered, with the problem of explanation covering the behaviour of not just one actor but all those in the situation, we enter the realm of social interaction as such. The other actors are not just situational, they are brought into the dynamical system, from an analytical standpoint. Person and other are treated jointly. It is a two-actor system, not a single-actor system with other actors' behaviours only as exogenous inputs. The problem here is to explain the emergence of patterns of interaction. In particular, as Homans makes clear, the fundamental problem of social interaction explanation is to account for enduring social bonds, not for ad hoc acts in isolated situations. That is, the recursion now extends over time and possibly space between multiple human beings whose behaviours provide inputs to each other. As in Parsons, the existence of anything like order in this interaction nexus is the theoretical problem. But here we seek to explain the various patterns of interaction that emerge by applying the behavioural principles to each act in each situation by each actor, over time and space — at least, in principle this is what we do.

Thus the level below the social behavioural consists of the 'social individual' and 'social interaction system' explanations. Since Homans treats social interaction as exchange, he is both generalizing and going far beyond economics. Economic theory applies ideas that simplify the complexity of social behaviour. It takes the actor's preferences as given rather than attempting to explain how they emerge and change in social interaction. In its scope restricted to idealized markets, it treats interaction as an isolated episode transiently relating a pair of actors. It is not concerned with the problematic character of endurance, of the build-up and continuity of social relations. This is the fundamental problem for Homans. Thus he is taking the existence of enduring social relations and patterns as problematic: in this respect he is not very far from Parsons' presumed locus for the fundamental problem of sociological theory, the problem of social solidarity. Whereas the generic social element (I) deals with the coordination of action, the solidary element (II) deals with the social bond — precisely the problematic element for Homans.

Simplifying somewhat, we can summarize this discussion with the assertion that for both Parsons and Homans the fundamental problem of *sociological* theory is to account for social bonds, for emergent patterns of enduring social relations, for solidarities. In both cases the explanations are grounded in a theory of action. It is not my purpose here to assess these ideas. Most readers will know that neither theory maintained widespread support among sociologists since the 1960s, a period of proliferation of new approaches and a widespread belief in the futility of general theorizing.

Recent Foundation Ideas: Alexander

In the 1980s there was a renewal of interest in general theory among sociological theorists. Alexander (1983) formulated a widely discussed pair of presuppositional problems that he used to analyze the history of sociological thought. A debate about such theory unfolded around such issues as micro-macro linkage and agency and structure. We can place Coleman's work, as perceived widely by other theorists in sociology, in terms of Alexander's formulation of the two presuppositional or foundational issues.

The two foundational problems that he sees emerging in the history of sociological theory each have two types of received solutions. In Alexander's critical terms, theorists have acted as if they must choose between one or the other of the two types. His own preferred solution is 'multidimensionality', in the sense of combining *elements* stressed in otherwise dichotomous thought that produces inadequate theorizing. Let us review this framework for looking at foundation problems as a way of locating Coleman's approach to the foundations of social theory.

The first of Alexander's two foundational problems concerns the nature of human action and how it is addressed in general terms. The solutions found in the history of social thought focus on how to treat rationality. One foundational solution is to presuppose that action is rational. This leads to the treatment of interaction as a matter of transactions with each actor engaged in goal oriented choices of instrumental means. Classical utility theory and the modern theory of games can be interpreted as adopting this solution. The other solution to the action problem posits that action is expressive communication having moral implications. This leads to the treatment of interaction as a matter of mutual interpretations, often involving reading of un-intended impressions given off by actors. Much of the work of Goffman can be inter-preted as adopting this solution. For instance, through acts that express deference, actors indicate that others are moral beings deserving of respect (Goffman, 1967). In these terms Alexander proposes that a general sociological theory must be based on a treatment of action as comprising elements of both types, rational (instrumental) and non-rational (expressive-moral). In his work Coleman (1990a) makes it clear that his action foundation adopts the first solution, not a combination solution favoured by Alexander or, before him, Parsons (1951) with his three types of action elements, instrumental, expressive and moral.

Alexander's second foundation problem that defines a presuppositional issue con-cerns the nature of social order. The two solutions here are framed by Alexander as individualistic and collectivistic. In the individualistic solution, social order is defined in terms of, and is a consequence of, actions of individuals. This is methodological individualism. Alexander rejects this solution because it presupposes socialized actors, hence social order, and hence cannot be a general solution to the problem of order. The second solution, the collectivistic type, treats the social level as non-reducible. Roughly speaking, Weber seems to represent the first solution and Durkheim the second. But these allocations of solutions are rather crude because of various strands of thought in any particular classic theorist's complete corpus.

Combining the two issues, each with two types of solutions, Alexander obtains four types of foundational approaches to social theory:

1 rational-individualist;
2 rational-collectivist;
3 non-rational-individualist;
4 non-rational-collectivist.

For Alexander, the fourth type is typified by Durkheim's approach (in his later 'idealist' work), the third by Blumer's, the second by Marx's, and the first by con-temporary rational choice theory in sociology.

Thus the resurgence of the rational choice approach to social theory is clearly located in this metatheoretical scheme derived from an analysis of classic and contem-porary sociological theory. The rational-individualist approach treats action as rational, placing expressive aspects of action in a residual category, implying their lesser signi-ficance for explanatory purposes; and it employs methodological individualism as a theory strategy. Coleman's foundation of social theory clearly represents this type. But since most contemporary sociological theorists see the whole point of classic socio-logical theory as getting beyond this prototypically 'economic approach', it is not surprising that the reviews of Coleman's book by theorists have often been very critical. In Alexander's terms, Coleman's foundational approach represents a failure to overcome the debilitating effects of not adopting a truly 'multidimensional' solution in the sense of *combining elements of all four types* in one theoretical foundation.

But this critique is not as powerful as it sounds. It is based on a neglect of the process of theory growth. In particular, it abstracts from the logic of theory extension and from allied notions to be described below. So let us now look more closely at Coleman's presuppositions and how he theorizes on their basis, in particular, the centrality of micro-macro linkage in his work, and the way in which this leads into the core of his social theory.

Coleman's Foundations: Metatheory

Let us look first at how Coleman treats explanation in social science; then, because of its centrality to his metatheory, we shall examine the rational choice context of his approach.

Explanation: Micro-Macro Logic

The most general and important metatheoretical principle that Coleman uses is that there must be a single model of action that applies to every explanatory situation. He sees sociologists as making a fundamental error here: when a macro level outcome appears quite 'emotional', such as a panic in a theatre, they invoke an emotion-driven actor; when a macro level outcome appears deliberate, they invoke a rational actor.

From his own standpoint, what Coleman has done is to implement this idea in a principle that action is *purposive* by contrast with *expressive*. Then the job of the theorist is to carry out this decision with unrelenting consistency, rather than to 'give up' and pass to an explanation in terms of emotions and of interpersonal 'influences' unmediated by rational choices.

We can best understand this conception of theory by asking three questions and looking at how Coleman frames the possible answers and adopts a particular one of them:

1 What is to be explained by social theory?
2 What form should explanation take?
3 How should we implement this type of explanation?

As to the first question, in principle we might be trying to explain individual behaviour or social system behaviour. For Coleman, the former aim is misplaced: it is not the job of social theory. However, a great deal of modern sociological research does just this when, for instance, it explains variation in voting behaviour by variations in social class background. The job of social theory is to account for social system phenomena. For instance, it might try to explain the institutionalization of a particular type of voting rule.

As to the second question, concerning the form of the explanation, there are two aspects of the problem. First, there can be a focus on the external properties of the individual or system. Second, there can be a focus on its internal mechanisms that produce the external aspects. Good scientific theory is based on formulating models of inner mechanisms. Since social theory deals with social system behaviour, it must formulate inner mechanisms of the social system itself. This means models treating the interdependence of actions of actors. It is misplaced explanatory focus to develop models of the internal mechanisms of individual actors as such. Such models will deal with the interdependence of psychological elements, introducing complexity at the level of the acting unit and making explanation of the social system phenomena cumbersome at best and probably inadequate from the standpoint of generating or showing how such phenomena are produced.

This takes us to the second aspect of the problem of the form of explanation, as treated by Coleman. This is the problem of micro–macro linkage. While Blau (1964) formulated the problem, his treatment of it left a gap: he was not successful in showing how the macro level phenomena could be explained on the basis of micro mechanisms. Later he turned to pure macro level theory (Blau, 1977). Coleman's discussion of the problem must have emerged by some reflection on this prior effort by Blau. In addition, excellent statements of the micro–macro problem from a meth-odological individualist standpoint have been given by other sociologists, such as Boudon (1981, 1987) and Wippler and Lindenberg (1987). As Coleman (1987, 1990a) formulates the problem, it is as follows.

Since social theory must explain systemic phenomena, one might think that the proper procedure (following Durkheim here) would be to explain 'social facts' (say, M1) in terms of other such social facts (say, M0). But the theoretical problem is to account for this very relationship, the relational fact that in systemic circumstances M0, we find systemic outcome M1. This implies a need to 'look inside' the system, to model the internal mechanisms leading from M0 to M1. Logically this requires three steps:

Step 1. Macro to micro. Pass from systemic initial conditions (M0) to the actor initial conditions (m0): for instance, indicate how the actor's preferences depend upon social position and how the actor's possible choices de-pend upon situational opportunities under the M0 conditions.

Step 2. Micro to micro. Given any actor's preferences and situational opportu-nities (and constraints), as specified through Step 1, show how a specific action (m1) is logically implied.

Step 3. Micro to macro. Show how the actions of all actors combine to pro-duce the systemic outcome (M1).

When these three steps are followed, we have an explanation of *how and why* the initial macro conditions (M0) lead to the macro outcomes (M1). We have explanation in the form of an inner mechanism because we have modelled the generation of actions and their interdependence leading to the systemic outcome.

Now let us turn to the third question: how shall we implement this form of explanation of social systemic phenomena? Here Coleman's purposive action presup-position is developed in two distinct contexts. One context is qualitative. The prin-ciple is simply that action is purposive-rational in a fairly broad and non-quantitative sense. The aim is to construct theory to explain as much as possible with this prin-ciple, admitting that this abstracts from the more complete character of human action. For instance, it eliminates immediate consideration of not only expressive behaviour, but also impulsive behaviour and self-destructive behaviour.

The other context is quantitative. Here a mathematical theory is to be developed based on the implementation of the purposive action presupposition in the following principle: the actor maximizes utility subject to constraints. This is an idealization, made for instrumental reasons (i.e., allowing a smooth micro-micro transition in the sense of deduction of action from the model of the actor in the situation of action). It is not intended as a literal depiction of action. In some ways, it should be compared with statements in physics about the treatment of bodies as mass-points or even as massless. The theorist is not saying that descriptively the entity's mass is all at its tiny inner core or that it has no mass (except for certain elementary particles). The theorist is idealizing and abstracting from the facts in order to gain explanatory leverage on a problem. In the present case a mathematical theory implementing adequate micro-macro linkage as just discussed will idealize the actor model to gain leverage in the treatment of the interdependence of actions and so on generating systemic outcomes under given systemic conditions. Moreover, intrinsic to mathematical theorizing is the idea of *extension of scope*, which widens applicability while capturing initial formulations as special cases. This is a very important phase of Coleman's work, as will be discussed later in this chapter.

Coleman's presuppositional choices include the rational-purposive model of human action as a starting point at the actor level. In this choice he places his theory within the 'umbrella' of rational choice theories in social science as a whole.

Rational Choice as an Umbrella Theory

Rational choice theory (RCT) is an umbrella theory for social science in a sense somewhat analogous to Darwinian theory for the life sciences. In both cases theorists begin any analysis by trying to comprehend the phenomenon to be explained in terms of the principle of the umbrella framework. Of special interest are phenomena that seem to be outright contradictions of the principle. For the life sciences, the existence of altruistic behaviour among animals is such a problem. How could a species exist if its genetically determined behavioural repertoire includes giving an alarm signal to others? By doing so, the animal makes itself especially observable to a predator. This means an increase in its chance of being killed and hence a decrease in the chance that its genes will be propagated to the next generation. Over evolutionary time such a behaviour should disappear. Thus we find theoretical model building about altruism exciting theoreticians in the life sciences, with new ideas such as inclusive fitness being invented to bring the phenomenon within the explanatory scope of the umbrella theory, in this case Darwin's theory. The result of the concept of inclusive fitness, for instance, is to broaden the scope of the concept of fitness and hence of the umbrella theory itself. Standard, non-inclusive fitness calculations are a special case of the broader notion.

Corresponding to fitness functions in evolutionary theory, we have utility functions in rational choice theory. Theorists attempt to comprehend any and all social phenomena under the umbrella of rational choice. But this ambition runs into phenomena that appear to contradict the fundamental framework-defining principle. As in biology, we find great interest in trying to bring these phenomena within the explanatory scope of the umbrella theory. These are explanatory problems of general-theoretic interest and not merely of historical or empirical interest.

One example is the existence of voting in a democratic election with a large electorate. A theoretical model of the rational choice of voting or not voting in such an election yields the deduction of not voting. This holds for each prospective voter, and hence there are no voters. This is contrary to fact. Hence the problem is to account for a commonplace phenomenon that appears contrary to the umbrella framework.

A second example is the pursuit of collective action to attain a shared goal. Sociologists used to assume, before the work of Olson (1965) on public goods, that if everyone agrees on the goal, there is little problematic about collective action. But if the number of individuals is large, and if the benefit can be obtained whether or not one participates in the collective action, then a theoretical model of the rational choice of contributing or not yields the deduction of not contributing: free riding. This holds for each prospective contributor, and hence there are no contributors. This is often contrary to fact, despite the generality of the deduction. Hence the problem is to account for another commonplace phenomenon: the self-organizing of individuals to pursue a common goal.

A final example occurs in the context of mixed motive situations, the standard Prisoner's Dilemma (PD) situation. As is well known, the rational actor will choose to defect rather than cooperate because this yields a better outcome whatever the other actor does. But in one sense, the very core of social life is a PD: the situation it models is a recurrent one at all levels and types of social organization. But then how is social order possible? What generates cooperation, at least some of the time?

In all these and other cases, what rational choice theorists have demonstrated is that a social phenomenon is incompatible with a direct and simple rational actor model. Thus they have defined a phenomenon that requires the extension of standard rational choice theory in the same sense that inclusive fitness extends standard Darwinian fitness. The logic of comprehensive theory building is to try to generalize the framework, not abandon it. Most sociologists have interpreted classic theory as an abandonment of the rational choice umbrella. But some have not, especially Boudon (1981), who argues that implicitly or explicitly Weber, Pareto and Durkheim were adopting a *generalized* rationality of action as a postulate. In the generalized version the subjective point of view of the actor is crucial to a rational choice explanation. The actor's beliefs matter, including subjective probabilities of outcomes that may or may not be well grounded in objective chances. The actor's preferences may not be readily assimilated to those that they 'should' be for the most efficient attainment of a goal. For that matter, the goal may be some transcendent state that is not even empirical. Emotions may affect these preferences, either in an abrupt and situated way or in some long-term cumulative way, building up commitments. In short, a generalized rational action principle broadens the scope of classic utility theory as a foundation of social theory: it widens the scope of the umbrella theory.

Let us try to clarify the logical and epistemological status of some of these RCT umbrella theory's accomplishments before its key premise is generalized. Let us say that by 'the RCT axiom' one means the principle that action is purposive-rational. This principle can be implemented in various ways, but mathematically it will usually involve a utility function that is maximized.

If the RCT axiom holds, then the following propositions are examples of derived theorems within various disciplinary traditions:

economic theory:
> competitive market economy → efficient resource allocation
standard game theory:
> PD situation → non-cooperative outcome

> *extended game theory*:
>> iterated PD situation → cooperation evolves
> *public choice theory*:
>> public goods in large groups → non-production of goods.

Logically each of these propositions is a theorem of the RCT umbrella theory. Each has the general macro-macro form (M0 implies M1). The reasoning that leads to the theorem exhibits the micro-macro logic explicated earlier with rational choice as the micro-to-micro step. (What is meant by 'extended game theory' is exemplified by the work of Axelrod, 1984.)

Empirically we ask how any such general derived theorem corresponds or applies to the social world. If observation shows that when the world approximately satisfies the first condition (call it M0, as in my discussion of micro-macro logic), it does not realize the derived outcome (M1), then a theoretical problem is generated for theorists to try to solve. An agenda for theorizing is generated.

This epistemological situation is similar to that framed by Toulmin (1953, 1961) in regard to other 'principles of natural order' in theoretical sciences. Such principles are not empirical generalizations but modes of representation or 'representation principles' (Fararo, 1989a: Ch. 1). Such a principle enables a mode of modelling the phenomena, including those that appear to be outright contradictions. The principle of natural order itself is chosen because it formulates something that the theorist will not try to explain but only to presuppose in all explanations. The idea of purposive-rational action is such a principle, corresponding to the intuitive sense that we have of making a choice, not merely mechanically reacting to a situation. Even where we do not find by introspection an explicit choice, we feel we could have stopped to make a choice. What we now are is simply the accumulation of the consequences of many small choices made over time and space. For the social sciences, the RCT mode of representation is a posited idealized form of natural order, a species characteristic and perhaps a wider characteristic of higher organisms generally. This idea is also central to the foundations of social theory we find in Homans. He also argued, adopting a perspective summarized recently by Herrnstein (1990), that behavioural psychology's principle of action is a generalized version of the utility theory implementation of the RCT axiom.

Thus the epistemological situation is very compatible with the analogy I have drawn between the Darwinian umbrella theory for the life sciences and the RCT umbrella theory for the social sciences. As in biology, the battle is over *how* to generalize the umbrella theory.

Parsons' foundation ideas also fit into this perspective, if we recall that in his earliest foundation statement (Parsons, 1937) he does not repudiate 'utilitarianism' so much as embed it within a broader frame of reference. In later critical commentary on Homans' theory, Parsons (1971) does not directly challenge the generalization of RCT adopted by Homans. Rather, he criticizes the restriction of its applications to the elementary forms of social behaviour, thereby failing to address other emergent levels of social organization. More recently, working within Parsons' framework, Rainer Baum (1976) has proposed a four-function family of rational choice formulations that is close in spirit to the approach I have taken toward the problem of synthesizing rational choice ideas with functional analysis (Fararo, 1993).

However, as indicated earlier, both the Parsonian and the Homans versions of the generalized umbrella theory had various unsatisfactory aspects, including the absence of continuity of method. The method must involve building explicit and idealized theoretical models that use the RCT axiom or its generalization logically to derive the outcomes to be expected at the system level given the initial conditions, the actor model and the way in which the actions combine. In short, their theoretical methods were deficient.

Coleman's Foundations: General Social Equilibrium

It is time to look at one of Coleman's key ideas: to generalize the economist's general equilibrium theory. One problem with Coleman's book is that he does not provide a general conceptual discussion of the logic of general equilibrium theory *as theory*. Thus it will be necessary to discuss what is meant by this type of theory, and, for sociologists, it is vital to see its relatedness to earlier work on the foundations of social theory within our discipline. For the latter purpose, I will discuss a key feature of Parsons' theory and then go on to discuss Coleman's use of a general equilibrium model.

General Equilibrium Theory

In the history of economic thought a vital distinction has emerged that has not played a correspondingly important role in sociological thought, namely the distinction between partial equilibrium and general equilibrium analysis. For a recent set of conceptual and mathematical discussions of the varieties of general equilibrium theory in economics, see Eatwell *et al.* (1989). The original mathematical theories were formulated by Arrow and Debreu (1954) and presented in elegant axiomatic form by Debreu (1959). For an historical and critical treatment, see Ingrao and Israel (1990). For present purposes, a brief authoritative statement will have to suffice. The contributors to *The MIT Dictionary of Modern Economics* (Pearce, 1986) put the matter as follows:

> Economists have traditionally adopted two approaches in analyzing economic systems. The simpler approach, associated with the name of A. Marshall, has been that of partial equilibrium, where only a part of the system is examined (e.g., the market for oranges), on the assumption of unchanged conditions in the rest of the economy. The second and more difficult approach, both in conception and in its use of mathematical tools, is general equilibrium analysis, which looks at an economic system as a whole and observes the simultaneous determination of all prices and quantities of all goods and services in the economic system.

In a corresponding distinction in sociology, general equilibrium analysis is required for any coherent answer to the problem of order. (For an interesting discussion of this idea by an economist, see Rowe, 1989.) If partial equilibrium analysis is employed, what we are showing is that a stable social equilibrium is possible — social order can exist — given a wider social environment. Thus social order as given is used to help account for embedded social order. This is a very different problem.

275

We can see this in the economic case. General economic equilibrium theory is characterized by an abstract representation of an entire economy so that there are no purely *economic* givens. It is true, of course, that there is no message from the inner nature of things that defines the economic category: economists have quarrelled about what is and what is not purely economic for centuries. But, given the conceptual structure based on one or another set of decisions, it remains true that the conceptual task of the general theorist is that of showing how economic order can exist in a given non-economic environment. In the standard formulation of this problem, preferences are givens, and laws regulating the meaning and exchange of property are givens. Producer decisions and consumer decisions are endogenous, determined by the efforts of the economic actors to realize their interests subject to the given constraints.

By analogy and generalization, to construct a general theory of social order requires that there be *no social givens* in the sense of exogenous social states. In turn, as in the economic case, this requires a precise conceptualization of 'the social', so that other aspects of action can be conceptualized as the non-social environment. Let us connect this key idea to the action framework of Talcott Parsons.

Parsons' Theory and General Social Equilibrium

What Parsons tried to do was to suggest social order theorems — since he did not have an adequate formal theory, he could never deductively demonstrate them. By analogy with the economic problem and general economic equilibrium, Parsons' general social equilibrium — social order — could not have social givens. This would be reasoning in a circle, invoking social order to account for social order. Parsons saw the task as one of conceptualizing 'the social' as a distinct class of states such that the givens for this class would be specified in the very act of conceptualization. Thus the adoption of an analytical concept of 'the social' as one among a set of analytical concepts is required.

Let us state a version of Parsons' four-function scheme:

L–state of action: cultural state
I–state of action: social state
G–state of action: motivational state
A–state of action: cognitive-operational state.

The social state of such a general system of action refers to its transient or enduring solution to problems of integrating individual actions, e.g., generating and sustaining coordination and cooperation and managing conflicts. A particular state may exhibit more or less harmony or conflict. Social order refers not to some ideal state but to a state that can endure, given the exogenous states that function as given conditions for the analysis of the social order problem: cultural, motivational and cognitive-operational conditions. In AGIL terms, the focus on the social-functional problem implies treating the I state as endogenous and L, G and A as exogenous, although connected to the social state in relations of 'interchange', generalized input-output relations.

The general theoretical problem — by analogy with the similar analytic focus in general equilibrium theory in economics — is the problematic character of the existence, uniqueness and stability of general social equilibrium. Also there is a comparative statics analytical problem, in which the particulars of any given general social equilibrium are shown to depend upon the parameters of the system, L, G and A states functioning as givens for the analysis (Fararo, 1989a: Ch. 3).

In addressing this sort of problem, Parsons refers to a constraint on the relation between culture and motivation as a necessary condition for general social equilibrium in his conjectured 'fundamental dynamic theorem of sociology' (Parsons, 1951: 42). The social state is described in terms of relational expectations held by the actors. Order exists to the extent that the interaction is governed by stabilized and meshing relational expectations. The necessary condition for such social order is that the social value parameters (L-states) and the motivational or interest parameters (G-states) are such that social value commitments shape or qualify what would otherwise be purely instrumental interests of the actors. This condition is interpreted to mean that the values are 'introjected' or 'internalized'. In the theoretically ideal case of 'perfect integration' this condition holds throughout the system of action. Implied in this treatment of an action system is that there are levels of speed of adjustment of processes. The cultural-level parameters change more slowly than the social state, while the motivational level interests — apart from 'natural' interests given for social interaction in general — change more rapidly. This rapid adjustment is the process of socialization to given social positions in a social structure, so that actors' interests come to reflect their location in the social order.

To summarize: in the Parsonian formulation, the general social equilibrium is in reference to a state of social interaction — defined in terms of relational expectations among actors — that is adjusted to normative cultural and motivational givens, i.e., adjusted to social value parameters and actor interest parameters.

While Parsons (1951) was careful to indicate a distinction between 'partial social systems' and 'a society', with the latter as the focus of the general problem of social order, he did not make any attempt to utilize the technical apparatus of either Marshall's partial equilibrium analytic method or Walras' general equilibrium analytic method. Only with the recent work of Coleman (1990a) do we find a sociologist making an explicit generalization of general equilibrium theory in economics.

Coleman's Theory and General Social Equilibrium

Coleman makes the formalism of this economic theory explicit as the starting point for his entire social theory, interpreted as an effort to generalize economic theory, the same enterprise undertaken earlier by Pareto, Parsons and Homans. So while he is totally committed to the same *end* as these writers — generalizing economic theory to a general social theory grounded in a general theory of action — the *means* differ in that he makes direct use of the formal apparatus of general economic equilibrium theory. Two important theoretical strategies are used in this process. First, the general economic equilibrium theory is given a new and generalized interpretation. Second, the theory is modified in ways that extend its scope. Let us briefly review each of these strategies.

First, the mathematical structure is abstracted from the economic interpretation and given a more general interpretation. Recall that the general equilibrium problem is defined in the context of a complete system of interdependent markets. The entities in the system are *economic actors* (producers and consumers) and commodities (goods and services) that we can also call *economic resources*, including intermediate producer goods and producer services. These entities are connected by two relations. First, each economic actor effectively controls a commodity bundle as an initial condition. Second, each economic actor has an evaluative orientation toward possible commodity bundles such that some bundles may be preferred by the actor to the given bundle. Consumers attempt to maximize utility subject to the constraint of not exceeding the worth of their current bundle. The latter is actually the wealth of the actor. Producers attempt to maximize profit subject to an analogous constraint. On this basis the actors are motivated to engage in exchanges. In the axiomatic theory (Debreu, 1959) it is made clear that there is an environment containing various givens, including, but not limited to, the preferences of the actors. What Coleman does is generalize from economic actors and economic resources to general actors and general resources, with the economic interpretation as a special case. The two relations connecting these entities are the same, namely control and interest.

The control relation is *endogenous* to the formal theory, while the interests are *given*. The former is spelled out in the mathematical theory as a matrix: each actor (row) controls a certain quantity of each resource (column). Thus the analytically *social state* is given by this matrix, denoted C. What the theory shows is how the initial state of C is transformed into an equilibrium, the general social equilibrium. The interests are also spelled out in the mathematical theory as a matrix: each actor has a certain interest in each resource. This is the matrix denoted X. Hence, X contains the given parameters and C contains the endogenous state of social action.

Analytically, the interests are implicitly defined in the utility function that Coleman posits (technically a Cobb–Douglas form): there are terms in it that represent the interests of the actor. When the actor attempts to maximize utility, this means attempting to realize these interests.

Control is also implicitly defined, not formally, but through a discursive presentation that we can interpret as formulating a set of meaning postulates on the control concept (see Fararo, 1993). The discussion makes clear that the C matrix entries are intended to refer to *rights to control* various resources. It is in virtue of such rights that actors have differential control and hence, given their interests, differential power.

The point is that matrix C, the analytically distinct social state in FST, refers to states of *normative control* over action, putting it into direct correspondence with the corresponding analytical social concept of Parsons, with its role expectations. In general social equilibrium, we can interpret Parsons as saying, these expectations have a normative or legitimate aspect, they embody claims that will be backed up by others in the collectivity. In a word, they are Coleman's rights (including the implied obligations of others to respect these rights).

Similarly, the *given* interest configuration, matrix X, corresponds to the G-level motivational orientations or action interests of actors. Some of these action interests are general elements of action — the need for social approval, say — whereas others are directly under the control of the social state, the role expectations (always including the general membership role as well as specialized roles). Purposive control comes under normative control. The relation is two-way: ultimate interests of human beings help shape and constrain possible social equilibria, but the structures that emerge as aspects of the equilibria normatively constrain purposes (as well as enable the attainment of them via acquired skills and opportunities).

Coleman uses his quantitative interest concept, along with the control concept, to find the power of each actor and the value of each resource implied in the existence of an equilibrium state of the system.

We turn now to the second strategy in Coleman's use of the general equilibrium framework of economics. This involves not just reinterpretation but creation of an analogous model and also logical extension. Thus two types of modifications of the theory are involved.

In the first type Coleman introduces the concept of *perfect social system*: an analogue of the perfect competitive market as in the general equilibrium starting point from microeconomics. The difference is that now divisible resources are replaced by indivisible *events* thought of as having various outcomes which are differentially favourable to the interests of various actors. Vote trading in legislatures is one instance for which the perfect social system is the idealized theoretical model functioning as the baseline.

In the second type of modification, the prior theoretical models are treated as idealized baseline models and we have *extensions* of them to treat aspects of social action systems such as interpersonal bonds, communication networks and event interdependencies as they affect the exchanges in otherwise perfect social systems.

Each extension is built on the methodological principle of introducing additional formal ideas and deriving new formulas or propositions, such that the original formal theory is a special case. All of this is in the spirit of extending the scope of some formulation within the context of the RCT umbrella theory. The following are examples of such extensions:

Psychic investment. Actors can have diffuse or intrinsic interests in other persons, psychic investments, as well as specific interests of instrumental relevance to the actor. A matrix of such investments is introduced, and the general equilibrium derivations are carried out. When this matrix is the identity matrix, so that only the actor's self is a social object of intrinsic interest, the original theory and its formal results are obtained as a special case. This extension is very important in terms of embedding concern for others in a rational choice framework, which might otherwise be accused of equating self-interest with selfish interests.

Dependence of events. Once events are introduced (as in a perfect social system), the possible outcomes of one event can have consequences for other event outcomes. A matrix of such event dependencies is introduced in such a way as to capture the original formulation as a special case.

Losses in exchange between actors and between resources. For instance, communication networks (as in the network exchange experiments discussed by various contributors in a special issue on the subject edited by Willer, 1992) constrain who can exchange with whom, and these are represented in the theory by extending it to allow barriers between actors. Similarly, barriers between resources may exist, as when laws forbid a direct exchange of money for a vote.

Dynamics. The original theory is a before-and-after formulation of the change in constitution of the social action system. In one extension there is a time path from the initial state of the constitution to the final state. A two-stage process is postulated, with a first-stage Walrasian pseudo-process in which there are virtual value changes over time until all markets can be cleared, and then in the second stage the re-distribution of resources is carried out by a series of assembled 'movements' over time instead of an instantaneous change of state. In another type of extension there is a postulated shift in the givens of control and interest, with a process of adjustment by which a new distribution of value and power is generated.

This concludes my discussion of the general equilibrium models developed by Coleman. I will close this essay with an assessment of *Foundations of Social Theory*.

Coleman's *Foundations*: Assessment

In this essay I have used Parsons' AGIL roster of dimensions of action to discuss foun-dation problems and to locate Coleman's ideas within a context of other systematic discourse about presuppositional issues in social theorizing. From this standpoint the key dimension for *social* theory is the integration of the actions of multiple actors (I). Roughly speaking, the general problem relates to the coordination of the actions of diverse actors. Then cultural (L), motivational (G) and cognitive-operational (A) conditions are relevant to fundamental social theory (so defined) as givens.

However, *action* theory takes all these states as endogenous and implicitly or explicitly has the problem of treating a generalized problem of order in which only biophysical parameters are givens. It embeds the coordination problem within a wider set of problems; for instance, the problem of the origins of preferences and the way that they emerge in repeated behavioural episodes that, however, are embedded in a dynamically evolving body of culture. Thus *social* theory is only one theory in the tree of theories that can be formulated under an action-theoretic umbrella.

Criticism: Social Integration Problem

Adopting the standpoint of Parsons and Homans, we can claim that *sociological* theory addresses a specific but highly general theoretical problem of the integration of actions of diverse actors: it is only one branch of social theory. As in the foundation work of Homans, such an analytical sociological theory treats the problem of the social integration of the diverse parts of a social system. This is the 'social integration' (II) problem, the problematic nature of enduring social bonds.

Any theoretical model that puts such bonds in the role of the givens may be an important theory, but it will not be addressing the fundamental problem of sociolog-ical theory, as framed in this analytical way. For an example of a recent theory that does put solidary bonds into the problematic endogenous role, see Collins (1988: Ch. 6). In Collins' synthesis of ideas from Durkheim, Goffman and others, the classical types of solidarity appear as special cases of outcomes of a recursive ritual interaction process.

Perhaps my main criticism of Coleman's book, viewed in this perspective, is that I do not see any explicit articulation of this problem. Where social bonds appear, they are in the context of 'social capital' available to the actor, i.e., the bonds are given. Of course, between primordial ties of old and modern social systems, there has been an historical shift: certain bonds that used to exist as social capital no longer can be counted upon to exist. But this historical fact is not the same as a general-theoretical comparative statics model. More importantly, it is vastly different from a general theoretical treatment of ties as problematic outcomes in systems of interaction in a fully dynamic model with the emergence of groups or other solidary units as macrosocial outcomes. (It was this idea that dominated my thinking in Fararo, 1989a.)

A similar problem exists with respect to the equality-inequality aspect of the social system. In most treatments of social structure there are two fundamental types of elements: what Blau (1977) calls nominal (horizontal) and graduated (vertical) aspects. From the present point of view the former has to do with the emergence of solidary ties and with conflict among actors in and between the emergent collectivities, while the latter has to do with the distribution of resources in the social system. Some resources are ultimate givens for social life, but others are emergent, especially those that function as symbolic media of social interaction. Coleman's constitution matrix is, in one sense, a static picture of a system of distributions, a kind of distributive complex. The model transforms an initial distributive complex into a final distributive complex. But in this process — and here we get a technical result from the Walrasian formulation of general equilibrium that Coleman employs — the wealth or power of the actor is invariant. Resources are redistributed, but subject to the constraint that no actor can end up with a bundle of rights of control over actions or events that exceeds the amount initially given. But if this is a correct analysis of the theory, then it provides no explanation of inequality, its existence or amount or the generalized way it may depend upon specified parametric givens. If this is true, the critical theory aspect of Coleman's foundation is rather severely undermined.

Further assessments of Coleman's theory can be highlighted by an analogous reference to the other dimensions of action, the cultural, the motivational and the behavioural.

Criticism: Culture and the Social Focus

Coleman's social action system is *culture-embedded* in the same sense that the economist's market has been analyzed as *social*-embedded. Ordinarily the latter is taken as a criticism (Granovetter, 1985), but this is a failure to maintain the analytical point of view. We do not want to make the same error in the assessment of Coleman's social theory, although there is also room for a valid critical point.

Coleman is a theorist concentrating on the *social* dimension. Appropriately, Coleman's theory places I-states in an endogenous position and (with an important exception to be discussed below) treats L-states, cultural entities and processes, as givens. This is an interpretation of the scope of the theory. But there are two problems here.

First, in terms of the empirical world, it is the cultural setting of the West (and usually of American society) which Coleman ordinarily presupposes. Of course, a foundation treatise should not be so scope-restricted in this empirical sense.

Second, in abstract terms this scope restriction is accompanied by the absence of any conceptual discussion of culture, despite the long history of ideas in twentieth century sociology and anthropology concerning the relation of culture to social systems. Yet a foundation of social theory should contribute a generalized response to this received conceptual problem. Thus it is a valid criticism that Coleman's book contains no explicit conception of culture and its relation to analytical social theory, although we grant that analytically defined cultural processes need not be treated as endogenous in a purely social theory. This remark leaves open exactly what such a cultural process is, a job for conceptual discussion of a foundation theory.

If we refer to Parsons' foundations once again, the cultural state variable L is differentiated into four substates: LL (religious and existential beliefs), LI (normative ideas), LG (expressive symbolization) and LA (cognitive symbolization). Implicitly Coleman's theory presupposes actors with certain unspecified but given levels of shared cognitive symbolization, accompanied by certain unspecified but given existential beliefs and expressive modes of symbolization. The theory by and large is not concerned with a generalized explanation of changes of state with respect to these types of culture, although Coleman is interested in them from the standpoint of historical change (i.e., changes of state in particular societies in the world in particular time periods, mostly contemporary with us).

However, his viewpoint toward normative culture is completely different. First, this aspect of culture is made explicit. Second, Coleman takes it as a fundamental theoretical problem to show how norms emerge. He defines norms as a species of rights, namely rights of control over an actor's action that are held by *other* actors in the system. Since everyone agrees that such norms (and other rights) are not *ultimate* givens, to show how they emerge is an important contribution. We can count this problem focus as one of the most important of the many topics treated in Coleman's book. However, the process he proposes seems to work best for conscious attempts to institute normative ideas in groups and perhaps less so for what Sumner called 'crescive' developments of folkways and mores in which, as Homans liked to put it, the 'is' becomes 'the ought'. So perhaps the RCT umbrella theory tends to favour theoretical models that underplay such crescive, more or less unconscious developments? Would this not be a serious scope limitation for a general theory?

Perhaps it would, but this judgment may be too hasty. We have to distinguish between the admittedly partial inroads Coleman has made on a large number of problems and really fundamental limitations. Because Coleman himself does not set out his problems in the systematic way that I have been using to interpret and assess his work, it is often difficult to judge which is the case: are we dealing with a fundamental limitation or merely a case of something on the agenda for further theorizing later? The next topic will illustrate the danger of a too hasty negative judgment.

Criticism: Motivation and the Social Focus

As indicated earlier, interests generally function in the theory as givens, but in his mathematical work, Coleman (1990a: Ch. 34) presents two beautiful theoretical results — that is, logically derived theorems — that show how interests of the *corporate* actor can be constructed from its members' interests. Unfortunately, Coleman does not follow the nice practice of theoretical economics where theorems are explicitly identified as such, i.e., labelled and offset as 'theorems'. Thus numerous readers may fail to find the core contributions amid the complex formula-laden presentation. One theorem says that within the RCT framework as employed by Coleman, in particular with Cobb-Douglas utility functions, a corporate actor's *interest* in a resource is the *value* of that resource as generated as a macro level emergent from exchanges among members. The second theorem is even more beautiful: if a corporate actor is composed of actors with Cobb–Douglas utility functions and it is a perfect social system internally, then the corporate actor itself has a utility function which is Cobb–Douglas.

Thus, in a very important sense, the interests of corporate actors can be treated as not simply given but as outcomes of internal processes; and this is to say, not merely as outcomes in some intuitive sense, but by deduction of a quantitative utility function at the collectivity level. Moreover, Coleman goes on to specify carefully the scope conditions under which this sort of beautiful theorem has validity; for instance, it applies only to resources that are the same for both the member actors and the corporate actor they comprise. This leads him into a question at the presuppositional level: does the construction not amount to creating an expressive action for the corporate actor? But how does this relate to various meanings of rational action? The general point is that readers who skip over Coleman's mathematical studies come away with a very limited and perhaps misleading understanding of Coleman's discrete contributions.

Coleman is less clear about another aspect of motivation relating to the concept of individual interest. This concept functions in fundamental social theory in two quite distinct analytical contexts: as ultimate given for the treatment of the problem of social order (Hobbesian interests, for instance), and as socialized motivation to membership and other roles in a given social system. Coleman provides no real discussion of the first or 'human nature' level interest parameters and how they play a role in constraining the generally possible social orders in a way that is conceptually distinct from the constraints introduced by the socially generated interests. A stronger treatment of this distinction might have led to a theoretical orientation closer to Parsons and Homans in the sense of drawing upon the theoretical resources of psychology in dealing with the social-motivational nexus.

On the positive side, not only is there the set of theorems about corporate actor interests described earlier, but also Coleman's original and important discussion of the problem of interpersonal comparison of utilities. Placing himself in opposition to most utility theorists and probably most other rational choice theorists, Coleman maintains that social processes provide a natural empirical basis for the combinatory operations required for valid interpersonal comparisons. The theorems about corporate actor interests arising out of member interests illustrate this conceptual point.

Criticism: Emotions and the Social Focus

From my point of view the problem at the behavioural level may be that Coleman has dismissed Homans' later work too readily, even while admitting (Coleman, 1971; Swedberg, 1990: 49) how much he was influenced by Homans' earliest theoretical formulation on the subject of social behaviour as exchange (Homans, 1958). There is an ad hoc and casual use by Coleman of terms referring to sentiments, emotions, learning. These terms refer to elements and processes central to Homans' work and, indeed, to the work of numerous other classic and recent theorists (e.g., Collins). Coleman may *appear* to be explaining numerous phenomena without reference to emotions (e.g., certain collective behaviours). But might not emotions be involved causally and not just epiphenomenally as producing such acts as 'transferring a right to control one's action to another person'? What produced the transfer decision, after all? Might the immediate situated utility terms of the actor be parametrized by an interest in survival that is communicated to others by an involuntary upsurge of fear and a readiness to run first, think later? Similarly, might a reluctance to become the only one to try to sanction a norm violator be grounded in a situationally generated fear of being hurt in some way? Coleman has no general conceptual discussion of how emotions and expressive action function in social life and how they relate to instrumental action. In taking up Homans' proposal that social behaviour is an exchange of rewards, Coleman has gone a certain distance forward, but there are gaps and cracks in the foundations. Nor is there any attempt to work out a relationship between the implied trial-and-error adaptive model (used informally by Homans) and the postulate of a situated actor with a given utility function to be maximized.

Conclusion

For all these reasons and others, relating to the various dimensions of action and to the fundamental problems of social and sociological theory, it is my belief that a sociology built upon Coleman's foundations still needs to turn to the work of classic theorists such as Weber and Pareto, of postclassic theorists such as Homans and Parsons, and of more recent theorists such as Alexander and Collins, to articulate and strengthen its foundations.

Taking into account not only this work on the foundations of social theory but also the other lasting contributions he has made, Coleman has a place in the history of sociology on at least an equal level with Weber, Durkheim and a few others: he is a master of sociological thought. The critical implications of my brief assessment are in a direction that Coleman himself encourages: further theoretical studies, striving for greater consistency of formulations and greater coherence in the connections among the parts of the theoretical edifice, connecting the work to other significant theoretical projects in contemporary sociology. The latter step would be another implementation of what I have called 'the spirit of unification' in sociological theory (Fararo, 1989b).

17 Rational Choice as Grand Theory: James Coleman's Normative Contribution to Social Theory

Adrian Favell

Introduction: Coleman's Rational Choice Theory as Grand Theory

Without doubt, the world of sociology has been correct to greet the publication of James Coleman's *Foundations of Social Theory* with the kind of fanfare reserved for very special works. Offering a complete and elegant extension of rational choice theory and methods across the full range of central problems in social theory, the work does indeed mark a return to the terrain of general sociological theory: a rival to the grand foundational works of Parsons and Merton, that will undoubtedly prove just as influential and formative, in particular since it is a work that reconnects sociology directly with the current debates and methodological concerns of analytical political science, policy studies and institutional economics, thereby restoring sociology to a central place in the social sciences. In this chapter I argue that its importance may not end there. Coleman can be read in the company of other authors: that is, to borrow the words of Quentin Skinner, as a 'grand theory', a work that can be read as a rival to the kind of grand philosophical works dominant in European social and political thought, alongside the likes of Habermas, Rawls, Luhmann and Gadamer (Skinner, 1985: 3–20). Such works offer foundational 'systematic theories of man and society', grounding normative political concerns and applications in the long philosophical tradition of modernity.

Coleman goes beyond the piecemeal and normally modest empiricism of most rational choice theorists to offer a comprehensive, humanistic rational choice theory in the long tradition of utilitarian social thought. As such, it is a welcome intervention in the disciplinary wars of the social sciences, countering charges of 'economics imperialism' with a theory that demonstrates the richness and subtlety of such an approach: a theory with philosophical breadth and depth that can nevertheless plug into the highly practical and effective apparatus of empirical quantitative research and methods. This contribution may indeed be its most significant: as a way of going beyond the tiresome disputes between 'theorists' or 'philosophers' in the social sciences and those engaged in empirical and quantitative work.

Coleman's work goes further on a number of fronts. It advances beyond the habitual normative reticence of positive social science, to offer a positive social theory that is yet designed to make strong normative statements about the society it studies. It offers a thoroughly liberal Enlightenment theory that can debate with Habermas and neo-Kantians such as Rawls, while drawing on far stronger empirical credentials;

superseding their explicitly normative philosophy with a political theory far richer in practical policy intervention. It makes important advances on the current limitations of economics as normative theory, revising some of the weaker micro-foundational aspects of welfare and institutional economics. And it offers itself as a grand unifying theory for the social sciences, reconnecting the common concerns of political science, economics and sociology, around a base in organizations theory and policy research: in Coleman's words, a 'new social science' fit for the social scientist's role in the conditions of the late twentieth century. I shall consider these claims, and read them as the mark of a grand theory, presenting the strongest case for considering Coleman the missing grand theorist in Skinner's collection.

The Virtues of an Explanatory Theory

The source of the power of *Foundations* is in its strict adherence to the virtues of empirically-based positive social research — Coleman's lifework as an applied sociologist — and its willingness to use this power to formulate a strong new normative prerogative for sociological research. As such, Coleman begins *Foundations* with a metatheory about explanation in the social sciences that states positive scientific concerns alongside philosophical ones about the nature of man and society (Coleman, 1990a: Ch. 1). It thus reconnects the case for methodological individualism and causal explanation in the social sciences with an older doctrine about the normative principles and consequences that follow from this: the early modern tradition of social thought from Hobbes through Locke and Rousseau.

Coleman first clearly distinguishes and characterizes the kind of theory a comprehensive social theory should be. It is not one concerned with the ad hoc explanation of individual behaviour, but with social phenomena, the aggregation of individuals as social systems. He thus distances the preoccupation of the sociologist from the internal focus of the psychologist, trying to explain the behaviour of individuals from their internal mental states; and from the social statistician, attempting to explain differences in individual behaviour solely through the external correlation of variable traits and social contexts. Once the focus becomes the explanation of social systems of behaviour, the external correlation of group characteristics with behavioural differences is not sufficient to explain the origins and dynamics of group behaviour: to reveal this, the system level behaviour needs to be broken down into its component parts, for which the natural unit of analysis is the individual and its relation to the collective grouping. Thus the siting of the object of study at the system level brings with it a mechanistic concern for the internal analysis of the system's parts.

The moral of all this is not only the positivistic one, of grounding the right approach and unified language of a workable empirical sociological theory; it is also the purchase this gives to a social analyst in being able to produce effective explanation for public purposes. Here the classically Popperian style of scientific explanation asserts its wider virtues: its claim to derive normative power from the strength of its conclusions. Coleman's methodological individualism here is aimed at the design of pared down, two-level, mechanistic models, testable according to empiricist criteria and operational through the basic building blocks laid out in the theory. The centrality of casting the essential explanatory question as the analytical movement from system to components and back (the micro-to-macro problem) is the explanatory *effectiveness* of such a method; an explanation being 'sufficiently fundamental for the purpose in hand if it provides a basis for knowledgable intervention than can change system behaviour' (Coleman, 1990a: 4).

Two essential points about the micro-to-macro model emerge. One is the rationale for using individual purposive action as the elementary currency of all individual social action. This is to keep the micro-to-micro move as simple as possible for combinatorial purposes across individuals, since the next aggregating move back up to the macro level is likely to be far more complex and integral to understanding the way in which social systems come to be formed. The key to this is the economics inspired prerogative of simplicity at the micro level for quantitative work to be possible: this, as we shall see, troubles Coleman, but he at least begins with accepting this as a sensible starting point. Individuals in themselves are not interesting: the differences between their particular mental states and motivations are for psychologists to worry about. Rather, it is the kind of common patterns generated across collections of individuals that the social scientist is to be interested in. Coleman compensates by emphasizing that the micro-to-macro transition must not be seen as simple aggregation in the manner of all Pareto inspired macro generalizations. What enters into the formation of social systems with complex internal organization and constitutions are important factors of relative power and interests in the process of working out institutional arrangements. Diagnosing the role of relative power and interests is, as we shall see, the key to the sociologist's role as social analyst.

Coleman's definition of a sufficient explanation immediately sets the tone for a social science grounded on pragmatist interventionist foundations; distanced from the classical idea of science, formulating covering laws with a realist correspondence doctrine of truth. Ironically, this takes the theory away from the strictly positivist concerns that such social science usually has. Thus Coleman's line on the weakness of functionalist theories rife in the social sciences is not restricted to their scientific weaknesses. Their explanations are deficient on several grounds. First, they locate the workings of social systems primarily not in the actions of individuals but in the under-analyzed notion of social norms guiding behaviour: promoting a social picture based habitually on unproblematic conformity, rather than the problematic individual to collective relation. Second, this leads to a tendency to postulate a purpose in social systems not reducible to the aggregated purposive acts of individuals: an absurdity in the literal sense. Third, there is thus a compensatory tendency to reify notions of culture and value, giving them a causal status irreducible to the micro level of individual action. Finally, functionalist explanations are weak because they read off predictions entirely from what exists and survives on an evolutionary basis, with no access to the inner workings that produced this situation and not another. They thus offer no purchase for counterfactual thinking, and the positive intervention made possible when the social scientist is armed with a model that can identify the essential elements causing a particular situation. As a result of these faults, the social scientist cannot distinguish between one kind of society and another if they both function in similar ways; such theories thereby miss a connection that Coleman dearly wants to reintroduce into sociology: a reconnection with the concerns of classical political philosophy in Hobbes, Locke and Rousseau. These philosophers pictured man as an individual free to choose and living in perpetual tension with the social structures he is constrained to live in: thus posing the essential question as to how and why an individual would give up his sovereignty to society and polity, and under what conditions such an act would make the social arrangement legitimate — the classic social contract.

Coleman makes this his second body of reference after the question of explanation in the social sciences: the normative concerns of contemporary moral philosophy and social choice theory. On the face of it, this is an unusual field of thought to be importing into sociology, which generally has had little interface with the works of contemporary political philosophy. Philosophers, however, have — through their use of rational choice theory and the tools of analytical political science — been closely linked with the work of economists, and with the derivation of social choice functions and distributive theories of justice. While endorsing their focus on purposive and freely choosing individuals as being a conducive picture of the relation of man to society, Coleman argues that the theories of contemporary moral and political philosophy offer precious little explanatory backup for the ideal derivations they propose (Coleman, 1974b; 1990a: 328–35, 384–7). A similar fault can be found in mainstream welfare economics models, using very simple mathematical aggregation to discover social choice functions, because they do not pay enough attention to the sociological factors that enter into the contracting of any social consensus. Coleman's aim is to wed the explanatory and the normative in the terms of his own theory; to offer a theory that is able to account for the real world working out of consensus arrangements, swayed by the relative weight of actors' power, interests and control, while holding on to the idea that a properly explanatory social mechanism will be able to identify and lay bare what he calls the 'internal morality' of such systems, to render them changeable and legitimate in the eyes of those who submit to them.

This challenge poses an important advance on the underlying Kantian component of theories such as Rawls' (1971) and Habermas' (1987), which in the final analysis derive their ideal or just normative models from the residual idea of a transcendental moral rationality, the inherent moral value of all persons, most commonly expressed in terms of the idea of foundational universal rights. Utilitarians have always been critical of this kind of bulwark to philosophical theories, and have sought to derive their conclusions from a combination of simple (and amoral) universally applied assumptions about choice and action, and the inherently egalitarian mathematical properties of social calculus. Where Coleman adds to this is in the case he makes for the explanatory function of a moral theory to be also considered necessary for any practical theory. It is telling that the Rawlsian theory has, as its philosophical assumptions have been exposed, dropped its original explanatory use of rational choice to derive its basic moral principles in favour of an interpretative Kantian constructivist model (Rawls, 1993). The conditions for its applying to the real world can thus be seen to rely on a kind of functionalism about the origin of moral consensus in society: the functionalism of transcendental rights or the inherent moral nature of persons, driving the pluralist social world towards moral 'overlapping consensus'. Rawls' root faith in the good faith of the moral person, able to articulate and adhere to the inherent moral principles found in all rationally tenable pictures of the good life, marks the important gap in social realism in Rawls' theory, a gap that in practice — and in the derivation of practical political imperatives from the original theory — leads inevitably towards either a critical idealism (a favourite of the Rawlsians on the left) or a legal formalism hinged on human rights.

Coleman's wager is that he can use the same language of voluntary association, individual freedom and contractual style relations to produce a fully social theory of rights (Coleman, 1976b; 1990a: Ch. 3; 1993c). Sociologically speaking, it makes no sense to say that rights are held (inviolably) by individuals before they enter into social relations with others. Rights, whatever their content may be, are things that are given by the social community to the individual; that is, by the social grouping coming to some kind of constitutional consensus about where the right to do something lies. This legal analogy can be extended across all kinds of social relations, such that all social grouping can be seen as the outcome of some collective process of bargaining, or aggregation of individual purposive action, about what can be formalized theoretically as the social organization of a constitution of rights to act. One need not stop with formal organizations with a written constitution and formal hierarchy; one can extend this picture across even those forms of collective behaviour most resistant to being seen as purposively enacted: crowd panics, mass movements, ethnic or cultural groupings. The challenge of the theory is to render all such forms equally transparent to the analysis of social organization as the formalized legal structures — the key role of the chapters on collective behaviour and the emergence of norms (Coleman, 1990a: Chs 9–11).

This is the explanatory challenge: before addressing the subtle and indirect ways Coleman draws normative conclusions from this way of picturing problems in social theory, it is worth nothing criticisms that have standardly been made: from sociologists on the one hand and philosophers on the other, from different backgrounds that share common concerns. The first is a charge of excessive individualism in the explanatory formulation and elementary building blocks of the theory, despite Coleman's own contention that he is seeking to reduce the individualistic component of methodological individualism via a more careful consideration of sociological factors in rational choice explanations. They ask: how is the root foundation of individual purposive action even possible conceptually, when — from a sociological point of view — individuals are always seen to be so thoroughly socialized by particular cultures, values, languages, etc. that to reduce their behaviour to intentionality or rational purpose is absurd (Smelser, 1990)? The second is a scepticism about the derivation of normative conclusions from an internal empirical analysis of social forms. They ask: how can any kind of moral conclusions be drawn from the theory if, as it claims, all social consensus thus described is shot through with power-weighted relations that inherently corrupt, and fail to match up to, what ideal just arrangements would look like? They point to the timeworn impossibility of interpersonal comparison of utility, and accuse the theory of exactly the fault it claimed to set out against: moral relativism (Frank, 1992).

A New Utilitarian Social Theory

Coleman's response needs to be considered as a whole, as a combination of philosophical and sociological argument, which amounts to a renaissance of utilitarian social theory; a development all the more remarkable since sociology since Durkheim has resolutely refused the precepts and language of utilitarian theory as 'unsociological': one has only to think of Parsons' (1937), and via him, Habermas' (1987) treatment of the individualism of contractual or instrumental style reasoning. Yet the potential gain of building a theory from a utility-based theory of action, and its immediate affinities with the reasoning of economics, are very large: rational choice theory, unlike the holistic and teleological theories of Parsons and Habermas, is designed for close application in distinct spheres of social life, and comes equipped with a ready functioning apparatus of quantitative methods that fit straight onto methodological individualist presuppositions. Building from this base, Coleman offers a theory that transcends the classic division of labour that philosophers and sociologists habitually use to build disciplinary walls between themselves: a moral and explanatory theory of rational institution building, put together through the operation of viewing all social systems as organizational in nature, that is, as potentially working according to the instrumentally purposive logic of formalized rational organization.

First, Coleman spells out the normative principles at the heart of the theory: the moral value of the individuals described in the theory (Coleman, 1990a: 531–2). This is based around the thought, not that the individuals of a methodological individualist theory building are real entities — solo, solipsistic choosers holding intentions and deciding as actually described — but that they theoretically *represent* in some sense the 'natural persons' on whose behalf social research is undertaken. In reality, of course, individuals are always embedded in social structures, and cannot be divided from the plurality of social consensus that determines their roles and their action, if explanation is to work. But they can — and must, for moral reasons — be at least conceivable theoretically as holding sovereignty over themselves, prior to its alienation or endowment in social structures. What counts as alienation and what counts as legitimate endowment is the crucial aspect in evaluating the social outcomes of individual action. The role of the social scientist thus becomes to lay bare the form and mechanism of the social structures individuals find themselves in, in order that they become recognizable and thus controllable to those individuals that constitute them. This has long been an explicit motivation in Coleman's sociological work (see Coleman, 1974c; 1982a). In Part IV of *Foundations* he describes the complex and circular feedback that links the social scientist's description of the social structures to the constitution of the social structures themselves, a feedback in which through the intervention of better social understanding — a more lucid and transparent picture of how society's mechanisms work — the individual will be able to grasp how social organization is constituted in part by his or her actions, and thus restore to him or herself a control of those rights to act s/he may have within the existing social structure.

Such a conception depends on the effectiveness of the theoretical language in translating an understanding of the state of affairs into the realization of the purposive freedom such knowledge may bring. Here Coleman uses Hirschman's (1970) famous terminology of exit and voice organizational forms to explore this thought, extending them across from firms and bureaucratic organizations to a variety of different 'corporate structures', such as adherence to the nation state or revolutionary movements (Coleman, 1990a: 463–6). Coleman argues how, in corporate structures such as firms, this perspective sets up an internal dynamic which connects the continued success and evolution of the corporate structure to its ability continually to inspire allegiance with the interests of the firm through permitting the exercise of democratic voice, thus avoiding that individuals take the exit option and leave. This dynamic, also known as the principal-agent problem in organizations theory, is said to reveal a moral dimension of evolving social forms: what Coleman calls the 'internal morality' of a social system (Coleman, 1990a: 172–4). Against the iron cage imagery of the Weberian model of bureaucracy, where agents are all automatons in service of the will and action of the principal, it asserts a progressive developmental picture of formal social organization that claims to have discovered how the internal process of identification of the agent's interests with those of the corporation takes place: that is, how firms evolve and grow following an open and stable logic of progressive corporation building, held together by the continual freedom of the agent to withdraw his assent to the role they play, and thus threaten the legitimacy and possibly the existence of the corporate body itself (Coleman, 1990a: Ch. 16). Coleman's hope is that this logic can be extended across other forms of social organization, such as constitutions and nation states, as a new kind of social choice theory that can reveal the optimal form of rational progressive institution building.

This ideal picture connects, and only makes sense, if put into the larger developmental picture that Coleman goes on to describe. In a strong echo of the Enlightenment story developed by Habermas, taking his theory from lifeworld to system, Coleman sets out his own picture of the transformation of the modern social world, a development, he argues, that necessitates the kind of social theoretical language he is proposing (Coleman, 1990a: Ch. 24; 1993b). The movement from older forms of community based on kinship and family to a modern society characterized by artifice and individuality has been accompanied by the steady erosion of the informal 'social capital' of the old forms of social structure that have given way to purposively built ones (he cites the decline of the family and the rise of public social services having the same purpose). One of the essential roles of the social scientist — as Habermas (1985) also underlines — is to provide research that can facilitate these changes, and thus recognize the positive developments of modern progress while dealing with the dysfunctions of social change. The essential contribution of the social scientist lies here, in the potential intervention he makes possible if he can correctly describe the new forms of social organization.

We have here a strong statement about the purpose and meaning of sociological research, and the central role that organizations theory plays in establishing this role. To make the strongest case for this use of theory, it is essential to develop the strongly pragmatist overtones that it relies on to found its picture of social reality. The theory's *Erkenntnisinteressen*, if not exactly emancipation in the critical theory sense (Habermas, 1978), is at least a faith in the restoration of democratic social control, potentially enabled by a better use of theory. The key contrast with Habermas is in its particularly American willingness to hitch the work and findings of social research to the positive formulation of social policy, and not merely the formal charms of law that rights-based philosophers usually adhere to (see Dworkin, 1986; Habermas, 1992). One interesting reference point in this connection is the theory developed by certain systems theorists, interested in describing the internal epistemological relation between theory making and policy formation: read as a kind of fictional language built up in order to make intellectual treatment of social problems possible (Teubner, 1993). One of the key reference points for this is the kind of argument developed on either side by law and economics scholars debating public and private interventions into market breakdowns. As has been mentioned before, the normative proof of the explanation being the right one is in its practical efficacy in establishing and fulfilling the terms of the theory. This sets an explicit epistemological rationale for the use of rational choice theory, in that its ultimate grounding lies in its contention that the picture of social mechanisms it provides is the best way the social sciences have of grasping and changing social reality.

Applications of the Rational Choice Approach

We begin to appreciate the force of Coleman's formulation when, as it must be, it is put to work in the contextualized fields of social policy-making. Coleman's work, unlike that of the philosophers, has come as the completion of a career as an empirical sociologist, not like Habermas and Rawls, as the tortuous application of a theory for years worked out only in the abstract. For example, when Coleman's work on education and inequality is mapped into the new grand framework, it offers a precise and explicit vocabulary for social policy debates that is able to go into the field and explain the shifting interests and power relations of state, local constituencies, families and pupils, and make informed and decisive contributions to the formulation and changing of social policy (Coleman, 1990b). The famous regression example from the *Coleman Report* that was instrumental in the introduction of compulsory busing in American schools in the 1960s is but one instance of the work that can be done with a fully worked out social theory that is clear about its direct relation to politics (see Sørensen and Spilerman, 1993).

Similar contributions can be made to debates about welfare and citizenship: what is important is that the key terms of evaluation, and the terms which picture the social situation and its causal elements, are ones that are as clear as possible of the heavily moralized tones in which most normative debate takes place. This compares very favourably with the language preferred by philosophical commentators: whether those using rights-based derivations, or the talk about the value of identity, community and solidarity found in the recent spate of republican communitarianism among self-styled normative sociologists in America (Etzioni, 1988; Bellah *et al.*, 1985, 1991; Selznick, 1992).

Since these voices are rather marginal to the determination of political debates, except perhaps in the way they influence the rhetoric of political argument, it is also worth noting how the sociological perspective Coleman develops also takes significant steps beyond the assumptions — and notoriously black boxes — at the base of public choice literature in the markets and hierarchies vein: debates that have certainly left their mark on the politics of the 1970s and 1980s (Dunleavy, 1991). These often argue on the (new right) assumption that before any kind of social calculus can be made, it has to be assumed that the property rights have already been distributed by tradition or convention. From this starting point an application of the Paretian or Coase theorem can then draw decisive conclusions about the distribution of resources (Milgrom and Roberts, 1992: Ch. 2). What Coleman contributes is a framework for explaining, and thus intervening in, the origins and formation of the rights themselves, such that there is a potential — given the democratic logic of the primacy of natural persons and their voluntary ability to give assent and legitimacy to the organization they are in — for justifying a progressive transformation of the conditions for social choice themselves.

Coleman's central contribution has been to capture and generalize what has become a growing tendency in applied American social research, applied in a manner very alien to the self-styled radicalism of so much European social theory, thoroughly disenchanted (and disconnected) from the political world it purports to study. Getting to the political heart of the matter — the justification of legal and institutional reform — has been a key concern in the recent progressive agenda underlying works like Jon Elster's *Local Justice* (1992), Cass R. Sunstein's *After the Rights Revolution* (1990), Susan

Ackerman's *Reforming the Progressive Agenda* (1992) or Gerald Rosenberg's *The Hollow Hope* (1991). Their message is a strongly positivistic one, in that they argue that the best hope of relevance for the social sciences must lie in cautiously building on the best formal empirical models to explain social phenomena. But it is also a message which does not deny the normative and politically engaged results of such work.

In one sense the liberal left is here merely getting onboard a waggon that the right, particularly in the guise of Chicago School economists, has been rolling for a long time: that it is a definitive step beyond rhetoric and ideology to ground arguments for policy in scientifically formulated and testable empirical hypotheses (Friedman, 1953). The sober and more impartial language of political debate that this kind of formulation encourages is a much more precise terrain for social policy than highly idealized debates about the bases of equality or fundamental rights. One need only remember the impasse that two perfectly respectable liberals, Rawls (1971) and Nozick (1974), reached through the application of their theories to equality of education (see Coleman, 1974b).

A marvellous test for exactly this kind of social policy debate, which also underlines the obsolescence of philosophical concerns about rights, is the American debate about race and social policy during the 1980s, particularly if viewed through the competing theories of Charles Murray (1984) and William Julius Wilson (1987). Murray, a spokesman of the Reaganite new right, uses rational choice theory to argue how the 'Great Society' reforms of the 1960s, building on some of the errors of civil rights oriented sociological research, changed the balance of incentives for the poor in society; such that it encouraged more laziness and family dissolution, with males 'rationally' choosing not to work or to leave their family, while collecting improved welfare payouts. Wilson, responding in kind, and admitting some of the negative sides of 1960s idealism (particularly that civil rights reform helped the black middle class to leave the ghetto but left the real black underclass untouched), sets out a different picture, in which numerous other physical, geographical and institutional factors moulded the behaviour of individuals in negative ways; a situation that can only be overcome with the positive and finely targetted intervention by the state.

What is important here is to see how a key political debate of the 1980s — through the voices of two key academics and national political advisors — is being contested around essentially epistemological and scientific terms; about which is the best theory for explanation, not about the symbolic interpretation of these or those fundamental rights, which is the usual rhetoric of political debate. Coleman's work makes it easier to appreciate how Murray's simplistic use of a rational choice frame that deliberately ignores wider institutional factors would be superseded and falsified by one using a much more complex model of aggregation and social formation that took on board the kind of reflexive and organizational elements central in Coleman's theory. Wilson's theory, which sticks resolutely to a strictly materialist and purposively instrumental picture — strongly refusing the introduction of cultural explanations (see Jencks, 1992) into the perpetuation of underclass social behaviour — fits much better with Coleman's: setting out its own convincing agenda for inner city intervention and new institution building.

The Limits of the Rational Choice Approach

The extensions of Coleman's work can fairly be said to fit the paradigm for social scientific policy research that he lays out in theory. Its operational rationale is complex enough to refute the claims of more sentimentally inclined normative sociologists that a rational choice theory overrationalizes the picture of society it provides, and is thus a reflection and apology of the selfish individualist society that arose with the new right in the 1980s. Rather, the effectiveness of the language it provides to applied social research ought to encourage sociologists with the prospect of new influence in progressive policy formation. In most cases, such as that of Wilson's work where the subject is a sensitive one about race and ethnicity, the sober and materialist frame it offers is a great improvement on normative social science saturated with reifications about culture and value: all the shrill talk of inviolable ethnic and cultural identities, collective norms so often obtuse to any kind of elementary analysis or breakdown to the individual level.

This cannot but be a good thing for the social sciences, and Coleman's lucid and crisp mechanistic model of social scientific explanation has a power that ought to render much verbose and jargon ridden social theory obsolete: with none more deserving than those still operating in the windy grand theoretical frame of Marxist, post-Marxist and post-structuralist thought. However, the rational choice project is an incomplete one in a number of ways, containing certain limitations and in-built design faults that hamper its progress towards the new social science it promotes.

A number of these limitations surface in Coleman's work, and it is important to see how Coleman addresses them: one of the marks of a grand theory status being its comprehensive ambition and the fact that certain faultlines are bound to exist and be revealing of future developments. One gets a clear idea of what happens at the points where rational choice theory is overstretched from the way Coleman feels bound to develop an account of the self within the terms of his theory, addressing deep questions of psychology and intentionality (Coleman, 1990a: Ch. 19). Traditionally in economics and rational choice theory, the self is a behavioural black box, with an order of exogenously formed preferences that can have no independent grounding within the theory. The structure of action of the individual can only be read off behaviourally from their revealed preferences, and each individual is thus necessarily pictured as choosing and following preferences in isolation. The justification for this kind of approach has always derived from the efficacy of modelling that this permits; and it is doubtful whether charges of it being fatally unrealistic hold, unless it can be shown that such assumptions destroy the possibility of sufficient explanation over a generalized number of cases. In fact, when the model is taken as a model of the average individual, a strong case can be made for the predictive realism of the theory (Shepsle, 1989).

Coleman, however, is dissatisfied with the excessively individualist assumptions that this places on the theory. He is, after all, a sociologist, and one of his key concerns is quite naturally going to be the socialization process: in other words, how individuals come to have the preferences they have. A solution to this problem has already been hinted at in the theory of corporate organizations; the idea that changes in the order of preferences or interests of individual agents are formed within the corporate actor by some self-constitution or identification with the corporate structure, an act of formalized role-taking which is also what sustains the organization as a rational institution.

Taking the organizational model as the base, Coleman feels the need to go back and extend this part of the organizational paradigm to the internal constitution of the self, as it becomes socialized into the basic collective groupings of social life. The learning of morality within the family is the key example, and Coleman wants to go back and see the rational model working at this level. It is interesting to note in passing that both Rawls and Habermas felt similarly constrained to import ideas from psychology to shore up their moral theories at this point (Rawls, 1971: Pt 3; Habermas, 1987). For Coleman, the key to remodelling the self in a way compatible with his wider theory is to split the self in the same way the corporation is split between principal and agent; between the acting and object self. Here Coleman uses Mead at key points to get at the idea that morality can somehow be pictured as the generalized other in this picture, extending outwards from concrete others with whom the self first identifies and transfers its interests. Coleman offers the idea of the looking-glass self, where the self's internal constitution is identically reflective of the pattern of significant others around, and then seeks to situate the actual self and the autonomy it must have at some remove from this (see Hollis, 1987).

It becomes clear that there are serious problems with this step beyond the bottom line of individually inviolate natural persons into a pseudo-psychological generalization about internal constitutions (something Coleman's original explanatory frame ruled out as necessary). The rational control being exercised to balance internal influences on the constitution of the self is most certainly not the same kind of rational control Coleman wishes to return to individuals making exit-voice decisions within purposive corporate structures. There is an absurdity in the thought that those primordial type social structures such as the family can be so wholly reduced to rights-based constitutions that offer possibilities of exit and so forth. This is a disconcerting stumbling block. As one extends the objection upwards to other so-called primordial relations, such as ethnic and national identities, the *reductio ad absurdum* unravelling of the rational choice approach starts going in an unconstructive and disappointing direction.

This need not be the outcome: it simply has to be admitted that the rational choice project is incomplete at this point, and is thus an inappropriate sort of language in which to discuss child socialization. As has been said, the choice of applying rational choice methods and language is an inherently normative question, because of the way it sets an epistemological agenda. When it comes to treating the study of ethnicities and national identities, the approach might be exactly what is required to go beyond current dogmas. But it is clear that the failure to extend the process of rational identification to internal processes of the self means that the mechanism of identification needs to be looked at further.

A second major problem with rational choice theory that Coleman struggles with is the circularity and dubious empirical status of the explanatory logic of economics used in many of the prominent examples from organizations theory that Coleman is inspired by. The problem is simple: there is a danger that Coleman's normative faith in the explanatory powers of a social science, and the feedback it can provide, can only work in a society in which individuals are indeed behaving in optimally purposive ways. The problem with economics making judgments about better or worse forms of organization (what counts as optimal) is always that it can only read off from those that survive over time. It will thus always read corporate success as a revealed preference for capitalist or liberal democratic forms (a common story about 1989 and the collapse of communism, for example).

In one sense this is but a similar instance of the necessary internal confidence progressives have to be able to affirm about modernity, if they are to picture it as an incomplete project guided by some 'ideal': we have already encountered this kind of logic in Rawls and Habermas, and identified as a form of functionalism. However, it is precisely the attack on the explanatory weakness of functionalist theories that is Coleman's launch pad, and such a functionalism within his theory would invalidate much of the positive practical contribution of the theory. Yet it returns in many places: not least in the picture of norms emerging as a natural development of co-ordination or cooperation, rather than being a contingent product of certain collectively problematic situations (Coleman, 1990b: Ch. 10). Elster has always been good at recognizing and cataloguing such limitations (Elster, 1989a, 1989b); but his solution within the rational choice paradigm has been to return to intentionality and psychology (Elster, 1993), reneging somewhat on the social scientific focus on social systems and the mathematical virtues of quantitative work — an integral part of Coleman's work. Coleman himself at times speaks of 'social optimum' in the blithe manner of economists grinding out their social choice functions, with efficiency as the prime mover (Coleman, 1990b: 38–43). Yet this circularity has always been the functionalist evolutionary element of revealed preference-based economics logic: it admits of no suboptimality and situations where people fail to make the optimal decisions, and misses situations where, as a result, individuals fail to be optimally free and purposive, and thus have their choices distorted by mystification and lack of information. This is exactly the source of substantively unfair inequality and hierarchy in organizational forms, and exactly why people lose an operational grip on rights that might constitutionally be theirs; why vested power interests, not individual purposive freedom, so often triumph in social life. The faith in the triumph of rationality thus appears to be just that; and Coleman simply lines up on this score with the philosophers of the Enlightenment, against the cynics, sceptics and nihilists who think that power always wins. Choosing between them becomes more a question of intellectual temperament than empirical verification.

Such criticism reveals the soft underbelly of Coleman's enlightened optimism about the efficacy of his theory as the basis of a new social science (see Coleman, 1993b): it is distinctly American, in its boldest moments guided by its normative urgency rather than its scientific prudence; although this might be why it looks at its best in the hands of academics happy with working for the government or one of the two main political parties. But a more robust and effective theory is going to need a better scientific base.

It is here that one of the most telling critiques and developments of the rational choice paradigm makes its challenge, a challenge associated most notably with the names of Harrison White (1990, 1992), Mark Granovetter (1985, 1992) and Alessandro Pizzorno (1986, 1991). What the inherent functionalism and normative limits of the rational choice paradigm most reveal is its inability to deal with situations that are a long way from embodying the working out of a stable rational consensus, situations of chaos, flux and change. Before the theory can begin confidently to picture individuals purposively acting, and collectively making optimal social choices, it has to be confident of the fact they have identified themselves coherently as a social system that is in a position (on feedback reflection) to make such choices for itself; that is, that it has some kind of self-identity.

This is the root problem exposed by the efficiency logic: within the terms of the theory, only social processes in which the elements remain essentially unchanged over time can be modelled in a meaningful way. The model of an agent identifying with a corporation does not capture the shifting identities at play in many social situations: the identities of 'employee' and 'the firm' are very clearly recognizable and established social forms, that remain the same before and after. The problem is that in many social processes the identities of both the individual and the collective structure have yet to be recognized as such: for example, in a nation state that is emerging as an identity from diverse and disparate individuals who do not yet know they are connected to one another. For some kind of mutual identity to emerge, a collective act of recognition has to take place; and this depends on some kind of bond or relation emerging between the individuals. In rational choice terms this would amount to asking how they come to see each other as behaving in rational, cooperative terms, understandable to all in these terms.

This is a problem that has been addressed by writers in the sociology of economics field, looking to see how a self-identifiable market emerges from diverse transactions, with trust, recognition and networks the key elements (White, 1981). The connection with Coleman's work, while retaining the strong emphasis on policy intervention and normative questions that his sociological critics are generally ready to drop, is suggested through his development of the analytical category of 'social capital' (Coleman, 1990a: Ch. 12). Social capital was, of course, the main currency in Coleman's historical story of the transformation from primordial to modern, although at this level it remains a somewhat metaphorical term. However, criticisms of its underdeveloped use within the theory have been ungenerous towards its potential. It is noteworthy that two of the other notable recent uses of the term, by Glenn Loury (1987) and Pierre Bourdieu (1986, 1993), have both developed it as a tool of both scientific and normative analysis in interesting ways.

In Coleman, social capital functions as a shorthand for the missing interpersonal dynamic revealed in the idea of social systems needing to self-identify themselves. Social capital, unlike the other term in economics literature — human capital — to which it is only superficially contiguous, is not something held by individuals in the way resources are held. It is rather something potential in the relations between people, something that must be recognized before it can be utilized. Coleman gives the example of someone who moves out of a local community on a clearly instrumental basis, losing nothing from the change, but who precipitates a collapse in the local social network that may have previously allowed two otherwise unconnected individuals to see themselves as connected and thus take the trouble to meet, or have allowed people to walk the street at night without fearing strangers. Explored in this way, it becomes a potential category for exactly the kind of thing we talk about when we talk of the emergence of morality or sociability: the propensity of people to recognize, trust and attribute rationality to one another, even when there is no formal context or instrumental reason for their doing so.

This becomes a key to describing those situations where a stable self-identity must be established before a social system, amenable to rational improvement, can get off the ground. This is what makes the term so suggestive, because it conceptualizes the identification of some currency — such as optimal utility — which can then be used as the criterion for evaluating the rationality of a purposive corporate system, and contribute a feedback analysis to the social agents self-identified as part of that system. White (1981) asks the question how markets come to recognize efficiency as their criterion of optimal operation; similar questions could be asked about how welfare in distribution questions, rights in law, or citizenship in the membership of a nation-state come to be the salient self-identified currencies. What social capital may offer is a social scientific language able to treat in both normative and scientific terms exactly these kinds of prior questions that ask how it is a certain institutional boundary and currency came into being: a critical addition to a rational choice framework, which too often assumes that individuals are always acting according to a recognizably common purposive motivation and that they always aggregate into recognizable social forms that admit of a macro-to-micro mechanistic explanation. In such a way, a number of those difficult questions for rational choice theory that arise from cultural or identity type analyses can be fitted back into the empirical rational choice framework.

Conclusion

There is every reason to hope that Coleman's theory will succeed in opening new lines of thinking in the social and political science that bring back normative questions into the heart of social scientific research, overcome some of the interdisciplinary infighting that hampers constructive progress, and offer serious food for thought to philosophers and social theorists inspired by writers more normally recognized as 'grand theorists'. Indeed, Coleman offers a lesson in how a comprehensive and paradigm setting theory can also be turned into fine-grained and effective empirical social science work. All of this, of course, is in addition to the dominant influence Coleman's work will continue to exercise within his own field in American sociology. It is to be hoped that more researchers in humanistic disciplines unaccustomed to the rigour and practical ambition of the 'new social science' might find James Coleman the ideal ambassador of this kind of work.

18 Constitutionalism versus Relationalism: Two Versions of Rational Choice Sociology

Siegwart Lindenberg

There is a clear paradigm shift going on in sociology. More and more, the central theoretical task of sociologists seems to consist in the specification of micro mechanisms that trace the relationship of individual action to macro phenomena. The question is: what theoretical base should be used for this task? The general answer that has emerged is: rational choice. But this answer is only satisfactory as a first approximation. Within the broad confines of what may be called 'rational choice sociology' there are important differences. Maybe the most important difference is how far you go in the introduction of cognitive limitations into rational choice theory. In this chapter this question will be pursued with a discussion of the central substantive issue of sociology: social order. There is no room to go into a general discussion of how social order has been treated in sociology: nor would this address the central issue. Rather, two positions within the rational choice camp will be contrasted. First, there is Coleman's argument about the relation of social structure to the requirements of social theory. Second, there is my own argument about the convergence of sociology and economics and its consequence for social theory. In the following, three crucial questions confronting any champion of a particular paradigm shift will be discussed: first, how can a shift be distinguished from a temporary fashion? second, in what way must the new paradigm be different from older paradigms? and, third, what is the direction of development of the paradigm? Given the limited space, it will be impossible to do full justice to either position; the interested reader is invited to take this exposition more as an invitation to help him or her through some of the rational choice literature.

Constitutionalism

Paradigm Shift or Temporary Fashion?

How does Coleman answer the first question?[1] Recently, Coleman (1990a) has argued that sociology is a reflexive discipline in the sense that it must be able to say something about its own role in society. 'The content of the theory must be such as to account for the action of engaging in the construction of social theory', he maintains (1990a: 610). Until now, however, the discipline could not furnish this account. What is Coleman's own suggestion? For him, there are two important transformations: from natural to constructed physical environment, and from natural to constructed social environment. It is the latter that is of interest here. At all times individuals have been surrounded by corporate actors; but one kind of corporate actor is not like the other corporate actor (1990a: 610). The constructed social environment consists of large corporate actors like firms, trade unions, professional organizations, large conglomerate schools, single-purpose voluntary organizations and governments. Natural or 'primordial' structures are family, extended family, neighbourhood and religious groups. The important difference between purposive and primordial corporate actors is that primordial structures are composed of individuals, whereas purposive corporate actors are made up of positions, with individuals being merely temporary occupants (1990a: 597). He argues that man–made (purposive) corporate actors greatly increased in number and importance relative to primordial structures with the result that a considerable asymmetry in power between corporate actors and individuals came into existence. The danger of this asymmetry lies in the fact that purposive corporate actors have acquired control over most events that individuals are interested in, thus possibly creating the vicious cycle of dependent populations, viz. loss of interest and a new shift of control away from the individual to the corporate actor. What is really withering away in this process is social capital, that is, normative structures which enforce obligations, guarantee trustworthiness, induce effort on behalf of others, and suppress free riding. Unless the asymmetry can be mitigated, the functions of social capital will be lost and actions of purposive corporate actors will be largely uninformed about the interests of individuals, both processes creating great inefficiencies from the point of view of the individuals. The supra-individual actors act like parasites on the individual actors.

A new science, one that can redress this asymmetry, is being increasingly demanded. It must extend its knowledge 'to the understanding of how natural persons can best satisfy their interests in a social system populated with large corporate actors' (Coleman, 1990a: 651). This entails that the new social science 'must provide a foundation for the purposive reconstruction of society' (1990a: 652). Coleman thus envisions sociology, properly conceived, as a *design science*, able to fill the void created by the erosion of primordial structures.

How Is the New Paradigm Different?

The second question was: in what way must the new paradigm be different from older paradigms?[2] Coleman's answer to this questions is twofold. First, whereas for most traditional approaches in sociology theorizing is kept to the level of entire social systems, for the understanding of and the intervention in the workings of these systems it is necessary to analyze their *internal* workings. This means analysis on the level of the individual or of the corporate actor, as the case may be. Second, whereas some traditional approaches in sociology use individual level theories, they do not all make use of the notion of *purposive* action. Why must this new science be based on a theory of purposive action? To begin with, theorizing is itself a purposeful activity and that fact alone would be incompatible with any theory that lets human behaviour be governed by inexorable forces. Because the corporate actors have been purposefully designed as purposeful actors, we would be caught in an even more serious paradox if we assumed that action were governed by inexorable forces. In response to the growing asymmetry between purposeful corporate actors and individuals,

Coleman furnishes an additional argument for a purposive theory. For individuals to redress the power imbalance *vis-à-vis* corporate actors, they need powerful arguments. These can come only from a science the results of which are convincing enough to create a broad consensus. This consensus is needed for individuals in order to battle the legitimacy of position (of corporate actors) by legitimacy of argument. To achieve this, the scientific results must uncover the causal connections between accepted valued states and particular policy moves (1990a: 641f). In turn, causal connections can only be uncovered convincingly if the theory deals with the level below the system that is being studied, and this is again the level of the individual or of corporate actors, both purposive.

The Direction of Paradigm Development

The third question concerns the direction of paradigm development. Coleman basically envisions the use of neo-classical microeconomics as the basis for the further development of the new science. The major reason is that such a basis should have analytical power and simplicity. Analytical power provides predictive power, but why simplicity? Simplicity is so crucial because, according to Coleman, there is an important trade-off in theory construction in the social science. Coleman distinguishes two kinds of elements of a social theory: the social organization components (macro-to-micro and the micro-macro component) and the individual action component. He assumes that there is a trade-off to be made. If you want more complexity in the social organization component (as any sociologist should want), then you need great simplicity in the individual action theory. The assumption of utility maximization used by economists has proven to be analytically powerful and simple, and for this reason Coleman uses it as the behavioural principle for his action theory.

This choice of neo-classical theory also proves very useful for the mathematical formulation of his exchange theory, especially for the calculation of equilibrium conditions, i.e., for the establishment of a 'true' macro-micro-macro sequence. The exchange theory follows the lead of economics, but it is more distinctly worked out as a theory of interaction than often found in economics, especially with regard to interest and control. People have interests in certain events and may or may not have control over these events. If they have control, they might be willing to give up this control (which is a right) in exchange for the control of an event that is of greater interest to them. People's available types of action are thus limited to three: first, exercising control; second, gaining control; third, giving away control. Institutional design on this basis consists first and foremost in reasoned suggestions for the allocation of control rights, leading to social optima. Development of the new science thus means refining the tools for making these suggestions (pure research) and coming up with the design suggestions themselves (applied research). In Coleman's own words the enterprise is quite close to the problems dealt with by the eighteenth century political philosophers Hobbes, Locke and Rousseau (1990a: 5).

Evaluation of Constitutionalism

Coleman uses the venerable arguments about *Gemeinschaft* and *Gesellschaft*, or about mechanical and organic solidarity, in a novel way by tying them to the explanation of the development of sociology. *Gemeinschaft* or mechanical solidarity (primordial structures) is waning, and *Gesellschaft* or organic solidarity is waxing. Durkheim too saw sociology as a science that should be able to suggest ways in which mechanical solidarity could be restored or replaced. What Coleman adds is the insistence that a design science *must* be based on internal analysis of the system and on the assumption of purposive action. On this basis he can place sociology in the design tradition of Hobbes, Locke and Rousseau, taking institutions to be mainly allocations of rights. In this way sociology comes to be placed in a venerable tradition that is quite different from its own. Part and parcel of this tradition is that it assumes that individuals are independent and they can jointly forge allocations of rights by consenting on a particular allocation (social contract). This position can be called 'constitutionalism' because the social contract forms a constitution for all interactions. Other economists and political scientists have made use of this classical constitutional tradition, but Coleman expands in two important respects: first, he refuses the fictitious assumption of equal weight of individuals in a social contract. Quite to the contrary, he argues, people mostly have different amounts of power, and any allocation of rights that does not reflect this difference is doomed to failure in terms of efficiency. In addition, Coleman incorporates norms as the precursors of formal constitutions (1990a: 327). Norms are informal allocations of rights to act. Sometimes such norms may be ineffective in satisfying the interests of the potential beneficiaries, and from a design point of view such norms can only be displaced by a purposefully created corporate actor (which itself is based on an allocation of rights).

The very important substantive contribution seems to be the consistent development of instruments. Norms, authority relations, collective behaviour and many other concepts are worked out in detail. What does surprise at first, however, is that there are so few suggestions for institutional reform, few designs for the replacement of primordial structures. Why is there so little design in a thick book that sells sociology as a design science?

There seem to be some problems. To begin with, there are problems with the answer to the first question. The analysis suggests that the new sociology came about through demand 'out there' by individuals seeking to redress the asymmetry *vis-à-vis* purposeful corporate actors. Whereas the asymmetry may be a good reason to do sociology, it certainly cannot be said that rational choice sociology has been established by popular demand. There must be something wrong with the sociology of knowledge part of Coleman's analysis.

Yet there is a much more serious problem to do with the major task of the new science: to find ways to fill the void left by the vanishing primordial structures. As far as I can see, Coleman's answer to the third question blocks an effective analysis of even the very functions of primordial structures that have to be replaced. His insistence that microeconomics be the basis for the new social science is taking its toll. Because of the methodological principle adopted by Coleman (in the third question), the model of man has to remain so simple that each individual has to be a sovereign chooser, by design. But for what does such a sovereign chooser need primordial structures?

The term 'social capital' hides much. Supposedly, it is responsible for normative structures that enforce obligations, guarantee trustworthiness, induce effort on behalf of others and suppress free riding. How does social capital do that? It seems that Coleman assumes that it is only structural interdependencies that will create these functions of primordial structures (1990a: 31). Which? What is the relation to the allocation of rights? There seems to be no answer. The strategy followed by Coleman seems to be dual. On the one hand, he keeps the theory of action simple. On the other hand, he adds on an ad hoc basis effects that have little to do with the simple version of the theory of action. For example, he lists a variety of deviations from the simple rationality assumed in microeconomics, such as framing effects and weakness of the will, and then he responds by observing: 'One justification for disregarding deviations from rationality in this book . . . is that they do not substantially affect the social theory developed here' (1990a: 506). Since his main mode of analysis derives from constitutionalism, a tradition that assumes independent, rational individuals, this conclusion may not be surprising. But then constitutionalism has no room for the functions of primordial structures.

Thus, in many of his concrete analyses, he adds complexities on an ad hoc basis. For example, concerning unselfishness he observes that 'most parts of the theory will assume that actors possess [it] . . . , although the assumptions are largely implicit' (1990a: 32). Child rearing is supposed to have created a good part of social capital before mothers decided to spend most of their time in the context of corporate actors (1990a: 584ff). What is it that child rearing actually achieves, and how does it relate to the theory of action? Social isolation is supposedly something that never occurred in functioning primordial structures. Why is it so damaging (1990a: 592)? Stigmatization and deference seem to work in the small groups of primordial structures and not in the larger groups of purposeful corporate actors (1990a: 657). Why did they work in small groups to begin with? Is the problem banished by calling these ad hoc additions 'social psychological'? In effect, it seems that the strategy of keeping the theory of action simple and adding only complexity in the constraints for action will not yield adequate analyses of primordial functions. Constitutionalism offers many interesting analyses but it cannot address the problem Coleman has described as his major concern; therefore, it is not really surprising that there are so few concrete institutional design suggestions made by Coleman.

Relationalism

Paradigm Shift or Temporary Fashion?

Sociology and economics had been diverging for at least a hundred years, with two very different models of humankind coexisting side by side: the *homo oeconomicus* and the *homo sociologicus*. The former is an all-informed, strongly consumption oriented maximizer, the latter is a socialized, norm oriented conformer. Interestingly enough, this difference has not been the source of serious debate or serious attempts to confront the models empirically. There was lively controversy, like the nature/nurture debate, but it bypassed the two models of humankind. Not even books remembered for their sociological critique of 'utilitarianism', such as Parsons' *Structure of Social Action* (1937), seriously confronted both models. Rather, they reinforced the stylized differences between sociology and economics. The reason the two models coexisted was that economics and sociology were locked into a curious division of labour in which economics would take the 'rational' or 'logical' side and sociology would take the (complementary) 'non-rational' or 'non-logical' side. It is my argument that this division of labour has been vital for the kind of development both sciences took, with the emphasis on model building in economics and with the emphasis on dealing with the 'dirty' social reality in sociology. For reasons which I will summarize below, the divergence has been reversed in the last twenty years, and just as the divergence was vital for the development before, so is the convergence now vital for virtually everything that happens in the socioeconomic sciences today.

The old division of labour worked well for both sides for quite some time. It exempted economists from gathering and analyzing data that their models could not have dealt with (such as data on religion, tradition, ideology, self-sacrifice, mass appeal, issues of fairness, norms, complex interactions, networks, power relations, self-conceptions and reference groups), and it exempted the sociologists for obvious reasons from formulating rigorous models. It also forced economists and sociologists alike to stay well within the boundaries of their discipline-defining subject matter (market versus non-market). Why did such a satisfying arrangement break down? Elsewhere (Lindenberg, 1985, 1990) I have described the process in some more detail.[3] I will mention only two main points here.

First, there was movement within sociology itself. Sociology had always been a debunking science directed at 'naive' explanations of social phenomena, especially biological explanations. These explanations were curiously popular in widely diverging types of societies. In traditional societies of Europe, social inequality was readily explained by heredity, and in individualistic societies, such as the United States, the ideology that human beings forge their own luck stressed individual differences as sources of social inequality. The main instrument used for debunking such views was *homo sociologicus*. For example, the 'native' view is that actions of an agent must originate in characteristics of this agent. Thus, if somebody is less successful in society than somebody else, he must lack talent or ambition or both. A group of people who rank low on the social ladder is thus a collection of individuals who lack talent and/ or ambition. Against this view the sociologist would maintain that people are entirely formed by learning integrated patterns of behavioural expectations (roles) and that what somebody aspires to is part of these patterns. Talent and ambition are thus not given traits but are parts of structurally produced roles. Groups of similarly situated people are thus not collections of people with similar traits but groups that are structurally reproduced.

The sociological battle against trait explanations proved to be very successful, so much so that by the 1960s Western culture had virtually absorbed the idea that trait explanations are naive. In Western countries, policies on race relations, on ethnic groups, on crime, on schooling, on welfare programs, etc. were all steeped in the basic sociological message. But a big irony began to appear. While *homo sociologicus* had been a good instrument for fighting trait explanations by debunking, it was a very bad instrument for explaining how people react to a changing environment. Sociologists could not accurately predict and explain the workings of the policies they themselves had helped into existence. For example, why would welfare programs sometimes work in the intended direction but then again sometimes also create the opposite effect, making people more, rather than less, apathetic? Some analysts even went so far as to blame sociologically inspired policies for an increase in crime (McKenzie and Tullock, 1985: 119). As a response, an increasing number of sociologists began to look for ways to deal with behaviour in changing circumstances, and some of them found 'purposeful behaviour' rather than role playing to be the answer. Quite naturally, microeconomics became an interesting box of tools, and soon one spoke of 'the economic program in sociology' (see Opp, 1985). One of the major forces of this program in the United States was Coleman himself. For others, the two hundredth anniversary of the *Wealth of Nations* by Adam Smith was a welcome occasion to rationalize a renewed interest in economics. The long trend of divergence of the two disciplines had reversed itself.

Second, this convergence was aided by a movement within economics itself, although this movement was heavily pushed by sociology's demise as a policy science. Rigorous model building was not easily compatible with analyzing institutions in any serious way, and institutional economists had always remained outside the mainstream. The increasing quest for a policy science that could come up with more detailed recommendations and evaluation programs drew an increasing number of daring mainstream economists into a terrain formerly assigned to sociology in the old division of labour. One of the main forces here was Gary Becker. One began to be willing to make concessions to formalism and move into virtually every area of the social sciences. The so-called 'economic imperialism' was just another name for the radical end to an old division of labour with sociology (see Frey, 1992; Siegers, 1990). Although we are probably dealing with a sea change and most certainly not with a temporary fashion, there was, and is, a long way to go to make this convergence work.

The upshot of this analysis is that what really drives research at the frontier of the social sciences is not the demand for a replacement of primordial structures per se, but problems that arise from the new convergence of the social sciences, and part of these problems has to do with the interface of formal and informal social structures, with utility and morality, with law and norms, etc. These issues simply represent problems of integrating the specific insights from both disciplines.

How Is the New Paradigm Different?

The level of the phenomena that social scientists want to explain is clearly the collective level. There is no particular interest in the individual or in clinical work. But the social sciences themselves are distinguished by very large incompleteness. This means that propositions on the macro level sometimes hold and sometimes not. This incompleteness is, among others, the result of the influence of human inventiveness (growth of knowledge and technology) on the relationship between macro variables. So far it has not been possible to isolate a sociological 'law' that would be largely invariant as to time and place. The best remedy to deal with incompleteness is to go to a level that offers more stable relationships. This level is the individual level of human nature.

Thus a sociological or an economic explanation directed at reducing the incompleteness of the macro level would have to contain an individual level theory suited for the explanation of phenomena on the macro level. Psychological theories are not suited for this purpose because they were made to explain phenomena on the individual or subindividual level and require too much information on the individual case. This also excludes learning theory for this purpose. So what individual level theory should one take? Given the failure of role theories as theories of action and the success economists had with the assumption that behaviour is largely governed by changing relative prices, *homo oeconomicus* would seem to be a good choice as a theory of action were it not for the fact that many of the economic analyses using this model of man are quite unrealistic.

The process of convergence between economics and sociology also presses for an action theory that can accommodate insights from both economics and sociology. This is no easy task, but it must be embedded in a much broader framework of dealing with the convergence. This framework has been worked out as the *method of decreasing abstraction* (see Lindenberg, 1992), in which model building is explicitly geared toward the possible integration of insights from sociology and economics, preserving the advantages of model building from economics and the advantages of realistic descriptions from sociological research.

The guiding principle of this method is that in order to have analytical power, a model should be as simple as possible, and in order to be realistic, the model should be as complex as necessary. Together, these maxims entail that model building consists of a series of models, each successive one being more complex and thus more realistic, but less simple and thus with less analytical power. The process should be stopped when additional complexity does not make the model more realistic. The important point for the theory of action is that it has to allow this sequential building of models. For this reason the following strategy seemed most promising.

A core theory of action is isolated by taking the five most relevant aspects of human nature to be found in the literature. The attributes are: resourceful, restricted, expecting, evaluating, maximizing (RREEM). For each aspect, bridge assumptions have to be made before the core can be used as a theory of action. For example, if we interpret 'resourcefulness' and 'expecting' as being completely informed about alternatives and prices, if we take 'evaluating' as preference functions for consumer goods, if 'restricted' refers to somebody's budget, and 'maximizing' refers to the technical meaning of choosing the package of goods that maximizes utility given price and budget constraints, then we have *homo oeconomicus* as most often encountered in economics textbooks. In most contexts, however, there would be reason to make the model more complex, for example by at first letting go of the assumption of market transparency in favour of subjective probabilities and by introducing social goods, such as 'social approval', with shadow prices under the heading of 'evaluating'.

The Direction of Paradigm Development

The direction of development is quite clearly delineated by the convergence. What needs to be done is to develop theory for the use of the method of decreasing abstraction. From economics, the major insight about the importance of relative prices (or relative scarcities) for behaviour has already been incorporated in the core. Regarding sociology, major traditional insights need to be reworked in such a way that they can be used in model building. I can identify at least four such (groups of) insights:

1   that the definition of the situation matters for the kind of action somebody takes;
2   that socialization teaches skills needed for managing delay of gratification — this skill cannot be taken for granted;

3   that relations between people matter both as dyads and as part of a network;
4   that social (dis)approval is the major coin in social interaction and that role expectations and conformity to these expectations create flows of social approval.

There are, of course, different ways in which these insights can be integrated into model building. Clearly, 'social embedding' (Granovetter, 1985) needs to be broken down into behavioural and structural components. What guided my own efforts in this direction was the wish to work out the integration in such a way that two goals would be served at once: to facilitate the method of decreasing abstraction, and to uncover the basic mechanisms of social order. In this vein I formulated a theory of framing (i.e., of the definition of the situation in a rational choice context) (Lindenberg, 1993), a theory of relations (Lindenberg, 1988), a theory of socialization in the family (1986, 1991), a theory of sharing groups and norms (1982, 1994). With a summary term, one can refer to the concert of these theories as *relationalism* because relations emerge as the single most important factor. This is quite different from constitutionalism in which the consensus of unrelated people is the basis of social order.

As mentioned above, for Coleman there will be norms if interdependencies cannot be worked out bilaterally. Such norms are consensual allocations of rights to act and they are enforced by sanctions within the group. For the individual, the existence of norms makes it possible to achieve goals not otherwise achievable and thus norms are a kind of 'social capital' for the individual. There are other forms of social capital, such as trustworthiness and mutual obligations. As we have seen above, it is exactly here, with the concept of social capital, that Coleman's analysis becomes ad hoc. He is caught in the belief that there is a trade-off regarding the locus of simplicity. Behavioural theory needs to stay simple, no matter what, in order to allow all the complexity in the structural component. Take, for example, his question: 'why do rational actors create obligations?' His best answer is: I am willing to create an obligation in you in situations in which your need is high and I can help you at low cost. It is rational to do so because then 'the favor is sufficiently great that you will be ready to repay me with a favor in my time of need . . .' (Coleman, 1990a: 309). Why are you willing to repay me if my favour to you was 'sufficiently high'? There is nothing in microeconomic price theory that would answer this question. To uncover the mechanisms that make social capital work would necessitate a behavioural theory more complex than price theory, and bound by his own trade-off principle, Coleman is unable to furnish this theory. Social order at the level of interacting individuals needs both more complex structural assumptions and more complex behavioural assumptions. For reasons of space, it is not possible to go into a detailed presentation of relationalism. Instead, I will list a number of important points that are different from Coleman's theory.

Some Major Points of Relationalism

First, social norms come about only when there are both positive and negative externalities, not just one or the other. Typically, the combination of positive and negative externalities exists when people share in consumption or production. The more there is being shared, the more norms are being produced in order to mitigate the negative externalities of sharing while keeping together to have the benefit of the positive externalities. A corollary of this is that with privatization in consumption and production, social norms will become more vague and regulate behaviour less.

Second, one of the most important goods for anybody anywhere is social approval in its various forms. Yet, because in most interactive situations one will not get social approval if the explicit aim is to make the other approve, people learn to pursue goals that yield social approval as a byproduct. The most important such goal is keeping a good relationship with relevant others. The more that is being shared with others, the more relevant these others are.

Third, people frame situations, they see situations through certain kinds of glasses. A frame is a major situational goal that helps select and order behavioural alternatives. In terms of rational choice, this means that people pay situationally particular attention to some cost/benefit aspects and less to some other cost/benefit aspects. For example, in a friendship relation, the most prominent cost/benefit aspects are related to rules of good friendship and the weight of, say, monetary costs and benefits is less than in other kinds of relationships. This also means that the impact of relative prices differs situationally. There is no super frame such as 'personal interest' that would allow maximization across all situations.

Fourth, the salience of a frame can vary with the strength of competing situational goals. A weak frame will be deposed by another frame. For example, if my frame is monetary gain, it may be weakened and even deposed by the goal to maintain a good relationship and vice versa.

Fifth, together with framing, an asymmetric utility function (identified by Kahneman and Tversky, 1979), which gives more weight to losses than to gains, is seen as a major mechanism creating reciprocity as a learned response. Because people react quite vehemently to loss (and most certainly, they withdraw social approval), others around them learn quickly to accommodate this fact. Loss generally leads to 'overreaction' for which the costs of the reaction exceed the original value of the loss. If I want social approval and other goods from another member of the group, I must avoid being seen as the source of loss. In bilateral transactions this means that I have to make sure the other does have the feeling of getting at least as much out of the transaction as he put in, in the rough units of social exchange rates. This is the rock bottom mechanism of reciprocity and relational signalling.

Sixth, given that things happen that were not intended, including things you did that hurt relevant others, it is important to keep signalling interest in a good relationship to relevant others. Only then can others interpret your intent and keep giving you social approval.

Seventh, a corollary of the last two points is that reactions to mishaps in relevant relationships are likely to be stratified. To use a means of control that is in the eyes of the other an 'overreaction' will trigger the experience of loss in the offender and thus create a spiral of negative reactions. For this reason you start control efforts by signalling to the offender that you believe he is interested in a good relation *although* he has just done something that does not look like it. If the response is not a clear relational signal, then you will either drop the whole thing in order not to escalate negative relational signals, or you will choose a stronger control remedy, such as outright complaining. At the end you may resort to legal means. But the price is high because to resort to legal means signals that other goals far outweigh the relationship. Ironically, when the rules most institutional economists deal with become applicable, the fabric of ongoing relationships has already ripped. This is also true for most of the rules Coleman talked about. In a study on how people in one neighbourhood treat law in various kinds of conflicts, Ellickson (1991) showed that control efforts are stratified in a way consistent with relational signalling. More importantly, Ellickson also showed that there is no calculation of legal versus relational means of control. Litigation is only expected for parties 'who lack the prospect of a continuing relationship' (1991: 274). People do not even know what their legal entitlements are until they come to the use of law after escalation of control efforts. This clearly points to framing effects. Also it is clear that the higher the stakes, the more likely that control efforts will escalate because then the frame will switch more easily from relational to, say, monetary concerns.

Eighth, norms as rights to act are only one kind of rule in an interacting group, and, as I shall argue, not even the most important kind. Social capital consists of many other kinds of rules. Let me briefly mention some of them.

Sharing rules. The most basic rules in sharing groups are rules that regulate the joint production or consumption (not the negative side effects). Thus, for the farmers, it is rules about cost sharing and rules concerning the timeshares for using the combine. In the case of neighbours, it is rules on property, especially delineating common property and allotting private property.

Mitigating rules. Relational signals allow in most cases quite a range of personal variance. If my cow eats your flowers, I can help you replant, or bring you a present, or help you dig a ditch around the flower bed. Still there must be some rules of a social grammar, specifying what range of actions is considered to be a relational signal for certain classes of situations. In addition, there are situations where no obvious signals are specified. For example, when people share small living quarters, it is quite important that the joint living room is relatively free to move about. What is the relational thing to do when one of you has a guest (which inevitably causes negative externalities)? Should everybody join in, or should you take him upstairs, or should you sit in a corner and talk quietly? No matter what you do, you might be giving the wrong signal. In such a case it is in your and everybody else's interest to agree on a preferred way of dealing with guests.

Externality rules. There not just norms and relational signals but also rules that deal with the recognition of negative externalities. For example, 'fish and guest stink after three days' conveys to those who might not know that one can easily overstay one's welcome. Of course, to recognize potential negative externalities before they occur is a way of dealing with them, and yet these rules are different from what Coleman or Ellickson would call a norm.

Another group of rules deals with the identification of the *producers of externalities*. This includes the classical question of tort already posed by Coase. For example, if my cattle graze on your land, did I not watch my cattle, or did you fail to fence your field? If this question is unsettled, there will be no clear relational signals possible, and the result will be escalation of conflict rather than agreement on borders or fence building.

Metarules. The more important it is that people behave cooperatively, i.e., the more there is being shared in the group, the more likely that there will be rules on a metalevel about the importance of having and showing a cooperative attitude (i.e., signals), of keeping promises and of sticking to rules.

All these rules indicate the prevalence of relations in social interaction. They can be considered social capital in Coleman's sense of the word. In the theory presented here they derive mainly from the combination of four ingredients: framing, the importance of social approval, the importance of loss, and the importance of sharing. The context in which this analysis has grown is the convergence of sociology and economics. None of these ingredients is an explicit part of Coleman's theory, although all of them can be considered important for the analysis of how primordial structures work and how they might, or might not, be endangered and how they might, or might not, be replaced by design.

Conclusion

There are two quite different ways of doing rational choice sociology. One is being strongly formed by microeconomics and by the economic analysis of institutions. In this approach consensus of independent people on the allocation of rights is the central order creating mechanism, and the name 'constitutionalism' aptly covers this source of social order. The fact that Coleman expanded constitutionalism with the assumption that power differences matter is an important advance, but it does not change the source of order. Sociology certainly has influenced Coleman's work but mainly with regard to problems and kinds of constraints. Because of the constitutionalist basis of social order, sociology cannot find its way into the theory of action itself. Contrasted with this approach is a way of doing rational choice sociology in which the convergence of economics and sociology is central. The importance of convergence presses for a methodology in which insights from sociology can exert their influence even in the theory of action.

The method of decreasing abstraction is meant to allow just that: preserve the analytical power of model building in the simpler versions of the model but allow increasing complexity in the very heart of the theory of action as you elaborate the models. The order of model building (from simple to complex) should, however, not be confused with the structure of social order. Relationalism means that the production of grass roots social order is complex and that we need a more enriched model of man for the analysis of primordial structures. By contrast, when we model institutional processes that are *built on top* of the grass roots order, we can indeed pretend that human beings create order by the weighted consensus of independent people, i.e., we can get away with a much simpler model of man. Ironically, then, constitutionalism is a much better approach when questions concerning primordial structures have already been solved, rather than an approach that can help us design replacements for primordial structures. Ultimately, both approaches have their legitimate place assigned to them by the method of decreasing abstraction *and* the structure of social order.

Notes

1 The arguments for the first question can be found in Coleman (1990a), especially in Chapters 23 and 24.

2 The arguments for the answers to the second and third questions can be found in Coleman (1990a), especially in Chapter 1.
3 There will be an asymmetry in the number of entries in the bibliography between Coleman (1) and Lindenberg (8). The reader should not forget, however, that Coleman's book has 1000 pages.

19 Analyzing the Economy: On the Contribution of James S. Coleman

Richard Swedberg

That James Coleman has made seminal contributions to such fields as the sociology of education, mathematical sociology and general sociology is well known. His work on economic topics is, however, less often mentioned, but well worthy of attention. In this chapter I shall outline Coleman's work in this latter area, discuss its high points and indicate the potential for future work along the lines suggested by Coleman. *Foundations of Social Theory* (1990) represents the key work in an undertaking of this sort. I will, however, not limit myself to a discussion of this work but also discuss Coleman's analyses of economic topics in his earlier work. In doing so, I will show how Coleman's sociology originates in the Columbia School of Sociology and that this type of sociology still informs his work very strongly. Indeed, the more general thesis of this article is that Coleman's rational choice sociology represents a creative and novel version of Columbia-style sociology, and that some critiques directed at *Foundations* as being too barren and non-sociological have failed to see the spirit that animates it. After having discussed the impact of Columbia-style sociology on Coleman when he was a graduate student in his 20s (Part 1) and how he later discovered rational choice (Part 2), I will present and comment upon what I see as some of Coleman's finest analyses of economic phenomena (Part 3). In the concluding remarks (Part 4), I will again stress that the key to Coleman's sociology is to be found in its creative mixture of Columbia-style sociology and rational choice.

Part 1: The Impact of Columbia (1951–55)

One reason that the link between Coleman's sociology and the Columbia School of Sociology has been missed in much of the current debate is that this school has been unduly neglected in the standard accounts of American sociology. The general tendency is to give full accounts of the Chicago School as well as of Harvard under Parsons, but only to devote a few lines to Merton and even less space to Lazarsfeld.[1] What is missing in the literature is first of all a realization that Columbia sociology constitutes a *school* in the full sociological sense of this word: a 'living being', as Schumpeter put it, made up of scholars and their students with an intellectual style or approach in common (see Table 19.1).[2]

What makes this lacuna in the historiography of American sociology of more than academic interest is that while Chicago sociology and Parsons' work are already well known — and to some extent also exhausted — the situation is just the opposite with Columbia sociology. Indeed, as the year 2000 approaches, Columbia-style sociology

Richard Swedberg

Table 19.1. A Brief Guide to the Columbia School of Sociology

Period: Mid-1940s to mid-1960s.

Intellectual leaders: Robert K. Merton and Paul Lazarsfeld

Key students and faculty members: Bernard Barber (faculty), Peter Blau (PhD 1952; later faculty), James Coleman (PhD 1955), Lewis Coser (PhD 1954), Rose Laub Coser (PhD 1957), Kingsley Davis (faculty), Amitai Etzioni (faculty), Alvin Gouldner (PhD 1953), Herbert Hyman (PhD 1942, later faculty), Elihu Katz (PhD 1956; later faculty), Seymour Martin Lipset (PhD 1949; later faculty), Morris Rosenberg (PhD 1953), Alice S. Rossi (PhD 1957), Peter Rossi (PhD 1951; later faculty), Philip Selznick (PhD 1947), Martin Trow (PhD 1957; later faculty).

Main thrust: 'Middle range sociology' which avoids abstract statements about society as much as narrowminded empiricism. The goal is to focus on some part of the social structure or on a social mechanism, which is of particular interest. Theory and facts should inform one another and be as close as possible.

Areas of interest: concept formation and measurement problems, bureaucracy and organization theory, market research, mass communication, public opinion, science, voting.

Research centre: Bureau of Applied Social Research.

Major works: Lazarsfeld, Berelson and Gaudet, *The People's Choice* (1944); Merton, *Social Theory and Social Structure* (1949, 1957, 1968); Selznick, *TVA and the Grass Roots* (1949); Gouldner, *Patterns of Industrial Bureaucracy* (1954); Blau, *The Dynamics of Bureaucracy* (1955); Katz and Lazarsfeld, *Personal Influence* (1955); Lipset, Trow and Coleman, *Union Democracy* (1956); and Coleman, Katz and Menzel, *Medical Innovation* (1966).

Note: I am grateful to Robert K. Merton for his comments on and additions to this table.

looks considerably more modern and interesting than its historical competitors — not the least in Coleman's own rational choice version.

When Coleman enrolled at Columbia University in June 1951, he was 25 years old and had worked for a while as a chemist at Eastman Kodak. However, he was discontented with his work and ready for a change. In an autobiographical sketch he divides his life into two periods, before and after Columbia, and it is clear that Columbia was to have a tremendous impact on his life. He describes his years as a graduate student between 1951 and 1955 as 'an intense four-year period in my life' (Coleman, 1985: 1). After the time at Columbia Coleman (1985: 1) says, 'I was a different person, with different goals, headed in a different direction'.

Among Coleman's fellow students at Columbia were Martin Trow, Elihu Katz and Sidney Morgenbesser. He took courses for and/or attended seminars with Merton, Lazarsfeld, Kingsley Davis, Herbert Hyman and Seymour Martin Lipset. The three people that influenced Coleman the most were Merton, Lazarsfeld and Lipset. Merton was by far the most important person to Coleman and imparted 'a sense of mission' to him (1990d: 29). That Coleman still cherishes the memory of Merton as a teacher is clear from the dedications in two of his most recent books, *Individual Interests and Collective Action* (1986) and *Foundations of Social Theory* (1990): 'To Robert K. Merton whose excitement with social theory started me along this path' and 'To Robert K. Merton, my teacher'.

Lazarsfeld often hired Coleman on his various projects, and it was here that Coleman was taught (and taught himself) a number of innovative sociological methods. Lipset was Coleman's thesis advisor, and his dissertation became part of the work that resulted in *Union Democracy*. One very important thing that Coleman says he learned from working with Lipset was that theory and facts come together only if one starts with a problem and lets there be 'a dominance of the problem over the data' (Coleman, 1985: 37).[3] Coleman later summarized the influence of his three teachers in this way: 'I worked *with* Lipset, worked *for* Lazarsfeld, and *worked to be like* Merton' (Coleman, 1990d: 31).

As an undergraduate at Purdue University, Coleman had not been very much interested in economics, and the only course that he took in this field made him think of economics as a truly 'dismal science'. At Columbia he audited a number of classes outside sociology, including one in microeconomics from George Stigler — but it failed to make an impression on him. In general, there was little interaction at Columbia between the departments of economics and sociology since it was tacitly agreed that the two were engaged in rather different enterprises. Lazarsfeld represented something of an exception on this score, mainly because he wanted to learn from the economists' methods and their general way of analyzing problems. Through his work for Lazarsfeld, Coleman came in contact with game theory (the famous Luce-Raiffa volume was written as part of one of Lazarsfeld's projects) and with economists such as Modigliani, Baumol and Vickrey. He also became interested in market research, which Lazarsfeld had introduced at Columbia and of which many sociologists disapproved.[4] Coleman sums up his attitude to economics during graduate school in the following way:

> So I read some economics at that time. Yet, I did not see much value in carrying over the economist's paradigm of rational action into sociology. That was in large part because I was essentially a Durkheimian, seeing the central problem of sociology in the study of how properties of a social system affect individuals within that system. (Coleman, 1990e: 49)

Part 2: Discovering Rational Choice (1960s–80s)

For a few years after he graduated in 1955 Coleman continued to work along the lines of the rather straightforward type of sociology that he had picked up at Columbia, and which he has described in the following way: the reality of the group differs from that of the individual, and what sociology deals with is the way that the group influences the actions of the individual. Coleman labelled this approach 'Durkheimian', and says that it was after his time at Columbia that he began to look at the other side of the coin, namely how individuals combine to form a group or a social structure. 'This is much more a Weberian orientation', he said later, 'that is, Weber was closer to a kind of action theory than probably any other major social theorist' (Coleman, 1990e: 50).

The first time that Coleman had a sense that he was onto something new and exciting after his time at Columbia was in 1957 or 1958 when he listened to a talk by George Homans, who suggested that one might see social interaction as a form of exchange (cf. Homans, 1958). This was the first event, Coleman has noted in retrospect, that was to make him interested in rational choice. But even though Homans' paper 'introduced . . . rational choice theory into sociology', it was far too psychological and small group oriented to Coleman's mind (Coleman, 1986b: 1311; Coleman and Lindenberg, 1989: 283). A second event that made him interested in rational choice — and which also made him feel that he could overcome the limitations to

Homans' approach — occurred in 1960 or 1961, when Coleman, as part of his research on education, began to experiment with games. The idea that now occurred to him was that social structure could be conceptualized as a number of positions with incentives as well as rules attached to them. A concrete social system would come into being when individuals filled these positions and when they acted rationally by following the rules and the incentives.

Eventually these ideas from the years 1957–61 were to develop into the full-blown theory for a rational choice sociology that can be found in *Foundations of Social Theory* (1990). It would, however, take more than twenty years for these ideas to mature, a period during which Coleman spent most of his energy writing on education and mathematical sociology. But simultaneously with these activities, which resulted in a number of seminal studies, Coleman also found time to read more in economics. What particularly interested him was the logic of economic reasoning, and he found some of the attempts to extend this reasoning to topics which traditionally belonged to political science extremely exciting. He read and worked with the ideas of such people as Kenneth Arrow, Anthony Downs, Gordon Tullock and James Buchanan, and by the mid-1960s he had become convinced that sociology was on the wrong track and ought to switch direction. He especially felt that the notion of an individual largely governed by norms was problematical. In a key article from 1964 he says that one should 'proceed in precisely the opposite fashion to that taken by the advocates of homo sociologicus', namely, 'start with an image of man as wholly free: unsocialized, entirely self-interested, not constrained by norms of a system, but only rationally calculating to further his own self interest' (Coleman, [1964] 1986: 16–17; see also Coleman, 1966a).

During the years between the mid-1960s and the 1980s Coleman continued to follow the attempts to extend the logic of economics to social topics. He, for example, became fascinated by the work of Gary Becker, who was in the process of applying the economic approach to a series of new topics, including discrimination, education and the family (cf. Coleman, 1993a). In the 1960s Coleman was one of the very few sociologists who followed what was going on in economics — and who published in journals such as *The American Economic Review* and *Public Choice* (see Coleman, 1966b, 1967a, 1968a, 1970b).

Coleman's fascination with the economists' approach was at this point considerably stronger than his interest in economic phenomena per se. Nonetheless, he wrote on economic phenomena occasionally, and when he did, the mixture of rational choice and Columbia-style sociology is obvious. One example is an interesting but neglected article from 1970 entitled 'Social Inventions', centred on the idea that 'sometimes a new form [of social organization] constitutes such a departure from existing modes of organization that it can be said to constitute a *social invention*' (Coleman, 1970c: 163; emphasis added). Among the various examples that Coleman discusses in this article there is one that is of special interest: the historical invention of 'the corporation as a legal actor'. The main novelty here, he says, was to conceive of the corporation as a non-physical actor — an idea that first emerged in Roman law and later in medieval law (Coleman, 1970c: 165–6).

Another important article where Coleman discusses economic phenomena is entitled 'Introducing Social Structure into Economic Analysis', which was published in 1984 in *The American Economic Review*. In reading this article one gets a distinct sense that Coleman was very close to a fully developed rational choice perspective on sociology. This, however, was not the main thrust of his article, but rather that economics can only progress if it broadens its analysis to include a truly social perspective. Up till now, Coleman says, economic analysis has been built on very narrow assumptions about social reality, even though these assumptions have helped economics to advance. 'Further progress', however, 'lies in modifying or discarding these assumptions' (Coleman, 1984b: 84).

To illustrate his point that economics needs to include a more sophisticated social perspective, Coleman discusses three major kinds of economic problems in his article from 1984: the role of trust in economic life, the way markets operate, and the behaviour of firms. Trust, Coleman says, can be very important to an economic enterprise; but it can also suddenly be withdrawn, leading to terrible panic — a truly social phenomenon. Some fairly innocuous action in the housing market (as Thomas Schelling has shown) may also have dramatic consequences — especially if the behaviour is interdependent or social in nature. And the workings of a firm become easily misinterpreted if the firm is conceptualized as a single individual who has all the power — thereby neglecting the fact that the firm is a social system in its own right. What prevents economics from being able to handle these three types of behaviour, Coleman says, is that individual behaviour usually goes through a qualitative change in the transition from the micro level to the macro level:

> What I have been describing [here] is the problem of moving from a model of individual behavior to a theory of the behavior of a system composed of these individuals, taking social organization explicitly into account in making this transition. *This, I believe, is the central intellectual problem in the social sciences.* But it is too often dealt with by fiat, as economists do when they invoke a representative agent to get from a micro level to a macro level. And it is too often ignored altogether, as quantitative sociologists do when they concentrate wholly on explaining individual behavior. (Coleman, 1984b: 86; emphasis added)

Part 3: Coleman on Economy and Society — Some Major Contributions

I shall now discuss what I see as some of Coleman's most important contributions to our understanding of economic phenomena. These contributions all illustrate the power of combining a rational choice perspective with a Columbia School approach to sociology. I have chosen to focus on three examples: the invention of the modern corporation, the relationship between Protestantism and capitalism, and the changing nature of the modern corporation.

The Social Invention of the Modern Corporation

One of the most interesting contributions that Coleman has made to the analysis of the economy has to do with the great importance that he attributes to the invention of the modern organization (including the modern corporation) — a topic that has been unduly neglected in contemporary organization theory. According to Coleman, the emergence of the modern organization represents 'one of the most important social inventions in history' (Coleman, 1990a: 170). What was new about the modern organization (or 'the corporate actor', to use Coleman's terminology) is that here, for the first time ever in history, a purposive unit came into being, which was (1) separate from the individuals, and (2) consisted of positions rather than of individuals. 'The essence of the concept of the corporate actor', Coleman (1990a: 540) says, 'lies in the existence of a separate set of rights and responsibilities, which can neither be allocated to a single physical person nor be allocated among a set of persons'.

What is so remarkable about the corporate actor is the impact that it has had on the development of human society. According to Coleman, there basically exist only two types of actors in society: 'natural persons' (or individuals) and 'corporate actors' (or organizations); and the corporate actor, especially in its modern version, has ever since its inception grown tremendously in power.[5] While in early history society grew mainly 'by accretion', it has now for a long time grown 'by design' (Coleman, 1990a: 650). Instead of living in a world which is dominated by the family and individuals (basically a 'constructed physical environment'), we today live in a world dominated by corporate actors (basically a 'constructed social environment'; see Coleman, 1990a: 650).

When, then, was the modern organization created? Coleman's way of answering this difficult question is quite ingenious. He argues that there must first have emerged a notion of an independent social unit, which was different as well as separate from the individual and therefore represented something novel in human affairs. Under the impact of social and economic circumstances, this notion would eventually come to a legal expression — and it is exactly at this point, according to Coleman, that we can access the development of the notion of the corporate actor.[6]

In his own brief history of the birth of the corporate actor Coleman mainly relies on the work of two famous legal historians, Otto Gierke and Frederic William Maitland (see especially Gierke, [1881] 1961, [1900] 1958; Pollock and Maitland, [1898] 1968). He notes that the idea of corporation existed already in Roman law (especially as *universitas*), but that it was not very developed at this point and also subordinate to the state. The real breakthrough came in the Middle Ages with 1243 as an important symbolic date: in this year the notion of *persona ficta* or 'fictitious person' was invented by the Italian jurist Sinibald Fieschi (Coleman, 1993b: 2).[7] During the following centuries further important events took place, as the notion of corporate actor became more modern and spread from encompassing religious and political actors to include economic actors. Much of this history, Coleman notes, still remains to be written.[8]

What Coleman primarily focuses on in his account of the 'social invention' of the corporate actor is the modern organization in general, as opposed to the modern economic corporation. Nonetheless, now and then he also touches on the latter topic, and when he does, there is one circumstance that he pinpoints as being particularly important to its development: the invention of the concept of limited liability. 'Through the law of limited liability', Coleman (1993b: 2) says, '[the idea of a fictitious person] became the vehicle that created the modern corporation'.

Coleman's idea to use law to trace the birth of the modern organization is quite brilliant — but is the historical account in his work also correct? The question may seem unnecessarily blunt, but anyone who has tried to use legal history for sociological purposes knows how exceedingly difficult it is to work with this type of material. For example, all the primary sources in this particular case are in medieval Latin.

Luckily enough, however, there does exist an easy way to check if the main lines of development, as sketched by Coleman, are correct; that is by confronting his account with that of Weber. Unbeknown to Coleman (to judge from the sources he cites), Weber asked more or less the same question as Coleman around the turn of the century — and Weber was a trained legal historian, read medieval Latin and had a superb grasp of Roman and medieval law. It is, therefore, of interest to note that the basic verdict of Weber is the same as that of Coleman: 'the rational concept of corporation . . . was produced in the confluence of Roman and medieval law' (Weber, [1922] 1978: 726; see also the rest of the section on 'the juristic personality' in *Economy and Society*).

Weber's account of the birth of the economic corporation parallels that of Coleman: the key event that liberated the firm from its individual members was the invention of limited liability. While Coleman's work only contains a brief reference to this development, however, Weber has dug deeper. The notion of limited liability, Weber says, grew out of the family, since the family constituted the first continuous trading unit (Weber, [1923] 1981: 223–9; cf. Coleman, 1990a: 558–9). As more people from outside the family became involved in these family trading units and — even more importantly, according to Weber — as the need for credit increased, it became increasingly imperative to separate the property of the firm from that of its individual members. The first time this was done, Weber says, was in fourteenth century Florence with the emergence of the concept of *corpo della compagnia* (Weber, [1923] 1981: 229). It would, however, not be until the nineteenth century that limited liability became the norm for business enterprises in England (Weber, [1922] 1978: 725).

Weber also notes that the great trading corporations of the seventeenth and eighteenth centuries (which Coleman mentions but does not discuss) played an important role in the later evolution of the firm, especially in popularizing the notion of the stock company. The shares in the Dutch and English East Indian companies were, however, not yet freely transferable; and until balances and inventories were generally required, many corporations easily went bankrupt. A number of smaller 'social inventions' were consequently needed, according to Weber, before the modern corporation could finally emerge in the form that it has today. Nonetheless, it should be clear, even from this brief account, that Weber essentially validates Coleman's approach and also underscores the fruitfulness of conceptualizing economic development in terms of 'social inventions'.[9]

The Relationship between Protestantism and Capitalism

While the discussion of the birth of the modern corporation illustrates one interesting theme in Coleman's sociology — the idea of 'social inventions' — the next example illustrates a different one, namely the importance that he attaches to what he calls 'the macro-micro-macro transition'. The general idea here is that instead of simply analyzing a phenomenon on the macro level, one should try to see how the macro level affects the individual (including the corporate actor) and how individuals, by interacting, create an effect on the macro level. The whole idea can be summarized in a diagram, which spells out the three steps involved (see Figure 19.1). Coleman stresses that it is the third step — '*the transformation problem*' — that is the most difficult one. 'The

Figure 19.1.   The Macro-Micro-Macro Scheme

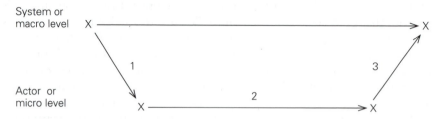

major theoretical obstacle to social theory built on a theory of action', he says, 'is not the proper refinement of the action theory itself, but the means by which purposive actions of individuals *combine* to produce a social outcome' (Coleman, 1986b: 1321).

In Coleman's writings from the 1980s and 1990s one can find several illustrations of his three-step model, some of which explictly deal with economic phenomena (see, e.g., Coleman, 1990b: 641–5). The case that Coleman uses the most often to illustrate his macro–micro–macro scheme, however, is Weber's famous study, *The Protestant Ethic*, and I shall therefore use it also for my discussion (see Coleman, 1986b: 1320–3; 1990a: 6–10). The fact that Norwegian sociologist Gudmund Hernes has challenged Coleman's analysis of Weber on this particular point also makes it especially interesting to discuss *The Protestant Ethic*.

According to Coleman, Weber makes some statements in *The Protestant Ethic* which are not anchored in individual behaviour and consequently should be seen as a kind of macro-to-macro argument. Most of Weber's analysis, however, is clearly intended to include the individual level and can be recast according to the macro-micro-macro scheme. If one does this, Coleman continues, one gets the following three propositions:

1   Protestantism generates certain values in its adherents;
2   these adherents develop certain attitudes to economic life, especially a duty-filled and methodical attitude to work (what Weber calls 'vocation'); and
3   these attitudes to work help bring about capitalism (see Figure 19.2).

According to Coleman, Weber failed to specify his third proposition, and this constitutes a great flaw in his analysis. 'What [Weber] fails to show', Coleman (1986b: 1323) stresses, 'is how individual orientations combined to produce the structure of economic organization that we call capitalism'.

Gudmund Hernes has challenged Coleman on precisely this point in an excellent article entitled 'The Logic of *The Protestant Ethic*', which appeared in 1989 in *Rationality and Society*. According to Hernes (1989a: 149), 'Coleman's critique of Weber is misplaced, as Weber carefully constructs a socio-logic whereby the ascetic Protestants jointly produce a new social structure'. The thrust of Hernes' own argument is that the Protestant ascetics did not so much produce a new economic institution as encourage a fierce and methodical sort of competition which led to a new stage of capitalism. The Protestant ascetics, Hernes says, saw themselves as isolated individuals (alone in their responsibility to God) and tried to gain religious points by surpassing one another in economic affairs. In a kind of positive Prisoner's Dilemma, the Protestant ascetics developed a brutal competition, first between themselves and then

Figure 19.2. Effects of Religious Doctrine on Economic Organization, According to Weber in
The Protestant Ethic

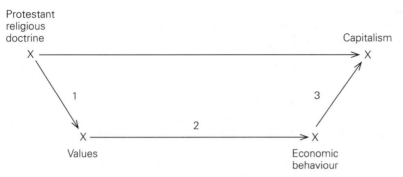

Source: Coleman, 1990a: 8.

between themselves and the rest of society, which ended up by generating capitalism. In brief, Weber had solved 'the transformation problem' through the notion of competition: when isolated individuals competed, they inadvertently created capitalism.

Coleman wrote a response to Hernes, which was published in a later issue of *Rationality and Society*, to which Hernes in his turn responded (see Coleman, 1989a; Hernes, 1989b). Coleman was not at all convinced by Hernes' argument that Weber had indeed provided an explanation for how the actions of individual and isolated Protestants had resulted in the creation of capitalism. He thought that Hernes' argument was 'ingenious' — especially the idea that the Protestant ascetics could 'succeed merely through the combined efforts of *separate* actors [rather than through] joint action and social organization' — but he also felt that this argument could not be found in the text of *The Protestant Ethic* and consequently was an invention by Hernes (Coleman, 1989a: 291). Weber, Coleman reaffirmed, had failed to supply an account of the mechanism through which individual Protestants produced the economic organization that we know as capitalism.

It should first be noted that Coleman is correct when he says that that certain parts of Hernes' solution to the transformation problem come more from Hernes than from Weber. While Weber, for example, mentions the competition between 'new' and 'old' entrepreneurs, this part of *The Protestant Ethic* plays a much more central role in Hernes (cf. Weber, [1904–05] 1958: 67–8). What both Coleman and Hernes have missed, however, is that Weber himself *did* provide a micro-macro link, and that he added to his analysis on this particular point after he had published *The Protestant Ethic*.

To see this, we must first adjust Coleman's analysis as represented in Figure 19.3. On the macro level we should replace 'Protestant religious doctrine' with 'Protestant ethic', and 'Capitalism' with 'Spirit of capitalism'. The former change may be of minor interest in this context, even though it was crucial to Weber's overall analysis in *The Protestant Ethic*.[10] The latter, however, is of great importance in this context: what Weber wanted to explain was not the emergence of the institutional structure of capitalism but its 'spirit'. That Weber in *The Protestant Ethic* was not interested in explaining the emergence of the various economic institutions that make up capitalism is clear from the fact that he explicitly says so (Weber, [1904–05] 1958: 64ff). The same point is also made repeatedly in Weber's many rebuttals to his critics as well

321

as in the secondary literature on *The Protestant Ethic* (see Weber, 1907: 244; 1908: 277; 1910: 200; see also, e.g., Marshall, 1982: 18–19, 59, 66–7). The 'spirit of capitalism' was defined by Weber in a very concrete manner as a specific kind of 'lifestyle' (*Lebensführung, Lebensstil*);[11] and the problem that Weber set himself in *The Protestant Ethic* was exactly the following:

> In order that a style of life so well adopted to the peculiarities of capitalism — [as that of Benjamin Franklin or the spirit of capitalism] — could be selected at all, i.e., should come to dominate others, it had to originate somewhere, and not in isolated individuals alone, but as *a way of life common to whole groups of men*. (Weber, [1904–05] 1958: 55; emphasis added)

From this quote we see that Weber was interested in what Coleman calls 'the transformation problem'; and that Weber's solution was the following: the ascetic Protestants, in forming 'whole groups of men', created a collective lifestyle — 'a way of life common to whole groups of men' — that was identical (minus its religious part) to the lifestyle of modern capitalism (or what Weber termed 'the spirit of capitalism'). Weber, it can be granted, was not explicit about 'the mechanism' involved in transforming individual religious volitions into a collective phenomenon. What is missing, in brief, is some kind of argument about how individuals come together into a group and orient their actions to one another. On the other hand, Weber's analysis does indicate a counterintuitive and surprising result of the various individual actions — the emergence of a new '*lifestyle*'.

It should also be emphasized that Weber, after having completed *The Protestant Ethic*, became fascinated by the way that this 'lifestyle' was strengthened by one particular social mechanism, viz. *the sect*. This part of Weber's argument can be found in his article, 'The Protestant Sects and the Spirit of Capitalism' (1906; revised for a 1920 publication).[12] A sect, Weber says here, 'breeds' or 'selects' certain qualities, primarily by making the individuals 'hold their own' in front of the other members of the sect. In this context it should also be noted that Hernes can be said to have been half right in stressing the role that *isolation* plays in motivating the ascetic Protestant to behave as 'social atoms'. As the following quote shows, Hernes missed the role that being together in a group — especially in a sect — played in fortifying the attitudes of the Protestants and in creating a lifestyle in common:

> It is not the ethical *doctrine* of a religion, but that form of ethical conduct upon which *premiums* are placed that matters. Such premiums operate through the form and the condition of the respective goods of salvation. And such conduct constitutes one's specific 'ethos' in the sociological sense of the word. For Puritanism, that conduct was a certain methodical, rational way of life which — given certain conditions — paved the way for the 'spirit' of modern capitalism. *The premiums were placed upon 'proving' oneself before God in the sense of attaining salvation . . . and 'proving' oneself before men in the sense of socially holding one's own within the Puritan sects. Both aspects were mutually supplementary and operated in the same direction: they helped to deliver the 'spirit' of modern capitalism.* (Weber, [1920] 1946: 321; emphasis added)

To conclude: 'The Protestant ethic' led to an 'individual religious ethic' (Step 1), which in its turn implied a 'methodical attitude to work (*vocation*)' (Step 2); and this

Figure 19.3. The Main Argument in Weber's *Protestant Ethic,* According to the Macro-Micro-Macro Scheme

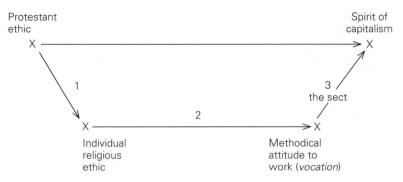

Figure 19.4. The Full Argument in Weber's *Protestant Ethic,* According to the Macro-Micro-Macro Scheme

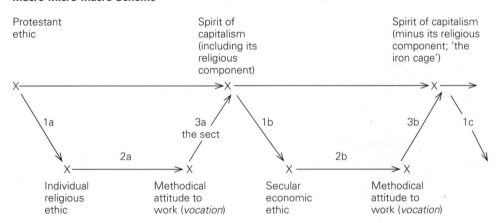

attitude to work helped to create — especially under the impact of the sect (Step 3) — a new 'lifestyle' that was similar to 'the spritit of capitalism'. For a corrected version of Coleman's argument, see Figure 19.3.

There is, of course, more to *The Protestant Ethic* than I have discussed. There is, in particular, the issue of how the capitalist lifestyle ('the spirit of capitalism') spread from religious groups to become the norm in Western society, something which Hernes discusses with great elegance in his article. It is probably possible to construct also this latter part of Weber's analysis with the help of the macro–micro–macro schedule. Hernes' argument can be conceptualized as in Figure 19.4, where the diffusion is represented by 1b–2b–3b–1c, etc.

Regardless of the way one may modify Coleman's analysis of *The Protestant Ethic,* the general point is simply the general fruitfulness of using Coleman's macro-micro-macro scheme. This approach can be used to tease out very complex explanations — even when, as I happen to think, Coleman's own application of his scheme to *The Protestant Ethic* happens to be incomplete. Coleman's macro–micro–macro scheme, in all brevity, is a most useful device, and it sets exemplary high standards for sociologists in analyzing economic phenomena.

The Nature of the Modern Corporation

The third example from Coleman's work is his analysis of the modern corporation. This example illustrates particularly well the usefulness of the principle of *rationality* in analyzing social phenomena, or of assuming that social action is interest-driven. Coleman's analysis of the modern corporation displays a great deal of originality and also represents a challenge to some strongly held opinions in contemporary organization theory.

The standard view of the modern corporation, Coleman says, is far too much under the influence of Weber's ideas on bureaucracy as the most rational and efficient form of organization. The whole notion of the organization as a kind of machine where everyone carries out orders from the top of the organization is, however, fundamentally wrong. The core of the problem with this type of analysis — or 'the Weberian flaw', as Coleman calls it — is that, according to this view, there is only one actor who follows his or her interest, viz. the one who is in charge of the bureaucracy (Coleman, 1990a: 422–5). All the other members of the organization essentially lack interests of their own and are supposed to act out of obedience; they are simply 'robots in the employ of the bureaucracy' (1990a: 197).

There do exist ways to correct the more obvious errors in Weber's analysis, Coleman says. Robert Michels, for example, has shown that the members of the leadership have special interests of their own. It has also been argued that *all* employees can only be induced to do what the corporation tells them to do, if they are being compensated well enough to give up their own interests (and if this compensation is less than what the corporation can get out of its employees). To some extent Coleman himself thinks along these lines, and he suggests the use of the following two concepts in analyzing the corporation: 'conjoint authority' (where the interests of the superordinate and the subordinate coincide) and 'disjoint authority' (where these interests do not coincide and where the subordinate has to be compensated for giving up his or her interests; see Coleman, 1990a: 74). A modern corporation is characterized primarily by 'disjoint authority'.

Despite the fact that Coleman supplies this novel and useful terminology for analyzing authority in the modern corporation, one gets a distinct impression that he would rather get rid of the notion of authority altogether and replace it with exchange. An attempt in this direction can also be found in Coleman's analysis of the corporation in terms of what he calls 'viability' (Coleman, 1990a: 426ff). The more direct and primitive form of viability is called 'reciprocal viability', and is defined as a situation where both parties benefit from an exchange. 'Independent viability' represents a higher form than 'reciprocal viability', and here there is an imbalance in the exchange which means that a third party has to compensate one of the parties. An employee that is involved in a non-reciprocal exchange with another individual (say a secretary with his or her boss), and where the corporation compensates for the unequal exchange, would constitute an example of independent viability. The advantage with independent viability, as compared to reciprocal viability, is that it allows you to cut down the number of exchanges that would normally be needed to accomplish the final, unbalanced exchange. This higher form of viability, in other words, makes organization possible by operating a little bit like money in comparison to barter: it simplifies things and allows for much more complex exchanges than otherwise would have been possible.

There also exists a form of viability that Coleman terms 'global viability' and which is characteristic of the modern corporation. In this case only one overarching account at the corporation has to be positive (plus that of all the subordinates); and one can consequently ignore all negative exchanges as long as there is a positive balance in the end. Global viability entails certain problems, Coleman says, but it also enables giant and very sophisticated organizations to exist.

In addition to criticizing the way that the corporation is analyzed in contemporary organization theory, it is clear that Coleman is very discontent with the way that the corporation functions in today's society. Any organization, he says, that is built on the idea of 'disjoint authority' — that is, a situation where the subordinate basically has no interest in what he or she is doing — is bound to suffer from certain structural weaknesses. Those who obey will not be energized and do a good job; and those who give orders will have a tendency to extend their authority in an illegitimate manner. Corporations also often exploit the weakness of will that can be found among people. Impulse buying and the use of credit cards (as opposed to, say, lay-away plans) are examples of the kind of economic *akrasia* that is encouraged in today's society. Coleman emphasizes that: 'The capacity of corporate actors to exploit weakness of will in persons is especially pronounced in the United States, where the rate of personal savings is lowest of any developed country and where credit-card pushing is higher than in any other country' (Coleman, 1990a: 549).

But according to Coleman there are also signs that a new concept of the corporation is beginning to emerge. Coleman cites three examples in this context: the emergence of quality circles in Japan; the decision in 1976 to introduce co-determination in Germany; and the growing tendency to share ownership of innovations in the United States. Quality circles show how one can rely less on orders from superiors in a corporation and instead let individuals assume responsibility on their own, within the context of his or her work group. Co-determination of the German type, Coleman says, represents one way for labour to have more of a say in the running of the corporation in relation to capital, something that is only appropriate since capital is becoming less and less involved in the everyday affairs of the corporation. Finally, the tendency for corporations and individuals to share the right to innovations, which can be found in high technology and biological industries, represents a positive tendency in that it leads to a much higher rate of innovations.

Coleman's own recipe for how to design tomorrow's corporation is fully in accordance with his rational choice approach to social theory. The most important thing is to see to it that people are in control over what is of interest to them, according to the following two principles:

1   Taking the technical interdependence of activities as given, discover for each position what other agents are directly affected by the actions of the occupants of that position.
2   Give those agents right of control over what interests that occupant, such as wage and promotions. (Coleman, 1990a: 448)

The tasks of the management would mainly be to design the system of the corporation in such a way that the above becomes possible and to supply resources. Through this 'rational reconstruction of the corporation' one would get as close as possible to a situation where the interests of the corporation and of the employees would presumably coincide.

Coleman's analysis of the modern corporation has many positive qualities. While it is true, for example, that Weber has been criticized for having a machine-like view of the modern corporation, Coleman's idea that Weber's main error consists of ignoring *the interests* of the subordinates represents an original insight. Coleman's vision of the new corporation as an organization with an incentive structure constructed according to the idea that the interests of the principal and the agent should coincide as much as possible, is convincing and shows the fruitfulness in viewing the corporation from a rational choice or interest-centred perspective.

Part 4: Concluding Remarks

The three examples from Coleman's work that have been discussed in this chapter — the invention of the modern corporation, the relationship between Protestantism and capitalism, and the concept of the modern corporation — have all been chosen to show the fruitfulness of using, as Coleman does, a Columbia-style sociology in combination with certain principles of rational choice, when one analyzes economic phenomena. Other examples from Coleman's work could have been used, such as social capital and the role of trust in economic life, but space limitations did not allow for this.

Finally, a few words need to be said about how Coleman himself views the potential of his rational choice sociology in analyzing economic phenomena. Since he recently completed an essay on this very topic, entitled 'A Rational Choice Perspective on Economic Sociology' (1994a), this is a rather simple task. It is, for example, clear from this article that Coleman is still critical of the tendency in mainstream economics to ignore social structure, and he keeps insisting that 'social organization and social structures are largely missing from neoclassical economics' (Coleman, 1994a: 166). He is definitely positive to the idea that one can use rational choice sociology in analyzing economic phenomena — but one can also sense a certain hesitation in his attitude. That rational choice sociology can be useful on this score, he says, may seem 'unlikely' since it has its own origin in various economic principles, such as methodological individualism and rationality. Nonetheless, Coleman concludes, rational choice sociology 'appears capable of making valuable contributions [to our understanding of economic phenomena]' (Coleman, 1994a: 172). On this last point, however, I would like to be much more affirmative than Coleman himself. In particular, I would hope that the earlier discussion in this chapter has shown that the fusion of Columbia-style sociology and rational choice analysis that one can find in Coleman's social theory makes it into a very powerful tool in analyzing economic phenomena.

Acknowledgment

I would like to thank Robert K. Merton and Cecilia Gil-Swedberg for helpful comments.

Notes

1 See Shils (1970), Bogardus (1973), Mullins and Mullins (1973), Martindale (1974), Coser (1976), Wells and Picou (1981), Mullins (1983), Vidich and Lyman (1985) and Turner

and Turner (1990). The literature on Merton is extensive and that on Lazarsfeld is growing — but neither one has much to say about Columbia-style sociology in general. I have been unable to locate one single work — be it an article, a book or a dissertation — directly devoted to the Columbia School of Sociology. According to Robert K. Merton (1994), in a letter to the author, 'there are still no extensive monographs focussed on that subject [that is, Columbia-style sociology]'.

2   According to Schumpeter (1954: 815), 'We must never forget that genuine [scientific] schools are sociological realities — living beings. They have their structures — relations between leaders and followers — their flags, their battle cries, their moods, their all-too-human interests'. Schumpeter's emphasis on a scientific school as a 'sociological reality' seems more fruitful than Sorokin's attempt to divide sociology into different schools according to what 'factor' they emphasize (cf. Sorokin, 1928). Not much has been written on the concept of 'school' in sociology: see, nonetheless, Mullins and Mullins (1973), Szacki (1973) and Tiryakian (1979).

3   The passage where Coleman talks about this issue deserves to be cited in full:

> Macro-social problems and sample survey techniques do not mix well in social research. How was Lipset able to bring about a successful mix [in *Union Demo-cracy*]? The answer, I believe, lies in the dominance of the problem over the data, a dominance buttressed both by the rich store of knowledge that Lipset had about the printer's union and in the rich fund of social and political theory bearing on the problem that he had at his fingertips. The result was that the problem was central, and the data subordinate. . . . Although quantitative analysis of the survey data can be found throughout the book and indeed are central to the book, this is the result of our finding ways to make the quantitative data bear on *a framework of ideas that came from social theory*. (Coleman, 1985: 37–8)

4   See Paul Lazarsfeld's comments about his colleagues' attitudes in 'Reflections on Business' (1959). The contribution of the Columbia School to the sociology of consumption is outlined in Frenzen, Hirsch and Zerillo (1994).

5   Coleman occasionally uses the term 'pre-modern corporate actor' and contrasts it with 'the modern purposive corporate actor' (see, e.g., Coleman, 1990a: 660). The former unit is based on 'primordial bonds', but it is not clear whether a family would qualify as one of these 'pre-modern corporate actors', or if the term should be reserved for early and incomplete forms of 'the modern purposive corporate actor', such as the early nation state. Whatever the answer to this question might be, the main thrust of Coleman's analysis is that 'the corporate actor' is synonymous with 'the modern purposive corporate actor'.

6   He also notes in this context that 'sociologists . . . have largely ignored law', something which obviously represents a handicap when it comes to analyzing the emergence of the modern corporation (Coleman, 1990a: 535).

7   Fieschi later became Pope Innocent IV (cf. Gierke's discussion of the discovery of the notion of 'persona ficta', which is the one that Coleman relies on; Gierke, [1990] 1958: xviii–xix).

8   This is also true for the emergence of the corporate actor within the army, a topic which Coleman does not discuss. There is some reason to suspect that the emergence of a separate military corporate actor antedates the emergence of religious and political actors by several centuries. (I am grateful for this comment to Cecilia Gil-Swedberg.)

9   See also Weber's statement in *Economy and Society*: 'It must . . . not be forgotten that forms of establishment and of the firm (*Betriebs- und Unternehmungsformen*) must, like technical products, be "invented"' (Weber, [1922] 1978: 200; cf. [1922] 1978: 687).

10   What mattered, according to Weber, were not abstract opinions of the type to the found in religious and theological writings but rather the 'practical impulses for action' that came

from Protestantism. See Weber's concept of 'economic ethic' (e.g., Weber, [1915] 1946: 267).

11 See Weber [1904–5] (1958): 52, 55, 58; or, for the German original, Weber (1920): 33, 37, 43.

12 See Weber [1906] (1985), [1920] (1946); see also Berger (1971).

20 Can Rational Action Theory Unify Future Social Science?

Randall Collins

Can rational action theory unify social science? Less ambitiously, can it unify sociology, or some significant slice of overlap among the discipline? This chapter will consider the question from two angles. The first part treats the analytical possibilities as to what might be accomplished along this line, grounded in what has happened thus far. The second part takes the viewpoint of the sociology of science, considering to what extent the multiple factions of the intellectual world are capable of uniting under a single theoretical banner.

The Antiquity and Analytical Diversity of Rational Action Theory

What we are dealing with under current terms such as 'rational choice' has comprised a variety of intellectual movements under different names. In one sense the approach is at least as old as the discipline of economics; and some view the current movement as simply economic imperialism. More broadly there is the utilitarian tradition in political philosophy, represented by such figures as Hobbes, Bentham and Mill.

In sociology there is an independent set of traditions. These began with examining social markets, starting from Willard Waller in the 1930s concerned with the process by which individuals discover their sexual and social attractiveness; from this developed a mainstay of the sociology of family, status homogamy and status trade-offs in marriage. The sociological concern is with barter markets and the particular links produced by exchanges rather than with aggregate characteristics of the market system as a whole. In recent decades this line has broadened into the study of the circulation of cultural capital in conversational exchanges and on this basis the structuring of status groups in everyday life. The theoretical approach associated with this movement in sociology has generally been called 'exchange theory'; this too has proved to be a heterogeneous and branching set of movements. Under Homans exchange theory became associated with a militant program for micro reduction proposing to ground sociology upon behaviourist psychology. On the other side exchange theory was developed by Blau to emphasize macro level patterns of interaction which constrain the individual; Blau's later work became virtually a counterpoint to Homans' reductionism in its emphasis upon structures. Coming out of exchange theory are the studies of exchange networks (another variant is Willer's Elementary Theory) which determine the power accruing to occupants of particular network nodes. We find in sociology affinities both with individualistic motivational principles and with the economics of markets, but diverging to explore the variety of exchange structures other than markets per se.

A parallel concern with the variety of exchange structures developed in game theory, focusing upon local processes of rational calculation among very small numbers of actors. Here interest has focused on particular types of games with paradoxical or other remarkable properties (of which the Prisoner's Dilemma is the archetype); not so much classical markets but exchange anomalies have become the centre of attention. Game theory provides a tool for representing and analyzing the varieties of social interactions; we arrive at a taxonomy of games within which markets are only a small part. Here game theory suggests a parallel with the tendency of sociological exchange theory to turn into the exploration of the varieties of social network structures.

Since about 1980 a movement has developed which is explicitly ecumenical, claiming a viewpoint applicable to problems across a wide swathe of social science. It is this self-consciousness of an intellectual movement that gave rise to the slogans 'rational choice' or 'rational action'. A relative of this broad movement has been the 'public choice' movement as a policy science rather a narrowly academic discipline. Coleman's *Foundations of Social Theory* appearing in 1990 is an emblem of the ambitious scope of these movements in the largest sense, combining analytical theory on every level of sociological analysis with a theory of social justice and application to central policy issues of modern society.

This range of movements and their recent energy suggest wide prospects for a rational action approach. At the same time its variety suggests difficulties in unifying a territory so divided within itself. Moreover, almost every part of this lineup has been subject to controversies and polemics, some from inside, some from external critics.

Let us take as the analytical core of the rational action approach, the principle that behaviour is motivated by maximization under constraint; i.e., what happens in social interaction is determined by the ratio between the rewards of alternative courses of action, and their costs. This abstract and general formulation leaves many things vague. It says nothing, for example, about how long it takes in real time for the benefit/constraint ratio to work itself out in behaviour; nor indeed whether such behaviour ever reaches a stable equilibrium. Nor does it settle the micro–macro relationship, since it could apply, abstractly stated as it is, primarily to the behaviour of larger units such as organizations and states rather than to individual human beings. And it says nothing about social–interactional micro processes by which such actors arrive at a line of behaviour; it does not explicitly state that it is done by rational calculation, or indeed that the benefits and costs are necessarily material, or that moral and emotional qualities are ruled out. Let us consider a few of these questions.

The Nature of Micro Processes

It is generally assumed that the actor in the constraints-benefits approach engages in calculations and choices, and furthermore that what looms largest in this motivational nexus are material incentives. Much of the critique of rational choice theory bores in on weaknesses in these specific models. It is not necessary, however, that the actor be so characterized. Rational action theory explains patterns of behaviour in the medium run; it implicitly assumes that actors face a series of opportunities among which they move according to constraints and benefits. In real life it takes considerable time to work through these possibilities, of the order of weeks, months or even years. The rational 'choice' within this period may be entirely metaphorical, since it is immaterial to the validity of the model whether individuals actually calculate the various possibilities or drift through by trial and error. The rational action model is oriented towards behavioural outcomes, not towards the process by which they come about. In this sense it is more of a meso sociological theory with points of contact to micro actors, than a micro theory in the sense of symbolic interaction, interaction ritual theory, or ethnomethodology, which are concerned with situational cognition and emotion. Thus the rational action theory needs to be supplemented with a model of micro processes.

Rational action models are supported by some empirical evidence on the micro situational level, but the nature of this research gives a misleading impression as to what it actually represents. Laboratory experiments (for instance, in the exchange network or Elementary Theory programs; e.g., Markovsky *et al.*, 1993) place several subjects in a bargaining network, where they carry out dozens or more token exchanges in a few hours or less. What may be represented is the process by which power is accumulated by an actor situated in a particular network node or holding a particular configuration of resources. In real life such a political bargaining process among politicians or organizational members would extend over a period of time several orders of magnitude longer than the laboratory situation. It would not comprise one situation at all. The appearance of calculation given by concentrating all the exchanges in a short period of time during which they are the exclusive focus of attention is an artifact of the experimental design. The laboratory experiment may correctly simulate the key structural features of networks and resource distributions which determine various kinds of exchange outcomes; but it is not an investigation of micro sociological processes in the way that conversation analysis or studies of interaction rituals are. Most such experiments are research in meso or even macro sociology, compressed in time and space by the laboratory design.

The same can be said about game theory experiments, especially iterated games by computer simulation. Here a huge number of interactions can be compressed in time. Again the experimental design focuses exclusive attention upon just those items of rational calculation which are of interest in the theoretical model. In the natural world the rewards and costs are spread out in time, and have to be brought into focus of attention from among all the other concerns of social life. I am not suggesting that they are thereby rendered inefficacious; but only that the cognitive and behavioural processes by which natural actors react to constraints and benefits can involve a great many other aspects than conscious calculation.

Research on micro situational cognition shows that actors rarely engage in much calculation, and that when they attempt it, the limits on individual rationality are apparent (see references in Collins, 1993). Ethnomethodology (which also describes itself as the study of everyday commonsense reasoning) and conversation analysis find that persons in the flow of ordinary life prefer to take social arrangements for granted; that they tend to acquiesce in whatever definitions of social reality are presented to them; and that they strenuously try to avoid breakdowns of superficial understandings which would require them consciously to consider the reasons for choosing various courses of action. Such findings are consistent with those produced by more explicitly positivistic investigations. Research on decision-making is famous for uncovering anomalies of choice. The school of organizational research concerned with informational flow under conditions of complexity produced as its most central formulation the concept of bounded rationality. The March-Simon formulation of satisficing and episodic trouble-shooting is consistent with the ethnomethodologist Garfinkel's emphasis upon the conservativeness of everyday rationality in maintaining taken-for-granted social conventions, and upon rapid repairs whenever breaches occur in order to re-establish normalcy as soon as possible.

The consistency among these various angles of empirical investigation points to a central aspect of micro situational cognition. Human beings, as individuals, operate within restricted cognitive limits, avoiding broad-ranging calculations and sticking conservatively within background assumptions. This result does not necessarily undermine the rational action perspective, provided that we see that its core formulation applies to the meso level of analysis, the medium-term drift of behaviour over a period of time (of the order of weeks and years), and that it leaves blank the micro situational processes by which such outcomes are produced. The abstractness of the formulation (medium-term maximization of the benefits/constraints ratio) leaves open two different ways in which such maximization may come about. The theoretical tendency to play up the calculation of rewards makes this process seem more anomalous when confronted with the micro evidence than it need be.

An alternative formulation is that actors can have hazy and only episodically conscious awareness of reward opportunities; but constraints take effect whether actors spend much effort focusing upon them or not. Behaviour in the medium term has a 'rational' drift, not because there is a great deal of conscious calculation, but because certain pathways come up against material constraints which make it impossible to pursue them further. It is for this reason that social life has an episodic, jerky trajectory, alternating between normalcy and crises during which rapid adjustments are made. As we shall see shortly, this aspect of the micro-to-meso implication of rational action theory is consistent with evidence on the macro level in the state breakdown model of revolutions and political change.

One is tempted to joke: the weakness of the approach is highlighted in the terms 'rational' and 'choice'. Insofar as 'rational' carries the connotation of explicit means-ends calculation, it does not fit well with micro situational evidence of actual behaviour; and 'choice' appears to be more what individuals in real life avoid than what they normally engage in. The terminology must be taken as metaphorical. What is rational is the motivational dynamics of the medium-term drift of behaviour; 'choice' is an overly individualized way of referring to the shaping effects of the opportunity structure upon behaviour.

Material Incentives, Emotions, Morals and Social Solidarity

Controversies surround the emphasis within rational action theory upon material incentives, in contrast to morality, altruism or values. More generally, a line of criticism holds that emotions interfere, perhaps fatally, with the rational pursuit of any goals whatsoever. One analytic strategy is to concede the territory but to declare it unimportant. Thus altruism exists, but it explains only a small proportion of behaviour — just as Lenski (1966: 45) estimated that altruism explains a very small proportion of the distribution of wealth.

If we take the home turf of rational action theory to be the meso and macro levels, it is easier to make the case that material incentives are causally overriding. Crises and change points, on the scale of state breakdowns and social revolutions, come about due to large shifts in material conditions, as in periods of acute strain in the economy of state resource extraction. During inter-crisis periods when macro/ organizational structures are stable, the 'normal' state of affairs is overlaid by beliefs as to its ideological legitimacy and the moral respectability of its figureheads. Such emotions and beliefs are generally a drag upon structural change; it is when organizational resources break down, and simultaneously when there is resource mobilization of oppositional interests, that periods of rapid social change are precipitated, in beliefs as well as in structures. A prominent objection to resource mobilization theory is that it fails to explain the directions which movements and revolutions take, and that ideologies and emotions must be reintroduced to account for the specific nature of the movement's action. Nevertheless, the difficulty with an ideal oriented theory is not that ideologies do not exist, but that there are so many of them, and that their salience shifts with great volatility. There is good evidence in the comparative theory of revolutions (see below) that ideologies not only do not precipitate breakdown points, but do not determine long-term outcomes very much either. The period of organizational crisis is a period of floundering this way and that, just what is to be expected if viable pathways are being found by trial and error. Histories are made by marching backwards into a future whose contours were not foreseen in the actors' ideologies.

Morals and emotions loom larger on the micro level of immediate interaction. Insofar as rational action theory is meso oriented, one could write off this level of detail as unnecessary, a trivial noise in the system. On the other hand, a strong theory, especially one with unifying ambitions, should deal with every level of analysis. One approach to the prevalence of emotional processes at the micro level is to treat emotions as dependent variables within a larger process of rationally motivated action. Kemper (1978, 1990) provides a comprehensive theory which derives specific emotions from combinations of actors' positions *vis-à-vis* one another along the dimensions of power and status interactions, together with power/status expectations built up from previous interactional experience. The emphasis here is on emotions as consequents of action; and that in turn has a rational, interest oriented structure insofar as individuals attempt to maximize power and status.

The limitation of this approach is that it is not clear that power and status, especially as they are manifested in micro interactional situations, are to be construed as material incentives. We lack direct evidence that micro situational behaviour is determined by calculation of material advantage; indeed, there is considerable evidence of the opposite. Conversation analysis, based on detailed study of recorded vocal interaction, shows a preference for agreement over disagreement (Heritage, 1984), a self-effacing of interest in favour of what can be described as ritual solidarity in the momentary situation. Homans' (1961: 316–34) principle that prolonged face-to-face interaction among equals generates conformity to local group practices is one of the foundation stones of social exchange theory. Homans interpreted this pattern as evidence that exchanges of rewards are taking place among these actors; the rider that actors must be equals buttresses the point insofar as unequals impose additional costs for some actors. The reward at hand is ubiquitous and non-material: social approval or solidarity. Given that Homans' formulation is perhaps the empirically best supported of micro interactional principles, social (I would say emotional) reward has good claim for pride of place among all other incentives.

There is a deeper reason why social emotion should be placed at the centre of the micro motivational scheme. One essential problem with the core model of motivation by constraints and benefits is the common denominator issue. By what metric can actors weigh alternative courses of action? In economic theory the problem is avoided by assuming the existence of a monetary standard of value, or simply positing an abstract utility function. In social interaction, however, actors must concretely decide among seeming incommensurables, say the trade-off between varying levels of family love and of patriotic fervour, between working and carousing, between religion and sex. There is no question that individuals actually apportion their time and efforts among such things, but by what cognitive process do they do so? There are various incommensurable scales, most of which have vague ordinal metrics at best; to multiply each of these by a metric of future expectations compounds the difficulty.

A radical solution (Collins, 1993) is to take emotions as primary over material incentives; and to recognize a common denominator within the realm of diverse emotions. This emotional common denominator is called emotional energy (EE); it is a continuum, measurable by non–verbal indicators, from confidence and enthusiasm at the high end down to depression at the low end. Specifiable variations in the structures of micro interactional situations give each actor a particular degree of emotional solidarity or feeling of group membership. Higher and lower emotional energies result from individuals' trajectories of movement through their chain of interactions; and these emotional energies, along with the cultural symbols charged by the conversational content of each interaction, provide the resources by which varying degrees of solidarity are negotiated in subsequent interactions.

The individual maximizes emotional energy in the sequence of situations by moving towards those which sustain or raise EE, and away from those which lower EE. Micro behaviour is determined by a market for interaction rituals (IRs). Individuals follow the opportunity structure of available sociable encounters. This is done, not primarily by conscious calculation of sociable payoffs; rather, locally EE maximizing outcomes result from individuals following their feelings of attraction to some interactions and lethargy or antipathy towards others. Emotions, far from being anti-rational, are the medium of rational action in moving through the opportunity structure at the micro level of sociability.

This model of emotional energy-seeking in the local market for IRs also implies a theory of individual thinking. The symbols with which conscious cognition takes place are for the most part circulated in the conversational market. Thinking is above all internalized conversation. The symbols which come most readily to mind in a given situation are those which are charged by the individual's trajectory of experiences in their personal chain of IRs. One thinks with symbols which are emblems of the group in which one has the strongest emotional resonance. Thinking thus occupies a peculiar place in the revised model of micro level rational action. Conscious thinking is not often rational in the sense of explicitly formulating the rewards and costs in the surrounding opportunity structure; indeed, the market for conversational interactions, internalized in individual thinking, tends to make most salient emotionally charged ideologies which often direct attention away from such explicit calculations. Behaviour as a whole remains consistent with rational action theory, insofar as the rational tendency of action manifests itself in the medium run. But it does shift the causal focus of attention quite drastically from the conventional image of rational choice: thinking is a dependent variable explained by the market for IRs, and not a major causal determinant of behaviour in that market.

Where then do material incentives enter? They do so in two ways: first, insofar as material objects themselves become symbols loaded with feelings of membership in interactional communities. Clothes, decor, styles of entertainment or of religious participation, even money can become items focused upon in conversational interactions; to the degree that social groups have high emotional solidarity, these material objects are valued by their participants. Second, material resources enter on the side of constraints. The pursuit of EE is possible only to the extent that material resources are available for assembling the group, focusing its emotional attention, and staging the rituals of interaction. Just as macro organizations break down due to resource depletion, local interaction rituals also break down when material conditions are not available to stage them. People's lives tend to fluctuate between their preferred high-emotion rituals (amorous, religious, political, leisured, etc.), and the necessity of material production to support their ritual participation. The social distribution of work energies can also be derived, insofar as emotional rituals can occur in work situations. When the conditions for high degrees of work group solidarity (including professional status enactment) are present, some persons become superproducers, so to speak; they are emotionally committed to material production, because of the opportunity structure of micro situations in their work *vis-à-vis* their non-work lives.

This line of argument unifies the emotional and moral side of interaction with rational action theory at what may seem too high a cost: taking the market for emotional solidarity as primary, and deriving the pursuit of material goods from it. On the other hand, I do not see how the common denominator problem can be overcome, and unification on the micro level effected, if one starts with the primacy of material incentives. There is some degree of convergence between this line of argument and the recent concern for a rational action theory of social solidarity. Coleman (1990a: Chs 10–11) weaves market and network considerations into a two-step argument. First, he shows how particular configurations on the meso level of interaction result in a demand for normative regulation of individual behaviour. Second, he proposes structural conditions affecting micro interaction which determine the extent to which this demand can be met. On this level there is some implicit convergence with the interaction ritual model: for Coleman, as for IR theory, it is assumed that social rewards are overridingly powerful; in both a key structure is a tightly focused local network which brings social rewards to bear, especially upon zealots whose actions put them in the centre of group attention. Coleman stresses that it is zealots' production of a good for the group which determines the reward they receive in social approval; IR theory stresses that whatever puts an individual into the centre of attention (it could sometimes happen by the route which Coleman describes) will make him/her into an emotional focal point and thus an emblem of group solidarity. The difference between the two models is largely a matter of how much explicit theoretical weight is given to the emotional processes which take place once the group becomes focused.

In Hechter's (1987) model of solidarity, the emotional and moral aspect is not played up. More emphasis is given to the degree of group control over the individual through the structure of material incentives and by variations in capacity for monitoring individual behaviour. Hechter's model of solidarity is couched at the level of meso organizational structures, and pays little attention to the processes taking place in micro interactional situations. It sidesteps emotions as a trivial part of a control process whose guts are in the material and coercive aspects of the incentive system. This work brings us up to a meso level, and is most conveniently considered in that context.

Meso Structures: Markets, Hierarchies and Other Organizational Forms

The rational action approach as a theoretical movement has picked up momentum as it has transcended a narrow market apparatus, and shifted attention to the variables which determine the kinds of interactional structures in which action takes place. Williamson (1975) led one prong of this advance, by formulating conditions under which transactions are carried out in hierarchies rather than markets. Williamson's conception of 'hierarchy' is simplistic, useful primarily as a bridge to the more sophisticated organizational research which has been accumulating since the 1920s. By the mid-1960s this work had mapped out the variations in organizational structure determined by task environments, technologies and informational linkages within the human organizational network (see overviews in Thompson, 1967; Stinchcombe, 1990). Conditions for integration of rational action theory with the organizational level of analysis are propitious insofar as the constraint side of the maximizing-under-constraint formulation has been extensively explored here.

Integration between rational action and organizational theory has occurred most extensively in regard to another topic. Organizational research from Bernard in the 1930s, through March and Simon, Blau and others in the 1950s, culminated in synthetic statements such as Etzioni (1961, 1975) giving the antecedents and effects of various forms of interpersonal control. Etzioni's category of normative control in his organizational theory has been polemically expanded in his later works into a critique of economistic theory in general. Thus it may seem perverse to cite Etzioni as part of a synthetic tendency in the organizational field, harmonizing with rational action theory. In his organizational synthesis Etzioni has shown the costs and benefits of material, coercive and normative incentives in various kinds of organizational task environments. Normative control is an effective form only within particular kinds of task situations, which in fact resemble those which Coleman characterizes as producing a structural demand for normative regulation. Coleman (1990a: Chs 7, 16–17) reworks much of this material into the framework of organizational incentive systems. A related version of this program for integrating organizational analysis into a rational action terminology is now carried out under the rubric of agency theory. This analyzes the divergences of interest between the 'principals' or top level of organizational property or power holders, and their subordinates, and shows how various kinds of incentive systems and control devices shape these conflicts of interest. Agency theory recapitulates many points of the earlier literature on organizational control and intra-organizational conflict. A broadening of the application of control theory has come about by the refinements introduced in Hechter's theory of solidarity. Kiser and his colleagues (Kiser and Barzel, 1991; Kiser and Schneider, 1994) have shown, for example, how historical variations in the power of the central state can be explained by the contingencies of extracting resources, through taxes and otherwise, under conditions of variation in the 'agency problem' of motivating and monitoring administrators.

Here we see a current tendency toward conceptual integration around organizational principles. Not only the internal processes within individual organizations, but linkages among organizations, are analyzed using the principles of control over resources under varying constraints. Organizations can be seen as a key building block for explaining dynamics on the largest macro level of societies. One such loosely structured complex of organizations that has been systematically theorized by a version of rational action theory is the sociology of religion. Stark and Bainbridge (1985, 1987) synthesize evidence on several levels of analysis. On the macro level, market principles enter most explicitly in the contrast between state-established monopolistic churches, and open markets for competing religious organizations; these macro structural conditions predict variations in the intensity of religious movements and in religious belief and commitment. On the meso level, Stark and Bainbridge synthesize a model of the dynamics of religious recruitment and disrecruitment among competing organizations, who array themselves in a religious commodity spectrum of varying degrees of tension between worldly and religious rewards. This integrative achievement in the theory of religion has many areas of overlap with both network theory and social movement theory, and thus points to potential theoretical integration across these fields.

Resource mobilization theory of social movements, with its focus upon the material resources available for bringing individuals into public action, has an affinity with rational action theory. Related to this on the short-term micro interactional level of collective behaviour is the analysis of network structures as they affect the propensity of individuals to leap from isolated vulnerability into the relative safety of collective action. Marwell and Oliver (1993) show how such tipping points are determined by the critical mass of potential actors. Such analysis meshes with Coleman's models (1990a: Ch. 9) predicting forms of collective behaviour from variations in focus of attention, heterogeneity and size of crowds. Thus we find rational action theory sketching in the variety of meso level structures, ranging from formal organizations to the more volatile structures of group mobilization.

Macro Sociology: State Building, State Breakdown and Revolution

One area of macro theory where progress in recent decades has amounted to a paradigm revolution is the theory of the state. Historical comparative research shows a tendency towards integrating disparate areas under a common frame of analysis. State formation can be seen as part of a larger continuum, which includes state breakdown and revolution, determined by a common set of processes.

The core of the state is its military organization, together with the administrative apparatus for extracting economic resources to support it. Once this apparatus was in existence, it could be used for other purposes as well (including economic regulation and infrastructure, welfare and cultural dissemination); this part of state organization became relatively large in most instances only very recently, building upon the core of organization servicing the military. The 'military revolution' of the sixteenth and seventeenth centuries escalated the size of military forces, along with their costs of equipment and their permanence and centralization of their control. Tilly (1990; see also Levi, 1988) shows that variations in the forms of state organization are explained by conditions affecting the kinds of resources which states can draw upon to support this military expansion. Where concentrated sources of capital (mainly urban trade economies) were available within their territories, rulers rented short-term military force in collaboration with capitalists, fostering shared power in urban oligarchies and federations, and laying down structural bases for republics. At the other extreme, dispersed economic resources (agricultural land) made landed conquest the route to state growth dominated by military aristocracies.

On the negative side of the state formation continuum, a key is the vulnerability of states and their rulers to crises of resource extraction, relative to state costs. Skocpol's (1979) pioneering formulation focused upon the material economy of the state; the state itself is an economic entity, which forms class interests in its own right. Primary among these are the state administrative class, whose economic interests favour the expansion of extractive capability. The principal class of opponents is the propertied elite (in agrarian societies the landowning nobles) whose interests are to evade exactions upon their resources. Insofar as these two classes are intertwined socially and politically, under conditions of state budgetary crisis conflicts break out within the elite. These conflicts, together with the financial aspect of the crisis itself which paralyzes or alienates the military forces, culminate in breakdown of the state at the top; and this opens the way to revolutionary forces from below.

Goldstone (1991) clarifies the model: state breakdown results from the combination of (1) state fiscal strain, (2) intra-elite conflicts which paralyze the government, and (3) popular revolt. Skocpol stresses military strain as the prime source of state fiscal/administrative crisis; the sources of such military strains, further along the causal chain, are specified by geopolitical theory. Goldstone adds causal paths to all three aspects of state crisis, focusing on the ways in which population pressures, mediated by prices, inflation and taxation, affect conditions (1–3). Goldstone argues against the Skocpolian emphasis upon military sources of (1) state fiscal strain, but the two causal chains are not mutually exclusive; in his own model the key to state breakdown is not population pressure per se, but the relative overall balance between state obligations and state resources. In other words, there are alternative pathways into the core conditions of state breakdown; various ancillary theories, including geopolitical theory, population dynamics and economic conditions, combine with the core model to produce the historical variety of trajectories towards state breakdown.

What we are seeing, in these and overlapping models of various aspects of state formation and state breakdown, is elaboration of a core model, plus a series of side conditions which bring about more specific scenarios. Not all state breakdowns are followed by revolutions, in the specific sense of wholesale transformation of the ruling elite accompanied by political and economic restructuring. Conversely, not all states grow the same way. This historical variety is not an obstacle to theory, insofar as we come to understand how an array of subprocesses feed into a core model of state resource demands and its constraints. On this level the affinity is apparent between the core model of state dynamics and the core of the rational action perspective.

This is hardly to say that this macro theoretical core of state resource extraction and strain has solved most problems, even in the restricted area of state dynamics. We understand much more about state breakdowns than we do about the revolutions which sometimes follow them; progress is in recognizing that these are two different analytical problems to be solved. Many other areas of macro sociology are still very far from theoretical convergence; the theory of economic development, or in a different direction the theory of democracy, show relatively little consensus, and progress consists mainly in recognition that the phenomena are multidimensional and the conditions are very complex. But all progress towards integration in social science is piecemeal, and we should be pleased with what degrees of integration in specific areas we can find.

How Much Analytical Synthesis?

Where do we stand in terms of the analytical achievements of rational action theory and its possibilities for unifying some portion of social science? I have argued that once we straighten out the micro/macro problem, a good deal starts to fall into place. The rational actor perspective is not principally a micro but rather a meso theory. It does not need to defend a model of the actor engaged in micro situational calculation, nor — this is no doubt even more controversial — the primacy of material incentives (although material constraints are indeed very central). I have suggested how rational action theory can be made compatible with the cutting edges of research on the most closely studied micro levels of interaction, including conversation analysis, interaction ritual and the sociology of emotions. The real strength of rational action theory is at the meso level. This includes the older sociology of barter markets for love and sex, marriage and friendship; as well as the dynamics of solidarity and zealotry in large groups; the dynamics of collective behaviour (especially in tipping phenomena determined by critical mass); and of the resource bases which determine the rises and falls of social movement mobilization (and within which we can include more broadly the patterns and turning points of religious recruitment and disrecruitment).

On the level of relatively permanent meso structures, rational action theory blends with an older accumulation of research findings on the forms of organizational control, and the structuring of the variety of organizations by the control resources and informational networks available in various task environments. Since organizations are a meso level building block for the macro sociology of long-term and society-wide change, this work has conceptual affinity with the recently emerging paradigm in the state-centred theory of revolution, and more broadly with the core determinants of the continuum of state building and state breakdown.

What is left out? Many institutional areas of sociology (sociology of education, of urban communities, etc.) are applications of two overarching analytical areas: theory of organizations, and stratification theory. Rational action theory has done well at integrating with organizational theory, and its prospects for further extension into specific institutional areas are good. On the other hand, I have said nothing directly about stratification. Here a huge division of efforts reigns. The chaotic quality of stratification theory and research comes in part because there are several different forms of stratification: economic classes, cultural status groups, power factions within organizations and communities; racial and ethnic groups as subcategories or combinations of these; gender stratification as an even more complex mix. Issues of opportunity and mobility vie for attention with issues of distribution (of wealth, income, cultural capital and many other things); questions of structural boundaries and group consciousness vie with questions of dynamics over time. Ideological perspectives

Randall Collins

abound and shape much of what researchers consider to be important questions. Some set the task of theory as bringing one's favoured analytical categories to the fore; many sociologists rest content with empirical descriptions designed to display the maximal degree of injustice to one's favourite group. There is very little focus on an analytical theory of stratification per se.

Since rational action theory is above all an analytical approach, it has not meshed well with most work on stratification. This is not to say such an application of rational action theory is impossible. In fact, the focus upon actors motivated by interests operating in a world of material resources and constraints fits well with conflict theory, in the sense of theory which focuses upon the generic properties of struggle over unequal resources. On the other hand, some ancestral versions of the rational actor tradition epitomized the opposite of conflict theory, namely functionalism. The most famous of this variety was the Davis-Moore theory of stratification, a rather simple application of a market model to explain inequalities of wealth as rewards necessary to motivate individuals to undertake onerous training for the most socially necessary services. The Davis-Moore theory is not very defensible, even from the point of view of a market model, without a number of dubiously restrictive assumptions; and in recent decades the analytical perspective of rational action has been used to derive a variety of conflict theories, ranging from state protection rent (Lane, 1979) to Marxian exploitation models (Roemer, 1986). What this illustrates is the extreme difficulty in stratification theory of separating the analytical parts from the ideological orientation which selects parts of reality for attention. I would conclude that rational action theory has a good deal to offer for stratification theory — as, indeed, it has to offer elsewhere — but that theory application here is rather like slogging one's way through a swamp; there is no way to do it without getting muddy.

A Sociology of Science Viewpoint on the Prospects for Theory Integration

Finally, a brief comment, not on whether the analytical prospects are there for the extension of rational action theory across many areas, but on the likelihood that social scientists are likely to be motivated to take up these possibilities. There are several good reasons why we should not expect any very widespread unification.

On one level there is the institutional structure of disciplines. Supposing it were simply a matter of applying economic theory straightforwardly to the issues traditionally treated by sociologists, political scientists and anthropologists. This would eliminate the ideological distinctiveness of these fields and create pressures within academic organizations to abolish departments and fold the remainder into economists' posts. Rational action theory itself suggests that the members of non-economic disciplines would resist this prospect, by attempting to further their intellectual distinctiveness. In fact, this scenario is not very likely. One of the main trends in the broader rational actor movement of recent decades has been to elaborate a core theory which does not depend upon the economists' technical apparatus for analyzing markets. A major analytical accomplishment has been to lay out the wider array of structural possibilities, within which markets are a restricted subset. Networks, organizational structures, social movement dynamics, geopolitical patterns all find their home in something other than strictly neo-classical economic turf. Inspiration flows across the disciplinary

340

boundaries, but the main trend is not methodological imperialism. The brand of mathematics which holds sway within economics, and which is virtually a totem of membership in that community, was developed to analyze markets. No other formalism comes near to displacing it from the central attention of the guild of practising economists; one might even say that the core professional territory of economists is that upon which such market formalisms can be straightforwardly applied. By the same token, we should expect that the expansion of the rational actor perspective into non-economic disciplines will go alone with attachment to methodological emblems which play up the distinctiveness of other concerns; thus we may find that network modelling will be increasingly central for sociologists of rational action.

There is the further question of the extent to which, within a particular discipline like sociology, the competing theoretical factions will give way to a single unifying perspective. Here again there are strong interests against unification. The social sciences have a large area of overlap with lay interests and ideologies; insofar as such social interest groups are in conflict, adherents within a field like sociology will also be in conflict. Partisans of various positions — liberal, radical, conservative, gay, ethnic-particularist, various stances of feminism — have no interest in ceasing their divisions or adopting a common analytical perspective. As I have argued in the case of stratification research, many sociologists have little interest in analytical questions at all, because ideological interests frame what they do. The proportion of sociologists who are primarily interested in analytical questions has always been a minority of the field, and I see little prospect that their proportion will drastically change.

Against these grounds for pessimism we can set at least one process, tending towards some degree of unification around rational action theory. Especially in sociology in the 1990s one can see a tendency towards simplification. In place of the extreme theoretical factionalism that has prevailed for the past twenty years, there are signs of polarization into a few camps. The growth of the militant anti-positivist movement, in its various manifestations as interpretive sociology, French structuralism and post-structuralism, cultural and historicist metatheory, and postmodernism, has provoked a counter-movement towards unification among the opponents of these movements. The Simmelian conflict dynamic operates: the increasing prominence of the postmodernist attack has brought a search for allies on the side of those who feel their central intellectual commitments threatened and degraded. The movement of rational action theory has become the organizational vehicle for a united front of those motivated to defend analytical social science. This alliance-making has already had consequences for the intellectual content of what goes under the banner of rational action. We see a broadening of the position, an effort to reconcile it with research on emotions and rituals, with conflict theory or world-systems theory, with the branches of macro historical sociology which resist particularist historicism. The narrower contours of rational choice theory in its earlier incarnations are being widened. The ongoing dynamics of conflict between megamovements, not just in sociology but across a wide swathe of the social sciences and humanities, may be expected to contribute, if not to overall unification, to a continuing growth of the alliance around rational action theory.

Among the things that the sociology of science perspective reminds us of is the fact that what we accomplish is done by a community of researchers. The community that today we refer to as rational action theory links us backwards across the generations, and forward into the future as well. James Coleman has moved within several branches of that network. His great synthetic work expresses the moment at which a critical mass was attained. That is why he has communicated, perhaps more than anyone, the sense of a broad and unified movement, full of energy in its upward trajectory of growth.

21　A Vision for Sociology

James S. Coleman

Editorial Foreword

In April 1994 James S. Coleman was the first scholar to receive the Phoenix Prize from the Social Sciences Division of the University of Chicago in recognition of his career achievements in expanding the research horizons of the social sciences. The presentation of the award was followed by a two-day conference on his work. 'A Vision for Sociology' — part retrospect, part prospect — was Jim Coleman's response to the award of the Phoenix Prize, and brings the main part of this volume to a conclusion. It is immediately followed by a slightly revised version of Robert K. Merton's presentation at the Phoenix Prize conference, entitled 'Teaching James Coleman'.

When I finished graduate school at Columbia in 1955, I had a proposal for a research project to study high schools. The proposal combined my vision for sociology with what I felt were my principal research skills. Let me go back a little way to explain. My years in graduate school, the early 1950s, constituted a kind of watershed for sociology, best exemplified by the contrast between community studies, which were dominant until then, and survey research, which was dominant after. One might think of the Lynds' *Middletown* as the typical community study, but there were many others. Some were part of the 'Chicago School' of sociology, including Drake and Cayton's *Black Metropolis*, Clemmer's *The Prison Community*, Zorbaugh's *The Gold Coast and the Slum*. The typical survey project could be exemplified by the Michigan voting studies, the first of which, titled *The Voter Decides*, studied the 1952 election, or earlier, Stouffer's *American Soldier* volumes.

The typical community study differed from the typical survey research project in two dimensions. One dimension concerns what is often called the unit of analysis. The unit of analysis in the community studies was the community itself, as a social system. Individual interviews and observations of actions were all directed toward the goal of characterizing the community, discovering the norms and values, the local status systems, social cleavages, and how all these shaped people's lives and the community's functioning.

In survey research, the unit of analysis is nearly always the individual. What is being explained is individual actions; in the Michigan studies, voting behavior is the action to be explained. In the American soldier studies, it was attitudes of American soldiers. In contrast to the community studies, there was always a dependent variable, such as the individual's action or attitude, and a framework of causation was introduced, with independent variables introduced to explain variations in the dependent variable. Social norms, values, and other aspects of social structure and culture do enter, but only as variables to explain individual behavior.

The second dimension along which community studies and survey research differed was in methods. Community studies were based on observation, qualitative interviews with people who occupy certain positions in the community and, quite generally, methods for learning about the community's functioning. All this information was combined to provide a narrative account, or 'picture' of the community's functioning.

Survey research was based on systematically gathered data from standardized interviews or questionnaires, often obtained via a randomly drawn sample from a well defined population of individuals. In contrast to community studies, where information from individuals was used, like a piece in a jigsaw puzzle to help fill out the overall picture, individuals were treated as independent in survey research. The data were combined via quantitative techniques, first cross-tabulations and later regression analysis and its extensions all directed to answering the causative question, accounting for individual actions or attitudes.

This watershed was very much in evidence at Columbia in the early 1950s. The two figures who symbolized the two sides of the watershed were Robert S. Lynd and Paul F. Lazarsfeld. Lynd, however, was in eclipse; it was the new survey research that captured students' attention. Yet what was most striking was that as this watershed was being crossed, moving from the community study side of the divide to the survey research side, most of the work having elements from the new survey research side also contained strong elements of the community study side. An early voting study exemplifies this. *The People's Choice*, by Lazarsfeld, Berelson and Gaudet, was a community study, conducted in Sandusky, Ohio. Its design included not only interviews with a panel of voters; it included information on unions, churches and other institutions in the community. Yet that information never led to a focus on community functioning. It did not deflect the research from its focus on individual voting behavior.

Other research did manage to use survey methods while keeping a focus on community functioning. The medical school studies by Merton and colleagues, published as *The Student-Physician*, used the quantitative methods of survey research, but were designed to study the medical school as a socializing institution. Similarly, Merton's housing study, which used systematic interviews and quantitative analysis, the tools of survey research, maintained its focus on the community as the unit of analysis, doing so by comparing two communities very different in what I would now call social capital. And I believe that *Union Democracy*, designed and executed by Seymour Martin Lipset, successfully combined the systemic focus (how did the International Typographical Union break the iron law of oligarchy?) with quantitative methods. Lipset's earlier *Agrarian Socialism* was a thesis written under Robert S. Lynd, in the pre-watershed mode. In *Union Democracy*, Lipset combined this orientation with the new methodological developments taking place at Columbia and elsewhere.

This struggle to combine the two sides was evident elsewhere as well. At Chicago, August Hollingshead had used some quantitative methods in his study *Elmtown's Youth*, and was relatively successful in maintaining a focus on the community. An even better example of the watershed was Lloyd Warner's Yankee City series, in which he used survey methods to study the stratification system of a small city in New England. This research was, from one perspective, *Middletown* with quantification, and from the other perspective a precursor to the studies in the 1970s and 1980s of status attainment.

The Yankee City series symbolizes not only the watershed in sociology; it symbolizes as well a watershed in American society. That work in stratification was nearly the last of its kind for a simple reason. Social stratification could no longer be studied in a single community. Labor markets transcended the community; and a principal avenue of social mobility was geographic mobility outside the community. One could even fault a book like *Elmtown's Youth* for not recognizing this, when the process of social mobility through leaving the community at the end of school was already well under way.

One might ask why, since there were in the 1950s examples of research which combined the new methodology with the pre-watershed substantive focus on social systems, there came to be such a decisive shift to a substantive focus on the individual as the unit of analysis. I believe that in part it was due to developments in statistics: sampling from a population of individuals, regarded as independent. Sampling theory could be applied to time sampling, or sampling of relationships, or of activities taking place in a sample of time-and-space units, or what has been called 'snowball sampling'. But all these are more difficult to design and implement than the straightforward idea of population sampling — which already had undergone development in the United States Census Bureau.

In part, the decisive shift was due to the increased prominence of government agencies in funding of applied social research. Governments are less interested in analysis of social system functioning than in descriptive statistics for well defined populations, such as the population for which they have some responsibility. Thus they will favor research which gathers data on a representative sample, from which inferences about the population can be rigorously drawn.

All this is background to the vision I had for sociology when I left graduate school. Sociology, as I saw it, should split the two dimensions which constituted the watershed. It should have the social system (whether a small system or a large one) as its unit of analysis, rather than the individual; but it should use quantitative methods, leaving behind the unsystematic techniques which lend themselves to investigator bias, fail to lend themselves to replication, and often lack an explanatory or causation focus. Why did I, and other students at Columbia at the time, have this vision? I believe it was the unique combination of Robert K. Merton and Paul Lazarsfeld, not just in the same department, but collaborating and teaching together. Lazarsfeld showed us the opportunities provided by the new quantitative methods, and Merton kept our eyes fixed on the theoretical problems that were central to the discipline. If the two of them could collaborate, then surely we could carry forward this combination, and transform the discipline.

Now what does all this have to do with my proposal to study high schools? Simply this, high schools seemed to be one of the few social contexts in modern society that constituted largely self-contained social systems. Most adolescents directed their attention inward. Status among the adolescents in the school was more important than status outside. The youth could not easily leave the system and choose a different one. This meant that the processes which generate norms, systems of status, cleavage and conflict, in short the community's functioning, were first of all internally generated (though with influences from school staff, parents and community), and second, they were effective in shaping the behavior of the members of the system.

Thus it seemed that a comparative study of high schools (it turned out to be ten high schools in Illinois, selected and studied during my first stay at the University of Chicago) would make possible the study of functioning social systems, and could be

carried out using the new methods of structured questionnaires analyzed quantita-
tively. My particular interest was causes and consequences of a pluralistic status system
in the school, one that offered many avenues to status, as compared to a monolithic
status system, in which only one activity brought status. As it turned out, the schools
I chose differed less among each other in their status systems than if I had gone further
afield in my sampling of schools. In addition, I found, as have many other researchers
who studied small numbers of social systems comparatively, that the ten systems of
my study differed in a number of other ways, making indeterminate the causes and
consequences of this one difference in which I was interested. As it turned out, the
research, published as *The Adolescent Society*, resulted in 'pictures' of the status systems
in the schools, along with some indication of the processes which generated the status
systems, but was unable to achieve the original goal. My study shared the defect of
some community studies, providing only a picture, not answering a cause-and-effect
question.

So this was my vision for sociology back in 1955, the study of social systems
by use of new quantitative methods which had been largely applied to the study
of behavior of individuals. Now let me move ahead thirty-nine years to a seminar
presentation of three weeks ago, to give some idea of my current vision for sociology.
The topic was again high schools, this time prompted by a long look at my own high
school yearbook from 1944. The yearbook made clear what I already knew: that football was the dominant activity in the school. This explained, for example, why not
only I, but also two of my friends, Bobby Shipp and David Armstrong, went out
for football in their first year although neither of the two had much promise in that
direction and both quit after the first year.

Looking at the yearbook, and being reminded of the way various members of
the class chose to invest their time in particular activities, I was struck by the difference between the way I then accounted for their doing well or badly in academic
pursuits than the usual way I and other researchers typically study achievement in
schools. Typically, we embrace both dimensions of the near side of the watershed.
The analysis is quantitative and the focus is on individual outcomes, such as mathematics achievement, as affected both by individual background differences and school
characteristics. This approach ignores altogether the fact that the adolescent is choosing how to invest his time, and that the choices depend greatly on the social system
surrounding him. It is oblivious to how the individual's investments of time and, subsequently, his social location, are determined by the fit of his capacities to the values
of the system and the social rewards he gets especially from those close to him, such
as friends and parents. Social researchers generally do not even measure those things,
and are far from attempting to model them. So my conclusion from the perusal of
the yearbook was that even if we are interested in accounting for individual actions,
we would do much better in this task if we first characterized the social system of
the high school, and then examined how that social system and his potential place in
it shaped the investments of time made in particular activities. More specifically, as
I went through the yearbook, explaining to myself why, for example, Nick Fetzer
invested little time in school activities, concentrating much more on social relations
in his neighborhood, or Willie Woo Sang invested so much effort in his studies, and
went on to become class valedictorian, I found myself using implicitly a theory quite
unlike the approach usually applied to account for student performance in school.

First of all, I began to see student performance in academic and other activities as resulting from choice about how they would invest their time and effort. A student's choice, in turn, depended on whose esteem or respect he wanted to gain most of all, for what kinds of achievement those significant others accorded esteem or respect, his own potential for achievement in each activity, and just how hard it was to succeed in each activity. This implicit theory involves movement back and forth between the level of the student making investment decisions and the level of the system within which competition for achievement was taking place — in this example, the school.

Explaining my 1944 classmates' performances in school activities is not, I hasten to say, my vision for sociology now. But it does offer some hints about that vision. It shares with my 1955 vision for sociology a focus on the social system and quantitative methods (though the latter are not apparent in what I have described), but it includes some additional points. First, it takes into account not only system behavior, but also individual actions as proper phenomena for sociological study and sees them as closely intertwined, individual actions that generate system behavior as well as system properties that, in turn, affect individual actions. This vision thus requires going beyond both the kind of analysis characteristic of the pre-watershed era, which concentrated on the social system and used individual actions primarily as indicators of system functioning, and analysis characteristic of the post-watershed era, which uses properties of the individual (and sometimes the 'context') to account for individual actions. It is in the way one goes beyond either of these approaches that I see sociology's greatest potential for learning from the field of economics. What distinguishes economics from the other social sciences is not its use of 'rational choice' but its use of a mode of analysis that allows moving between the level of individual action and the level of system functioning. By making two assumptions, that persons act rationally and that markets are perfect with full communication, economic analysis is able to link the macro level of system functioning with the micro level of individual actions. Never mind that neither the assumption that people act perfectly rationally nor the assumption that the social structure is fully connected so that markets are perfect is fully valid; never mind that macroeconomic theory is not really well articulated with microeconomic theory. The achievement is an important one for social science. As Kenneth Arrow and Frank Hahn wrote in 1971, 'Whatever the source of the concept, the notion that a social system moved by independent actions in pursuit of different values is consistent with a final coherent state of balance, and one in which the outcome may be quite different from those intended by the agents, is surely the most important intellectual contribution that economic thought has made to the general understanding of social processes'. It is not as if no other social science had discovered the unintended consequences of purposive action, as any sociologist who has read Robert K. Merton's work knows. And it is not as if sociologists were not concerned with social equilibria resulting from purposive action, as any reader of Talcott Parsons's work can testify. But the additions made by economic theory are two: first, the development of a formal apparatus to make the transition between interdependent actions and their systemic consequences, and second, the demonstration that this can lead to a balance or equilibrium at the system level. Now the domain within which economics has done this is narrow indeed; the 'balance' of which Arrow and Hahn write is ordinarily merely an equilibrium price.

It is here where sociology parts company with economics. Community studies like *Middletown* or *Black Metropolis* are concerned with very different aspects of the community's equilibrium, the norms and values that have come into existence, the level of trust in the community, the stable lines of cleavage, the voluntary associations through which much action in the community takes place, the distribution of status and the system of stratification, the social organization of crime and deviance. To do for these aspects of social equilibria what economists have done for price is no small order; but it is, I submit, our first order of business.

How then does my vision for sociology differ from the vision I had when, in graduate school, I was straddling the watershed sociology and society had reached? Somewhat surprising to me, it does not differ greatly. For example, a few weeks ago in my mathematical sociology seminar, I presented a sketch of a theory of the distribution of investments of time by high school students, involving rewards of esteem from significant others. James Heckman pointed out that these significant others had limited amounts of esteem, and that one could expand the model by recognizing that they were endowed with esteem budgets, which they could allocate to draw forth investments in particular activities. This suddenly took me back to 1962 when I developed what I called, in an unpublished paper, 'The social system of the high school and the game of adolescence'. There teachers, parents and students all had 'bank accounts of esteem' from which they could award esteem to others. I had forgotten this, but Heckman's comment made me realize that the theory which grew out of my 1994 perusal of the 1944 yearbook had been developing over a long period of time.

One of the most important stages in this development was my work with social simulation games in the 1960s at Johns Hopkins University in Baltimore. More than any other activity, it was this which led me to change my theoretical orientation from one in which properties of the system are not only determinants of action (à la Emile Durkheim's *Suicide* study), to one in which they are also consequences of actions sometimes intended, sometimes unintended. In constructing the rules of a game, I engaged in an activity not greatly different from that which I held appropriate for social theorists: not to bother about a theory of the actions of players, except to assume that given the goals and constraints and the actions of other players, they would act 'reasonably' or 'rationally'. The task of the game designer was to formulate the rules so that reasonable persons, as players, would act so as to generate system behavior that simulated the functioning of real social systems. The task of the social theorist, as I came to see it, was to discover in real social systems implicit rules and norms, constraints and goals, and the way in which the actions they generate combine and interact to produce system functioning. I have found that in order to pursue that vision, I needed to assume a theory of action rather than focus, as Durkheim did, on social and moral density as the prime mover. In the tradition of Max Weber and Talcott Parsons, and in common with economists, I have chosen the simplest such foundation, that of rational, or if you prefer, purposive action. The most formidable task of sociology is the development of a theory that will move from the micro level of action to the macro level of norms, social values, status distribution and social conflict. This is a still unrealized goal, although the beginnings have been made. Some of my colleagues are working in that direction, Kazuo Yamaguchi and Ronald Burt among them. Their work combines rational action with social networks to generate systemic consequences in non-fully-connected social systems. Others are Mary Brinton, who shows how gender stratification in Japan is held in place by actions on each player's part that are rational given the actions of other players, and Gary Becker, who extends economic analysis to social institutions, particularly the family. Some graduate students are contributing to realization of this vision, such as Jaehyuck Lee's work on equilibrium levels of trust in a community when persons place trust optimally, and Hua-Ying Wang's model of the systemic consequences of social exchange operating under a norm of equity.

There is, I should say, another component of my vision for sociology. This concerns sociology and social policy. Harold Lasswell invented the term 'policy sciences', one of which is sociology. But sociology has only sporadically addressed itself to social policy, most prominently in the areas of demography and criminology.

Sociology has tools with which it can address issues in social policy: empirical data and social theory. The first, empirical data, has been the more frequently used tool; it is the one I have used on several occasions. Social theory, by contrast, has been seldom used in relation to social policy. This is not a healthy state of affairs. One of the criteria for judging work in social theory is its potential usefulness for informing social policy. For example, there is theoretical work on the conditions under which a stable and effective norm, with a particular content, will be brought into existence. Knowledge of these conditions would be extremely valuable in the design of organizations. For example, norms regarding expenditure of effort toward schoolwork develop among the students in most high schools. Often these are norms opposed to working hard, norms which act to suppress effort.

Sometimes, however, the norms go in the opposite direction, toward encouraging strong efforts and high achievement. What are the conditions that determine the strength and direction of this norm? The question arises in workplaces other than schools as well. At least since the Western Electric studies of the 1930s, with the differences between the Relay Assembly Groups and the Bank Wiring Room, it has been apparent that such norms can be strong in a plant or a work group and that their direction may be toward increased output or decreased output. Roethlisberger and Dickson not only made empirical observations; they developed theoretical points as well. Yet the theory has not been sufficient to ensure, over fifty years after publication of their work, that organizations (especially schools and workplaces) be designed to bring about norms that encourage production rather than discouraging it. It is not difficult to see the practical importance for education and for the economy of a comprehensive theory of norm emergence which would inform the design of organizations.

Why should such applications be a concern for an academic discipline like sociology? For a simple reason. Sociology, in its research and in development of theory, exists on the sufferance of society. If society's support for this research and theory development is to continue, there must be some reciprocation. Some benefits must flow from the discipline to the rest of society. It may well be true that the contraction of social and financial support for sociology in recent years and the lack of growth of the discipline is a consequence of a perceived lack of benefits from the discipline to society.

Taken all together, this then is my vision for sociology. One part of that vision is to combine the substantive focus on the social system that characterized the pre-watershed period with quantitative methods and models developed and used since the watershed. This implies the use of a theory of action, because it involves a micro to macro transition. In some cases, it may involve formal modelling as well, since the linkage between individual action and system behavior is a complex one. A second part of that vision is increased utility of social theory for the ongoing functioning of society.

Appendix 1: Teaching James Coleman

Robert K. Merton[1]

When invited to join in celebrating the first award of the Phoenix Prize to James S. Coleman, I was asked to tell what it was like to have been his sometime teacher. For an anxious moment, I took this to be an invitation to describe my influence on the young Jim Coleman at Columbia. But I soon realized that that momentary inference was plainly absurd. For we sociologists have ample cause to know, as Simmel taught us long ago, that social (and I would add, cognitive) interaction always involves some degree of reciprocal influence, no matter how unequal participants may be in terms of rank, power or institutionalized authority. And in the case of the student Jim, that was surely the case. When he first set foot in Columbia, what probably began as the usual asymmetry of influence between teacher and graduate student moved with un-accustomed speed first toward a symmetry of mutual influence and then developed into a new asymmetry which had the student sometimes teaching the teacher more than he the student. Nor is this simply a nostalgic reconstruction summoned up for this grand occasion. Rather, it is a sober résumé of Jim Coleman's evolving place at Columbia and not long afterward in the discipline of sociology at large.

(I see Jim squirming embarrassedly in his seat and sense that he is engaged in denying all that. For as we know, though Jim has a sturdy enough ego, he is afflicted with an abiding and incorrigible modesty which, on occasions such as this one cele-brating his unrivalled accomplishments, leads him to deny what he must know was actually the case. What, then, *was* the case back then?)

So far as an episodic memory allows me to say, Paul Lazarsfeld and I spotted Jim as a sociological talent within months after he came to the Department. Indeed, in fairly short order we were at first unwittingly and then quite overtly competing for his attention. At least, we came dangerously close to such rivalry. The question was: which one of us had rightly identified the quintessential Jim? Paul confidently claimed that Jim was of course destined to be a methodologist and mathematical sociologist of the first rank, while, with equal assurance, I claimed that he was destined to be a phenomenal theorist who would draw upon his systematic empirical research to greatly deepen and extend our basic sociological understanding. I don't recall when it came to pass that Paul and I finally saw the light and recognized that we were both right: Jim was bound to be all that — and more. Plainly, he would be both an extra-ordinary sociological theorist and an extraordinary methodologist, endowed with a keen sense of the practical and policy implications of sociological inquiry. That last quality made for a further elective affinity among the three of us. For Paul had long been committed to what he liked to describe as '*applied* social research' and had re-cruited my at-first reluctant self into the Department's research arm, which, tellingly enough, was extended from the Office of Radio Research to the Bureau of *Applied* Social Research.

Let it be said that when Jim arrived at Columbia in 1951, he did not come upon a dry-as-dust Department of Sociology. It was a place sparkling with intellectual excitement. Vastly expanding the educational opportunity structure, the GI Bill had done much to quicken the flood of budding sociological talent that had come to our doors. And so it was that Jim entered a sociocognitive micro environment and a student subculture of the first intellectual magnitude. A detailed list of the destined luminaries among students of the 1940s and the 1950s would try your patience and exhaust my time, but even a greatly delimited specimen list would surely include, in roughly chronological order, Daniel Bell, Philip Selznick, Peter M. Blau, Seymour Martin Lipset, Milton Gordon, Alvin W. Gouldner, E. Digby Baltzell, Patricia Kendall, Nathan Glazer, Rose Laub Coser, Dennis Wrong, Natalie Rogoff-Ramsoy, Charles Glock, Louis Schneider, Peter Rossi, Lewis A. Coser, Alex Inkeles, Alice Kitt Rossi, Charles Wright, David L. Sills, Charles Kadushin, Denise Bystryn Kandel, Hanan Selvin, Morris Rosenberg, Martin Trow, Barney Glaser, Suzanne Keller, Maurice Stein, Elihu Katz, Immanuel Wallerstein, Juan Linz, Terence Hopkins and Richard Hamilton.

Why do I dwell upon this directory of talent in Jim's time and before? Only to remind us that such an array of talented and vibrant graduate students surely provided an evocative sociocognitive environment for each of them and, no doubt, for their teachers as well. In such environments, the education of students comes as much from the interaction among themselves as with their teachers. Now, I don't want to be so self-abnegating as to suggest that that micro environment would have been the same had we teachers not also been there, but I do mean to suggest that had the other students — and, as in the case of Marty Lipset, a onetime student become faculty — not been there as well, Jim would probably have taken a longer time and possibly a different path to become what, to no one's surprise, he did become.

As I say, it was a time of great excitement back then during Jim's cohort of the early 1950s. A time of intense cognitive interaction in which students and teachers were engaged — variously but significantly engaged — in what we took to be a modest common enterprise, one that called merely for the remaking of modern sociology in terms of theoretically grounded empirical research that would feed back into an enlarged theoretical understanding. Research of a kind that would be demanding enough to provide serious answers to the enduring question: what kind of evidence leads you to think that what you declare is so, really is so? that leads you to conclude that it is social reality, not merely social appearance? There we were trying to abide by demanding rules of evidence which, as we know, Jim Coleman has abided by ever since. And there was Jim in the midst of this sociological galaxy and, to the collective eyes of fellow students and teachers alike, clearly the first among equals, truly *primus inter pares*.

Jim spent a good deal of time interacting with Paul Lazarsfeld and me just as he did with those somewhat younger collaborators, Marty Lipset and Marty Trow. As he has intimated or stated in reflective autobiographical accounts of his life as a student at Columbia,[2] and as we would expect from the theory of sociological ambivalence, Jim (sometimes? often?) experienced mixed feelings about his teachers. In one of those retrospectives, he expresses great respect and esteem for Paul's unyielding commitment to work on a wide array of intellectual problems which he regarded as consequential and co-opting others to work on some of them as well; problems, Jim notes, which were chiefly methodological and substantively psychological rather than sociological. Jim goes on to express great frustration over Paul's not being content 'to see his protégés and colleagues solve problems that others outside felt were important, but was only satisfied when a problem *he* saw as important was solved, and solved in a way that made sense to *him*'. In another retrospective, Jim expresses generous regard for my having transformed sociology 'into a calling' for him and fellow students in the course of analyzing 'the *process* of theory construction in sociology' in an effort to show how theoretical work interacts with systematic empirical research. But, in authentic ambivalent style, Jim then goes on to express the despair he and fellow students felt when I would subject their finest efforts to what he describes as exceedingly detailed critiques that often left them on edge and with a sense that they had failed to meet (impossible) demands.

Now one would expect from the notion of sociological ambivalence that Jim's grateful teachers would in turn have had their share of ambivalent feelings about him as a most exacting student. I cannot speak for his other teachers, but I can for myself. And try as I might, Jim, I cannot recall or find documentary evidence of any such mixed feelings. As I've said, soon after your arrival on Morningside Heights, Paul and I found ourselves competing for your attention — this, mind you, while *you* thought yourself engaged in trying to gain more of *our* attention. But if I can't find evidence of ancient negative feelings about you, I can easily summon up evidence of distinctly positive feelings. And so, Jim, knowing how much weight you place on objective evidence, I've brought along four documents, three of them attesting to the way I felt about you then, and have ever since.

To begin with, I ask you to recall the paper on 'The Theory of Social Isolation' which you wrote in 1952 for that course of mine on the logic of theory construction, the one bearing the rather odd title, 'Social Theory Applied to Social Research'. You describe that paper in one of your retrospectives as 'the theoretical piece of which I was most proud during my days in graduate school'. You then report having become persuaded that I had simply lost the paper and that it then languished further until you managed to lose *your* copy of it as well. But cheer up, Jim, all is not really lost. For here, carefully retained these forty-two years in obviously prescient fashion, is the original and appreciatively annotated manuscript of that supposedly forgotten paper.

The second exhibit moves us from that distant past to the immediate now as I present you with a volume entitled *Social Science Quotations* which your onetime fellow graduate student David Sills and I recently put together as Volume 19 of the *International Encyclopedia of the Social Sciences*. To our dismay, it was outrageously priced at a hundred dollars a copy and so David and I insisted on a more widely accessible freestanding edition. You have your choice of either edition — or, better still, here are both. If you will now turn to pages 40 and 41 in either of them, you will find sandwiched between quotations from the British historian, economist and sociologist, G.D.H. Cole, and from the French philosopher and sociologist, Auguste Comte, a great array of quotations from the US sociologist James S. Coleman. Should you leisurely browse through that encyclopedic volume, you will discover that the quotations from that US sociologist rightly outnumber the quotations drawn from any other living sociologist.

The third exhibit, Jim, is one that I had quite mysteriously asked your permission to read on this occasion. I can now explain that it is included here in accord with Morgan Forster's noble precept: 'Only connect!' And so to signal the enduring connection between a long-ago student and a long-ago teacher, I turn to what may be the most remarkable letter ever written about a dedication to a book. Sent from the

Department of Sociology at the University of Chicago and dated 25 March 1987, it is addressed to

Dear Bob:

This, you will find, is a strange letter. It is a letter to apologize for dedicating a book to you. There is a book coming in the mail, published last fall, titled *Individual Interests and Collective Action*, published by Cambridge University Press, which has a dedication, set in very small type, 'To Robert K. Merton/whose excitement with social theory/ started me along this path'.

I apologize not because this is not true, nor because the dedication is unintended, nor because the book is a bad one, nor because of the small type, but because this is a dedication intended for a different book, one not yet finished, a book which you know about from an occasional letter describing my progress — in short, the book that I intend to be my magnum opus.

My intention was not to let you know of that dedication until the book was printed (I had told Harriet about it earlier), and then to surprise you with it. I had written out a couple of possible dedications, trying them on, so to speak, and somehow one that I had retained found its way to Cambridge University Press and onto the pages of this book — purely without intention on my part. I saw this only today, and was made speechless when I saw it. I didn't send it to them, except in error (and somehow things from the one book apparently got mixed up with the manuscript of the other), and I didn't see it in proof. (I guess they didn't send me some of the front matter, and since I hadn't dedicated the book to anyone, I didn't look for the dedication.)

So this lets the cat out of the bag, in a most peculiar way, informing you that I intend to dedicate the big book to you. I don't think you'll mind the present dedication, because the book, though it is composed primarily of papers published earlier, does have a coherence and focus, and is more than a collection of essays. But the important dedication is yet to come.[3]

Sincerely,

James S. Coleman
University Professor

No words of mine, Jim, could possibly compare with this testament to friendship. Still, your beautiful story of the inadvertent twin dedications leads directly to the story of another, far less imposing, dedication that the Fates have kindly allowed me to present as the fourth and final exhibit this day. Here, then, are the proofs of Part I of a little monograph bearing the title *Opportunity Structure* followed by what your austere self may decide is the rather overextended subtitle (in the seventeenth century mode): *The Emergence, Diffusion, and Differentiation of a Sociological Concept, 1930s–1950s*.

The coda to that monograph reads this way:

As Paul Lazarsfeld and I happily recognized at the time, and as I have had occasion to note here almost half-a-century later, the intellectually exciting micro-environment constituted by the Columbia Department of Sociology and its Bureau of Applied Social Research owed much to the remarkable flow of talented students in the 1940s and 1950s (and, as we shall see in Part II of this paper, in later decades as well). A sizable number of those students were destined to become sociological luminaries of the first rank. That scholarly stature has since been symbolically attested for some of them by *Festschriften* paying tribute not only by their students but by one of their ancient teachers as well. But alas, on this lone occasion, circumstance and inept planning have prevented me from getting even a short tributary paper to the *Festschrift* for the polymathic and consequential sociologist, James Samuel Coleman.

Belatedly, I do so now. As another old hand in a neighboring social science precisely and tellingly observed in a tribute to a student of his own: 'One of the great pleasures in academic life is to see a younger savant develop, evolving into a colleague . . . — and then, best of all, is the rare sight of the companion at arms who forges ahead of you as you were able to do at the inflection point of your own career'. As often before, Paul A. Samuelson speaks for me once again. It is with that singular kind of pleasure that I think back on Jim Coleman's 25-or-so books and countless seminal articles; in particular, of course, the vastly consequential *Coleman Report*, fittingly described as 'the most powerful empirical critique of the myths (the unquestioned basic assumptions, the socially received beliefs) of American education ever produced', and the climactic *Foundations of Social Theory*, that *magnum opus* that merges *homo œconomicus* and *homo sociologicus* in demanding and evocative theoretical style. And so, I conclude as I began by dedicating this retrospective study to

James S. Coleman
my onetime student,
longtime colleague,
enduring friend
and teacher.

Notes

1 Presented 15 April 1994 at the conference celebrating the first award of the Phoenix Prize of the University of Chicago to James S. Coleman in recognition of his fundamental contributions to social science.

2 For James S. Coleman's retrospectives on that micro environment, see his 'Research Chronicle: *The Adolescent Society*' (Coleman, 1964c); 'Paul F. Lazarsfeld: The Substance and Style of His Work' (Coleman, 1980b); 'Robert K. Merton as Teacher' (Coleman, 1990d); 'Columbia in the 1950s' (Coleman, 1990f); and 'A Vision for Sociology' (Coleman, 1994b, also reprinted as Chapter 21 above). For other word portraits of that Columbia micro environment set forth by participant-observers in those early cohorts, see the accounts by Peter M. Blau, Phillip E. Hammond, Herbert M. Hyman, Seymour Martin Lipset and Charles Wright, in P.E. Hammond (ed.), *Sociologists at Work* (Hammond, 1964); and the accounts by Dennis Wrong, Nathan Glazer, Alice Rossi and Cynthia Fuchs in B.M. Berger (ed.), *Authors of Their Own Lives* (Berger, 1990). See also the accounts by Alice Rossi and Lewis Coser in Matilda White Riley (ed.), *Sociological Lives* (Riley, 1988); David L. Sills, 'Paul F.

Lazarsfeld' (Sills, 1987); and Chapter 7 of Everett M. Rogers, *A History of Communication Study* (Rogers, 1994).

3 *Editor's Note*: The dedication to *Foundations of Social Theory* reads: 'To Robert K. Merton, my teacher'.

Appendix 2: Transcripts of Drafts for a Concluding Chapter, by James S. Coleman with a Commentary by Zdzislawa A. Coleman

Contexts of Transcripts 1, 2 and 3
Zdzislawa A. Coleman

It is hard for me to write this account and I do so for one reason only. Had Jim been able, he would have written the concluding chapter for this volume. It would have been an original piece inspired partly by the work of the authors contributing to the volume, partly inspired by his own vision of his life-work, and by his agenda for the future reaching beyond *Foundations* and opening up still another unfinished debate. I cannot do justice to what Jim Coleman would have written, but I can try to illuminate the context of this work-in-progress.

For Jim work in sociology was never a finished business, it was always an ongoing enterprise. One research project led to another. Projects of diverse substantive contents were carried out simultaneously, and new ideas percolated at all times. His academic entrepreneurship and mulling over new ideas were evident even while he was combatting the last stages of the disease.

Although he considered *Foundations of Social Theory* his most important work to date, by no means did he believe that his work was finished. On the contrary, he set out to construct another short-term agenda, and a long-term agenda as well.

His short-term agenda was this: one important enterprise was to conduct empirical research that would follow the framework explicated in *Foundations*. During the free time away from the Department made possible by a Fulbright Fellowship, which we spent in Florence, Italy, Jim developed a conceptual framework for an empirical project, to be carried out later. Upon returning to the United States in 1993 with Barbara Schneider as co-author and co-investigator, he began an empirical study at the National Opinion Research Center and the University of Chicago. That project was to examine schools and school design as output-driven systems, or in the original version as output-driven organizations. The project is now in its final stage of data analysis and preparation of the book is underway.

Jim felt very strongly about the discipline of sociology as a whole. He was convinced that sociology was in dire need of change — theoretical, methodological and empirical — if it were to move into the twenty-first century. *Foundations* would provide the theoretical guideposts; the Coleman-Becker seminar at the University of Chicago would provide a rigorous and closely scrutinized display of work-in-progress; the journal *Rationality and Society*, a forum for ideas; the new section for Rational

Choice of the American Sociological Association, a vehicle for organizing topical sessions at the annual meetings; and far from last, there would be an updating of the curriculum for graduate students in sociology at the University of Chicago. To that end, and despite his failing health, he was determined to teach and did teach the main introductory sociology course for first year graduate students in the fall quarter of 1994. He greatly enjoyed teaching the course. Whether he had the premonition that his time was limited, I do not know, but he put everything he believed important into it in an effort to twist anew the minds of incoming students to the essentials of the discipline. Jim was truly delighted when he received a card from the students sent in the winter of 1995, when they learned his health was getting worse, for the messages showed that some of his teachings had sunk in. Here are some selected excerpts:

Remember: you put the 'social' back in sociology.

Super-duper-super-duper-super-duper-social science!

Professor Coleman, your initial encouragement to share our life experiences has carried through to almost all my work, and definitely to the work that I enjoy. I continue to think about ideas from your class. Thank you for broadening my horizon — hope you feel better soon.

Seriously, it was good that I could talk about my experiences before going into big theories. I could have been lost in the theoretical forest.

Prof. Coleman, you gave us a great send-off into our graduate careers. Thank you. Sociology Rules!

Going beyond *Foundations* was the next item on his short-term agenda. Jim felt that Part V, its mathematical section, was never fully understood, discussed or put to rigorous test. Yet it was an intrinsic part of the theory he had laid out. To this end, he wanted to have the linear system of action models subjected to far greater scrutiny than they had received. A possible forum was the Mathematical Sociology Seminar he was conducting at the University. In fact, the line-up for the spring quarter of the seminar, which he was still preparing just days before he died, already included a couple of presentations related to his models, with the first scheduled for Monday, 27 March 1995, to be given by Tony Tam, his former graduate student now at Harvard University.

While hoping to remedy the lack of interest in the mathematics of *Foundations*, Jim began to consider further ideas that had to be addressed as a result of what had been laid out in *Foundations*. These were, in broad compass:

1   basic problems in theory;
2   empirical research as it should be.

In theory the focus was on the dynamics of decision-making mostly at the individual level and on the question whether decision-making at that level should be taken as axiomatic, as economists do, or rather rethought as actions embedded in the social structure of choice, with norms as the ethos of choice, rights as the legitimation of choice, and social systems or social organizations as the outcome of choice.

The most readily discernible empirical observations are outcomes. Whether these are at the individual level or at the system level is not as important, unless bad statistics or bad aggregating procedures disallow the description of the outcomes, for example, students' grades and evaluation of teachers' performance. Unless within-school outcomes are described properly, the between-school outcomes are meaningless.

This brings me to the last item on Jim's short-term agenda: writing the concluding chapter for this volume. As Jon Clark reports in Chapter 1, the structure of the volume evolved over time. It incorporated the social reality of Jim's past work, and it concludes with the social reality that began to unfold with his death.

Jim had read all the papers in this volume. Some of the papers he had re-read. Others, he was still discussing. After a stay in the hospital in winter 1995 coping with a bout of pneumonia, he recuperated at home. It was an uphill battle to get going, but he did manage, and began the 1995 winter quarter as usual. He conducted the Mathematical Sociology Seminar at home, and met with students and faculty as well. Debbie Milton, his secretary, provided a wonderful liaison, and the chapter for this volume was on his mind most of the time. Whenever he worked, whether in the livingroom, diningroom or bedroom, the papers were laid out for a volume in progress. At first, he used the original table of contents.[1] Then he began to rethink it all. And we talked. One day, I found the chapters arranged in a different order.[2] Only then did he begin to write.

There were many false starts and he would destroy the pages he had written. His writing began to be less legible, and Debbie brought him a tape-recorder to dictate the chapter. He tried, did not like what he heard, and decided not to use it. With the demands of chemotherapy and a more complicated time at home, he decided to try to establish a schedule for writing, perhaps an hour or two a day, depending on how he felt. There was no discipline involved, nor was it written in stone, but it was important to Jim that he continue to work. Transcript 1, dated 18 March, was the first result from attempting this schedule. Transcript 2, the next day, 19 March, resulted from the second attempt. In the meantime physical matters were going from bad to worse. No matter. He was still in business. On Tuesday, 21 March, Jim felt pretty good. And so we discussed the chapter again. The third and last transcript is from that day. He was sitting in an armchair writing on his lap as usual. He felt good about it, and said: 'Now I know what to write'. On Thursday morning, I took him to the hospital and on Saturday, 25 March 1995 at 12:15 p.m., Jim died.

1 June 1995

Acknowledgments

I am grateful to Robert K. Merton, James Heckman and Lynne Pettler for their comments and help in the preparation of this text.

Appendix 2

Editor's Notes

1 The original order of chapters was: Kandel, Husén, Alexander/Entwisle, Sørensen, Heyns, Boocock, Heckman/Neal, Bulmer, Kilgore, Bartholomew, Abell, Inbar, Zablocki, Fararo, Favell, Swedberg, Lindenberg, Collins.
2 The re-arranged order of chapters proposed by Jim Coleman was: Husén, Kandel, Heyns, Alexander/Entwisle, Heckman/Neal, Bulmer, Kilgore, Zablocki, Boocock, Bartholomew, Abell, Sørensen, Swedberg, Inbar, Fararo, Favell, Lindenberg, Collins.

Transcript 1   18 March 1995

The first two chapters in this book by Denise Kandel and Torsten Husén address youth and adolescence. In so doing, they have chosen between at least two foci, the one they have focused on, and another, which is the way that small, relatively closed social systems form and the effect of that system upon those inside it.

The first independent research I carried out, published as *The Adolescent Society*, carried both of these foci, and I had an interest in both. It was not accidental that the work which grew from *The Adolescent Society* addressed the first focus more than the second. Even my description of the second, above, is simpler and more straightforward than the first ('adolescent development'). And if I can't make clear my aim, as with the second ('the way that small, relatively closed social systems form and the effect on those inside it').

Why do I go into this extensive illustration? It is because of a difficulty that has beset my work since the outset. My major interest is in the way social systems (or subsystems) function, not in the way individuals' actions are shaped. Yet my methodological skills, as well as my conceptual framework, lead me to make use of information at the level of individual actions, which must be somewhere combined to. . . .

Torsten Husén has provided, in his essay, a rich perspective on the growth of 'adolescence' and 'youth' as distinct stages in life. He has pointed to the work of those pioneer social scientists like G. Stanley Hall and Charlotte Bühler, whose identification of these stages provided the conceptual base for those of us (including himself and including me) who have studied these stages of life more recently.

In placing my own work within this context, Husén has imposed a greater order on this work than it deserves, and I hasten to reintroduce some of the fits and starts which in fact marked this work.

I began the research that led to *The Adolescent Society* not primarily with a special interest in adolescence as a stage in life, but with a special interest in studying relatively closed social systems. I saw the high school as the closest approximation in modern society to a closed social system, but only, of course, if one studied not the school (as teachers or parents conceived it), but as the setting within which adolescents created a social system for themselves.

Thus I did not see my work as contributing to understanding of human development or life stages, but as contributing to an understanding of how social systems function. Yet I found myself to some degree captured by those very aspects which had been incidental to my choice of research settings. The research results themselves focused my interest on the special circumstance of youth in modern society, in particular the segregation of its social world from that of the adults with whom it shared living quarters.

I will not discuss the controversy, which Husén points to (but does not take a stand on), about whether there was indeed segregation of social worlds between adolescents and youth on one hand, and adults on the other. But I will acknowledge that this view that there is in modern society an age segregation of social worlds between youth and their parents has had a strong impact on my subsequent work. It has had a direct impact on the framing of *Youth: Transition to Adulthood*, on my joint work with Husén in the OECD report, *Becoming Adult in a Changing Society*, and on my theoretical work about macro social change, in *Power and the Structure of Society* and *The Asymmetric Society*.

Altogether, then, although I never set out to study adolescence and youth for its own sake, the research results have greatly shaped my subsequent work.

This is an extraordinary set of papers! It is not a festschrift, consisting of papers by former students, colleagues and associates presenting some of their own work that is more or less related to that of the honoree. With few exceptions, it consists of analyses of portions of my work, relating this portion to other parts of my work and to other work in social science.

Any response on my part to each of these papers, to be in any way responsible, would require another volume of comparable size. I will not attempt this. Rather, I will look back over my work and attempt to answer the question, 'What was I trying to do?' In some cases I will also attempt to answer, 'How will I succeed, using both evidence from the papers and my own evaluation?'

Some of the papers do not lend themselves to this approach, because of their more tenuous relation to my own work. Depending on the paper, I will comment in a way that seems useful.

Behavior of Social Systems, Not Behavior of Individuals

Sociology has had two dominant problematics. One is the explanation of behavior of social systems and the second the explanation of individual behavior. By the behavior of social systems, I refer to the equilibrium conditions that can be specified about a set of persons, but not about a single person, such as a set of norms governing dress; and to the non-equilibrium conditions that can be specified about a set of persons, such as a panic in a crowded theater.

The second problematic, the explanation of individual behavior, came into full flower during my period in graduate school, with the development of survey research. Although survey research came to be the dominant research technique used in sociology, and has been the method I have used in much of my research, I have attempted to pervert this method to the study of the behavior of social systems. In my estimation, the second problematic, for which survey research has been primarily used, is not a proper part of sociology, and belongs elsewhere.

My first work beyond graduate school, published as *The Adolescent Society* (and a series of papers), constitutes a first attempt in this direction. This study of ten high schools in Northern Illinois was not based on a sample survey; it was a *census* of students, parents and teachers. The questions asked were not merely about the respondent, but about the respondent's relations with others: who were friends, whom did the respondent want to be like or be friends with, who was in the leading crowd in the school, and so on. This all assumed, of course, that the school was a relatively self-contained or closed social system; and the analysis was designed to characterize the school as a social system, to make possible its comparison with the nine other schools.

These deviations from standard survey methods suggest how the method is not intrinsically tied to the problematic; I will not, however, go into the difficulties of applying survey methods to the study of the behavior of social systems.

The description I have given indicates the basis for the design of this first research: high schools as small 'manageable' closed social systems with well defined positions; stable occupants of these positions; and information not merely about persons, but about relations between them. In the forty years since the design of this research, some progress has been made toward applying survey methods to the study of the behavior of social systems (see, for example, Bryk and Raudenbusch, 1992), but a sustained attempt to apply these methods in this way has yet to be carried out.

I have described the character of the ten social systems whose behavior was to be under study, but not the content of the research. As it happened, it was the content of the research which captured my attention for the next several years, as well as that of the authors of several of the papers. My applied research throughout most of my career has been connected in one way or another with high schools, and more particularly with achievement of high school students.

Two of the authors, Denise Kandel and Torsten Husén, have focused specifically on this emerging period of social and physical development, coming closest to the content interests in the role of youth in modern society that motivated my study of high schools. Although the use of adolescents in high schools was somewhat adventitious, as I have described earlier, my interest did not decline. Nine of the nineteen papers (Kandel, Husén, Alexander and Entwistle, Sørensen, Heyns, Boocock, Heckman, Bulmer and Kilgore) in this volume are about schools and youth.

Appendix 3: In Memoriam James S. Coleman (1926–1995); Speeches Given at the Memorial Service, 19 May 1995, in the Rockefeller Memorial Chapel, Chicago

1 *Marta Tienda*
Chair, Department of Sociology, University of Chicago

Good afternoon. On behalf of Zdzislawa Coleman and the entire Coleman family, it is my privilege to welcome friends and colleagues of James S. Coleman to this Memorial Service.

We are assembled to celebrate and to remember the many ways Jim Coleman's profound scholarship influenced those present today, and thousands more who, though unable to travel, have shared their sentiments about Jim's inspiration. Our speakers represent Jim's reach as a mentor; as a social theorist; as a social analyst in the service of public policy; and as a world-class influence on social sciences throughout the world.

Without any further ado, I will turn the program over to our first speaker.

2 *Mark Siegler, MD*
University of Chicago Hospitals

Zdzislawa, Tom, John, Steven, and Daniel, Ladies and Gentlemen:

Jim was my friend but he was *far more* than a friend — he was a squash partner. Jim and I were among the crazed handful who would play squash all summer long indoors on unairconditioned courts when even mad dogs, Englishmen and tennis players would be playing tennis outdoors in the midday sun.

For almost twenty years, we played one or two matches a week, matches memorable for their intensity and vigor as well as for the feature of having two left-handers — unusual in squash — trying to figure out ricochet angles — as we struggled for court position. I'll never forget: Jim hit a squash ball harder than anyone I have ever seen — God, he could hit hard!

I still remember the first time Jim and I *ran into* each other on the old squash courts at Bartlett Gym — I don't mean encountered each other, I mean literally ran into one another. (It was in our first match and it never happened again — I think it was the lefty-lefty thing.) I ended up flat on my back and only later did someone tell me that Jim had developed his physical solidity in the boxing ring, where he had enjoyed a distinguished career as an amateur fighter.

You learn a lot about people on the squash court, and Jim was a brilliant competitor unequalled in drive and determination. But at the same time he was the cleanest, most generous and most polite opponent — someone for whom the game provided an opportunity for intense competitiveness but always within a structure of rules that assured civility. These are the remarkable qualities that led to our long-term friendship.

It was from our interactions on the squash court that Jim and I gradually — over a period of ten years — forged our other relationship, that of patient and physician. As I think back on it, I now believe that we built our friendship in the squash court encounter and solidified it in the medical encounter.

Perhaps we worked so well together in the medical sphere because we agreed about so many aspects of the doctor-patient relationship. Jim and I agreed that the ideal medical relationship is a relationship of friends rather than strangers. This kind of medical relationship is not always possible because our society's mobility discourages long-term relationships; because medicine is very complex and no single doctor can function adequately without calling on specialists for help; and because our health care institutions are often large and impersonal bureaucracies. While all this is true in general, sometimes a medical relationship of friends *is* doable and there is a better chance of doing it in a geographically and intellectually coherent community like our university community, where the Colemans live next door to Ralph Muller, the president of the hospital, and where Jim and Zdzislawa's son, Daniel, and my daughter, Jessica, were on the same swim team.

In Jim's view, the *physician's* role in this medical relationship of friends was to help by serving first as medical advisor — occasionally as debating partner — and finally as an administrator who could gain access to medical services within the system that might benefit the patient. This brings us to the role of the *patient* as Jim understood it. The patient clearly was the one in charge. The patient had responsibility for gathering information, analyzing it, and applying it to make the right choices for himself.

Jim had a clear sense that no one understood his values and utilities better than he did himself and that because he had the most to risk, his body and his life, it was only right that he made the crucial choices.

Jim's perspective was clearly evident in his analysis of new treatment approaches for prostate cancer. I remember that early on Jim set up a meeting with Sam Broder, the director of the National Cancer Institute, to get an overview of the state of prostate cancer research. Later, he met and corresponded with the leading prostate cancer researchers in Chicago, Boston, New York, Washington, Houston and Seattle. He knew everything that was known about the problem, and often he had the latest treatment data even before it was presented by the investigators as abstracts at scientific meetings. Jim was helped in his investigations, and, of course, in his treatment, by his oncologist, Dr Nick Vogelzang. But both Nick and I are quick to concede that Jim's scientific quest for information about prostate cancer was unprecedented. And in every respect, he was the leader and we were his assistants. For Jim, this search for good data that could be used to make reasonable personal decisions was the culmination of an intellectual pilgrimage and perhaps even the ultimate test of a theory of rational choice.

It was so typically like Jim that from these personal experiences he crafted a brilliant analytic essay entitled: 'Phase I Cancer Trials: The Patient's Perspective'. I won't say more about this incisive paper because I know Ed Laumann will refer to it in his remarks later.

From all that I've said about Jim's response to his illness, you understand that Jim was not a *typical* patient; the original meaning of the word *patient* was 'one who suffers or faces illness with resignation'. All of us who knew Jim throughout his life, or knew him during his illness, understand that *this* concept of *patient* was foreign to him. I have never known anybody who was more *impatient* about being a *patient*. And by his example, Jim *taught* us a new model of patienthood.

The qualities that marked Jim as a friend and as a squash partner — fierce dedication, generosity, genius, all-out energy, full confrontation within the rules of the game — 'God, he could hit hard . . .' — these qualities also summarize his attitude toward his illness and his life.

He was a rare friend and squash partner and a great teacher. He taught all of us till the end.

3   *Seymour Martin Lipset*
Institute of Public Policy, George Mason University

If we believe as the ancient Greeks did, or as Jews do in a very different way, Jim is alive and with us. For the Greeks thought that the dead go down to Hades, where their vitality depends on their being remembered and discussed by those above. Today especially we remember, and Jim lives. And given his importance, his creativity as a teacher and scholar, many will remember him for eons to come. Fortunately, he had time to finish his great book on social theory.

Those concerned with education, with opportunity, with race, with political systems, with trade unions, with the way people behave in different contexts, will remember him. And beyond his fame in the scholarly and policy worlds, the teachers and youth of Israel have cause to remember him. For Jim Coleman, who clearly was not of the seed of Abraham and Sarah, was a dedicated friend of Israel, one of the band of Gentile Zionists. He went frequently to Israel and collaborated with many of its social scientists, seeking especially to find ways to improve the education of deprived youth, much as he did in our own country. He found a Polish wife who gave him love and support, as he did her. And her native land, like Israel, benefitted much from his enthusiasms. The sociologists and people of Poland remember him as well.

But above all, we, his colleagues, friends, teachers and especially students, re-member him. And we can safely say, his memory, his name, will not fade as long as there are efforts to apply sociological theory and methods to the task of interpreting and improving our country, our world.

I will remember him. I had the good fortune of being with him from the start of his sociological endeavors. (Before that he had a brief but successful career as an engineer.) I knew him as a student, as a thesis advisee, as a research collaborator, as a fellow activist in the American Sociological Association, as a poker player at the Center for Advanced Study in the Behavioral Sciences at Stanford, but above all as a friend. He excelled in all those roles.

I worked with him most closely when he was a student and I, a young faculty member, in that memorable, now almost mythical, Columbia sociology department and Bureau of Applied Research, in the early 1950s. Paul Lazarsfeld and Bob Merton were leading us to the promised land of theoretically and methodologically scientific sociology. We believed we were involved in a truly revolutionary effort, one which would not only change social science, but by so doing would provide a basis for re-organizing society. Jim, Martin Trow and I produced *Union Democracy*, a study which I thought incorporated and illustrated all the analytic sophistication which our mentors gave us. It sought to specify the conditions for democracy not only in organizations but in the larger polity as well. Collaborating with Jim, I learned how hard a creative person could work. He regularly put in eighteen-hour workdays and returned for more. When the foundation money to pay him ran out, he did not stop. And this was a pattern he followed all his life.

I remember the education study, the famous *Coleman Report*. It, like his later work, had a major impact on school systems here and abroad. He wrote it as a report mandated for the US Congress in under two months, but, almost unchanged, it then became a major book. And, of course, he more than delivered as a theorist, with his magnum opus, a book on rational choice which already has had a major impact on sociology and political science.

Jim was the greatest, the most innovative of the offspring of the Golden Age of Columbia. He also, as you of Chicago were fortunate to know, was a superb and conscientious teacher, a dedicated departmental colleague, and to you, as to the rest of us, a good friend.

For all this and much more, we remember him; his memory and knowledge of his works will stay on. And we pray that God above will remember, reward, and preserve him, in the place He has reserved for great minds. We ask this of the God of Abraham, Sarah, and Hagar, of Isaac and Ishmael, of Moses and of Jesus.

4   *Edward L. McDill*
Department of Sociology, Johns Hopkins University

James Coleman was the pre-eminent sociologist of his generation, both as theoretician and empirical researcher. The breadth and depth of his voluminous contributions to the substance and method of both his own and cognate disciplines are monumental. His reach and grasp were remarkable, producing seminal contributions to problems as diverse as community conflict, social exchange theory, the social organization of schools, social network theory, social structure, rational choice theory, and stochastic process models, which, incidentally, were a major influence on the development of quantitative, sociological methods.

In these and other areas of research, Jim's scholarship was guided by two principles: first, Charles Sanders Peirce's dictum that science embodies the epitome of man's intellectual development; and second, the philosophers of pragmatism core belief that science is a form of adjustive intelligibility and action that is useful in guiding society.

Coleman was a man of extraordinary *intellectual vision*. To paraphrase the famous hockey player Wayne Gretzky: Jim always skated to where the puck was going to be, not where it had been. Second, he was a person of remarkable *ambition*, in the most positive sense of that term. He always took giant steps because he understood David Lloyd George's pithy aphorism that the most dangerous thing in the world is to leap a chasm in two jumps. Third, Coleman was a man of *unbridled determination*. Nowhere was this asset documented better than in his completion on schedule, against overwhelming odds, of the *EEO* report, the most important educational document of the post-war period.

As superb a scholar as Coleman was, he was also a wonderful person and colleague. I am going to relate a few anecdotes about my relationship with Jim during twelve years at Johns Hopkins University, where he was first my mentor, then my senior colleague and, most importantly, my close friend. First, I remember Jim as the friendly but fiercely competitive athletic type. Two of our favorite pastimes were playing squash together and arm wrestling. One day in the spring of 1962 we literally collided at the mail boxes during the lunch hour when the departmental office was closed. Almost immediately we were lying on the floor locked in fierce arm-wrestling combat with our bald heads as red as beets. Shortly thereafter the secretaries returned from lunch and almost went into a state of apoplexy, fearing that one or other of us was about to have a heart attack.

Second, Jim was a person of enormous and focused *intellectual and physical energy*. He never wasted a moment and was intolerant of dawdling. If he wasn't engaged in his own research agenda, he was giving counsel or advice to junior colleagues and students on both personal and academic matters. He was a very generous and supportive man who was never personal or unfair in his criticism of the intellectual work of students or junior colleagues. He understood that students, like children, have more need of models than of critics. Students and junior colleagues learned from him primarily by active participation in the research process and by observing him in action. He was an exemplar par excellence.

A third of Jim's most likeable characteristics was his *unassuming nature*. He was one of the least pretentious academicians I have ever met. This unassuming quality manifested itself in several delightful ways. For example, he was an inveterate but modest beer drinker and a heavy consumer of hard shell crabs. During the numerous times he visited Baltimore after he moved to Chicago, his favorite treat was spending an evening voraciously consuming crabs and sipping local beer.

Another manifestation of his unpretentious manner, which could have been misinterpreted as affectedness, was his lack of interest in clothes. Sartorial elegance was not Coleman's strong suit. Neat dresser yes! Fancy dresser no! Clothes for him played a strictly utilitarian role. He was especially insensitive to the matter of rotating his footwear. When Jim purchased a pair of shoes, he wore them continuously, without ever shining them, until they had to be discarded. I remember once in the late 1960s I purchased a pair of ugly, snub-toed, high-top shoes which immediately made my feet ache. Shortly thereafter I was at a departmental party where I gratuitously insulted Jim for continuing to wear a pair of totally exhausted oxfords. He informed me that he had been unable to find the time to visit the shoe store. His second response was to suggest seriously that I 'loan' him my 'handsome' shoes. On the spot my charitable spirit overwhelmed me and I gladly donated to him the painful clodhoppers which, in turn, made it unnecessary for him to visit the shoe store for at least another year.

A fourth personal characteristic, related to Jim's unpretentiousness, was a sense of *humility*, which is all the more remarkable given his superior intellect and scholarly accomplishments. He clearly understood the relevance of humility as a social scientist because he knew that a halo has to fall only a few inches to become a noose. He was very approachable, friendly and warm.

Finally, Jim Coleman *persevered* in the face of adversity, whether working on a gargantuan research project such as the EEO survey, or refusing to yield to the ravages of cancer. Although I saw him only twice after he became seriously ill, on both occasions he manifested that same indomitable spirit and determination which had led him to the apex of his profession. He followed FDR's advice: 'When you come to the end of your rope, tie a knot and hang on'.

For us at JHU, Jim Coleman was 'a man for all seasons' — a gifted and original scholar and social researcher, a wonderful colleague, a cherished friend, and *the* one person who made immeasurable contributions to the Department of Sociology and to the educational R and D Center as academic enterprises. We at Hopkins miss him deeply. We mourn his passing.

5   *Sally B. Kilgore*
Hudson Institute, Indianapolis

James S. Coleman was my teacher and friend. He was also one of my intellectual fathers. As such I took the liberty of calling him 'Daddy-rabbit number three' (My father having been the first). As is fitting, Jim was more concerned about the fact that I had ranked him number three than by my use of either the term 'Daddy' or 'rabbit'. Number three was not a ranking Jim took lightly.

While James S. Coleman's work will be known and respected by thousands for decades to come, I come today to honor his character — those habits of his mind and heart that will endure in the daily lives of his students.

When a student first met Jim, he or she would be struck, successively, by several things. First, he was seldom on time for anything — except, perhaps squash games and that required an alarm on his wrist watch.

In time a student would learn about a second truth: why Jim was always late. Jim was always late because he was available — in his office, on the midway, on the phone. In each instance, he gave equal attention to the concerns of those who approached him: concerns profound or mundane, concerns intellectual or personal. He was never too busy for his students, his West Virginia neighbors, or a local high school that needed a judge for a mathematics competition on Saturday morning. Jim's accessibility could easily obscure a third and more essential trait: Jim was extremely disciplined in his use of time. Once, during our work on the public and private school study, Jim called me from a pay telephone. A phone began ringing in the distance and Jim excused himself. I learned that Jim had taken over a row of pay phones where, one by one, he had placed calls to other people, leaving them, with luck, an open line to him. Only with such forethought could Jim have been not only a colleague to the many, but a scholar with few peers.

Knowing Jim as teacher brought new insights: Jim was almost too careful in his efforts to make his thinking accessible to others. Jim's vast knowledge of economics, science and mathematics was never used as a means of intimidating students. In graduate classes he would present his work without mathematical notations — sometimes at the risk of oversimplification and excessive pausing. His famous 'uh . . . uh' came when he tried to generate a simplified version of one of his mathematical formulations.

Jim became a colleague to a student when one began attending his numerous —

and his family must think too numerous — non-credit seminars. The very fact that Jim held 'non-credit' seminars — usually every week — communicated to students the dedication he had to — and the hunger he maintained for — exploring new ideas. Such seminars were important to students who availed themselves of the opportunity in other respects: Jim opened up the profession — its routine and responsibilities — to his students. We learned the process of reviewing manuscripts, presenting papers, criticizing and evaluating. And we learned of his standards. Michael White recalls the review of an important manuscript for the *American Journal of Sociology*. The students worked diligently on the review of the submitted work. It was a paper that eventually had substantial impact on the field. Michael, however, remembers best the last session when Jim read aloud, as he wrote on the review form: 'This is an outstanding paper, but it needs major revision'.

Thus, as colleague, Jim promoted many norms for the profession. I valued most his demand that he — and others — understand what was being said. At almost every presentation Jim attended, one could count on him to rub his bald head and say with his usual modesty: 'I don't understand'. When I was in the audience, I usually breathed a sigh of relief; at least I was not alone in my confusion. When I was the presenter, I had to anticipate this comment. It required that I truly understand every mathematical formulation I presented, every number I reported. Anything less would lead to total, albeit kind, humiliation. Requiring such clarity served as a powerful reminder of who I was and what I was doing: To be a teacher required that one communicate, enlighten — not intimidate or obscure.

Finally, a few students were fortunate to learn from him as we wrote with him. Those who wrote with Jim learned that his ability to produce findings that withstood the test of time and reanalysis was not accidental or lucky — as many would have us believe. Rather, Jim's analysis stood the test of time because he was very careful. Any given set of numbers might appear to be the result of one regression equation, but, in fact, Tom Hoffer and I know that any given table was the result of hundreds of regression runs — alternative specifications to evaluate the stability of the results. Jim knew before we published whether our conclusions were sufficiently robust to withstand the alternative interpretations that critics might impose.

Jim expected his co-authors to review and critique his first drafts, as he did ours. The fact that we could actually improve upon Jim's work gave us self-confidence. The fact that such drafts required revision gave us insight into the process one followed to achieve excellence. The fact that he welcomed and incorporated those comments gave us a different appreciation for the nature of great men.

As we wrote with Jim, we also learned of Jim's respect for truth seeking and the obligations that imposed. No person in my lifetime better exemplified the call of Albert Einstein: 'The right to search for truth implies also a duty: One must not conceal any part of what has recognized to be true'.

For those of us who had that opportunity to not only write with Jim, but were also allowed to struggle in heated debates with him, we learned how to concede points forthrightly and gracefully; that bitterness and outrage had no place in truth seeking; and that a passion for excellence brought life's greatest joy. Jim not only sought excellence in his own work, but had an unaffected admiration for excellence wherever he found it: he was as pleased to admire it in others as to achieve it himself.

With Jim, students came to appreciate Richter's claim that I paraphrased here: 'In later life as in earlier, only a few persons influence the formation of our character;

the multitude pass us by like a distant army. One friend, one teacher, one beloved, one dining table, one work table, are the means by which the spirit of a nation and university affect the individual'.

For your teaching and work table, I thank you Jim Coleman.

6   *Edward O. Laumann*
Department of Sociology, University of Chicago

Recently Jim wrote a little inscription for the flyleaf of his magnum opus, *Foundations of Social Theory* (1990), which said:

> To Ed, My friend, my colleague and my intellectual co-conspirator and much more.

I would like to reflect and amplify on that comment — it is a useful way into a remarkably productive personal and intellectual journey with a colleague who profoundly shaped my own work and the work of our students, sociology as a discipline, the social sciences more generally and even public policy. As some of you may know, I have been known to talk about Talcott Parsons, my mentor, on at least some occasions. My first exposure to Jim's writings was when I read in the early 1960s as a graduate student his lengthy critique of Parsons' paper on 'the concept of influence'. And it really made me angry. Already Jim was flirting with rational choice explanations and, as many of you will appreciate, such explanations sorely offend the sensibilities of most sociologists as somehow conceding far too much to our arch rivals, the economists. For such heresy, I promptly dismissed him from my concerns.

It was only in 1973 when I decided to accept the Chicago offer that I discovered that Jim was also joining the faculty here as a university professor. He had just completed a fourteen-year stint at the Johns Hopkins University as the founding chair of the Department of Social Relations. I don't recall that Morris Janowitz, then chair of the department, who was actively recruiting me and knew my theoretical prejudices, ever mentioned Jim's likely arrival as — to use Jim's lingo — a 'positive incentive' for my coming here. But shortly after my arrival, Jim called to say that he heard that I played squash — would I like a game? Thus began a weekly encounter that provided an important thread in stitching together our personal and professional lives. This athletic forum was regular and inevitable — nothing on either side, not faculty meetings, administrative chores, visiting dignitaries, urgent consultations, was permitted to interfere with a scheduled game. And with Jim's legendary travel plans and commitments and my growing administrative responsibilities, there were many challenges to that commitment. The unanticipated benefit of these predictable encounters was that we had each other's undivided attention for the inevitable in-game sidebar discussions of our research ventures as well as our mutual commitments to students, the university and faculty business. These meetings, then, helped forge a formidable shared intellectual and professional agenda that played itself out in many ways over the years.

Jim and I shared many characteristics that greatly facilitated the growth of our strong personal feelings of trust and friendship. We both came from small towns in the Ohio River Valley and are Protestant in background — the driven variety, of course. Perhaps most important, we both were alike in having highly competitive personalities, however we might try to disguise them. What could have expressed itself as an intense intellectual rivalry between two camps in sociological thinking was diverted into highly stylized competition on the court. But I certainly didn't ignore our intellectual disagreements, and neither did he. We, however, conducted the dialogue through our students, who were expected to broker and integrate our in-congruent expectations and explanations as best they could. And we shared many students — foreign and domestic — over the years. Just quickly counting those for whom we chaired or co-chaired dissertations, I come up with eighteen, an impressive number of whom have gone on to pursue outstanding scholarly careers at leading institutions both here and abroad. Jim, of course, was a wonderful and dedicated teacher who attracted hundreds of students, graduate and undergraduate alike, through-out his long career. His legacy is large and richly variegated because he never insisted on a party line, but pushed his students to pursue their own understanding. His sole, unfailing requirement was that they meet universal standards for intellectual incisive-ness and clarity of thought.

Jim understood better than most the critical importance of building a community around an innovative and controversial intellectual program if one hoped to exert an impact on the way a field would develop over the long haul. And he devoted himself unflaggingly to the cultivation of this community. Despite his staggering round of off-campus, often out of the country, professional commitments, he offered annually, in addition to his regular teaching duties, a year-long weekly seminar on mathematical sociology that brought his students and potential recruits together to discuss the latest path-breaking work on a catholic range of topics. The biweekly Becker/Coleman faculty seminar on rational choice, begun in 1984, proved itself to be a vital, decade-long workshop that achieved an international reputation for the quality and excitement of its Tuesday night meetings. Many distinguished scholars vied for the honor to be grilled by an exacting and highly interactive audience of regulars. Jim's efforts to build strong intellectual and social bonds among his students and the much broader com-munity of scholars, both here at Chicago and internationally, featured many informal social occasions for socializing at picnics, competitive sporting events and parties at his home. The very regularity of these events helped institutionalize an easy-going aware-ness of each other as people as well as scholars with shared interests.

Despite our closeness, it is rather surprising that we rarely read, in detail, each other's work. I can think of only one or two occasions when I did so for Jim and he for me — although we were very current with each other's work through the student intermediaries. Informal talk was far more important. One incident concerns my efforts to formulate a network monitoring strategy in assessing the AIDS count nationally. Jim called me at 10 o'clock one night to say that he had been thinking about the problem since our talk at the gym that afternoon. He suggested that I ask about some other rare but well counted population events, like homicides or suicides, so that I could triangulate on the performance of my measure in estimating the AIDS count. It was a brilliant suggestion: elegant, simple, effective — the hallmark of the Coleman intellectual style.

Another distinguishing feature of the Coleman style was unrelenting intellectual honesty and the courage to address controversial subjects without fear or favor. Others today are sharing some reflections on some of the famous public controversies on busing and white flight in which he was embroiled. I want to recount an example closer to home. Jim learned of his prostate cancer some five years ago. He immediately began to read exhaustively the relevant medical research literature on the disease process and medical interventions and their likely outcomes. Soon he was an active collaborator with his physicians in making choices among treatment options. Initially hesitant in telling me and others outside the family about his health situation because he didn't want to burden us with his personal problems, he was persuaded that this was appropriate to share with those who cared about him. Soon I was vicariously participating in an intellectual journey of discovery about the state of medical knowledge and ignorance. Despite its dread consequences for him as an individual patient, and my own imaginings of the difficulties of sorting through the personal and the general in this case, I watched him at some level transcend the personal to find a general lesson for us all. I have never been so proud to know someone as when I observed him, with a glint in his eye, lead a seminar in clinical medical ethics based on his paper entitled 'Phase 1 Trials: The Patient's Perspective', some ten months before his own death. In attendance, among many others, were the oncologists who were treating him and who were also in charge of the university's Phase 1 cancer trials, in which he had been asked to participate.

I cannot reveal all of our political collusion over academic initiatives and policies here at the university — some are still in process — but again these grew out of our regular get-togethers for a beer after the squash matches. I hasten to add that none of our discussions of what was best for the department, the division, the university or the field were anything less than finely motivated and argued assessments of intellectual promise and efforts to sniff out exciting new directions. Never have I heard Jim rest his judgment on ad hominem considerations — his optimism, overall cheerfulness and engagement, and 'can do' personal style tolerated no such mingy mean-spiritedness, even for those erstwhile friends who castigated and reviled him for his willingness to change views when his empirical work told him he must. Despite his strong commitments to his own intellectual agenda, he was doggedly open-minded about the errors of others, including my own. I don't know whether our students would say it was always fun, but our collegial and personal friendship was a continuing source of challenge and inspiration to all of us. And we shall sorely miss him.

7 Gudmund Hernes
Minister of Education, Research and Church Affairs, Oslo, Norway

Vitality — if James S. Coleman is to be encapsuled in one term, 'vitality' is the one for me. He had an exceptional drive and energy, stamina and, as was demonstrated during the last years of his life, fortitude.

Vitality manifest as curiosity — in the capacity to detect what others have seen often but yet have overlooked. He could become fascinated with a swarm of mosquitoes, an assembly of individual actions yet with a collective shape, seemingly random actions yet apparent in a definite aggregate form. Or by the logic underlying freely forming human groups. He was trained as an engineer. But he found that since he did not think about his job after hours, since it did not engage his curiosity, it was not worth spending his life on. He became a sociologist, and his experiences, both those he sought by large-scale data collections as well as those distilled from incidental encounters, became raw material for his thinking. Talking to him you could always expect the unexpected question. And he had the guts to find the simplest and most intuitive illustrations for profound relations, such as the giving of an extra scoop to a friend in an ice-cream parlor epitomizing the principal-agent relation. Jim's eyelids would get very heavy when his curiosity was not engaged — and his mind instantly set on red alert when it was kindled.

Curiosity — and *originality*. Jim Coleman had a unique capacity to see patterns and to uncover the processes generating them. His mind combined the two faculties that made for ingenious and inventive theorizing: a sensitivity to form that gave him hunches, and a dogged will to pursue his intuitions with the tools of mathematics: a keen eye for qualities and soft observations combined with a wonderful talent for translating them into formal language and hard logic to develop rich concepts. He had an equally well developed talent for finding data that were relevant, and for squeezing them imaginatively to put his theories to the test. He loved constructing social theories — but he did not vanish into the edifices he built: he became impatient if they did not depict and divulge something about the real world. He never forgot what his models should be models *of*. His originality can also be put this way: what he touched in his profession, he transformed — and he touched so much: diffusion theory, conflict theory, educational sociology, medical sociology, mathematical sociology, probability theory, political theory, moral philosophy. He became no prefix-sociologist: he was so curious about everything that he traversed the whole field. He was a sociologist — period.

Perseverance. He would never let go of a problem that he had posed until he had worked it out to his satisfaction. Nay, a problem would not let *him*. Not having solved it left him dissatisfied and restless. So he would try again and again, over and over, attempt to roll the boulder to the top in a labour of Sisyphus. What he called his 'big book' started as a comment on Talcott Parsons' paper, 'On the Concept of Influence', in 1962. A breakthrough came as hunch at a concert in Vienna in 1965, when in a flash he saw the interrelations between actors' control over and interest in events and the derived concepts of value and power. The 'big book' was announced to be published in 1973 under the title *A General Theory of Action*. It only came out in 1990 as *Foundations of Social Theory*, after years and years of intellectual strain and struggle. The same tenacity was seen in the way he confronted his terminal illness: he used all his imagination and stamina to understand it — as well as the social organization of advanced medical research and treatment.

Courage. He had the pluck to change his views and put his ideas to new tests when he had an inkling that they did not square with new data. This of course meant that he generated controversy, that he was disowned and denounced by former allies and embraced and applauded by former opponents — none of them quite appreciating that his loyalty was to truth as he found it, not to doctrines held by true believers, some of them based on insights he had won. Some of his colleagues moved to have him ostracized from the American Sociological Association at one point when he changed his views and announced that the earth moved.

Action. Jim Coleman was not just a student of man, but a man of action — a sociologist who wanted to see theory put to use, and saw important parts of social science as policy research, providing guidelines for action. But he fit into no simple mould as liberal or conservative. He had, however, strong convictions on important issues: that there should be equality of opportunity and that social organization could foster or frustrate it. Hence he was all the time concerned not just with positive theory, but with normative theory. Indeed, he looked upon social research as a political resource and became increasingly interested in moral philosophy. Marx's last thesis on Feuerbach fits him: 'The philosophers have only interpreted the world in various ways, the point however, is to change it'.

Joy. Jim's zest stood out not just in exercising his mind, but also in using his body, his muscles and bones, and engaging his friends in games and play and sometimes in pranks. He could resist everything but a challenge. He loved life and used his skill and drive to shape a society which becomes ours when we change it. His is an admonition to us all to use life while we have it. For Jim left his fingerprint not just on American social science and American social life, but on many other countries as well. To take but one example: Norwegian schools have adopted as guidelines for actions, principles Jim formulated in his essay, 'How Do the Young Become Adults?'

No one is indispensable. But when Jim is gone, life is recast for his family. When Coleman is gone, the profession takes another course — the country as well, yours and mine. His family will have another life, the field will take another track. For he set his imprint on his environment, in the close circle of relatives and friends, in the wider ring of colleagues at home and abroad.

Vitality. So Jim will live on: first in our memories, in the many details we remember, such as the rubber bands he would sometimes keep on his wrist for days on end; then in his contributions, which we will return to again and again. Not only because they provide us with insights and solutions, but because they are a source of questions, a lasting agenda for research. Most of all he will live in his theories, which have become ours, our concepts and our language, over a wide range, spanning from 'contagious poisson' to 'school effects', from 'corporate actors' to 'conjoint action'.

He has left us, but he has left us with important problems not yet solved and ideas not yet worked out. He has left us with tasks to do and directions for where to go. He remains an intellectual principal for whom we will remain agents.

We halt and bow our heads, in loss, in sorrow, in mourning. But also in veneration, in appreciation, in gratitude and indeed in joy: for what he made and what he gave, for what he invented and what he created — for what he left us with when he left us.

8   *Senator Daniel Patrick Moynihan*

In the spring of 1966 Seymour Martin Lipset walked into a reception at the Harvard faculty club, came over to me (it happened I was there), and said, 'You know what Coleman is finding, don't you?' I said, 'What?' He said, 'All family'. I said, 'Oh. Lord'.

The next day I called the assistant to the then Secretary of Health, Education and Welfare to say that the findings of the largest social science research project in history were about to arrive in the secretary's office and he was not going to like them and they had best get ready for that. They were anything but, and a kind of stalemate ensued as to what to do with the report. It was typical of Jim to find a solution. He said you can write anything you wish about what you decide I have found, or we have found, as long as you publish the data. And indeed they wrote exactly as they wished and released the document for the Saturday papers of the 4 July weekend. It had become a non-event.

That fall, we arranged a faculty seminar at Harvard, thinking a half dozen or so dons might stay with the subject through the winter. One evening the next spring, the entire second floor of the Harvard faculty club was taken up with a hundred odd physicists, lawyers, statisticians, ministers, what you will, who had learned that something new had appeared. In the great honor of the scientists in particular, they came and said, 'Do you mean to tell us there is something about schooling that you don't understand? Now that's interesting'.

But of course to say that things were not understood was to say that things were not as they had been held to be and this was not welcome. In very short order, as Dr Becker will recount [in the next contribution, Editor], Jim was the object of vicious attacks in a mode very much as Hannah Arendt once observed of the superiority of the totalitarian elites of the 1920s and the 1930s in Europe — the ability immediately to dissolve every statement of fact into a declaration of purpose.

A crisis of liberalism occurred. It is with us still, unresolved and in some large measure still not fully understood. That Coleman bore all this with equanimity is known to everyone here. I wondered in thinking of these remarks how much those of the generation that followed him might understand this and so I asked the assistant secretary of what is now the Department of Health and Human Services, a sociologist charged with policy planning, what his views would be of the life of this extraordinary man. Back came by fax this no less extraordinary statement: 'There are a very small number of people who end up defining a major part of the intellectual agenda for their times. Their work is both so powerful and so well argued, and their conclusions so important that others are inspired to focus on these same issues. An even tinier group of thinkers influence both intellectual and policy debate. James Coleman's work formed the bedrock for scholarship and policy in education and sociology for a generation'.

Yeats once wrote of a man that he was blessed and had the power to bless. Such was Jim Coleman. *We* are blessed to have shared his company and to share this parting.

9 Gary S. Becker
Departments of Economics and Sociology, University of Chicago

Jim and I both returned to Chicago in the early 1970s as university professors. I do not remember much contact with him until 1974 and 1975 when he gave two papers in our Workshop on Applications of Economics. One was his controversial study of white flight from compulsory busing of black students into what had been mainly white schools. Using a simple model of rational choice, he concluded that whites moved out of public schools in massive numbers from communities with busing programs.

I was highly impressed by the study, even though it was criticized for some of its statistical techniques. It showed an imaginative use of rational choice theory to analyze an immensely important and politically charged subject. My respect for Jim's talents and character grew rapidly after that. But some leading members of the American Sociological Association were so upset by the conclusions of his study that they moved to have him expelled from the association. Fortunately the move failed, but for many years Jim refused to go to the annual meetings of this association because that episode bothered him enormously.

Jim and I had only a modest amount of direct contact after that until he shyly asked in 1984 whether I would consider a joint appointment in sociology. He appeared to expect that I would turn him down, but I was happy to accept for several reasons. It was an excellent department, and in this way I would have more contact with Jim. Shortly afterwards, we decided to start an interdisciplinary evening seminar on rational choice in the social sciences. This seminar succeeded beyond our wildest expectations. We attracted outstanding faculty and students from many disciplines who attended on a regular basis.

The seminar soon acquired a world-wide reputation as a center for hard-hitting probing discussions of both the strengths and weaknesses of rational choice theory in interpreting social, political, economic and other behavior. We began to receive far more requests each year than we could accommodate from scholars who wanted the opportunity to give a paper and be attacked at the seminar. But we sometimes had to admonish speakers not to interrupt too often, so that the discussion among the participants could proceed more smoothly.

Jim was quite active during the discussions. He was sympathetic to the speaker's point of view, and yet critical when that was called for. Our comments were usually in agreement, but occasionally we had sharp differences of opinion. But these differences never for a moment affected our personal relations.

Of course, in planning and running the seminar, Jim and I had frequent contact. He was tough-minded and stubborn, yet at the same time was appropriately flexible. In more than ten years of running the seminar we seldom disagreed on who was worth inviting and whether a seminar failed or succeeded. I was pleasantly surprised how similar our views were on most issues, from national and university politics to the evaluation of economic and sociological research.

When the seminar began, his theoretical interests were moving rapidly toward rational choice, and he began to work on his magnum opus, *Foundations of Social Theory*. In this work Coleman takes over the basic assumption of rational choice theory as developed in economics; namely, that individuals choose those actions that maximize their utility, considering both benefits and costs of the actions. But Jim makes a major advance by incorporating social structure into the theory. He shows how individual choices are greatly affected by social norms, peer pressure, a desire to emulate leaders and other group influences.

Jim was not content simply to take social structure as given. He recognized that it was desirable to try to build up the structure from the interactions among the choices of individuals and other actors. He attempted to explain the development of norms and other social structures through aggregating the behavior of individual and corporate actors. He called this the micro to macro problem in sociology, and believed it was the major challenge to be overcome before there would be a satisfactory theory of social behavior.

Foundations, published in 1990, is already a classic and deservedly so. It contains a rich mixture of imaginative theorizing and common examples of social behavior. The theory is developed both verbally and with mathematics in order to reach the many potentially interested readers who lack sufficient mathematical tools, and also to attract those who prefer a more concise formal statement. His decision to use both modes of expression was wise, for it not only widened the audience, but also enriched the book since each part contains many insights that are not fully captured by the other part.

He considers individual actors and corporate actors, as in collective action through voting and interest group politics. He has exciting chapters on norms and social capital — the concept of social capital is already being extensively applied by economists and sociologists to explain the influence of communities on behavior. Social capital is an aspect of human capital — and Jim first presented his work on social capital at the 1987 meetings of the American Economics Association that I organized. Social capital describes a class of interdependencies among individuals that arise from community structure. For example, I benefit when my neighbors are alert to strangers who may be trying to break into my house.

As the other speakers have made clear, Jim was no ivory tower theorist removed from the real world. Although *Foundations* contains less systematic quantitative evidence of the type found in many of his other studies, it does have a stimulating dialogue between theory and evidence. The theory is used to explain, among other things, bank runs, fads and fashions, acquisitive crazes, behavior in communes, trust in business and social relations, management practices — including quality circles — voting, the organization of schools, and peer pressure on students.

I claimed on the jacket of *Foundations* that this is 'the most important book in social theory in a long time'. Its impact has strongly confirmed this judgment. The book is having an especially large influence on the slowly growing number of younger sociologists interested in rational choice theory, and the more rapidly expanding number of younger economists and political scientists who are beginning to appreciate the importance of social structure for economic and political behavior.

Jim greatly influenced my own work as it shifted during the past decade toward greater attention to social influences on behavior. Jim said that I was becoming a sociologist. He meant it, and I took it as a fine compliment. I will forever be indebted to Jim for this impact on my approach to explaining behavior.

Jim was a truly outstanding and innovative sociologist; in my judgment he was the most creative sociologist of his generation. He was also a better analyst of real economic problems than most economists who know far more economic theory. He had a working knowledge of economic theory and public choice theory, along with his mastery of sociological theory. In addition, he had a vast command of evidence, examples and the social science literature.

Throughout his long career Jim was concerned both with improving sociological theory by placing it on a more rigorous and firmer foundation, and with the quantitative analysis of behavior in social situations. He combined exceptional ability with fertile imagination, and courage to go against received opinion and bear vicious attacks. This helps to explain his enormous contributions to sociology and social science more generally.

I would like to end on a more personal note. My wife Guity heard me often repeat how much I liked and admired Jim. I looked forward to our time together, not only because I learned so much from him, nor because our views and prejudices about the world were so similar. He was loyal and generous as well as creative, and willing to stand up and be counted for what he believed. This is an extremely rare trait in academia, and probably in most other fields as well.

It is common at memorial services to indicate that the world has lost an outstanding person, but in Jim Coleman's case that is no exaggeration. There is no way anyone can express the loss to his family, close friends and colleagues. Fortunately, the impact of his work and personality, and the memories of our association with him, cannot be taken away.

10   *Marta Tienda*
Chair, Department of Sociology, University of Chicago

On behalf of the Department of Sociology, the Social Science Division, National Opinion Research Center, and the university community, I would like to thank the speakers for their inspiring comments; we have all been enriched by this event and by the privilege of knowing James Coleman.

I would like to thank Jim's students, Hua-Ying Wang, Seh-Ahn Lee, Katie Schiller, Steven Plank and Michael Rosenfeld, for serving as ushers. We are especially grateful for Debra Milton's dedicated service in orchestrating this celebration for Jim's life.

Willie Jasso, a former Hopkins student of Jim's, was unable to attend, but like so many others who sent their condolences and private eulogies, she is here in spirit. Her words are a fitting close. I quote: 'In every scholar's life, there are a few teachers who shape forever one's perspective, who provide a sense of the important and interesting questions, who enlarge one's vision and one's toolbox. Coleman did all of these things for countless [scholars], including [those] as yet unborn'.

This Memorial Service on Jim's behalf was made possible through the generous support of the Office of the Provost, the Division of Social Sciences, the National Opinion Research Center, and the Coleman family, who cordially invite you to a reception at the Quadrangle Club. Thank you kindly for your presence.

Appendix 4: Curriculum Vitae and Publications of James S. Coleman, Compiled by Debra A. Milton

Date of Birth: 12 May 1926
Place of Birth: Bedford, Indiana

Education

1944 DuPont Manual High School, Louisville, Kentucky
1949 BS, Purdue University
1955 PhD, Columbia University (Sociology)

Academic and Research Experience

1953–55 Research Associate, Bureau of Applied Social Research, Columbia University
1956–59 Assistant Professor, Department of Sociology, University of Chicago
1959–73 Associate Professor, Professor, Department of Social Relations, Johns Hopkins University
1973– Professor, Department of Sociology, University of Chicago; Researcher, National Opinion Research Center (NORC)

Awards and Activities

Fellow, Center for Advanced Study in the Behavioral Sciences, 1955–56
American Academy of Arts and Sciences, 1966
National Academy of Education, 1966
Guggenheim Fellow, 1966
John Dewey Society Award for Distinguished Service to Education, 1969
Honorary Doctor of Laws, Purdue University, 1970
Nicholas Murray Butler Medal in Silver, Columbia University, 1970
American Philosophical Society, 1970
President's Science Advisory Committee, 1970–73
National Academy of Sciences, 1972
Phi Beta Kappa, 1972
Honorary Doctor of Science, State University of New York, 1974
Honorary Professor of Sociology, University of Vienna, 1978

Fellow, Wissenschaftskolleg zu Berlin, 1981–82
Honorary Doctor of Humane Letters, State University of New York at Albany, 1984
Royal Swedish Academy of Sciences, 1984
Doctor Philosophiae Honoris Causa, Hebrew University of Jerusalem, 1986
Honorary Doctor of Laws, University of Southern California, 1987
Doctor Honoris Causa, Vrije Universiteit Brussels, 1987
Honorary Doctorate in Economics and Sociology, University of Erlangen-
    Nuremberg, Nuremberg, West Germany, 1988
Doctor Philosophiae Honoris Causa, University of Haifa, 1992
Honorary Doctor of Laws, Marquette University, 1991
President, American Sociological Association, 1991–92
Fulbright Senior Scholar, European University Institute, 1993
Honorary Member, Polish Sociological Association, 1994
Phoenix Prize, University of Chicago, 1994
Honorary Doctor of Laws, University of Notre Dame, 1994

Memberships

American Sociological Association
Sociological Research Association

Publications

Books and monographs.
   1   *Union Democracy.* Seymour M. Lipset, Martin A. Trow and James S. Coleman.
       New York: The Free Press of Glencoe, 1956.
   2   *Community Conflict.* New York: The Free Press of Glencoe, 1957.
   3   *Social Climates in High Schools*, Cooperative Research Monograph No. 4, US
       Department of Health, Education, and Welfare, 1961.
   4   *The Adolescent Society.* New York: The Free Press of Glencoe, 1961.
   5   *Introduction to Mathematical Sociology.* New York: The Free Press of Glencoe,
       1964.
   6   *Models of Change and Response Uncertainty.* Englewood Cliffs, NJ: Prentice-Hall,
       1964.
   7   *Adolescents and the Schools.* New York: Basic Books, 1965.
   8   *Equality of Educational Opportunity.* Washington, D.C.: US Government Printing
       Office, 1966. (With E.Q. Campbell, C.J. Hobson, J. McPartland, A.M. Mood,
       F.D. Weinfeld and R.L. York.)
   9   *Medical Innovation*, James S. Coleman, Elihu Katz and Herbert Menzel.
       Indianapolis: Bobbs-Merrill, 1966.
  10   *Macrosociology: Research and Theory*, James S. Coleman, Amitai Etzioni and John
       Porter. Boston: Allyn and Bacon, 1970. 'Properties of Collectivities', pp. 5–101.
  11   *Resources for Social Change: Race in the United States.* New York: John Wiley,
       1971.
  12   *Information Systems and Performance Measures in Schools*, James S. Coleman and
       Nancy L. Karweit. New Jersey: Educational Technology Publications, 1972.

13 *The Mathematics of Collective Action*. London: Heinemann Educational Books, 1973.

14 *Youth: Transition to Adulthood*. Report of the Panel on Youth of the President's Science Advisory Committee, June 1973, James S. Coleman, Chairman, *et al*. Washington: US Government Printing Office, 1973; Chicago: University of Chicago Press, 1974.

15 *Power and the Structure of Society*. New York: W.W. Norton, 1974.

16 *Qualitative and Quantitative Social Research: Papers in Honor of Paul F. Lazarsfeld*. Robert K. Merton and Peter Rossi, eds. New York: The Free Press, 1979.

17 *Longitudinal Data Analysis*. New York: Basic Books, 1981.

18 *The Asymmetric Society*. Syracuse, NY: Syracuse University Press, 1982.

19 *High School Achievement: Public, Catholic, and Private Schools Compared*. New York: Basic Books, 1982. (With Thomas Hoffer and Sally Kilgore.)

20 *Becoming Adult in a Changing Society*. Paris: OECD, 1985. (With Torsten Husén.)

21 *Approaches to Social Theory*. Russell Sage Foundation, 1986. (Edited with Siegwart Lindenberg and Stefan Nowak.)

22 *Individual Interests and Collective Action*. Cambridge: Cambridge University Press, 1986.

23 *Public and Private High Schools: The Impact of Communities*. New York: Basic Books, 1987. (With Thomas Hoffer.)

24 *Foundations of Social Theory*. Cambridge, MA: Harvard University Press, 1990.

25 *Equality and Achievement in Education*. Boulder, CO: Westview Press, 1990.

26 *Social Theory for a Changing Society*. Boulder, CO: Westview Press; New York: Russell Sage Foundation, 1991. (Edited with Pierre Bourdieu.)

27 *Rational Choice Theory: Advocacy and Critique*, Volume 7: Key Issues in Sociological Theory. Newbury Park, CA: Sage Publications, 1992. (Edited with Thomas J. Fararo.)

28 *Parents, Their Children, and Schools*. Boulder, CO: Westview Press, 1993. (Edited with Barbara Schneider.)

Papers and chapters.

1 'An Expository Analysis of Some of Rashevsky's Social Behavior Models,' Ch. 3, pp. 105–65, in *Mathematical Thinking in the Social Sciences*, P.F. Lazarsfeld (ed.). New York: The Free Press of Glencoe, 1954.

2 'Social Cleavage and Religious Conflict,' *Journal of Social Issues*, Vol. 12, No. 3, 1956, pp. 44–56.

3 'Multidimensional Scale Analysis,' *American Journal of Sociology*, Vol. 63, No. 3, November 1957, pp. 253–63.

4 'The Diffusion of an Innovation among Physicians,' James S. Coleman, Elihu Katz and Herbert Menzel, *Sociometry*, Vol. 20, No. 4, December 1957, pp. 253–70.

5 'A Program of Research in Mass Dynamics,' James S. Coleman and William N. McPhee, *PROD*, Vol. 1, No. 4, March 1958, pp. 6–10.

6 'Relational Analysis: The Study of Social Organization with Survey Methods,' *Human Organization*, Vol. 17, No. 4, 1958, pp. 28–36.

7 'Social Processes in Physicians' Adoption of a New Drug,' Herbert Menzel, Elihu Katz and James S. Coleman, *Journal of Chronic Diseases*, Vol. 9, No. 1, January 1959, pp. 1–19.

8 'Dimensions of Being Modern in Medical Practice,' James S. Coleman, Elihu Katz and Herbert Menzel, *Journal of Chronic Diseases*, Vol. 9, No. 1, January 1959, pp. 20–40.

9 'Academic Achievement and the Structure of Competition.' *Harvard Educational Review*, Vol. 29, No. 4, Fall 1959, pp. 330–51.

10 'Style and Substance in American High Schools.' *College Admissions 6*, New York: College Entrance Examination Board, 1959, pp. 9–21.

11 'The Adolescent Subculture and Academic Achievement.' *American Journal of Sociology*, Vol. 65, No. 4, January 1960, pp. 337–47.

12 'Electronic Processing of Sociometric Data for Groups up to 1000 in Size,' James S. Coleman and Duncan MacRae, Jr., *American Sociological Review*, Vol. 25, No. 5, October 1960, pp. 722–7.

13 'A Sociologist Suggests New Perspectives,' in *The Adolescent Citizen*, Franklin Patterson (ed.). New York: The Free Press of Glencoe, 1960.

14 'The Mathematical Study of Small Groups,' Part 1, pp. 7–149, in *Mathematical Thinking in the Measurement of Behavior*, Herbert Solomon (ed.), New York: The Free Press of Glencoe, 1960.

15 'Analysis of Social Structures and Simulation of Social Processes with Electronic Computers,' *Educational and Psychological Measurement*, Vol. 21, No. 1, Spring 1961, pp. 203–18.

16 'The Competition for Adolescent Energies,' *Phi Delta Kappan*, Vol. 42, No. 6, March 1961, pp. 231–6.

17 'The Equilibrium Size Distribution of Freely-Forming Groups,' *Sociometry*, Vol. 24, No. 1, March 1961, pp. 36–45.

18 'Athletics in High Schools,' *The Annals of the American Academy of Political and Social Science*, Vol. 338, November 1961, pp. 33–4.

19 'Comment on Three "Climate of Opinion" Studies,' *Public Opinion Quarterly*, Vol. 25, Winter 1961, pp. 608–10.

20 'Community Disorganization,' Part 12, pp. 553–604, in *Contemporary Social Problems*, Robert K. Merton and Robert A. Nisbet (eds), New York: Harcourt, Brace and World, 1961.

21 'Teen-agers and Their Crowd,' *The PTA Magazine*, Vol. 56, No. 7, March 1962.

22 'Strengthening the Behavioral Sciences,' *Science*, Vol. 136, No. 3512, 20 April, 1962, pp. 233–41. Behavioral Sciences Subpanel of the President's Science Advisory Committee.

23 'Transformation of the Young,' *The Johns Hopkins Magazine*, May–June 1962.

24 'Comment on Harrison White, "Chance Models of Systems of Causal Groups",' *Sociometry*, Vol. 25, No. 2, June 1962, pp. 172–6.

25 'Can Consumer Pressures Improve the Quality of Medical Practice?' *Journal of Chronic Diseases*, Vol. 15, June 1962, pp. 1069–76.

26 'Reward Structures and the Allocation of Effort,' Ch. 8, pp. 119–32, in *Mathematical Methods in Small Group Processes*, Criswell, Soloman and Suppes (eds), Stanford: Stanford University Press, 1962.

27 'Comment on "On the Concept of Influence",' *Public Opinion Quarterly*, Vol. 27, Spring 1963, pp. 63–82.

28 'Surplus Youth: A Future Without Jobs,' *The Nation*, 25 May 1963, pp. 439–43.

29 'High School Social Status, College Plans, and Interest in Academic Achievement: A Panel Analysis.' *American Sociological Review*, Vol. 28, No. 6, December 1963, pp. 905–18.

30 'Comments,' pp. 158–61, in *The Discipline of Education*, James L. Kuethe and John Walton (eds). Madison: University of Wisconsin Press, 1963.

31 'Collective Decisions,' *Sociological Inquiry*, Spring 1964, pp. 166–81.

32 'Implications of the Findings on Alienation,' Response to Melvin Seeman's 'Alienation and Social Learning in a Reformatory,' *American Journal of Sociology*, Vol. 70, No. 1, July 1964, pp. 76–84.

33 'Research in Autonomy and Responsibility in Adolescents.' *Journal of the National Association of Women Deans and Counselors*, Vol. 27, No. 1, Fall 1964, pp. 2–9.

34 'Computers and Election Analysis: The *New York Times* Project,' James S. Coleman, Ernest Heau, Robert Peabody and Leo Rigsby, *Public Opinion Quarterly*, Vol. 28, Fall 1964, pp. 418–46.

35 Research Chronicle: 'The Adolescent Society,' pp. 184–211, in *Sociologists at Work*, Phillip E. Hammond (ed.), New York: Basic Books, 1964.

36 'Mathematical Models and Computer Simulation,' Ch. 27, pp. 1027–62, in *Handbook of Modern Sociology*, Robert E.L. Faris (ed.), Chicago: Rand McNally and Company, 1964.

37 'The Coming Crisis in Secondary Education,' Response to Ivor Kraft, *The Bulletin of the National Association of Secondary-School Principals*, Vol. 49, No. 298, February 1965, pp. 49–60.

38 'Social Change — Impact on the Adolescent,' *The Bulletin of the National Association of Secondary-School Principals*, Vol. 49, No. 300, April 1965, pp. 11–14.

39 'Family and Peer Influences in College Plans of High School Students,' Edward L. McDill and James S. Coleman, *Sociology of Education*, Vol. 38, No. 2, Winter 1965, pp. 112–26.

40 'The Use of Electronic Computers in the Study of Social Organization,' *European Journal of Sociology*, Vol. 6, No. 1, 1965, pp. 89–107.

41 'Some Sociological Models,' Ch. 3, pp. 175–212, in *Mathematics and Social Sciences*, Saul Sternberg, V. Capecchi, T. Kloek and C.T. Leenders (eds), Paris: Mouton, 1965.

42 'Studies of Changes in Response Over Time — Changes in Belief in the Weeks Following the Assassination,' pp. 256–268, in *The Kennedy Assassination and the American Public: Social Communication in Crisis*, Bradley S. Greenberg and Edwin B. Parker (eds), Stanford: Stanford University Press, 1965.

43 'Foundations for a Theory of Collective Decisions,' *American Journal of Sociology*, Vol. 71, No. 6, May 1966.

44 'Games with Simulated Environments in Learning,' Sarane S. Boocock and James S. Coleman, *Sociology of Education*, Vol. 39, No. 3, Summer 1966.

45 'Individual Interests and Collective Action,' pp. 49–62, in *Papers on Non-Market Decision-Making*, Gordon Tullock (ed.), Charlottesville, VA: Thomas Jefferson Center for Political Economy, University of Virginia, 1966.

46 'Equal Schools or Equal Students?' *The Public Interest*, No. 4, Summer 1966.

47 'Female Status and Premarital Sexual Codes,' *American Journal of Sociology*, Vol. 72, No. 2, September 1966.

48 'Introduction: In Defense of Games,' Part 1, *American Behavioral Scientist*, Vol. 10, No. 2, October 1966.

49   *Simulation Games and Learning Behavior*, Parts 1 and 2, Special Issues of *American Behavioral Scientist*, J.S. Coleman, S. Boocock and E.O. Schild (eds), October and November 1966.

50   'The Possibility of a Social Welfare Function,' *American Economic Review*, Vol. 56, No. 5, December 1966, pp. 1105–22.

51   'Peer Cultures and Education in Modern Society,' pp. 244–69, in *College Peer Groups*, Theodore M. Newcomb and Everett K. Wilson (eds), Chicago: Aldine, 1966.

52   'Learning through Games,' *NEA Journal*, Vol. 56, No. 1, January 1967.

53   'Toward Open Schools,' *The Public Interest*, No. 9, Fall 1967.

54   'Game Models of Economic and Political Systems,' pp. 30–44, in *The Study of Total Societies*, Samuel Z. Klausner (ed.), New York: Anchor Books, 1967.

55   'Games — New Tools for Learning,' *Scholastic Teacher*, Vol. 15, No. 8, 9 November 1967.

56   'Mathematical Models in Sociology,' in *Transactions of the Sixth World Congress of Sociology*, Evian, 4–11 September 1966. Vol. 2 (International Sociological Association, 1967).

57   'Formalisierung und Simulation von Interaktionen in einer Drei-Personen-Gruppe,' Ch. 9, pp. 169–90, in *Formalisierte Modelle in der Soziologie*, Renate Mayntz (ed.), Berlin: Herman Luchterland Verlag, 1967.

58   'The Possibility of a Social Welfare Function: Reply,' *American Economic Review*, Vol. 17, No. 5, December 1967, pp. 1311–17.

59   'The Concept of Equality of Educational Opportunity,' *Harvard Educational Review*, Vol. 38, No. 1, Winter 1968, pp. 7–22.

60   'Academic Games and Learning,' *Proceedings of the 1967 Invitational Conference on Testing Problems*. Princeton, NJ: Educational Testing Service, 1968.

61   'The Mathematical Study of Change,' pp. 428–78, in *Methodology in Social Research*, Hubert M. and Ann B. Blalock (eds), New York: McGraw-Hill, 1968.

62   'Review Symposium of Harold Garfinkel, *Studies in Ethnomethodology*,' *American Sociological Review*, Vol. 33, No. 1, February 1968, pp. 126–30.

63   'Equality of Educational Opportunity: Reply to Bowles and Levin.' *Journal of Human Resources*, Vol. 3, No. 2, Spring 1968, pp. 237–46.

64   'Benefits, Costs, and Equity,' *The Public Interest*, No. 11, Spring 1968, pp. 118–22.

65   'Responsibility of Schools in the Provision of Equal Educational Opportunity.' *The Bulletin of the National Association of Secondary School Principles*, Vol. 52, No. 328, May 1968, pp. 179–90.

66   'Social Processes and Social Simulation Games,' pp. 29–51, in *Simulation Games and Learning*, Sarane S. Boocock and E.O. Schild (eds), Beverly Hills, CA: Sage Publications, 1968.

67   'The Marginal Utility of a Vote Commitment,' *Public Choice*, Vol. 5, Fall 1968, pp. 39–58.

68   'Equality of Educational Opportunity.' *Integrated Education*, Vol. 6, No. 5, September–October 1968, Issue 35.

69   'Educational and Urbanism: An Introductory Statement,' *Education and Urban Society*, Vol. 1, No. 1, November 1968, pp. 5–8.

70   'Interne Machtstruktur und Handlungsfähigkeit von Körperschaften,' (Control of Collectivities and the Power of a Collectivity to Act), *AIAS Informationen*, Part 1: 2, 1968/69, pp. 139–51; Part 2: 5/6, 1969, pp. 379–408.

71 'A Symposium: Evaluating Educational Programs,' *Urban Review*, Vol. 3, No. 4, February 1969, pp. 6–8.

72 'The Methods of Sociology,' pp. 86–114, in *A Design for Sociology: Scope, Objectives, and Methods*, Monograph No. 9, Robert Bierstedt (ed.), Philadelphia: American Academy of Political and Social Science, April 1969.

73 'Questions and Answers: Some Good Things, Some Bad,' Interview in *Southern Education Report*, Vol. 4, No. 10, June 1969.

74 'Games as Vehicles for Social Theory,' *American Behavioral Scientist*, Vol. 12, No. 6, July–August 1969, pp. 2–6.

75 'The Symmetry Principle in College Choice.' *College Board Review*, No. 73, Fall 1969, pp. 5–10.

76 'Incentives in American Education,' *Educate*, Vol. 2, No. 4, September 1969, pp. 18–24.

77 'Equality of Educational Opportunity, Reexamined.' *Socio-Economic Planning Sciences*, Vol. 2, 1969, pp. 347–54.

78 'Beyond Pareto Optimality,' pp. 415–39, in *Philosophy, Science, and Method: Essays in Honor of Ernest Nagel*, Sidney Morgenbesser, Patrick Suppes and Morton White (eds), New York: St Martin's Press, 1969.

79 'Race Relations and Social Change,' pp. 274–341, in *Race and the Social Sciences*, Irwin Katz and Patricia Gurin (eds), New York: Basic Books, 1969.

80 'A Brief Summary of the Coleman Report,' pp. 253–9, in *Equal Educational Opportunity*. Cambridge, MA: Harvard University Press, 1969.

81 'The Struggle for Control of Education,' Ch. 5. pp. 64–88, in *Education and Social Policy: Local Control of Education*, C.A. Bowers, I. Housego and D. Dyke (eds), New York: Random House, 1970.

82 'The Social Basis of Markets and Governments,' pp. 37–49, in *Urban Processes as Viewed by the Social Sciences*. Washington: The Urban Institute, 1970.

83 'Education in Cities,' pp. 202–19, in *The Conscience of the City*, Martin Meyerson (ed.), New York: George Braziller, Daedalus Library, 1970.

84 'Schools Look to Society as a Resource,' *The New York Times Annual Education Review*, Monday, 12 January 1970, p. 66.

85 'Reply to Cain and Watts,' *American Sociological Review*, Vol. 35, No. 2, April 1970, pp. 242–9.

86 'The Benefits of Coalition,' *Public Choice*, Vol. 8, Spring 1970, pp. 45–61.

87 'Political Money,' *American Political Science Review*, Vol. 64, No. 4, December 1970, pp. 1074–87.

88 'Social Inventions,' *Social Forces*, Vol. 4, No. 2, December 1970, pp. 163–73.

89 'Interpretations of Adolescent Culture,' pp. 20–29, in *The Psychopathology of Adolescence*, Joseph Zubin and Alfred M. Freedman (eds), New York: Grune and Stratton, 1970.

90 'Comments on Conference,' pp. 174–5, in *Do Teachers Make a Difference?* Washington: US Government Printing Office, 1970.

91 'Clustering in N Dimensions by Use of a System of Forces,' *Journal of Mathematical Sociology*, Vol. 1, No. 1, January 1971, pp. 1–47.

92 'New Incentives for Schools,' Ch. 5, in *New Models for American Education*, James W. Guthrie and Edward Wynne (eds), Englewood Cliffs, NJ: Prentice-Hall, 1971.

93 'Education in Modern Society,' Ch. 4, in *Computers, Communications, and the*

Public Interest, Martin Greenberger (ed.), Baltimore, MD: Johns Hopkins Press, 1971.

94 'Multivariate Analysis for Attribute Data,' in *Sociological Methodology: 1970*, Edgar F. Borgatta and George W. Bohrnstedt (eds), San Francisco: Jossey-Bass, 1971.

95 'Conflicting Theories of Social Change,' *American Behavioral Scientist*, Vol. 14, No. 5, May–June 1971, pp. 633–50.

96 'Internal Processes Governing Party Positions in Elections,' *Public Choice*, Vol. 11, Fall 1971, pp. 35–60.

97 'Social Systems,' in *Hierarchically Organized Systems in Theory and Practice*, Paul A. Weiss (ed.), New York: Hafner, 1971.

98 'The Role of Modern Technology in Relation to Simulation and Games of Learning,' in *To Improve Learning: An Evaluation of Instructional Technology*, Sidney G. Tickton (ed.), New York: Bowker, 1971.

99 'Analysis and Simulation of Reference Group Processes,' (with Frank Waldorf), in *Computer Simulation of Human Behavior*, J.M. Dutton and W.H. Starbuck (eds), New York: Wiley, 1971.

100 'Increasing Educational Opportunity: Research Problems and Results,' in *The Conditions for Educational Equality*, Sterling M. McMurrin (ed.), New York: Committee for Economic Development, 1971.

101 'Control of Collectivities and the Power of a Collectivity to Act,' in *Social Choice*, B. Lieberman (ed.), London: Gordon, 1971.

102 'The Children Have Outgrown the Schools,' *Psychology Today*, Vol. 5, No. 9, February 1972.

103 'The Evaluation of Equality of Educational Opportunity,' in *On Equality of Educational Opportunity*, Frederick Mosteller and Daniel P. Moynihan (eds), New York: Random, 1972.

104 'The Positions of Political Parties in Elections,' in *Probability Models of Collective Decision Making*, Richard G. Niemi and Herbert F. Weisberg (eds), Columbus, OH: Charles E. Merrill, 1972.

105 'Paul Lazarsfeld's Work in Survey Research and Mathematical Sociology,' pp. 395–410, in *Qualitative Analysis*, Paul F. Lazarsfeld, Boston: Allyn and Bacon, 1972.

106 'White and Black Careers during the First Decade of Labor Force Experience. Part 1: Occupational Status,' (with Z.D. Blum, A.B. Sørensen and P.H. Rossi), *Social Science Research*, Vol. 1, No. 3, September 1972, pp. 243–70.

107 'White and Black Careers during the First Decade of Labor Force Experience. Part 3: Occupational Status and Income Together,' (with C.C. Berry and Z.D. Blum), *Social Science Research*, Vol. 1, No. 3, September 1972, pp. 293–304.

108 'Integration of Sociology and the Other Social Sciences through Policy Analysis', Monograph No. 14, James C. Charlesworth (ed.), Philadelphia: American Academy of Political and Social Sciences, October 1972.

109 'Systems of Social Exchange,' *Journal of Mathematical Sociology*, Vol. 2, 1972, pp. 145–63.

110 'Flow Models for Occupational Structure,' pp. 80–93, in *Input-Output Techniques*, A. Brody and A.P. Carter (eds), Amsterdam: North-Holland, 1972.

111 'Social and Cultural Integration and Educational Policy,' pp. 125–32, in *Rethinking Urban Education*, H.J. Walberg and A.K. Kopan (eds), San Francisco: Jossey-Bass, 1972.

112 'Collective Decisions and Collective Action,' in *Philosophy, Politics and Society*, P. Laslett, W.G. Runciman and Q. Skinner (eds), Oxford: Basil Blackwell, 1972.

113 'Policy Research in the Social Sciences.' New Jersey: General Learning Press, 1972.

114 'How Do the Young Become Adults?' *Review of Educational Research*, Vol. 42, No. 4, 1972; *Phi Delta Kappan*, December 1972; and in *Changing Schools: Alternatives from Educational Research*, M.C. Wittrock (ed.), Englewood Cliffs, NJ: Prentice-Hall, 1973.

115 'Loss of Power,' *American Sociological Review*, Vol. 38, No. 1, February 1973, pp. 1–17.

116 'Equality of Opportunity and Equality of Results,' *Harvard Educational Review*, Vol. 43, No. 1, 1973, pp. 129–37. Review of Jencks *et al.*, *Inequality*.

117 'Review Symposium of Jencks *et al. Inequality*,' *American Journal of Sociology*, Vol. 78, No. 6, May 1973.

118 'The University and Society's New Demands upon It,' pp. 359–399, in *Content and Context: Essays on College Education*, Carl Kaysen (ed.), A Report prepared for the Carnegie Commission on Higher Education. New York: McGraw-Hill, 1973.

119 'Theoretical Bases for Parameters of Stochastic Processes,' pp. 17–28, in *The Sociological Review Monograph No. 19: Stochastic Processes in Sociology*, P. Halmos and R.E.A. Mapes (eds), University of Keele, July 1973.

120 'The Hopkins Games Program: Conclusions from Seven Years of Research,' *Educational Researcher*, Vol. 2, No. 8, August 1973, pp. 3–7.

121 'A Model for the Mutual Effects of Attributes,' in *Logic, Methodology and Philosophy of Science IV*, P. Suppes, L. Henkin, A. Joja and G.C. Moisil (eds), Amsterdam: North Holland, 1973.

122 'The Transition from Youth to Adult,' *New York University of Education Quarterly*, Vol. 5, No. 3, Spring 1974, pp. 2–5.

123 'Processes of Concentration and Dispersal of Power in Social Systems,' *Social Science Information*, Vol. 13, No. 2, April 1974, pp. 7–18.

124 'Urban System Performance.' Erik Van Hove, James S. Coleman, Kenneth Rabben and Nancy Karweit, pp. 153–174, in *Evaluating Educational Performance*, Herbert J. Walberg (ed.), Berkeley, CA: McCutchan, 1974.

125 'Inequality, Sociology, and Moral Philosophy,' *American Journal of Sociology*, Vol. 80, No. 3, November 1974, pp. 739–64.

126 'Comments on Responses to *Youth: Transition to Adulthood*.' *School Review*, Vol. 83, No. 1, November 1974, pp. 139–44.

127 'Recent Developments in American Sociological Methods,' *Polish Sociological Bulletin*, No. 2, 1974.

128 'What Is Meant by "An Equal Educational Opportunity"?' *Oxford Review of Education*, Vol. 1, No. 1, 1975, pp. 27–9.

129 'Analysis of Occupational Mobility by Models of Occupational Flow,' pp. 319–34, in *Social Indicator Models*, Kenneth C. Land and Seymour Spilerman (eds), New York: Russell Sage Foundation, 1975.

130 'Recent Trends in School Integration,' *Educational Researcher*, Vol. 4, No. 7, July–August 1975, pp. 3–12.

131 'Methods and Results in the IEA Studies of Effects of School on Learning,' *Review of Educational Research*, Vol. 45, No. 3, Summer 1975, pp. 335–86.

132 'Trends in School Segregation, 1968–73,' James Coleman, Sara Kelly and John Moore. Washington, D.C.: The Urban Institute, August 1975.

133 'Racial Segregation in the Schools: New Research with New Policy Implications,' *Phi Delta Kappan*, Vol. 57, No. 2, October 1975.

134 'Social Research and Advocacy: A Response to Young and Bress,' *Phi Delta Kappan*, Vol. 57, No. 3, November 1975, pp. 166–9.

135 'Equality and Liberty in Education.' *Education Tomorrow: For Whom: Why?* Address given in the plenary sessions at the 1975 National Forum, College Entrance Examination Board, pp. 16–22.

136 'Problems of Conceptualization and Measurement in Studying Policy Impacts,' in *Public Policy Evaluation*, Kenneth M. Dolbeare (ed.), Beverly Hills, CA: Sage Publications, 1975, pp. 19–40.

137 'Legitimate and Illegitimate Use of Power,' pp. 221–36, in *The Idea of Social Structure*, Lewis A. Coser (ed.), New York: Harcourt, Brace, Jovanovich, 1975.

138 'Social Structure and a Theory of Action,' *Polish Sociological Bulletin*, No. 1–2, 1975.

139 'Social Structure and a Theory of Action,' in *Approaches to the Study of Social Structure*, Peter M. Blau (ed.), New York: The Free Press, 1975, pp. 76–93.

140 'Liberty and Equality in School Desegregation.' *Social Policy*, Vol. 6, No. 4, January/February 1976, pp. 9–13.

141 'A Reply to Green and Pettigrew.' *Phi Delta Kappan*, Vol. 57, No. 7, March 1976, pp. 454–5.

142 'Rawls, Nozick, and Educational Equality.' *The Public Interest*, Vol. 43, Spring 1976, pp. 121–8.

143 'The Ways of Socialization.' *The Center Magazine*, Vol. 9, No. 3, May/June 1976, pp. 3–10.

144 'Regression Analysis for the Comparison of School and Home Effects.' *Social Science Research*, Vol. 5, 1976, pp. 1–20.

145 'Social Science: The Public Disenchantment. A Symposium.' *The American Scholar*, Summer 1976.

146 'Response to Professors Pettigrew and Green.' *Harvard Educational Review*, Vol. 46, No. 2, May 1976, pp. 217–24.

147 'Differences between Experiential and Classroom Learning,' pp. 49–61, in *Experiential Learning: Rationale, Characteristics, and Assessment*, Morris T. Keton and Associates (eds), San Francisco: Jossey-Bass, 1976.

148 'Education' with S. Kelly, pp. 231–80, in *The Urban Predicament*, W. Gorham and N. Glazer (eds), Washington, D.C.: The Urban Institute, 1976.

149 'Individual Rights and the State: A Review Essay.' *American Journal of Sociology*, Vol. 82, No. 2, September 1976, pp. 422–8.

150 'Reply to Klees and Strike.' *American Journal of Sociology*, Vol. 82, No. 1, July 1976, pp. 201–5.

151 'Reply to Condon.' *American Journal of Sociology*, Vol. 82, No. 1, July 1976, pp. 217–18.

152 'The Emergence of Sociology as a Policy Science,' pp. 253–61, in *The Uses of Controversy in Sociology*, L. Coser and O. Larsen (eds), New York: The Free Press, 1976.

153 'Robert Nozick's Anarchy, State, and Utopia.' *Theory and Society*, Vol. 3, 1976, pp. 437–58.

154 'Policy Decisions, Social Science Information, and Education,' *Sociology of Education*, Vol. 49, October 1976, pp. 304–12.

155 'Reply to Hayduk,' *American Sociological Review*, Vol. 41, December 1976, pp. 1080–82.

156 'Social Action Systems,' pp. 11–50, in *Problems of Formalization in the Social Sciences*. Ossolineum, 1977.

157 'Notes on the Study of Power,' pp. 183–97, in *Power, Paradigms, and Community Research*, Beverly Hills, CA: Sage Publications, 1977.

158 'Population Stability and Equal Rights.' *Society*, Vol. 14, No. 4, May/June 1977, pp. 34–6.

159 'Constitutional Power in Experimental Health Service and Delivery Systems.' *Public Choice*, Vol. 29, Summer 1977, pp. 1–19.

160 'Can We Revitalize Our Cities?' *Challenge*, Vol. 20, No. 5, November/December 1977, pp. 23–43.

161 'Introduction: Choice in American Education', pp. 1–12, in *Parents, Teachers, and Children: Prospects for Choice in American Education*, San Francisco, CA: Institute for Contemporary Studies.

162 'The Balance between Rights Individually Held and Rights Collectively Held.' *Arizona Law Review*, Vol. 19, No. 1, 1978.

163 'Social Processes and Social Policy in the Stable Metropolis,' pp. 43–62, in *The Mature Metropolis*, Charles L. Leven (ed.), Lexington, MA: D.C. Heath and Company, 1978.

164 'The Corporate Structure of the Economy and Contributions to Income Inequality,' pp. 99–125, in *Mathematische Ansätze zur Analyse sozialer Macht*. Duisburg, Germany: Verlag der sozialwissenschaftlichen Kooperative, 1978. (With Anthony Babinec.)

165 'The Corporate Structure of the Economy and Its Effects on Income.' *Zeitschrift für Soziologie*, Jg. 7, Heft 4, October 1978, pp. 335–46.

166 'New Incentives for Desegregation.' *Human Rights*, Vol. 7, No. 3, Fall 1978, pp. 10–15.

167 'Sociological Analysis and Social Policy,' pp. 677–700, in *A History of Sociological Analysis*, Tom Bottomore and Robert Nisbet (eds), New York: Basic Books, 1978.

168 'A Theory of Revolt within an Authority Structure.' The Papers of the Peace Science Society, Vol. 28, 1978.

169 'Paul F. Lazarsfeld,' in *International Encyclopedia of Statistics*, William H. Kruskal and Judith M. Tanur (eds), New York: The Free Press, 1979.

170 'Presentation to Massachusetts Legislature — March 30, 1976,' pp. 111–24, in *New Perspectives on School Integration*, Murray Friedman, Roger Meltzer and Charles Miller (eds), Philadelphia: Fortress, 1979.

171 'The Measurement of Societal Growth,' pp. 61–75, in *Societal Growth*, Amos H. Hawley (ed.), New York: The Free Press, 1979.

172 'Some Issues Confronting American Education: Summation,' pp. 156–62, in *Educating All Our Children: An Imperative for Democracy*, Doxey A. Wilkerson (ed.), Westport, CN: Mediax, 1979.

173 'Future Directions for Work in Public Choice,' pp. 287–90, in *Collective Decision Making*, Clifford S. Russell (ed.), Baltimore, MD: Johns Hopkins University Press, 1979.

174 'Conflicts between Policy Research and Decision Making,' pp. 14–21, in *Scientific Expertise and the Public: Conference Proceedings*, Hans Skoie (ed.), Oslo: Studies in Research and Higher Education, September 1979.

175 'Purposive Actors and Mutual Effects,' in *Qualitative and Quantitative Social Research: Papers in Honor of Paul F. Lazarsfeld*, Merton, Coleman, and Rossi (eds), New York: The Free Press, 1979.

176 'Destructive Beliefs and Potential Policies in School Desegregation,' pp. 5–12, in *Detroit Metropolitan City-Suburban Relations*, John W. Smith (ed.), Detroit: Occasional Papers of the Henry Ford Community College, 1979.

177 'The Use of Social Science in the Development of Public Policy.' *IHS-Journal*, Vol. 3, Issue 2, 1979, pp. B13–B19.

178 'Paul F. Lazarsfeld: The Substance and Style of His Work,' pp. 153–74, in *Sociological Traditions from Generation to Generation*, Robert K. Merton and Matilda White Riley (eds), New Jersey: Ablex Publishing Company, 1980.

179 'Rational Actors in Macrosociological Analysis,' pp. 75–91, in *Rational Action: Studies in Philosophy and Social Science*, Ross Harrison (ed.), New York: Cambridge University Press, 1979.

180 'Equilibrating Processes in Social Networks: A Model for Conceptualization and Analysis,' pp. 257–300, *Perspectives in Social Network Research*. Center for Advanced Study in the Behavioral Sciences, 1979.

181 'The Life, Death, and Potential Future of PSAC.' *Technology in Society*, Vol. 2, Nos 1 and 2, 1980, pp. 131–41.

182 'The Structure of Society and the Nature of Social Research.' *Knowledge*, Vol. 1, No. 3, March 1980, pp. 333–50.

183 'Authority Systems.' *Public Opinion Quarterly*, Vol. 44, No. 2, Summer 1980, pp. 143–63.

184 'Conflicts between Policy Research and Policymaking,' pp. 85–93, in *Law and Equality in Education*, Stephen Goldstein (ed.), Jerusalem: The Van Leer Jerusalem Foundation, 1980.

185 'An Introduction to Privacy in Economics and Politics: A Comment.' *Journal of Legal Studies*, Vol. 9, December 1980, pp. 645–8.

186 'Applied Social Research as Evidence in Litigation,' Arthur F. Konopka, Robert J. Hallisey and James Coleman, *The Use, Nonuse, Misuse of Applied Social Research in the Courts*, Michael J. Saks and Charles H. Baron (eds). Abt Books, 1980.

187 'The Role of Incentives in School Desegregation,' pp. 182–93, in *Race and Schooling in the City*, A. Yarmolinsky, L. Liebman and C. Schelling (eds), Cambridge, MA: Harvard University Press, 1981.

188 'Rational Behavior in Panic Situations,' pp. 91–106, in *Toward a Science of Politics*, Gordon Tullock (ed.), Papers in Honor of Duncan Black. Public Choice Center, Virginia Polytechnic Institute and State University, 1981.

189 'Paul F. Lazarsfeld: Inhalt und Wirkung Seines Werkes.' *Kölner Zeitschrift für Soziologie und Sozialpsychologie* (Sonderdruck aus Sonderheft 23/1981), pp. 404–13.

190 'The Role of Policy Research in Social Decision.' Paper presented at the conference on 'Limits to the Future' for the tenth anniversary of the Netherlands Institute for Advanced Study in the Humanities and Social Sciences (NIAS), June 1981.

191   'Responses to Page and Keith.' *Educational Researcher*, September 1981.

192   'Quality and Equality in American Education: Public and Catholic Schools.' *Phi Delta Kappan*, November 1981, pp. 159–63.

193   'Policy, Research, and Political Theory,' in *The Social Sciences: Their Nature and Uses*, William H. Kruskal (ed.), Chicago: University of Chicago Press, 1982. Originally presented as the 375th Convocation Address, University of Chicago, 18 December 1979.

194   'Introduction', in *The Varied Sociology of Paul F. Lazarsfeld*, Patricia K. Kendall (ed.), New York: Columbia University Press, 1982.

195   'Summer Learning and School Achievement.' *The Public Interest*, Vol. 66, Winter 1982, pp. 140–4.

196   'Experiential Learning and Information Assimilation: Toward an Appropriate Mix.' *Child and Youth Services*, Vol. 4, No. 3/4, 1982, pp. 13–20. (Reprinted with permission of the *Journal of Experiential Education*, Spring 1979.)

197   'Systems of Trust: A Rough Theoretical Framework.' *Angewandte Sozialforschung* (Jahrgang 10, 3, 1982), pp. 277–99.

198   'The Use of "Ability" Measures as Controls for Concurrent or Subsequent Achievement.' *American Sociological Review*, Vol. 47, No. 6, December 1982, pp. 819–24. (Comment on Alexander *et al.*, *ASR*, October 1981.)

199   'Free Riders and Zealots,' *Ökonomische Erklärungen sozialen Verhaltens*, Berichte und Diskussionen, Internationale Wissenschaftliche Fachkonferenz, 11–13 March, 1982, in the Werner-Reimers-Stiftung, Bad Homburg, pp. 135–68.

200   'Cognitive Outcomes in Public and Private Schools.' *Sociology of Education*, Vol. 55, No. 2/3, April–July 1982, pp. 65–76. (With Thomas Hoffer and Sally Kilgore.)

201   'Achievement and Segregation in Secondary Schools: A Further Look at Public and Private School Differences.' *Sociology of Education,* Vol. 55, No. 2/3, April–July 1982, pp. 162–82.

202   'Income Testing and Social Cohesion,' pp. 67–88, in *Income-Tested Transfer Programs: The Case For and Against*, Irwin Garfinkel (ed.), New York: Academic Press, 1982.

203   'Recontracting, Trustworthiness, and the Stability of Vote Exchanges.' *Public Choice*, Vol. 40, 1983, pp. 89–94.

204   'Response to Tauber-James, Cain-Goldberger, and Morgan.' *Sociology of Education*, Vol. 56, No. 4, October 1983, pp. 219–34.

205   'Predicting the Consequences of Policy Changes: The Case of Public and Private Schools,' pp. 273–93, in *Evaluating the Welfare State: Social and Political Perspectives*. New York: Academic Press, 1983.

206   'Die Zukunft für Kinder und Jugendliche.' *Jugendzeit-Schulzeit*, Friedrich Schweitzer and Hans Thiersch (eds), Beltz Verlag, Weinheim und Basel, 1983.

207   'Schooling and Equality,' pp. 85–90, in *Open Session IEA General Assembly 1983*, T.J.H.M. Eggen (ed.), Twente University of Technology, Department of Education, December 1983.

208   'Micro Foundations and Macrosocial Behavior,' in *Angewandte Sozialforschung*, Vol. 12, 1/2, 1984, pp. 25–37.

209   'Stochastic Models for Market Structures,' pp. 189–213, in *Stochastic Modelling of Social Processes*. Orlando, FL: Academic Press, 1984.

210 'How Might Policy Research in Education Be Better Carried Out?', pp. 15–20, in *Improving Education: Perspectives on Educational Research*. National Academy of Education, 1984.

211 'The Transition from School to Work,' pp. 27–59, in *Research in Social Stratification and Mobility*, Volume 3, JAI Press, 1984.

212 'Interdependence among Qualitative Attributes,' *Journal of Mathematical Sociology*, Vol. 10, No. 1, 1984, pp. 29–50.

213 'Introducing Social Structure into Economic Analysis,' pp. 84–8, in *American Economic Review: Papers and Proceedings*. American Economic Association, May 1984.

214 'Issues in the Institutionalization of Social Policy,' pp. 131–41, in *Educational Research and Policy: How Do They Relate?*' Torsten Husén and Maurice Kogan (eds), Oxford: Pergamon Press, 1984.

215 'Responsibility in Corporate Action: A Sociologist's View,' pp. 69–91, in *Corporate Governance and Directors' Liabilities*, Klaus J. Hopt and Gunther Teubner (eds), Berlin: Walter de Gruyter, 1985.

216 'Norms of Equal Opportunity: When and Why Do They Arise'? *Angewandte Sozialforschung*, Jahrgang 13, 1, 1985, pp. 55–60.

217 'International Comparisons of Cognitive Achievement,' *Phi Delta Kappan*, February 1985, pp. 403–6.

218 'Schools and the Communities They Serve,' *Phi Delta Kappan*, April 1985, pp. 527–32.

219 'Achievement Growth in Public and Catholic High Schools,' *Sociology of Education*, Vol. 58, No. 2, April 1985, pp. 74–97. (With Thomas Hoffer and Andrew Greeley.)

220 'Sports in School,' *Sports and Education*, Vol. 1, Winter 1985, pp. 6–10.

221 'Schools, Families, and Children,' The 1985 Ryerson Lecture, University of Chicago.

222 'Becoming Adult in a Changing Society'. *OECD*, Paris 1985. (With Torsten Husén.)

223 'Social Theory, Social Research, and a Theory of Action'. *American Journal of Sociology*, Vol. 91, No. 6, May 1986, pp. 1309–35.

224 'Social Structure and the Emergence of Norms among Rational Actors,' pp. 55–83, in *Paradoxical Effects of Social Behavior: Essays in Honor of Anatol Rapoport*, A. Dickmann and P. Mitter (eds), Vienna: Physica-Verlag, 1986.

225 'Psychological Structure and Social Structure in Economic Models.' *Journal of Business*, Vol. 59, 1986, pp. S365–9.

226 'Equality.' *The New Palgrave: A Dictionary of Economics*. London: Macmillan, October 1987, pp. 49–58.

227 'Norms as Social Capital,' pp. 133–55, in *Economic Imperialism*, Gerard Radnitzky and Peter Bernholz (eds), Paragon Press, 1987.

228 'The Relation between School and the Social Structure,' pp. 177–204, in *The Social Organization of Schools: New Conceptualizations of the Learning Process*, Maureen T. Hallinan (ed.), New York: Plenum Press, 1987.

229 'Free Riders and Zealots,' pp. 59–82, in *Social Exchange Theory*, Karen S. Cook (ed.), New York; Sage Publications, 1987.

230 'Actors and Actions in Social History and Social Theory: Reply to Sewell.' *American Journal of Sociology*, Vol. 93, No. 1, July 1987, pp. 172–5.

231 'The Role of Social Policy Research in Society and in Sociology.' *The American Sociologist*, Vol. 18, No. 2, Summer 1987, pp. 127–33.

232 'Families and Schools.' *Educational Researcher*, Washington, D.C.: American Educational Research Association, Vol. 16, No. 6, August–September 1987, pp. 32–8.

233 'Catholic High School Effects on Achievement Growth,' pp. 67–88, in *Comparing Public and Private Schools, Volume 2: School Achievement*, Edward H. Haertzel, Thomas James and Henry M. Levin (eds), New York: Falmer Press, 1987.

234 'Microfoundations and Macrosocial Behavior,' pp. 153–73, in *The Micro-Macro Link*, Jeffrey C. Alexander, Bernhard Giesen, Richard Münch and Neil J. Smelser (eds), Berkeley, CA: University of California Press, 1987.

235 'Science Advice and Social Science Advice to Government,' pp. 90–4, in *Science and Technology Advice to the President, Congress, and Judiciary*, William T. Golden (ed.), Oxford: Pergamon Press, 1988. pp. 90–94.

236 'Equality and Excellence in Education,' pp. 376–92, in *Surveying Social Life: Papers in Honor of Herbert H. Hyman*, Herbert J. O'Gorman (ed.), Connecticut: Wesleyan University Press, 1988.

237 'Free Riders and Zealots: The Role of Social Networks.' *Sociological Theory 88*, Vol. 6, No. 1, Spring 1988, pp. 52–7.

238 'The Problem of Order: Where Are Rights to Act Located?' *Journal of Institutional and Theoretical Economics*, Vol. 144, No. 2, April 1988, pp. 367–73.

239 'Social Capital in the Creation of Human Capital.' Supplement to *American Journal of Sociology*, Vol. 94, 1988, pp. S95–S120.

240 'The Creation and Destruction of Social Capital: Implications for the Law,' *Notre Dame Journal of Law, Ethics and Public Policy*, Vol. 3, No. 3, 1988.

241 'Social Organization of the Corporation,' pp. 93–111, in *The US Business Corporation: An Institution in Transition*, John R. Meyer and James M. Gustafson (eds), New York: Harper and Row, 1988.

242 'Social Capital, Human Capital, and Schools.' *Independent School*, Fall 1988, pp. 9–16.

243 'The Corporation versus the Family: Consequences for Persons.' *Innovation* (Wein), 1988, pp. 527–41.

244 'Introduction,' pp. 1–9, in *Education in a Comparative Context: Studies of Israeli Society*, Vol. 4. Ernest Krausz (ed.), Transaction Publishers, 1989.

245 'Why Catholic Schools Outperform All Others.' *US Catholic*, July 1989, pp. 6–12.

246 'Do Students Learn More in Private Schools Than in Public Schools?' *Florida Policy Review*, Vol. 5, No. 1, Summer 1989, pp. 9–14.

247 'Simulation Games and the Development of Social Theory.' *Simulation and Games*, Vol. 20, No. 2, June 1989, pp. 144–64.

248 'Linear Systems Analysis: Macrolevel Analysis with Microlevel Data,' pp. 395–422, with Lingxin Hao. *Sociological Methodology*, Vol. 19. Washington: American Sociological Association, 1989.

249 'Weber and the Protestant Ethic: A Comment on Hernes.' *Rationality and Society*, Vol. 1, No. 2, October 1989, pp. 291–4.

250 'Schools and Communities.' *Chicago Studies*, Vol. 28, No. 3, November 1989, pp. 232–44.

251 'The Family, the Community, and the Future of Education,' pp. 169–85, in

Education and the American Family: A Research Synthesis, William J. Weston (ed.), New York: New York University Press, 1989.

252 'Rational Organization.' *Rationality and Society*, Vol. 2, No. 1, January 1990, pp. 94–105.

253 'Commentary: Social Institutions and Social Theory.' *American Sociological Review*, Vol. 55, No. 3, June 1990, pp. 333–9.

254 'Do Students Learn More in Private Schools Than in Public Schools?' *The Madison Papers*, No. 4. Tallahassee, FL: James Madison Institute for Public Policy Studies, 1990, pp. 1–14.

255 'Loosening the Ties That Bind.' *Noteworthy*. Aurora, CO: Mid-Continent Regional Educational Laboratory, Spring 1990, pp. 26–9.

256 'The Emergence of Norms,' pp. 35–59, in *Social Institutions: Their Emergence, Maintenance, and Effects*, Michael Hechter, Karl-Dieter Opp and Reinhard Wippler (eds), New York: Aldine de Gruyter, 1990.

257 'How Worksite Schools and Other School Reforms Can Generate Social Capital.' *American Educator*, Summer 1990, pp. 35–6.

258 'Robert K. Merton As Teacher,' pp. 25–32, in *Robert K. Merton: Consensus and Controversy*, Jon Clark, Celia Modgil and Sohan Modgil (eds), London: Falmer Press, 1990.

259 'Rational Action, Social Networks, and the Emergence of Norms,' pp. 91–112, in *Structures of Power and Constraint: Papers in Honor of Peter M. Blau*, Craig Calhoun, Marshall W. Myers and W. Richard Scott (eds), Cambridge: Cambridge University Press, 1990.

260 'Norm-Generating Structures,' pp. 250–81, in *The Limits of Rationality*, Karen S. Cook and Margaret Levi (eds), Chicago: University of Chicago Press, 1990.

261 'Forms of Rights and Forms of Power,' pp. 119–49, in *Generalized Political Exchange*, Bernd Marin (ed.), Frankfurt am Main: Campus Verlag; and Boulder, CO: Westview Press, 1990.

262 'On the Self-Suppression of Academic Freedom.' The Sidney Hook Memorial Award Address. *Academic Questions*, Vol. 4, No. 1, Winter 1990–91, pp. 17–22.

263 'Choice, Community and Future Schools,' pp. ix–xii, in *Choice and Control in American Education. Volume 1: The Theory of Choice and Control in Education*. London: Falmer Press, 1990.

264 'Toward a Rational Theory of Constitution Construction,' pp. 209–26, in *Philosophy of Social Choice*, Piotr Ploszajski (ed.), Nowy Swiat: Poland, IFiS Publications, 1990.

265 'Natural Persons, Corporate Actors, and Constitutions.' *Constitutional Political Economy*, Vol. 2, No. 1, 1991, pp. 81–106.

266 'Matching Processes in the Labor Market.' *Acta Sociologica*, Vol. 34, 1991, pp. 3–12.

267 'Pseudo Social Networks for the Study of Social Processes,' pp. 25–36, in *Disziplin und Kreativität: Sozialwissenschaftliche Computersimulation: Theoretische Experimente und praktische Anwendung*, Henrik Kreutz and Johann Bacher (eds), Opladen: Leske and Budrich, 1991.

268 'What Constitutes Educational Opportunity?' *Oxford Review of Education*, Vol. 17, No. 2, 1991, pp. 155–9.

269 'Sport As an Educational Tool.' *School Sports and Education*, National Conference Issue, Institute for Athletics and Education, 1991, pp. 3–5.

270 'Parental Involvement in Education.' *Policy Perspectives*, Office of Educational Research and Improvement, US Department of Education, 1991, pp. 1–24.

271 'Prologue: Constructed Social Organization,' pp. 1–14, in *Social Theory for a Changing Society*, Pierre Bourdieu and James S. Coleman (eds), Westview Press/ Russell Sage Foundation, 1991.

272 'Reflections on Schools and Adolescents,' pp. 62–70, in *Reflections*, Derek L. Burleson (ed.), Bloomington, IN: Phi Delta Kappa Educational Foundation, 1991.

273 'Les Choix Collectifs Portant sur des Questions d'Intérêt Public.' *Politiques et Management Public*, Vol. 9, No. 2, June 1991, pp. 15–26.

274 'Comment on Douglas Long's "Taking Interests Seriously",' *Rationality and Society*, Vol. 3, No. 4, October 1991, pp. 500–2.

275 'Changes in the Family: Implications for the Common School.' *The University of Chicago Legal FORUM*, Volume 1991, pp. 153–70.

276 'Introductory Remarks,' Challenges to Pluralism and Democracy in Eastern Europe: Views from Inside and Outside. *Sisyphus Sociological Studies*, Vol. 7, 1991, pp. 151–2.

277 'Concluding Remarks,' Challenges to Pluralism and Democracy in Eastern Europe: Views from Inside and Outside. *Sisyphus Sociological Studies*, Vol. 7, 1991, pp. 172–3.

278 'Constructed Organization: First Principles.' *Journal of Law, Economics and Organization*, Vol. 7, Special Issue, 1991, 23.

279 'Democracy in Permanently Divided Systems.' *The American Behavioral Scientist*, Vol. 35, Nos 4 and 5, March/June 1992, pp. 363–74.

280 'The Problematics of Social Theory.' *Theory and Society*, Vol. 21, 1992, pp. 263–83.

281 'The Economic Approach to Sociology,' pp. 133–48, in *Universal Economics: Assessing the Achievements of the Economic Approach*, Gerard Radnitzky (ed.), New York: International Conference on the Unity of Sciences, 1992.

282 'Democracy in Permanently Divided Systems,' pp. 17–26, in *Reexamining Democracy: Essays in Honor of Seymour Martin Lipset*, Gary Marks and Larry Diamond (eds), Newbury Park, CA: Sage Publications, 1992.

283 'Parents' Rights in Choice of School,' pp. 1–10, in *Ernst Fraenkel Vorträge zur Amerikanischen Politik, Wirtschaft, Gesellschaft und Geschichte*, Vol. 6. Berlin: John F. Kennedy-Institut für Nordamerikastudien, 1992.

284 'Some Points on Choice in Education.' *Sociology of Education*, Vol. 65, No. 4, October 1992, pp. 260–2.

285 'Research and the Illumination of Christian Education.' *Journal of Research on Christian Education*, Vol. 1, No. 1, Autumn 1992, pp. 7–9.

286 'Effective Schools and Educational Choice,' pp. 5–18, in *School Effectiveness and Improvement*, Joseph Bashi and Zehava Sass (eds), Proceedings of the Third International Congress for School Effectiveness, Van Leer Jerusalem Institute, Jerusalem, 1990. Jerusalem: Magness Press, 1990.

287 'Foreword,' p. iii, in *Reclaiming Our Schools: A Handbook on Teaching Character, Academics, and Discipline*, by Edward A. Wynne and Kevin Ryan. New York: Macmillan, 1993.

288 'The Vision of Foundations of Social Theory.' *Analyse and Kritik*, Vol. 15, December 1992, pp. 117–28.

289 'The Rational Reconstruction of Society.' *American Sociological Review*, Vol. 58, No. 1, February 1993, pp. 1–15.

290 'Comment on Preston and Campbell's "Differential Fertility and the Distribution of Traits".' *American Journal of Sociology*, Vol. 98, No. 5, March 1993, pp. 1020–32.

291 'The Role of Rights in a Theory of Social Action.' *Journal of Institutional and Theoretical Economics*, Vol. 149, No. 1, March 1993, pp. 213–32.

292 'Racjonalna Rekonstrukcja Skpoteczeństwa.' *Studia Socjologiczne*, Nr 1/128, 1993, pp. 7–28.

293 'Reply to Blau, Tuomela, Diekmann and Baurmann.' *Analyse und Kritik*, 15, September 1993, pp. 62–9.

294 'The Impact of Gary Becker's Work on Sociology.' *Acta Sociologica*, Vol. 36, No. 3, 1993, pp. 169–78.

295 'Algunas Cuestiones sobre la "Libre Eleccion" de la Escuela.' *Grade*, Notas Para El Debate/9, 1993, pp. 98–101.

296 'The Design of Organizations and the Right to Act.' *Sociological Forum*, Vol. 18, No. 4, December 1993, pp. 527–46.

297 'Properties of Rational Organizations,' pp. 79–90, in *Interdisciplinary Perspectives on Organization Studies*, Siegwart Lindenberg and Hein Schreuder (eds), Oxford: Pergamon Press, 1993.

298 'Family Involvement in Education,' pp. 23–37, in *School, Family and Community Interaction*, Cheryl L. Fagnano and Beverly Z. Werber (eds), Boulder, CO: Westview Press, 1994.

299 'Social Capital, Human Capital, and Investment in Youth,' pp. 34–50, in *Youth Unemployment and Society*, Anne C. Petersen and Jeylan T. Mortimer (eds), Cambridge: Cambridge University Press, 1994.

300 'Parental Involvement: Implications for Schools,' pp. 19–31, in *Restructuring Education: Issues and Strategies for Communities, Schools, and Universities*, Robert J. Yinger and Kathryn M. Borman (eds), Cresskill, NJ: Hampton Press, 1994.

301 'A Rational Choice Perspective on Economic Sociology,' pp. 166–80, in *The Handbook of Economic Sociology*, Neil J. Smelser and Richard Swedberg (eds), Princeton, NJ: Princeton University Press, 1994.

302 'A Vision for Sociology.' *Society*, Vol. 32, No. 1, November/December 1994, pp. 29–34.

303 'Redesigning American Public Education.' *On the Horizon*, Vol. 3, No. 2, December 1994/January 1995, pp. 1–2, 5.

15 March 1995

Bibliography

Abell, P. 1987. *The Syntax of Social Life*. Oxford: Oxford University Press.

Abell, P. 1992. 'Is rational choice theory a rational choice of theory?', in J.S. Coleman and T.J. Fararo (eds), *Rational Choice Theory: Advocacy and Critique*. Newbury Park, CA: Sage.

Abell, P., Khalaf, H. and Smeaton, D. 1995. 'An exploration of entry to and exit from self-employment', Centre for Economic Performance Discussion Paper, London School of Economics.

Abell, P., Samuels, J. and Cranna, M. 1994. 'Managerial motives in the market for corporate control', Centre for Economic Performance Discussion Paper, London School of Economics.

Ackerman, S. 1992. *Reforming the Progressive Agenda*. Cambridge, MA: Harvard University Press.

Acs, Z.J., Audretsch, D.B. and Evans, D.S. 1992. 'The Determinants of Variations to Self-Employment Rates across Countries and over Time', Cambridge, MA: National Economic Research Associates.

Aldrich, H., Rosen, B. and Woodward, W. 1986. 'A social role perspective of entrepreneurship: preliminary findings from an empirical study', mimeo, University of North Carolina.

Alexander, J.C. 1983. *Theoretical Logic in Sociology*, Vols 1–4. Berkeley, CA: University of California Press.

Alexander, K. and Entwisle, D. 1988. 'Achievement in the first two years of school: patterns and processes', *Monographs of the Society for Research in Child Development*, 53, Serial No. 218.

Alexander, K. and Entwisle, D. 1994. 'Educational tracking during the early years: first grade placements and middle school constraints'. Paper presented at the Conference on Institutions and Careers, Duke University, 10–11 April.

Alexander, K., Entwisle, D. and Bedinger, S. 1993. 'On the efficacy of performance expectations: differences by race and SES'. Paper presented at the Annual Meeting of the Southern Sociological Society, New Orleans, LA.

Alexander, K., Entwisle, D. and Dauber, S. 1993. 'First grade classroom behavior: its short- and long-term consequences for school performance', *Child Development*, 64: 801–14.

Alexander, K., Entwisle, D. and Dauber, S. 1994. 'Children in motion: school transfers and elementary school performance'. Unpublished manuscript, The Johns Hopkins University.

Alexander, K., Entwisle, D. and Thompson, M. 1987. 'School performance, status relations, and the structure of sentiment: bringing the teacher back in', *American Sociological Review*, 52: 665–82.

Alexander, K. and Pallas, A.M. 1983. 'Private schools and public policy: new evidence on cognitive achievement in public and private schools', *Sociology of Education*, 56: 170–81.

Altonji, J. and Dunn, T. 1990. 'The effects of school and family characteristics on the returns to education', June 1990, revised December 1994. Mimeo, Department of Economics, Northwestern University.

Alwin, D. and Thornton, A. 1984. 'Family origins and the schooling process: early versus late influence of parental characteristics'. *American Sociological Review*, 49: 784–802.

Amemiya, T. 1985. *Advanced Econometrics*. Cambridge, MA: Harvard University Press.

Arrow, K.J. and Debreu, G. 1954. 'Existence of an equilibrium for a competitive economy', *Econometrica*, 22: 265–90.

Asch, S.E. 1957. *Social Psychology*. Englewood Cliffs, NJ: Prentice-Hall.

Audretsch, D.B. and Acs, Z.J. 1990. 'Innovation as a means of entry: an overview', in P.A. Geroski and J. Schwalbach (eds), *Entry and Market Contestability: An International Comparison*. Berlin: SSRC.

Auerback, A.J. (ed.) 1988. *Corporate Takeovers: Causes and Consequences*. Chicago, IL: University of Chicago Press.

Axelrod, R. 1984. *The Evolution of Cooperation*. New York: Basic Books.

Bannock, G. 1981. *The Economics of Small Firms: Return from the Wilderness*. Oxford: Blackwell.

Bar, R. and Dreeben, R. 1983. *How Schools Work*. Chicago, IL: University of Chicago Press.

Bar-Hillel, M. 1991. 'Commentary on Wolford, Taylor, and Beck: the conjunction fallacy?', *Memory and Cognition*, 19: 412–14.

Bar-Hillel, M. and Neter, E. 1993. 'How alike it is versus how likely it is: a disjunction fallacy in probabilistic judgements', *Journal of Personality and Social Psychology*, 65: 1119–31.

Bateson, G. and Bateson, M.C. 1987. *Angels Fear: Toward an Epistemology of the Sacred*. New York: Macmillan.

Baum, R.C. 1976. 'Introduction to Part IV: generalised medica in action', in Jan J. Loubser, Rainer C. Baum, Andrew Effrat and Victor Meyer Lidz (eds), *Exploration in General Theory in Social Science: Essays in Honour of Talcott Parsons*, Volume 2, New York: The Free Press, pp. 448–69.

Baumol, W.J. 1993. *Entrepreneurship, Management and the Structure of Payoffs*. Cambridge, MA: MIT Press.

Baumol, W.J., Panzer, J.C. and Willig, R.D. 1982. *Contestable Markets and the Theory of Industry Structure*. New York: Harcourt, Brace and Jovanovich.

Beksiak, J., Chmielecka, E. and Grzelonska, U. 1992. *Academic Economic Education in Change*. Economic Research Program for Central and Eastern Europe. Warsaw: Stefan Batory Foundation.

Bellah, R. with Madsen, R., Sullivan, R., Swidler, A. and Tipton, S. 1985. *Habits of the Heart: Individualism and Commitment in American Life*. Berkeley and Los Angeles, CA: University of California Press.

Bellah, R., *et al.* 1991. *The Good Society*. New York: Knopf.

Berelson, B. and Steiner, G.A. 1964. *Human Behavior: An Inventory of Scientific Findings*. New York: Harcourt, Brace and World.

Berger, B.M. (ed.) 1990. *Authors of Their Own Lives*. Berkeley, CA: University of California Press.

Berger, S.D. 1971. 'The sects and the breakthrough into the modern world: on the centrality of the sects in Weber's Protestant ethic thesis', *Sociological Quarterly*, 12: 486–99.

Berk, R. 1974. *Collective Behavior*. Dubuque: William C. Brown.

Berlin, I. 1953. *The Hedgehog and the Fox*. New York: Simon and Schuster.

Betts, J. 1995a. 'Does schooling quality matter? Evidence from the National Longitudinal Survey of Youth', *Review of Economics and Statistics*, 77 (2): 231–50.

Betts, J. 1995b. 'Is there a link between school inputs and earnings? Fresh scrutiny of an old literature', forthcoming in C. Burtless (ed.), *Does Money Matter? The Link between Schools, Student Achievement and Adult Success*. Washington: The Brookings Institution.

Bierstedt, R. 1990. 'Merton's systematic theory', in J. Clark, C. Modgil and S. Modgil (eds), *Robert K. Merton: Consensus and Controversy*. London: Falmer Press.

Birley, S. 1987. 'New ventures and employment growth', *Journal of Business Venturing*, 2: 155–65.

Birley, S. and Norburn, D. 1987. 'Owners and managers: the Venture 100 vs the Fortune 500', *Journal of Business Venturing*, 2: 351–63.

Black, J., de Meza, D. and Jeffreys, D. 1992. 'House prices, the supply of collateral and the enterprise economy', Centre for Economic Performance, London School of Economics.

Blanchflower, D.G. and Freeman, R.B. 1993. 'Did the Thatcher reforms change British labour market performance?', Centre for Economic Performance, London School of Economics.

Blanchflower, D.G. and Meyer, B. 1990. 'An empirical analysis of self-employment in Australia and the US', Centre for Economic Performance, London School of Economics.

Blanchflower, D.G. and Oswald, A.J. 1990. 'Self-employment and Mrs Thatcher's enterprise culture', in R. Jowell *et al.* (eds), *British Social Attitudes: 1990 Report*, Aldershot: Gower.

Blau, P.M. 1964. *Exchange and Power in Social Life*. New York: Wiley.

Blau, P.M. 1977. *Inequality and Heterogeneity: A Primitive Theory of Social Structure*. New York: The Free Press.

Blumer, H. 1953. 'Collective Behavior', in A.M. Lee (ed.), *Principles of Sociology*. New York: Barnes and Noble.

Bogardus, E.S. 1973. 'Twenty-five years of American sociology: 1947 to 1972', *Sociology and Social Research*, 57 (2): 150–61.

Bogenhold, D. and Staber, U. 1990. *The Revival of Independent Entrepreneurship*. Cologne: University of Cologne.

Boocock, S.S. 1968. 'From luxury item to learning tool: an overview of the theoretical literature on games', in Boocock and Schild (1968), pp. 53–64.

Boocock, S.S. and Coleman, J.S. 1966. 'Games with simulated environments in learning', *Sociology of Education*, 39 (Summer): 215–36.

Boocock, S.S. and Schild, E.O. (eds) 1968. *Simulation Games in Learning*. Beverly Hills, CA: Sage Publications.

Borjas, G. 1986. 'The self-employment of immigrants', *Journal of Human Resources*, 21: 485–506.

Bott, D.M. and Hargens, L.L. 1991. 'Are sociologists' publications uncited? Citation rates of journal articles, chapters, and books', *The American Sociologist*, 22: 147–58.

Boudon, R. 1981. *The Logic of Social Action*. Boston, MA: Routledge.

Boudon, R. 1987. 'The individualistic tradition in sociology', in J.C. Alexander, B. Giesen, R. Münch and N.S. Smelser (eds), *The Micro-Macro Link*. Berkeley, CA: University of California Press.

Bourdieu, P. 1986. 'The forms of capital', in J.G. Richardson (ed.), *Handbook of Theory and Research for the Sociology of Education*. New York: Greenwood Press.

Bourdieu, P. (ed.) 1993. *La misère du monde*. Paris: Seuil.

Bowles, S. 1970. 'Toward an educational production function', in W.L. Hansen (ed.), *Education Income and Human Capital*. New York: Columbia for NBER Press.

Bowles, S. and Levin, H. 1986. 'The determinants of scholastic achievement — an appraisal of some recent evidence', *Journal of Human Resources*, 2 (1).

Bracey, G. 1991. 'Why can't they be like we were?' *Phi Delta Kappan*, 73: 104–17.

Brenner, R. 1987. *Rivalry in Business, Science, among Nations*. Cambridge: Cambridge University Press.

Brockhaus, S.R. 1982. 'The psychology of the entrepreneur', in C.A. Kent *et al.* (eds), *Encyclopaedia of Entrepreneurship*. Englewood Cliffs, NJ: Prentice-Hall.

Brook, J.S., Brook, D.W., Gordon, H.S., Whiteman, M. and Cohen, P. 1990. 'The psychosocial etiology of adolescent drug use: a family interactional approach', in *Genetic, Social and General Psychology Monograph*, 116: 111–267.

Brown, B.B. 1992. 'The meaning and measurement of adolescent crowd affiliation', *SRA Newsletter*, 6: 1.

Brown, B.B., Mounts, N., Lambourn, S.D. and Steinberg, L. 1993. 'Parenting practices and peer group affiliation in adolescence', *Child Development*, 64: 467–82.

Brown, R. 1965. *Social Psychology*. New York: The Free Press.

Brummelle, S.L. and Gerchak, Y. 1982. 'The structure of indices of social mobility and inheritance', *Journal of Mathematical Sociology*, 8: 251–64.

Bryk, A.S. and Raudenbusch, S.W. 1992. *Hierarchical Linear Models: Applications and Data Analysis Methods*. Newbury Park, CA: Sage.

Bühler, C. 1921. *Das Seelenleben des Jugendlichen*. Jena: Fischer.

Bulmer, M. (1983). 'The methodology of early social indicators research: William Fielding Ogburn and Recent Social Trends, 1993' plus William Fielding Ogburn, 'A note on method: an unpublished memorandum on the methodology of the President's Research Committee on Recent Social Trends, 1929–1933', *Social Indicators Research*, 13: 109–30.

Bulmer, M. (1993). 'Independent social research institutes', in W. Sykes, M. Bulmer and M. Schwerzel (eds), *Directory of Social Research Organisations in the United Kingdom*. London: Mansell.

Burch, J. 1986. *Entrepreneurship*. New York: Wiley.

Burrows, R. 1980. 'A socio-economic anatomy of the British petty bourgeoisie', mimeo, University of Surrey.

Burt, R. 1992. *Structural Holes*. Cambridge, MA: Harvard University Press.

Cable, J. and Schwalbach, J. 1990. 'International comparisons of entry and exit', in P.A. Geroski and J. Schwalbach (eds), *Entry and Market Contestability: An International Comparison*. Berlin: SSRC.

Cadigan, D., Entwisle, D., Alexander, K. and Pallas, A. 1988. 'First-grade retention among low achieving students: a search for significant predictors', *Merrill-Palmer Quarterly*, 34: 71–88.

Cain, G. and Watts, H. 1970. 'Problems in making inferences from the Coleman Report', *American Sociological Review*, 35: 228–42.

Campbell, D.T. 1987. 'The experimenting society', in D.T. Campbell (ed.), *Methodology and Epistemology for Social Science: Selected Papers*. Chicago, IL: University of Chicago Press, pp. 290–314.

Campbell, M. and Daly, M. 1992. 'Self-employment: into the 1990s', *Employment Gazette*, June.

Canetti, E. 1966. *Crowds and Power*. New York: Viking.

Card, D. and Krueger, A. 1992a. 'School quality and black–white relative earnings: a direct assessment', *Quarterly Journal of Economics*, 107 (1): 151–200.

Card, D. and Krueger, A. 1992b. 'Does school quality matter: returns to education and the characteristics of public schools in the United States', *Journal of Political Economy*, 100 (1): 1–40.

Card, D. and Krueger, A. 1994. 'The economic return to school quality: a partial survey'. Princeton, NJ: Industrial Relations Section, Princeton University.

Carlson, B.W. and Yates, J.F. 1989. 'Disjunction errors in qualitative likelihood judgement', *Organisation Behaviour and Human Decision Processes*, 44: 368–79.

Carlson, E. 1967. 'Games in the classroom', *Saturday Review*, 15 April: 62–4, 82–3.

Casson, M.C. 1982. *The Entrepreneur*. Totowa, NJ: Barnes and Noble.

Ceci, S. 1991. 'How much does schooling influence general intelligence and its cognitive components? A reassessment of the evidence', *Developmental Psychology*, 5: 703–22.

Chell, E. 1985. 'The entrepreneurial personality: a few ghosts laid to rest', *International Small Business Journal*, 3: 37–62.

Cherryholmes, C.H. 1966. 'Some current research on effectiveness of education simulations: implications for alternative strategies', *American Behavioral Scientist* 10 (October): 4–7.

Chubb, J.E. and Moe, T.M. 1990. *Politics, Markets and America's Schools*. Washington, DC: The Brookings Institution.

Cohen, D.K. and Garet, M.S. 1975. 'Reforming educational policy with applied social research', *Harvard Educational Review*, 45 (1): 17–43.

Cohen, D.K. and Weiss, J.A. 1977. 'Social science and social policy: schools and race', in C.H. Weiss (ed.), *Using Social Research in Public Policy Making*. Lexington, MA: D.C. Heath.

Cohen, J. 1979. 'High school subcultures and the adult world', *Adolescence*, 14 (5): 491–502.

Cohen, J. 1983. 'Peer influence on college aspirations with initial aspirations controlled', *American Sociological Review*, 48: 728–34.

Cohen, L.J. 1979. 'On the psychology of prediction: whose is the fallacy?', *Cognition*, 7: 385–407.

Cohen, L.J. 1981. 'Can human irrationality be experimentally demonstrated?', *Behavioural and Brain Sciences*, 4: 317–70.

Coleman, J.S. 1957. 'The diffusion of an innovation among physicians', *Sociometry*, 20: 253–70.

Coleman, J.S. 1961a. *The Adolescent Society*. Glencoe, IL: The Free Press.

Coleman, J.S. 1961b. *Social Climates in High Schools*. Cooperative Research Monograph No. 4. US Department of Health, Education and Welfare, Office of Education. Washington, DC: US Government Printing Office.

Coleman, J.S. 1961c. 'The equilibrium size distribution of freely forming groups', *Sociometry*, 24: 36–45.

Coleman, J. 1964a. *Models of Change and Response Uncertainty*. Englewood Cliffs, NJ: Prentice-Hall.

Coleman, J. 1964b. *Introduction to Mathematical Sociology*. London: Collier-Macmillan and the Free Press of Glencoe.

Coleman, J.S. 1964c. 'Research chronicle: *The Adolescent Society*', in P.E. Hammond (ed.), *Sociologists at Work*. New York: Basic Books.

Coleman, J.S. [1964] 1986. 'Collective decisions', in J.S. Coleman, *Individual Interests and Collective Action*, Cambridge: Cambridge University Press, pp. 15–32.

Coleman, J.S. 1965. *Adolescents and the Schools*. New York: Basic Books.

Coleman, J.S. 1966a. 'Individual interests and collective action', in G. Tullock (ed.), *Papers on Non-Market Decision-Making*. Charlottesville, VA: Thomas Jefferson Center for Political Economy, University of Virginia, pp. 49–62.

Coleman, J.S. 1966b. 'The possibility of a social welfare function', *American Economic Review*, 56 (5): 1105–22.

Coleman, J.S. 1966c. 'In defense of games', *American Behavioural Scientist*, 10 (October): 3–4.

Coleman, J.S. 1967a. 'The possibility of a social welfare function: reply', *American Economic Review*, 57 (5): 1311–17.

Coleman, J.S. 1967b. 'Toward open schools', *The Public Interest*, 9: 20–7.

Coleman, J.S. 1968a. 'The marginal utility of a vote commitment', *Public Choice*, 5 (Fall): 39–58.

Coleman, J.S. 1968b. 'Social process and social simulation games', in Boocock and Schild (1968).

Coleman, J.S. 1968c. 'The concept of equality of educational opportunity', *Harvard Educational Review*, 38 (1): 7–22.

Coleman, J.S. 1968d. 'The mathematical study of change', in H. Blalock and A.B. Blalock (eds), *Methodology in Social Research*. New York: McGraw-Hill.

Coleman, J.S. 1969a. 'A brief summary of the Coleman Report', in *Equal Educational Opportunity*. Cambridge, MA: Harvard University Press, pp. 253–9.

Coleman, J.S. 1969b. 'Equality of educational opportunity reexamined', *Socio-Economic Planning Sciences*, 2: 347–54.

Coleman, J.S. 1970a. 'Interpretations of adolescent culture', in J. Zubin and A.M. Freedman (eds), *The Psychopathology of Adolescence*. New York: Grune and Stratton.

Coleman, J.S. 1970b. 'The benefits of coalition', *Public Choice*, 8 (Spring): 45–61.

Coleman, J.S. 1970c. 'Social inventions', *Social Forces*, 49 (2): 163–73.

Coleman, J.S. 1970d. 'Properties of collectivities', in J.S. Coleman, A. Etzioni and J. Porter (eds), *Macrosociology: Research and Theory*. Boston, MA: Allyn and Bacon, pp. 5–101.

Coleman, J.S. 1970e. 'Reply to Cain and Watts', *American Sociological Review*, 35 (2): 242–9.

Coleman, J.S. 1971. 'Collective decisions', in H. Turk and R.L. Simpson (eds), *Institutions and Social Exchange: The Sociologies of Talcott Parsons and George C. Homans*. New York: Bobbs-Merrill.

Coleman, J.S. 1972a. *Policy Research in the Social Sciences*. Morristown, NJ: General Learning Press.

Coleman, J.S. 1972b. 'The evaluation of equality of educational opportunity', in Mosteller and Moynihan (1972), pp. 146–67.

Coleman, J.S. 1973a. 'Information processing and experience learning', in S.A. Livingston, G.M. Fennessy, *et al.*, *The Hopkins Games Program: Final Report on Seven Years of Research*, Report No. 155. Baltimore, MD: The Johns Hopkins University, Center for Social Organisation of Schools.

Coleman, J.S. 1973b. *Youth: Transition to Adulthood*. Report of the Panel on Youth of the President's Science Advisory Committee. Washington, DC: US Government Printing Office.

Coleman, J.S. 1973c. *The Mathematics of Collective Action*, Chicago, IL: Aldine.

Coleman, J.S. (ed.) 1974a. *Youth: Transition to Adulthood*. Chicago and London: University of Chicago Press.

Coleman, J.S. 1974b. 'Review essay: inequality, sociology and moral philosophy', *American Journal of Sociology*, 80: 739–64.

Coleman, J.S. 1974c. *Power and the Structure of Society*. New York: Norton.

Coleman, J.S. 1975a. 'Policy decisions, social science information and education', *Sociology of Education*, 49 (October): 304–12.

Coleman, J.S. 1975b. 'Games as vehicles for social theory', in C.S. Greenblat and R.D. Duke (eds), *Gaming-Simulation: Rationale, Design, and Application*. New York: Sage Publications/Wiley.

Coleman, J.S. 1975c. 'Collective decisions', in C.S. Greenblat and R.D. Duke (eds), *Gaming-Simulation: Rationale, Design, and Applications*. New York: Sage Publications/Wiley.

Coleman, J.S. 1975d. 'What is meant by an equal educational opportunity?', *Oxford Review of Education*, 1: 27–9.

Coleman, J.S. 1976a. 'The emergence of sociology as a policy science', in L.A. Coser and O.N. Larsen (eds), *The Uses of Controversy in Sociology*. New York: The Free Press.

Coleman, J.S. 1976b. 'Rawls, Nozick and educational equality', *The Public Interest*, 43: 121–8.

Coleman, J.S. 1976c. 'Policy decisions, social-science information, and education', *Sociology of Education*, 49 (4): 304–12.

Coleman, J.S. 1978. 'Sociological analysis and social policy', in T.B. Bottomore and R.A. Nisbet (eds), *A History of Sociological Analysis*. London, Heinemann.

Coleman, J.S. 1979a. 'Purposive actors and mutual effects', in R.K. Merton, J.S. Coleman and P. Rossi (eds), *Qualitative and Quantitative Social Research: Papers in Honor of Paul F. Lazarsfeld*. New York: The Free Press.

Coleman, J.S. 1979b. 'Presentation to the Massachusetts Legislature, 30 March 1976', in M. Friedman, R. Meltzer and C. Miller (eds), *New Perspectives on School Integration*. Minneapolis, MN: Fortress Press, pp. 111–24.

Coleman, J.S. 1979c. 'Destructive beliefs and potential policies in school desegregation', in J.W. Smith (ed.), *Detroit Metropolitan City-Suburban Relations*. Occasional Papers, Henry Ford Community College, 3: 5–12.

Coleman, J.S. 1980a. 'The structure of society and the nature of social research', *Knowledge*, 1 (3): 333–50.

Coleman, J.S. 1980b. 'Paul F. Lazarsfeld: the substance and style of his work', in R.K. Merton and M. White Riley (eds), *Sociological Traditions from Generation to Generation*. Totowa, NJ: Ablex, pp. 153–74.

Coleman, J.S. 1981a. 'Pulblic schools, private schools and the public interest', *The Public Interest*, 64: 19–28.

Coleman, J.S. 1981b. 'The role of incentives in school desegregation', in A. Yarmolinsky, L. Liebman and C. Schelling (eds), *Race and Schooling in the City*. Cambridge, MA: Harvard University Press.

Coleman, J.S. 1982a. *The Asymmetric Society*. New York: Syracuse University Press.

Coleman, J.S. 1982b. 'Policy, research, and political theory', in W.H. Kruskal (ed.), *The Social Sciences: Their Nature and Uses*. Chicago, IL: University of Chicago Press.

Coleman, J.S. 1984a. 'Issues in the institutionalisation of social policy', in T. Húsen and M. Kogan (eds), *Educational Research and Policy: How Do They Relate?* Oxford: Pergamon Press.

Coleman, J.S. 1984b. 'Introducing social structure into economic analysis', *American Economic Review*, 74 (2): 84–8.

Coleman, J.S. 1984c. 'The transition from school to work', in D.J. Treiman and R.V. Robinson (eds), *Research on Stratification and Mobility*. Greenwich, CT: JAI Press, pp. 27–59.

Coleman, J.S. 1985. *Autobiographical Sketch, I–II*. Unpublished manuscript. Second draft. Partly published as 'Columbia in the 1950s', in B.M. Berger (ed.), *Authors of Their Own Lives*. Berkeley, CA: University of California Press, 1990.

Coleman, J.S. 1986a. *Individual Interests and Collective Action*. Cambridge: Cambridge University Press.

Coleman, J.S. 1986b. 'Social theory, social research, and a theory of action', *American Journal of Sociology*, 91 (6): 1309–35.

Coleman, J.S. 1987. 'Microfoundations and macrosocial behaviour', in J.C. Alexander, B. Giesen, R. Münch and N.S. Smelser (eds), *The Micro-Macro Link*. Berkeley, CA: University of California Press.

Coleman, J.S. 1988a. 'Social capital in the creation of human capital', *American Journal of Sociology*, 94: 95–120.

Coleman, J.S. 1988b. 'The creation and destruction of social capital: implications for the law', *Notre Dame Journal of Law, Ethics and Public Policy*, 3: 375–404.

Coleman, J.S. 1988c. 'Free riders and zealots', *Sociological Theory*, 6: 52–7.

Coleman, J.S. 1989a. 'Weber and the Protestant ethic: a comment on Hernes', *Rationality and Society*, 1 (2): 291–4.

Coleman, J.S. 1989b. 'Response to the Sociology of Education Award', in *Footnotes: The Newsletter of the American Sociological Association*, 17 (1): 4–5. Also in *Academic Questions*, 4 (1).

Coleman, J.S. 1990a. *Foundations of Social Theory*. Cambridge, MA: Harvard University Press.

Coleman, J.S. 1990b. *Equality and Achievement in Education*. Boulder, CO: Westview Press.

Coleman, J.S. 1990c. Preface to (1990b).

Coleman, J.S. 1990d. 'Robert K. Merton as teacher', in J. Clark, C. Modgil and S. Modgil (eds), *Robert K. Merton*. London: Falmer Press, pp. 25–32.

Coleman, J.S. 1990e. 'Interview: James S. Coleman', in R. Swedberg, *Economics and Sociology*. Princeton, NJ: Princeton University Press, pp. 47–62.

Coleman, J.S. 1990f. 'Columbia in the 1950's', in B. Berger (ed.), *Authors of Their Own Lives*. Berkeley, CA: University of California Press.

Coleman, J.S. 1990g. 'The Sidney Hook memorial award address: on the self-suppression of academic freedom', *Academic Questions*, 4 (1).

Coleman, J.S. 1992. 'Sociology of Education in the Year 2000', *Sociology of Education*, Official Newsletter of the Sociology of Education Section of the American Sociological Association, Winter, p. 4.

Coleman, J.S. 1993a. 'The impact of Gary Becker's work on sociology', *Acta Sociologica*, 36: 167–78.

Coleman, J.S. 1993b. 'The rational reconstruction of society', *American Sociological Review*, 58 (1): 1–15.

Coleman, J.S. 1993c. 'The role of rights in a theory of social action', *Journal of Institutional and Theoretical Economics*, 149 (1): 213–32.

Coleman, J.S. 1994a. 'A rational choice perspective on economic sociology', in N.J. Smelser and R. Swedberg (eds), *Handbook of Economic Sociology*. Princeton and New York: Princeton University Press and the Russell Sage Foundation.

Coleman, J.S. 1994b. 'A vision for sociology', *Society*, 32 (1): 29–34.

Coleman, J.S. 1994c. 'What goes on in school: a student's perspective', unpublished manuscript, University of Chicago.

Coleman, J.S. and Fararo, T.J. (eds) 1992. *Rational Choice Theory: Advocacy and Critique*. Newbury Park, CA: Sage.

Coleman, J.S. and Hoffer, T. 1987. *Public and Private High Schools: The Impact of Communities*. New York: Basic Books.

Coleman, J.S. and Husén, T. 1985. *Becoming Adult in a Changing Society*. Paris: OECD.

Coleman, J.S. and Lindenberg, S. 1989. 'In memoriam: George Homans', *Rationality and Society*, 1 (2): 283–4.

Coleman, J.S. and McPhee, W.N. 1958. 'A program of research in mass dynamics', *PROD*, 1: 6–10.

Coleman, J.S., Boocock, S.S. and Schild, E.I. (eds) 1966a. 'Simulation games and learning behaviour, Part I', Special issue of *American Behavioural Scientist*, 10 (October).

Coleman, J.S., Boocock, S.S. and Schild, E.I. (eds) 1966b. 'Simulation games and learning behaviour, Part II', Special issue of *American Behavioural Scientist*, 10 (November).

Coleman, J.S., Campbell, E.Q., Hobson, C.J., McPartland, J., Mood, A.M., Weinfeld, F.D. and York, R.L. 1966. *Equality of Educational Opportunity*. Washington, DC: US Government Printing Offfice.

Coleman, J.S., Hoffer, T. and Kilgore, S. 1982. *High School Achievement: Public, Catholic, and Private Schools Compared*. New York: Basic Books.

Coleman, J.S., Katz, E. and Menzel, H. 1966. *Medical Innovation*. Indianapolis, IN: Bobbs-Merrill.

Coleman, J.S., Kelly, S. and Moore, J. 1975. *Trends in School Segregation, 1968–1973*. Washington DC: The Urban Institute.

Collins, R. 1988. *Theoretical Sociology*. San Diego, CA: Harcourt Brace Jovanovich.

Collins, R. 1993. 'Emotional energy as the common denominator of rational choice', *Rationality and Society*, 5: 203–30.

Converse, J. 1987. *Survey Research in the United States: Roots and Emergence 1890–1960*. Berkeley, CA: University of California Press.

Coser, L. 1976. 'Sociological theory from the Chicago dominance to 1965', *Annual Review of Sociology*, 2: 145–60.

Crain, R.L. and Mahard, R.E. 1979. *The Influence of High School Racial Composition on Black College Attendance and Test Performance*. Washington, DC: Government Printing Office.

Cremin, L.A. 1951. *The American Common School*. New York: Knopf.

Cromie, S. and Johns, S. 1983. 'Irish entrepreneurs: some personal characteristics', *Journal of Occupational Behaviour*, 4: 317–24.

Cross, M. 1981. *New Firm Formation and Regional Development*. Farnborough: Gower.

Crouchley, R., Abell, P. and Smeaton, D. 1994. 'An analysis of the aggregate time series of self-employment in GB', Centre for Economic Performance Discussion Paper, London School of Economics.

Curran, J. 1986. *Bolton Fifteen Years On*. London: Small Business Research Trust.

Curran, J. and Burrows, R. 1988. *Enterprise in Britain*. Mimeo.

Daly, M. 1991. 'The 1980s — a decade of growth in enterprise', *Employment Gazette*, March.

Dauber, S., Alexander, K. and Entwisle, D. 1993. 'Characteristics of retainees and early precursors of retention in grade: Who is held back?', *Merrill-Palmer Quarterly*, 39: 326–43.

David, J. 1974. *Follow Through Summer Study: A Two-Part Investigation of the Impact of Exposure to Schooling on Achievement Growth*. EdD Dissertation, Harvard Graduate School of Education.

David, J. and Pelavin, S. 1978. 'Secondary analysis in compensatory education programs', *New Directions for Program Evaluation*, 4: 31–44.

Davis, J.A. 1978. 'Studying categorical data over time', *Social Science Research*, 7: 151–79.

Debreu, G. 1959. *The Theory of Value: An Axiomatic Analysis of Economic Equilibrium*. New Haven, CT: Yale University Press.

Dewey, J. 1916. *The School and Society*. Chicago, IL: University of Chicago Press.

Dishion, T.J., Patterson, G.R., Stoolmiller, M. and Skinner, M.L. 1991. 'Family, school, and behavioural antecedents to early adolescent involvement with antisocial peers', *Developmental Psychology*, 27: 172–80.

Dishion, T.J., Ray, J. and Capaldi, D. 1992. 'Parenting precursors to male adolescent substance use'. Presented at symposium on Family Processes and Adolescent Substance Use, Society of Research in Adolescence, Washington, DC, March.

Duncan, O.D. 1985. 'New light on the 16-fold table', *American Journal of Sociology*, 91: 88–129.

Dulany, D.E. and Hilton, D.J. 1991. 'Conversational implicature, conscious representation, and the conjunction fallacy', *Social Cognition*, 9: 85–110.

Dunleavy, P. 1991. *Democracy, Bureaucracy and Public Choice: Economic Explanations in Political Science*. Hemel Hempstead: Harvester.

Dworkin, R. 1986. *Law's Empire*. London: Fontana.

Eatwell, J., Milgate, M. and Newman, P. (eds) [1987] 1989. *The New Palgrave: General Equilibrium*. New York: Norton.

Eccles, J. and Midgley, C. 1990. 'Changes in academic motivation and self-perception during early adolescence', in R. Montemayor, G. Adams and T. Gulotta (eds), *From Childhood to Adolescence: A Transitional Period?* Newbury Park, CA: Sage, pp. 134–55.

Elder Jr., G. 1974. *Children of the Great Depression: Social Change in Life Experience*, Chicago, IL: University of Chicago Press.

Elder, Jr., G.H., Liker, J.K. and Cross, C.E. 1984. 'Parent-child behaviour in the Great Depression: life course and intergenerational influences', *Life Span Development and Behaviour*, 6: 109–58.

Elkin, F. and Handel, G. 1989. *The Child and Society*. 5th ed. New York: Random House.

Ellickson, R.C. 1991. *Order Without Law. How Neighbors Settle Disputes*. Cambridge, MA: Harvard University Press.

Elliott, D.S., Huizinga, D. and Ageton, S.S. 1985. *Explaining Delinquency and Drug Use*. Newbury Park, CA: Sage.

Elster, J. 1989a. *Nuts and Bolts for the Social Sciences*. Cambridge: Cambridge University Press.

Elster, J. 1989b. *Solomonic Judgements: Studies in the Limitations of Rationality*. Cambridge: Cambridge University Press.

Elster, J. 1992. *Local Justice: How Institutions Allocate Scarce Goods and Necessary Burdens*. New York: Russell Sage.

Elster, J. 1993. *Political Psychology*. Cambridge: Cambridge University Press.

Entwisle, D. and Alexander, K. 1988. 'Factors affecting achievement test scores and marks received by black and white first graders', *The Elementary School Journal*, 88: 449–71.

Entwisle, D. and Alexander, K. 1989. 'Early schooling as a "critical period" phenomenon', in K. Namboodiri and R. Corwin (eds), *Sociology of Education and Socialisation*, Vol. 8. Greenwich, CT: JAI Press, pp. 27–55.

Entwisle, D. and Alexander, K. 1990. 'Beginning school math competence', *Child Development*, 61: 454–71.

Entwisle, D. and Alexander, K. 1992. 'Summer setback: race, poverty, school composition, and educational stratification in the United States', *American Sociological Review*, 57: 72–84.

Entwisle, D. and Alexander, K. 1993. 'Entry into schools: the beginning school transition and educational stratification in the US', *Annual Review of Sociology*, 19: 401–23.

Entwisle, D. and Alexander, K. 1994. 'Winter setback: school racial composition and learning to read', *American Sociological Review*, 59: 446–60.

Entwisle, D. and Hayduk, L. 1982. *Early Schooling: Cognitive and Affective Outcomes*. Baltimore, MD: Hopkins Press.

Entwisle, D., Alexander, K., Cadigan, D. and Pallas, A. 1987. 'Kindergarten experience: cognitive effects or socialisation?', *American Educational Research Journal*, 24: 337–64.

Entwisle, D., Alexander, K., Pallas, A. and Cadigan, D. 1989. 'A social psychological model for the schooling process over first grade', *Social Psychology Quarterly*, 51: 173–89.

Ericsson, K.A. and Simon, H.A. 1980. 'Verbal reports as data', *Psychological Review*, 87: 215–51.

Erikson, E. 1968. *Identity, Youth and Crisis*. New York: Norton.

Erikson, R. and Goldthorpe, J.H. 1992. *The Constant Flux*. Oxford: Clarendon Press.

Etzioni, A. [1961] 1975. *A Comparative Analysis of Complex Organisations*. New York: The Free Press.

Etzioni, A. 1988. *The Moral Dimension: Towards a New Economics*. New York: Macmillan.

Evans, D.S. and Jovanovic, B. 1989. 'Estimates of a model of entrepreneurial choice under liquidity constraints', *Journal of Political Economy*, 97: 808–27.

Evans, D.S. and Leighton, L.S. 1989. 'Some empirical aspects of entrepreneurship', *American Economic Review*, 79: 519–35.

Evans, W. and Schwab, R. 1994. 'Finishing high school and starting college: do Catholic schools make a difference?' Mimeo, University of Maryland.

Fararo, T.J. 1989a. *The Meaning of General Theoretical Sociology*. ASA Rose Monograph. New York: Cambridge University Press.

Fararo, T.J. 1989b. 'The spirit of unification in sociological theory', *Sociological Theory*, 7: 175–90.

Fararo, T.J. 1993. 'General social equilibrium: toward theoretical synthesis', *Sociological Theory*, 11 (3): 291–313.

Featherman, D. and Stevens, G. 1982. 'A revised socioeconomic index of occupational status: application in analysis of sex differences in attainment', in R. Hauser, D. Mechanic, A. Haller and T. Hauser (eds), *Social Structure and Behaviour: Essays in Honor of William Hamilton Sewell*. New York: Academic Press.

Feller, W. 1950. *Probability Theory and Its Applications*. Vol. 1. New York: Wiley.

Fiedler, K. 1988. 'The dependence of the conjunction fallacy on subtle linguistic factors', *Psychological Research*, 50: 123–51.

Frank, J. 1973. *Persuasion and Healing*. Baltimore, MD: The Johns Hopkins University Press.

Frank, R.H. 1992. 'Melding sociology and economics: James Coleman's *Foundations of Social Theory*', *Journal of Economic Literature*, 30: 147–70.

Frenzen, J., Hirsch, P.M. and Zerillo, C. 1994. 'Consumption, preferences and changing lifestyles', in N.J. Smelser and R. Swedberg (eds), *Handbook of Economic Sociology*. Princeton and New York: Princeton University Press and Russell Sage Foundation.

Freud, S. 1971. *Group Psychology and the Analysis of the Ego*. New York: Bantam.

Frey, B.S. 1992. *Economics as a Science of Human Behavior*. Boston/Dordrecht/London: Kluwer.

Friedman, M. 1953. 'The methodology of positive economics', in M. Friedman, *Essays in Positive Economics*. Chicago, IL: University of Chicago Press.

Gavanski, I. and Roskos-Ewoldsen, D.R. 1991. 'Representativeness and conjoint probability', *Journal of Personality and Social Psychology*, 61: 181–94.

Geroski, P.A. and Schwalbach, J. (eds) 1990. *Entry and Market Contestability: An International Comparison*. Berlin: SSRC.

Gierke, O. [1881] 1961. 'The idea of corporation', in T. Parsons *et al.* (eds), *Theories of Society*, Glencoe: The Free Press.

Gierke, O. [1900] 1958. *Political Theories of the Middle Age*. Translated with an introduction by F.W. Maitland. Boston, MA: Beacon Press.

Gigerenzer, G. 1991. 'How to make cognitive illusions disappear: beyond "heuristics and biases"', *European Review of Social Psychology*, 2: 83–115.

Gilmore, J.B. 1972. *An Investigation of Selected Entrepreneurial Models*, PhD, University of Oklahoma.

Glaser, R. and Chi, M.T.H. 1988. 'Overview', in M.T.H. Chi, R. Glaser and M.J. Farr (eds), *The Nature of Expertise*. Hillsdale, NJ: Lawrence Erlbaum Associates.

Glass, D.V. (ed.) 1954. *Social Mobility in Britain*, London: Routledge and Kegan Paul.

Gmytrasiewicz, E. 1993. *Edukacja a szansa rozwoju gospodarki* [Education and Economic Growth]. Warsaw.

Goffman, E. 1967. *Interaction Ritual*. New York: Doubleday.

Goffman, E. 1974. *Frame Analysis*. New York: Harper.

Goldberger, A.S. and Cain, G.G. 1982. 'The causal analysis of cognitive outcomes in the Coleman, Hoffer and Kilgore Report', *Sociology of Education*, 55: 103–22.

Goldstone, J. 1991. *Revolution and Rebellion in the Early Modern World*. Berkeley, CA: University of California Press.

Goldstone, J.A. 1994. 'Is revolution individually rational? Groups and individuals in revolutionary collective action', *Rationality and Society*, 6: 139–66.

Goldthorpe, J.H. 1987. *Social Mobility and Class Structure in Modern Britain*. Oxford: Clarendon Press.

Goode, E. and Nachman, B.-Y. 1994. 'Moral panics: culture, politics and social construction', *Annual Review of Sociology*, 20: 149–71.

Goodman, N. 1983. *Fact, Fiction and Forecast*. 4th ed. Cambridge, MA: Harvard University Press.

Gould, A. and Keeble, D. 1984. 'New firms and rural industrialisation in East Anglia', *Regional Studies*, 18: 189–201.

Granovetter, M. 1973. 'The strength of weak ties', *American Journal of Sociology*, 78: 1360–80.

Granovetter, M. 1978. 'Threshold models of collective behavior', *American Journal of Sociology*, 83: 1420–43.

Granovetter, M. 1982. 'The strength of weak ties revisited', in P.V. Marsden and N. Lin (eds), *Social Structure and Network Analysis*. Beverly Hills, CA: Sage.

Granovetter, M. 1985. 'Economic action and social structure: the theory/problem of embeddedness', *American Journal of Sociology*, 91: 481–510.

Granovetter, M. and Swedberg, R. (eds) 1992. *The Sociology of Economic Life*. Boulder, CO: Westview Press.

Greenblat, C.S. 1975a. 'Gaming as applied sociology', in C.S. Greenblat and R.D. Duke (eds), *Gaming-Simulation: Rationale, Design, and Applications*. New York: Sage Publications/Wiley.

Greenblat, C.S. 1975b. 'Teaching with simulation games: a review of claims and evidence', in C.S. Greenblat and R.D. Duke (eds), *Gaming-Simulation: Rationale, Design and Applications*. New York: Sage Publications/Wiley.

Greenblat, C.S. 1989. 'Extending the range of experience', in D. Crookall and D. Saunders (eds), *Communications and Simulation*. Clevedon: Multilingual Matter.

Greve, A. and Foss, L. 1990. 'Networks and entrepreneurship', mimeo, University of Oslo.

Grice, P. 1989. *Studies in the Way of Words*. Cambridge, MA: Harvard University Press.

Grossman, G. 1984. 'International trade, foreign investment and the formation of the entrepreneurial class', *American Economic Review*, 74: 605–14.

Habermas, J. 1978. *Knowledge and Human Interests*. London: Heinemann.

Habermas, J. 1985. 'Law as medium and law as institution', in G. Teubner (ed.), *Dilemmas of Law in the Welfare State*. New York: Walter de Gruyter.

Habermas, J. 1987. *Theory of Communicative Action*. 2 vols. Oxford: Polity Press.

Habermas, J. 1992. *Faktizität und Geltung: Beiträge zur Diskurstheorie des Rechts und des demokratischen Rechtsstaats*. Frankfurt: Suhrkamp.

Hacking, I. 1995. *The Logic of Statistical Inference*. Cambridge: Cambridge University Press.

Hagan, J., Merkens, H. and Boehnke, K. 1994. 'Delinquency and disdain: social capital and the control of right wing extremism among East and West Berlin youth', Presented at the thirteenth meeting of the Society for the Study of Behavioural Development. Amsterdam, July.

Hakim, C. 1989. 'New recruits to self-employment in the 1980's', *Employment Gazette*, 97: 286–98.

Hall, G.S. 1904. *Adolescence I–II*. New York and London: Appleton and Co.

Hall, G.S. 1922. *Life and Confessions of a Psychologist*. New York: Appleton and Co.

Hamblin, C.L. [1970] 1986. *Fallacies*. Virginia: Vale Press.

Hamilton, R.T. 1989. 'Unemployment and business formation rates: reconciling time series and cross section evidence', *Environment and Planning*, 21: 249–55.

Hammack, F. 1986. 'Large school systems' dropout reports: an analysis of definitions, procedures, and findings', *Teachers College Record*, 87: 324–41.

Hammond, P. and Frechtling, J. 1979. 'Twelve, nine and three month achievement gains of low and average achieving elementary school students', paper presented at AERA Annual Meeting, San Francisco, 8 April.

Hammond, P.E. (ed.) 1964. *Sociologists at Work*. New York: Basic Books.

Hannan, M.T. 1992. 'Rationality and robustness in multilevel systems', in Coleman and Fararo (1992).

Hanushek, E. 1968. *The Education of Negroes and Whites*. Unpublished PhD Thesis, Department of Economics, Massachusetts Institute of Technology.

Hanushek, E. 1972. *Education and Race*. Cambridge, MA: Ballinger Press.

Hanushek, E. 1991. 'When school finance reform may not be a good policy', *Harvard Journal on Legislation*, 28 (2).

Hanushek, E. 1994. *Making Schools Work: Improving Performance and Controlling Costs*. Washington, DC: The Brookings Institution.

Hanushek, E. and Harbison, R. 1992. *Educational Performance of the Poor: Lessons from Northeast Brazil*. New York: Oxford University Press.

Hanushek, E.A. and Kain, J.F. 1972. 'On the value of equality of educational opportunity as a guide to public policy', in F. Mosteller and D.P. Moynihan (eds), *On Equality of Educational Opportunity*. New York: Random House.

Harvard Education Letter. 1992. 'The seventh-grade slump and how to avoid it', *Harvard Education Letter*, January–February: 1–4.

Harvard Educational Review. 1968. 'A special issue: equality of educational opportunity', *Harvard Educational Review*, 38: 3–175.

Hauser, R.M. 1978. 'On "a reconceptualisation of school effects"', *Sociology of Education*, 51 (1): 86–73.

Hauser, R.M., Sewell, W.H. and Alwin, D.F. 1976. 'High school effects on achievement', in W.H. Sewell, R.M. Hauser and D.L. Featherman (eds), *Schooling and Achievement in American Society*. New York: Academic Press.

Hayes, D. and Grether, J. 1969. 'The school year and vacations: when do students learn?', Paper presented at the annual meeting of the Eastern Sociological Association, New York (subsequently published in *Cornell Journal of Social Relations*, 17, 1983: 56–71).

Hechter, M. 1987. *Principles of Group Solidarity*. Berkeley, CA: University of California Press.

Heckman, J. 1992. 'Randomization and social program evaluation', in C. Manski and I. Garfinkel (eds), *Evaluating Welfare and Training Programs*. Cambridge, MA: Harvard University Press.

Heckman, J. and Robb, R. 1985. 'Evaluating the impact of treatments on outcomes', in J. Heckman and B. Singer (eds), *Longitudinal Analysis of Labor Market Data*. Cambridge: Cambridge University Press.

Heckman, J. and Smith, J. 1995. 'Assessing the case for randomized evaluations of job training programs', *Journal of Economic Perspectives*, April.

Heckman, J., Layne-Farrar, A. and Todd, P. 1995. 'Does measured schooling quality really matter?', in G. Burtless (ed.), *Does Money Matter? The Link between Schools, Student Achievement and Adult Success*. Washington: The Brookings Institution.

Heckman, J., Layne-Farrar, A. and Todd, P. (forthcoming) 1996. 'The Schooling Quality-Earnings Relationship: Using Economic Theory to Interpret Functional Forms Consistent with the Evidence,' *Review of Economics and Statistics*.

Heirich, M. 1971. *The Spiral of Conflict: Berkeley 1964*. New York: Columbia University Press.

Heritage, J. 1984. *Garfinkel and Ethnomethodology*. Cambridge: Polity Press.

Hernes, G. 1989a. 'The logic of *The Protestant Ethic*', *Rationality and Society*, 1 (1): 123–62.

Hernes, G. 1989b. 'Response to Coleman', *Rationality and Society*, 1 (2): 295–9.

Herrnstein, R.J. 1990. 'Rational choice theory: necessary but not sufficient', *American Psychologist*, 45: 356–67.

Herrnstein, R.J. and Murray, C. 1994. *The Bell Curve: Intelligence and Class Structure in American Life*. New York: The Free Press.

Hess, R. and Holloway, S. 1984. 'Family and school as educational institutions', in R. Parke (ed.), *Review of Child Development Research Vol. 7: The Family*, Chicago, IL: University of Chicago Press, pp. 179–222.

Heyns, B. 1978. *Summer Learning and the Effects of Schooling*. New York: Academic Press.

Heyns, B. 1986. 'Summer programs and compensatory education: the future of an idea', working paper prepared for the National Institute of Education, Chapter One Study Team, Conference on the Effects of Alternative Designs in Compensatory Education, Washington, DC, June.

Heyns, B. 1987. 'Schooling and cognitive development: is there a season for learning?' *Child Development*, 58: 1151–60.

Hill, P.T. 1980. 'Evaluating education programs for federal policy-makers: lessons from the NIE compensatory education study', in J. Pincus (ed.), *Educational Evaluation in the Public Policy Setting*. Santa Monica, CA: RAND R-2502-RC.

Hirschman, A.O. 1970. *Exit, Voice and Loyalty: Responses to Decline in Firms, Organisations and States*. Cambridge, MA: Harvard University Press.

Hoaglin, D.C., Light, R.J., McPeek, B., Mosteller, F. and Stoto, M.A. 1982. *Data for Decisions*. Cambridge, MA: Abt Books.

Hodgson, G. 1973. 'Do schools make a difference?', *The Atlantic*, 231: 35–46.

Hoffman, P.J. 1960. 'The paramorphic representation of clinical judgement', *Psychological Bulletin*, 57: 116–31.

Hollis, M. 1987. *The Cunning of Reason*. Cambridge: Cambridge University Press.

Homans, G.C. 1950. *The Human Group*. New York: Harcourt, Brace and World.

Homans, G.C. 1958. 'Social behaviour as exchange', *American Journal of Sociology*, 63: 597–606.

Homans, G.C. [1961] 1974. *Social Behaviour: Its Elementary Forms*. Rev. ed. New York: Harcourt Brace Jovanovich.

Homans, G.C. 1967. *The Nature of Social Science*. New York: Harcourt, Brace and World.

Hope, K. 1978. 'Indicators of the state of society', in M. Bulmer (ed.), *Social Policy Research*. London: Macmillan.

Hornaday, J.S. and Bunker, C.S. 1970. 'The nature of the entrepreneur', *Personnel Psychology*, 23: 47–54.

Huizinga, J. 1955. *Homo Ludens*. Boston, MA: Beacon Press.

Husén, T. 1944. *Adolescensen*. Stockholm: Almqvist and Wiksell.

Husén, T. 1969. *Talent, Opportunity and Career*, Stockholm: Almqvist and Wiksell.

Husén, T. 1979. *The School in Question: A Comparative Study of the School and Its Future in Western Societies*. London and New York: Oxford University Press.

Husén, T., Tuijnman, A. and Halls, W.D. (eds) 1992. *Schooling in Modern European Society*. Oxford: Pergamon Press.

Inbar, M. (forthcoming) 1995. *The Critical Assessment of Argument: Elements of a Conceptual Framework of Analysis*.

Inbar, M. and Stoll, C.S. 1968. 'Autotelic behaviour in socialization', Baltimore, MD: The Johns Hopkins University, Center for Social Organisation of Schools Report No. 29.

Ingrao, B. and Israel, G. 1990. *The Invisible Hand: Economic Equilibrium in the History of Science*. Cambridge, MA: MIT Press.

Institute for Scientific Information, Inc. 1956–94. *SSCI: Social Sciences Citation Index*. Philadelphia, PA: Institute for Scientific Information.

Jencks, C. 1972. 'The Coleman Report and conventional wisdom', in F. Mosteller and D. Moynihan (eds), *On the Equality of Educational Opportunity*. New York: Vintage Books.

Jencks, C. 1985. 'How much do high school students learn?', *Sociology of Education*, 58: 128–53.

Jencks, C. 1992. *Rethinking of Social Policy*. Cambridge, MA: Harvard University Press.

Jencks, C., Smith, M., Acland, H., Bane, M.J., Cohen, D., Gintis, H., Heyns, B. and Michelson, S. 1972. *Inequality: A Reassessment of the Basic Effect of Family and Schooling in America*. New York: Basic Books.

Johnson, G. and Stafford, F. 1973. 'Social returns to quantity and quality of schooling', *Journal of Human Resources*, 8: 139–55.

Johnson, P.S. 1986. *New Firms: An Economic Perspective*. London: Allen and Unwin.

Johnson-Laird, P.N. 1983. *Mental Models*. Cambridge: Cambridge University Press.

Johnson-Laird, P.N. 1988. *The Computer and the Mind: An Introduction to Cognitive Science*. Cambridge, MA: Harvard University Press.

Johnson-Laird, P.N. 1993. *Human and Machine Thinking*. Hillsdale, NJ: Lawrence Erlbaum Associates.

Jugend zwischen 15 und 24. 1954–55. German Shell Foundation.

Jugend, Bildung und Freizeit. 1965. German Shell Foundation.

Jugend zwischen 13 und 24. 1975. German Shell Foundation.

Jugend in Europa: Ihre Eingliederung in die Welt der Erwachsenen. 1977. German Shell Foundation.

Kahneman, D. 1981. 'Who shall be the arbiter of our intuitions?', *Behavioral and Brain Sciences*, 4: 339–40.

Kahneman, D. and Tversky, A. 1979. 'Prospect theory: an analysis of decision under risk', *Econometrica*, 47: 263–91.

Kahneman, D. and Tversky, A. 1982. 'On the study of statistical intuitions', in Kahneman, Slovic and Tversky (1982).

Kahneman, D., Slovic, P. and Tversky, A. (eds) 1982. *Judgement under Uncertainty: Heuristics and Biases*. Cambridge: Cambridge University Press.

Kanbur, S.M.R. 1982. 'Entrepreneurial risk taking, inequality and public policy: an application of inequality decomposition analysis to the general equilibrium effects of progressive taxation', *Journal of Political Economy*, 90: 1–22.

Kandel, D.B. 1978. 'Homophily, selection and socialisation in adolescent friendships', *American Journal of Sociology*, 84: 427–36.

Kandel, D.B. 1995. 'The parental and peer contexts of adolescent deviance: an algebra of interpersonal influences', in H. White (ed.), *Empirical Validity of Theories of Drug Abuse*, Special issue of *Journal of Drug Abuse* (in press).

Kandel, D.B. and Andrews, K. 1987. 'Processes of adolescent socialisation by parents and by peers', *International Journal of the Addictions*, Special Issue, 22: 319–42.

Kandel, D.B. and Lesser, G. 1972. *Youth in Two Worlds*. San Francisco, CA: Jossey Bass, Foreword by James S. Coleman.

Karl, B.D. 1987. *The Uneasy State*. Chicago, IL: University of Chicago Press.

Katz, E. and Lazarsfeld, P. 1955. *Personal Influence*. Glencoe, IL: The Free Press.

Kemper, T. 1978. *A Social Interactional Theory of Emotions*. New York: Wiley.

Kemper, T. 1990. *Research Agendas in the Sociology of Emotions*. Albany: SUNY Press.

Kerckhoff, A.C. 1993. *Diverging Pathways: Social Structure and Career Decisions*. New York: Cambridge University Press.

Kidder, S.J. 1971. 'Emotional arousal and attitude change during simulation games', Baltimore, MD: The Johns Hopkins University, Center for Social Organisation of Schools, Report No. 111.

Kihlstrom, R.E. and Laffont, J.J. 1979. 'A general equilibrium entrepreneurial theory of the firm formation based on risk aversion', *Journal of Political Economy*, 87: 719–48.

Kirzner, I.M. 1973. *Competition and Entrepreneurship*. Chicago, IL: University of Chicago Press.

Kiser, E. and Barzel, Y. 1991. 'The origins of democracy in England'. *Rationality and Society*, 3: 396–422.

Kiser, E. and Schneider, J. 1994. 'Bureaucracy and efficiency in taxation in early Prussia', *American Sociological Review*, 59: 187–204.

Knight, F. 1921. *Risk, Uncertainty and Profit*. New York: Houghton Mifflin.

Kraus, P. 1973. *Yesterday's Children*. New York: John Wiley.

Lane, F.C. 1979. *Profits from Power: Readings in Protection Rent and Violence-Controlling Enterprises*. Albany, NY: SUNY Press.

Lang, K. and Lang, G. 1961. *Collective Dynamics*. New York: Thomas Crowell.

Lareau, A. 1987. 'Social class differences in family-school relationships: the importance of cultural capital', *Sociology of Education*, 60: 78–85.

Lazarsfeld, P. 1959. 'Reflections on business', *American Journal of Sociology*, 65: 1–31.

Lazarsfeld, P. 1978. 'Some episodes in the history of panel analysis', in D. Kandel (ed.), *Longitudinal Research in Drug Use: Empirical Findings and Methodological Issues*. Washington, DC: Hemisphere-John Wiley.

Le Bon, G. 1952. *The Crowd*. London: Ernest Benn.

Lee, H. 1960. *To Kill a Mockingbird*. New York: Warner.

Leff, N.H. 1979. 'Entrepreneurship and economic development: the problem revisited', *Journal of Economic Literature*, 17: 46–64.

Lenski, G.E. 1966. *Power and Privilege: A Theory of Stratification*. New York: McGraw-Hill.

Lever, J. 1978. 'Sex differences in the complexity of children's play and games'. *American Sociological Review*, 43: 471–83.

Levi, M. 1988. *Of Rule and Revenue*. Berkeley, CA: University of California Press.

Levin, H. 1970. 'A new model for school effectiveness', in US Department of Health, Education and Welfare (ed.), *Do Teachers Make a Difference?* Washington, DC: US Department of Health, Education and Welfare.

Levine, D. and Bane, M. 1975. *The 'Inequality Controversy': Schooling and Distributive Justice*. New York: Basic Books.

Lichbach, M. 1994. 'Rethinking rationality and rebellion: theories of collective action and problems of collective dissent', *Rationality and Society*, 6: 8–39.

Lindenberg, S. 1982. 'Sharing groups: theory and suggested applications', *Journal of Mathematical Sociology*, 9: 33–62.

Lindenberg, S. 1985. 'Rational choice and sociological theory: new pressures on economics as a social science', *Journal of Institutional and Theoretical Economics (ZgS)*, 141: 244–55.

Lindenberg, S. 1986. 'The paradox of privatization in consumption', in A. Diekmann and P. Mitter (eds), *Paradoxical Effects of Social Behavior. Essays in Honor of Anatol Rapoport*. Heidelberg/Wien: Physica Verlag, pp. 297–310.

Lindenberg, S. 1988. 'Contractual relations and weak solidarity: the behavioral basis of restraints on gain maximization', *Journal of Institutional and Theoretical Economics*, 144: 39–58.

Lindenberg, S. 1990. 'Homo socio-oeconomicus: the emergence of a general model of man in the social sciences', *Journal of Institutional and Theoretical Economics*, 146: 727–48.

Lindenberg, S. 1992. 'The method of decreasing abstraction', in J.S. Coleman and T.J. Fararo (eds), *Rational Choice Theory: Advocacy and Critique*. Newbury Park, CA: Sage, pp. 3–20.

Lindenberg, S. 1993. 'Framing, empirical evidence and applications', *Jahrbuch für Neue Politische Ökonomie*. Tübingen: Mohr (Siebeck).

Lindenberg, S. 1994. 'Norms and the power of loss: Ellickson's theory and beyond', *Journal of Institutional and Theoretical Economics*, 150: 101–13.

Lipset, S.M., Trow, M. and Coleman, J.S. 1956. *Union Democracy*. New York: The Free Press.

Livingston, S.A. 1972. 'The academic games program: summary of research results (1967–1972)'. Baltimore, MD: The Johns Hopkins University, Center for Social Organisation of Schools, Report No. 146.

Livingston, S.A., Fennessey, G.M., Coleman, J.S. *et al.* 1973. 'The Hopkins games program: final report on seven years of research'. Baltimore, MD: The Johns Hopkins University, Centre for Social Organisation of Schools, Report No. 155.

Lofland, J. 1985. *Protest: Studies of Collective Behavior and Social Movements*. New Brunswick, NJ: Transaction.

Lopez, L.L. 1981. 'Decision-making in the short run', *Journal of Experimental Psychology*, (7): 377–85.

Loury, G. 1987. 'Why should we care about group inequality?', *Social Philosophy and Policy*, 5: 249–71.

Lucas, R.E. 1978. 'On the size distribution of firms', *Bell Journal of Economics*, 9: 508–23.

Lynd, R.S. and Lynd, H.M. 1937. *Middletown in Transition*. New York: Harcourt Brace.

McClelland, D.C. 1961. *The Achieving Society*. Princeton, NJ: Princeton University Press.

McDill, E.L. and Coleman, J.S. 1965. 'Family and peer influences in college plans of high school students', *Sociology of Education*, 38: 112–26.

McGuire, J.W. 1976. 'The small enterprise in economics and organisation theory', *Journal of Contemporary Business*, 115–38.

McKenzie, R. and Tullock, G. 1985. *The New World of Economics*. 4th ed. Homewood, IL: Irwin.

McPhail, C. 1991. *The Myth of the Madding Crowd*. New York: Aldine.

McPhail, C. and Wohlstein, R. 1983. 'Individual and collective behaviors within gatherings, demonstrations and riots', *Annual Review of Sociology*, 9: 579–600.

March, J.G. 1978. 'Bounded rationality, ambiguity, and the engineering of choice', *Bell Journal of Economics*, 9: 587–608.

Markovsky, B., Skvoretz, J., Miller, D., Lovaglia, M.J. and Erger, J. 1993. 'The seeds of weak power: extending network exchange theory', *American Sociological Review*, 58: 197–209.

Marshall, G. 1982. *In Search of the Spirit of Capitalism: An Essay on Max Weber's Protestant Ethic Thesis*. London: Hutchinson.

Martindale, D. 1974. 'American sociology since World War Two', *International Journal of Contemporary Sociology*, 11 (2–3): 165–73.

Marwell, G. and Oliver, P. 1993. *The Critical Mass in Collective Action*. Cambridge: Cambridge University Press.

Mason, C. 1990. 'Spatial divisions of enterprise', mimeo, University of Southampton.

Massey, D. and Denton, N. 1993. *American Apartheid: Segregation and the Making of the Underclass*. Cambridge, MA: Harvard University Press.

Mead, G.H. 1934. *Mind, Self and Society*. Chicago, IL: University of Chicago Press.

Mead, M. 1943. *Coming of Age in Samoa: A Study of Adolesence and Sex in Primitive Societies*. Harmondsworth: Penguin.

Mead, M. 1970. *Culture and Commitment*. New York: Natural History Press-Doubleday.

Meager, N. 1992. 'Does unemployment lead to self-employment?', *Small Business Economics*, 4: 87–103.

Merton, R.K. 1968. *Social Theory and Social Structure*. New York: The Free Press.

Merton, R.K. 1994. Letter to R. Swedberg, 28 July.

Milgrom, P. and Roberts, J. 1992. *Economics, Organisation and Management*. Englewood Cliffs: Prentice-Hall International.

Morier, D.M. and Borgida, E. 1984. 'The conjunction fallacy: a task specific phenomenon', *Personality and Social Psychology Bulletin*, 10: 243–52.

Mosakowski, E.M. and Carroll, G.R. 1985. 'The career dynamics of entrepreneurship: an empirical analysis of self-employment in the Federal Republic of Germany', mimeo, University of Cologne.

Mosteller, F. and Moynihan, D.P. 1969. *Equality of Educational Opportunity*. Boston, MA: Harvard University Press.

Mosteller, F. and Moynihan, D.P. (eds) 1972. *On the Equality of Educational Opportunity*, Papers deriving from the Harvard University Faculty Seminar on the Coleman Report. New York: Random House.

Moynihan, D.P. 1969. *Maximum Feasible Misunderstanding*. New York: Basic Books.

Moynihan, D.P. 1993. 'Educational goals and political plans', in A.B. Sørensen and S. Spilerman (eds), *Social Theory and Social Policy: Essays in Honor of James S. Coleman*. New York: Praeger.

Mullins, N. 1983. 'Theories and theory groups revisited', *Sociological Theory*, 1: 319–37.

Mullins, N. and Mullins, C. 1973. *Theories and Theory Groups in Contemporary American Sociology*. New York: Harper and Row.

Murnane, R. 1975. *The Impact of School Resources on the Learning of Inner City Children*. Cambridge, MA: Ballinger.

Murnane, R., Newstead, S. and Olsen, R.J. 1985. 'Comparing public and private schools: the puzzling role of selection bias', *Journal of Business and Economic Statistics*, 3: 23–35.

Murnane, R., Willett, J.B. and Levy, F. 1995. 'The growing importance of cognitive skills in wage determination', *Review of Economics and Statistics*, forthcoming.

Murray, C. 1984. *Losing Ground: American Social Policy 1950–1980*. New York: Basic Books.

Nathan, R. 1988. *Social Science in Government: Uses and Misuses*. New York: Basic Books.

Natriello, G., McDill, E. and Pallas, A. 1990. *Schooling Disadvantaged Children: Racing against Catastrophe*. New York: Teachers College Press.

Neal, D. 1994. 'The effect of catholic secondary schooling on educational attainment', Chicago, IL: University of Chicago, Centre for the Study of the Economy and the State, Working Paper No. 95.

Newell, A. 1990. *Unified Theories of Cognition*. Cambridge, MA: Harvard University Press.

Nisbett, R.E. and Bellows, N. 1977. 'Verbal reports about causal influences on social judgements: private access versus public theories', *Personality and Social Psychology*, 35: 613–24.

Nisbett, R.E. and Wilson, T.D. 1977. 'Telling more than we can know: verbal reports on mental processes', *Psychological Review*, 84: 231–59.

Noell, J. 1982. 'Public and catholic schools: a reanalysis of public and private schools', *Sociology of Education*, 55: 123–32.

Nozick, R. 1974. *Anarchy, State and Utopia*. New York: Basic Books.

Oberschall, A.R. 1994. 'Rational choice in collective protests', *Rationality and Society*, 6: 79–100.

OECD. 1986, 'Cyclical sensitivity of self-employment', *OECD Outlook*. Paris: OECD.

OECD. 1994. *Report on Poland*. Paris: OECD.

Ogbu, J. 1988. 'Class stratification, racial stratification, and schooling', in L. Weis (ed.), *Class, Race and Gender in American Education*. Albany, NY: State University of New York Press.

Ogbu, J. 1992. 'Understanding cultural diversity and learning', *Educational Researcher*, November.

Oliver, P. 1993. 'Formal models of collective action', *Annual Review of Sociology*, 19: 271–300.

Olson, M. 1965. *The Logic of Collective Action: Public Goods and the Theory of Groups*. Cambridge, MA: Harvard University Press.

Opp, K.-D. 1970. 'Theories of the middle range as a strategy for the construction of a general sociological theory', *Quantity and Quality*, 4 (2): 243–53.

Opp, K.-D. 1985. 'Sociology and economic man', *Journal of Institutional and Theoretical Economics*, 141: 213–43.

Paley, V.G. 1984. *Boys and Girls: Superheroes in the Doll Corner*. Chicago, IL: University of Chicago Press.

Pallas, A.M. 1993. 'Schooling in the course of human lives: the social context of education and the transition to adulthood in industry society', *Review of Educational Research*, 63: 409–47.

Pallas, A., Entwisle, D., Alexander, K. and Cadigan, D. 1987. 'Children who do exceptionally well in first grade', *Sociology of Education*, 60: 257–71.

Pallas, A., Entwisle, D., Alexander, K. and Stluka, M. 1994. 'Ability-group effects: instructional, social or institutional?', *Sociology of Education*, 67: 27–46.

Papert, S. 1980. *Mindstorms: Children, Computers, and Powerful Ideas*. New York: Basic Books.

Pareto, V. [1920] 1935. *The Mind and Society*. Translation by A. Bongiorno and A. Livingston. New York: Harcourt Brace.

Parker, S., Greer, S. and Zuckerman, B. 1988. 'Double jeopardy: the impact of poverty on early child development', *Pediatric Clinics of North America*, 35: 1227–40.

Parsons, T. 1937. *The Structure of Social Action*. New York: The Free Press.

Parsons, T. 1951. *The Social System*. New York: Free Press.

Parsons, T. 1970. 'Some problems of general theory in sociology', in J.C. McKinney and E.E. Tiryakian (eds), *Theoretical Sociology*. New York: Appleton-Century-Crofts, pp. 28–68.

Parsons, T. 1971. 'Levels of organisation and the mediation of social interaction', in H. Turk and R.L. Simpson (eds), *Institutions and Social Exchange: The Sociologies of Talcott Parsons and George Homans*. New York: Bobbs-Merrill.

Parsons, J.E., Adler, T.F. and Kaczak, C.M. 1982. 'Socialisation of achievement attitudes and beliefs: parental influences', *Child Development*, 53: 322–39.

Patterson, G.R., Reid, J.B. and Dishion, T.J. 1992. *Antisocial Boys*. Eugene, OR: Castalia.

Pearce, D.W. (ed.) 1986. *The MIT Dictionary in Modern Economics*. Cambridge, MA: MIT Press.

Pelavin, S. and David, J. 1977. *Evaluating Long-Term Achievement: An Analysis of Longitudinal Data from Compensatory Educational Programs*. Prepared for Office of the Assistant Secretary for Education, Department of Health, Education and Welfare.

Pickles, A.R. and O'Farrell, P.N. 1987. 'An analysis of entrepreneurial behaviour from male work histories', *Regional Studies*, 21: 424–44.

Pizzorno, A. 1986. 'Some other kinds of otherness: a critique of rational choice theories', in A. Foxley *et al.* (eds), *Development, Democracy and the Art of Trespassing: Essays in Honor of A.O. Hirschman*. Notre Dame, IN: Notre Dame University Press.

Pizzorno, A. 1991. 'On the individualist theory of social order', in J.S. Coleman and P. Bourdieu (eds), *Social Theory for a Changing Society*, Boulder, CO: Westview Press.

Plous, S. 1993. *The Psychology of Judgement and Decision-Making*. New York: McGraw-Hill.

Pollock, F. and Maitland, F.W. [1898] 1986. *History of English Law*. 2 vols. Cambridge: Cambridge University Press.

Prais, S.J. 1955. 'Measuring social mobility', *Journal of the Royal Statistical Society A*, 118: 56–66.

Quarantelli, E. and Hundley, J. 1969. 'A test of some propositions about crowd formation and behaviour', in R. Evans (ed.), *Readings in Collective Behavior*. Chicago. IL: Rand McNally.

Raser, J.R. 1969. *Simulation and Society: An Exploration of Scientific Gaming*. Boston, MA: Allyn and Bacon.

Ravitch, D. 1993. 'The Coleman Reports and American education', in A.B. Sørensen and L. Spilerman (eds), *Social Theory and Social Policy: Essays in Honor of James S. Coleman*. Westport, CT: Greenwood.

Rawls, J. 1971. *A Theory of Justice*. Cambridge, MA: Harvard University Press.

Rawls, J. 1993. *Political Liberalism*. New York: Columbia University Press.

Raz, J. 1978. 'Reasons for action, decisions and norms', in J. Raz (ed.), *Practical Reasoning*. Oxford: Oxford University Press.

Recent Social Trends. 1933. *Recent Social Trends: The Report of the President's Committee on Recent Social Trends*. New York: McGraw-Hill.

Rees, H. and Shah, A. 1986. 'An empirical analysis of self-employment in the UK', *Journal of Applied Econometrics*, 1: 95–108.

Riley, M.W. (ed.) 1988. *Sociological Lives*. Newbury Park, CA: Sage Publications.

Robinson, P. 1994. 'The British labour market in historical perspective — changes in the structure of employment and unemployment', CEP discussion paper, London School of Economics.

Roemer, J. 1986. *Analytical Marxism*. Cambridge: Cambridge University Press.

Rogers, E.M. 1994. *A History of Communication Study*. New York: The Free Press.

Rose Ackerman, S. 1992. *Reforming the Progressive Agenda: The Reform of the American Regulatory State*. New York: Free Press.

Rosenberg, G.N. 1991. *The Hollow Hope: Can Courts Bring About Social Change?* Chicago, IL: University of Chicago Press.

Rosenfeld, F.H. 1975. 'The educational effectiveness of simulation games: a synthesis of recent findings', in C.S. Greenblat and R.D. Duke (eds), *Gaming-Simulation: Rationale, Design, and Applications*. New York: Sage Publications/Wiley.

Rossi, P. 1964. 'Researchers, scholars and policymakers: the politics of large-scale research', *Daedalus*, 92: 1142–61.

Rowe, N. 1989. *Rules and Institutions*. Ann Arbor, MI: University of Michigan Press.

Rudé, G. 1964. *The Crowd in History 1730–1848*. New York: Wiley.

Sampson, R. and Laub, J. 1993. *Crime in the Making: Pathways and Turning Points through Life*. Cambridge, MA: Harvard University Press.

Sander, W. and Krautmann, A. 1994. 'Catholic schools, dropout rates and educational attainment', *Economic Inquiry*, forthcoming.

Saxe, G. 1989. 'Cultural practices in Brazil and children's mathematics', paper prepared for Biennial Meeting of SRCD, Kansas City.

Schneider, B. and Coleman, J.S. 1993. *Parents, Their Children and Schools*. Boulder, CO: Westview Press.

Schultz, T.W. 1980. 'Investment in entrepreneurial ability', *Scandinavian Journal of Economics*, 82: 437–48.

Schumpeter, J.A. 1939. *Business Cycles: A Theoretical, Historical and Statistical Analysis of the Capitalist Process*. New York: McGraw-Hill.

Schumpeter, J.A. 1954. *History of Economic Analysis*. London: George Allen and Unwin.

Schwarz, N., Strack, F., Hilton, D. and Naderer, G. 1991. 'Base rates, representativeness, and the logic of conversation: the contextual relevance of "irrelevant information"', *Social Cognition*, 9: 67–84.

Searle, J.R. 1970. *Speech Acts*. Cambridge: Cambridge University Press.

Selznick, P. 1992. *The Moral Commonwealth*. Berkeley, CA: University of California Press.

Shapero, A. 1971. *An Action Program for Entrepreneurship*. Austin, TX: Multi-Disciplinary Research Press.

Shellow, R. and Roemer, D. 1969. 'The riot that didn't happen', in R. Evans (ed.), *Readings in Collective Behavior*. Chicago, IL: Rand McNally.

Shepsle, K.A. 1989. 'Studying institutions: some lessons from the rational choice approach', *Journal of Theoretical Politics*, 1: 131–49.

Shils, E. 1970. 'Tradition, ecology, and institution in the history of sociology', *Daedalus*, 99 (4): 760–825.

Shirts, R.G. 1970. 'Games students play', *Saturday Review*, 16 May: 81–2.

Shorrocks, A.F. 1978. 'The measurement of mobility', *Econometrica*, 46: 1013–24.

Siegers, J.J. 1990. 'Towards the construction of interdisciplinary theoretical models to explain demographic behaviour', in C.A. Hazeu and G.A.B. Frinking (eds), *Emerging Issues in Demographic Research*. Amsterdam: Elsevier.

Sills, D.L. 1987. 'Paul F. Lazarsfeld', in *Biographical Memoirs No. 56*. Washington, DC: National Academy Press.

Simmel, G. 1950a. *The Sociology of Georg Simmel*, translated and edited by K. Wolf. Glencoe, IL: The Free Press.

Simmel, G. 1950b. 'Sociability: an example of pure or formal sociology', in Simmel (1950a).

Simon, H.A. 1986. 'The information processing explanation of Gestalt phenomenon', *Computers in Human Behaviour*, 2: 241–55.

Simon, H.A. and Kaplan, C.A. 1989. 'Foundations of cognitive science', in M.I. Posner (ed.), *Foundations of Cognitive Science*. Cambridge, MA: MIT Press.

Skinner, Q. (ed.) 1985. *The Return of Grand Theory in the Human Sciences*. Cambridge: Cambridge University Press.

Skocpol, T. 1979. *States and Social Revolutions*. New York: Cambridge University Press.

Slaughter, D. and Epps, E. 1987. 'The home environment and academic achievement of black American children and youth: An overview', *Journal of Negro Education*, 56: 3–20.

Smelser, N. 1962. *Theory of Collective Behavior*. New York: The Free Press.

Smelser, N. 1990. 'Can individualism yield a sociology?', *Contemporary Sociology*, 19: 778–83.

Smith, M. 1972. 'Equality of educational opportunity: the basic findings reconsidered', in F. Mosteller and D. Moynihan (eds), *On the Equality of Educational Opportunity*. New York, Vintage Books.

Sokal, M.M. 1987. *Psychological Testing and American Society, 1890–1930*. New Brunswick, NJ: Rutgers University Press.

Sommers, P.M. and Conlisk, J. 1979. 'Eigenvalue immobility measures for Markov chains', *Journal of Mathematical Sociology*, 6: 253–76.

Sørensen, A.B. and Hallinan, M.T. 1977. 'A reconceptualisation of school effects', *Sociology of Education*, 50: 522–35.

Sørensen, A.B. and Spilerman, S. (eds) 1993. *Social Theory and Social Policy: Essays in Honour of James S. Coleman*. Westport, CT: Greenwood.

Sorokin, P. 1928. *Contemporary Sociological Theories*. New York: Harper and Row.

Spencer, H. 1873. *The Principles of Psychology*, Vol. 11. New York: Appleton.

St John, N.H. 1975. *School Desegregation: Outcomes for Children*. New York: Wiley.

Stanworth, M.J.K. and Curran, J. 1976. 'Growth and the small firm: an alternative view', *Journal of Management Studies*, 13: 95–110.

Stark, R. and Bainbridge, W.S. 1985. *The Future of Religion*. Berkeley, CA: University of California Press.

Stark, R. and Bainbridge, W.S. 1987. *A Theory of Religion*. New York: Lang.

Steinberg, L., Darling, N., Fletcher, A., Brown, B.B. and Dornbusch, S.M. 1993. 'Authoritative parenting and adolescent adjustment: an ecological journey', presented at the Urie Bronfenbrenner symposium, Cornell University, Ithaca, New York, 24–26 September.

Steinmitz, H. and Wright, D. 1989. 'The fall and rise of the petty bourgeoisie: changing patterns of self-employment in post war United States', *American Journal of Sociology*, 94: 973–1008.

Stinchcombe, A. 1990. *Information and Organisations*. Berkeley, CA: University of California Press.

Stipek, D. 1984. 'The development of achievement motivation', in R. Ames and C. Ames (eds), *Research on Motivation in Education*, Vol. 1. New York: Academic Press, 1968.

Stoll, C.S. 1968. 'Player characteristics and strategy in a parent–child simulation game', Baltimore, MD: The Johns Hopkins University, Center for Social Organisation of Schools. Report No. 23.

Stoll, C.S., Inbar, M. and Fennessey, J.J. 1968a. 'Game experience and socialisation — an exploratory study of sex differences', Baltimore, MD: The Johns Hopkins University, Center for Social Organisation of Schools, Report No. 30.

Stoll, C.S., Inbar, M. and Fennessey, J.J. 1968b. 'Socialization and games: an exploratory study of race differences', Baltimore, MD: The Johns Hopkins University, Center for Social Organisation of Schools, Report No. 31.

Storey, D.J. 1982. *Entrepreneurship and the New Firm*. London: Croom Helm.

Storey, D.J. 1991. 'The birth of new firms — does unemployment matter?', *Small Business Economics*, 3: 167–78.

Stouffer, S. 1949. *The American Soldier*. Princeton, NJ: Princeton University Press.

Strauss, A. 1947. 'Research in collective behavior: neglect and need', *American Sociological Review*, 12: 352–64.

Sunstein, C.R. 1990. *After the Rights Revolution: Reconceiving the Regulatory State*. Cambridge: Cambridge University Press.

Sutton, J. 1992. *Sunk Costs and Market Structure*. Cambridge, MA: MIT Press.

Swedberg, R. 1990. *Economics and Sociology. Redefining Their Boundaries: Conversations with Economists and Sociologists*. Princeton, NJ: Princeton University Press.

Szacki, J. 1973. '"Schools" in sociology', *Social Science Information*, 12 (4): 173–82.

Teubner, G. 1993. *Law as an Autopoietic System*. Oxford: Blackwell.

Thompson, J.D. 1967. *Organisations in Action*. New York: McGraw-Hill.

Thompson, M., Alexander, K. and Entwisle, D. 1989. 'Household composition, parental expectations, and school achievement', *Social Forces*, 67: 424–51.

Thompson, M., Entwisle, D., Alexander, K. and Sundius, M. 1992. 'The influence of family composition on children's conformity to the student role', *American Educational Research Journal*, 29: 405–24.

Tilly, C. 1978. *From Mobilization to Revolution*. Reading, MA: Addison-Wesley.

Tilly, C. 1990. *Coercion, Capital and European States, AD 990–1990*. Cambridge: Blackwell.

Timpane, M., Abromowitz, S., Berryman Bobrow, S. and Pascal, A. 1975. *Youth Policy in Transition*. Santa Monica, CA: Rand Corporation.

Tiryakian, E.A. 1979. 'The significance of schools in the development of sociology', in W.E. Snizek *et al.* (eds), *Contemporary Issues in Theory and Research*. London: Aldwych.

Tolstoy, L. 1957. *War and Peace*. Translated by R. Edmonds. Baltimore, MD: Penguin.

Toulmin, S. 1953. *The Philosophy of Science*. London: Hutchinson.

Toulmin, S. 1961. *Foresight and Understanding: An Enquiry into the Aims of Science*. New York: Harper.

Trotti, L. 1943. *The Oxbow Incident*. Los Angeles, CA: Twentieth Century Fox.

Trow, M. 1979. 'Reflections on youth problems and policies in the United States', in M. Gordon (ed.), *Youth Education and Unemployment Problems*. Washington, DC: Carnegie Foundation for the Advancement of Teaching.

Tullock, G. 1989. *The Economics of Special Privilege and Rent Seeking*. Boston, MA: Kluwer.

Turkle, S. 1984. *The Second Self: Computers and the Human Spirit*. New York: Simon and Schuster.

Turner, S.P. and Turner, J. 1990. *The Impossible Science: An Institutional Analysis of American Sociology*. London: Sage.

Turner, V. 1969. *The Ritual Process*. Chicago, IL: Aldine.

Tushnet, M.V. 1994. *Making Civil Rights Law: Thurgood Marshall and the Supreme Court, 1936–1961*. New York: Oxford University Press.

Tversky, A. and Kahneman, D. 1982. 'Judgements of and by representativeness', in D. Kahneman, P. Slovic and A. Tversky (eds), *Judgement under Uncertainty: Heuristics and Biases*. Cambridge: Cambridge University Press.

Tversky, A. and Kahneman, D. 1983. 'Extensional versus intuitive reasoning: the conjunctive fallacy in probability judgement', *Psychological Review*, 90: 293–315.

Vidich, A.J. and Lyman, S.M. 1985. *American Sociology*. New Haven, CT: Yale University Press.

Von Neumann, J. and Morgenstern, O. 1953. *Theory of Games as Economic Behaviour*. 3rd ed. New York: Wiley.

de Vries, Kets M.F.R. 1977. 'The entrepreneurial personality: a person at the crossroads', *Journal of Management Studies*, 12: 34–57.

Wachtel, P. 1976. 'The effects of earnings of school and college investment expenditures', *Review of Economics and Statistics*, 58: 326–31.

Weber, M. [1904–05] 1958. *The Protestant Ethic and the Spirit of Capitalism*. Translated by Talcott Parsons. New York: Charles Scribner's Sons.

Weber, M. [1906] 1985. '"Churches" and "sects" in North America: an ecclesiastical socio-political sketch', *Sociological Theory*, 3 (2): 7–13.

Weber, M. 1907. 'Kritische Bemerkungen zu den vorstehenden "Kritische Beiträgen"', *Archiv für Sozialwissenschaft und Sozialpolitik*, 25: 243–9.

Weber, M. 1908. 'Bemerkungen zu der vortstehenden "Replik"', *Archiv für Sozialwissenschaft und Sozialpolitik*, 30: 176–202.

Weber, M. 1910. 'Antikritisches zum "Geist des Kapitalismus"', *Archiv für Sozialwissenschaft und Sozialpolitik*, 30: 176–202.

Weber, M. [1915] 1946. 'The social psychology of world religions', in H.H. Gerth and C.W. Mills (eds), *From Max Weber*. New York: Oxford University Press.

Weber, M. 1920. *Gesammelte Aufsätze zur Religionssoziologie*. Vol. 1. Tübingen: J.C.B. Mohr.

Weber, M. [1920] 1946. 'The Protestant sects and the spirit of capitalism', in H.H. Gerth and C.W. Mills (eds), *From Max Weber*. New York: Oxford University Press.

Weber, M. [1922] 1978. *Economy and Society*. Edited by G. Roth and C. Wittich. Berkeley, CA: University of California Press.

Weber, M. [1923] 1981. *General Economic History*. Translated by F. Knight. New Brunswick, NJ: Transaction Books.

Weber, M. 1949. *On the Methodology of the Social Sciences*. Translated by E. Shils and H. Finch. Glencoe, IL: The Free Press.

Weick, K.E. 1974. 'Middle range theories of social systems', *Behavioural Science*, 19: 357–67.

Weiss, C.H. 1986. 'The many meanings of research utilization', in M. Bulmer *et al.* (eds), *Social Science and Social Policy*. London: Allen and Unwin.

Welch, F. 1966. 'Measurement of the quality of schooling', *American Economic Review Papers and Proceedings*, 56: 379–92.

Welch, F. 1967. 'Labor market discrimination: an interpretation of income differences in the rural South', *Journal of Political Economy*, 75 (3): 225–40.

Welch, F. and Light, A. 1987. *New Evidence on School Desegregation*. Washington, DC: US Government Printing Office, US Commission on Civil Rights, Clearinghouse Publication 92.

Wells, R.H. and Picou J.S. 1981. *American Sociology: Theoretical and Methodological Structure*. Washington, DC: University Press.

White, H. 1981. 'Where do markets come from?', *American Journal of Sociology*, 87 (3): 517–47.

White, H. 1990. 'Control to deny chance, but thereby muffling identity', *Contemporary Sociology*, 19: 783–8.

White, H. 1992. *Identity and Control: A Structural Theory of Social Action*. Princeton, NJ: Princeton University Press.

Whyte, W.F. 1943. *Street Corner Society*. Chicago, IL: University of Chicago Press.

Wieckowski, S. 1994. 'Interview with Wojciech Starzynski', *Edukacja i Dialog*, 3 (56): 3–10.

Willer, D. (ed.) 1992. 'Special double issue: location of power in exchange networks', *Social Networks*, 14 (3–4).

Williams, J.D. 1985. 'Catholic-school effects on academic achievement: new evidence from the High School and Beyond follow-up study', *Sociology of Education*, 58: 98–114.

Williamson, O. 1975. *Markets and Hierarchies*. New York: The Free Press.

Willms, J.D. and Jacobsen, S. 1990. 'Growth in mathematics skills during the intermediate years: sex differences and school effects', *International Journal of Educational Research*, 14: 157–74.

Wilson, J.Q. 1994. 'From welfare reform to character development', 1994 Wriston Lecture at the Manhattan Institute.

Wilson, W.J. 1987. *The Truly Disadvantaged: The Inner City, the Underclass and Public Policy*. Chicago, IL: University of Chicago Press.

Wippler, R. and Lindenberg, S. 1987. 'Collective phenomena and rational choice', in J.C. Alexander, B. Giesen, R. Münch and N.S. Smelser (eds), *The Micro-Macro Link*. Berkeley, CA: University of California Press.

Wolford, G., Taylor, H.A. and Beck, J.R. 1990. 'The conjunction fallacy?', *Memory and Cognition*, 18: 47–53.

Yamaguchi, K. and Kandel, D.B. 1985a. 'On the resolution of role incompatibility: life event history analysis of family roles and marijuana use', *American Journal of Sociology*, 90: 1284–325.

Yamaguchi, K. and Kandel, D.B. 1985b. 'Dynamic relationships between premarital cohabitation and illicit drug use: a life event history analysis of role selection and role socialisation', *American Sociological Review*, 50: 530–46.

Yamaguchi, K. and Kandel, D.B. 1993. 'Marital homophily on substance use among young adults', *Social Forces*, 72: 505–28.

Yaniv, I. and Foster, D.F. 1993. 'Graininess of judgement under uncertainty: an accuracy-informativeness tradeoff'. Working paper, Center for Decision Research, Graduate School of Business. Chicago, IL: University of Chicago.

Yasuda, S. 1964. 'A methodological inquiry into social mobility', *American Sociological Review*, 29: 16–23.

Zablocki, B. 1980a. *The Joyful Community*. Chicago, IL: University of Chicago Press.

Zablocki, B. 1980b. *Alienation and Charisma: A Study of Contemporary American Communes*. New York: The Free Press.

Zablocki, B. 1993. 'Rational models of charismatic influence', in A. Sørensen and S. Spilerman (eds), *Social Theory and Social Policy*. Westport, CT: Praeger.

Zald, M. and McCarthy, J. (eds) 1979. *The Dynamics of Social Movements: Resource Mobilization, Social Control and Tactics*. Cambridge: Winthrop.

Zhou, X. 1993. 'Unorganized interests and collective action in communist China', *American Sociological Review*, 58: 54–73.

List of Contributors

Peter Abell is Professor, Interdisciplinary Institute of Management, Centre for Economic Performance and Department of Sociology, London School of Economics and Political Science, UK.

Karl L. Alexander is Professor, Department of Sociology, The Johns Hopkins University, USA.

David J. Bartholomew is Professor, Department of Statistical and Mathematical Sciences, London School of Economics and Political Science, UK.

Sarane S. Boocock is Professor, Department of Educational Theory, Policy and Administration, Rutgers University, USA.

Martin Bulmer is Professor, Department of Sociology, University of Surrey, UK.

Jon Clark is Professor of Industrial Relations, Department of Sociology and Social Policy, and Dean of Social Sciences, University of Southampton, UK.

Randall Collins is Professor, Department of Sociology, University of California Riverside, USA.

Doris R. Entwisle is Professor, Department of Sociology, The Johns Hopkins University, USA.

Thomas J. Fararo is Professor, Department of Sociology, University of Pittsburgh, USA.

Adrian Favell is a Research Student, Department of Political and Social Sciences, European University Institute, Florence, Italy.

James J. Heckman is Professor, Department of Economics, University of Chicago, USA.

Barbara Heyns is Professor, Department of Sociology, New York University, USA.

Torsten Husén is Professor Emeritus, Institute of International Education, Stockholm University, Sweden.

Michael Inbar is Barbara and Morton Mandel Professor Emeritus of Cognitive Social Psychology and Education, Department of Sociology and Social Anthropology, Hebrew University of Jerusalem, Israel.

Denise B. Kandel is Professor, Department of Psychiatry and School of Public Health, College of Physicians and Surgeons, Columbia University, USA.

Sally B. Kilgore is Senior Fellow, Hudson Institute, Indianapolis, USA.

Siegwart Lindenberg is Professor, Department of Sociology, University of Groningen, The Netherlands.

Derek Neal is Assistant Professor, Department of Economics, University of Chicago, USA.

Aage B. Sørensen is Professor, Department of Sociology, Harvard University, USA.

List of Contributors

Richard Swedberg is Professor, Department of Sociology, Stockholm University, Sweden.

Benjamin Zablocki is Professor, Department of Sociology, Rutgers University, USA.

Author and Name Index

Note: This index covers all authors and individuals named in the volume with several exceptions. The Notes following certain chapters, Appendix 4 and the Bibliography are not indexed. Entries in this index under 'Coleman, J.S.' indicate references to specific works by Coleman; in addition, in the subject index there are detailed subentries under 'Coleman, J.S.' to particular aspects of his work.

Subject Index